Comparative International Law

Comparative International Law

EDITED BY

ANTHEA ROBERTS

PAUL B. STEPHAN

PIERRE-HUGUES VERDIER

MILA VERSTEEG

OXFORD
UNIVERSITY PRESS

OXFORD
UNIVERSITY PRESS

Oxford University Press is a department of the University of Oxford. It furthers the University's objective of excellence in research, scholarship, and education by publishing worldwide. Oxford is a registered trademark of Oxford University Press in the UK and certain other countries.

Published in the United States of America by Oxford University Press
198 Madison Avenue, New York, NY 10016, United States of America.

Library of Congress Cataloging-in-Publication Data

Names: Roberts, Anthea, editor. | Stephan, Paul B, editor. | Verdier, Pierre-Hugues, editor. |
    Versteeg, Mila, 1983– editor.
Title: Comparative international law / edited by Anthea Roberts, Paul B. Stephan,
    Pierre-Hugues Verdier, Mila Versteeg.
Description: New York : Oxford University Press, 2018. | Includes bibliographical references
    and index.
Identifiers: LCCN 2017021780 | ISBN 9780190697570 ((hardback) : alk. paper)
Subjects: LCSH: International and municipal law. | International law. | Comparative law.
Classification: LCC KZ1263 .C66 2017 | DDC 341—dc23
LC record available at https://lccn.loc.gov/2017021780

9 8 7 6 5 4 3

Printed by Sheridan Books, Inc., United States of America

Note to Readers
This publication is designed to provide accurate and authoritative information in regard to the subject matter covered. It is based upon sources believed to be accurate and reliable and is intended to be current as of the time it was written. It is sold with the understanding that the publisher is not engaged in rendering legal, accounting, or other professional services. If legal advice or other expert assistance is required, the services of a competent professional person should be sought. Also, to confirm that the information has not been affected or changed by recent developments, traditional legal research techniques should be used, including checking primary sources where appropriate.

*(Based on the Declaration of Principles jointly adopted by a Committee of the
American Bar Association and a Committee of Publishers and Associations.)*

**You may order this or any other Oxford University Press publication
by visiting the Oxford University Press website at www.oup.com.**

CONTENTS

CONTRIBUTORS

Daniel Abebe is Deputy Dean and Harold J. and Marion F. Green Professor of Law at The University of Chicago.

Tomer Broude is Associate Professor, Faculty of Law and Department of International Relations and Sylvan M. Cohen Chair in Law at Hebrew University of Jerusalem.

Congyan Cai is Professor of International Law at Xiamen University (China).

Mathilde Cohen is Professor of Law at the University of Connecticut and Research Fellow at the CNRS.

Kevin L. Cope is a Research Assistant Professor in the School of Law and a faculty affiliate with the Department of Politics at the University of Virginia. He is also a PhD Candidate in Political Science at the University of Michigan.

Ashley S. Deeks is Professor of Law at the University of Virginia.

Shai Dothan is Associate Professor of International and Public Law, University of Copenhagen Faculty of Law; affiliated with iCourts, the Danish National Research Foundation's Centre of Excellence for International Courts.

Mathias Forteau is Professor at the University of Paris Ouest (Nanterre-La Défense) and a former member of the International Law Commission.

Tom Ginsburg is Leo Spitz Professor of International Law, Ludwig and Hilde Wolf Research Scholar, and Professor of Political Science at the University of Chicago.

Jill I. Goldenziel is Associate Professor of International Law and International Relations at Marine Corps University—Command and Staff College.

Yoram Z. Haftel is Associate Professor of International Relations and the Giancarlo Elia Valori Chair in the Study of Peace & Regional Cooperation at Hebrew University of Jerusalem.

Neha Jain is Associate Professor of Law at the University of Minnesota.

Alec Knight is Development Associate, International Center for Transitional Justice.

Nico Krisch is Professor of International Law, Graduate Institute of International and Development Studies, Geneva, and Research Program Coordinator, Institut Barcelona d'Estudis Internacionals, Barcelona.

Katerina Linos is Professor of Law at the University of California, Berkeley.

Lauri Mälksoo is Professor of International Law at the University of Tartu (Estonia).

Makane Moïse Mbengue is Associate Professor of International Law, University of Geneva, Faculty of Law and Affiliated Professor, Sciences Po Paris (School of Law).

Christopher McCrudden FBA is Professor of Human Rights and Equality Law, Queen's University Belfast, and William W. Cook Global Professor of Law at the University of Michigan.

Hooman Movassagh is Principal Education Specialist and Visiting Lecturer in International Human Rights Law, University at Albany, SUNY; formerly, Lecturer, Shahid Beheshti University School of Law.

Emilia Justyna Powell is an Associate Professor of Political Science and concurrent Associate Professor of Law at the University of Notre Dame.

Anthea Roberts is Associate Professor at Australian National University.

Alejandro Rodiles is Associate Professor of International Law, ITAM, Mexico City.

Stefanie Schacherer is a PhD candidate at the Universities of Geneva and Vienna, and a Teaching and Research Assistant, University of Geneva, Faculty of Law.

Paul Stephan is John C. Jeffries, Jr., Distinguished Professor of Law and John V. Ray Research Professor of Law at the University of Virginia.

Alexander Thompson is Associate Professor of Political Science at Ohio State University.

Bakhtiyar Tuzmukhamedov is Professor of International Law and a retired Appeals Judge at the United Nations International Criminal Tribunals for Rwanda and for the former Yugoslavia.

Pierre-Hugues Verdier is E. James Kelly, Jr.—Class of 1965 Research Professor of Law at the University of Virginia.

Mila Versteeg is Professor of Law at the University of Virginia.

Masaharu Yanagihara is Professor of International Law at the Open University of Japan.

ACKNOWLEDGMENTS

The chapters of this volume were presented at the twenty-seventh and twenty-eighth Sokol Colloquia on Private International Law, held at the University of Virginia School of Law in September 2014 and November 2015. The editors and authors sincerely thank Ronald Sokol and the Sokol Colloquium Fund, Deans Paul Mahoney and Risa Goluboff of the University of Virginia School of Law, and the UK Leverhulme Trust for their support.

Benedict Kingsbury consistently supported the project, suggested several contributors, and gracefully offered to publish some of the contributions in a special issue of the *American Journal of International Law*. We thank him and his editorial team.

John Harrison, John Norton Moore, John Setear, and Ann Woolhandler of the University of Virginia School of Law contributed to the two Colloquia as panel chairs or commentators, as did several of the authors whose chapters are included in this volume.

Judy Ellis did indispensable work in planning the Colloquia and editing this volume. Ashley Angelotti, Joseph Betteley, Virginia Blanton, and Christian Truman provided excellent research and editorial assistance.

Introduction

1

Conceptualizing Comparative International Law

ANTHEA ROBERTS, PAUL B. STEPHAN, PIERRE-HUGUES
VERDIER, & MILA VERSTEEG*

I. INTRODUCTION

At first glance, "comparative international law" might sound like an oxymoron. By definition, international law—at least when it arises from multilateral treaties or general custom—applies to all treaty parties or states equally. It is perhaps the one area of law where cross-country comparisons seem inappropriate, because the same rules ostensibly govern all states. Accordingly, internationalist Hersch Lauterpacht concludes that "international law is the only branch of law containing identical rules administered as such by the courts of all nations."[1] Likewise, comparativist Harold Gutteridge explains that employment of the comparative method with respect to international law "would at first sight appear to be excluded, because rules which are avowedly universal in character do not lend themselves to comparison."[2]

Real-world international legal practice, however, does not always follow this classical conception. Many scholars and practitioners have noted that international law is often understood, interpreted, applied, and approached differently in different settings. David Kennedy, a US international lawyer, observes that international

---

* We would like to thank participants of the 2014 and 2015 Sokol Colloquia for helpful comments and suggestions. This chapter is a revised and expanded version of our short introduction to the July 2015 American Journal of International Law symposium on comparative international law: Anthea Roberts, Paul Stephan, Pierre-Hugues Verdier & Mila Versteeg, *Comparative International Law: Framing the Field*, 109 AM. J. INT'L L. 467 (2015).

1. Hersch Lauterpacht, *Decisions of Municipal Courts as a Source of International Law*, 10 BRIT. Y.B. INT'L L. 65, 95 (1929).

2. H.C. Gutteridge, *Comparative Law and the Law of Nations*, in INTERNATIONAL LAW IN COMPARATIVE PERSPECTIVE 13 (W.E. Butler ed., 1980).

law is "different in different places."[3] B.S. Chimni, an Indian international lawyer, explains that "location matters" when it comes to international law, "be it in terms of the issues that are addressed or the ways in which these are approached."[4] Likewise Xue Hanquin, the Chinese Judge at the International Court of Justice, observes that: "Notwithstanding its universal character, international law in practice is nonetheless not identically interpreted and applied among States."[5]

On issues from treaty interpretation to the content of customary international law, different states and international bodies may set forth different interpretations of the same rules, sometimes strategically, other times unaware of the differences. In some cases, these varying interpretations may subsist with minimal attention, while in others they may change or destabilize the international rules themselves. The field of *comparative international law* studies these phenomena and, in the process, brings together two fields—international law and comparative law—that often sit alongside each other but rarely interact.[6] It utilizes insights and methods from comparative law in order to identify, analyze, and explain similarities and differences in how international law is understood, interpreted, applied, and approached by different national and international actors.

Although the use of comparative approaches in international law finds important antecedents in earlier scholarship,[7] distinct attention to "comparative international

3. David Kennedy, *The Disciplines of International Law and Policy*, 12 LEIDEN J. INT'L L. 9, 17 (1999).

4. B.S. Chimni, *The World of TWAIL: Introduction to the Special Issue*, 3 TRADE L. & DEV. 14, 22 (2011).

5. XUE HANQIN, CHINESE CONTEMPORARY PERSPECTIVES ON INTERNATIONAL LAW: HISTORY, CULTURE AND INTERNATIONAL LAW 16 (2012).

6. Mireille Delmas-Marty, *Comparative Law and International Law: Methods for Ordering Pluralism*, 3 U. TOKYO J.L. & POL. 44, 44 (2006) ("the two disciplines tend to ignore each other, isolated by their own specific languages, rites, dogma and clergy."); Colin B. Picker, *International Law's Mixed Heritage: A Common/Civil Law Jurisdiction*, 41 VAND. J. TRANSNAT'L L. 1083, 1086 (2008) ("most international law scholars are not comparatists" and "most comparatists study domestic legal systems, primarily their private law dimensions, and not the international legal system").

7. *See, e.g.,* Emmanuel G. Bello, *How Advantageous Is the Use of Comparative Law in Public International Law*, 66 REVUE DE DROIT INTERNATIONAL, DE SCIENCES DIPLOMATIQUES ET POLITIQUES 77 (1988); Eric Stein et al., *International Law in Domestic Legal Orders: A Comparative Perspective*, 91 ASIL PROC. 289 (1997); Eric Stein, *International Law in Internal Law: Toward Internationalization of Central-Eastern European Constitutions?*, 88 AM. J. INT'L L. 427 (1994); Eric Stein, *National Procedures for Giving Effect to Governmental Obligations Undertaken and Agreements Concluded by Governments*, in RAPPORTS GÉNÉRAUX AU IXᵉ CONGRÈS INTERNATIONAL DE DROIT COMPARÉ 581 (1977); Luzius Wildhaber & Stephan Breitenmoser, *The Relationship Between Customary International Law and Municipal Law in Western European Countries*, 48 ZEITSCHRIFT FÜR AUSLÄNDISCHES ÖFFENTLICHES RECHT UND VÖLKERRECHT 163 (1988). Other early comparative work on international law included debates on competing Western and Soviet approaches. *See, e.g.,* PERESTROIKA AND INTERNATIONAL LAW: CURRENT ANGLO-SOVIET APPROACHES TO INTERNATIONAL LAW (Anthony Carty & Gennady Danilenko eds., 1990). On the attitude of newly-independent states to the international legal order, see, for example, FELIX CHUKS OKOYE, INTERNATIONAL LAW AND THE NEW AFRICAN STATES (1972); T. O. ELIAS, AFRICA AND THE DEVELOPMENT OF INTERNATIONAL LAW (1972). On the contribution of non-Western legal

law" as an emerging, or re-emerging, phenomenon has grown in recent years.[8] Some scholars describe distinctive contemporary approaches of particular states or regions toward international law, such as US, Chinese, and EU approaches to international law.[9] Others offer historical accounts of specific regional approaches to international law, such as Latin American approaches during the nineteenth and early twentieth centuries,[10] or rival Western and Soviet approaches during the Cold War.[11] Some explore how different national actors, such as domestic courts, interpret and apply international law in diverse ways.[12] Others identify similarities and

systems to international law, see, for example, C. G. WEERAMANTRY, ISLAMIC JURISPRUDENCE: AN INTERNATIONAL PERSPECTIVE (1988).

8. *See, e.g.,* THE INTERPRETATION OF INTERNATIONAL LAW BY DOMESTIC COURTS: UNIFORMITY, DIVERSITY, CONVERGENCE (Helmut Philipp Aust & Georg Nolte eds., 2016); Martti Koskenniemi, *The Case for Comparative International Law*, FINN. Y.B. INT'L L. (2009); Anthea Roberts, *Comparative International Law? The Role of National Courts in Creating and Enforcing International Law*, 60 INT'L & COMP. L.Q. 57, 61–64 (2011); Boris N. Mamlyuk & Ugo Mattei, *Comparative International Law*, 36 BROOK. J. INT'L L. 385, 389 (2011); Abdulqawi Yusuf, *Diversity of Legal Traditions and International Law: Keynote Address*, 4 CAMB. J. INT'L & COMP. L. 681 (2013); *Symposium on Comparative International Law*, 109 AM. J. INT'L L. 467 (2015). A spate of recent conferences also evidence renewed interest in this area. For example, in addition to the 2014 and 2015 Sokol Colloquia on Comparative International Law at the University of Virginia, at which the contributions to this volume were presented, there were a 2010 conference organized by the Toronto Group for the Study of International, Transnational, and Comparative Law, which included a panel entitled "Stories of the Gently Civilized: National Traditions in International Law"; a 2013 Cambridge Journal of International and Comparative Law conference entitled "Legal Tradition in a Diverse World"; and a 2015 Duke University-Geneva Conference on Comparative Foreign Relations Law.

9. *See, e.g.,* Anu Bradford & Eric A. Posner, *Universal Exceptionalism in International Law*, 52 HARV. INT'L L.J. 1 (2011); XUE, *supra* note 5 (Chinese approaches); Yasuaki Onuma, *A Transcivilizational Perspective on International Law*, 342 RECUEIL DES COURS 1 (2009) (Asian approaches); Francesco Messineo, *Is There an Italian Conception of International Law?*, 4 CAMB. J. INT'L & COMP. L. 681, 879 (2013).

10. *See, e.g.,* Arnulf Becker Lorca, *International Law in Latin America or Latin American International Law? Rise, Fall, and Retrieval of a Tradition of Legal Thinking and Political Imagination*, 47 HARV. INT'L L.J. 283 (2006); Arnulf Becker Lorca, *Universal International Law: Nineteenth-Century Histories of Imposition and Appropriation*, 51 HARV. INT'L L.J. 475 (2010); Liliana Obrégon, *Completing Civilization: Creole Consciousness and International Law in Nineteenth-Century Latin America, in* INTERNATIONAL LAW AND ITS OTHERS 247 (Anne Orford ed., 2006).

11. *See, e.g.,* Paul B. Stephan, *The Impact of the Cold War on Soviet and US Law: Reconsidering the Legacy, in* THE LEGAL DIMENSION IN COLD WAR INTERACTIONS: SOME NOTES FROM THE FIELD 141 (Tatiana Borisova & William B. Simons eds., 2012).

12. *See, e.g.,* INTERNATIONAL LAW AND DOMESTIC LEGAL SYSTEMS: INCORPORATION, TRANSFORMATION, AND PERSUASION (Dinah Shelton ed., 2011); NEW PERSPECTIVES ON THE DIVIDE BETWEEN NATIONAL AND INTERNATIONAL LAW (Janne E. Nijman & Andre Nollkaemper eds., 2007); Eyal Benvenisti, *Judicial Misgivings Regarding the Application of International Law: An Analysis of Attitudes of National Courts*, 4 EUR. J. INT'L L. 159 (1993); Eyal Benvenisti, *Reclaiming Democracy: The Strategic Uses of Foreign and International Law by National Courts*, 102 AM. J. INT'L L. 241 (2008); Roberts, *supra* note 8, at 61–64.

differences in the textbook and scholarly traditions of international law academics in different states.[13]

Building on these earlier works, the purpose of this volume is to bring together contributors who are engaged in different aspects of the comparative international law phenomenon to give some sense of the contours of this emerging field. By its nature, we believe that the field of comparative international law benefits from collective endeavors. Any particular comparative international law analysis necessarily will be partial. One may compare the approaches of two or more states to international law. Or one may examine how multiple authoritative actors have interpreted or applied a particular international law rule or principle. Or one might theorize about how and why similarities and differences arise across states and among lawmakers. Only by combining multiple perspectives and approaches to the topic can one begin to develop a sense of the field of comparative international law as a whole.

Our project thus has three goals: to establish comparative international law as a field of research in a way that has some coherence but remains sufficiently broad to embrace a variety of perspectives and approaches; to identify various theoretical perspectives and methodological approaches that scholars have brought, or might bring, to bear on this subject; and to conduct an initial array of comparisons across issue-areas and legal systems to illustrate some of the types of projects that can be conducted, and range of insights that might be derived, from this field. To these ends, we first explain what we mean by comparative international law (Part II), how one might go about finding and analyzing similarities and differences (Part III), what hypotheses have been suggested for explaining similarities and differences (Part IV), and what some of the normative challenges and implications of this field might be (Part V).

II. WHAT IS COMPARATIVE INTERNATIONAL LAW?

As a newly emerging field, the contours of comparative international law necessarily are fluid and contingent. Aware of these difficulties, we offer only a provisional definition: *comparative international law entails identifying, analyzing, and explaining similarities and differences in how actors in different legal systems understand, interpret, apply, and approach international law.*[14] Although the field is primarily descriptive and explanatory, it also brings to the fore normative and theoretical questions, such as whether divergence or convergence should be celebrated or feared, encouraged or discouraged, and what findings of similarities and differences might mean for how one conceptualizes international law.

In order to provide a framework for analysis, we identify three ways in which comparative law insights might be particularly helpful in the field of international law.

---

13. *See, e.g.,* ANTHEA ROBERTS, IS INTERNATIONAL LAW INTERNATIONAL? (2017); Antony Carty, *A Colloquium on International Law Textbooks in England, France and Germany: An Introduction,* 11 EUR. J. INT'L L. 615 (2000); Guglielmo Verdirame, *"The Divided West": International Lawyers in Europe and America,* 18 EUR. J. INT'L L. 553 (2007).

14. *See* Roberts et al., *supra* note *, at 469.

First, comparative law methods may be relevant in *identifying* the substantive content of international law. International lawyers are called on to engage in comparative analyses when they seek to identify custom, which requires a review of state practice and *opinio juris* from different states, and general principles, which may require an analysis of whether certain principles are common to many, or the main types of, legal systems. For instance, as Mathias Forteau shows, the International Law Commission (ILC) engages in comparative analysis of different understandings, interpretations, and applications of international law in determining whether and how to codify or progressively develop international law.[15] Likewise, as Neha Jain demonstrates, international criminal tribunals have drawn on comparative studies of national legal systems in seeking to identify general principles that might apply in criminal trials.[16]

Comparative approaches can also be useful in identifying outlier approaches, which may be characterized as violations of existing international law or as innovative attempts at progressive development. For instance, Alec Knight examines the way in which the Convention on the Elimination of Discrimination Against Women (CEDAW) Committee encourages what it views as progressive interpretations of the CEDAW Convention while discouraging what it views as regressive attempts to limit the Convention's application.[17] Similarly, Makane Mbengue and Stefanie Schacherer examine the Pan-African Investment Code from a comparative perspective, showing how the treaty departs from existing approaches propagated by developed states because it was drafted from the perspective of developing and least-developed countries with the aim of fostering sustainable development.[18]

Second, comparative law approaches are relevant in identifying, analyzing, and explaining similarities and differences in the *interpretation and application* of international law. For instance, as some of our contributors show, common treaty provisions may be interpreted in similar or different ways by national, regional, and international courts.[19] Different interpretations of international law norms may be put forward by executives from different states in a range of settings, including in the formulation of treaty reservations and understandings and corresponding

---

15. *See* Mathias Forteau, *Comparative International Law Within, Not Against, International Law: Lessons from the International Law Commission* (this volume).

16. *See* Neha Jain, *Comparative International Law at the ICTY: The General Principles Experiment*, 109 Am. J. Int'l L. 486 (2015).

17. Alec Knight, *An Asymmetric Comparative International Law Approach to Treaty Interpretation: The CEDAW Committee's Tolerance of the Scandinavian States' Progressive Deviation* (this volume).

18. Makane Moïse Mbengue & Stefanie Schacherer, *Africa and the Rethinking of International Investment Law: About the Elaboration of the Pan-African Investment Code* (this volume).

19. *See* Christopher McCrudden, *CEDAW in National Courts: A Case Study in Operationalizing Comparative International Law Analysis in a Human Rights Context* (this volume); Jill I. Goldenziel, *When Law Migrates: Refugees in Comparative International Law* (this volume); Shai Dothan, *Comparative Views on the Right to Vote in International Law: The Case of Prisoners' Disenfranchisement* (this volume).

objections,[20] and claims about whether international law applies to areas such as espionage and, if so, what it requires.[21] The content of international legal obligations might also be domesticated similarly or differently by legislatures in different states.[22]

Third, methods from comparative law and politics provide a useful way of understanding and explaining different *approaches* to international law. For instance, states differ in the degree and types of power and influence they enjoy, which may affect whether they function primarily as exporters or importers of international law norms.[23] They differ in their fundamental ideological commitments, which may affect their interpretations of central international law notions such as sovereignty and human rights. Pierre-Hugues Verdier and Mila Versteeg further show how states also differ in their constitutional structures, legal traditions, and rules on the reception of international law and its application by domestic legal institutions.[24] These differences empower different domestic actors, which may help to explain similarities and differences in the understanding, interpretation, or application of international law by those states. Finally, as Nico Krisch and Anthea Roberts show, states also have different legal academies with their own norms and incentive systems, which may affect how international law is conceptualized, taught, and written about in those states.[25]

While these categories provide a useful typology of comparative international law inquiries, we should not understand them as exhaustive or hermetically sealed. In some cases, similarities or differences in the way in which international law is interpreted and applied might affect what is identified as international law. Likewise, similar or different approaches to international law might result in similar or different interpretations and applications of international law with respect to particular issues.

A. Distinguishing Comparative International Law from Related Fields

As explored in more detail by Christopher McCrudden and Paul Stephan, these comparative international law inquiries relate to, but are distinct from, several

---

20. *See* Tom Ginsburg, *Objections to Treaty Reservations: A Comparative Approach to Decentralized Interpretation* (this volume).

21. *See* Ashley S. Deeks, *Intelligence Communities and International Law: A Comparative Approach* (this volume).

22. *See* Kevin L. Cope & Hooman Movassagh, *National Legislatures: The Foundations of Comparative International Law* (this volume).

23. *See* ROBERTS, *supra* note 13.

24. Pierre-Hugues Verdier & Mila Versteeg, *International Law in National Legal Systems: An Empirical Investigation* (this volume).

25. Nico Krisch, *The Many Fields of (German) International Law* (this volume); ROBERTS, *supra* note 13.

existing bodies of scholarship, most notably those dealing with the fragmentation of international law, comparative constitutional law, and comparative foreign relations law.[26]

The fragmentation literature typically looks at how different understandings of international law are adopted in different subfields of international law (e.g., human rights and humanitarian law) or by different international bodies (e.g., the International Court of Justice and the International Criminal Tribunal for the former Yugoslavia). Comparative constitutional law examines how different states interpret and apply particular constitutional norms, which are sometimes drawn from or influenced by international instruments, such as human rights treaties. Comparative foreign relations law looks at the rules, institutions, and practices in different states with respect to how that state conducts relations with foreign states and other actors.

Unlike the fragmentation debate, comparative international law focuses primarily, though not exclusively, on interpretations of international law put forward by states and substate actors, such as national courts, rather than on interpretations put forward by different international actors. Our definition does not, however, limit the focus of inquiry to different national actors, as both national and international actors might put forward interpretations of the same norms. For example, Jill Goldenziel's chapter compares interpretations of the Refugee Convention adopted by Australian, American, and EU courts,[27] while Knight contrasts the CEDAW Committee's interpretations of the Convention and those of several state parties.[28]

Unlike comparative constitutional law, comparative international law looks primarily at cross-national understandings, interpretations, applications, and approaches to international law rather than constitutional law. However, as both may implicate common issues, such as human rights, there is often overlap between the two. For instance, Verdier and Versteeg argue that national constitutional rules governing treaty-making and the domestic status of international law may influence how states interpret and apply their international law obligations, and Alejandro Rodiles situates his analysis of the dialogue within the Inter-American human rights system as emerging from a merger of national constitutional law and international law.[29]

Our definition is also broad enough to include certain aspects of comparative foreign relations law that concern similarities and differences in how states understand, interpret, apply, and approach international law. For instance, Stephan examines how the movement to develop a field of foreign relations law differed significantly between the United States and the United Kingdom.[30] In the former, it

26. Christopher McCrudden, *Comparative International Law and Human Rights: A Value-Added Approach* (this volume); Paul B. Stephan, *Comparative International Law, Foreign Relations Law and Fragmentation: Can the Center Hold?* (this volume).

27. Goldenziel, *supra* note 19.

28. Knight, *supra* note 17.

29. Verdier & Versteeg, *supra* note 24; Alejandro Rodiles, *The Great Promise of Comparative Public Law for Latin America: Towards* ius commune americanum? (this volume).

30. Stephan, *supra* note 26.

was promoted by scholars who were skeptical about international law and wanted to emphasize the role of domestic law constraints on international law entering the US legal system. In the latter, it was developed by courts and scholars who wished to use international law to confine the Crown Prerogative, which had formerly walled off much executive conduct with respect to foreign relations from judicial oversight. The recent decision of the Supreme Court on the process for leaving the European Union confirms the growing importance of the field.[31]

B. The Unit of Analysis

The effort to conceptualize comparative international law also calls attention to the appropriate unit of analysis. In studying similarities and differences in understanding, interpreting, applying, and approaching international law, to which actors should scholars turn? Cross-national studies can have multiple potential units of analysis, including: states as unitary actors, domestic state institutions (such as courts, legislatures, and executives), and nonstate actors (such as academics, nongovernmental organizations, and social and political movements). Comparative international law studies may also focus on the understandings, interpretations, applications, and approaches of various international actors, such as the ILC and international courts, which sometimes coincide, and at other times conflict, with each other and with national approaches. Thus, our definition of comparative international law includes both horizontal (state-to-state) and vertical (state-to-regional and state-to-international) studies.

The bulk of existing scholarship on comparative international law has focused on states (as unitary actors) or decisions of domestic courts (as substate actors). Domestic courts constitute a natural object of comparative international law analysis because of their dual relationship with international law: on the one hand, they are often called upon to implement international law (as impartial law enforcers), while on the other, they are in a position to shape international law through their interpretations (as partial law creators).[32] However, other state actors, such as legislatures, executives, and administrative bodies, also interpret and apply international legal rules in ways that may help to enforce or create international law.[33] Focusing too heavily on court decisions tends to skew comparative international law analysis

---

31. Miller v. Ministry of Justice [2017] UKSC 5.

32. *See* Roberts, *supra* note 8. As an example of a court-centered approach, see the recent edited volume on international law in domestic courts by Helmut Aust and George Nolte, *supra* note 8.

33. For instance, the executive arms of the United States and Russian governments have produced different national security statements that have a bearing on the interpretation and application of the use of force. *Compare* NATIONAL SECURITY STRATEGY OF THE UNITED STATES OF AMERICA (2010) *with* Концепция Внешней Политики РоссийскойоФедерации [Foreign Policy Concept of the Russian Federation, 2000], Jun. 28, 2000. Likewise, a number of states have adopted the international prohibition on genocide in their domestic law but have made its definition broader or narrower than the Rome Statute's definition. See W.N. FERDINANDUSSE, DIRECT APPLICATION OF INTERNATIONAL CRIMINAL LAW BY NATIONAL COURTS 5 (2006).

toward consideration of certain states, particularly Western, common law, English-speaking states;[34] and certain issues that arise before courts, such as human rights and refugee law.[35]

Conscious of these biases, this volume includes contributions by Congyan Cai, Neha Jain, Bakhtiyar Tuzmukhamedov, and Lauri Mälksoo that provide more detailed consideration of court practices in certain non-Western states (China, India, and Russia) that often receive less attention in international law scholarship on domestic courts.[36] The book also features contributions that focus on other international and national actors, including Forteau's chapter on the ILC, Ashley Deeks's analysis of different executive approaches to espionage, Knight's study of executive practice before the CEDAW Committee and the Committee's responses to such practice, Tom Ginsburg's review of executive practice with respect to reservations to the International Covenant on Civil and Political Rights and objections to such reservations, and Kevin Cope and Hooman Movassagh's study of domestic legislatures.[37]

We also highlight the way in which cross-national similarities and differences may be reflected in and shaped by the practices of nonstate actors. For example, international law academics, whose writings constitute a subsidiary source for the determination of international law, may play an important role in creating uniform or diverse constructions of the field. To the extent that distinct national or regional "epistemic communities"[38] of international lawyers exist, as suggested by Krisch and Roberts, this may reflect and perpetuate national differences in the interpretation and application of international law.[39] Rodiles takes up this idea in his study of the idea of a *ius constitutionale commune* in Latin America by tracing debates in regional academic and judicial dialogues.[40] The interpretation and application of international law across countries may also be shaped by other nonstate actors, including

---

34. ROBERTS, *supra* note 13.

35. *Cf.* Congyan Cai, *International Law in Chinese Courts During the Rise of China* (this volume) (noting that Western international lawyers often focus on national courts applying human rights treaties, which Chinese courts almost never do, but that certain non-Western courts might be more active in applying international law in other contexts, such as private international law).

36. *Id.*; Neha Jain, *The Democratizing Force of International Law: Human Rights Adjudication by the Indian Supreme Court* (this volume); Lauri Mälksoo, *Case Law in Russian Approaches to International Law* (this volume); Bakhtiyar Tuzmukhamedov, *Doing Away with Capital Punishment in Russia: International Law and the Pursuit of Domestic Constitutional Goals* (this volume).

37. Forteau, *supra* note 15; Deeks, *supra* note 21; Knight, *supra* note 17; Ginsburg, *supra* note 20; Cope & Movassagh, *supra* note 22.

38. Peter Haas, *Epistemic Communities and International Policy Coordination*, 46 INT'L. ORG. 1 (1992); David Kennedy, *One, Two, Three, Many Legal Orders: Legal Pluralism and the Cosmopolitan Dream*, 31 N.Y.U. REV. L. & SOC. CHANGE 641 (2007).

39. ROBERTS, *supra* note 13.

40. Rodiles, *supra* note 29.

nongovernmental organizations, social and political movements, and the public at large.[41]

III. THE METHODS OF COMPARATIVE INTERNATIONAL LAW

A necessary first step in most comparative international law enquiries is descriptive, and involves identifying similarities and differences in how international law is understood, interpreted, applied, and approached across different legal systems. Several contributors to this volume undertake this descriptive task by mapping common and divergent approaches to international norms in areas such as espionage, refugees, and women's rights, among others. A possible next step, undertaken by some contributors, is to seek to explain similarities and differences: Why do different legal systems set forth similar or different interpretations and applications of international legal rules?[42]

In this section, we consider what lessons and insights might be brought to comparative international law from the related fields of comparative law and comparative politics. From comparative law, we suggest that scholars' long-standing preoccupation with the functional method, appropriate benchmarks for comparison, and classifications of the world's legal systems into families or traditions can inform comparative international law inquiries. With respect to methods, we suggest that comparative politics and other social science fields offer valuable insights on topics such as case selection and the relative merits and drawbacks of different approaches, such as detailed qualitative case studies versus large-N quantitative studies.

A. Lessons from Comparative Law

One of the core insights from comparative law is that seemingly different legal rules and doctrines may have similar functions and produce similar outcomes.[43] Thus, when taking into account the actual operation of rules in particular legal systems, we may find that facially different rules are in fact functional equivalents. To illustrate, the constitutions of the United States and the United Kingdom look very different from one another (one is written and the other unwritten), and yet, both serve to coordinate and constrain government behavior. Likewise, facially similar rules might actually serve different functions in different domestic contexts. For

---

41. *See, e.g.*, BETH A. SIMMONS, MOBILIZING FOR HUMAN RIGHTS: INTERNATIONAL LAW IN DOMESTIC POLITICS (2009); KATERINA LINOS, THE DEMOCRATIC FOUNDATIONS OF POLICY DIFFUSION: HOW HEALTH, FAMILY, AND EMPLOYMENT LAWS SPREAD ACROSS COUNTRIES (2013).

42. *See* John C. Reitz, *How to Do Comparative Law*, 46 AM. J. COMP. L. 617, 626–27 (1998).

43. For an overview, see Ralf Michaels, *The Functional Method in Comparative Law*, *in* THE OXFORD HANDBOOK OF COMPARATIVE LAW (Mathias Reimann & Reinhard Zimmermann eds., 2006); *see also* Mathias Reimann, *The Progress and Failure of Comparative Law in the Second Half of the Twentieth Century* 50 AM. J. COMP. L. 671, 679 (2002) (describing functionalism as the requirement to "analyze not only what rules say, but also what problems they solve in their respective legal system").

example, while many nations protect the freedom of expression in similar terms, the actual meaning given to these provisions differs substantially across countries.[44] Functionalist scholars in comparative law thus emphasize the need to look not merely at formal similarities and differences, but also at functional ones.

The functional method is intuitively appealing for comparative international law inquiries. As a general matter, international law does not dictate how states implement their international legal obligations as long as they comply with the relevant rule.[45] For example, while international law provides that states are immune from the jurisdiction of foreign courts for their acts *de jure imperii*, it is usually immaterial whether that rule is implemented by statute, applied directly by courts, or secured by executive decree. In this sense, international law is usually concerned with results rather than means; it insists on functional rather than formal similarity. From this perspective, comparative international law could consist of studying the ways in which different states implement a given international obligation in their respective legal systems. Indeed, this functionalist impulse may help explain why comparative international law has not yet emerged as a systematic field of enquiry. As long as outcomes are the same—or at least represent satisfactory compliance with the rule—there is no need for international lawyers to dig deeper.

However, although the functional method is prominent in traditional comparative law scholarship, it does not lack critics.[46] The most common criticism is that, in its focus on functional equivalence, this method neglects interesting and important differences both in the details of each legal system and in the relevant economic, social, and cultural context.[47] Indeed, an important insight from the comparative law debates over the functional method is that functional analyses tend to result in more observed similarities than do formal analyses. In turn, this can understate important differences in how the rule truly functions in different legal systems. Thus, critics of the functional method suggest that instead of searching for similarities, convergence, and globalization, comparative law should focus on difference, divergence, and diversity.[48]

This suggests alternative approaches for comparative international law. First, researchers could deliberately search for functional differences, thus emphasizing cases where differences in interpretation and application produce substantively different outcomes across different states, which may include non-compliance with the relevant international rule. Another approach is to search not just for functional

---

44. *See* Frederick Schauer, *The Exceptional First Amendment, in* AMERICAN EXCEPTIONALISM AND HUMAN RIGHTS 29 (Michael Ignatieff ed., 2005).

45. ANTONIO CASSESE, INTERNATIONAL LAW 218 (2d ed. 2005) ("States are only interested in the final result: fulfilment or non-fulfilment of an obligation. They show no interest in the factors that brought about that result.... [T]his state of affairs reflects the individualistic structure of the international community and the paramount importance of respect for other States' internal affairs.").

46. For a summary, see MATHIAS SIEMS, COMPARATIVE LAW 37–39 (2014).

47. *See, e.g.,* William Twining, *Globalization and the Common Law,* 6 MAASTRICHT J. EUR. & COMP. L. 217 (1999).

48. Reimann, *supra* note 43, at 681.

differences, but for formal ones as well. Even if the states compared ultimately comply with the relevant international legal rule—thus reaching the same functional outcome—the fact that they use formally different ways of getting there can be interesting and worthy of study in its own right. Finally, analyses could search for functional differences in the face of formal similarities. Here, the focus would be on states that invoke formally identical treaty or customary norms, but use these to achieve different functions in their domestic legal systems. For instance, Jain argues that the Supreme Court of India's invocations of international human rights law often serves—and is shaped by—domestic political objectives.[49]

A second, and related, debate in comparative law involves identifying the appropriate benchmark for comparison. The seemingly simple question, "[w]hat is going to be compared to what?" has stirred substantial controversy in practice.[50] In order for comparison to be possible, the units of comparison—usually countries or legal systems—need to have something in common. Comparative law scholars have suggested that any comparative analysis requires a *tertium comparationis*, which is a common point of departure, typically "a real-life problem or an ideal."[51] For a functionalist, the *tertium* may be a functional outcome (e.g., the legal protection of private property rights); for a formalist, a formal rule (e.g., a constitutional clause prohibiting expropriation); for those engaged in normative analyses, an ideal (e.g., the importance of protecting private property). Whether one finds similarities or differences depends in part on what the *tertium* is, and the level of generality with which it is defined.[52] As a rule, the higher the level of generality, the fewer the differences. For comparative international law, the benchmark for comparison could be the international legal rule itself, as it is common to the legal systems under study.[53] Yet, even with a seemingly clear point of departure, the degree to which international law is interpreted and applied similarly or differently across national systems depends on whether one looks for functional, formal, or normative similarities or differences. We do not privilege any particular approach but believe that it is important for comparative international law studies to be explicit about their benchmark for comparison.

Another potentially useful idea from comparative law is that of dividing the world into legal families or traditions. The main distinction is usually between the common law and the (Romanist, Germanic and Nordic) civil law, with smaller

---

49. See Jain, *supra* note 36.

50. Reitz, *supra* note 42, at 620.

51. *Id.* at 623.

52. *See* Katerina Linos, *Methodological Guidance: How to Select and Develop Comparative International Law Case Studies* (this volume).

53. There is some debate in comparative law regarding whether single country studies of foreign systems count as comparative law, the objection being that a description of a foreign system does not entail a comparison. *See, e.g.,* Reitz, *supra* note 42, at 618–19; Hirschl, *infra* note 73, at 126. The fact that international law offers a benchmark of comparison, however, suggests that single-country comparative international law studies do arguably count as comparative. Indeed, a number of our contributors perform single-country studies that we believe qualify as comparative work.

groups of countries classified as Confucian systems, Islamic legal systems, Hindu systems, and (prior to the 1990s) socialist systems.[54] Many other groupings exist as well, such as Ugo Mattei's distinction between the "rule of professional law," the "rule of political law," and the "rule of traditional law."[55] While the specific features of such classifications and their usefulness remain controversial, they may be relevant to comparative international law scholarship. For example, the chapter by Verdier and Versteeg suggests that states in different legal families might approach the relationship between international and domestic law differently.[56] Roberts's work suggests that legal families might influence transnational flows of students, legal ideas, and materials in ways that create distinct epistemic communities of international lawyers.[57]

Among political scientists, Beth Simmons's work finds that common law states are less likely to ratify international human rights treaties and more likely to add reservations.[58] Sara Mitchell and Emilia Powell argue that legal traditions inform states' approaches to international adjudication, including their support for the International Court of Justice, the International Criminal Court, and the UN Convention on the Law of the Sea (UNCLOS).[59] In her chapter on Islamic law states and UNCLOS, Emilia Powell examines in some detail how Western and non-Western international law notions might overlap or diverge and what consequences might follow.[60] She highlights the Islamic international law concept of *siyar*, which regulates the behavior of Islamic law states and individuals in the international arena and provides a parallel to Western conceptions of international law. After observing that Islamic law states have signed onto UNCLOS, which includes compulsory dispute resolution, at a much higher rate than other treaty regimes with dispute resolution, Powell examines whether a possible cause might be that UNCLOS expresses principles that have historically been present in Islamic law.

In employing such classifications, it is important to be mindful of the insights from comparative law regarding the strengths and weaknesses of relying on any

54. For prominent classifications, see ZWEIGERT & KÖTZ, AN INTRODUCTION TO COMPARATIVE LAW 67–68 (3d ed. 1998); H. PATRICK GLENN, LEGAL TRADITIONS OF THE WORLD (5th ed. 2014); MARTIN SHAPIRO, COURTS: A COMPARATIVE ANALYSIS (1986). For an overview of different classifications, see SIEMS, *supra* note 46, at 75–80.

55. Ugo Mattei, *Three Patterns of Law: Taxonomy and Change in the World's Legal Systems*, 45 AM. J. COMP. L. 5 (1997).

56. Verdier & Versteeg, *supra* note 24.

57. ROBERTS, *supra* note 13.

58. SIMMONS, *supra* note 41, at 83–84.

59. SARA MCLAUGHLIN MITCHELL & EMILIA JUSTYNA POWELL, DOMESTIC LAW GOES GLOBAL: LEGAL TRADITIONS AND INTERNATIONAL COURTS (2011). *See also* DANA ZARTNER, COURTS, CODES AND CUSTOM: LEGAL TRADITIONS AND STATE POLICY TOWARD INTERNATIONAL HUMAN RIGHTS AND ENVIRONMENTAL LAW (2014).

60. Emilia Powell, *Not So Treacherous Waters of International Maritime Law: Islamic Law States and the UN Convention on the Law of the Sea* (this volume).

particular taxonomy. First, classifications are ideal-types.[61] They always involve simplifications, and they have been criticized for "overemphasizing the differences between categories, underemphasizing the differences within these categories and ignoring hybrids."[62] Second, these classifications are not static and exogenous, but dynamic and subject to change. For example, while many countries became members of a legal family through colonial imposition,[63] some of the pathways this established continue to have considerable contemporary influence.[64] There is substantial debate over whether common law systems and civil law systems have converged.[65] Transplanted rules may also take on unique meanings as they interact with indigenous norms and traditions.[66] Indeed, to capture this dynamism, some comparative lawyers have suggested that the term legal *tradition* is more appropriate than that of a legal *family*.[67] Thus, while classifications can suggest important insights for comparative international law research, scholars should recognize their limitations and be careful when attributing specific similarities and differences to putative general characteristics of legal traditions. As the field of comparative international law develops, scholars will likely rely on additional classifications, such as Western and non-Western states, liberal and illiberal states, or democratic and authoritarian states.[68]

B. Lessons from Comparative Politics

As described above, comparative law offers important substantive insights that may be useful in comparative international law inquiries. However, in recent years comparative law has come under criticism for its lack of concern with methodology in the social scientific sense of the word. In assessing the successes and failures of comparative law in the second half of the twentieth century, Matthias Reimann

61. *See* Reimann, *supra* note 43, at 677.

62. SIEMS, *supra* note 46, at 80.

63. ALAN WATSON, LEGAL TRANSPLANTS: AN APPROACH TO COMPARATIVE LAW 21–22 (1974); Pierre Legrand, *The Impossibility of 'Legal Transplants'*, 4 MAASTRICHT J. EUR. & COMP L. 111, 116–18 (1997).

64. *See, e.g.*, Holger Spamann, *Contemporary Legal Transplants: Legal Families and the Diffusion of (Corporate) Law*, 2009 BYU L. REV. 1813, 1851 (2009).

65. *See, e.g.*, John Merryman, *On the Convergence (and Divergence) of the Civil Law and the Common Law*, 17 STAN. J. INT'L L. 357 (1981).

66. Legrand, *supra* note 63; SALLY ENGLE MERRY, HUMAN RIGHTS AND GENDER VIOLENCE: TRANSLATING INTERNATIONAL LAW INTO LOCAL JUSTICE (2006); Sally Engle Merry, *Transnational Human Rights and Local Activism: Mapping the Middle*, 108 AM. ANTHROPOLOGIST 38, 39 (2006).

67. Reimann, *supra* note 43, at 678; GLENN, *supra* note 54.

68. *See* ROBERTS, *supra* note 13; Anne-Marie Slaughter, *International Law in a World of Liberal States*, 6 EUR. J. INT'L L. 503 (1995).

concludes that "attempts to develop even a moderately sophisticated method of comparison have been exceedingly rare, and, as far as I can see, happily ignored."[69] In practice, traditional comparative law research tends to consist either of detailed doctrinal comparison (as epitomized by the European project of searching for a "common core" in private law)[70] or studies inspired by anthropological approaches, which view comparative law as a "way of life"[71] requiring immersion in a foreign system's culture, language, and legal tradition.[72]

More recently, scholars have drawn on social science disciplines, including comparative politics, to inject greater methodological rigor into comparative law studies. A decade ago, political scientist Ran Hirschl raised the issues of case selection, causal inference, and controlled comparisons in comparative constitutional law.[73] For example, comparative constitutional studies tended to rely on a limited set of cases, mainly English-speaking common law systems, without any justification for the case selection.[74] While focusing on a limited set of cases might allow scholars to reflect upon their own system, this approach does not allow them to set forth causal explanations on why certain types of provisions are adopted, or what their impact is.[75] Hirschl's call is by no means universally embraced today, but it did influence the methodological standards in comparative constitutional law, and such methodological guidance may also prove useful in comparative international law.

Many comparative international law researchers may choose to conduct qualitative case studies, a method that is relatively familiar to legal scholars. While this approach has significant merits, the focus on a limited number of cases raises the issue of how these cases are selected. Katerina Linos's contribution draws on comparative politics to discuss principles of case selection that allow researchers to make general claims.[76] She cautions against "convenience sampling," which consists of selecting cases that are easily accessible or that the researcher is familiar with, and suggests that sampling choices be theoretically informed. This requires defining "important traits that could explain the phenomenon of interest," based on which the researcher can "select among the many countries in each theoretically defined

---

69. Reimann, *supra* note 43, at 689.

70. Holger Spamann, Empirical Comparative Law (Manuscript 2015) (noting that "in practice, however, classical comparative law has been almost exclusively doctrinal").

71. David Kennedy, *The Methods and the Politics, in* COMPARATIVE LEGAL STUDIES: TRADITIONS AND TRANSITIONS (Pierre Legrand & Roderick Munday eds., 2002) (quoting William Twining).

72. *See, e.g.,* Reitz, *supra* note 42, at 628, 631–33; Merry, *supra* note 66.

73. Ran Hirschl, *The Question of Case Selection in Comparative Constitutional Law*, 53 AM. J. COMP. L. 125 (2005). *See also* Ran HIRSCHL, COMPARATIVE MATTERS: THE RENAISSANCE OF COMPARATIVE CONSTITUTIONAL LAW 224–81 (2014).

74. Sujit Choudhry, *Bridging Comparative Constitutional Law and Comparative Politics: Constitutional Design in Divided Societies, in* CONSTITUTIONAL DESIGN FOR ETHNICALLY DIVIDED SOCIETIES 1, 8 (Sujit Choudhry ed., 2008).

75. Hirschl, *supra* note 73, at 132.

76. *See* Linos, *supra* note 52.

category."[77] Through theoretically informed sampling, researchers can make statements about how general a practice is. For example, if one wants to show that a legal principle is "fundamental to our notion of the rule of law," one could point out that this principle is found in legal systems that otherwise differ in many respects, such as "in ancient Egypt and modern Germany as well as in tribal Afghanistan."[78]

This example illustrates one approach to case selection, which consists of looking at the "most different" cases to establish commonalities. If one is trying to prove that a general rule exists, finding that this rule holds with respect to states that might otherwise be considered very different is probative, as illustrated above. By contrast, if one is trying to identify a relevant difference and its causes, it can help to look for evidence through comparisons between states that are otherwise "most similar." Thus, Deeks's work on international law and intelligence communities examines the very different approaches adopted by two states that might otherwise be considered similar: the United Kingdom and the United States.[79] After identifying these divergent approaches, she then analyzes some of the differences between these states that might explain them, such as whether domestic or regional courts require their governments to justify the conformity of their actions with international law.

Qualitative case studies can also be used to make more general causal claims about what explains differences or similarities in formal rules or outcomes across legal systems. As Linos notes, qualitative techniques are particularly well-suited "to the development and testing of mid-range theories that seek to develop causal mechanisms that apply under particular conditions."[80] For example, Ran Hirschl relies on in-depth case studies of the establishment of judicial review in Israel, New Zealand, South Africa, and Canada to set forth the theory that elites who fear losing political power establish judicial review to protect through the judiciary values they can no longer advance through the political process.[81] Making causal claims, however, requires careful case selection. We refer to Linos's contribution for a discussion of relevant selection techniques, such as the use of most-similar and most-different cases, and the use of critical and deviant cases.[82]

Further methodological pressure on comparative law has come from economists who have taken the field's classic legal families and examined their impact on outcomes such as economic growth, the structure and equity of debt markets, judicial independence, and the content and quality of corporate law.[83] This body of research

77. *Id.* at 43.

78. *Id.* at 49. *See also* Saul Levmore, *Rethinking Comparative Law: Variety and Uniformity in Ancient and Modern Tort Law*, 61 TULANE L. REV. 235 (1986).

79. Deeks, *supra* note 21.

80. Linos, *supra* note 52, at 39.

81. HIRSCHL, *supra* note 73.

82. Linos, *supra* note 52.

83. *See, e.g.,* Rafael La Porta et al., *Law and Finance*, 106 J. POL. ECON. 1113 (1998); Paul G. Mahoney, *The Common Law and Economic Growth: Hayek Might Be Right*, 30 J. LEG. STUD. 503 (2001). For an

has resulted in calls for "large-sample, quantitative research design" in comparative law.[84] While the quantitative approach has by no means replaced traditional
methods,[85] large-N research designs are becoming more common. Mathias Siems's
2014 comparative law textbook devotes an entire chapter to numerical approaches,
and Holger Spamann recently announced the field of "empirical comparative law."[86]
Examples of this new empirical scholarship include (re-)coding and classifying
legal systems as well as mapping the extent to which higher courts cite each other.[87]
Comparative constitutional law has also seen a wave of large-N studies that map
global developments and (to varying degrees) rely on social science methods to
make causal claims.[88]

Likewise, comparative international law inquiries could benefit from the use of
large-N samples and statistical analysis in appropriate cases. Such research designs
are particularly useful in systematically mapping differences and similarities across
a large number of legal systems, evaluating how common a practice is, and showing how it has changed over time. Verdier and Versteeg introduce an original data
set for 101 countries for the period 1815–2013 that captures numerous features of
national approaches to international law, including treaty-making procedures, the
status of treaties, and the reception of customary international law. It is only because
they study a large number of systems over time that they are able to show several
long-term trends, such as the increase in legislative approval requirements for ratification of more treaties in more countries, the increasing prevalence of direct
application and hierarchical superiority of treaties over domestic statutes, and the
subordination of customary international law to domestic legislation.[89]

Quantitative approaches can also be useful to explore possible explanations
for observed similarities and differences through the use of regression analysis.[90]

---

overview of the voluminous literature spurred by this research agenda, see Rafael La Porta et al., *The Economic Consequences of Legal Origins*, 46 J. ECON. LIT. 285 (2008).

84. Holger Spamann, *Large-Sample, Quantitative Research Designs for Comparative Law?*, 57 AM. J. COMP. L. 797 (2009). *See also* Mathias Siems, *Numerical Comparative Law: Do We Need Statistical Evidence in Order to Reduce Complexity?*, 13 CARDOZO J. INT'L & COMP. L. 521 (2005).

85. Ralf Michaels, *Comparative Law by Numbers? Legal Origins Thesis, Doing Business Reports and the Silence of Traditional Comparative Law*, 57 AM. J. COMP. L. 765 (2009).

86. SIEMS, *supra* note 46, ch. 7; *see also* Spamann, *supra* note 70. A similar development is taking place in international law. *See* Gregory Schaffer & Tom Ginsburg, *The Empirical Turn in International Legal Scholarship*, 106 AM. J. INT'L L. 12 (2012).

87. *See, e.g.*, Martin Gelter & Mathias Siems, *Networks, Dialogue or One-Way Traffic? An Empirical Analysis of Cross-Citations Between Ten of Europe's Highest Courts*, 8 UTRECHT L. REV. 88, 98 (2012); Martin Gelter & Mathias Siems, *Language, Legal Origins, and Culture Before the Courts: Cross-Citations Between Supreme Courts in Europe*, 21 SUP. CT. ECON. REV. 215, 215 (2013).

88. *See, e.g.*, ZACHARY ELKINS ET AL., THE ENDURANCE OF NATIONAL CONSTITUTIONS (2009).

89. Verdier & Versteeg, *supra* note 24.

90. *But see* Spamann, *supra* note 70 (expressing skepticism of the ability of empirical comparative studies to make causal claims).

Regression analysis allows researchers to examine the relationship between two variables of interest while controlling for confounding factors. For example, one can explore the relationship between national treaty ratification procedures and the number of treaties a country ratifies, while holding constant other factors such as the country's level of economic development or democracy.[91] While such methods help make causal claims more plausible, regression analysis using cross-country data also raises complex methodological challenges, such as controlling for unobservable confounding factors and establishing the direction of causation.[92]

However, it is worth emphasizing that large-N studies do not necessarily require the use of statistical methods: as illustrated by the Verdier and Versteeg chapter, the systematic mapping of differences and similarities can be illuminating in its own right, painting a larger picture that could not be discerned from traditional qualitative case studies. Likewise, Tomer Broude, Yoram Haftel, and Alexander Thompson conduct a large-N analysis of how states have renegotiated investor-state dispute settlement provisions in their investment agreements over time, providing an overall picture of the substantive trends and of cross-regional variations that can inform legal analysis and policy debates.[93] Chris McCrudden's extensive analysis of domestic court decisions interpreting and applying CEDAW, although not quantitative in nature, shows how a large-N sample can reveal meaningful similarities and differences in national approaches.[94]

IV. EXPLAINING SIMILARITIES AND DIFFERENCES

As noted above, once similarities and differences have been identified, a further step for comparative international law analyses is to explain them. Indeed, an important objective of this volume is to encourage scholars to move beyond traditional descriptive accounts and toward articulating and supporting hypotheses to explain similarities and differences in how international law is understood, interpreted, applied, and approached by different actors. To this end, this section introduces several explanatory accounts that may assist in such efforts. These accounts are general in nature, and as such do not provide ready-made explanations for any specific case. However, because they emphasize different actors and mechanisms, their central ideas can be deployed as the building blocks for theoretically coherent and empirically validated accounts of cases or issue-areas of interest to comparative international law.[95]

---

91. *See* Pierre-Hugues Verdier & Mila Versteeg, Domestic Law and the Credibility of Treaty Commitments (working paper 2017).

92. *See* Spamann, *supra* note 70 (discussing these challenges).

93. Tomer Broude, Yoram Z. Haftel & Alexander Thompson, *Who Cares About Regulatory Space in BITs? A Comparative International Approach* (this volume).

94. McCrudden, *supra* note 19; Verdier and Versteeg, *supra* note 24.

95. It goes without saying that these explanations are not exhaustive, not is our classification the only possible one. In his chapter, Daniel Abebe proposes theoretical conjectures about comparative international law arising from three schools of international relations theory: realism, institutionalism, and liberalism—a classification that in some respects overlaps with, and in others departs from,

A. Geopolitical Factors

A first set of explanatory factors is geopolitical in nature. In such accounts, the interpretation and application of international law may vary along the lines of power
divides and competitive relationships in the international system. In the past two
decades, analyses of the effect of power dynamics on international law emphasized
the hegemonic role of the United States.[96] More recently, as the "unipolar moment"
has receded, scholars have turned to analyzing the effect of shifting power configurations on international law. Thus, Paul Stephan proposes:

> [A] powerful state will seek to impose its own version of international law. If
> the international system contains multiple great powers, each will offer up a
> distinct and competing version of the subject. Symmetry in power promotes
> selectivity in international law. As a corollary, a single superpower will pro-
> vide an exclusive vision, even if its claims face a critical response and calls for
> reform. Asymmetry in power promotes universality in international law.[97]

He contends that in periods with two or more great powers (more symmetry),
such as during the Cold War, it is possible to recognize greater selectivity—and
more comparativism—in the approach of great powers to international law.[98] By
contrast, in the 1990s, the emergence of the United States as a unipolar power
(greater asymmetry) coincided with attempts to project a more universal—and
less comparative—theory of international law. In a similar vein, Roberts argues
that comparative international law was more salient when the two Cold War super-
powers held conflicting visions of international law, and is likely to rise again as the
world moves into a period of greater multipolarity.[99]

The effect of shifting power configurations on international law is attracting
increasing attention. Scholars such as Congyan Cai and William Burke-White
have outlined the ways in which international law is likely to change as Old Great
Powers, namely Europe and the United States, decline and New Great Powers,
including Brazil, China, India, and Russia, emerge.[100] Lauri Mälksoo has studied

the one we propose below. Daniel Abebe, *Why Comparative International Law Needs International
Relations Theory* (this volume).

96. *See, e.g.,* UNITED STATES HEGEMONY AND THE FOUNDATIONS OF INTERNATIONAL LAW
(Georg Nolte & Michael Byers eds., 2003); Nico Krisch, *International Law in Times of Hegemony:
Unequal Power and the Shaping of the International Legal Order*, 16 EUR. J. INT'L L. 369 (2005).

97. Paul B. Stephan, *Symmetry and Selectivity: What Happens in International Law When the World
Changes*, 10 CHI. J. INT'L L. 91, 107 (2009).

98. Similarly, Anu Bradford and Eric Posner identify the European Union, China, and the United
States as international law powerhouses that promote distinct interpretations of international law
based on their own preferences. *See* Bradford & Posner, *supra* note 9.

99. Roberts, *supra* note 13.

100. Congyan Cai, *New Great Powers and International Law in the 21st Century*, 24 EUR. J. INT'L L.
755 (2013); William W. Burke-White, *Power Shifts in International Law: Structural Realignment and
Substantive Pluralism*, 56 HARV. INT'L L.J. 1 (2015).

how Russian approaches to international law have changed since the end of the Cold War and the dissolution of the USSR.[101] A number of commentators are now focusing on Chinese and/or Russian approaches to international law and how these differ from Western conceptions or approaches.[102] These analyses draw on developments in state practice, such as the "Declaration of the Russian Federation and the People's Republic of China on the Promotion of International Law" issued in June 2016.[103]

The diversity of approaches within this tradition makes it difficult to articulate general features, but two recurring themes can be identified. First, geopolitical explanations give a central place to the role of power relationships in explaining similarities and differences in approaches to international law. Power-based explanations feature in the work of those working in the "realist" tradition of international relations, but also in Critical Legal Studies and historical analyses of the international system. Second, scholars within this tradition often focus on states (or geopolitical blocks of states) as the central unit of analysis, downplaying the role of substate actors (such as national courts) and nonstate actors (such as academics and NGOs). To the extent they include an analysis of substate actors, these may be viewed as "national actors seeking to create and shape international norms"[104] to advance their state's interests rather than as independent actors faithfully implementing international legal rules. Third, geopolitics implies the persistence of the boundary between international law and domestic law, both formally (through dualist doctrines) and informally (through doctrines that avoid engagement with international law when important state interests are involved).[105] Finally, geopolitical approaches tend to regard state interests as generally consistent and stable, which suggests that differences in approaches to international rules and doctrines—and to international law in general—are likely to be persistent, shifting only when the balance of power of the system as a whole shifts.

101. Lauri Mälksoo, *The History of International Legal Theory in Russia: A Civilizational Dialogue with Europe*, 19 EUR. SOC'Y INT'L L. 211 (2008); LAURI MÄLKSOO, RUSSIAN APPROACHES TO INTERNATIONAL LAW (2015).

102. *See, e.g.*, Anthea Roberts, *Crimea and the South China Sea: Connections and Disconnects Among Chinese, Russian and Western International Lawyers* (this volume); Anne Peters, *After Trump: China and Russia Move from Norm-Takers to Shapers of the International Legal Order*, EJIL: Talk! (Nov. 10, 2016), http://www.ejiltalk.org/after-trump-china-and-russia-move-from-norm-takers-to-shapers-of-the-international-legal-order/; Lauri Mälksoo, *Russia and China Challenge the Western Hegemony in the Interpretation of International Law*, EJIL: Talk! (Jul. 15, 2016), http://www.ejiltalk.org/russia-and-china-challenge-the-western-hegemony-in-the-interpretation-of-international-law/; Ingrid Wuerth, *China, Russia, and International Law*, LAWFARE (Jul. 11, 2016), https://www.lawfareblog.com/china-russia-and-international-law.

103. The Declaration of the Russian Federation and the People's Republic of China on the Promotion of International Law (June 25, 2016), http://www.mid.ru/en/foreign_policy/position_word_order/-/asset_publisher/6S4RuXfeYlKr/content/id/2331698.

104. Roberts, *supra* note 8, at 60.

105. *See* Benvenisti, *Reclaiming Democracy*, *supra* note 12.

B. Domestic Institutions and Politics

Another set of explanations draws attention to domestic institutions and politics. In such accounts, the principal unit of analysis shifts from the unitary state to the multiple domestic institutions—including courts, legislatures, executives, and regulatory agencies—that engage with international law.[106] At an institutional level, this approach requires examination of the fundamental structural features of the relevant legal system, such as constitutional rules that govern the reception of international law and allocate responsibility for interpreting and applying it.[107] At a political level, this approach requires consideration of the incentives and constraints that shape the relationship of domestic institutions with international law, and how they may affect the interpretation and application of international rules.[108] Several contributions, such as those by Cope and Movassagh, Deeks, Goldenziel, and Jain, reflect on how domestic incentives and constraints may shape how different arms of government engage with international law.[109]

For example, at an institutional level, "dualist" legal systems that present the domestic legislature with an opportunity to introduce interpretations or modifications to international obligations when adopting implementing legislation may tend to produce more competing interpretations of international law.[110] By contrast, "monist" legal systems where courts are empowered to interpret and apply international laws directly may produce more convergence, as courts may be less likely to introduce political considerations in their reasoning and more likely to follow precedent set by international and foreign cases.[111] Beyond these formal institutional

---

106. This is a central theme of the "liberal" school of international relations theory. *See* Andrew Moravcsik, *Liberal Theories in International Law, in* INTERDISCIPLINARY PERSPECTIVES ON INTERNATIONAL LAW AND INTERNATIONAL RELATIONS: THE STATE OF THE ART (Jeffrey L. Dunoff & Mark A. Pollack eds., 2012).

107. *See* Verdier & Versteeg, *supra* note 24; Stephan, *supra* note 26. More generally, this work overlaps to some extent with the emerging field of comparative foreign relations law, which is being developed by scholars such as Curtis Bradley, Karen Knop, and Campbell McLachlan. *See* CAMPBELL MCLACHLAN, FOREIGN RELATIONS LAW (2014); Curtis Bradley's project on "Comparative Foreign Relations Law and Democratic Accountability," supported by a Carnegie Fellowship; and Karen Knop's new course at University of Toronto entitled "Foreign Affairs and the Canadian Constitution," which according to the syllabus aimed at "help[ing] to inaugurate foreign affairs and the Canadian constitution as a field of legal inquiry in Canada."

108. Oona A. Hathaway, *Between Power and Principle: An Integrated Theory of International Law*, 72 U. CHI. L. REV. 469 (2005).

109. Jain, *supra* note 36; Deeks, *supra* note 21; Goldenziel, *supra* note 19; Cope & Movassagh, *supra* note 22.

110. Cope & Movassagh, *supra* note 22.

111. *See* Eyal Benvenisti & George W. Downs, *National Courts, Domestic Democracy, and the Evolution of International Law*, 20 EUR. J. INT'L L. 59 (2009). These ideas have affinities with earlier theories, such as George Scelle's notion of "dédoublement fonctionnel" under which domestic judges play a dual role as national and international officials when interpreting and applying international law. Antonio Cassese, *Remarks on Scelle's Theory of Role Splitting (dedoublement fonctionnel) in International Law*, 1 EUR. J. INT'L L. 210 (1990).

differences, political incentives and constraints may also play an important role. For instance, domestic courts that benefit from effective independence from the political branches of government may be more faithful implementers of international law than politicized courts, so that consistency is more likely among states with independent courts.[112]

While this type of analysis has primarily focused on domestic courts, scholars should not neglect the role of executives or legislatures. Legislatures have an important role in implementing treaty obligations, especially in dualist systems or where non-self-executing treaties are concerned.[113] Executives are often required to interpret international law in the realm of executive powers, such as warfare, national security, and international affairs.[114] Executives and legislatures thus routinely engage with international law, and, as with courts, their incentive structures are likely to vary in predictable ways across countries. For example, legislatures and executives in parliamentary systems are subject to different incentives and constraints than those in presidential systems, and legislatures and executives in proportional representation systems with grand coalitions are likely to be subject to different incentives and constraints than those that operate in first-past-the-post systems.[115] Likewise, regulatory agencies may attempt to use international standard-setting to increase their independence or discretion from their political principals.[116]

Beyond these examples, several other features of legal systems may affect the interpretation and application of international law. As noted above, at a general level, different legal traditions may differ in their approaches to international law. At a more specific level, different legal systems may privilege different interpretive approaches (textual, systematic, intent-based, teleological) in the domestic context, and may tend to apply their favored approach to the interpretation of treaties—perhaps disregarding ostensibly uniform interpretive rules provided by the Vienna Convention on the Law of Treaties (VCLT).[117] Indeed, a recent edited volume on VCLT usage finds that most domestic courts do not explicitly rely on the VCLT principles of treaty interpretation, although most domestic approaches are

---

112. *See, e.g.,* Yonatan Lupu, *Best Evidence: The Role of Information in Domestic Judicial Enforcement of International Human Rights Agreements,* 67 INT'L ORG. 469 (2013) (finding that countries with independent courts implement the International Covenant on Civil and Political Rights more successfully).

113. Cope & Movassagh, *supra* note 22.

114. *See* Deeks, *supra* note 21.

115. On the incentives of legislatures, see Cope & Movassagh, *supra* note 22.

116. *See* Pierre-Hugues Verdier, *The Political Economy of International Financial Regulation,* 88 IND. L.J. 1405 (2013).

117. Vienna Convention on the Law of Treaties art. 31–33, May 23, 1969, 1155 U.N.T.S. 331 [hereinafter VCLT]. *See* Helmut Phillip Aust, Alejandro Rodiles & Peter Staubach, *Unity or Uniformity? Domestic Courts and Treaty Interpretation,* 27 LEIDEN J. INT'L L. 75 (2014); INTERPRETATION OF INTERNATIONAL LAW BY DOMESTIC COURTS (Helmut Phillip Aust & Georg Nolte eds., 2016).

nonetheless broadly consistent with these principles.[118] National constitutional traditions also differ considerably, with some more concerned about maintaining the
domestic separation of powers (or its distribution among federal units), and others
about established interpretations of rights and freedoms or the primacy of religious
law. In some legal systems—such as in Russia—there may be a strong tradition
of deference to the executive in interpreting and applying international law, with
courts taking a secondary role.[119] All of these features may help explain similarities
and differences in interpretation, application, and approaches to international law.

C. Transnational Communities and Norms

Another approach draws attention to communities that transcend national boundaries and through which norms or attitudes toward international law diffuse. The
idea that international behavior is formed in part through interactions in epistemic
communities has its roots in sociological and constructivist scholarship.[120]

A growing literature on diffusion explores empirically how norms and policies
diffuse from one country to another and tries to identify the social and political
processes at play.[121] A related strand of scholarship emphasizes the role of experts
and "disaggregated" state actors increasingly interacting with each other in the international sphere, pursuing global interests that transcend their national affiliations,
and contributing to the formation and implementation of international rules and
standards.[122] For example, scholars have studied judicial networks through which
cosmopolitan judges interact with one another and converge upon the same interpretations, which are then adopted in national court decisions.[123] Others have studied the role of "norm entrepreneurs," such as human rights activists, who mobilize
support for international normative change.[124]

---

118. Kevin L. Cope & Mila Versteeg, *Book Review: The Interpretation of International Law by Domestic Courts,* 111 Am. J. Int'l L. 538 (2017) (reviewing Interpretation of International Law by Domestic Courts, *supra* note 117).

119. *See* Mälksoo, *supra* note 36.

120. *See* Peter M. Haas, *Epistemic Communities and International Policy Coordination,* 46 Int'l Org. 1 (1992).

121. *See, e.g.,* Beth A. Simmons et al., *The Global Diffusion of Public Policies: Social Construction, Coercion, Competition, or Learning,* 33 Ann. Rev. Soc. 1, 449 (2007); Linos, *supra* note 41; Benedikt Goderis & Mila Versteeg, *The Diffusion of Constitutional Rights,* 39 Int'l Rev. L. & Econ. 1 (2014).

122. *See* Anne-Marie Slaughter, *Sovereignty and Power in a Networked World Order,* 40 Stan. J. Int'l L. 283 (2004).

123. *See* Anne-Marie Slaughter, *A Global Community of Courts,* 44 Harv. Int'l L.J. 191 (2003)

124. *See, e.g.,* Margaret E. Keck & Kathryn Sikkink, Activists Beyond Borders: Advocacy Networks in International Politics (1998); Abraham L. Newman, *Building Transnational Civil Liberties: Transgovernmental Entrepreneurs and the European Data Privacy Directive,* 62 Int'l Org. 103 (2008).

Epistemic communities are sometimes thought to be global in nature. Oscar Schachter famously described the existence of an "invisible college" of international lawyers who are "dispersed throughout the world" yet "engaged in a continuous process of communication and collaboration."[125] As Roberts and Krisch show, however, distinct national communities of international law academics exist that are frequently characterized by different legal training, publishing profiles, and professional experiences.[126] These differences may contribute to and perpetuate differences in the interpretation and application of international law within different national contexts, as evidenced by the starkly different debates within different communities of international lawyers over Russia's actions with respect to Crimea in 2014 and the legitimacy of the South China Sea arbitral award and China's reaction to it in 2016.[127]

Likewise, the social processes by which norms and practice travel across borders that are emphasized in the diffusion literature may operate more intensely among groups of states that share common characteristics, such as language, legal origins, colonial histories, ideological commitments, economic conditions, or political arrangements.[128] For example, court decisions from former colonial states may have disproportionate influence in their former colonies, due to their availability in a common language, the familiarity of their legal reasoning, and the links among their legal elites.[129] Constitution-makers borrow primarily from countries with the same legal origins, because constitution-makers are most familiar with those foreign constitutions that are written within the same legal tradition and the same language.[130] Rodiles's work on the relationship between ideas of a *ius constitutionale commune* that emerged in Europe and Latin America represents an example of such analysis.[131]

In the same vein, we might expect that countries facing specific challenges, such as encouraging foreign investment or revising their investment treaties to better protect regulatory space, may learn from and adopt the interpretations of international law advanced by similarly situated states, especially when those approaches are seen as successful. Thus, while sociological diffusion processes are often assumed

---

125. Oscar Schachter, *The Invisible College of International Lawyers*, 72 Nw. U. L. Rev. 217, 217 (1977).

126. Roberts, *supra* note 13; Krisch, *supra* note 25.

127. Roberts, *supra* note 102.

128. *See* Zachary Elkins & Beth Simmons, *On Waves, Clusters and Diffusion: A Conceptual Framework*, 598 Annals Am. Academy Pol. & Soc. Sci. 33, 43–44 (2005); Beth A. Simmons & Zachary A. Elkins, *The Globalization of Liberalization: Policy Diffusion in the International Economy*, 98 Am. Pol. Sci. Rev. 171 (2004); Benedikt Goderis & Mila Versteeg, *The Diffusion of Constitutional Rights*, 39 Int'l Rev. L & Econ. 1 (2014).

129. *See* Holger Spamann, *Contemporary Legal Transplants—Legal Families and the Diffusion of (Corporate) Law*, 2009 BYU L. Rev. 1813 (2010).

130. Goderis & Versteeg, *supra* note 128.

131. Rodiles, *supra* note 29.

to favor the development of a "world society" in which states converge on global norms and standardized patterns of behavior,[132] they may also create segmentation among different groups of states, which might result in differing approaches. For instance, Broude, Haftel, and Thompson engage in a comparative analysis of the different ways in which states have engaged in renegotiating their bilateral investment treaties, with certain modifications gaining popularity in Western Europe and others being pioneered in North America.[133] Mbengue and Schacherer's analysis of the Pan-African Investment Code provides one such example.[134]

Some national traditions may also have a disproportionate impact in shaping the approaches of various international institutions. For instance, Mathilde Cohen argues that the dual English-French language policy of a number of international courts has far-reaching consequences on which individuals work at and appear before these courts, and in which national legal cultures they are trained.[135] While she focuses on the disproportionate influence wielded by the French legal culture, others, such as Michael Bolhander, have focused on the dominant role played by Anglo-American legal sources and approaches in various international courts and tribunals.[136] Apart from the language policies of these international courts, a number of scholars have pointed to common educational backgrounds as an explanation for these patterns, given that many elite international lawyers have completed at least part of their legal education in France, the United Kingdom, or the United States.[137]

V. NORMATIVE QUESTIONS AND IMPLICATIONS

International lawyers often resist emphasizing local, national, or regional approaches because these are seen as threatening to the field's universalist assumptions and aspirations.[138] Unlike domestic law, which we might expect to differ between states,

132. *See* John W. Meyer et al., *World Society and the Nation-State*, 103 AM. J. SOC. 144, 163 (1997); John W. Meyer & Brian Rowan, *Institutionalized Organizations: Formal Structure as Myth and Ceremony*, 83 AM. J. SOC. 340 (1977); Paul J. DiMaggio & Walter W. Powell, *The Iron Cage Revisited: Institutional Isomorphism and Collective Rationality in Organizational Fields*, 48 AM. SOC. REV. 147, 147–60 (1983).

133. Broude, Haftel & Thompson, *supra* note 93.

134. Mbengue & Schacherer, *supra* note 18.

135. Mathilde Cohen, *On the Linguistic Design of Multinational Courts: The French Capture*, 14 I•CON 498, 501 (2016); Mathilde Cohen, *The Continuing Impact of French Legal Culture on the International Court of Justice* (this volume).

136. Michael Bohlander, *Language, Culture, Legal Traditions, and International Criminal Justice*, 12 J. INT'L CRIM. JUST. 491 (2014); Michael Bohlander & Mark Findlay, *The Use of Domestic Sources as a Basis for International Criminal Law Principles*, 2 GLOB. COMMUNITY Y.B. INT'L L. & JURISPRUDENCE 3 (2002).

137. *See, e.g.,* Gleider I. Hernandez, *On Multilingualism and the International Legal Process, in* 2 SELECT PROCEEDINGS OF THE EUROPEAN SOCIETY OF INTERNATIONAL LAW 441 (Hélène Ruiz Fabri, Rüdiger Wolfrum & Jana Gogolin eds., 2010); ROBERTS, *supra* note 13.

138. *See* Kennedy, *supra* note 38.

international law is often premised on an assumption that it is a common law that binds all states. Highlighting national differences might be seen as running the risk of undermining the existence and unity of international law, potentially resulting in an excessive focus on the particular in a way that obscures the general.[139] In addition, many of the concepts that international lawyers celebrate rest on universalist ideologies, such as human rights and the rule of law.[140] Recognizing differences between national approaches to these issues might undermine claims to universality in these areas.

However, we believe that comparative international law should not be understood as having an implicit normative agenda or predetermined ideological commitments, for three reasons. First, comparative international law inquiries involve studies looking for both *similarities* and *differences*. In some cases, cross-national comparisons can highlight a lack of divergence, as shown by Chris McCrudden's study of substantive interpretations of CEDAW adopted by different national courts.[141] Such studies are important because they can provide a useful check on the tendency of commentators to focus on a handful of high profile cases of disagreement and dialogue that might not be representative of the greater universe of cases where common approaches or a lack of cross-national contestation may pass unremarked.

Second, because international law is often premised on an assumption of uniformity, many comparative international law studies will focus on examples of divergence that test the field's prevailing self-image. But such inquiries are not necessarily premised on a normative assumption that divergence is good or that all interpretations of international law are equally valid. Many comparative international law studies are descriptive or explanatory in nature; they seek to identify and account for differences without celebrating or validating them. One can note different interpretations of international law, but still conclude that some are more or less persuasive under international law's interpretive framework or according to a particular normative framework. International law also has its own mechanisms for working out how to respond to divergent interpretations and practices, as explored by Forteau's contribution on the ILC's strategies for codifying and progressively developing the law.[142]

Similar fears were expressed about the threat of international law's fragmentation in the 1990s and early 2000s, but the international system has learned to live with some degree of divergence without descending into crisis.[143] Instead of ignoring

---

139. *See* Forteau, *supra* note 15.

140. Bruce G. Carruthers & Terence C. Halliday, *Negotiating Globalization: Global Scripts and Intermediation in the Construction of Asian Insolvency Regimes*, 31 LAW & SOC. INQUIRY 521, 546 (2006).

141. McCrudden, *supra* note 19.

142. Forteau, *supra* note 15.

143. Rep. of the Int'l Law Comm'n, 58th Sess., May 1–June 9, July 3–Aug. 11, 2006, U.N. Doc. A/ 61/10; GAOR, 61st Sess., Supp. No. 10 (2006).

differences, comparative international law projects examine when similarities and differences arise and prompts questions about how international lawyers should approach them. Given the decentralized nature of international law, some differences should be expected. And given that international law is often based on the actions and interpretations of states, differences may prove helpful in spurring its evolution over time. Moving past the assumption of universality in order to look at the facts on the ground is not the same as endorsing an "anything goes" approach. Nor does it involve any sort of prejudgment about how international law or international lawyers should respond to differences or similarities that they observe.

Third, comparative international law studies are not ideologically committed to supporting the agenda of international law's left or right. This can be seen in some of the early writers who have explored the idea of comparative international law, who hail from both the right (such as Eric Posner) and the left (such as David Kennedy). Realist scholars and Critical Legal Scholars have in common a desire to look behind the law to uncover power dynamics that privilege certain actors and their preferred interpretations. While realist scholars tend to celebrate these power differentials as providing the key to understanding international law as an apology for state power, Critical Legal Scholars often highlight them as a part of a call to disrupt and counter these power differentials in the name of pursuing a different world order.

For instance, Anu Bradford and Eric Posner explore the idea of comparative international law as part of a claim that all powerful states and entities engage in exceptionalist behavior with respect to international law.[144] In seeking to counter the notion of American exceptionalism, they highlight the existence of European and Chinese exceptionalism as a way of normalizing and legitimizing US exceptionalism. They argue that international law is best understood as an overlapping consensus of the otherwise "exceptional" views of the great powers, which would mean that it has a small, core content, outside of which conflicting views exist. This example of comparative international law scholarship sits squarely within the realm of realism and can be readily associated with new sovereigntist attempts to limit the scope of international law.

At the other end of the political spectrum, Critical Legal Scholars, such as Martti Koskenniemi and David Kennedy, and scholars who adopt Third World Approaches to International Law, such as Antony Anghie and B.S. Chimni, engage in comparative international law scholarship when they emphasize how the universalist rhetoric of international law masks its Western, and largely European, origins.[145] For instance, Koskenniemi highlights the Eurocentrism of international law, arguing that the "view that there is a single, universal international law with a homogeneous history and an institutional-political project emerges from a profoundly Eurocentric view of the world."[146] Anghie, meanwhile, draws attention to the importance of the

---

144. Bradford and Posner, *supra* note 9.

145. *See, e.g.,* ANTONY ANGHIE, IMPERIALISM, SOVEREIGNTY AND THE MAKING OF INTERNATIONAL LAW (2005); B.S. Chimni, *Third World Approaches to International Law: A Manifesto,* 8 INT'L CMTY. L. REV. 3 (2006).

146. Koskenniemi, *supra* note 8, at 4.

"telling of alternative histories" of international law, which include "histories of resistance to colonial power" and "history from the vantage point of peoples who were subjugated to international law."[147]

An example of using a comparative international law approach to tell alternative histories is Masaharu Yanagihara's contribution on the status of the Ryukyu Kingdom from the 1600s to the 1800s, in which he compares two concepts that were commonly used in East Asia during the relevant period, "shioki" (control) and "fuyo" (dependency), with those of "sovereignty" and "independence" propagated by modern European international law.[148] He argues that East Asia had its own unique international law concepts during the relevant period and that international law should not be retroactively universalized by applying ideas developed in one region (Europe) at one time to another region (East Asia) at a different time.

Daniel Abebe's contribution further illustrates how comparative international law can accommodate a variety of normative projects.[149] In his account, acknowledging that domestic institutional design affects how states interpret and apply international law raises the prescriptive question of which interpretations should be preferred and what institutional designs should be adopted. This is where the normative dimension of international relations theories comes in. Abebe suggests that different theories—realism, institutionalism, and liberalism—point to different prescriptions, because they privilege different normative goals. Thus, comparative international law can help researchers draw connections between international relations theory and institutional design, without itself privileging particular proposals.

We have not engaged in a comparative international law project in order to further normative goals, nor should we shy away from normative questions about the costs and benefits of looking for and finding similarities and differences. For instance, Stephan argues that foreign relations law and comparative international law help to ensure that international law remains relevant to problems of international cooperation in an increasingly challenging world,[150] whereas Forteau warns of the dangers of focusing excessively on national differences in ways that overlook similarities or undermine international law's broader legitimacy.[151] It may also be that costs and benefits differ across issue-areas or types of instruments. For instance, do some treaty formulations permit greater flexibility in interpretation than others, and is this a good or bad thing in particular contexts, such as human rights law?

An example of a scholar considering such issues is Shai Dothan whose contribution focuses on examining how the European Court of Human Rights applies its margin-of-appreciation doctrine.[152] He shows that the legislative regimes and court

---

147. ANGHIE, *supra* note 145, at 6–12 (2005)

148. Masaharu Yanagihara, *"Shioki (Control)," "Fuyo (Dependency)," and Sovereignty: The Status of the Ryukyu Kingdom in Early-Modern and Modern Times* (this volume).

149. Abebe, *supra* note 95.

150. Stephan, *supra* note 26.

151. Forteau, *supra* note 15.

152. Dothan, *supra* note 19.

decisions in different states evidence diverging approaches to the voting rights of prisoners, and that these differences can be traced to fundamentally different conceptions about the right to vote. Dothan shows how the European Court of Human Rights invokes the Emerging Consensus doctrine as a mechanism for balancing between divergence and convergence in the application of a human rights treaty. In this way, he demonstrates a link between comparative international law and the approaches adopted by international courts, and in the process raises important questions about whether and when international courts should bridge differences or permit them to subsist.

Another example is Alec Knight's examination of the way in which the CEDAW Committee tolerates certain minority views about the meaning of the Convention and not others. He finds that the CEDAW Committee permits, if not encourages, Scandinavian feminist states to adopt interpretations of CEDAW that go beyond the margin of appreciation in a politically progressive direction, while simultaneously criticizing predominantly Muslim states for deviations from the text that seek to bend the Convention in a politically conservative direction.[153] This asymmetric approach raises questions about whether deviation should be permitted when it is seen as progressively developing a treaty rather than attempting to regressively limit its application. As this chapter and others show, the field of comparative international law spurs participants to ask important normative questions, but it does not provide preordained answers to those questions.

VI. CONCLUSION

This edited collection is intentionally eclectic. It showcases a range of contributions that reflect different aspects of the comparative international law phenomenon and begins laying a theoretical and methodological foundation for this field. Conceptualizing comparative international law as a distinct field allows us to better connect the work of different scholars on different continents and across different generations and to focus greater attention on the field's historical evolution and future trajectory. In particular, situating the current surge in comparative work in the context of a longer tradition allows us to consider how it can—and often does—innovate, for example, by considering a more diverse array of countries and legal systems, devoting more attention to the causes and consequences of different national and regional approaches, and drawing on social sciences methods. In sum, by encouraging international law scholars to pursue comparative projects and engage with the fundamental theoretical and methodological questions they raise, we hope to further the development of comparative international law and to thereby contribute to a better understanding of international law.

153. Knight, *supra* note 17.

PART ONE

Comparative International Law and Related Fields

Comparative Politics, Foreign Relations Law, and International Relations

2

Methodological Guidance

How to Select and Develop Comparative International Law Case Studies

KATERINA LINOS*

I. INTRODUCTION

To develop arguments about international law we often must study how different countries act. For example, to assess whether a practice constitutes international custom, it is essential to understand whether the practice is widespread or rare. Similarly, to evaluate compliance with a treaty, it is very helpful to know how different governments understand its key terms. International courts, casebook and textbook authors, and other scholars often reference the practices of foreign states. International lawyers are well aware of the need of comparison. What we lack is the toolkit to select and develop these comparative analyses. As a result, our comparisons often focus on a handful of countries that share strong linguistic, cultural, legal, and political ties, which is not always analytically ideal.[1]

Where should courts, casebook authors, and researchers start their comparisons? How can we know whether we are cherry-picking examples that favor our preferred conclusions? When is it best to develop examples from countries that

* This chapter draws heavily on my piece *How to Select and Develop International Law Case Studies: Lessons from Comparative Law and Comparative Politics*, 109 Am. J. Int'l. L. 475 (2015), and includes additional examples and techniques. I thank Adam Chilton, Stavros Gadinis, Benedict Kingsbury, Aila Matanock, Alison Post, Anthea Roberts, Paul Stephan, Pierre-Hugues Verdier, and Mila Versteeg, as well as participants at the 2014 Berkeley Faculty Retreat and the 2014 Sokol Colloquium at the University of Virginia for very helpful comments. Jerome Hsiang and Melissa Carlson provided excellent research assistance.

1. For some examples, and a critique, of international courts drawing on unsystematically chosen country examples, see Neha Jain, *Comparative International Law at the ICTY: The General Principles Experiment*, 109 Am. J. Int'l L. 486 (2015) (discussing the development of general principles of law in the jurisprudence of the ICTY).

are very different from one's own, and when should one focus on similar ones? How should one define similarity? And finally, which aspects of foreign systems are most relevant for particular inquiries? The fields of comparative law and comparative politics have made tremendous progress on each of these questions. This chapter synthesizes their key findings, and applies them to fundamental questions in international law.

International lawyers recognize three main sources of legal authority: treaties, custom, and general principles.[2] Cross-country comparisons are deeply embedded in the very definitions of two of these three sources. To establish international custom, an international lawyer must show that a very broad range of states consistently engages in a certain practice out of a sense of legal obligation. To establish a general principle, an international lawyer must show that it is "recognized by civilized nations"; in practice this requires that the principle be found in diverse legal families. Treaty interpretation does not necessitate cross-country comparison as a matter of definition: in theory, the text of the treaty itself could provide the requisite answers. However, in practice, international and domestic courts are frequently faced with ambiguous treaty terms. To interpret them, they often turn to the jurisprudence of states, and to subsequent state practice,[3] thus, implicitly, beginning a comparative inquiry. In sum, comparative international law is useful for identifying and applying international law, as this volume's Introduction explains.

But international law scholars often take on additional tasks: we seek to establish not only what international law is as a matter of current doctrine, but also try to assess how it operates in practice, and what directions it should take in the future. Cross-national comparisons are also critical in performing these tasks, and are needed both to evaluate important enforcement and implementation challenges and to design reform alternatives. After all, international rules and institutions are intended to govern conduct in many countries that face diverse challenges.

Traditional legal training provides important rules on how to choose and analyze cases. But these traditional rules aim to focus lawyers' attention on cases and propositions that have a high degree of legal authority within a domestic legal system. These traditional rules can be less helpful, and even misleading, to international lawyers seeking to make either doctrinal claims involving cross-country generalizations, or causal inferences about how law interacts with economic and social forces. For example, traditional legal training prompts a lawyer to ask whether the case comes from a lower court or a higher court. The higher the court, the greater the domestic authority it has, and thus the more relevant the case is likely to be to the development of a doctrinal argument within the particular jurisdiction. However, while cases from higher courts are more authoritative legally than cases from lower courts, they are also subject to much stronger selection biases, as George Priest and

---

2. Statute of the International Court of Justice art. 38, June 26, 1945, 33 U.N.T.S. 993. As a subsidiary source, "judicial decisions and the teachings of the most highly qualified publicists *of the various nations*" can be used (emphasis added).

3. Vienna Convention on the Law of Treaties art. 31(3)(b), May 23, 1969, 1155 U.N.T.S. 331.

Benjamin Klein have famously argued.[4] That is, because only a subset of parties have the willingness, the resources, and, sometimes, the legal right or court permission to appeal a case after having lost, it is likely that cases before high courts are atypical. Cases before higher courts are more likely to involve novel issues, issues over which there is significant uncertainty, and at least one well-resourced party. If a principle of law is well established in a country, it is likely to be rarely litigated, and when litigated, unlikely to be appealed all the way to the country's highest court. International lawyers seeking to establish international custom or general principles of law are often looking for such well-established principles. So a first idea might be to look beyond the case law of a country's highest court to locate such well-established rules.

Traditional legal training also leads us to ask which jurisdiction the case comes from. But while lawyers know that cases from one's home jurisdiction are likely to have greater authority than cases from other jurisdictions before domestic courts, we often receive little training in how to select among foreign cases. To conduct cross-country comparisons, international lawyers usually turn to a handful of familiar jurisdictions. In a study of international law casebooks and textbooks from around the world, Anthea Roberts highlights that citations to foreign cases in very different countries, including casebooks and textbooks from Australia and South Africa, but also France and China focus overwhelmingly on two English-speaking jurisdictions: the United States and the United Kingdom.[5] Cases from other rich Western courts, notably France, Israel, and Canada, also elicited a good number of citations, but citations to cases from outside the West were extremely rare.[6] There are certainly plausible sociological explanations for these patterns, such as the importance of case law in the common law tradition, and the centrality of the United States and the United Kingdom in the legal training of academics from around the world. However, these citation patterns are at odds with international law principles that call for surveys of a broad range of countries—not comparisons of a handful of similarly situated states. The tendency to cite predominantly to a handful of rich Western democracies is not limited to the authors of international law casebooks and textbooks: both domestic US courts,[7] and even European regional courts[8] show similar, though somewhat less pronounced, biases.

Likewise, focusing on similar countries to assess claims about how international law operates in practice and what alternatives might work better is also likely to lead to inferential errors. At the most basic level, focusing on one part of the world can lead us to miss important problems that crop up in different regions of the world,

4. George L. Priest & Benjamin Klein, *The Selection of Disputes for Litigation*, 13 J. LEGAL STUD. 1 (1984).

5. ANTHEA ROBERTS, IS INTERNATIONAL LAW INTERNATIONAL? (2017).

6. *Id.*

7. David Zaring, *The Use of Foreign Decisions by Federal Courts: An Empirical Analysis*, 3 J. EMPIRICAL LEGAL STUD. 297 (2006).

8. Erik Voeten, *Borrowing and Nonborrowing Among International Courts*, 39 J. LEGAL STUD. 547 (2010).

and to ignore promising solutions that have been tried out elsewhere. But social scientists argue that case selection can bias research answers in unexpected ways as well. For example, if one didn't select cases on the basis of familiarity and convenience, but chose instead to concentrate on instances of success or failure, this too could easily lead to wrong answers.[9]

This mismatch between international law rules and social science methodologies that require systematic cross-country comparisons, and the actual citation patterns of international law textbooks, domestic courts, and even international courts, is cause for consternation. To date, international lawyers have proposed two types of solutions. The first involves changing fundamental international law rules to simplify the comparative exercise. For example, the International Law Association's Committee on Formation of Customary International Law has proposed that the very definition of custom be changed, so that lawyers will only have to establish one fact, rather than two, about any jurisdiction. This proposal suggests that we should redefine custom by studying state practice alone, rather than also having to document *opinio juris*—states' subjective beliefs that particular practices are required by law.[10] The second type of approach—which I call the brute force approach—involves adding more country cases and moving from the United States and the United Kingdom to 10, 20, or even 30 or 40 examples. This second approach is time-consuming, and often unconvincing as there is no guarantee that additional cases that are unsystematically selected will allow us to confirm or disconfirm important principles.

Where should authors, courts, and researchers start their comparisons? How can they know whether they are cherry-picking examples that favor their preferred conclusions? When is it best to develop examples from countries that are very different from one's own, and when should one focus on cases that are very similar? How should one define similarity? And finally, which aspects of foreign systems are most relevant for particular inquiries? The fields of comparative law and comparative politics have made tremendous progress on each of these questions. This chapter synthesizes their key findings, and applies them to fundamental questions in international law. The goal of this chapter is to briefly present ideas that are very well developed in other fields, and to illustrate why they might prove useful to the development of international law claims. The interested reader can then turn to the cited works for a more extensive treatment of techniques that seem potentially useful.

The ideas that follow have much in common with principles that the empirical legal studies movement has brought to the legal academy in the last few years. But because the empirical legal studies movement has primarily focused on US law (and been predominantly quantitative), it is helpful to highlight some comparative advantages of cross-national research. Today, cross-national research is both quantitative and qualitative; the two sets of techniques have distinct advantages, and are

9. Barbara Geddes, *How the Cases You Choose Affect the Answers You Get: Selection Bias in Comparative Politics*, 2 POL. ANALYSIS 131 (1990).

10. International Law Association, London Conference, Final Report of the Committee, Statement of Principles Applicable to the Formation of General Customary International Law 33–34 (2000).

often best employed in combination. Quantitative methods can be especially useful to establish how common a practice is, to test general claims that apply over a broad range of cases, and to identify how much a particular factor contributes to an outcome of interest.[11] Qualitative techniques, on the other hand, may be better suited to the development and testing of mid-range theories that seek to develop causal mechanisms that apply under particular conditions.[12] For legal scholars interested in policy-relevant work, the advantages of qualitative research can thus be significant. For one, policymakers are often not looking for general theories, but rather for mid-range claims they can apply to the problem at hand. For another, regulators must often act quickly on the basis of very limited information; waiting for the accumulation of large amounts of information suitable to quantitative analysis is often too slow. In turn, comparative techniques are essential for international lawyers, both because fundamental international law doctrines require comparative analysis and because any international agreement is likely to function better if its drafters have some sense of whether it will be workable in diverse contexts. More generally, looking beyond a single country's domestic laws can greatly help with the identification of very diverse regulatory options, and with an assessment of their costs and benefits.

The rest of this chapter explores how one might seek to identify particularly helpful cases to develop and test generalizations and theories, and which aspects of these cases one might want to highlight. For now, I structure the analysis around two tasks that are central to the development of international law doctrine and research: selecting the appropriate country cases depending on one's research goal, and analyzing these cases to make doctrinal and also social-scientific claims.

II. SELECTING CASES TO ESTABLISH GENERALITY

Establishing that a practice is commonplace among diverse legal systems is critical to the development of claims about international custom and general principles of law. It can also be very helpful for the purpose of treaty interpretation, and the development of claims linking international law doctrine to diverse domestic societies. At the same time, establishing that many countries' legal systems share a feature or flaw is very difficult. For one, the amount of research necessary to canvas approximately 200 sovereign states' legal systems is enormous. And even if one had all this data at one's fingertips, complicated differences in countries' legal architectures would make it hard to figure out exactly what to look for, and what legal rules to consider sufficiently similar. Two concepts that have been extensively refined in social science and comparative law analysis, sampling and functional analysis respectively, can prove very useful to international lawyers.

Practicing lawyers, legal academics, and casebook and textbook authors might choose to include cases from different countries for a variety of reasons, including

11. *See* ALEXANDER L. GEORGE & ANDREW BENNETT, CASE STUDIES AND THEORY DEVELOPMENT IN THE SOCIAL SCIENCES 19–34 (2004).

12. *Id.*

a particularly gripping set of facts, an inherently important historical conflict, or a clearly written opinion. They might chose to focus on a shocking legal conclusion, or a beautiful turn of phrase. Cases selected for such reasons, however, may not be especially useful for the establishment of general patterns. Indeed, they might often be anomalous exceptions, rather than cases that help establish general rules.

This is not to say that intriguing cases, or cases one happens to be familiar with, have no analytic utility: they are critical to the generation of new ideas, and to the development of theories. That is, instead of (or in addition to) deriving a theory deductively, from first principles, a scholar might note an unusual pattern in a specific case, and perhaps even derive a set of logically connected propositions. One could go a step further, and suggest that unsystematically selected case studies could serve as plausibility probes for a theoretical claim, suggesting that it could conceivably occur under the right circumstances.[13] But to establish a general pattern, or test a theory, one usually needs to turn to additional cases, beyond the ones used to develop the theory.

How should one go about selecting additional cases to establish generality? Sometimes, relevant evidence on the entire universe of cases—approximately 200 sovereign states—is available. For example, international lawyers often turn to vote counts following General Assembly resolutions, and to treaty ratification patterns, to argue that a principle enjoys very widespread acceptance among governments, and thus constitutes international custom. This approach has the major advantage that important information on all or almost all sovereign states can be easily ascertained—thus, one need not worry much about case selection and sampling. At the same time, there are important limitations to the type of evidence voting and ratification patterns offer. For example, many international lawyers argue that while votes in the General Assembly are helpful in establishing *opinio juris*, or states' beliefs, the big gap between what states say and what states do requires much further research into state practice, the other element of the definition of international custom.[14] Moreover, on many issues that potentially constitute international custom, and on even more that potentially constitute general principles, there are few relevant resolutions and treaties. Thus, careful thinking about case selection and sampling is often required to establish both states' practices and states' beliefs.

Tireless scholarly research groups, and major international bodies, are in the process of collecting and publicizing data on important aspects of hundreds of countries' legal systems that can help fill some of these gaps.[15] For example, in this

13. Jack S. Levy, *Case Studies: Types, Designs, and Logics of Inference*, 25 CONFLICT MGMT. & PEACE SCI. 1, 6–7 (2008).

14. *See* Anthea Roberts, *Traditional and Modern Approaches to Customary International Law: A Reconciliation*, 95 AM. J. INT'L L. 757 (2001).

15. Databases international lawyers might find especially useful include the United Nations Treaty Collection, treaties.un.org (last visited Mar. 29, 2015), the Comparative Constitutions Project, comparativeconstitutionsproject.org (last visited Mar. 29, 2015), the World Bank's Doing Business Data, doingbusiness.org (last visited Mar. 29, 2015), and the Correlates of War Project, correlatesofwar.org (last visited Mar. 29, 2015). See Holger Spamann, *Empirical Comparative Law*, 11 ANN. REV. L. & SOC. SCI. 131 (2015), for a very helpful review of the quantitative literature in comparative law.

volume, Tom Ginsburg draws on existing data compiled by the United Nations to explore reservation patterns.[16] Also in this volume, Pierre-Hugues Verdier and Mila Versteeg take on an even more ambitious challenge: they compile a novel database of how different domestic systems approach international law, including treaty-making procedures, the status of treaties in domestic law, and the reception of customary international law.[17] Through a multi-year, grant-funded effort involving many coders, they have been able to complete data on over 100 (but far from the universe) of national systems. Sometimes, limiting a claim to a certain region of the world (e.g., to Europe or to Latin America) makes it possible to examine every country case. For example, in this volume, Shai Dothan surveys (almost) all members of the Council of Europe, to highlight significant variations in countries' willingness to grant the right to vote to prisoners.[18] But critical information is not yet available on countless aspects of legal systems that interest international lawyers.[19] And even if one had ample data at one's fingertips, complicated differences in countries' legal architectures would make it hard to figure out exactly what to look for, and what legal rules to consider sufficiently similar.

Three broad types of sampling strategies are commonly used: convenience sampling, random sampling, and theoretically informed sampling. Convenience sampling, as the term suggests, is perhaps the easiest technique to implement. Just as international lawyers often turn to a handful of familiar jurisdictions with easy-to-access records, so social scientists sometimes start their inquiry with respondents who are easy to contact. At the same time, while convenience sampling is the starting point for much research, it is considered the least rigorous of sampling methods, and the most likely to lead to results that lack generalizability.[20] Worries about convenience sampling are also widespread in law: here, the most publicized concern is that lawyers will cherry-pick cases that fit their predetermined conclusions.[21] To take one example, Chief Justice Roberts has famously criticized the use of foreign law in US constitutional jurisprudence by claiming that "looking to foreign law for support is like looking out over a crowd and picking out your friends."[22]

---

16. Tom Ginsburg, *Objections to Reservations: A Comparative Approach to Decentralized Interpretation* (this volume).

17. Pierre-Hugues Verdier & Mila Versteeg, *International Law in National Legal Systems: An Empirical Investigation*, 109 AM. J. INT'L L. 514 (2015) (also in this volume).

18. *See* Shai Dothan, *Comparative Views on the Right to Vote in International Law: The Case of Prisoners' Disenfranchisement* (this volume).

19. *See* Mathias Forteau, *Comparative International Law Within, Not Against, International Law: Lessons from the International Law Commission*, 109 AM. J. INT'L L. 498 (2015) (also in this volume).

20. *See, e.g.,* Martin N. Marshall, *Sampling for Qualitative Research*, 13 FAM. PRAC. 522 (1996).

21. *See, e.g.,* JEREMY WALDRON, "PARTLY LAWS COMMON TO ALL MANKIND": FOREIGN LAW IN AMERICAN COURTS 171–75 (2011).

22. *Confirmation Hearing on the Nomination of John G. Roberts Jr. to be Chief Justice of the United States Before the S. Comm. on the Judiciary*, 109th Cong. 200-01 (2005).

Random sampling involves choosing a sample of units (e.g., countries) from a larger population (e.g., the list of UN Member States) at random, so that each unit has the same probability of being chosen. This technique, used widely by quantitative social scientists, can be excellent for establishing generality with little prior knowledge of the population in question, as long as certain conditions are met. Random sampling produces some striking efficiencies: for example, it allows us to find out the opinions of hundreds of millions of Americans with a high degree of accuracy by asking only hundreds or thousands of randomly chosen respondents. Some scholars advocate for the use of random sampling in cross-country comparisons, as it has a key advantage over other types of sampling: namely, that researchers cannot cherry-pick cases that support their claims.[23]

At the same time, random sampling for cross-country research has been heavily criticized. Quantitatively oriented social scientists suggest that even if one were to draw a relatively large sample of countries at random, the types of countries that are likely to have missing data are not randomly chosen, but tend to be poorer states with less ability to keep good records, which limits one's ability to generalize.[24] Qualitatively oriented scholars point to more significant limitations of random sampling. More specifically, to develop case studies, one often has to trade breadth for depth. If one must investigate a country's legal institutions in some detail, as explained below, this might require limiting the number of countries chosen to just a handful of cases. Choosing these at random is very likely to produce a widely unrepresentative set of cases.[25]

A third technique, theoretically informed sampling, requires the researcher to choose cases in light of some knowledge of the underlying population of cases. For example, a survey researcher might want to interview enough members of different ethnic groups, a task that requires some knowledge of a society's ethnic composition.[26] Theoretically informed sampling is thus both more difficult to carry out than random sampling and more likely to allow the researcher to introduce some biases, perhaps inadvertently. At the same time, it is the preferred technique for comparative researchers, as it is likely the strongest of available alternatives.

In theoretically informed sampling, the researcher starts by defining important traits that could influence the phenomenon of interest. Legal families, geographic regions, and levels of economic development are traits likely to be important across a broad range of legal fields. Other traits are likely to be critical in particular legal fields: for example, if one wanted to investigate customary practices related to the

23. See, e.g., James D. Fearon & David D. Laitin, Integrating Qualitative and Quantitative Methods, in OXFORD HANDBOOK OF POLITICAL METHODOLOGY 758 (Janet M. Box-Steffensmeier et al. eds., 2008).

24. See, e.g., David A. Freedman, Do the N's Justify the Means?, 6 QUALITATIVE & MULTI-METHOD RES. 4 (2008).

25. See, e.g., John Gerring, Techniques for Case Selection: A Response to David Freedman, 6 QUALITATIVE & MULTI-METHOD RES. 10 (2008).

26. Theoretically informed sampling, also known as purposive sampling, bears important similarities to stratified random sampling.

law of the sea, one might also focus on whether a country is coastal or landlocked, and whether or not it has important fisheries, a large navy, and/or extensive maritime commerce.

To establish generality, the researcher would then pick country-cases that show great diversity in terms of the theoretically chosen traits. For example, one would want to make sure to include common law and civil law countries from different regions of the world as well as countries at different levels of development. Multiple countries should exist within each of the theoretically defined categories—after all, if one puts in place a theoretical scheme so complex that each sovereign state is in its own category, one loses the efficiency gains of sampling, and ends up studying the universe of states.

Theoretical and practical considerations can help the researcher select among the many countries in each theoretically defined category. For example, there might be multiple former French colonies in Africa at relatively low levels of development with relevant laws. If the researcher knows that a country experienced a set of particularly idiosyncratic legal developments, or that this country's legal records are effectively unavailable, it might make sense to pick a similar country with a more typical history and more accessible information.[27] To decide whether to study additional cases within each theoretically defined category, the scholar can consider processes such as legal transplantation. If it turns out that multiple former French African colonies copied the French legal code in a particular issue area, and have not amended it much, then multiple case studies are likely to be repetitive. If instead the area of law was subject to rapid change driven by country-specific forces, additional case studies are likely to generate valuable information. Having selected a manageable number of cases that are diverse in terms of theoretically important traits, the researcher must then analyze these, a question addressed in Sections IV and V.

III. SELECTING CASES TO ESTABLISH CAUSATION

While establishing that a practice is widespread is necessary for claims about international custom and general principles, it is not necessarily sufficient. By most accounts, these doctrines require the legal scholar to explore why it is that different countries have adopted similar rules. It is much easier to establish that a widespread practice constitutes international custom if many countries engage in this practice *because of* a sense of legal obligation, rather than for their own idiosyncratic reasons.[28] Conversely, if countries are highly varied in their rationales, and the similarity in their rules is coincidental, it will be much harder to assert that a widespread practice constitutes an international legal obligation. Causal claims are also essential

27. *See* JOHN GERRING, CASE STUDY RESEARCH (2007); Jason Seawright & John Gerring, *Case-Selection Techniques in Case Study Research: A Menu of Qualitative and Quantitative Options*, 61 POL. RES. Q. 294 (2008), for a more extensive discussion.

28. As noted *supra*, the continued relevance of *opinio juris* is debated; while the US Restatement emphasizes *opinio juris*, other authorities are more flexible. Relatedly, some scholars argue that to establish a general principle, deductive, natural-law-like reasoning is appropriate.

to the application of international (as well as domestic) law doctrine. For example, a common task in international law is to assess whether a state should be held legally responsible for a particular event—for example, whether Russia bears any responsibility for the downing of Malaysian Airlines Flight 17. To make this assessment, lawyers must develop a theory—a series of logically interconnected propositions— and identify facts relevant to each of these propositions. In the case of Malaysian Airlines Flight 17, to continue with this example, one might want to know the answers to several questions: whether pro-Russian separatists or Ukrainian soldiers operated the anti-aircraft missile that downed the plane, whether Russia trained and supplied the rebels with the missile, and what exactly the legal standard is for the attribution of conduct to a state, to name a few.[29]

Causal arguments are also needed to assess how international law operates in practice. To take one example, questions about compliance are central to international law debates because international society lacks the thick institutional infrastructure and enforcement machinery that characterizes many modern states. Theoretically interesting claims about compliance typically involve causation rather than mere correlation. For example, while it might be interesting to find out that richer states comply more frequently with international obligations than poorer states, international lawyers typically want to know why this is the case, and what can be done about it. Is it because richer states tend to have better technical knowledge and bureaucratic capacity, in which case technology transfer is critical to improving compliance?[30] Is it because richer states get to draft international rules in ways that favor their interests, and thus a redesign of international institutions is necessary?[31] Or might this correlation be entirely spurious, caused by some third factor that leads both to prosperity and to respect for legal obligations, such as British legal origin?[32]

Causation is an extensively studied topic in both law and social science, and I could not possibly hope to synthesize this literature. The paragraphs that follow have a more modest aim: to introduce to international lawyers some analytic techniques that are (1) not part of the standard legal curriculum on causation, and (2) particularly helpful in the establishment of causal claims that involve cross-country comparisons.

---

29. *See* Jens David Ohlin, *Control Matters: Ukraine & Russia and the Downing of Flight 17*, Opinio Juris (Jul. 23, 2014), http://opiniojuris.org/2014/07/23/control-matters-ukraine-russia-downing-flight-17/, for more details on this example.

30. *See, e.g.,* Abram Chayes & Antonia H. Chayes, *On Compliance*, 47 Int'l Org. 175, 175–76, 178 (1993).

31. *See, e.g.,* Nico Krisch, *International Law in Times of Hegemony: Unequal Power and the Shaping of the International Legal Order*, 16 Eur. J. Int'l L. 369 (2005).

32. *See, e.g.,* Rafael La Porta et al., *The Economic Consequences of Legal Origins*, 46 J. Econ. Lit. 285 (2008).

A. Most Different and Most Similar Cases

A good place to start is John Stuart Mill's methods of similarity and difference—they have guided much of comparative scholarship in the social sciences, and can also prove useful to the development of international law claims. Mill's method of similarity—or the comparison of most different systems—could prove very useful to international lawyers. In this technique, countries that are very different in critical respects are compared, to identify features they all share, and thus regularities about the world. The comparison of most-different systems can thus begin with modern sampling methods described in Section II above. To move from a descriptive to a causal claim, Mill suggests that one seek to find a similarity shared by these very different countries. This shared similarity then becomes a plausible causal factor. For example, international lawyers must often establish whether a certain principle constitutes international custom. If very different countries' navies refuse to capture fishing boats as prizes of war, and do so for one shared reason—their belief that international law prohibits this—this would be a paradigmatic case of international custom.[33] That said, Mill's method of similarity has important analytical limitations in a world in which the same phenomenon can have multiple causes, and the same cause can produce different effects depending on the context, and is rarely used on its own.[34]

Mills method of difference—or the comparison of most-similar systems—is more commonly used to test social scientific claims. In comparative scholarship, two countries that are similar in every way but the one that is being examined are often chosen, so that any effects can be traced back to the single, isolated difference. For example, the United States is often paired with the United Kingdom, as they share a language, the common law system, cultural similarities, a large diplomatic corps, and more. So if the United States and the United Kingdom take a radically different approach to the international law governing spying, to take one example, one can set aside language, culture, and the common law as plausible explanations for their divergence, and look for other possible causes.[35] Ashley Deeks further investigates this question in this volume.[36] The comparison of most-similar systems is analogous to the controlled comparisons underpinning multivariate regression.[37] That said, the comparison of most-similar systems also has important limitations when applied to cross-country research, as even well-matched countries typically differ in many respects. To overcome these limitations, a scholar might start with Mill's methods for case selection, and then combine these with "within-case analysis," which is discussed in Section V below.

---

33. *See* The Paquete Habana, 175 U.S. 677 (1900).

34. *See* George & Bennett, *supra* note 11.

35. Ashley Deeks, *Intelligence Communities and International Law: A Comparative Approach* (this volume).

36. *Id.*

37. *See* Gary King et al., Designing Social Inquiry 168 (1994).

B. Critical Cases, Deviant Cases, Necessary and Sufficient Cases

Another helpful conceptual tool is the focus on critical cases.[38] A critical case is one in which a hypothesis would be least likely to hold true, as a matter of theory, and would thus prove especially powerful evidence in support of the hypothesis. For example, to establish that customary international law prohibits the use of chemical weapons, one could survey the practice and *opinio juris* of hundreds of states. Indeed, the International Committee of the Red Cross has attempted to do exactly this, and thus codify international custom on the laws of war.[39] Yet even this leading study, which took almost a decade to complete, mostly drew upon a few dozen countries. Focusing on critical cases where international rules were most likely to be violated could provide a useful shortcut. For example, in the laws-of-war context, critical cases might be those that involve authoritarian states fighting total wars in which they are about to be defeated. If it turns out that even Adolf Hitler or Saddam Hussein refrained from using cost-effective weapons out of a sense that these were prohibited by international law, even when faced with the prospects of imminent and total defeat, this evidence is likely to be very helpful for the argument that international custom prohibited these weapons' use. Such evidence might well be more persuasive than a much larger number of cases of non-use of controversial weapons by democratic governments that might have their own, domestic reasons, to avoid these weapons.

Least-likely case design has been used to great effect in prominent academic scholarship. For example, in US Supreme Court scholarship, Gerald Rosenberg's *The Hollow Hope* stands out because it employs a variant of least-likely case design.[40] That is, Rosenberg analyzes two very prominent Supreme Court cases—*Roe v. Wade* and *Brown v. Board of Education*—to argue that the Court had a limited impact on public opinion and policy debates.[41] Had Rosenberg focused on cases where his argument was more plausible a priori—perhaps appellate or lower court cases on highly technical matters—it would not have generated the attention it did. Similarly, in this volume, Neha Jain uses a variant of least-likely case design to explain her focus on the Indian Supreme Court.[42] She argues that even a Court known for its openness to international law, and for landmark decisions invoking international law in both the fundamental rights and environmental arenas, in fact operates in pursuit of primarily domestic goals. This claim would have been far less interesting

---

38. *See* Harry Eckstein, *Case Studies and Theory in Political Science, in* 7 HANDBOOK OF POLITICAL SCIENCE 79–138 (Fred Greenstein & Nelson Polsby eds., 1975), for further analysis of whether a case might be more or less likely to confirm a theory.

39. JEAN-MARIE HENCKAERTS & LOUISE DOSWALD-BECK, CUSTOMARY INTERNATIONAL HUMANITARIAN LAW (2005).

40. GERALD N. ROSENBERG, THE HOLLOW HOPE: CAN COURTS BRING ABOUT SOCIAL CHANGE? (1991).

41. *Id.*

42. Neha Jain, *The Democratizing Force of International Law: Human Rights Adjudication by the Indian Supreme Court* (this volume).

if she had focused on a court people never associate with active internationalism—a court such as the US Supreme Court, for example.

Another helpful concept is that of the deviant or outlier case: this is a case that should have been especially likely to confirm a theory, but turns out to offer no evidence in its support.[43] Deviant cases, in turn, can help not only with the falsification of earlier theories, but also with the development of new theories.[44] For example, in my own work exploring why governments fail to comply promptly with EU social policy directives, I was initially convinced that conflict between employers and labor unions would explain cross-national variation, just as it explains so many domestic social policy disputes.[45] So I was very surprised when labor union leaders in countries experiencing very significant problems with directive implementation did not blame business as the main culprit for stagnant social policy.[46] Follow-on conversations helped me identify a different factor—the role of bureaucratic obstacles—as central to compliance with EU law, and allowed me to develop and test a different theory about state capabilities.

A further potentially useful principle is the formulation of necessary and sufficient conditions, though these are generating some controversy within social scientific disciplines at present. That said, if claims can be usefully formulated not in probabilistic terms, but in terms of absolute requirements, then a handful of cases can be used to confirm (and especially to disconfirm) a claim. For example, if, for the establishment of an international custom, all specially affected states must conform to a practice, focusing first on specially affected states might be a useful way to eliminate plausible customary rules that turn out not to have binding force.

After selecting country cases in a principled way, what should one look for in each country? Sections IV and V below turn to this question of case analysis.

IV. ANALYZING CASES TO ESTABLISH GENERALITY— COMPARISONS ACROSS CASES

What should one look for in different countries' laws to establish whether a practice is widespread or rare? A core—though controversial—insight from comparative law is the concept of functionalism. Functionalism begins with the idea that doctrines and rules that are formally different might all have the same function, and yield similar legal conclusions in response to the same real-world facts.[47] For

---

43. *See* Ronald Rogowski, *The Role of Theory and Anomaly in Social-Scientific Inference*, 89 Am. Pol. Sci. Rev. 467, 468 (1995).

44. *See* George & Bennett, *supra* note 11, at 20–21.

45. The power resources thesis emphasizes the role of organized labor and organized business opposition to labor in the development of modern welfare states. *See, e.g.,* David Bradley et al., *Distribution and Redistribution in Postindustrial Democracies*, 55 World Pol. 193 (2003).

46. *See* Katerina Linos, *How Can International Organizations Shape National Welfare States?: Evidence from Compliance with European Union Directives*, 40 Comp. Pol. Stud. 547, 561 (2007).

47. *See generally* Ralf Michaels, *The Functional Method of Comparative Law*, in Oxford Handbook of Comparative Law 342 (Mathias Reimann & Reinhard Zimmermann eds., 2006).

example, comparativists highlight that, while there are large formal differences between legal systems that require handover of physical possession to transfer property, and legal systems that only require the parties' consent, answers to specific fact patterns can be surprisingly similar across these diverse systems.[48] Thus, a key idea for international lawyers searching for general practices is to allow for the possibility that formally different legal rules may in fact provide very similar answers to the same problems.

A key challenge in applying functionalist analysis is the choice about the appropriate level of generality. The more generally one defines a rule or problem, the more likely one is to find functional equivalents in diverse legal systems. For example, while many comparativists view trusts and consideration to be among the most distinctive features of common law systems, other comparativists have identified their functional equivalents in the civil law.[49] That said, international lawyers are often interested in establishing generality to advance a particular type of claim, and argue, for example, that a rule is so common in domestic legal systems that it should also apply in relations between states.[50] For this purpose, rules expressed in very abstract terms are less likely to help advance international legal claims than rules phrased more precisely. Therefore, international lawyers often have strong incentives to avoid defining concepts abstractly when looking to establish a rule governing relations between states, and instead look for narrowly-defined functional analogues that are nevertheless widespread. For example, the rule that necessity, defined abstractly, can justify a breach of an international obligation, is widely accepted as international custom. However, the fact that necessity had not been specifically defined outside the context of war and natural disaster led arbitral tribunals to disagree in assessing whether Argentina's severe economic crisis in 2000–2001 met the necessity threshold, and thus justified Argentina's violations of promises made to foreign investors.[51] In short, while functional equivalents are easy to find at high levels of generality, international lawyers often have strong incentives to define concepts more specifically, in order to advance particular claims that allow or preclude specific behaviors.

Functionalist analysis faces major epistemological and normative critiques. Social scientists have extensively critiqued the assumption that functional purposes

48. See id. at 373. See also F. Vinding Kruse, What Does "Transfer of Property" Mean with Regard to Chattels? A Study in Comparative Law, 7 AM. J. COMP. L. 500 (1958).

49. See, e.g., Henry Hansmann & Ugo Mattei, The Functions of Trust Law: A Comparative Legal and Economic Analysis, 73 N.Y.U. L. REV. 434 (1998); Arthur T. von Mehren, Civil-Law Analogues to Consideration: An Exercise in Comparative Analysis, 7 AM. J. COMP. L. 500 (1959).

50. See generally BIN CHENG, GENERAL PRINCIPLES OF INTERNATIONAL LAW AS APPLIED BY INTERNATIONAL COURTS AND TRIBUNALS (2d ed. 2006).

51. Compare LG&E Energy Corp. v. Argentine Republic, ICSID Case No. ARB/02/1, Decision on Liability, ¶229, 245 (Oct. 3, 2006), and Continental Casualty Co. v. Argentine Republic, ICSID CASE No. ARB/03/9, Award, ¶168, 233 (Sep. 5, 2008) (excusing Argentina's conduct because Argentina found itself in a state of necessity), with CMS Gas Transmission Co. v. Argentine Republic, ICSID Case No. ARB/01/8, Award (May 12, 2005) (holding that the requirements of necessity had not been met).

determine the origin and persistence of institutions. And legal scholars have found some of the normative projects connected with functionalism, such as the unification of the world's legal systems, utopian at best, and highly troubling at worst.[52] At the same time, the core idea of functionalism, that we should not focus on doctrinal structures alone, but study these rules' effects and identify possible functional equivalents, is critical for international lawyers eager to identify whether particular practices are rare or widespread. Moreover, as a practical matter, major international institutions such as the World Bank,[53] the EU,[54] and the OECD[55] are resuscitating functionalist analysis, and collecting extensive data on how different countries' legal systems treat the same problems. International lawyers could thus use both the methodologies of functionalism and the newly available data to answer important questions about the generality or rarity of legal practices.

V. ANALYZING CASES TO ESTABLISH CAUSATION—WITHIN-CASE ANALYSIS OF MULTIPLE EMPIRICAL IMPLICATIONS

While case selection principles and the search for functional equivalents are useful starting points, they are unlikely to fully confirm or disconfirm a causal claim involving cross-country comparisons. This is because countries are highly idiosyncratic; it is rarely possible to construct the perfect counterfactual in which all factors but one stay the same.

Within-case analysis can be a very helpful supplementary tool. Within-case analysis requires a theoretical framework with multiple interconnected propositions, and the testing of each of these individual propositions. For example, the doctrine of general principles requires not only that a rule be found in diverse legal families, but also that rules be so fundamental to our notion of the rule of law that any country lacking them would not be considered a "civilized nation." One possible general principle is that of extinctive prescription—the notion that a claim may be extinguished if a claimant does not raise it in a timely fashion. One could start by identifying very diverse cases—as described above—and see if such a rule could be found in ancient Egypt and modern Germany as well as in tribal Afghanistan. Noting that the United States, the United Kingdom, and Canada all share the principle would be much less useful in establishing its generality. If this principle was commonly found in diverse domestic legal systems, one could then look for an additional implication of the theory of general principles—namely the legislators' intent in including such a rule. Sometimes legislative preambles will be very helpful in this task, and at other times, more research will be needed. If it turns out that different countries

---

52. See Michaels, *supra* note 47, at 343–63, for a more extensive treatment of these critiques.

53. The World Bank, Doing Business: Measuring Business Regulations, www.doingbusiness.org.

54. *See, e.g.,* THE HARMONISATION OF EUROPEAN CONTRACT LAW (Stefan Vogenauer & Stephen Weatherill eds., 2006).

55. *See, e.g.,* OECD, ANTI-CORRUPTION ETHICS AND COMPLIANCE HANDBOOK FOR BUSINESSES (2013), http://www.oecd.org/corruption/anti-corruption-ethics-and-compliance-handbook-for-business.htm.

inserted such a rule in their laws for highly idiosyncratic reasons—for example, to prevent disfavored individuals from bringing particular claims—it would be harder to argue that this constitutes a general principle of law. If instead, very different legislators saw prescription as fundamental to fairness, predictability, and stability, this would help establish prescription as a general principle. This search for multiple implications would then continue. One might want to know whether the principle of extinctive prescription is applied in similar ways to similar claims and claimants; if not, it is less likely to constitute a general principle.

The identification of multiple empirical implications depends critically on how well-theorized a concept is. If for example, custom is well-theorized in international law, while jus cogens is less fully specified, the logic of multiple empirical implications should apply more straightforwardly to the former concept.

VI. CONCLUSIONS AND NEXT STEPS

In recent years, international law scholars and practitioners have proposed diverse, novel, and important theories. To advance further, and test and refine theoretical propositions, this chapter introduces some social science techniques that may be of relevance to international lawyers. By testing claims and moving from highly general theories to mid-range theories that specify clearly under what conditions particular results obtain, scholars can do work that is both theoretically rich and more relevant to policymakers and practitioners.

This chapter outlines some useful tools to help international lawyers test whether a particular theory is supported or disconfirmed by comparative evidence. I have focused on case selection techniques, as it is here that legal scholars often get stumped—we often pick cases that are familiar to us, even when we suspect we might need to look further afield. And we try hard to select as many cases as possible—moving from two to five to twenty to a hundred, even though what we should be doing is working smarter, rather than harder, through sampling techniques. I have also focused on within-case analysis techniques, as these are the essential complement of careful case selection. That is, however carefully one matches country cases, it is very likely that they will differ on more than one critical dimension. As a result, top scholars develop theoretically interconnected propositions, and look for their implications within each country case.

This brings me to another take-away point: although this chapter has been framed as an empirical one, often what we need to better assess a theory is a better theory—a theory that is better spelled out, or a theory that is more appropriate for our goals. For example, moving from highly general theories to mid-range theories that specify clearly under what conditions particular results are likely to hold will also likely make this research of greater relevance to policymakers and practitioners, a key goal for much of international legal research. One component of policy-relevant research is the inclusion of variables the decision-maker can influence. To take an example from medicine, it may be useful to know, as a theoretical matter, that genetic factors are the major determinants of a disease's progression. But even if nutrition plays a relatively small role in the progress of a disease, a patient may be eager to know exactly what to eat and not eat, simply because she has much more control over her food intake than over her genes. Similarly, to return to the foreign policymaking context, it may be important for decision-makers to know that the current state of military technology, and an adversary's geography, wealth, and domestic political structure, primarily determine whether a dispute will escalate or not. But research on levers that decision-makers can actually move—for example, small carrots or small threats that are likely to be credible—may be far more policy-relevant.

Similarly, if the evidence neither fully confirms, nor fully disconfirms, one's initial theory, one might need to rewrite this theory. The logics of scope conditions developed in comparative (and other) scholarship can usefully be extended to international law claims. Scope conditions limit broad-ranging propositions, and specify the circumstances under which they apply. For example, when international lawyers start to look for near universal obligations that states take on—but only find them in a particular region—they may seek to establish claims about regional custom. To take another example, international law distinguishes between ordinary times (during which international obligations must be respected) and extraordinary times (during which states may be able to use concepts such as the ability to derogate from key obligations or the defense of necessity to suspend compliance). Comparativists can offer useful lessons on how to circumscribe claims to particular times and places, and how to study institutions that may interact with one another, or serve as substitutes.

For reasons of time and space, this chapter has only previewed a few techniques, and articulated how they can be applied to problems of interest to international lawyers. For the scholar interested in additional reading of accessible social-scientific treatises, Gary King, Robert Keohane, and Sidney Verba have a very useful introduction to quantitative methods,[56] while Alexander George and Andrew Bennett,[57] and Andrew Bennett and Jeffrey Checkel offer particularly useful guides to qualitative techniques.[58] Useful shorter works applying these social scientific techniques to challenges specific to legal scholarship include Ran Hirschl's writings on case selection,[59] and Katerina Linos and Melissa Carlson's writings on case study research.[60] This work presents, in significantly more detail, various techniques for testing legal principles empirically. In short, for the curious international legal scholar, arbitrage opportunities exist; there is much in recent social scientific work that can be fruitfully and relatively straightforwardly applied to problems that have troubled international lawyers for decades, if not centuries.

---

56. GARY KING, ROBERT O. KEOHANE & SIDNEY VERBA, DESIGNING SOCIAL INQUIRY: SCIENTIFIC INFERENCE IN QUALITATIVE RESEARCH (Princeton Univ. Press 1994).

57. GEORGE & BENNETT, *supra* note 11.

58. PROCESS TRACING: FROM METAPHOR TO ANALYTIC TOOL (Andrew Bennett & Jeffrey T. Checkel eds., 2014).

59. Ran Hirschl, *The Question of Case Selection in Comparative Constitutional Law*, 53 AM. J. COMP. L. 125 (2005).

60. Katerina Linos & Melissa Carlson, *Qualitative Methods for Law Review Writing*, 84 U. CHI. L. REV. 213 (2017).

3

Comparative International Law, Foreign Relations Law, and Fragmentation

Can the Center Hold?

PAUL B. STEPHAN*

This chapter considers the rise of foreign relations law as a way of thinking about the legal dimensions of international relations. It connects this development to the emergence of comparative international law and anxieties about fragmentation in international law. Each of these fields challenges conventional ways of thinking about international law and thus seems to bolster those who would dismiss international law as irrelevant or ineffectual. But these challenges instead may reinvigorate international law. As a normative matter, none of these emerging fields needs be unwelcome.

Foreign relations law focuses on the domestic institutions that conduct a state's relations with foreign actors, whether states, international organizations, or foreign persons. One of its tasks is to intervene between international and domestic law.[1]

---

* I am grateful for comments from participants in workshops at All Souls College, Oxford, the Saarland University Europa-Institut, and Georgetown University Law Center regarding an earlier version of this chapter. All errors and misjudgments remain mine alone.

1. *See, e.g.,* Louis Henkin, Foreign Affairs and the Constitution 188 (1972):

It is principally the President, "sole organ" of the United States in its international relations, who is responsible for the behavior of the United States in regard to international law, and who participates on her behalf in the indefinable process by which customary international law is made, unmade, remade. He makes legal claims for the United States and reacts to the claims of others; he performs acts reflecting views on legal questions and justifies them under the law, in diplomatic exchange, in judicial or arbitral proceedings, in international organizations or in the public forum. Congress, state legislatures and even state officials also impinge on foreign relations governed by law, for example in determining and giving effect to the rights of aliens in the United States or of foreign vessels off our coasts; and Federal and state courts are major makers of international law when they determine what that law requires in order to decide a

Comparative International Law. Edited by Anthea Roberts et al. © Anthea Roberts, Paul B. Stephan, Pierre-Hugues Verdier, Mila Versteeg 2018. Published 2018 by Oxford University Press.

This function makes us think about international law as embraced and implemented by states (or not), rather than the workings of the international community (whatever that may be). Foreign relations law takes us at least one step away from the conventional conception of international law as a uniform and universal body of rules and standards. At the most general level, foreign relations law provides part of an explanation for the similarities and differences in the practice, methodology, and ideology of international law among states that comparative international law studies.

Some see the contemporary version of foreign relations law as an attempt to undermine the significance and power of international law. Perhaps the same critique could be directed at comparative international law as well as at the fragmentation literature. This chapter takes up the normative challenge. It defends both foreign relations law and comparative international law as ways of ensuring that international law remains relevant to problems of international cooperation and the advancement of human flourishing in an increasingly challenging world.

The discussion proceeds in three sections. The first describes contemporary foreign relations law as a distinct field that emerged in the United States in the late 1990s and developed independently in parts of the British Commonwealth and Europe. It traces the parallels with and differences between foreign relations law and comparative international law. The second section considers the possibility that these complementary trends, as well as new concerns about fragmentation in international law, pose a threat to international law as conventionally conceived. Are all three of these developments different aspects of a general turn away from international law? The third section responds to these concerns. It argues that all these challenges may strengthen international law as a resilient and helpful means for meeting the growing and greater demands that the contemporary world places on it.

I. THE RISE OF FOREIGN RELATIONS LAW

Foreign relations law encompasses the legal standards and rules that govern dealings between a state and outsiders, whether international actors, other states, or nonstate foreign actors.[2] Every state, as well as supranational organizations that exercise sovereignty, might be thought of as having its own variety of foreign relations law. Part of this law's job is to define and implement the relationship between international law and a state's domestic legal system. As definition means limitation, foreign relations law necessarily qualifies the impact of international law on domestic law. Emphasis on limitations, rather than empowerment, has characterized the

case before them. But these other actors play on the domestic scene only; the President represents what they do to the rest of the world and can seek to justify them under international law or confess violation.

2. *See* Curtis A. Bradley, *What Is Foreign Relations Law?*, *in* COMPARATIVE FOREIGN RELATIONS LAW (Curtis A. Bradley ed., forthcoming 2018) ("For purposes of the book, the term is used to encompass the domestic law of each nation that governs how that nation interacts with the rest of the world.")

contemporary version of the field, both academic and practice, that has emerged over the last two decades.

The term goes back at least to the 1950s, when the American Law Institute (ALI) launched the first Restatement of the Foreign Relations Law of the United States (due to odd ALI naming conventions, this was called the Second Restatement, and its successor the Third).[3] Both the Second and Third Restatements presented international law as uniform and universal. They explored the peculiarities of the ways in which the United States embraced and fulfilled its international obligations, including the portals through which international law entered the domestic legal system. But neither project suggested that domestic legal structures, constitutional or otherwise, might affect what we thought of as international law.

Even so, the Third Restatement contained the seeds of contemporary foreign relations law, if only in the dialectical sense. It proposed a robust role for US judges in the exposition and implementation of international law, and indicated that the application of international law could override various kinds of domestic law, including earlier-enacted statutes and all law adopted by the states of the Union.[4] It even hinted at the use of international law as a means of modifying the country's constitutional settlement.[5] Its project, and to a large extent its achievement, was to make international law influential in the US legal system in a way that it had not been before.

These moves had two significant consequences for the field of foreign relations law. First, the Third Restatement provoked challenges to the ways in which it characterized US law, in particular its account of the points of entry of international law into the domestic legal system.[6] Second, by inviting US judges to apply international law, it led them to make claims about the content of international law. Because

---

3. RESTATEMENT (SECOND) OF THE FOREIGN RELATIONS LAW OF THE UNITED STATES (1965); RESTATEMENT (THIRD) OF THE FOREIGN RELATIONS LAW OF THE UNITED STATES (1987) [hereinafter RESTATEMENT THIRD]. Louis Henkin, a professor at Columbia Law School, was the principal reporter of the Third Restatement, assisted by Andrea Lowenfeld, a professor at NYU Law School, and Louis Sohn and Detlev Vagts, then professors at Harvard Law School. Henkin's earlier treatise, *supra* note 1, focused more on U.S. domestic legal institutions, specifically the Constitution, and less on international law as such. For a discussion of the evolution in Henkin's thinking between the publication of his treatise and his work on the Restatement, see Paul B. Stephan, *Courts, the Constitution, and Customary International Law—The Intellectual Origins of the Restatement (Third) of the Foreign Relations Law of the United States*, 44 VA. J. INT'L L. 33 (2003).

4. See RESTATEMENT THIRD, *supra* note 3, §§ 111(1) & comments c–e, reporters' notes 3–5; 115(a)(2) comments c–e.

5. *Cf. id.* §§ 701–02; 721 comments b, k; 722 comments a–b.

6. An early instance, which provoked an extended debate among specialists, was Curtis A. Bradley & Jack L. Goldsmith, *Customary International Law as Federal Common Law: A Critique of the Modern Position*, 110 HARV. L. REV. 815 (1997). A search of the Westlaw database indicates that US federal courts have cited this piece at least 15 times. Judicial criticism of the Third Restatement includes United States v. Stuart, 489 U.S. 353, 375 (1989) (Scalia, J., dissenting) (characterizing project as "proposal for change rather than a restatement of existing doctrine"); United States v. Yousef, 327 F.3d 56, 99–103 (2d Cir. 2003) (criticizing Restatement Third as advocacy rather than reflecting state practice).

US judges are generalists and most lack experience with the discipline, some were induced to assert interpretations that foreign observers (and others) largely found implausible.[7] These events drove the dialectic of critique and opposition.

Foreign relations law as a field that expresses this critique emerged in the United States around the turn of the century.[8] The dispute over the domestication of international law gained even greater significance with the 9/11 attack and the US government's response. The law of war and the new meme of lawfare suddenly became a matter of general interest and considerable consequence.[9] New courses on foreign relations law appeared on the curriculum of the leading law schools, bolstered by new casebooks and treatises.[10] Scholars began to distinguish themselves as experts in foreign relations law, rather than simply as international lawyers. Government lawyers as well as the private bar began to focus on the technicalities of translating international law into domestic legal obligations, often to resist claims about international law emanating from nongovernmental actors.[11]

---

7. *E.g.*, Arrest Warrant of 11 April 2000 (Dem. Rep. Congo v. Belg.), 2002 I.C.J. 3, 63, ¶ 48 (Feb. 14) (joint separate opinion by Higgins, Kooijmans, Buergenthal, JJ.) (indicating that US judicial practice regarding universal jurisdiction "has not attracted the approbation of States generally"); Jones v. Ministry of the Interior of the Kingdom of Saudi Arabia, [2006] UKHL 26, ¶ 20 (US decisions on universal jurisdiction do not "express principles widely shared and observed among other nations.")

8. A key moment in the emergence of this field was a conference organized by Curtis Bradley, then at the University of Colorado, later published as a special issue of the University of Colorado Law Review. *Symposium—A New American Foreign Affairs Law*, 70 U. Colo. L. Rev. 1089 (1999). For Bradley's later account of the field, see Curtis A. Bradley, International Law in the U.S. Legal System (2d ed. 2015).

9. *See, e.g.*, Hamdan v. Rumsfeld, 548 U.S. 557, 595–613 (2006) (plurality opinion); Bruce A. Ackerman, Before the Next Attack: Preserving Civil Liberties in an Age of Terrorism (2006); Eric A. Posner & Adrian Vermeule, Terror in the Balance: Security, Liberty, and the Courts (2007); Saikrishna Prakash, Imperial from the Beginning: The Constitution of the Original Executive (2015); Michael D. Ramsey, The Constitution's Text in Foreign Affairs (2007); The Constitution in Wartime: Beyond Alarmism and Complacency (Mark Tushnet ed., 2005); Richard H. Pildes, *Conflicts Between American and European Views of Law: The Dark Side of Legalism*, 44 Va. J. Int'l L. 145 (2003); Jed Rubenfeld, *Unilateralism and Constitutionalism*, 79 N.Y.U. L. Rev. 1971 (2004).

10. *E.g.*, Curtis A. Bradley & Jack L. Goldsmith, Foreign Relations Law: Cases and Materials (1st ed. 2003); Phillip R. Trimble, International Law: United States Foreign Relations Law (2002). Earlier casebooks on national security law overlapped to some extent with these later works, but had less of a focus on US judicial practice. An early outlier was Thomas M. Franck & Michael J. Glennon, Foreign Relations and National Security Law: Cases, Materials and Simulations (1987), the most recent (fourth, 2012) edition of which is authored by Michael J. Glennon, Sean D. Murphy, and Edward T. Swaine. This book, like Henkin's 1972 treatise, concentrates more on US legal institutions as such and less on foreign relations law as a constraint on the internalization of international law.

11. *See, e.g.*, Supplemental Brief for the United States as Amicus Curiae in Partial Support of Affirmance, Kiobel v. Royal Dutch Petroleum Co., 133 S. Ct. 1659 (2013) (No. 10–1491); Brief for the United States as Respondent Supporting Petitioner, Sosa v. Alvarez-Machain, 542 U.S. 692 (2004) (No. 03–339).

An important part of the foreign-relations-law project focuses on particular domestic legal debates, such as the nature and scope of federal common law, the effect of the supremacy clause on treaties, and the proper defaults for judicial interpretation of statutes and treaties. These tasks, however, inevitably invite a general invidious comparison. A key move in the turn to foreign relations law involves skepticism about, if not outright disparagement of, international law.

The rules of international law, these scholars argue, can be both indeterminate and illegitimate.[12] They can be indeterminate because the compromises necessary to achieve agreement across wide divides of culture and interest rob the rules of clarity and specificity. Rather, too many function as delegations to downstream decision-makers to do what their judgment deems best. Moreover, too many are illegitimate because they rest on the claims of domestic and international bureaucrats and civil-society advocates, rather than democratically accountable political actors. Arguments for narrowing the portals for international law thus rest in part on concerns about international law itself, at least as a source of rules that independent judges might apply in concrete cases.[13]

Pushing back against international law is not, of course, the only possible response to these charges. Within the traditional international law field, many contemporary scholars seek to reform international lawmaking to address these concerns. They draw on both international human rights law and domestic concepts of administrative due process to propose the fashioning of a body of global administrative law.[14]

The point here, however, is that most contemporary foreign-relations-law scholars do not make this move. Rather, they see the shortcomings of international law as we find it as a reason for clarifying and strengthening the domestic institutions that filter international law as it seeks entry into domestic law. Whether this is the wisest choice is not my concern. What matters for the purpose of this chapter is that contemporary foreign relations law emerged bearing a critique of international law.

The latest Restatement of Foreign Relations Law, of which I am a co-coordinating reporter, does not disparage international law. It does, however, emphasize the domestic sources of the law in question. For example, the current preliminary draft does not repeat claims made in the Third Restatement about the existence of particular rules of international law said to limit a state's exercise of prescriptive and adjudicative jurisdiction. Rather, it seeks to embrace these limits but ground them

12. *See, e.g.,* BRADLEY & GOLDSMITH, *supra* note 10, at 857–59.

13. A concrete expression of this skepticism is Section 6(a)(2) of the Military Commission Act of 2006, 10 U.S.C. § 948a (2006), which provides: "No foreign or international source of law shall supply a basis for a rule of decision in the courts of the United States in interpreting the prohibitions enumerated in [18 U.S.C. § 2442(d), dealing with war crimes in conflicts governed by Common Article 3 of the Geneva Conventions]."

14. *E.g.,* Benedict Kingsbury, Nico Krisch & Richard Stewart, *The Emergence of Global Administrative Law,* 68 L. & CONTEMP. PROBS. 15 (2005); Ruti Teitel & Robert Howse, *Cross-Judging: Tribunalization in a Fragmented but Interconnected Global Order,* 41 N.Y.U. J. INT'L L. & POL. 959 (2009); *Symposium: Through the Lens of Time: Global Administrative Law After 10 Years.* 13 I. CON: INT'L J. CONST. L. 463 (2015).

in domestic legal sources. The effect is not to diminish the stature of international law so much as to limit its domain.[15]

Developments outside the United States bear noting. In the British Commonwealth, foreign relations law also has emerged as a field. Its path and project, at first glance, seems different from what has happened in the United States. Rather than ousting international law, foreign relations law there seeks to fill a legal vacuum. Commonwealth scholars, in particular Campbell McLachlan, see it as a concept that shrinks the scope of the Crown Prerogative.[16] The Prerogative, as traditionally conceived, walls off particular issues, especially the conduct of foreign relations, from judicial oversight. Foreign relations law seeks to bring judicially administered discipline to the conduct of foreign affairs.

Because courts and scholars have looked to international law as a source for the legal rules that can confine the Prerogative, Commonwealth foreign relations law seems to expand the role of international law, not limit it. Thus in *Kuwait Airways Corp. v. Iraqi Airways Co.*, the House of Lords refused to give legal effect to an Iraqi decree nationalizing the plaintiff's property.[17] Even though normal rules of conflict of law would have required recognizing the validity of that decree, the court relied on customary international law governing the use of force to override the Iraqi confiscation.[18]

Commonwealth courts have recognized, however, that domestic law also can rein in the Prerogative, sometimes at the expense of international law. For example, the Supreme Court of the United Kingdom in *Treasury v. Ahmed* struck down the Treasury's implementation of the asset-freezing orders issued by the UN Security Council's Sanctions Committee. It held that the United Nations Act 1946, the enactment that fulfills UK obligations under the UN Charter, does not provide the executive unlimited discretion to apply a UN freezing order as it wished.[19] Basic principles of respect for individual rights, including the imposition of a substantial evidentiary burden on the state to justify substantial restrictions of individual liberty and allowing an opportunity to challenge the order through effective judicial oversight, required negation of the orders. The United Kingdom's obligation under Article 25 of the Charter to implement Security Council resolutions, no matter what other international legal obligation might apply, did not justify interpreting the 1946 Act as giving the government carte blanche to enforce the UN orders in

---

15. *Compare* RESTATEMENT THIRD, *supra* note 3, §§ 401–03, 421–23 (1987) (ascribing limits on exercise of prescriptive and adjudicative jurisdiction of states to customary international law) *with* RESTATEMENT (FOURTH) OF THE FOREIGN RELATIONS LAW OF THE UNITED STATES— JURISDICTION §§ 201–05, 301–06 (Tent. Draft No. 2, Mar. 22, 2016) (restating domestic law limits on exercise of prescriptive and adjudicative jurisdiction).

16. CAMPBELL MCLACHLAN, FOREIGN RELATIONS LAW (2014).

17. Kuwait Airways Corp. v. Iraqi Airways Co. [2002] UKHL 19.

18. *Id.* ¶ 22. *See also Habib v Commonwealth* (2010) 183 FCR 62 (Austl.) (breach of preemptory norms of international law precludes act-of-state defense).

19. HM Treasury v. Ahmed [2010] UKSC 2.

any manner it chose.[20] Most recently, litigation over the necessity of parliamentary approval of withdrawal from the European Union thrust the British courts into the center of a high stakes debate over the limits of the Prerogative.[21]

As *Ahmed* indicates, Commonwealth foreign relations law may limit, as well as expand, the domestic effect of international law. There are reasons to suspect that this tendency might gather force in the future. As judicial supervision of matters traditionally left to the executive becomes more common, these countries will encounter pressure to root that supervision in domestic rather than international law. The movement to reform international lawmaking from within, although a wonderful source of scholarship, is not likely to gain much traction in the world of affairs. As a result, the same concerns about the indeterminacy and illegitimacy of international law that influence US academics, policymakers, and judges will come to affect their Commonwealth counterparts. More generally, as judicial supervision becomes more consequential, one might expect national lawmakers to want more control, rather than less, over its content.[22]

One can detect the most subtle of hints of this possible future in the decision of the Court of Appeals in *Mohammed v. Secretary of State*.[23] The court relied on jurisprudence developed by the European Court of Human Rights and embraced by the Supreme Court of the United Kingdom to rule that a person held by British troops for more than four days after his capture in combat in Afghanistan may maintain a cause of action in tort for violation of his rights. While asserting that earlier Supreme Court precedent demanded this outcome, the opinion seems to suggest that the result is problematic and that the Supreme Court would be well advised to revise its jurisprudence. The Supreme Court in turn ruled that the domestic act of state doctrine rendered the claim nonjusticiable. Its holding thus sidelined the asserted substantive rule of international law by disabling courts from applying it in the context of an overseas armed conflict.[24]

Although the use of domestic foreign relations law to obstruct international law is furthest along in the United Kingdom, other European countries also have done this. Even supposedly monist countries such as Austria, Germany, and Italy see their constitutional law as a potential check on the enforceability of their international

---

20. *Id.* ¶ 76.

21. Miller v. Ministry of Justice [2017] UKSC 5.

22. A harbinger of increased political interest in these decisions was the ferocious press response to the High Court's decision in the Brexit controversy. Although the press received the Supreme Court's judgment with appropriate respect and deference, Lord Neuberger stated in a BBC interview that politicians did not speak out quickly or clearly enough to defend the High Court and that unjustified attacks on the judiciary undermined the rule of law. *Attacks on Judges Undermine Law—Supreme Court President*, BBC NEWS (Feb. 16, 2017), http://www.bbc.com/news/uk-38986228.

23. Mohammed v. Secretary of State [2015] EWCA Civ. 843.

24. Rahmatullah (No 2) v. Ministry of Defense [2017] UKSC 1.

commitments. The most vivid instance involves the 2014 decision of the Italian Constitutional Court striking down a statute meant to implement the International Court of Justice's judgment in *Jurisdictional Immunities of the State (Germany v. Italy)*. The Italian court ruled that Italy could not comply with the customary international law of sovereign immunity because its constitution guarantees access to civil justice in instances of grave violations of human rights, no matter what international law requires in the way of state immunity.[25]

Finally, one might note that European (i.e., EU) law increasingly controls the way international law enters into the legal systems of the states that the EU comprises. The *Kadi* jurisprudence represents the most vivid instance of European law, as interpreted and applied by EU courts, interposing itself between states and their international legal obligations as conventionally conceived.[26] The ongoing controversy over the validity of bilateral investment treaties (BITs) in light of the acquis communautaire provides another example.[27] In each case, a kind of foreign relations law derived from European law filters the impact of international legal obligations on both the European Union and its constituent states.

II. THE THREAT TO INTERNATIONAL LAW

Anthea Roberts reports that a leftist international law scholar once characterized contemporary US foreign relations law as a conservative attempt to strip international law of its normative power and its capacity to promote human rights.[28] Valid or not, the claim captures something important in the contemporary US debate. Human rights lawyers were used to being the good guys, the people who harness law's expressive power to fight the greatest of evils on behalf of the most appealing of victims. Foreign relations law throws up roadblocks. If nothing else, foreign relations law tends to make it harder to invoke international law to protect persons from the worst excesses of the state. Because bad states may face few constraints other than those found in international law, this seems an intolerable outcome. The move is all the more upsetting because these barriers rest on arguments about judicial craft and the rule of law.

The political-agenda assertion does have more than a whiff of Manicheanism in it. One may find its reductionism unhelpful. Without denying the basic insight that

25. Corte Cost., 22 ottobre 2014, Foro it. 2015, I, 1152 (It.), *translated in Judgement No. 238—Year 2014*, Corte Constituzionale, http://www.cortecostituzionale.it/documenti/download/doc/recent_judgments/S238_2013_en.pdf. *See* Jurisdictional Immunities of the State (Ger. v. It.), Judgment, 2012 I.C.J. 99 (Feb. 3); Paul B. Stephan, *The Political Economy of Jus Cogens, in* The Political Economy of International Law: A European Perspective (Alberta Fabricotti ed., 2016).

26. Case C-402/05, Kadi v. Council, 2008 E.C.R. I-6351; Case C-584/10, Kadi v. Council, 2013 E.C.R. I-518.

27. *See, e.g.*, Case C-118/07, Commission v. Finland, 2009 E.C.R. I-10, at 899.

28. Anthea Roberts, Is International Law International? xx (2017).

foreign relations law complicates the international human rights project, I want to explore other ways that the move threatens international law generally. This inquiry exposes the link between contemporary foreign relations law, comparative international law, and fragmentation in international law.

First, as a doctrinal matter foreign relations law operates in direct opposition to the fundamental principle of international law that domestic law cannot excuse a failure to obey international law.[29] The salience of this principle is, if anything, more important in the contemporary world, as a growing number of renegade states have enacted domestic measures to thwart their international legal obligations. To the extent that more reputable states invoke their domestic law of foreign relations to justify the dishonoring of their obligations, states already inclined to undermine the rule of law gain greater freedom of movement.[30]

Second, the challenge posed by foreign relations law, as well as by the rise of comparative constitutional law and anxieties about fragmentation, differs significantly from earlier critiques of international law. For much of the last century academic critics portrayed the field of international law as an undemocratic mask for particular interests. In the recent past such charges emanated from groups such as the Critical Legal Studies (CLS) and the Third World Approaches to International Law (TWAIL) movements.[31] Earlier expressions of the same impulse include Soviet scholars' initial position that existing international law represented only the reified power grabs of capitalists and imperialists.[32]

---

29. *See, e.g.,* Vienna Convention on the Law of Treaties art. 27, *opened for signature* May 23, 1969, 1155 U.N.T.S. 331. Article 46 of that instrument recognizes an exception to this principle in instances where domestic law deals with the competence to make a treaty.

30. To consider just one example, a recent decision of the Constitutional Court of the Russian Federation handed down at the government's request an advisory opinion upholding the general principle that Russia could rely on its Constitution as a basis for disregarding certain international legal obligations. The court cited the practice of the Constitutional Courts of Austria, Germany, and Italy, as well as the Supreme Court of the United Kingdom, as support for its decision. Postanovlenie Konstitutsionnogo Suda Rossiiskoi Federatsii ot 14 iulya 2015 g. No. 21-P [Judgement of the Russian Federation Constitutional Court of July 14, 2015]. The Russian legislature responded with legislation requiring domestic judicial review of all orders of international human rights courts. Federal'nyi Zakon Rossiiskoi Federatsii o Vnesenii Izmenenii v Federal'nyi Konstitusionnyi zakon o Konstitusionnom Sude Rossyiskoi Federatsii [Federal Constitutional Law of the Russian Federation on Amendments to the Federal Constitutional Law on the Constitutional Court of the Russian Federation], Rossiiskaia Gazeta [Ros. Gaz.] Dec. 16, 2015.

31. *See, e.g.,* Antony Anghie, *Finding the Peripheries: Sovereignty and Colonialism in Nineteenth-Century International Law,* 40 Harv. Int'l L.J. 1 (1999); David Kennedy, *A New Stream of International Legal Scholarship,* 7 Wis. Int'l. L.J. 1 (1988); Makau Mutua, *What Is TWAIL?,* 94 Am. Soc'y Int'l L. Proc. 31 (2000); Nigel Purvis, *Critical Legal Studies in Public International Law,* 32 Harv. Int'l L.J. 81 (1991).

32. *See, e.g.,* E.A. Korovin, Mezhdunarodnoe Pravo Perekhodnogo Vremeni [International Law in the Period of Transition] (1924).

Each of these earlier challenges, however, also recognized the field's potential for transformation in the service of humanity's broader needs, once the right people took over the project. The threats discussed in this chapter seem more in the nature of an existential challenge to the discipline than an effort to displace one establishment with another. Foreign relations scholars, as well as those drawing attention to comparative international law and fragmentation, are not jousting for power within the field, but rather drawing into question whether it's worth talking about "international law" as a singular or universal field at all.

Foreign relations law acknowledges international law but shifts our focus to domestic legal systems. It intimates that at least some of the work, and perhaps the most important work, of international law takes place within, rather than among, nation-states. To understand how international law affects state behavior as well as the lives of people, we must learn how international law operates as part of domestic law. But to do this, we must understand how the relevant domestic law works. International law, at least that part that we should care about, becomes a hybrid. As it enters domestic law, it responds to the demands of the domestic legal system in ways that change its content, and ultimately its identity.

This intimation, however logical, is also subversive. It suggests that international law, rather than imposing uniform and universal rules on states, shifts shape as it encounters the states on which it is supposed to act. Accordingly, international law, stripped of its character as uniform and universal and thus becoming relative rather than absolute, may lose its majesty and capacity to compel our respect.

The problem is grave exactly because international law anticipates, and perhaps even requires, variation in domestic law. If all states were largely alike in their fundamental institutional settlements, and if these fundamentally similar inputs were to lead to largely interchangeable outputs, there should be few international differences to bridge, or at least none of great importance. It is profound differences among states that give international law its salience. But if these differences also affect the domestic arrangements that foreign relations law studies, then the relativity of international law should increase with the significance of the matter at issue.

To appreciate better the challenge that foreign relations law presents to international law, one must consider two other tendencies in recent scholarship. Fragmentation and comparative international law also convey a sense that international law, far from being uniform and universal, is more often contingent, local, and to some degree inevitably various. Each of these developments undermines the stature of international law as something transcendent and compelling. Independent of but largely parallel to the rise of contemporary foreign relations law, they also challenge the traditional conception of international law.

Take fragmentation first. Since the end of World War II, and especially since the collapse of the bipolar regime of US-Soviet rivalry, the international system has witnessed the emergence of institutions both resting on and charged with administering international law. The bodies around the United Nations, including the International Court of Justice, are the first and best instances, but the proliferation of regional governance, the rise of powerful international structures such as the World Trade Organization, and the growth of judicial bodies, both permanent and ad hoc, to resolve international disputes also have great contemporary salience. The insight of the fragmentation literature is that, far from developing a unified body of standards and rules, these institutions create discrete and even hermetic bodies of law. What international law applies to which actors and transactions depends to a large extent on how those actors and transactions affect the jurisdiction of particular international institutions. The differences among these international laws are great, perhaps so profound as to undermine one's confidence that the concept of general international law retains any meaning.[33]

Some international lawyers respond to the challenge posed by fragmentation by positing an internal hierarchy, with human rights norms dominating all other forms of international law.[34] Others argue that international law contains (or might be seen as containing) a body of conflict-of-law rules that are themselves coherent and authoritative.[35] To many, however, these moves seem more wishful than persuasive. The claim for human rights dominance rests on normative ideals that, however attractive, function externally to international law as a legal system. Moreover, these responses are aspirational and have, at best, a shaky basis in contemporary practice.

The field of comparative international law, the subject of this book, has arisen more recently and raises many of the same questions.[36] It focuses on variations in national and regional practice regarding international law. More empirical than theoretical, the scholarship documents the significant differences in the training, promotion, and use of international lawyers as part of a general inquiry into differences in the content and methodology of international law. Like fragmentation, this field looks at departures from the conventional ideal of uniform and universal international law, but uses states, substate actors, and supranational structures, rather than international institutions, as the main unit of analysis. Like foreign relations law, it

---

33. Tomer Broude, *Fragmentation(s) of International Law: Normative Integration as Authority Allocation*, *in* THE SHIFTING ALLOCATION OF AUTHORITY IN INTERNATIONAL LAW: CONSIDERING SOVEREIGNTY, SUPREMACY AND SUBSIDIARITY (Tomer Broude & Yuval Shany eds., 2008); Eyal Benvenisti & George W. Downs, *The Empire's New Clothes: Political Economy and the Fragmentation of International Law*, 60 STAN. L. REV. 595 (2007); Jonathan Charney, *Is International Law Threatened by Multiple Tribunals?*, 271 REC. DES COURS 101 (1998); Martti Koskenniemi & Päivi Leino, *Fragmentation of International Law? Postmodern Anxieties*, 15 LEIDEN J. INT'L L. 553 (2002).

34. Rep. of the Study Group of the Int'l Law Comm'n, Fragmentation of International Law: Difficulties Arising from the Diversification and Expansion of International Law, Fifty-Eighth Session, U.N. Doc. A/CN.4/L.682 (2006), as corrected, U.N. Doc. A/CN.4/L.682/Corr.1 (2006) (finalized by Professor Martti Koskenniemi).

35. *See, e.g.*, Harlan Grant Cohen, *Finding International Law, Part II: Our Fragmenting Legal Communities*, 44 N.Y.U. J. INT'L L. & POL. 1049 (2012).

36. Anthea Roberts, Paul B. Stephan, Pierre-Hugues Verdier & Mila Versteeg, *Comparative International Law—Framing the Field*, 109 AM. J. INT'L L. 467 (2015). Central works include this volume, as well as a monograph authored by Anthea Roberts just published this year, *see supra* note 28, and Martti Koskenniemi, *The Case for Comparative International Law*, FINN. Y.B. INT'L L. (2009). For my own earlier effort to link the field to a theory of international relations, see Paul B. Stephan, *Symmetry and Selectivity: What Happens in International Law When the World Changes*, 10 CHI. J. INT'L L. 91 (2009).

takes as its subject differences in how states make, interpret, and apply international law, but has a wider field of vision that goes beyond the impact of domestic law on the application and interpretation of international law.[37]

Notwithstanding their differences, these fields have commonalities that undergird their challenge to international law. First, each claims to be empirical rather than normative. Workers in each talk about contemporary practice rather than motivating norms, although each has an eye out for those practices that disrupt the traditional conception of international law. Second, each emphasizes relativism in international law. What the law is depends on who and where you are. This simple insight undermines the distinction between international and domestic law. Third, each moves us away from a normative vision with universal aspirations. By concentrating on what we get rather than what we want, each suggests that international law's moral center may not matter all that much, if indeed it exists at all. Fourth, by documenting the departures of international law practice from uniformity and universalism, each implies a critique of conventional accounts of international law. The traditional international lawyers, it seems, have missed out on the big story, even if we can't agree on what the big story is.

Consider some examples. Over the last two decades, British courts have refused to implement particular decisions of the European Court of Human Rights, not only because foreign relations law can impose a barrier to implementation of the Strasbourg judgment, but because they believe the Strasbourg court misinterpreted the Convention. The most visible conflict between the courts involves the scope of the Convention's limits on qualifications for voting. The European Court has determined that UK bans on voting by felons violate the Convention.[38] British courts have pushed back, partly on the ground that the Strasbourg court has misapplied the concept of proportionality.[39] A less prominent, but no less entrenched, dispute involves a British statute allowing a limited exception to the hearsay rule in criminal cases.[40] Even earlier the courts had skirmished over the validity of the British law of adverse possession, although the European Court then had backed down.[41]

37. Anthea Roberts, Paul B. Stephan, Pierre-Hugues Verdier & Mila Versteeg, *Conceptualizing Comparative International Law* (this volume).

38. Hirst v. United Kingdom (No. 2), 2005-IX Eur. Ct. H.R. 187; Greens v. United Kingdom, 2010-VI Eur. Ct. H.R. 57; Firth v. United Kingdom, App. No. 47784/09 (Eur. Ct. H.R. Dec. 15, 2014); McHugh v. United Kingdom, App. No. 51987/08 (Eur. Ct. H.R. Feb. 10, 2015).

39. Chester v. Secretary of State for Justice [2013] UKSC 63; Moohan v. Lord Advocate [2014] UKSC 67.

40. *Compare* Al-Khawaja v. United Kingdom, 2011-VI Eur. Ct. H.R. 191, *with* Regina v. Horncastle [2009] UKSC 14, *and* Regina v. Ibrahim [2012] EWCA (Crim) 837 (Eng.). *See* Paul B. Stephan, *The Political Economy of Judicial Production of International Law, in* THE POLITICAL ECONOMY OF INTERNATIONAL LAW: A EUROPEAN PERSPECTIVE 202 (Alberta Fabricotti ed., 2016).

41. *Compare* J.A. Pye (Oxford) Ltd. v. United Kingdom, 2007-III Eur. Ct. H.R. 365, *with* Ofulue v. Bossert [2008] EWCA (Civ) 7 (Eng.).

One might dismiss each of these tussles as exercises in distinction rather than as outright conflicts. A fair reading of the cases, however, indicates that British courts perceive a greater margin of appreciation, and thus greater tolerance of entrenched national practice, in the Convention than does the Strasbourg court. These cases illustrate how domestic factors—institutional structure, cultural traditions, configurations of political and economic interests—may drive a wedge between nominally disinterested judicial institutions confronted with the same international instrument. Both foreign relations law and comparative international law thus recognize—and possibly breed—heterogeneity in the interpretation and application of international obligations.

How destructive is all this? Should international lawyers double down on the field's fundamental norms, insisting that what the new fields have uncovered is epiphenomenal rather than significant? Perhaps the perceived variations in international law attributable to domestic foreign relations law, fragmentation, and comparative law represent early false starts. Perhaps, as people come to appreciate the promise of international law more, a better and unified version will prevail. A few decades from now, practitioners and jurists may wonder what all the fuss was about.

The doubling-down approach, however, suggests denial more than engagement. Empirical challenges demand responses. The mounting evidence, viewed from different perspectives and by different observers, points in the same direction. As the scope and significance of international law have become greater, so have systematic and salient differences in the methodology and content of international law. The more we have asked it to settle, the less it provides consistent answers. This presents a problem.

III. PLURALISM IN INTERNATIONAL LAW

To frame a response, I start with several fundamental questions: Is uniformity and universality essential for international law to survive as a distinct field? Would international law still command our respect even if it were to concede its instability and contingency? Can one do international law if one cannot guarantee a reliable fit-for-all-purposes product?

My answers, in short, are no, yes, and yes. These answers depend on a particular understanding of what it means to do international law, and thus of the work that international law does. To put it in reductive terms, I urge international lawyers to embrace diversity and pluralism by making clear distinctions among the multiple roles that international law can play. We need not abandon the invisible college, but we do have to admit that the college has many departments and serves multiple functions, as captured by Roberts's notion of the "divisible college of international lawyers."[42]

---

42. *Compare* Oscar Schachter, *The Invisible College of International Lawyers*, 72 Nw. U.L. Rev. 217 (1977) *with* Roberts, *supra* note 28, at 2.

International law has lots of jobs, each with its own set of tasks, customs, participants, and institutions.[43] To use the jargon of contemporary social science, each has a distinct hermeneutic community. The basic question is whether to see each of these functions and communities as part of a greater whole (i.e., to synthesize) or instead to focus on their differences and boundaries (i.e., to analyze). The discipline traditionally has tied all these tasks together in a general international law enterprise. This synthetic approach accepts the distributed, rather than centralized, nature of the process of making and applying international law but seeks to compensate for it.[44] Because international law comes at us from many places and many directions, making sense of the field requires assimilating and making sense of all instances where international law pops up.

The analytic perspective, in contrast, argues that context dominates content. Rather than positing metaphysical principles to unify the field, or torturing the data to exclude dissonance, we should accept that international law serves different communities. It is perfectly natural for international law to behave differently depending on what each community expects of it and what tools each can bring to bear to the task at hand.

This approach is not merely analytical, but also functional. It assumes that the complex relationship between a legal system and the society in which it operates should command our attention, at the expense of ideas as such. It marries analysis with induction and privileges engagement with social behavior over reason and imagination as ends in themselves.

What kind of case can be made for a distributed, localized, and relativistic system of international law? Two types of arguments occur to me. First, understanding how international law works in the world in which we find ourselves is useful, and not nihilist. Second, the alternative is worse. Considering international law as the province of advanced thinkers, untethered by local commitments of the sort that states and other political institutions embody, invites comparison to historically significant dystopias.

First, the positive case. Approaching international law as a tool that people may use to solve problems focuses the mind on human needs. People who find themselves governed by particular legal rules might tolerate specific requirements that vary according to circumstances, if they accept that the variations that dictate different outcomes rest on defensible distinctions.

Take an example about which I have written elsewhere.[45] Several international and domestic courts have articulated rules specifying when an actor (either a state or a legal person) should bear responsibility for others who, as a formal matter, are legally distinct from the actor but, as a practical matter, act to some degree under the

---

43. *See* Paul B. Stephan, *The Law and Economics of International Law Enforcement*, in OXFORD HANDBOOK OF LAW AND ECONOMICS (Francesco Parisi, ed., 2016); *Disaggregating Customary International Law*, 21 DUKE J. COMP. & INT'L L. 191 (2010).

44. *See, e.g.*, Laurence R. Helfer, *Nonconsensual International Lawmaking*, 2008 ILL. L. REV. 71.

45. Stephan, *supra* note 40, at 222–23.

actor's influence. Responsibility under international law turns on the rule chosen. Solutions vary between a strict standard of command and control, making it harder to attribute responsibility, versus one of general supervision, which makes attribution easier.[46] Unless context can justify this, the existence of these different rules of attribution seems evidence of international law's incoherence.

A functional perspective might indicate that each expression of the rule fits its purpose. In the case of the International Court of Justice, a strict rule makes it more difficult to hold a state accountable for the objectionable behavior of others. The International Court of Justice acts against a background of state suspicion of its jurisdiction and concern that the rules it expresses in principle apply to all parties who might appear before it. The ease of withdrawing from the International Court of Justice's jurisdiction makes these concerns significant. Caution serves the goal of protecting the Court's authority from diminution by dubious states.

In the case of the International Criminal Tribunal for the former Yugoslavia, by contrast, no downstream threats to jurisdiction exist. The court's authority already is circumscribed both geographically and temporally. Any changes in its jurisdiction must go through the Security Council. In this context, a broader rule of attribution poses no threat to powerful actors, and thus to the court.

As for US courts working within the framework of the so-called Alien Tort Statute, the disparate practice of the international tribunals might lead them to focus on the particular requirements and purposes of that statute. Asserting that international law "provides" a rule of attribution leads to lazy thinking about the basis and purpose of these tort suits. The range of outcomes we have seen to date suggests some recognition of this challenge, although lazy thinking is not completely absent.[47]

The attribution example illustrates a general phenomenon. Plausible, if not necessarily compelling, reasons explain differences in domestic institutional arrangements that affect the domestication of international law, fragmentation within the international legal system, and state approaches generally to the field. These reasons may allow us to distinguish between plausible variation, on the one hand, and naked opportunism, on the other. They suggest a project for understanding international law as a complex social phenomenon with real if complicated constraints, rather than as an empty practice of ex post rationalization. To give way to heady optimism, a functional approach to international law—as illustrated by foreign relations law, fragmentation, and comparative international law—can help us find matches between particular legal regimes and human needs.

Next, the negative case. The alternative to a functional and thus relativistic approach to international law is one that rests on overarching ideas about justice, decency, and human flourishing. Such ideas cannot emanate solely from official

46. *Compare, e.g.,* Military and Paramilitary Activities in and Against Nicaragua (Nicar. v. U.S.), Judgment, 1984 I.C.J. Rep. 392, ¶ 115, *with* Prosecutor v. Tadić, Case No. IT-94-1-A, Judgment, ¶ 120 (Int'l Crim. Trib. for the former Yugoslavia Jul. 15, 1999).

47. *See, e.g.,* Presbyterian Church of Sudan v. Talisman Energy, Inc., 582 F.3d 244 (2d Cir. 2009); Aziz v. Alcolac, Inc., 658 F.3d 388 (4th Cir. 2011); Doe I v. Nestle USA, Inc., 766 F.3d 1013 (9th Cir. 2014).

actors such as states, as these institutions necessarily have local interests that can blind them to the needs of humanity. Indeed, democratic politics, organized through states, leans toward the marginalization of the concerns of outsiders. One might consider this alternative vision of international law as a strong conception of the invisible college. Particular persons, through their exemplary powers of reasoning, expression, and moral example, illuminate a vision of a better life that inspires many and should move all of us. These people make international law, if not in all instances then at the level of fundamentals.

Normative attraction does not take place in a vacuum, but rather depends on the work of norm entrepreneurs. What these entrepreneurs do is make us all aware of the needs of humanity and therefore of the requirements of international law. Enough acclaim among a sufficiently large group of relevant actors suffices to elevate them to the level of international law's arbiters and the fabricators of its fundaments.

One difficulty I have with this strong conception of the invisible college is the unhappy history of past efforts to construct and impose transnational norms. Going back half a millennium in European history, the universal Catholic Church claimed the authority to articulate the standards and rules that would govern the conduct of princes both with respect to each other and with regard to their subjects. The Reformation put paid to that claim, and Westphalia codified its demise. In the past century, both International Socialism, led if not necessarily controlled by the Soviet Union, and National Socialism, incarnated in Italian Fascism, the German Reich, and Spanish Falangism, among others, posited a set of scientific principles and inspirational ideals that operate above the level of existing state structures. Both of these movements, which attracted many of the era's leading thinkers, constructed international networks of supporters who regarded adherence to the movement's principles and guidance as more important than loyalty to status-quo political institutions, nation-states in particular. Neither turned out well.

It would be a mistake to reject the strong conception of the invisible college on the basis of the flaws found in earlier manifestations of the institution. Indeed, the postwar international legal establishment included many actors whose lives were disrupted by either International or National Socialism, including all four of the Reporters of the Third Restatement.[48] My point is only that persons worried about the Scylla of international law nihilism implied by excessive functionalism must also acknowledge the Charybdis of ideological absolutism implied by a universal normative system.

At the end of the day, we should embrace the turn toward foreign relations law, comparative international law, and fragmentation. It does not threaten international law so much as challenge it. Each of these developments asks international law to ground its work on richer, more empirical, and more functional foundations.

48. Henkin's family were refugees from the Soviet Union who brought him to the United States in 1923. Lowenfeld's family were German refugees from Nazism who brought him to the United States in 1938. Sohn was a Pole who came to the United States weeks before Nazi Germany invaded his country, and remained exiled after the establishment of a Soviet-dominated regime there in 1945. Vagts's family were German refugees from Nazism who brought him to the United States in 1933.

These demands do complicate the task of international lawyers, largely by demanding mastery of a greater range of disciplines. By breaking down the barrier between public international lawyers, comparative constitutional lawyers, and comparativists generally, it forces specialists to talk to a wider range of experts and to learn the tricks of other trades. This may be hard, but I don't see how it can hurt. The alternative may well be irrelevance.

4

Why Comparative International Law Needs International Relations Theory

DANIEL ABEBE

Realism, institutionalism, and liberalism are unhelpful for the study of comparative international law. After all, they are narrow international relations theories that purport to explain how states behave in international politics, nothing more. Comparative international law, in contrast, "entails identifying, analyzing, and explaining similarities and differences in how actors in different legal systems understand, interpret, apply, and approach international law."[1] Reductionist theories focused on power, preferences, or domestic incentives are simply inapposite to the careful, subtle analyses of the comparative international law project. The conventional wisdom is clear: international relations theory has nothing to offer scholars interested in comparative international law.

But this is much too simple. Analyzing the similarities and differences in the way states apply international law—the core of comparative international law—not only requires an understanding of national actors, but also an appreciation of how states pursue their goals in international politics. For example, imagine a comparative international law scholar ("comparativist") who thinks that some form of realism best describes the way that states operate in international politics. Imagine further that this comparativist is trying to explain differences between the United States' and France's understanding of international law, say Article 51's self-defense provisions of the United Nations (UN) Charter. She would view and explain any interpretive differences, such as they exist, in terms of US power and global commitments; the variance in the interpretation and application of international law would be viewed as a function of international politics.

In contrast, consider the comparativist who subscribes to a liberal theory of international politics. He would view interpretive differences through a very

---

1. Anthea Roberts, Paul B. Stephan, Pierre-Hugues Verdier & Mila Versteeg, *Conceptualizing Comparative International Law* (this volume).

Comparative International Law. Edited by Anthea Roberts et al. © Anthea Roberts, Paul B. Stephan, Pierre-Hugues Verdier, Mila Versteeg 2018. Published 2018 by Oxford University Press.

different lens, namely the incentives, constraints, and interests of subnational actors. International politics, in this story, is not the primary or even secondary explanatory variable. At bottom, background assumptions about international relations theory shape the comparativist's inquiry into analyzing and explaining differences in the way national actors interpret international law.

In destabilizing the conventional wisdom, this chapter argues that comparativists should not underestimate the value of international relations theory in explaining how and why certain states adopt particular interpretations of international law. International relations theory cannot explain the evolution of specific doctrines but, as I describe below, it can be very useful in understanding the general approaches to international law that states embrace. Perhaps more importantly, I argue that comparative international law's descriptive goal cannot be easily divorced from the normative questions that flow from it. Let me explain. Building from the previous example, assume that a comparativist finds that the United States interprets Article 51 more expansively than other members of the UN—permitting the United States to use force more often—and attributes that view to the role of the president in foreign affairs. Great. But the inquiry does not (and should not) end there. The next question is whether the United States' interpretation of international law is appropriate and, if not, how to encourage the United States to adopt the proper interpretation.

At this step of the analysis, it becomes clear how international relations theory becomes relevant to the prescriptive component of the comparative international law project. Comparativists with realist inclinations might view the United States' interpretation as normatively attractive—it permits a greater use of US power— and would endorse a substantial role for the president in the interpretation and application of international law. In contrast, the comparativist who embraces liberalism might find the United States' interpretation problematic—it deviates from the proper interpretation shared by the bulk of the international community—and argue for a reduced role for the president to ensure that the United States complies with international law.

In other words, the descriptive project is inextricably linked with an implicit normative view about the proper interpretation and application of international law and the proper arrangement of subnational entities to achieve that goal. Comparativists have normative preferences, just like all other international law scholars. Without linking the explanatory to the normative, comparative international law risks being a wholly descriptive project, one that produces knowledge about state practices but leaves the most salient prescriptive questions unanswered.

Comparativists, international law scholars, and international relations theorists with normative views about how states should behave and apply international law—whether drawn from realism, liberalism, or institutionalism—should also care about the distribution of interpretive authority for international law within states. The prescriptive ambitions of those international relations theories can only be fully realized with an understanding of how and why states vary in their application of international law. Comparativists who subscribe to each theory (or any other) should prefer, and design, subnational institutional arrangements that promote their normative goals.

Comparativists from the realist perspective would likely endorse the centralization of foreign affairs authority in the branch, department, agency, or commission that is most likely to produce interpretations and applications of international law consistent with realism. Liberals should prefer allocating interpretive authority to the subnational entity most congenial to compliance with international law, while institutionalists should favor arrangements that are more likely to produce applications of international law that maximize national public welfare. In short, I argue that, regardless of paradigm, scholars of all types should care deeply about institutional design and its consequences for the interpretation and application of international law—comparative international law.

The sections below outline the connection between subnational design and the interpretation and application of international law on one side, and realism, institutionalism, and liberalism on the other. Greater consideration of the relationship among power, domestic institutional arrangements, and international relations theory paradigms will not only prove fruitful for the comparative international law project but also for those thinking about the aims of international law and the operation of international politics.

I. INTERNATIONAL RELATIONS THEORY AND COMPARATIVE INTERNATIONAL LAW

Comparative international law is the study of the interpretation and application of international law by domestic and international actors. But, as the provisional definition in the introductory chapter suggests, comparative international law also includes explaining, identifying, and analyzing different approaches to international law by various actors in international politics. Given the breadth of this definition, it is hard to see what wouldn't be relevant for comparative international law, ranging from more abstract international relations theory paradigms to more parochial domestic theories of statutory interpretation. However, as the field is evolving and its limits are still undefined, beginning with a broad provisional definition and narrowing over time is a sound approach. For purposes of this chapter, I will focus on the interpretation and application of international law in the foreign affairs and security context.

International law is a product of treaties and customary international law. Treaties are formal agreements between states, while customary international law is a product of the consistent and widespread state practice performed out of a sense of legal and moral obligation (*opinio juris*).[2] Though all states are bound by customary international law and their treaty commitments, it is unsurprising that the heterogeneity in regime type, power, and domestic institutional design of states would lead to variance in the way international commitments and obligations are interpreted, applied, enforced, and fulfilled. Comparative international law helps explains the reasons for the variance and permits normative inferences to be drawn.

---

2. *See* David J. Bederman, International Law Frameworks 15–16 (2001).

A. Realism and Structure

Realism is an international relations theory that attempts to describe state behavior in international politics.[3] Although there are several variants of realism,[4] nearly all realist theories begin with a set of core assumptions about states and the structure of the international system and, from those assumptions, make predictions about how the great powers will behave. Realism begins with the assumption that states are unitary actors pursuing their self-interest in an anarchic world without a central enforcement mechanism—a world with no global policeman to enforce international law or protect small states from big ones.[5] The world is anarchic[6]—in realist parlance—because there is no formal hierarchy, or world government with a monopoly on violence governing all states. In an anarchic world, states privilege survival over everything else and, given this concern, states prioritize military and economic strength to guarantee their security. States might vary in their material capabilities but their interest in self-preservation is relatively stable. In short, states will try to maximize material power (up to a point) to survive.[7]

Although this description of realism is certainly under-nuanced, realism offers a theory to explain the reasons that the great powers—the world's most powerful states—fight wars, seek peace, and form alliances, among other things. The key takeaway is that realism's domain is narrow: it is a theory that explains security competition among a small number of very powerful states. Realism doesn't purport to explain the evolution of international law,[8] the rise of international organizations[9]

3. *See generally* JOHN J. MEARSHEIMER, THE TRAGEDY OF GREAT POWER POLITICS (2001) (outlining a theory of offensive realism to explain the expansionary behavior of states in the international system); KENNETH N. WALTZ, THEORY OF INTERNATIONAL POLITICS (1979) (discussing a neorealist theory of state behavior); HANS J. MORGENTHAU, POLITICS AMONG NATIONS: THE STRUGGLE FOR POWER AND PEACE (1985) (articulating the realist framework for international power politics); NUNO P. MONTEIRO, THEORY OF UNIPOLAR POLITICS (2014) (examining the effects of a unipolar system within the context of realist theory).

4. MEARSHEIMER, *supra* note 3, at 5–6 (detailing the theory of offensive realism and emphasizing the zero-sum nature of the power struggle in international politics); STEPHEN M. WALT, THE ORIGINS OF ALLIANCE (1990) (articulating that state behavior depends not only on power politics, but also on the intentions of other state actors); WALTZ *supra* note 3, at 127 (outlining defensive realism by using security concerns to explain state actions).

5. MEARSHEIMER, *supra* note 3, at 30 (explaining that realist theory is founded on anarchy as an ordering principle).

6. The term "anarchic" does not mean chaotic in the traditional sense, but rather that sovereignty in the international system does not reside in a central, supranational government. *Id.*

7. *See id.* at 80–81 (stating that the ultimate goal of a state actor is to achieve regional hegemony to maximize security).

8. *See generally* Eyal Benvenisti & George W. Downs, *National Courts, Domestic Democracy, and the Evolution of International Law*, 20 EUR. J. INT'L L. 59 (2009) (describing the growth in domestic application of international law).

9. *See* Jenny S. Martinez, *Towards an International Judicial System*, 56 STAN. L. REV. 429 (2003) (discussing the expansion of international organizations and tribunals).

and tribunals,[10] or the prevalence of international human rights treaties.[11] It doesn't say anything about courts, legislatures, or executives, or the virtues of a parliamentary or a presidential system.[12] Realism in its purest form is a parsimonious and reductionist theory explaining the logic of security competition among the world's great powers.

If realism's scope is so narrow, why should we think it has anything to say about comparative international law? On first glance, it doesn't appear to offer anything useful for the comparativist. Realism focuses on states as unitary actors and examines outcomes, not processes. It doesn't matter if the president, prime minister, or even the chief justice of the Supreme Court directs a state's foreign affairs; the anarchic structure of the international system forces states to act in predictable ways regardless of which domestic institution—or person—actually makes the decision. Structure is dispositive. In this light, realism seems like a bit of a dead end for those who care about domestic institutional design or the interpretation and application of international law by states.[13]

But, on further examination, realism's core assumptions permit certain inferences to be drawn about how international law is interpreted and applied, both domestically and in international organizations, and speak directly to the comparative international law project. Realist scholars would argue that international organizations will likely reflect the interests of the powerful states that create them[14] and, if the organizations begin to drift from the preferences of the powerful states—or if new powerful states emerge to challenge the status quo—the international organizations will lose relevance.[15] They would expect the interpretation and application of international law to replicate the interests of the great powers. For example, the League of Nations failed in responding to Italy's invasion of Ethiopia and the

10. *See* KAREN J. ALTER, THE NEW TERRAIN OF INTERNATIONAL LAW (2014) (examining the proliferation of binding international courts).

11. *See generally* BETH A. SIMMONS, MOBILIZING FOR HUMAN RIGHTS: INTERNATIONAL LAW IN DOMESTIC POLITICS (2009) (arguing for increased application of human rights treaties; *but see* ERIC A. POSNER, THE TWILIGHT OF HUMAN RIGHTS LAW (2014) (contending that international human rights law is not as effective as a foreign aid model).

12. *See* TOM GINSBURG, JUDICIAL REVIEW IN NEW DEMOCRACIES: CONSTITUTIONAL COURTS IN ASIAN CASES (2003) (examining the origins of judicial power); David S. Law & Mila Versteeg, *The Evolution and Ideology of Global Constitutionalism*, 99 CALIF. L. REV. 1163 (2011) (discussing the patterns in the global development of national constitutions); Rosalind Dixon & Eric A. Posner, *The Limits of Constitutional Convergence*, 11 CHI. J. INT'L L. 399 (2010) (describing the impacts of globalization on domestic legal structures).

13. *See* FAREED ZAKARIA, FROM WEALTH TO POWER: THE UNUSUAL ORIGINS OF AMERICA'S WORLD ROLE (1998); JACK SNYDER, MYTHS OF EMPIRE: DOMESTIC POLITICS AND INTERNATIONAL AMBITION (1991).

14. *See* John J. Mearsheimer, *The False Promise of International Institutions*, 19 INT'L SECURITY 5 (1994) (contending that international institutions do not impact state behavior).

15. *See id.* at 13–14.

rise of Nazi Germany,[16] tasks made altogether more difficult without the United States as a member,[17] and eventually collapsed.[18] The movement away from the General Agreement on Tariffs and Trade[19] and the formation of the World Trade Organization (WTO)—the creation, application, and enforcement of a new body of international law—by the United States, the European Union (EU), and Japan[20] reflected their collective power and dominance in international trade.

At the same time, the WTO's current difficulties are at least partially attributable to the rise of new economic powers with different preferences on the interpretation and application of international trade law.[21] The United States, despite being the primary impetus behind the creation of the UN,[22] ignored the UN during the 1999 bombing of Kosovo[23] and more recently during the run-up to the 2003 invasion of Iraq.[24] The International Criminal Court (ICC) has faced several challenges as the United States, China, India, and Russia declined to ratify the Rome Statute,[25]

---

16. See MARK MAZOWER, NO ENCHANTED PALACE: THE END OF EMPIRE AND THE IDEOLOGICAL ORIGINS OF THE UNITED NATIONS 193 (2009) (discussing the shortcomings of the League of Nations).

17. See generally JOHN MILTON COOPER, BREAKING THE HEART OF THE WORLD: WOODROW WILSON AND THE FIGHT FOR THE LEAGUE OF NATIONS (2001).

18. See generally F.S. NORTHEDGE, THE LEAGUE OF NATIONS: ITS LIFE AND TIMES, 1920–1946 (1986).

19. See Jose E. Alvarez, The WTO as Linkage Machine, 96 AM. J. INT'L L. 146 (2002) (noting that select states sought to make the GATT more favorable to their preferences); Andrew T. Guzman, Global Governance and the WTO, 45 HARV. INT'L L.J. 303 (2004) (providing a history of the WTO and the transition from the GATT); Alan O. Sykes, Protectionism as a "Safeguard": A Positive Analysis of the GATT "Escape Clause" with Normative Speculations, 58 U. CHI. L. REV. 255 (1991) (discussing the public choice theory behind the escape clauses in the GATT).

20. See Richard H. Steinberg, In the Shadow of Law or Power? Consensus-Based Bargaining and Outcomes in the GATT/WTO, 56 INT'L ORG. 339, 351 (2002) (describing the origins of GATT/WTO).

21. See generally Erik M. Dickinson, The Doha Development Dysfunction: Problems of the WTO Multilateral Trading System, 3 GLOBAL BUS. L. REV. 229 (2013) (articulating that bilateral trade agreements have certain advantages over multilateral agreements).

22. See MAZOWER, supra note 16, at 95–97 (stating that the United States led the charge to create the United Nations).

23. See Christopher Greenwood, International Law and the NATO Intervention in Kosovo, 49 INT'L & COMP. L.Q. 926 (showing that United States and NATO actions violated the UN Charter).

24. See Thomas M. Franck, What Happens Now? The United Nations After Iraq, 97 AM. J. INT'L L. 607 (2003) (arguing that the United States undermined UN provisions).

25. See Jack Goldsmith, The Self-Defeating International Criminal Court, 70 U. CHI. L. REV. 89 (2003) (asserting that the ICC is not aligned with the United States' interests, but dependent on the United States to succeed); Lydia Polgreen, Arab Uprisings Point Up Flaws in Global Court, N.Y. TIMES, July 7, 2012 (discussing the lack of support from world powers and its consequences).

meaning the world's two biggest economies,[26] two most populous countries,[27] and two largest nuclear powers[28] have rejected the ICC's jurisdiction (or simply rejected the interpretation and the application of international criminal law). Although this list is clearly intended to be illustrative rather than comprehensive, these international political outcomes involve great powers pursuing their self-interest in the security and trade areas and are generally consistent with realist predictions about the operation of international organizations. At bottom, the variance in the applications of international law could be explained, in part, by examining the interpretive differences through a realist perspective.

Similarly, realists would predict that most states would comply with international law most of the time[29] because the rules of international law reflect the interests of the powerful states, and those states have tools to coerce the weaker states into compliance. And, as international law covers a range of substantive areas well outside the security domain, realists would also expect to see reasonably high levels of compliance in those areas, but would not be surprised to see powerful states violating international law to advance their own interests when national security concerns predominate. As new great powers rise, the process repeats itself and a new equilibrium is reached.

Realism is essentially reductionist because it treats all states as rational, self-interested, unitary actors with relatively stable and predictable preferences but varying capabilities. Realism's parsimony permits an easy application of theory within the domain of security competition among great powers, but realism's narrow scope limits its applicability. Any inquiry into the vagaries of domestic institutional design, so the argument goes, is effectively moot because outcomes will reflect realism's predictions regardless of the decision-making locus within the state.

B. Institutionalism and State Preferences

This dark picture seemingly closes the door on the utility of realism for thinking about how states interpret and apply international law. The most extreme versions of realism, after all, assume a unitary state and are unconcerned with the activities of subnational entities. But a related framework for thinking about international law—institutionalism—brings some realist ideas to the study of international and comparative law. Institutionalists start with simple assumptions about rational,

---

26. *See* The World Bank Group, GDP at Market Prices (last updated 2013), http://data.worldbank.org/indicator/NY.GDP.MKTP.CD.

27. *See* The World Bank Group, Total Population (last updated 2013) http://data.worldbank.org/indicator/NY.GDP.MKTP.CD.

28. *See Nuclear Weapons: Who Has What?*, CNN, http://www.cnn.com/interactive/2013/03/world/nuclear-weapon-states/ (last updated Jan. 6, 2015).

29. *See* Kenneth N. Waltz, *Structural Realism After the Cold War*, 25 INT'L SECURITY 5, 27 (2000) (stating that international law is typically obeyed).

self-interested states pursuing their preferences in an anarchic world with the goal of maximizing national welfare. They study the conditions under which states are likely to comply with international law, and examine the role of incentives, reciprocity, reputation costs, and retaliation in facilitating international cooperation among states.[30] Unlike realism, this approach can be applied in almost every area of international law and can yield crisp predictions about the likelihood of mutually beneficial international cooperation.[31]

Institutionalism can be applied to the study of comparative international law. One variant suggests that differences in the domestic interpretation and application of international law by states would be predictable, as each state would apply international law to suit its interests. For example, the most powerful states in the world, including China, the United States, and the EU, have different sets of interests and incentives—varying along historical, economic, military, rule of law, institutional design, and geostrategic dimensions—and would naturally endorse their distinct visions of international law. Similarly, they would interpret international law in a manner consistent with their preferences.[32] Smaller states will also interpret and apply international law in a self-interested way, even though they lack the power to promote their own visions of international law. However, smaller states will have to consider the views and the coercive capacity of the most powerful states when they interpret and apply international law, particularly in the substantive areas of law where the great powers take the most interest. The fear of retaliation or sanctions from powerful states will shape how smaller states treat international law within their domestic legal systems. This approach suggests that all states are likely to apply international law according to their preferences, and the most powerful states will also attempt to impose their discrete visions or exceptionalist views of international law on the broader international community.

Institutionalism picks up where realism stops. It is more nuanced than realism and embraces the comparative international law project by accepting the challenge of explaining the variance in the interpretation and application of international law by states. It generates more carefully developed predictions than realism, namely that powerful states will present distinct visions of international law and will apply the law domestically consistent with their preferences. It is more useful in that it tries to understand the domestic foundations for the exceptionalist visions of

---

30. *See* ANDREW T. GUZMAN, HOW INTERNATIONAL LAW WORKS: A RATIONAL CHOICE THEORY (2008) (describing how rational choice strengthens the international legal system); ERIC A. POSNER & ALAN O. SYKES, ECONOMIC FOUNDATIONS OF INTERNATIONAL LAW (2012) (providing a framework for international law amongst rational state actors); ROBERT E. SCOTT & PAUL B. STEPHAN, THE LIMITS OF LEVIATHAN: CONTRACT THEORY AND THE ENFORCEMENT OF INTERNATIONAL LAW (2006) (examining enforcement mechanisms to promote international cooperation).

31. *See* POSNER & SYKES, *supra* note 30, at 19–20 (discussing the mutual gains that result from cooperation).

32. *See* Anu Bradford & Eric A. Posner, *Universal Exceptionalism in International Law*, 52 HARV. INT'L L.J. 1 (2011) (arguing that major state actors approach international law in a self-beneficial manner).

international law by powerful countries. Stated succinctly, China, the United States, and the EU have different visions of international law because they have different domestic policy preferences and different institutions, shaped by their own historical circumstances. And, as they have different self-interested visions, they will interpret and apply international law consistent with their policy preferences.

Despite institutionalism's consideration of domestic preferences, it doesn't tell us how variation in institutional design, political structures, and legal systems within a state affects its interpretation and application of international law. Institutionalism focuses on the narrow relationship between preferences and outcomes, but it doesn't directly consider how different governance structures could affect the interpretation of international law. The inquiry appears to end here. By at least considering domestic preferences (and their formation), institutionalism provides a framework to move beyond realism's focus on structure, but it still leaves the comparativist searching for a deeper understanding of state governance mechanisms.

C. Liberalism and Domestic Governance

Liberalism appears to provide the answer. Liberalism[33] is in many ways the antithesis of realism. Both realism and liberalism try to explain state behavior in international politics but they differ on the level of analysis.[34] As we already know, realists posit that the absence of a world central enforcement mechanism forces states to pursue power and act in certain predictable ways. The level of analysis is generally the structure of the international system.

In contrast, liberalism suggests that state behavior in international politics is a reflection of the myriad incentives, constraints, and interests that shape the internal decision-making institutions within states. The level of analysis is the state or the regime type,[35] not the structure of the international system. Liberalism completely rejects realism's unitary state model and hypothesizes that subnational factors explain state behavior.

What does liberalism capture that realism misses? For example, realists predicted that the United States and the Soviet Union would engage in stable patterns of behavior during the Cold War because of the bipolar structure of the

---

33. *See* ANDREW MORAVCSIK, LIBERALISM AND INTERNATIONAL RELATIONS THEORY (1992) (presenting the framework for liberal theory in international relations).

34. *See* J. David Singer, *The Level-of-Analysis Problem in International Relations*, 14 WORLD POL. 77 (1961) (discussing the differences resulting from varying levels of analysis); KENNETH N. WALTZ, MAN, THE STATE, AND WAR: A THEORETICAL ANALYSIS (2001) (delineating three levels for analyzing international relations).

35. A variant of liberalism is democratic peace theory, which purports to explain the occurrence of war between democratic regimes and between democratic and authoritarian regimes. As this theory's scope is narrow and only focuses on war, it is not always considered a general theory of state behavior. For a discussion of democratic peace theory, see Michael W. Doyle, *Kant, Liberal Legacies, and Foreign Affairs*, 12 PHIL. & PUB. AFF. 205 (1983); BRUCE RUSSETT, GRASPING THE DEMOCRATIC PEACE: PRINCIPLES FOR A POST-COLD WAR WORLD (1993).

international system.[36] However, realism couldn't predict that the United States would create certain kinds of international organizations to engage in international governance—the UN and the Bretton Woods[37] institutions, for example—because realism generally does not focus on the subnational features that might motivate state behavior. Liberalism would suggest that the United States, because of its general rule-of-law tradition, democratic regime type, and emphasis on constitutionally enshrined rights, would try to create a rule-based "constitutional order"[38] to manage world politics. As some forms of realism minimize the role of domestic factors in state decision-making, it couldn't predict the rise of international human rights,[39] the proliferation of international organizations, the creation of supranational entities such as the EU,[40] or the use of humanitarian intervention and nation building as features of American foreign policy.[41] Although realists would respond that powerful states often use whatever tools are available to pursue their interests, including international law and organizations, liberalism is much more nuanced in its ability to capture the distinctive institutional features of states and draw conclusions about the effects of such features on state behavior.

Given this micro focus, liberalism also easily generates hypotheses about comparative international law. For example, a state's compliance, *vel non*, with international law rules might be influenced by its subnational features, including regime type and judicial independence. Similarly, variance in the interpretation and application of international law by states should likely be explained by differences in their political, legal, and institutional characteristics. Liberal approaches to the comparative international law project would require a comprehensive examination of the state's subnational features, including the incentives, constraints, and design of courts, legislatures, and executives; the consequences of parliamentary and presidential systems on the application of international law; and the effects of proportional or majoritarian structures on the interpretation of a state's international obligations. Any strong claim about the effect of any single design variable on the interpretation and application of international law is well beyond the scope of this

---

36. See WALTZ, *supra* note 3, at 170 (noting the two nations' strategic focus on each other).

37. The World Bank and the International Monetary Fund. *See generally* EDWARD S. MASON & ROBERT E. ASHER, THE WORLD BANK SINCE BRETTON WOODS (1973).

38. *See* G. JOHN IKENBERRY, AFTER VICTORY: INSTITUTIONS, STRATEGIC RESTRAINT, AND THE REBUILDING OF ORDER AFTER MAJOR WARS (2009) (outlining the United States' efforts to create a rule-based international system).

39. *See* JACK DONNELLY, INTERNATIONAL HUMAN RIGHTS (4th ed. 2012) (sketching the evolution of international human rights since World War II).

40. *See* J.H.H. WEILER, THE CONSTITUTION OF EUROPE (1999) (characterizing the European Union as a triumph of liberal order); *but see* Sebastian Rosato, *Europe's Troubles: Power Politics and the State of the European Project*, 35 INT'L SECURITY 45 (2011) (asserting that the stability of the European Union is strained).

41. *See generally* JAMES F. DOBBINS, IAN O. LESSER & PETER CHALK, AMERICA'S ROLE IN NATION-BUILDING: FROM GERMANY TO IRAQ (2003).

short chapter. At bottom, heterogeneity in institutional design, not power or self-interest, is the key variable to explain the variance in the interpretation and application of international law.

So where does this leave us? Realism is a structural theory generally inapplicable to subnational behavior, institutionalism focuses on domestic preferences, and liberalism emphasizes the role of domestic institutions. As the three theories begin with different core assumptions and units of observation, they don't naturally lead to common research questions and shared hypotheses to explain interpretive variance among states. Intra-theoretical discourse triumphs over inter-theoretical discourse.

II. THE NORMATIVE FOUNDATION OF COMPARATIVE INTERNATIONAL LAW

Although there exist myriad differences between these paradigms, this chapter argues that there are profitable yet unrealized opportunities for theoretical engagement. Realism, institutionalism, and liberalism are descriptive theories with clear normative implications for the interpretation and application of international law. As comparativists, like all other scholars who care about international law and international politics, have normative views about how states should interpret and apply international law, they should care about the arrangement of subnational entities. And, to the extent that comparativists embrace the normative aims of the international relations theories discussed above, they should aim to optimize state domestic arrangements to fit their prescriptions. As I argue below, we can simultaneously explain why states vary in the way they interpret and apply international law and offer normative prescriptions. Comparative international law provides the descriptive basis to draw tentative normative conclusions about institutional design to achieve particular outcomes.

A. Realism and Its Normative Ends

Comparative international law naturally borrows from the various paradigms common to international relations theory. Realism, institutionalism, and liberalism are descriptive theories about how states behave in international politics. Although each theory examines different features of international politics to understand state behavior—the structural factors, preferences, and regime type—they also describe how states actually behave and prescribe how they should behave in international politics. The choice of paradigm through which to view international relations naturally affects how one would understand the normatively preferable interpretation of international law or the ideal design of international organizations.

Let me illustrate the point with realism and then apply the insight to liberalism and institutionalism. Realist assumptions about state compliance with international law have descriptive and prescriptive elements. The structure of the international system (anarchic) forces states to compete and maximize security through power. States maximize security because, in a world without a global policeman or world government, survival is at risk. In such a world, international law can't protect a state from threats, only power can. States that fail to appreciate the role of power and structure—and refuse to adopt polices accordingly—suffer.

Now imagine a comparativist with realist inclinations engaging in a project of institutional design. To be sure, an unreconstructed, diehard realist might not care at all about institutions—structure always trumps. But that is the least charitable understanding of realism. We can also imagine realists who focus on structure but concede that, on the margin, domestic factors might have some explanatory power, even if they are not the most important causal variables. In fact, many realists make exactly that move. For those realists, domestic institutional design might very well matter under some conditions. If so, realism's descriptive elements now have a normative valence. Like-minded comparativists should care about the allocation and distribution of foreign affairs power within states; the distribution of authority might have significant consequences for the interpretation and application of international law.

More concretely, our comparativist should care about the institutional design of the foreign affairs decision-making apparatus, if not the entire government structure. That comparativist should want the subnational entity most likely to generate realist outcomes in international law to have policymaking authority. Every institutional design question related to the application and interpretation of international law in the foreign affairs context—the power to go to war, the power to sign and terminate treaties, and the power to comply with and disregard international law—should be at the forefront of realist concerns.

A few examples are illustrative. In the context of foreign policy, the growth of realist, expansionary military behavior by the United States in the late nineteenth century has been attributed in large part to the growth of the executive branch relative to the legislature and judiciary.[42] More recently, the willingness of France, Germany, Belgium, Spain, and England to prosecute international human rights violations under universal jurisdiction statutes appears to depend on the level of executive control over prosecutorial decisions and the potential international relations costs of pursuing normative goals over realist ends.[43] For these states, the willingness to interpret and apply international criminal law is a function, to a significant degree, of subnational constitutional arrangements.

Similarly, it has been argued that national executives today are more inclined than national courts to disregard multilateral treaties and international law in the security context to the point that national courts have tried to coordinate to ensure greater

---

42. See ZAKARIA, supra note 13, at 40 (noting the increase in state autonomy as a result of the shift in power from the legislative to the executive).

43. See Maximo Langer, The Diplomacy of Universal Jurisdiction: The Political Branches and the Transnational Prosecution of International Crimes, 105 AM. J. INT'L L. 1 (2011) (outlining the incentive structures in a universal jurisdiction enforcement regime). For a critique of universal jurisdiction and a discussion of the tension between normative and strategic (realist) goals, see Henry Kissinger, The Pitfalls of Universal Jurisdiction, 80 FOREIGN AFF. 86, 95 (2001) ("The role of the statesman is to choose the best option when seeking to advance peace and justice, realizing that there is frequently a tension between the two and that any reconciliation is likely to be partial.")

fidelity to international law.[44] Others claim that national executives have tried to weaken or fragment international law through the creation of international institutions with overlapping jurisdictions, limiting the subject matter scope of treaty commitments, and minimizing the oversight role of international courts.[45] Still others counter that, at least in the United States, the executive branch has been no less friendly to international law than the courts.[46] Though much more research is necessary, the insight is neither that national executives are always realist and trying to disregard international law, nor that national courts are liberal and predisposed to international law; rather, the claim is that the allocation of foreign affairs authority likely has consequences for the pursuit of realist goals. Stated in the language of comparative international law, the variance in the interpretation and application of international law is directly related to subnational institutional design. At the very least, to the extent that domestic factors affect some aspects of state behavior—even if the structure predominates—the comparativist interested in realism must take seriously, as a normative matter, the domestic arrangement of decision-making authority.

By now it is clear that the allocation of decision-making authority might have consequences for many questions of comparative international law. One place to start is the interpretive process in international law. Among other things, interpretation includes the exercise of discretion by states to harmonize the often general and ambiguous language of international law and treaties with the similarly complicated language of domestic statutes, administrative regulations, and executive orders. The interpretive discretion is lodged in the relevant subnational decision-making entity and, with nearly 200 hundred countries in the world, we would expect a certain level of variance in how international law is interpreted and enforced. A simple structure might be the following: courts consider decisions of the International Court of Justice (ICJ) in light of domestic constitutional law, executives evaluate the terms of specific treaty obligations in developing foreign policy, and legislatures assess the effect of domestic implementing legislation for treaties on federal law. The greater the interpretive discretion permitted by the construction of a particular international law rule, for example, "make all reasonable efforts," or "undertakes to comply," the greater the latitude for the state decision-making apparatus—courts, legislatures, executives, administrative agencies, commissions, etc.—to make its own determination on the meaning of international law.

Allocation of authority, in some cases, matters. In fact, it is conceivable that the comparativist with realist views would actually prefer the executive to answer all

44. *See* Eyal Benvenisti, *Reclaiming Democracy: The Strategic Uses of Foreign and International Law by National Courts*, 102 AM. J. INT'L L. 241 (2008) (explaining how national courts can coordinate policies to respond to global standards).

45. *See* Benvenisti & Downs, *supra* note 8, at 63; Eyal Benvenisti & George W. Downs, *The Empire's New Clothes: Political Economy and the Fragmentation of International Law*, 60 STAN. L. REV. 595 (2007) (arguing that the fragmentation of international law heavily favors stronger state actors).

46. *See* Daniel Abebe & Eric A. Posner, *The Flaws of Foreign Affairs Legalism*, 51 VA. J. INT'L L. 507 (2011) (finding that foreign affairs legalism in the United States would obstruct international law).

interpretive and application questions related to international law to ensure fidelity with realist thinking. Or, hypothetically, maybe the comparativist would prefer the legislature to make such decisions in a dualist system because, after study, it is clear that the legislature is more likely to be realist than an executive in a monist system. Without running through all the permutations, the point is that the comparativist should look beyond the doctrine and think much more about the structure, incentives, and constraints that shape institutional design, the application and interpretation of international law, and executive decision-making in foreign affairs.

B. Institutionalism and Efficiency

The same logic applies to institutionalism. As we know, institutionalism treats states as rational, self-interested actors pursuing their preferences in a world without a central enforcement mechanism. It is not an international relations theory designed to prescribe state behavior. Nonetheless, institutionalism rests on normative claims about efficiency and the goal of maximizing social welfare. Whether operating within international organizations, negotiating international treaties, or pursuing ends in international politics, states should engage in mutually beneficial cooperation that maximizes national welfare for their citizens, and avoid commitments that reduce public welfare.

The implications for comparative international law are quite clear. States negotiate treaties with the full knowledge that there is no world government with the coercive power to enforce international legal obligations. In light of this, states can choose not to comply with their obligations if they are willing to bear the cost of noncompliance, ranging from reputational costs to economic or military retaliation. Thus, states can and do ignore international tribunals under certain conditions— the ICJ's decision in *Avena*[47] and the United States Supreme Court's response in *Medellin*[48] is an instructive example. In *Medellin*, the Supreme Court refused to give effect to the ICJ's judgment in *Avena*, which required the United States to permit the review and reconsideration of convictions of 52 foreign nationals who were not informed of their right to communicate with their national consulate in violation of Article 36 of the Vienna Convention on Consular Relations (VCCR).[49] The United States not only refused to enforce the ICJ's judgment, but also withdrew from the Optional Protocol to the VCCR providing the ICJ with final decision-making authority regarding the convention.[50] Noncompliance was not free—the United States surely suffered some form of reputational harm in the international

47. Case Concerning Avena and Other Mexican Nationals (Mex. v. U.S.), 2004 I.C.J. 12 (Mar. 31).

48. Medellin v. Texas, 522 U.S. 491 (2008).

49. *Id.* at 502.

50. *Id.* at 500.

community[51]—but the United States evidently concluded that the benefits of non-compliance outweighed the costs.

Noncompliance is not only the province of the United States. In *Kadi*,[52] the European Court of Justice (ECJ) refused to enforce United Nations Security Council ("UNSC") resolutions, which have binding status on UN Member States under Article 103 of the UN Charter, because the resolutions conflicted with EU law. In that case, the ECJ concluded that the UNSC's inclusion of Kadi on a list of alleged supporters of al-Qaeda and the subsequent freezing of his assets violated Kadi's fundamental rights under EU law because he was not informed of the basis of the designation.[53] Simply put, the ECJ concluded that its own law trumps international law. *Medellin* and *Kadi* are but two prominent examples of states refusing to enforce international laws that conflict with their domestic preferences. Of course, states also negotiate and sign treaties, but they ratify them with reservations,[54] refuse to pass the requisite implementing legislation,[55] or withdraw from the jurisdiction of international tribunals.[56] It is certainly clear that national courts can and do enforce international law, but national courts can also circumvent, disregard, or narrowly interpret international legal commitments. In the end, states sometimes ignore international law, though they are subject to informal enforcement by other states through retaliation, sanctions, and reputation costs.[57]

That states can and do exercise discretion in choosing which international commitments to fulfill has significant implications for institutionalism and domestic governance. Institutionalism has efficiency and the maximization of national welfare as prescriptive ends. Normatively speaking, states should make compliance decisions based on the welfare prospects for its citizens, not exclusively on a deontological belief in adherence to international law. While institutionalism might lead to high levels of compliance with international law, it also leaves the door open for states to disregard international commitments when the welfare benefits are great.

---

51. *See* John Quigley, *The United States' Withdrawal from International Court of Justice Jurisdiction in Consular Cases: Reasons and Consequences*, 19 DUKE J. COMP. & INT'L L. 263 (2009) (discussing the criticisms of the United States' withdrawal from the ICJ).

52. Joined Cases C-402/05 P & C-415/05 P, *Kadi & Al Barakaat v. Council*, 3 C.M.L.R. 41 (2008).

53. *Id.* at para. 348.

54. *See* Eric Neumayer, *Qualified Ratification: Explaining Reservations to International Human Rights Treaties*, 36 J. LEGAL STUD. 397 (2007) (providing data on reservations attached by states to various international human rights treaties).

55. *See* Jann K. Kleffner, *The Impact of Complementarity on National Implementation of Substantive International Criminal Law*, 1 J. INT'L CRIM. JUST. 86 (2003) (examining national implementation processes for the ICC).

56. *See* Quigley, *supra* note 51; Ernst-Ulrich Petersmann, *Constitutionalism and International Adjudication*, 31 N.Y.U. J. INT'L L. & POL. 753, 756 (1999) (noting France's withdrawal from compulsory ICJ jurisdiction).

57. *See* Rachel Brewster, *Unpacking the State's Reputation*, 50 HARV. INT'L L.J. 231 (2009) (articulating that concerns regarding state reputation tend to result in compliance).

Thus, comparativists who care about institutionalism should embrace a deep engagement with the design features of subnational entities. Presumably, they would argue that decisions about compliance with treaties, customary international law, and the judgments of international tribunals should be made by the branch, agency, or department that is most likely to maximize national welfare. Or, in the alternative, domestic governance structures for the interpretation and application of international law should be designed to promote the general welfare. If trade liberalization is welfare enhancing for a particular state, the authority to make determinations about international trade, tariffs against foreign goods, and other non-tariff measures should be reposed in the entity best suited to make trade-liberalizing decisions. Gridlock between the protectionist Congress and the pro-trade president—a common trope in American politics—should not exist if domestic design decisions are linked to normative, welfarist goals. Many aspects of domestic governance have implications for the pursuit of certain ends and, if institutionalism has a prescriptive component, comparativists who believe in it should look beyond domestic preferences and more closely consider the design of subnational entities.

C. Liberalism and the Rule of Law

By this point, it might appear that liberalism is the most useful tool for the comparativist. Unlike realism and institutionalism, liberalism already engages with the complex domestic governance questions that impact the application and interpretation of international law by states. The focus has been on courts[58] but the unit of observation could be executives, legislatures, administrative agencies, commissions, or any other department of government charged with interpreting and applying international law.

At the same time, liberalism, like realism and institutionalism, has a normative component. Liberalism, though not a fully developed theory of state behavior, tends to view the promotion of democracy, rule of law, and fidelity to international law as prescriptive ends.[59] In a world increasingly filled with democratic regimes, adherence to international law, not the self-interested pursuit of power or preferences, is the best route to achieving the cosmopolitan will of the international community. The study of comparative international law and the lessons drawn from it are key to achieving liberalism's normative ends. Unlike the other theoretical approaches, liberalism carefully links the creation, design, and implementation of domestic governance structures to the realization of its prescriptive goals: state compliance with international law. Comparative international law, in one view, describes the process through which states interpret and apply international law with the implicit goal of encouraging some form of harmonization.

---

58. *See generally* Karen Knop, *Here and There: International Law in Domestic Courts*, 32 N.Y.U. J. INT'L L. & POL. 501 (2000).

59. *See generally* Anne-Marie Slaughter, *International Law in a World of Liberal States*, 6 EUR. J. INT'L L. 503 (1995).

The story might seem complete. Realism and institutionalism don't pay enough attention to comparative international law—despite my entreaties—while liberalism is perfectly situated to examine it. But liberalism is not without its faults. In fact, liberalism's determination to locate variation in the interpretation of international law solely in domestic design features obscures the role of external, or international political, factors in shaping domestic decision-making. As I have argued in other places,[60] under certain conditions the structure of international politics and power can, and should, affect the way states arrange their domestic governance and interpret and apply international law.

Let me start with the structure of the international system and its consequences for state conceptions of international law. Let's say that the world is generally bipolar or multipolar,[61] meaning that there are either two or several great powers with competing preferences and foreign policy goals. Now imagine that three of the great powers—GP1, GP2, and GP3—are economic, political, and military competitors. Fearful of war, one of the great powers, GP1, decides to modify its domestic institutional arrangements to restrict the executive's ability to initiate hostilities unilaterally and violate the laws of war. With the new constraint in place—a greater role for the legislature in foreign affairs—GP1's president acts in compliance with domestic and international law.

From a comparative international law perspective, the liberal comparativist might attribute GP1's willingness to comply with the international laws of war to features of domestic design, namely the significant role of the legislature in foreign affairs. Thus, the takeaway for other states would be to allocate decision-making authority in foreign affairs to the legislature to ensure fidelity with international law. But this would be too simple a conclusion. GP1, in this example, is already constrained by the presence of GP2 and GP3, the other great powers. Even without the modification of institutional arrangements, GP1's president was already forced to consider the costs of potential military conflict with GP2 and GP3 and might very well have elected not to engage in hostilities or violate the laws of war. The domestic institutional design change might have been helpful, but the structure of the international system already helped constrain GP1's president.

Now let's consider a unipolar[62] world with one superpower.[63] The liberal, having incorrectly learned from GP1's experience that allocating more foreign affairs authority to the legislature constrains the president and results in greater compliance with international law, encourages the superpower to make similar changes.

60. See generally Daniel Abebe, The Global Determinants of U.S. Foreign Affairs Law, 49 STAN. J. INT'L L. 1 (2013); Daniel Abebe, Rethinking the Costs of International Delegations, 34 J. INT'L L. 491 (2013).

61. See JACK DONNELLY, REALISM AND INTERNATIONAL RELATIONS 17 (2000).

62. See generally MONTEIRO, supra note 3; William C. Wohlforth, Unipolarity, Status Competition, and Great Power War, 61 WORLD POL. 28 (2009); Jeffrey W. Legro, The Mix That Makes Unipolarity: Hegemonic Purpose and International Constraints, 24 CAMBRIDGE REV. INT'L AFF. 185 (2011).

63. For an extended discussion of unipolarity and the United States, see G. JOHN IKENBERRY, AMERICA UNRIVALED: THE FUTURE OF THE BALANCE OF POWER (2002).

But, like the example above, this conclusion is only partially correct. In a unipolar world, the external constraints on the superpower are minimized because there are, by definition, no other great powers. In effect, the president of the superpower doesn't have to consider the costs of potential conflict with competing great powers because they don't exist. Compared with the executive in GP1, the president of the superpower is much less constrained by the structure of the international system. Thus, if the goal is to constrain the superpower's president in foreign affairs to ensure fidelity with international law, replicating the institutional arrangements in GP1 might not be enough; perhaps even more foreign affairs authority should be allocated to the legislature to make up for the lack of external constraints on the superpower.[64]

The point of these two highly stylized examples is that variation in the interpretation and application of international law is not just a function of domestic institutional features; rather it is related to power and the structure of the international system as well. The takeaway here is that the comparativist who is solely focused on liberalism might, under certain conditions, miss the impact of external features—power and the structure of the international system—on domestic institutional design and the interpretation of international law. Drawing conclusions about design choices without considering the unique international political circumstances of each state leaves out key variables that are relevant to understanding why and how states interpret international law.

III. CONCLUSION

Realism, institutionalism, and liberalism each contribute to our understanding of international relations theory and international politics. They provide a theoretical approach to comparative international law by using a unit of analysis—power, preferences, and institutions—to help explain variation in the application and interpretation of international law. But as this chapter has argued, realism, institutionalism, and liberalism also have normative components, and comparativists should be sensitive to these in considering questions of domestic institutional design. As this volume clearly demonstrates, comparativists provide rich descriptions of state interpretive practices; this chapter encourages them to embrace international relations theory and connect state practice with normative ends. Comparative international law has the potential to not only explain variation in the interpretation of international law but also help link international relations theories with domestic governance.

64. *See* Abebe, *Global Determinants, supra* note 60, at 39 (discussing how Congress can limit presidential foreign affairs power in the absence of external constraints).

PART TWO

International Lawyers, the Academy, and Competing Conceptions of International Law

5

The Many Fields of (German) International Law

NICO KRISCH[*]

International law has long been imagined as a universal project, one in which difference featured largely as an aberration from the idea of an international rule of law. As a matter of doctrine, international legal norms were in any event imagined as uniform across the countries and actors they applied to. Comparison finds little place in such a picture—speaking of American, Russian, Chinese, Indian, German, Brazilian international law would always only be an analysis of deviance, an exploration of the ways in which particular countries have left the common path for their particularist policies.[1]

Yet in recent years, owing much to the turn to context, history, and politics in the study of international law, interest in comparative approaches has grown (again),[2] and the present volume seeks to reflect and shape this emerging area of research. This chapter contributes to this endeavor with a focus on the particularities of academic international law in Germany, but also with an interest in methodology and a broader argument for attention to a particular set of factors behind differences in the interpretation and application of international law. Using sociological insights, it focuses on the professional contexts in which the different interpreters are embedded—the social and professional "fields" in which they operate—and suggests connections

* I am grateful to Tània Foix and Konstantin Kleine for their valuable research assistance. I wish to also thank the editors of this volume, Jochen von Bernstorff, Christoph Möllers, Matthias Ruffert, and Ed Swaine as well as the participants in the Sokol Colloquium at the University of Virginia and the International Law Cyber-Colloquium for their helpful comments.

1. *But see, e.g.,* INTERNATIONAL LAW IN COMPARATIVE PERSPECTIVE (William E. Butler ed., 1980), albeit with a primary focus on the uses of comparison for the identification and codification of international law.

2. On the origins of this turn, see Boris N. Mamlyuk & Ugo Mattei, *Comparative International Law*, 36 BROOKLYN J. INT'L LAW 385 (2011).

between the shape of those contexts and the methodological and substantive commitments with which these interpreters approach international law.

This chapter is exploratory; it does not present a full analysis of all relevant fields,
nor of the rich landscape of international law in Germany. It hopes to provide a
basis from which we can explore the practice of international law in greater depth,
and some initial illustrations of where we may find reasons for, and expressions
of, difference in the comparative endeavor. The examples for this are drawn from
Germany—the legal and academic system I am most familiar with, but also one that
provides many structural differences to the way international law is taught and practiced elsewhere. The chapter begins with a brief sketch of the theoretical framework
and an outline of the different fields at play in international law, and then turns to a
deeper exploration of the fields that relate to international law in Germany.

I. FIELDS OF INTERNATIONAL LAW

Four decades ago Oscar Schachter depicted the "invisible college" of international
lawyers as the expression of a largely unified discipline.[3] Problematic already then,
such a portrayal would appear far-fetched today. The proliferation of specialized
areas in international law and the expansion of practitioners and scholars of international law in the domestic sphere have augmented the circle of "international lawyers" radically—and have included many in it for whom international law is only a
small aspect of their work.

If we want to understand how international law is construed (and why) by those
different interpreters, we have to take a step back and inquire into who they are
and what the context is in which they operate and through which they define their
approach to law. In order to do so, I propose here to adopt a sociological approach
based on the concept of "social fields" and to explore in which fields the relevant
interpreters are embedded, what their position in these fields is, what the standard
assumptions in them are, and how this affects the practice of interpretation.

A. Social Fields

The idea of social fields has become increasingly widespread over the last few
decades and has found reflection, in different forms, in organizational theory, social
movement studies, and economic sociology as well as historical institutionalism
in political science.[4] It has found its most prominent expression as a general struc-
turing device in sociology in the work of Pierre Bourdieu and, more recently, Neil
Fligstein, and Doug McAdam.[5] A field, in Bourdieu's characterization, is a place
for struggle between different agents: a "network, or a configuration, of objective
relations between positions." These positions are defined "by their present and

3. Oscar Schachter, *The Invisible College of International Lawyers*, 72 Nw. U. L. Rev. 217 (1977).

4. *See* Neil Fligstein & Doug McAdam, A Theory of Fields 3–8 (2012).

5. *See* Pierre Bourdieu & Loïc J.D. Wacquant, An Invitation to Reflexive Sociology
(1992); Fligstein & McAdam, *supra* note 4.

potential situation ... in the structure of the distribution of species of power (or capital) whose possession commands access to the specific profits that are at stake in the field, as well as by their objective relation to other positions."[6] Yet agents are not determined by the structure of the field: they have internalized the structure in the form of a "habitus," a "socialized subjectivity,"[7] which provides them with a sense of the "game" they play yet does not remove the rules of the game from potential contestation. Unlike in a game of chess, the rules of a field are always "in play," never entirely settled.[8]

When studying the ways in which international lawyers position themselves, we will want to inquire into the fields in which they operate, the rules that structure these fields, the distribution of capital in the field, and the positions actors occupy in it. In particular, we need to know about the relations *among* fields: the degree to which different fields are dependent or independent, and hierarchically or reciprocally ordered.[9]

B. Fields of International Law

Which social fields are then relevant for an understanding of international law? In the following, I outline a number of potential fields that may have a bearing on how international law is studied and interpreted and may help us to understand variation in approaches to international law. This list is not exhaustive—for each agent, various other fields may be relevant—but aims at mapping out the most important.

Transnational academic international law. Probably the most emblematic of academic fields in international law, the transnational academic field encompasses agents and academic production with a global ambition, straddling territorial boundaries and leaving behind particular national origins. It is currently centered on English-language work and United States (US) and United Kingdom (UK) institutions: academic institutions such as the New York University Law School or the Lauterpacht Centre for International Law in Cambridge; publishing houses such as Oxford University Press and Cambridge University Press; journals such as the *American Journal of International Law* and the *European Journal of International Law*; and associations such as the American Society of International Law, which brands itself as "the world's leading association for scholars, practitioners, and students of international law."[10] Other sites, especially in Africa, Asia, and Latin America, are perceived as more peripheral.[11]

6. BOURDIEU & WACQUANT, *supra* note 5, at 97.

7. *Id.* at 126.

8. PIERRE BOURDIEU, ÜBER DEN STAAT: VORLESUNGEN AM COLLÈGE DE FRANCE 1989–1992 175–80 (2014).

9. *See* FLIGSTEIN & MCADAM, *supra* note 4, at 59–64.

10. ASIL Membership Brochure, http://asil.org/sites/default/files/ASILmemberBrochure.pdf (last visited Dec. 29, 2015).

11. *See, e.g.,* the "periphery series" of the *Leiden Journal of International Law* and the reflection on the role of the periphery in the universalization of international law in Arnulf Becker Lorca, *Universal*

Transnational international law practice. The continuing professionalization of international law, and especially the proliferation of international judicial bodies, has led to the growth of a distinct set of practitioners. Foreign ministries' legal advisors, judges at international courts, legal officers in international organizations, or international law specialists in globalized law firms today form a structure that maintains links with academic international law but is generally distinct from it (and itself internally differentiated). Bridging institutions—such as the International Law Commission, or the Institut de Droit International—have lost some of the clout they may have had half a century ago.

National academic international legal fields. Even though universality is a typically voiced ambition of international legal studies, much of the academe is organized along national (in part also linguistic) lines. Many countries have their own learned societies—the *Société française pour le droit international* or the *Asociación Argentina de derecho internacional* are examples. They also have their own journals; some of these, perhaps most notably the *Indian Journal of International Law*, have achieved influence well beyond national boundaries. To what extent the social capital in this national field is linked to that in other fields, especially the transnational, will be one of the guiding questions in my more detailed case study in the next section.

National academic legal fields. Institutionally, academic international lawyers are typically part of universities' law faculties and they are thus deeply embedded in the broader national field of legal academia. Their status and reputation will often—though with significant variation across countries—depend on recognition in this broader field. Think only of the US system where international law scholars often seek to publish in generalist (student-edited) law reviews whose reputation typically surpasses that of top international law journals by a large measure.[12] The boundaries between international lawyers and others are also becoming blurred in some contexts. As international law increasingly affects the domestic sphere, scholars of national law, especially national constitutional and administrative law, face (and solve) interpretative and structural questions at the boundary between domestic and international law. The frames they use for this engagement—typically borrowed from their domestic work—will significantly shape the way international law is understood in a national context.

National professional legal fields. With the greater domestic salience of international law, many government departments (environment, finance, economy, etc.) today have their own specialized international lawyers, and many other officials deal with and interpret international law. This includes judges: they usually do

---

International Law: Nineteenth-Century Histories of Imposition and Appropriation, 51 HARV. INT'L L.J. 475 (2010).

12. *See also* ANTHEA ROBERTS, IS INTERNATIONAL LAW INTERNATIONAL? (2017). In the ranking of the Washington & Lee Law School Library for 2014, the first international law journal—the *Harvard International Law Journal*—appears at number 43, after a host of generalist law reviews (many obscure to the outsider). The *American Journal of International Law* comes 66th, and the *European Journal of International Law* 136th. *See* http://lawlib.wlu.edu/LJ/index.aspx (last visited Dec. 29, 2015).

not specialize in international legal matters but many are faced with them in their practice—on issues of human rights, trade, or even criminal law at times. As with national academics, we can expect that the frames they use will differ from the ones that characterize the transnational international law field. The effect of this "domesticated" international law may then also carry over into the academic field, depending on the proximity between the two.

Issue areas: transnational/national academic and professional fields. Many international lawyers today define themselves primarily as specialists—as trade, environmental, or human rights lawyers—and their main audience is among their peers in these particular groups. Within those fields—probably best seen as "nested"[13] in the broader fields of international law—particular forms of capital count: they have particular associations, journals, educational focal points, etc.; connections with fields of practice in the same issue area will often be tighter, and links to disciplinarily adjacent fields, especially to those related to policy or science in the same issue areas, will be valued. Certain issue areas thus seem to have produced fields of a distinct complexion—with their own rules and forms of capital and particular links between academic and professional, national and transnational fields.

C. Analyzing Fields and Their Relations

When we engage in an analysis of the different fields—and we might include others potentially relevant in certain contexts—the focus will be on a set of characteristics: (1) the scope and boundaries (and existence) of the fields in question, (2) the rules that structure the field, (3) the forms of social capital relevant to the field, (4) the identity of dominant actors (incumbents) and challengers, (5) the internal governance units, and (6) the degree of settlement of the field. Yet much of our interest will be devoted not only to the internal structure of each field, but also to the *relations* among the different fields. The fields I have introduced all have some connection to each other, but the intensity of these connections and their nature are not always clear, and they are likely to vary across countries and issue areas.

What relevance these characteristics of social fields and their relations have for understanding the interpretation and application of international law is eventually an empirical question. However, choosing this particular focus follows the insight that embeddedness in a social field often has a significant bearing on an individual's own positioning—as individuals are part of, and seek to gain a position in, their professional context, the "rules of the game" of that context are likely to have a major impact. This does not exclude the possibility that in many instances, other factors will play a significant role also in shaping the rules and forms of capital of a particular field. Focusing on the structure of the relevant fields should allow us to analyze the relation of endogenous and exogenous factors more directly.

13. FLIGSTEIN & McADAM, *supra* note 4, at 58.

II. INTERNATIONAL LAW IN GERMANY: AN APPROXIMATION

This chapter begins to inquire into the shape and interactions of the different fields of international law by reflecting on the particularity of academic international law in Germany. Rather than presenting a conclusive picture, it aims at identifying characteristics and categories that can help us to structure our further inquiry. The inquiry is based on an analysis of career paths and publication activities of academic international lawyers in Germany, triangulated with the author's own (semi-participant)[14] experience and the observations of others.

A. A Particular Focus

In substance, German international law scholarship has a number of characteristic traits. The first, and most frequently noted, is the orientation toward *doctrine and system*. As in many other countries of continental Europe, doctrinal analysis is seen as the core of the discipline. The technical mastery of the substance of the law and the ability to systematize large amounts of positive law and jurisprudence are key attributes of successful scholars.[15] This obviously presupposes that international law *can* indeed be regarded as a "system," and it reflects a particular "systemic mindset." As Eyal Benvenisti has put it, it embodies "a vision of international law as an ordered system, with rules of recognition that determine relationships between different areas of law and governing principles that set at least some kind of hierarchy amongst norms and ensure that no treaty is 'self-contained.'"[16]

Envisaging this kind of system is a constructive effort, and German scholars have often been associated with the "attempt to use general principles to develop, out of a multiplicity of single norms which may seem disparate and full of gaps, an overall, coherent normative order."[17] This is not just an epistemological choice, but also reflects an ethical standpoint from which "fostering and maintaining systematic coherence undergirds the ideas of legal certainty, equality, and, thereby, justice."[18]

---

14. I studied and did my PhD in Germany, then worked in the United States and the UK for eight years before returning to teach in Germany (though not at a law faculty) from 2009 to 2013.

15. Eyal Benvenisti, *The Future of International Law Scholarship in Germany: The Tension Between Interpretation and Change*, 67 ZEITSCHRIFT FÜR AUSLÄNDISCHES ÖFFENTLICHES RECHT UND VÖLKERRECHT 585 (2007); Anne Peters, *Die Zukunft der Völkerrechtswissenschaft: Wider den Epistemischen Nationalismus*, 67 ZEITSCHRIFT FÜR AUSLÄNDISCHES ÖFFENTLICHES RECHT UND VÖLKERRECHT 721, 771 (2007); Armin von Bogdandy, *General Principles of International Public Authority: Sketching a Research Field, in* THE EXERCISE OF PUBLIC AUTHORITY BY INTERNATIONAL INSTITUTIONS 730 (Armin von Bogdandy et al. eds., 2010); Andreas Zimmermann, *Zur Zukunft der Völkerrechtswissenschaft in Deutschland*, 67 ZEITSCHRIFT FÜR AUSLÄNDISCHES ÖFFENTLICHES RECHT UND VÖLKERRECHT 799, 805 (2007).

16. Benvenisti, *supra* note 15, at 588–89.

17. Zimmermann, *supra* note 15, at 805.

18. Armin von Bogdandy, *The Past and Promise of Doctrinal Constructivism: A Strategy for Responding to the Challenges Facing Constitutional Scholarship in Europe*, 7 INT'L J. CONST. L. 364, 379 (2009) (with a view to constitutional law scholarship).

The orientation towards doctrine and system has led to a particular emphasis on certain types of publications. Massive efforts such as the *Encyclopedia of Public International Law* under the aegis of the Heidelberg Max Planck Institute or the comprehensive commentaries on the UN Charter or the Statute of the International Court of Justice[19] are the fruit of this orientation (and are made possible by favorable material conditions).[20]

This general orientation also finds reflection in the design of scholarly inquiry. A recent example is the project on the exercise of public authority by international institutions, anchored at the Max Planck Institute. In explicit contrast to "external" approaches originating in the United States, it aims at developing an "internal" account that establishes a common framework and general principles for international public authority[21]—"an overarching theory and doctrine of public law."[22] The framers of the project recognize that the possibility of such an overarching frame is not self-evident, and they justify their doctrinal endeavor (in exceptionally frank terms) with the hope of contributing to "a better, more peaceful and more integrated world of closely and successfully cooperating polities governed by public international institutions."[23]

Much German scholarship is sustained by similar sensitivities and a broadly *internationalist* spirit. A decade ago, Jan Klabbers described German international law as "embarked on sheer idealism interlaced with a dose of almost intuitive sociology," as "characterized by a clear sense of advocating the right thing."[24] He went on to observe that

> ... there is probably not a country in the world where the concept of *erga omnes* obligations has received such a warm welcome as precisely in Germany; there is hardly a country in the world more jubilant about the *jus cogens* concept than Germany; and there is not a country in the world where the UN Charter is so steadfastly and seriously regarded as a constitution for the international community as Germany.[25]

19. THE CHARTER OF THE UNITED NATIONS: A COMMENTARY (Bruno Simma et al. eds., 3d ed. 2012); THE STATUTE OF THE INTERNATIONAL COURT OF JUSTICE: A COMMENTARY (Andreas Zimmermann et al. eds., 2012).

20. Many German law professors benefit from the ready availability of pre- and postdoctoral assistants as well as secretarial staff.

21. Armin von Bogdandy et al., *Developing the Publicness of Public International Law: Towards a Legal Framework for Global Governance Activities, in* THE EXERCISE OF PUBLIC AUTHORITY BY INTERNATIONAL INSTITUTIONS 3 (Armin von Bogdandy et al., eds., 2010).

22. von Bogdandy, *supra* note 15, at 741.

23. von Bogdandy et al., *supra* note 21, at 32.

24. Jan Klabbers, *Book Review*, 16 LEIDEN J. INT'L L. 201, 201–02 (2003) (reviewing ULLA HINGST, AUSWIRKUNGEN DER GLOBALISIERUNG AUF DAS RECHT DER VÖLKERRECHTLICHEN VERTRÄGE (2001)).

25. *Id.* at 202–03.

Such internationalism has, of course, been quite characteristic of many international lawyers across the globe,[26] yet its German variant may be of particular intensity. Going back to the interwar period, in particular Hans Kelsen's cosmopolitanism,[27] it found a strong expression in different strands of scholarship after World War II. Alfred Verdross's influential "universal international law," grounded in natural-law ideas, reflects much of this internationalist ethos, as does Hermann Mosler's 1974 lecture on "the international society as a legal community" at The Hague Academy.[28] Most German scholarship during the Cold War was less expansive, perhaps more pragmatic and focused on concrete problems in the interpretation and development of international law. Still, it typically depicted the international legal order in a positive light; further legalization, and the implementation of existing international law, were welcomed, and more fundamental critique remained marginal.[29] In the 1990s, The Hague lectures by Christian Tomuschat, Jochen Frowein, and Bruno Simma took the internationalist orientation further and established a highly distinguishable—and influential—vision of the international legal order.[30] Even if developments in the post-2001 world may have provoked greater doubts, such a vision remains strong among many German scholars today.[31] It is captured in the discourse of international constitutionalism, very much associated with German origins;[32] in the notion of an international community that embodies a particular

26. David Kennedy, *The International Style in Postwar Law and Policy*, 1 UTAH L. REV. 7 (1994).

27. *See* JOCHEN VON BERNSTORFF, THE PUBLIC INTERNATIONAL LAW THEORY OF HANS KELSEN: BELIEVING IN UNIVERSAL LAW (2010).

28. HERMANN MOSLER, THE INTERNATIONAL SOCIETY AS A LEGAL COMMUNITY 140 (1980); ALFRED VERDROSS & BRUNO SIMMA, UNIVERSELLES VÖLKERRECHT: THEORIE UND PRAXIS (1976).

29. *See* JOCHEN VON BERNSTORFF, DIE DEUTSCHE VÖLKERRECHTSWISSENSCHAFT UND DER "POSTCOLONIAL TURN" VOELKERRECHTSBLOG (2014), http://voelkerrechtsblog.com/2014/09/09/die-deutsche-volkerrechtswissenschaft-und-der-postcolonial-turn/.

30. Christian Tomuschat, *Obligations Arising for States Without or Against Their Will*, 241 RECUEIL DES COURS 195 (1993); Jochen A. Frowein, *Reactions by Not Directly Affected States to Breaches of Public International Law*, 248 RECUEIL DES COURS 345 (1994); Bruno Simma, *From Bilateralism to Community Interest in International Law*, 250 RECUEIL DES COURS 217 (1994). See also the more critical discussion in ANDREAS L. PAULUS, DIE INTERNATIONALE GEMEINSCHAFT IM VÖLKERRECHT (2000).

31. See the accounts in Andreas L. Paulus, *Zur Zukunft der Völkerrechtswissenschaft in Deutschland: Zwischen Konstitutionalisierung und Fragmentierung des Völkerrechts*, 67 ZEITSCHRIFT FÜR AUS-LÄNDISCHES ÖFFENTLICHES RECHT UND VÖLKERRECHT 695 (2007); Armin von Bogdandy, *Constitutionalism in International Law: Comment on a Proposal from Germany*, 47 HARV. INT'L L.J. 223 (2006). But see also the more cautious approach in Georg Nolte, *Kosovo und Konstitutionalisierung: Zur humanitären Intervention der NATO-Staaten*, 59 ZEITSCHRIFT FÜR AUS-LÄNDISCHES ÖFFENTLICHES RECHT UND VÖLKERRECHT 941, 958 (1999).

32. *See* BARDO FASSBENDER, UN SECURITY COUNCIL REFORM AND THE RIGHT OF VETO: A CONSTITUTIONAL PERSPECTIVE (1998); Anne Peters, *Are We Moving Towards Constitutionalization of the World Community?*, *in* REALIZING UTOPIA: THE FUTURE OF INTERNATIONAL LAW 118 (2012); ALFRED VERDROSS, DIE VERFASSUNG DER VÖLKERRECHTSGEMEINSCHAFT (1926).

set of common values; and in the liberal idea that the international order is ultimately based on the individual, not the state.[33]

If the *constitutionalist* discourse has a strong internationalist side, it also has a recognizably domestic side. It reflects an orientation toward "fundamental principles of the constitutional state"[34] and the image of an "international legal order which acknowledges and has creatively appropriated principles and values of domestic constitutionalism."[35] As Andreas Paulus puts it, through "the constitutionalization thesis[,] German international legal academia translates its experiences with its own constitution and with European law to the sphere of international law."[36] This can lead to ambivalences, especially when key tenets of domestic constitutionalism—for example, human rights—come into conflict with international law, as was the case in the much-discussed *Kadi* cases in the European courts. Even if the constitutional is thought of as universal, the actual tension between the constitutional as particular and the (different) international is a constant focus of scholarly attention.[37] Mostly, however, potential conflicts are interpreted as conflicts *within* the universal, resolvable through an emphasis on common values and liberal principles that align international law with domestic constitutional standards.[38]

International legal thought in Germany is, of course, not uniform. It has, for example, long had a more statist strand,[39] and for some scholars closer to that tradition, the commitment to constitutionalism may well lead to a retreat into the national order when international law does not conform to the demands of the German constitution—the constitution then becomes a "firewall against the dumbing down of nationally guaranteed liberties."[40]

---

33. Andreas L. Paulus, *Whether Universal Values Can Prevail over Bilateralism and Reciprocity*, in REALIZING UTOPIA: THE FUTURE OF INTERNATIONAL LAW 89 (Antonio Cassese ed., 2012); SUPRASTAATLICHE KONSTITUTIONALISIERUNG (Bardo Fassbender & Angelika Siehr eds., 2012); Anne Peters, *Humanity as the A and Ω of Sovereignty*, 20 EUR. J. INT'L L. 513 (2009).

34. Stefan Kadelbach, *Völkerrecht als Verfassungsordnung? Zur Völkerrechtswissenschaft in Deutschland*, 67 ZEITSCHRIFT FÜR AUSLÄNDISCHES ÖFFENTLICHES RECHT UND VÖLKERRECHT 599, 621 (2007).

35. Peters, *supra* note 32, at 118.

36. Paulus, *supra* note 31, at 701.

37. *See, e.g.*, Christian Walter, *Grundrechtsschutz gegen Hoheitsakte internationaler Organisationen*, 129 ARCHIV DES ÖFFENTLICHEN RECHTS 39 (2004).

38. Kirsten Schmalenbach, *Bedingt kooperationsbereit: Der Kontrollanspruch des EuGH bei gezielten Sanktionen der Vereinten Nationen: Zum Urteil des EuGH vom 3. 9. 2008, Rs. C 402/05 u. C 415/ 05—Kadi und Al Barakaat*, 64 JURISTENZEITUNG 35 (2009).

39. *See, e.g.*, KARL DOEHRING, VÖLKERRECHT: EIN LEHRBUCH (2004).

40. Stefan Talmon, *Die Grenzen der Anwendung des Völkerrechts im deutschen Recht*, 68 JURISTENZEITUNG 12–21 (2013). *See also, e.g.*, FRANK SCHORKOPF, GRUNDGESETZ UND ÜBERSTAATLICHKEIT: KONFLIKT UND HARMONIE IN DEN AUSWÄRTIGEN BEZIEHUNGEN DEUTSCHLANDS (2007).

B. International Lawyers, Not So International

German international law is recognizable in its substance, and it certainly has an audience well beyond its geographical and linguistic borders. However, taking into account the size of the field and the significant resources at its disposal, its projection into the transnational field of international legal academia appears to be relatively limited. Two indicators may suffice to illustrate this. One is the presence at The Hague Academy of International Law—at least traditionally, being selected to lecture in one of its summer courses has been regarded as a sign of transnational reputation. Yet in the last 10 sessions, only one public international law scholar based at a German university held a course there—far fewer than scholars from several other European countries.[41] This limited presence is not a historical novelty: between 1970 and 1989, for example, (West) German scholars accounted for only 4 of the 197 published courses on public international law at the Academy.[42]

A second indicator is the limited visibility in "international" journals. From 836 articles in four internationally-oriented, English-language journals published between 2004 and 2013, only 45 are from scholars based in Germany, compared with 245 from scholars in the United Kingdom or 78 from scholars in the (much smaller) Netherlands.[43] This picture is shown in Table 5.1 below.

Table 5.1. PUBLICATIONS IN INTERNATIONAL JOURNALS, 2004–2013

	D	UK	NL	Total articles
American Journal of International Law	1 (1%)	8 (7%)	2 (2%)	111
European Journal of International Law	19 (7%)	65,5 (24%)	11,5 (4%)	272
Leiden Journal of International Law	18,83 (8%)	42,5 (19%)	55,9 (25%)	223
International & Comparative Law Quarterly	6 (3%)	129,25 (56%)	8,75 (4%)	230
Sum	44,83 (5%)	245,25 (29%)	78,15 (9%)	836

41. This figure counts summer programs at the Academy from 2007 to 2016. Scholars from the Netherlands held 2, from France 11, from the UK 6, and from Switzerland 5 courses. The only German course was by Rudolf Dolzer in 2010; Bruno Simma held the general course in 2009 but he was a judge at the ICJ then. Here and in the following, I count as "nationals" scholars at academic institutions of the respective country, unless otherwise noted.

42. A further course was given by Bernhard Graefrath from the German Democratic Republic.

43. We have counted articles published between 2004 and 2013 of more than 20 pages in length in the *American Journal of International Law*, the *European Journal of International Law*, the *International and Comparative Law Quarterly*, and the *Leiden Journal of International Law*—by many accounts, the (English-language) international law journals most read in Europe. Coauthorships have been weighted.

This limited projection is reflected in the self-perception of German international lawyers. Stefan Oeter, for example, laments the "limited presence in international discourses" and finds reasons for it in linguistic barriers, but also (and perhaps mainly) in the relative weakness of international law in legal education and the fact that academic careers in Germany are built on the back of achievements in national public law, not international law.[44] Georg Nolte and Andreas Zimmermann make similar observations, pointing out that because of the way law faculties are structured, scholars of international law typically need to be generalists, covering domestic constitutional or administrative law and European Union law as well.[45] The one chair dedicated solely to (European and) international law, held in Munich by Bruno Simma, was converted back into the typical "mixed" public law/international law chair upon his departure in 2003. Thus, international lawyers in Germany typically only teach half or less than half of their courses in international law; much or even most of their teaching is in constitutional or administrative law. This stands in stark contrast with their colleagues in other European countries, such as France, the Netherlands, or the United Kingdom, or also the United States, where international lawyers teach primarily in their discipline. The German model certainly does not encourage specialization or a sustained presence in the transnational discourses of international law.[46]

The weakness of international law in most faculties stems in large part from the fact that international law is an optional subject, with a relatively small number of course offerings, in a system of legal education that is both heavily state-regulated and geared towards domestic legal practice.[47] LLM programs—elsewhere a main focus of teaching in international law—are small (in many faculties, nonexistent). This has repercussions not only for the design of academic posts but also for the overall number of professors in international law. In many smaller faculties, there is only one position covering international as well as European law; in bigger faculties, the two subjects may be separated, with 1 or 2 (out of around 30 faculty) focusing on international law alongside domestic constitutional or administrative law. Compare this with the situation in the United Kingdom where in many top law departments international lawyers make up around 10 percent of the faculty (and teach in large part, or even exclusively, international law subjects).

44. Stefan Oeter, *Zur Zukunft der Völkerrechtswissenschaft in Deutschland*, 67 ZEITSCHRIFT FÜR AUSLÄNDISCHES ÖFFENTLICHES RECHT UND VÖLKERRECHT 675, 691 (2007).

45. Georg Nolte, *Zur Zukunft der Völkerrechtswissenschaft in Deutschland*, 67 ZEITSCHRIFT FÜR AUSLÄNDISCHES ÖFFENTLICHES RECHT UND VÖLKERRECHT 657, 668 (2007); Zimmermann, *supra* note 15, at 805.

46. An exception is the Max Planck Institute for Comparative Public and International Law in Heidelberg, a publicly funded research institution at which many German international lawyers have worked as doctoral or postdoctoral fellows. Its directors do not have formal teaching obligations.

47. For a critical overview of German legal studies and scholarly practices, see the report by the German Council of Science and Humanities, WISSENSCHAFTSRAT, PROSPECTS OF LEGAL SCHOLARSHIP IN GERMANY CURRENT SITUATION, ANALYSES, RECOMMENDATIONS (2012) http://www.wissenschaftsrat.de/download/archiv/2558-12_engl.pdf.

In many ways, then, international law in Germany is a subfield of public law with relatively little differentiation. It has its own posts, journals (mainly the *Zeitschrift für ausländisches öffentliches Recht*, the *Archiv des Völkerrechts*, and the *German Yearbook of International Law*) and an association, the German Society of International Law, which has a long history and includes scholars from Austria and Switzerland as well as private international lawyers. Yet the main patterns and career paths are structured by the broader public law field, with the result that international lawyers invest significantly into work on domestic law issues to gain social capital (be hired, read, etc.). This contrasts with the situation in many other European countries—for example, the Netherlands, Switzerland, or the United Kingdom.[48] Even in France, where career and publication patterns are remarkably "national,"[49] scholars build their reputation primarily as experts in *international* law.

The German particularity is well reflected in scholars' curricula vitae. In the following, I analyze the curricula of 11 prominent public international lawyers working in Germany.[50] The career paths of these scholars are remarkably similar. All originally from Germany—German law faculties remain largely closed to foreigners[51]—they have gone through German legal education (at a variety of universities). All have spent a year abroad during their studies (typically in Europe, a majority in Geneva or Lausanne); two hold an LLM degree from a US university (both from Harvard). All but one have also completed their "second law degree," involving two years of practice (mostly clerking at courts or interning at law firms) and qualifying them as attorneys. All have done their doctoral degrees and their postdoctoral *Habilitation* at German universities. Notably, 7 out of the 11 worked for an extended period of time, in preparation of the doctoral thesis or the *Habilitation*, at the Max Planck Institute in Heidelberg, reflecting the central role of the Institute in German international law (as well as its extraordinary resources). Three of the 11 clerked for a judge at the Federal Constitutional Court. Typically, and following the customs of the field, only one of their two theses—for the doctorate and the *Habilitation*—had its focus in international law; the other concerned issues in domestic law, usually constitutional law, sometimes from a comparative angle, sometimes also with a focus on the EU. Of the 11 scholars analyzed here, 7 worked on international law for their doctoral degree; only 3 for their (longer and more weighty) *Habilitation*.

---

48. *See* ROBERTS, *supra* note 12.

49. *Id.*

50. Membership in the Council of the German Society of International Law is used as a proxy for prominence. The scholars analyzed here—Armin von Bogdandy (Max Planck Institute, Heidelberg), Ulrich Fastenrath (Dresden), Meinhard Hilf (Bucerius Law School, Hamburg), Stephan Hobe (Cologne), Rainer Hofmann (Frankfurt), Thilo Marauhn (Gießen), Georg Nolte (Humboldt University, Berlin), Stefan Oeter (Hamburg), Anne Peters (Max Planck Institute, Heidelberg), Christian Walter (LMU, Munich), and Andreas Zimmermann (Potsdam)—mostly enjoy a high reputation in the field.

51. Only 1.9 percent of law professorships are held by foreigners: see WISSENSCHAFTSRAT, *supra* note 47, at 45, 91.

All of them are thus firmly grounded in German (public) law—through their basic legal education, their pre- and/or postdoctoral work, the environments they worked in, and the posts they hold and the courses they teach. They also typically continue to publish in domestic public law as well as European and international law, but their visibility outside Germany is often limited. From 2010 to 2015, only 3 of the 11 scholars under analysis have had articles published in top international law journals; 3 others have had occasional pieces out in specialized international journals; and the remaining 5 have practically not published in international journals at all (or only the odd piece in rather obscure outlets). In part, this may reflect the generally lower emphasis on journal publications, as compared to edited volumes or commentary entries, in German legal scholarship.[52] The three monographs on international law arising out of *Habilitationen*, in part because they were all written and published in German, also did not attract much international attention, at least in terms of citations.[53]

This may be changing. Scientific institutions in Germany are calling for a greater internationalization of legal scholarship,[54] and younger international lawyers seem to aim more for international journals and publishers and to foster more transnational ties, as for example through the European Society of International Law. Seventy percent of the articles counted in Table 5.1 above have been authored by scholars under 40 years of age; only 8 percent by scholars above 50.[55] If we look more closely at the curricula of the younger generation—those below 50 with permanent international law positions at German universities—we can observe change, but not of a radical kind. Foreign degrees, especially LLM degrees, are now relatively common and held by a majority (62 percent) of the 13 scholars considered.[56] Some in this group have a more clearly international profile—three have turned their doctoral dissertation or *Habilitation* into monographs with top English-language publishers, one other is regularly publishing in highly visible journals in international economic law; one has, while being a constitutional court judge, suspended his previously very internationally oriented publication activity. But less than half (38 percent) publish the majority of their publications in English; 3 of the 13 only a small minority (less than 20 percent); and most are not aiming at journals but publish their English-language pieces mostly in edited collections. Less than a third

---

52. *See id.* at 22–23, 67–71.

53. On Google Scholar, the three works, published between 1991 and 2000, are listed with 93 citations in total.

54. WISSENSCHAFTSRAT, *supra* note 47.

55. See the information on the journals above. The author's age could be identified (with reasonable certainty) in 91 percent of the cases; only these are included in the calculation.

56. They include Andreas von Arnauld (Kiel), Jochen von Bernstorff (Tübingen), Sigrid Boysen (University of the Armed Forces, Hamburg), Philipp Dann (Humboldt University, Berlin), Markus Kotzur (University of Hamburg), Heike Krieger (Free University Berlin), Nele Matz-Lück (Kiel), Kerstin Odendahl (Kiel), Andreas Paulus (Göttingen and German Constitutional Court), Anja Seibert-Fohr (Göttingen), Pierre Thielbörger (Bochum), Christian Tietje (Halle-Wittenberg), and Silja Voeneky (Freiburg).

of those who have completed both a doctorate and Habilitation have a significant
international law element in both works; the traditional emphasis on at least one
of these concerning primarily domestic, German law largely remains in place. In
fact, in this generation some of the more transnationally oriented scholars with a
German academic background can be found abroad, occupying academic posts in
places such as Amsterdam, Cambridge, Geneva, Glasgow, Leiden, Miami, Rio de
Janeiro, and Sankt Gallen. Some of them are more visible in the transnational field
than their counterparts in Germany—this may point to the greater space afforded
to international law specializations in other academic systems, but it also highlights
the trade-offs between the domestic and the international that continue to characterize the role of international lawyers at German universities.

C. A Dependent Field: The Impact of German Public Law Academia

While international law in Germany leads a certain life of its own, it is to a large
extent dependent on the field of German public law. This dependence is enacted
mainly through the structures of career paths—the fact that academic posts always
also cover public law, that hiring decisions are largely taken by the public lawyers
on a faculty, and that at least one of the two theses should cover domestic (exceptionally European) constitutional or administrative law. In this way, the rules of the
public law field become central for the international law field as well.

The contrast with, for example, UK academia could not be stronger. In the United
Kingdom, most posts are primarily or exclusively advertised for international law;
hiring decisions for junior faculty (who may then progress through the ranks) are
heavily influenced, if not determined, by the international lawyers already on the
faculty; and the scholarship that counts most is that in international law. Even if
international lawyers are still embedded in broader faculty structures (e.g., through
promotion procedures), the dependence of the field is far lower. This is also true,
though to a lesser extent, in France: French international lawyers are recruited in a
competition that involves all disciplinary orientations within French law, but they
are primarily assessed on the basis of work in their own field.[57] Dependence comes
in degrees, but the German case is on the high end of the spectrum.

In Germany, high dependence is compounded by the particular level of integration of the public law field.[58] While in other countries, degrees of organization
in public law—and in academia generally—are low and diversity in directions
higher, in Germany the field is tight and centered on an institution (a "governance
unit"),[59] the Association of German Public Law Scholars (*Vereinigung der deutschen
Staatsrechtslehrer*). Practically all those who are eligible (only those who have passed
the *Habilitation* in public law) are organized in the Association, which is seen as

57. *See* ROBERTS, *supra* note 12.

58. *See generally* STAATSRECHTSLEHRE ALS WISSENSCHAFT (DIE VERWALTUNG BEIHEFT 7)
(Helmuth Schulze-Fielitz ed., 2007).

59. *See* FLIGSTEIN & MCADAM, *supra* note 4, at 77–78.

"representative for German public law scholarship," as "practically without compe-tition," and its meetings as "the central forum for formal and informal academic exchanges" in constitutional and administrative law.[60] As Armin von Bogdandy notes, it "largely determines points of scholarly focus in its annual meetings. Europe seems to have no other scientific association with this level of organization and the-matic influence."[61] An invitation to give a lecture at one of its meetings—with a topic predefined by the Association's board—is an important honor, and the recep-tion of this lecture is regarded as so important for one's further career that it is some-times described as a "third state exam."[62] The Association has long been seen as highly hierarchical and seniority-oriented; though slowly changing, it is still strong at reproducing established standards and codes.[63]

In a field with such a high degree of institutional integration and a very clearly structured career path, socialization effects are bound to be high. Helmuth Schulze-Fielitz, a German public law scholar himself, notes that the "academic recruit-ment of public law scholars through two state exams, the doctoral thesis and the *Habilitation*, linked to traditions of constitutional and administrative law prac-tice, rewards positions at the center of society, close to dominant opinions."[64] The German Science Council recently noted, in a report on the "prospects of legal scholarship in Germany," that the long process of socialization—especially the long proximity to, and dependence on, a supervisor—creates the risk that junior scholars "draw nearer to the intellectual positions of 'their' professors ... and that recruit-ment structures remain rather homogeneous."[65]

One effect of the resulting disciplinary integration is a high degree of con-tinuity and homogeneity in the understanding of the core of the field. While in other countries, the study of constitutional and administrative law has branched out widely—especially in the direction of the social sciences—in Germany (and some other continental European countries) the focus on doctrine has remained largely intact, even if Europeanization and internationalization begin to present a greater challenge.[66] Doctrine may be understood broadly, including a high degree

60. Helmuth Schulze-Fielitz, Staatsrechtslehre als Mikrokosmos: Bausteine zu einer Soziologie und Theorie der Wissenschaft des Öffentlichen Rechts 8 (2013); *see also* Walter Pauly, *Wissenschaft vom Verfassungsrecht: Deutschland, in* Handbuch Ius Publicum Europaeum vol. II 463, 481 (Armin von Bogdandy, Pedro Cruz Villalón & Peter M. Huber eds., 2008).

61. von Bogdandy, *supra* note 18, at 390.

62. German legal education is structured by two state examinations.

63. Michael Stolleis, *Die Vereinigung der Deutschen Staatsrechtslehrer. Bemerkungen zu ihrer Geschichte*, 80 Kritische Vierteljahresschrift für Gesetzgebung und Rechtswissenschaft 339 (1997).

64. Schulze-Fielitz, *supra* note 60, at 14.

65. Wissenschaftsrat, *supra* note 47, at 47.

66. *See, e.g.*, Pauly, *supra* note 60, at 477; Schulze-Fielitz, *supra* note 60, at 5; Wissenschaftsrat, *supra* note 47, at 38.

of theoretical engagement, but it remains wedded to the idea of devising a coherent system, "a careful and complete account of existing positive law, . . . and of the creation of order through a set of general concepts and principles."[67] This leads to relatively tight links with judicial practice—doctrinal efforts often aim to influence this practice but, in order to be successful, they have to operate within the bounds of what is acceptable in judicial practice.[68] The doctrinal focus has also engendered a "constitutional court positivism"[69] that sees its primary goal in the systematization of constitutional jurisprudence, yet makes it difficult to see beyond, or behind, the constitutional court's practices and normative universe.[70] As a result, questions that are central to public law scholarship elsewhere—for example those about the legitimacy of constitutional review—figure less prominently in German discourse.[71] Under the reign of doctrine, external critique necessarily remains marginal; progress can only be achieved on the terms of the existing order.

It is thus easy to see why *international* law in Germany would also be characterized by a doctrinal, system-building approach that emphasizes the logical over the political elements in legal construction. Being dependent on the field of public law, it largely shares the main frames through which law and legal scholarship are construed in the latter (other kinds of scholarship are easily dismissed as non-legal, or belonging in the field of political science). This may lead to tensions resulting from the fact that such an approach faces greater hurdles in international law because of the structure of its normative (and political) space,[72] or tensions because the transnational field of international law operates differently and grants doctrinal efforts less weight.

The dependence on public law may also help to explain the popularity of the constitutional frame among many German international lawyers. Embedded as they are in constitutional discourses at home—ones that, because of the dominant doctrinalism, are generally couched in positive terms—their thinking about the global space will often be shaped by these discourses. If a domestic legal argument can only be successful if it invokes, or operates in the boundaries of, "democracy" or "the rule of law" as understood in constitutional law discourse, it is a small step to employ these categories also beyond the state.

---

67. Armin von Bogdandy, *Vergleich, in* Handbuch Ius Publicum Europaeum, vol. II 807, 817 (Armin von Bogdandy, Pedro Cruz Villalón & Peter M. Huber eds., 2008).

68. Schulze-Fielitz, *supra* note 60, at 16.

69. Bernhard Schlink, *Die Entthronung der Staatsrechtswissenschaft durch die Verfassungsgerichtsbarkeit,* 28 Staat 161 (1989).

70. *See* von Bogdandy, *supra* note 18, at 377.

71. *See* Christoph Möllers, *Legalität, Legitimität und Legitimation des Bundesverfassungsgerichts, in* Das entgrenzte Gericht. Eine kritische Bilanz nach sechzig Jahren Bundesverfassungsgericht 281, 283 (M. Jestaedt et al. eds., 2011).

72. Benvenisti, *supra* note 15.

D. Caught in the Middle?

German international law, then, is in many ways caught in the middle between transnational international law and national public law, and it is often drawn more toward the latter. It is, perhaps more than elsewhere, busy translating and mediating between the different fields.[73] Comparatively, this may differ from the situation in the United Kingdom or in the Netherlands, where international legal academia appears to be significantly more independent and, as a result, has been able to tighten its links with (and influence on) the transnational field of international law. In some respects, it might not be so different from other countries in which career paths are determined, for the most part, in national frames—France may be an example, but also the United States where hiring decisions depend on faculties as a whole and reputation is closely tied to domestic institutions in legal education, publishing, and the world of practice.[74] However, despite this relatively national orientation, and somewhat in contrast with the German example, both French and US international law scholarship seem to have been able to maintain a greater projection beyond national boundaries (with different emphases and certainly for different reasons).

The relations of the different fields—and especially the dependence on the domestic public law field—may help us to understand some of the particularities of the German approach to international law, such as its doctrinal, system-oriented outlook and its constitutionalist sensitivities, as well as the relatively limited presence of German international lawyers in transnational discourses. They may also alert us to broader continuities with German scholarship construing international law through the lens of state law concepts at earlier times, for example in the influential international law theories of Georg Jellinek and Heinrich Triepel in the late nineteenth century.[75]

The focus on field relations does, however, raise a number of further questions. These concern, on the one hand, the factors that can account for the ability of the national public law field to maintain its dominant position in the face of diverging tendencies in a number of other countries.[76] These factors may be related to the (largely state-controlled) structure of legal education, especially the degree to which academic law teaching in Germany is oriented toward domestic (judicial) practice, and the limited scope and economic importance of LLM programs, which tend to favor international subjects. They may also relate to environmental factors, such as the country's size and economic strength as conditions for the sustainability of a relatively insular academic market.

Other questions concern the reach of this account—the dependence on the public law field does not explain everything in German international law. Tracing general trends, it can certainly not explain all individual cases—some, such as that

---

73. See also Nolte, *supra* note 45, at 660.

74. See ROBERTS, *supra* note 12.

75. VON BERNSTORFF, *supra* note 27, at 15–42.

76. On the decoupling of international and constitutional law in Finland, for example, see Martti Koskenniemi, *The Case for Comparative International Law*, 20 FINNISH Y.B. INT'L L. 1, 7 (2009).

of Bruno Simma whose career has a remarkably transnational orientation, may simply count as outliers. More importantly, perhaps, the dependence on the public law field has difficulties accounting for the internationalism of much international law scholarship during the Cold War, which may be seen to contrast with the relative statism of domestic constitutional law theory (and practice).[77] Germany's geopolitical situation may have played an important role here, and it may have urged stronger links of international legal discourses with foreign policy orientations. The aim of providing a positive image of Germany as a "good international citizen" with a relatively low profile, in contrast with the revisionist stance of the Third Reich, is likely to have favored a pragmatic approach to international law, mostly in line with the (Western) mainstream. It may also have contributed to the widespread emphasis on community and values in German international law, while the more self-confident assertion of a value-oriented constitutionalist approach after the end of the Cold War may have been facilitated by the general ideological climate of the 1990s as well as the greater *marge de manoeuvre* of the reunified Germany.

In the space of this chapter, I cannot inquire conclusively into the relative weight of competing accounts, or the importance of linkages of German international law with other fields, especially the link with foreign policy (which is partly institutionalized through the German foreign ministry's academic advisory council on international law). The most plausible account will involve a range of factors and linkages. Among these, factors such as geopolitics or domestic institutions (as suggested in the framing chapter) are likely to play a role, but a very different one than, for example, for German diplomats or judges on German courts—a role that can only be understood when we relate the dynamics of the academic field of German international law to the pathways of outside influence, and especially the linkages with other fields in both academia and politics. The configuration of these linkages, and their differences across countries, can take us some way toward understanding how the particularities of international law academia in certain contexts have come about.

III. FIELDS, COMPARISON, AND INTERNATIONAL LAW: A CONCLUSION

In this chapter, I have tried to suggest a frame of analysis for the comparative effort in international law. I have focused on "fields" as sites of social action—fields built around common rules and power relations that structure the positions and dispositions of the agents in a field, which are not stable and sealed, but are conceived of as dynamic and interrelated with many other social fields. I have used this framework to map the potential fields that make up, and have a bearing on, international law, in its transnational and national, academic and professional, generalist and issue-area-specific forms. In the application to the particular case of Germany we have seen how German academic international law is intimately related to—dependent on— the German public law field, how this conditions its methodological and substantive outlook as well as its relative distance from the transnational international law field, and how it shapes responses to factors of a broader political and cultural nature.

---

77. *See* CHRISTOPH MÖLLERS, STAAT ALS ARGUMENT (2d ed. 2011).

This approach, as we have seen, cannot explain everything, but it helps us to structure our investigation and focus on the context in which individual interpreters operate—the structures that shape their understanding of what is normal, appropriate, and desirable; the actors that occupy key positions in a field; and the particular (sometimes distant, sometimes proximate) relations with other fields. This should help us to map and understand national differences to quite some extent, in particular by providing us with a better grip on the pathways through which particular factors influence some fields and not others. It also highlights that focusing primarily on the national *vel* transnational orientation of interpreters in a given field may show us only part of the picture; sometimes, as in the case of Germany, we need to inquire into the *kinds* of links with different national fields to gain a fuller understanding.

The focus in this chapter has been on academia, but inquiries into the practice of international law would benefit from a similar approach. The many interpreters of international law—in foreign ministries, courts, and private practice—are all embedded in different contexts, the structures of which condition the form and substance of interpretation. To use an obvious example, a country's strategic interest will enter the interpretative exercise of a diplomat in a very different way than that of a judge, following the norms of the professional fields they inhabit. In the German case, the often-proclaimed *Völkerrechtsfreundlichkeit* (sympathetic consideration of international law) is likely to have a different complexion in executive positions than in the jurisprudence of the constitutional court.[78] When we seek to establish differences in interpretation across countries, we will do well to take these norms and structures (and their cross-national variation) into account—all the more so with respect to countries whose social and political structures differ more fundamentally from those we are accustomed to.

Many inquiries along such lines lie ahead in the fertile valleys of comparative international law. Some of these may be comparative not only along territorial but also other lines: institutional (comparing judicial and executive interpretations, for example), issue areas (comparing the interpretations of international law in investment with those in human rights law), potentially also historical lines—we may, for example, wonder how today, in an age of global governance, the relationship of the different fields in question differs from that half a century ago. As with all comparisons, though, these inquiries will have to proceed carefully and avoid facile generalizations.[79] Understanding difference means not only comparing the ways particular norms are interpreted in different places, and correlating this to a number of variables we may happen to find in databases. It requires an engagement with the cultural experiences, cognitive frames, and normative understandings that shape social action and make us see international law differently, depending on the place (and field) we find ourselves in.

---

78. On the continuing statism of the latter, see the contributions by Schorkopf and Fastenrath in DER "OFFENE VERFASSUNGSSTAAT" DES GRUNDGESETZES NACH 60 JAHREN: ANSPRUCH UND WIRKLICHKEIT EINER GROSSEN ERRUNGENSCHAFT (Thomas Giegerich ed., 2010).

79. Günter Frankenberg, *Critical Comparisons: Re-thinking Comparative Law*, 26 HARV. INT'L L.J. 411 (1985); Pierre Legrand, *How to Compare Now*, 16 LEGAL STUD. 232 (1996).

6

Crimea and the South China Sea

Connections and Disconnects among Chinese, Russian, and Western International Lawyers

ANTHEA ROBERTS

When asked to reflect on the professional community of international lawyers, Oscar Schachter memorably described it as an "invisible college" whose members were "dispersed throughout the world" yet "engaged in a continuous process of communication and collaboration."[1] However, it may be better to understand international lawyers as constituting a "divisible college" whose members hail from different states and regions and often form distinct, though sometimes overlapping, communities with their own understandings and approaches, as well as their own incoming influences and outgoing spheres of influence.[2]

The divisible college of international lawyers was starkly illustrated by the different responses by Western and Russian international lawyers to Crimea's annexation by, or reunification with, Russia in 2014. As a general rule, these two groups accepted different accounts of the facts, put forward different understandings of the law, and reached diametrically opposed conclusions on both the legality and legitimacy of what transpired. While Western international lawyers typically condemned Russia's illegal annexation of Crimea, Russian international lawyers generally celebrated Crimea's exercise of self-determination and lawful decision to reunify with Russia.

Part of what was striking about these debates was that they largely occurred in parallel silos: Russian international lawyers primarily published in Russian in Russian journals while citing other Russian scholars, whereas Western international lawyers primarily published in English in Western outlets while citing other Western scholars. These two communities of international lawyers found very few points of connection and commonality. They often did not communicate with each other and,

---

1. Oscar Schachter, *The Invisible College of International Lawyers*, 72 Nw. U. L. Rev. 217, 217 (1977).

2. Anthea Roberts, Is International Law International? 1-2 (2017).

Comparative International Law. Edited by Anthea Roberts et al. © Anthea Roberts, Paul B. Stephan, Pierre-Hugues Verdier, Mila Versteeg 2018. Published 2018 by Oxford University Press.

even when they did, they rarely found common ground. Instead, they largely existed in two separate communities with their own understandings of the law and facts.

To understand how these divisions come about, it is helpful to be aware of how these different communities are constituted.[3] Russian international lawyers have frequently completed all of their legal education in Russia, primarily using Russian-language materials. They have their own international law textbooks, they publish the vast majority of their academic works in the Russian language in Russian journals, and most of the authorities they cite are Russian. Dissent may also be difficult, particularly on issues that strike at core national interests, such as Russia's relationship with its near abroad. Although their subject is "international," this community of international lawyers is largely national.

On the other side of the equation, few Western international lawyers speak Russian or study in Russia. Western international lawyers have their own textbooks, publish the vast majority of their articles in Western languages in Western outlets, and primarily cite other Western scholars. Although many of these Western scholars transcend their national communities, the broader transnational community of which they form a part tends to be dominated by actors from, or at least educated in, other Western states. These international lawyers may not be caught in a national bubble in the same way as their Russian counterparts, but they largely operate within a Western context that transcends the national without being fully international.

A slightly different picture emerges if one looks at the reactions of Chinese and Western international lawyers to the *South China Sea* arbitral award by a tribunal constituted under the UN Convention on the Law of the Sea (UNCLOS) in 2016.[4] Chinese scholars were virtually unanimous in declaring that the tribunal lacked jurisdiction, although a handful dissented on whether the Chinese government adopted the right approach in refusing to appear before the tribunal. Western international lawyers split on whether the tribunal was right to take jurisdiction, but tended to be critical of China's failure to participate in the arbitration and to reject China's claim that it was not bound by the resulting award.

As with the Crimean example, the divergent approaches between the Chinese and Western international lawyers reflect many differences in their processes of socialization and incentive structures. In both cases, the two communities of international lawyers were exposed to very different government and media portrayals of the case and were subject to different levels of academic freedom. One striking difference in comparing these two cases, however, was how many Chinese international lawyers wrote about the South China Sea arbitration in English-language outlets, both published in China and abroad, thereby facilitating the consideration of diverse perspectives within a single debate. But there was less evidence of critical voices, whether Chinese or Western, appearing in Chinese outlets.

---

3. *Id.* ch. 3. The phrase "Western" in this chapter is used to refer to lawyers coming from states in the Western Europe and Others Group at the United Nations.

4. *See* The South China Sea Arbitration (Phil. v. China), PCA Case No. 2013–19, Award (July 12, 2016), http://www.pcacases.com/web/view/7.

The ability and motivation of Chinese international lawyers to bridge this divide owes much to their language skills, educational backgrounds, and incentive structures. It is common for high-profile Chinese international lawyers to have completed a second or third law degree abroad, usually in a Western state, thereby building their language skills and transnational connections. They are given incentives to publish in foreign journals and in foreign languages. Their outwardly-orientated advocacy aligned with the Chinese government's worldwide public relations campaign to popularize its viewpoint on the South China Sea. At the same time, explicit and implicit censorship played a role in limiting the presentation of diverse viewpoints in domestic Chinese debates.

In this chapter, I draw on these two recent, high profile controversies as case studies to help illustrate four broader points. First, instead of constituting a single, uniform field, international law is an amalgamation of multiple, partially overlapping fields. Debates about fragmentation have focused on divisions within international law with respect to different subfields (such as trade and human rights) and different international institutions (such as the International Court of Justice and the International Criminal Tribunal for the Former Yugoslavia). Comparative international law, by contrast, focuses attention on analogous divisions among international lawyers located in, coming from, or educated in different states or geopolitical groupings.[5]

Second, it is possible to identify examples of significant similarities in the understandings and approaches of international lawyers coming from the same state or geopolitical grouping, as well as substantial differences in those coming from different states and geopolitical groupings. I do not claim that all lawyers from the same community approach international legal questions in an identical way or that no common ground exists among international lawyers coming from different states and regions. Neither statement would be true. However, the contours of the "mainstream" debate in different international law communities can differ in significant ways, which can result in self-reinforcing echo chambers, particularly where the communities remain relatively self-contained.

Third, there are many possible causes for divergent viewpoints among different communities. Some might derive from different incentive structures, such as the level of academic freedom in different states and whether international lawyers feel able to dissent from their governments' positions without fearing costs or retribution. Others might reflect more subtle processes of socialization, such as divergent facts that are reported, or narratives that are developed, in different media sources. In these scenarios, one cannot prove that X causes Y. But, as international lawyers are shaped in different national environments, it is not unreasonable to surmise that differences in their national contexts might influence the way in which they understand and approach international law, so it is worth paying attention to these differences.

---

5. *See* Anthea Roberts, Paul Stephan, Pierre Verdier & Mila Versteeg, *Conceptualizing Comparative International Law* (this volume); Anthea Roberts, Paul Stephan, Pierre Verdier & Mila Versteeg, *Comparative International Law: Framing the Field*, 109 Am. J. Int'l L. 467, 469 (2015).

Fourth, if international lawyers want to develop well-rounded perspectives on international law issues, they should make it a priority to read varied sources and develop diverse networks in order to see international law disputes through different eyes and, in so doing, adopt a more critical eye with respect to their own assumptions and arguments. The surprising 2016 election in the United States and the unexpected UK vote to Brexit have focused attention throughout the world on the problem of different communities creating their own silos in which shared views are reinforced in echo chambers. One of the lessons that many people have taken from this experience is the need to view more diverse media sources to understand how others with whom they disagree might be viewing a common problem or issue. This chapter suggests taking a parallel approach in international law.

Consciously taking a more diverse approach is particularly important in the modern era given that the locus of geopolitical power is shifting from unipolarity towards greater multipolarity and the era of Western-led international law appears to be giving way to an era of greater competition, and increased need for cooperation, among various Western and non-Western states.[6] This makes it increasingly important for international lawyers from different states and geopolitical groupings to forge connections with, and overcome disconnects among, those coming from unlike-minded states.

I. THE MANY FIELDS OF INTERNATIONAL LAW

As a complex product of social construction, international law can be understood through the sociological notion of fields developed by scholars such as Pierre Bourdieu.[7] A field is a social sphere made up of objective relations between different agents who interact and compete. The position of agents within a field is determined by the different forms of "capital" they possess, which may include markers of prestige such as where they studied, where they work, and what and where they publish. The amount of capital different agents possess determines their potential to influence the functioning of the field.

A field's "habitus" provides agents within that field with a socially founded sense of the "game" they are playing, but the rules of the game are never set and are always open to challenge. Habitus helps to structure individuals' understandings of the field and what amounts to their "best" interests within it. Bourdieu's concepts of "doxa" and "opinion" denote a society's or field's taken-for-granted, unquestioned truths, on the one hand, and the sphere of what may be openly contested and discussed, on the other hand. The line between doxa and opinion may differ significantly among societies and fields.

---

6. *See, e.g.,* Ian Buruma, *The End of the Anglo-American Order*, N.Y. Times Mag., Nov. 29, 2016; Mercy A. Kuo, *The End of American World Order*, The Diplomat, Nov. 10, 2016.

7. *See* Pierre Bourdieu & Loïc J. D. Wacquant, An Invitation to Reflexive Sociology (1992); Pierre Bourdieu, *The Force of Law: Toward a Sociology of the Juridical Field*, 38 Hastings L.J. 805 (Richard Terdiman trans., 1987). *See also* Neil Fligstein & Doug McAdam, A Theory of Fields (2012).

Scholars have applied Bourdieu's insights to describe dynamics in the emergence, operation, and change of transnational legal fields.[8] This work calls attention to the role of legal experts, including academics and practitioners, in building and legitimating markets for their expertise at the transnational level. Agents often operate in both national and transnational fields. What counts as doxa, opinion, and capital may vary among different national communities, and may also vary between the national and international levels. The "national" plays an important role in constituting the "international" since typically agents are largely socialized in national settings, so transnational forums often become spaces where different national models vie for influence.

International lawyers typically exist at the intersection of two communities: a transnational community of international lawyers and a domestic community of national lawyers. When international lawyers are compared with their domestic peers, their international orientation often seems obvious. But comparing international lawyers from one state with their peers in other states makes it possible to identify certain national differences as well. One of these differences is the extent to which the international lawyers in different states are socialized and incentivized to engage transnationally (for instance, by studying abroad or publishing in foreign or transnational journals) or to focus their primary attention domestically (for instance, by only studying, and primarily publishing, in that state).

In *Is International Law International?*, I looked for patterns in this regard in the profiles of international law academics at elite universities in the five permanent members of the UN Security Council: the People's Republic of China, the French Republic, the Russian Federation, the United Kingdom of Great Britain and Northern Ireland, and the United States of America.[9] I examined various forms of nationalizing, denationalizing, and westernizing influences on these international law academics. The concepts of "nationalizing" and "denationalizing" influences capture the extent to which academics from different states are encouraged to focus on their domestic community or their transnational community. The concept of "westernizing influences" captures the extent to which some denationalizing influences involve a Western orientation.[10]

Education and publishing provide helpful illustrations.[11] As a general rule, students who study law in their home state only are less likely to develop transnational perspectives and connections than students who study law in more than one state. However, as many students who pursue foreign legal degrees head to the United Kingdom, the United States, and France, this sort of denationalization

---

8. For a description of a range of work applying insights from Bourdieu to international legal fields, see Mikael Rask Madsen, *Transnational Fields and Power Elites: Reassembling the International with Bourdieu and Practice Theory*, in PERSPECTIVES FROM INTERNATIONAL POLITICAL SOCIOLOGY: TRANSVERSAL LINES IN INTERNATIONAL RELATIONS 106 (Tugba Basaran et al. eds., 2016).

9. ROBERTS, *supra* note 2.

10. *Id.*, ch. 2.

11. *Id.*, ch. 3.

often introduces or confirms a westernizing influence. Similarly, academics who are encouraged to publish primarily or exclusively in domestic journals are more likely to be focused on their domestic community than ones who are given incentives to publish in foreign and transnational journals. However, as many (though not all) transnational international law journals are edited primarily by Western academics, these denationalizing influences are often westernizing.

Common educational and publishing patterns differ significantly among states. For instance, the United Kingdom and the United States are both Western, English-speaking, common law states, however, the profiles of their elite international law academics differ significantly. Most US international law academics study law only in the United States and are encouraged to publish primarily in US journals. By contrast, many international law academics at UK law schools have studied law in two or more states, and a significant number are foreign nationals who came to the United Kingdom after originally studying law in their home states. They are also given incentives to publish in foreign and transnational journals, which tend to embed them more in their transnational community than their US counterparts.

The stronger the nationalizing influences within a given state, the more likely it is that international lawyers in that state will operate as a relatively self-contained domestic community, while the opposite is true with respect to denationalizing influences.[12] However, international lawyers from different states also have different abilities to access and influence the transnational community. For instance, as many of the leading transnational international law journals are published in English, native English speakers have greater access to publishing in these journals than non-English speakers and nonnative English speakers. Some domestic outlets also have a more significant transnational influence than others. For instance, one would expect a French international law journal to have a wider audience than an international law journal of a former French colony.

How might these notions of fields play out in international law debates about controversies such as Crimea's annexation by, or reunification with, Russia and the legality and legitimacy of the South China Sea arbitral award? The next section examines these debates, paying particular attention to how these discussions played out in online sources given that there was a lot of contemporaneous commentary on these disputes and, at least in the latter case, it is too early for many published academic articles to have appeared.

II. DEBATES ABOUT CRIMEA

A revolution in February 2014 ousted the pro-Russian Ukrainian president Viktor Yanukovych and sparked a political crisis in Crimea. Opposition parties and defectors from the old government put together a caretaker government to control Ukraine until new presidential and parliamentary elections could be held. This new government was recognized internationally but not by Russia, which viewed the revolution as a "coup d'état" and the caretaker government as illegitimate.

12. *Id.*, ch. 5.

A pro-Russian government formed in Crimea and held a referendum on reunifying Crimea with Russia, which passed overwhelmingly. However, many states questioned the legitimacy of the referendum given the Russian presence within Crimea during the vote.

International law debates about the legality and legitimacy of what happened in Crimea were largely conducted in two parallel bodies of scholarship: one by Russian international lawyers, which was primarily written in Russian and published in Russia;[13] and the other by Western international lawyers, which

13. *See, e.g.,* С. Бабурин [S. Baburin], Ялтинские договоренности великих держав в 1945 г. и их уроки для международного права [1945 Yalta Agreement of the Great Powers and Their Lessons for International Law], 43 Вестник Омского университета, Серия "Право" [Rev. Omsk Univ., "Law" Series] 54 (2015); О.Г. Деревянко [O.G. Derevianko], Сравнительный конституционно-правовой анализ проведения АТО РФ на Северном Кавказе и Украиной в Луганской и Донецкой областях [Comparative Constitutional Analysis of Russia's Counter-Terrorism Operation in the North Caucasus and Ukraine's Counter-Terrorism Operation in Luhansk and Donetsk Regions], 51 Вестник Международного юридического института [Rev. Int'l Legal Inst.] 52 (2014); Инсур Фархутдинов [Insur Farkhutdinov], Евразийская интеграция и испытание украинской государственности в системе международного права [Eurasian Integration and a Test of Ukrainian Statehood in International Law], 79 Евразийский юридический журнал [Eurasian L.J.] (2014); А. Ибрагимов [A. Ibrahimov], Воссоединение Крыма и Севастополя с Российской Федерацией в призме международного права и мировой политики [Reunification of Crimea and Sevastopol with Russian Federation Through the Prism of International Law and World Politics], 4 Юридический вестник ДГУ [L. Rev. of Dagestan St. Univ.] 75 (2014); О.Н. Хлестов [O.N. Hlestov], Украина: право на восстание [Ukraine: The Right to Rebel], Международный правовой курьер [Int'l Legal Herald], www.inter-legal.ru/ukraina-pravo-navosstanie; А. Кудряшова [A. Kudriashova], Международно-правовые проблемы возвращения Крыма в состав России [International Legal Problems of Crimea's Return to Russia], Труды БрГУ. Серия: Гуманитарные и социальные проблемы развития регионов Сибири [Works of Fraternal State University, Series: Humanitarian and Social Problems of Siberia's Development] 26 (2014); В.А. Кряжков [V.A. Kriazhkov], Крымский прецедент: конституционно-правовое осмысление [Crimean Precedent: Reflections on Constitutional and Legal Aspects], 5 Сравнительное конституционное обозрение [Comp. Const. Rev.] (2014); Ю. Курилюк, И. Семеновский [Y. Kuriliuk and I. Semenovskiy], Правовой аспект вхождения Крыма и Севастополя в состав России [Legal Aspects of Crimean and Sevastopol's Joining Russia], 2 Научные записки молодых исследователей [Res. Notes Young Scholars] (2014); В. Самигуллин [V. Samigullin], Крым: историко-правовой аспект [Crimea: Historical and Legal Aspects], 3 Проблемы востоковедения [Problems Oriental Stud.] 13 (2014); К.П. Саврыга [K.P. Savryga], Украинский кризис и международное право: вооруженный конфликт на Востоке Украины и сецессия Крыма [Ukrainian Crisis and International Law: Armed Conflict in East of Ukraine and Crimean Secession], 187 Право и политика [Law & Pol.] 945 (2015); К. Сазонова [K. Sazonova], Международное право и украинский конфликт: что было, что будет, чем сердце успокоится [International Law and Ukrainian Conflict: What Has Happened, What Will Happen, How to Comfort Heart], 1 NB: Международное право [NB: Int'l L.] 1 (2014); Н. Свечников, М. Богданова [N. Svechnikov and M. Bogdanova], Крымский референдум—некоторые аспекты политико-правового анализа [Crimean Referendum: Several Aspects of Political and Legal Analysis], Вестник Пензенского государственного университета [Rev. of Penza St. Univ.] 28 (2014); К. Б. Толкачев [K.V. Tolkachev], "Крымский вопрос" и современное право: к дискуссии о легитимности референдума ["Crimean Question" and Contemporary Law: re Discourse on Referendum's Legitimacy], 72 Евразийский юридический журнал [Eurasian L.J.]

was primarily written in English and published in Western outlets.[14] These two scholarly communities engaged in very little interaction, subject to a

(2014); В.Л. Толстых [V.L. Tolstykh], Воссоединение Крыма с Россией: правовые квалификации [Reunification of Crimea and Russia: The Legal Qualifications], 72 Евразийский юридический журнал [Eurasian L.J.] 40 (2014); В.Л. Толстых [V.L. Tolstykh], Воссоединение Крыма и России: факты, квалификации, риторика [Reunification of Crimea and Russia: Facts, Qualification, and Rhetoric], 92–93 Новосибирский Юристъ: газ. Новосиб. юрид. ин-та (фи-ла) ТГУ [Novosibirsk's L.: Mag. Novosibirsk >L. Sch. (branch) Tomsk St. Univ.] 6 (2015); В.А. Томсинов [V.A. Tomsinov], "Крымское право" или Юридические основания воссоединения Крыма с Россией ["Crimean Law" or Legal Bases for the Reunification of the Crimea and Russia], Зерцало-М [ZERTSALO-M] (2015); В.А. Томсинов [V.A. Tomsinov], Международное право с точки зрения воссоединения Крыма с Россией [International Law from the Perspective of Crimean Reunification with Russia], Законодательство Номер 6 [LEG., VOL. 6] (2014); Г. Цыкунов [G. Tsykunov], Историко-правовые основы вхождения Крыма в состав Российской Федерации [Historical and Legal Foundations for Crimean Reunification with Russia], 25 Известия Иркутской государственной экономической академии [News ST. Acad. Econ. Irkutsk] 550 (2015); Г.М. Вельяминов [G.M. Veliaminov], Воссоединение Крыма с Россией: правовой статус [Reunification of Crimea with Russia: A Legal Perspective], Институт Государства и права РАН [Inst. St. & L. Russian Acad. Sci.] 12 (2014); В.Д. Зорькин [V.D. Ziorkin], Право силы и сила права [The Law of Power and the Power of Law], Российская газета [Russian Gazette] (May 28, 2015); В.Д. Зорькин [V.D. Ziorkin], Право—и только право, О вопиющих правонарушениях, которые упорно не замечают [Law—and Only Law. On Egregious Violations That Go Unnoticed], Российская газета [Russian Gazette], Mar. 23, 2015.

14. *See, e.g.,* THOMAS D. GRANT, AGGRESSION AGAINST UKRAINE: TERRITORY, RESPONSIBILITY, AND INTERNATIONAL LAW (2015); Veronica Bilkova, *The Use of Force by the Federation in Crimea,* 75 ZEITSCHRIFT FÜR AUSLÄNDISCHES ÖFFENTLICHES RECHT UND VÖLKERRECHT [Heidelberg J. Int'l L.] 27 (2015); Thomas D. Grant, *Current Developments: Annexation of Crimea,* 109 AM. J. INT'L L. 68 (2015); Christian Marxsen, *Territorial Integrity in International Law: Its Concept and Implications for Crimea,* 75 ZEITSCHRIFT FÜR AUSLÄNDISCHES ÖFFENTLICHES RECHT UND VÖLKERRECHT [Heidelberg J. Int'l L.] 7 (2015); Oleksandr Merezhko, *Crimea's Annexation by Russia: Contradictions of the New Russian Doctrine of International Law,* 75 ZEITSCHRIFT FÜR AUS-LÄNDISCHES ÖFFENTLICHES RECHT UND VÖLKERRECHT [Heidelberg J. Int'l L.] 167 (2015); Ilya Nuzov, *National Ratification of an Internationally Wrongful Act: The Decision Validating Russia's Incorporation of Crimea,* 12 EUR. CON. L. REV. 353 (2016); Peter M. Olsen, *The Lawfulness of Russian Use of Force in Crimea,* 53 MIL. L. & L. WAR REV. 17 (2014); Alisa Gdalina, Note, *Crimea and the Right to Self-Determination: Questioning the Legality of Crimea's Secession from Ukraine,* 24 CARDOZO J. INT'L & COMP. L. 531 (2016); Trevor McDougal, Comment, *A New Imperialism? Evaluating Russia's Acquisition of Crimea in the Context of National and International Law,* 2015 B.Y.U.L. REV. 1947 (2015); Ashley Deeks, *Russian Forces in Ukraine: A Sketch of the International Law Issues,* LAWFARE, Mar. 2, 2014; Robert McCorquodale, *Ukraine Insta-Symposium: Crimea, Ukraine and Russia: Self-Determination, Intervention and International Law,* OPINIO JURIS, Mar. 10, 2014; Anne Peters, *Sense and Nonsense of Territorial Referendums in Ukraine, and Why the 16 March Referendum in Crimea Does Not Justify Crimea's Alteration of Territorial Status under International Law,* EJIL: *Talk!,* Apr. 16, 2014; Ben Saul, *The Battle for Legal Legitimacy in Crimea,* THE DRUM, Mar. 3, 2014; Jure Vidmar, *Crimea's Referendum and Secession: Why It Resembles Northern Cyprus,* EJIL: *Talk!,* Mar. 20, 2014; Marc Weller, *Analysis: Why Russia's Crimea Move Fails Legal Test,* BBC NEWS, Mar. 7, 2014; Daniel Wisehart, *The Crisis in Ukraine and the Prohibition of the Use of Force: A Legal Basis for Russia's Intervention?,* EJIL: *Talk!,* Mar. 4, 2014.

handful of exceptions.[15] Indeed, the *Heidelberg Journal of International Law* editors created a symposium that brought together Russian and Western scholars because they recognized that:

> Hardly any "Western" politician or scholar deems Russia's political course justifiable and justified under the precepts of international law. Inversely, from what we can perceive from the outside, Russian politicians and scholars seem confident to be able to properly justify the incorporation of Crimea within the framework of the existing international legal order. *The crisis is matched by the absence of a serious legal dialogue among international legal scholars of both camps.*[16]

Western scholars tended to treat the issue as one of Russia's illegal annexation of Crimea and unlawful use of force in, and violation of the territorial integrity of, Ukraine. This is obvious even from the titles of these Western articles, which include "Territorial Integrity in International Law: Its Concept and Implications for Crimea," "The Use of Force by the Russian Federation in Crimea," "Crimea's Annexation by Russia: Contradictions of the New Russian Doctrine of International Law," "Analysis: Why Russia's Crimea Move Fails Legal Test," and "Aggression against Ukraine: Territory, Responsibility, and International Law."

By contrast, the Russian international lawyers typically analyzed the situation as one of self-determination, focusing on Crimea's voluntary and lawful decision to reunify with its mother country Russia, with titles such as " 'Crimean Law' or Legal Bases for the Reunification of Crimea and Russia," "Reunification of Crimea and Russia: Legal Qualifications," "Legal Aspects of Crimean and Sevastopol's Entering into Russia," "Historical and Legal Foundations for Crimean Reunification as Part of Russia," "Reunification of Crimea and Sevastopol with Russian Federation

---

15. Exceptions include: Vladislav Tolstykh, *Letter to the Editors: Reunification of Crimea with Russia: A Russian Perspective*, 13 Chinese J. Int'l L. 879 (2014); Letter from Anatoly Kapustin, President of the Russ. Ass'n of Int'l Law, to Executive Council, Int'l Law Ass'n, June 5, 2014, http://www.ilarb.ru/html/news/2014/5062014.pdf (last visited Feb. 5, 2017) [hereinafter *Kapustin Letter to ILA*]; Boris Mamlyuk, *Mapping Developments in Ukraine from the Perspective of International Law*, Cambridge Int'l L.J. Blog, Mar. 12, 2014; Anton Moiseienko, *Guest Post: What Do Russian Lawyers Say About Crimea?*, Opinio Juris, Sept. 24, 2014.

16. Christian Marxsen et al., *Introduction, Symposium: The Incorporation of Crimea by the Russian Federation in the Light of International Law*, 75 Zeitschrift für ausländisches öffentliches Recht und Völkerrecht [Heidelberg J. Int'l L.] 3, 3 (2015) (emphasis added). For examples of contributions by Russian scholars to this symposium, see Anatoly Kapustin, *Crimea's Self-Determination in the Light of Contemporary International Law*, 75 Zeitschrift für ausländisches öffentliches Recht und Völkerrecht [Heidelberg J. Int'l L.] 101 (2015); Alexander Salenko, *Legal Aspects of the Dissolution of the Soviet Union in 1991*, 75 Zeitschrift für ausländisches öffentliches Recht und Völkerrecht [Heidelberg J. Int'l L.] 141 (2015); Vladislav Tolstykh, *Three Ideas of Self-Determination in International Law and the Reunification of Crimea with Russia*, 75 Zeitschrift für ausländisches öffentliches Recht und Völkerrecht [Heidelberg J. Int'l L.] 119 (2015).

through the Prism of International Law and World Politics," "Reunification of Crimea and Russia: Facts, Qualification, and Rhetoric," "International Law from the Perspective of Crimean Reunification with Russia," "Reunification of Crimea with Russia: A Legal Perspective," "Ukraine: The Right to Rebel," "Crimea's Self-Determination in the Light of Contemporary International Law," and "Three Ideas of Self-Determination in International Law and the Reunification of Crimea with Russia."

Not all Russian scholars held identical views, nor did all Western scholars. But the commonalities within these groups were strong, whereas the divergence between them was palpable. The two groups of international lawyers generally evidenced divergent understandings of the facts. Russian international lawyers frequently asserted that: there had been a "military," "unconstitutional" "coup d'état" in Kiev in which the legitimate head of state was overthrown; the United States and the European Union were guilty of intervening in the internal affairs of Ukraine to foment this coup and to support the installation of an illegitimate regime that then engaged in grave human rights violations, including "extrajudicial killings," "kidnappings," and "beatings" of Russians, Russian speakers, and those who opposed the new regime. The Western international lawyers tended not to characterize the conflict as a coup, did not lay the blame for it on the West, accepted the legitimacy of the interim government, and tended to dismiss claims that Russians and Russian speakers were being targeted as based on unsubstantiated propaganda spread by Russia and the Russian media.

Russian and Western international lawyers also mostly divided on their approach to key legal questions. According to the Russian international lawyers, the coup resulted in a dissolution of Ukraine into those who supported the coup and those who opposed it. Some argued that the latter returned to their "natural state" and received the right to enter into a new social contract or join an existing contract. Others argued that the Crimean people had been politically disenfranchised in Ukraine and had their human rights violated, and thus their lack of internal self-determination gave rise to their right to external self-determination. The Crimean people exercised this right through a lawful referendum in which they overwhelmingly voted to join Russia in recognition of the strong historical, cultural, and language ties between these peoples. By contrast, the Western scholars largely viewed Crimea as remaining a part of Ukraine, were unconvinced that the Crimean people's internal right to self-determination had been violated seriously enough to justify an external right to self-determination, and considered the referendum to have been illegitimately called and unsoundly conducted. Whereas the Russians portrayed the presence of Russian forces during the referendum as designed to safeguard the voting process, Western scholars viewed it as a threatening way of influencing the outcome and curtailing freedom of speech and assembly.

To the extent that the Russian international law scholars accepted that Russian forces were on Ukrainian territory, they attempted to justify their deployment as necessary to protect Russian citizens and "compatriots" (that is, ethnic Russians and Russian speakers), justified under the doctrine of humanitarian intervention, and based on consent because they were there at the invitation of the legitimate leaders of Ukraine and Crimea. By contrast, Western international lawyers debated whether international law permits a state to use force to defend its nationals abroad but generally found no legal basis for Russia to protect "compatriots" and no humanitarian catastrophe of the sort that would justify humanitarian intervention. Moreover, any argument based on invitation or consent was flawed because the ousted leader of Ukraine lacked effective control over the state, and the Crimean government, as a substate entity, lacked the right to issue such an invitation. Western scholars often worked hard to distinguish NATO's use of force in Kosovo and Kosovo's declaration of independence, while Russian scholars routinely cited the advisory opinion of the International Court of Justice (ICJ) on Kosovo's declaration of independence and the positions taken by Western states with respect to Kosovo.

As can be seen, some of the differences between these communities turned on questions of facts (e.g., whether serious human rights violations had occurred) while others turned on understandings of the law (e.g., whether states are permitted to use force to protect citizens and compatriots abroad). Put together, they resulted in very different debates about and conclusions as to the legality and legitimacy of what transpired.

III. DEBATES ABOUT THE SOUTH CHINA SEA ARBITRATION

In 2013, the Philippines launched an arbitration against China under UNCLOS.[17] Rather than seek a ruling on which state had sovereignty over certain maritime features, the Philippines requested a determination of the nature of those features (for example, which were islands, rocks, or neither) and which maritime rights they gave rise to (for example, an exclusive economic zone, a territorial sea, or neither). China objected to the tribunal's jurisdiction on various grounds, including that the Philippines was de facto litigating issues of sovereignty, which are precluded under UNCLOS; that the Philippine claims required delimitation of maritime boundaries, which China had excluded from its acceptance of UNCLOS dispute resolution; and that the Philippines had failed to exhaust peaceful means of settling the dispute to which it had previously agreed.[18] China refused to participate in the arbitration and the tribunal adopted a broad ruling that was very favorable to the Philippines.[19]

Chinese international lawyers, including scholars, have been almost uniform in supporting the Chinese government's view that the South China Sea tribunal lacked jurisdiction. A key example was the statement issued by the Chinese Society of International Law, entitled "The Tribunal's Award in the 'South China Sea Arbitration' Initiated by the Philippines Is Null and Void" ("CSIL Statement"), which was published on the website of the Chinese Ministry of Foreign Affairs.[20]

---

17. *See* The South China Sea Arbitration (Phil. v. China), PCA Case No. 2013–19, Award, para. 4 (July 12, 2016), http://www.pcacases.com/web/view/7.

18. *See id.* para. 13.

19. *Id.* paras. 13–14, 1203.

20. Chinese Soc'y of Int'l Law, *The Tribunal's Award in the "South China Sea Arbitration" Initiated by the Philippines Is Null and Void*, June 10, 2016, http://www.fmprc.gov.cn/mfa_eng/zxxx_662805/t1371363.shtml (last visited Feb. 5, 2017) [hereinafter CSIL Statement].

After referring to the Chinese government's position paper setting out China's arguments as to why the tribunal lacked jurisdiction, the CSIL Statement provides: "The Chinese Society of International Law strongly supports the positions of the Chinese Government."[21]

The CSIL Statement and the positions taken by the Chinese government and Chinese officials are mutually reinforcing. For example, in a Statement of the Ministry of Foreign Affairs, the Chinese government stated that the Tribunal's award on jurisdiction was "null and void" and had "no binding effect on China."[22] Likewise, the CSIL Statement explained that the jurisdictional award was groundless in both fact and law and thus was "null and void," which meant that any decision on the substantive issues would have "no legal effect."[23] The CSIL Statement concluded that "China's non-acceptance of and non-participation in the Arbitration and its non-recognition of any award" made by the tribunal have a "solid legal basis" and are "acts of justice to maintain and uphold international law."[24] Similarly, Liu Xiaoming, China's ambassador to the United Kingdom, argued that by "not accepting or recognizing the ruling, China is not violating but upholding the authority and dignity of international law."[25]

Perhaps the Chinese Society of International Law's support for the Chinese government should not come as a surprise. The Chinese Society is more closely associated with its government than, say, the American Society of International Law. The Chinese Society is a national academic group that has a Secretariat located in the China University of Foreign Affairs, which is governed by the Ministry of Foreign Affairs.[26] The Society receives "guidance" from the Ministry of Foreign Affairs,[27] and its current president (Li Shishi) is a top official with the National People's Congress and was formerly a top legal official of the State Council.[28] With this background,

---

21. *Id.*

22. Ministry of Foreign Affairs, Statement of the Ministry of Foreign Affairs of the People's Republic of China on the Award on Jurisdiction and Admissibility of the South China Sea Arbitration by the Arbitral Tribunal Established at the Request of the Republic of the Philippines, Oct. 30, 2015, http://www.fmprc.gov.cn/mfa_eng/zxxx_662805/t1310474.shtml (last visited Feb. 5, 2017).

23. CSIL Statement, *supra* note 20.

24. *Id.*

25. Liu Xiaoming, *South China Sea Arbitration Is a Political Farce*, CHINA DAILY, July 25, 2016 (first published on the *Daily Telegraph* website on July 23, 2016).

26. See 中国国际法学会 [The Chinese Society of International Law], http://www.csil.cn/News/Detail.aspx?AId=16 (last visited Feb. 5, 2017).

27. 中国国际法学会 [The Chinese Society of International Law], art. 4, http://www.csil.cn/News/Detail.aspx?AId=19 (last visited Feb. 5, 2017).

28. 中国国际法学会会长致辞 [Speech by President of the Chinese Society of International Law], http://www.csil.cn/News/Detail.aspx?AId=17 (last visited Feb. 5, 2017). For biographical information on Li Shishi, see http://cn.chinagate.cn/politics/2008-03/14/content_12631668.htm (last visited Feb. 5, 2017) and http://www.npc.gov.cn/delegate/viewDelegate.action?dbid=121680 (last visited Feb. 5, 2017).

it would be hard to imagine the Society taking a view that was critical of or distinct from the Chinese government, particularly on a pressing issue of national importance. Of course, one cannot assume that the views of the Chinese Society of International Law reflect the views of all Chinese international lawyers.

The CSIL Statement is not an isolated example, however. Similar statements have been issued by the All China Lawyers Association,[29] the Chinese Law Society,[30] and the Chinese Society of the Law of the Sea.[31] Again, some of these groups are closely tied to the government, such as the All China Lawyers Association, which comes under the auspices of the Ministry of Justice.[32] At a meeting in China, 300 Chinese legal experts gathered to discuss the case and unanimously agreed that China was right to abstain from participating in the case because the tribunal lacked jurisdiction and that China had a legitimate right under international law to reject the arbitration.[33] Young Chinese PhD students in the Netherlands wrote an open letter endorsing China's legal position on the case, which reportedly received more than 20,000 signatures.[34] Prominent Chinese international law scholars who often write in foreign and transnational international law journals, such as Sienho Yee and Congyan Cai, have also criticized the tribunal's decision finding jurisdiction.[35]

Although Chinese international lawyers have been virtually unanimous, at least publicly, as to the tribunal's lack of jurisdiction, they have disagreed somewhat over whether the government adopted the right strategy in failing to appear before the tribunal to argue the case. Some academics who did not agree with the government's approach to this issue remained silent on the matter, explaining privately that it was "not easy, actually impossible" for Chinese scholars located in China to publish this view in Chinese journals.[36] But this view was expressed by at least one prominent

29. *All China Lawyers Association Issues Statement on South China Sea Arbitration Initiated by the Philippines*, XINHUA, June 7, 2016.

30. *China Law Society Issues Statement on South China Sea Arbitration Initiated by the Philippines*, XINHUA, May 5, 2016.

31. *Chinese Society of the Law of the Sea Issues Statement on South China Sea Arbitration Initiated by the Philippines*, XINHUA, June 2, 2016.

32. 中华全国律师协会 [All China Lawyers Association], art. 4, http://www.acla.org.cn/zhangchen.jhtml (last visited Feb. 5, 2017).

33. *Chinese Legal Experts Refute Philippine Claim in South China Sea*, CCTV AMERICA, May 7, 2016.

34. *20,000 Sign Open Letter on South China Sea Ruling*, XINHUA, July 13, 2016; *An Open Letter on the South China Sea Arbitration*, CHINA DAILY, July 12, 2016; *Young Scholars to Launch Open Letter Against South China Sea Arbitration*, XINHUA, July 7, 2016.

35. *See, e.g., China Offers Philippines Talks if South China Sea Court Ignored: China Daily*, REUTERS, July 5, 2016 (citing Sienho Yee: "Objectively the tribunal has no jurisdiction over the dispute" because "[n]egotiation has been agreed upon as the way to resolve the dispute"); *Interview: South China Sea Arbitration Abuses International Law: Chinese Scholar*, XINHUA, July 12, 2016 (citing Cai Congyan: "The Philippines' unilateral request for arbitration on the South China Sea could be deemed as abuse of international law, at least not in good faith" and "the arbitral tribunal did not conduct adequate review or a reasonable judgment on the legal role of negotiation in this case").

36. Email on file with author.

Chinese legal academic, Bing Ling, who was educated in both China and the United States and who holds an academic position in Australia rather than mainland China. Ling argued that China would have had a better chance of winning on jurisdiction if it had participated in the case, at least during the jurisdictional phase.[37] He suggested that China should have learned from the US approach in the ICJ *Nicaragua* case where the United States appeared in order to contest jurisdiction and, when it lost on that point, refused to participate in the merits.[38]

For their part, Western international lawyers have split on the correctness of the tribunal's decision on jurisdiction. Before the jurisdictional award, Julian Ku at *Opinio Juris* argued that there was "no basis for the ITLOS to assert jurisdiction over this dispute, without China's consent"[39] and that the Philippines would face a "huge challenge to get any arbitral tribunal to assert jurisdiction here."[40] By contrast, Diane Desierto at EJIL: *Talk!* concluded that there were no persuasive reasons that would justify denying the tribunal jurisdiction over the Philippines' narrowly framed Statement of Claim.[41] But the tribunal's decision to take jurisdiction in the case did not generate many blog posts and, by the time the award on the merits was released, the focus of the blogs had largely shifted to the award's substantive findings and to China's reaction to it.[42] Regardless of whether the tribunal was correct

---

37. 凌兵 [Ling Bing], 为什么中国拒绝南海仲裁有损中国的权益 [Why China's refusal to participate in the South China Sea Arbitration is detrimental to China's interests], 中国国际法促进中心, [Chinese Initiative on International Law], Dec. 18, 2015; 凌兵 [Ling Bing], 厘清南海仲裁案"不参与不接受"的几个问题 [Clarifying several problems with not participating in the South China Sea arbitration], 中国国际法促进中心 [Chinese Initiative on International Law], Dec. 28, 2015.

38. *Id.*

39. Julian Ku, *Why the Philippines Has No Chance of Making China Go to Court*, Opinio Juris, Apr. 17, 2012. *See also* Natalie Klein, *Some Lessons from Mauritius v. UK for Philippines v. China*, ILA Reporter, Apr. 16, 2015 ("it is, in my view, impossible to separate any consideration of entitlements from the question of who is so entitled" and the "territorial sovereignty dispute is the real heart of the problem in *Philippines v. China*").

40. Julian Ku, *Game Changer? Philippines Seeks UNCLOS Arbitration with China over the South China Sea*, Opinio Juris, Jan. 22, 2013.

41. Diane Desierto, *The Jurisdictional Rubicon: Scrutinizing China's Position Paper on the South China Sea Arbitration–Part I*, EJIL: *Talk!*, Jan. 29, 2015; *See also* Diane Desierto, *The Jurisdictional Rubicon: Scrutinizing China's Position Paper on the South China Sea Arbitration–Part II*, EJIL: *Talk!*, Jan. 30, 2015.

42. *See, e.g.*, Diane Desierto, *The Philippines v. China Arbitral Award on the Merits as a Subsidiary Source of International Law*, EJIL: *Talk!*, July 12, 2016; Julian Ku, *Short, Quick Take on the Philippines' Sweeping Victory in the South China Sea Arbitration*, Lawfare, July 12, 2016; Robert Williams, *Tribunal Issues Landmark Ruling in South China Sea Arbitration*, Lawfare, July 12, 2016. There were exceptions, such as Douglas Guilfoyle on EJIL: *Talk!*, who concluded that the tribunal's jurisdictional finding was "not eccentric or bizarre" and that arguments to the contrary ignore well-known scholarship. *See* Douglas Guilfoyle, *Philippines v China: First Thoughts on the Award in the South China Seas Case*, EJIL: *Talk!*, July 12, 2016. *See also* John E. Noyes, *In re Arbitration Between the Philippines and China*, 110 Am J. Int'l L. 102 (2016).

in asserting jurisdiction, the Western scholars almost all viewed China as bound by the decision.[43]

The big stories in the West were about China's decision not to appear in the arbitration, whether China would abide by the resulting award, and what that meant about whether a rising China would accept the international rule of law or challenge the existing international order. These questions generated significantly more attention than whether China's jurisdictional objections were well grounded. Moreover, regardless of whether the tribunal was correct in asserting jurisdiction, Western scholars almost all agreed that China was bound by the tribunal's decision.[44] They typically reasoned that UNCLOS—to which China is a party—gives tribunals jurisdiction to determine their own jurisdiction, so there could be no credible argument that the merits decision was null and void and without legal effect even if China disagreed with the tribunal's decision to take jurisdiction.[45]

Unlike the Crimean debates, which largely took place in parallel silos, the South China Sea debates offered many examples of Chinese officials and scholars crossing the divide to make their case in English to foreign audiences through statements, position papers, speeches, letters to foreign newspapers, advertisements in foreign papers, and even videos played in New York City's Times Square.[46] The CSIL Statement and the Statement of the China Law Society were issued in English or with English translations. The open letter by the Chinese students in the Netherlands was written in English, Dutch, and Chinese in order to "spread it far and wide to gather as much support as possible."[47] Chinese scholars have published on the disputes in English-language books,[48] transnational journals,[49] and Western blogs.[50]

43. *See, e.g.,* Julian Ku, *China's Ridiculously Weak Legal Argument Against Complying with the South China Sea Arbitration Award,* LAWFARE, June 6, 2016 [hereinafter Ku, *China's Ridiculously Weak Legal Argument*]. *But see* Stefan Talmon, Opinion, *Final Award in Sea Arbitration Will Be Flawed,* CHINA DAILY, July 9, 2016 (arguing that problems with the tribunal's jurisdictional ruling "provide China with good legal arguments to reject the tribunal's final award.").

44. *See, e.g.,* Ku, *China's Ridiculously Weak Legal Argument, supra* note 43; Julian Ku, *China's Legal Scholars Are Less Credible After South China Sea Ruling,* FOREIGN POLICY, July 14, 2016.

45. For a possible exception, see Talmon, *supra* note 43.

46. In addition to the examples given above, see also Letters to the Editor, *China-Philippines Dispute over South China Sea,* N.Y. TIMES, July 28, 2015; Letters to the Editor, *The South China Sea Dispute: Beijing's View,* N.Y. TIMES, May 31, 2016; *South China Sea Video Displayed at NY Times Square,* XINHUA, July 27, 2016.

47. *Young Scholars to Launch Open Letter Against South China Sea Arbitration,* XINHUA, July 7, 2016 (citing comments by Wang Zhili).

48. *See, e.g.,* ARBITRATION CONCERNING THE SOUTH CHINA SEA: PHILIPPINES VERSUS CHINA (Shicun Wu & Keyuan Zou eds., 2016); UN CONVENTION ON THE LAW OF THE SEA AND THE SOUTH CHINA SEA (Shicun Wu et al. eds., 2015).

49. *See, e.g.,* Gao Jianjun, *The Obligation to Negotiate in the Philippines v. China Case: A Critique of the Award on Jurisdiction,* 47 OCEAN DEV. & INT'L L. 272 (2016); Gao Zhiguo & Jia Bing Bing, *The Nine-Dash Line in the South China Sea: History, Status, and Implications,* 107 AM. J. INT'L. L. 98 (2013).

50. *See, e.g.,* Liu Haiyang, *The Lawfare over South China Sea: Exceptional Rules vs. General Rules,* OPINIO JURIS, July 14th, 2016.

The *Chinese Journal of International Law* played an important role in facilitating this sort of exchange.[51] This journal describes itself as an "independent, peer-reviewed research journal edited primarily by scholars from mainland China" that is published in association with the Chinese Society of International Law and Wuhan University's Institute of International Law.[52] From the outset, this journal adopted an English-only language policy with the express aim of communicating viewpoints and materials from and about China to the rest of the world.[53] The journal has published multiple pieces by Chinese authors, including ones questioning the tribunal's jurisdiction,[54] which has facilitated more Chinese voices to enter into English-speaking debates than was true of Russian voices in the Crimean debates. For example, Oxford University Press includes Debate Maps that link to English-language sources on particular topics. For "Ukraine Use of Force," the debate map only includes one Russian author, and that author was critical of Russia.[55] For "Disputes in the South and East China Seas," the debate map includes multiple Chinese authors who have generally supported China's stance.[56] The journal also published pieces by Western authors that were critical of the tribunal's jurisdiction, such as Chris Whomersley (former Deputy Legal Adviser in the UK's Foreign and Commonwealth Office) and Stefan Talmon (University of Bonn).[57]

In addition to writing in English, Chinese officials, media, and scholars often cite foreign international lawyers whose views are seen as supportive of China's position and whose Western origins are expressly referenced. For instance, Liu Xiaoming, China's ambassador to the United Kingdom, argued in a UK paper that

51. For another example of a Chinese journal that is published in English, see *China Legal Science*, which is sponsored by the China Law Society and published by China Legal Science Journals Press. For an explanation of the motivation behind founding this journal, see Chen Jiping, *Forward to the First Edition of China Legal Science*, 1 CHINA LEGAL SCI. 3 (2013).

52. *See About the Journal: Chinese Journal of International Law*, OXFORD JOURNALS, http://www.oxfordjournals.org/our_journals/cjilaw/about.html (last visited Feb. 5, 2017).

53. Wang Tieya & Sienho Yee, *Foreword*, 1 CHINESE J. INT'L L. iii, iii (2002). The *Chinese Journal of Comparative Law*, founded in 2013, is also English-only. *See About the Journal*, CHINESE J. COMP. LAW, http://cjcl.oxfordjournals.org/ (last visited Feb. 5, 2017).

54. *See, e.g.*, Sienho Yee, *The South China Sea Arbitration (The Philippines v. China): Potential Jurisdictional Obstacles or Objections*, 13 CHINESE J. INT'L L. 663 (2014); Michael Sheng-ti Gau, *The Agreements and Disputes Crystalized by the 2009–2011 Sino-Philippine Exchange of Notes Verbales and Their Relevance to the Jurisdiction and Admissibility Phase of the South China Sea Arbitration*, 15 CHINESE J. INT'L L. 417 (2016).

55. *Debate Map: Ukraine Use of Force*, OXFORD PUB. INT'L L., http://opil.ouplaw.com/page/ukraine-use-of-force-debate-map (last visited Feb. 5, 2017).

56. *Debate Map: South China Sea*, OXFORD PUB. INT'L L., http://opil.ouplaw.com/page/222/debate-map-disputes-in-the-south-and-east-china-seas (last visited Apr. 1, 2017).

57. *See, e.g.*, Stefan A.G. Talmon, *The South China Sea Arbitration: Observations on the Award on Jurisdiction and Admissibility*, 15 CHINESE J. INT'L L. (2016); Chris Whomersley, *The South China Sea: The Award of the Tribunal in the Case Brought by Philippines Against China—A Critique*, 15 CHINESE J. INT'L L. (2016).

the "recklessly partial tribunal" created more problems than it resolved, and intensified rather than solved disputes, before noting: "No wonder a former [Foreign and Commonwealth Office] legal advisor Chris Whomersley believes that the tribunal is potentially destabilizing the overall stability of international relations."[58] Chinese newspapers have cited Talmon's work and noted that he is an international law professor at the University of Bonn.[59] The CSIL Statement also cites a number of Western scholars in favor of some of its general points, expressly noting their Western origins.[60]

These attempts to bridge the divide between Chinese and Western debates on the South China Sea involve two important asymmetries. First, in many more instances Chinese scholars chose to publish in English than foreign scholars chose to publish in Chinese. This asymmetry reflects and reinforces the increasing dominance of English as international law's lingua franca.[61] In a few cases, Western international lawyers wrote articles for Chinese newspapers, but they were written in English and were generally critical of the tribunal's jurisdiction and did not present a view antithetical to China to a Chinese audience.[62] These differences likely result from language difficulties (few non-Chinese scholars are able to write in Mandarin), academic incentives (Western scholars are more likely to be rewarded for publishing in Western outlets than non-Western ones), and China's press censorship (which would typically prevent dissenting views being expressed in the mainstream media).

Second, although Chinese scholars' publicly expressed opinions were virtually uniform, there were some splits within the Western camp. Chinese officials and scholars can point to Western scholars whose viewpoints support their own, but their Western counterparts generally cannot do the same in reverse. Still, the uniformity of these Chinese opinions also works to undermine their credibility. As Ku concluded: the "remarkably and suspiciously uniform" support of China's legal position has "injured the reputation of Chinese universities" and "damaged the credibility of Chinese legal scholars," undermining the persuasiveness of their scholarship on the issue outside China.[63] Similarly, Bing Ling implored the Chinese government to "stop treating academics

---

58. Liu, *supra* note 25.

59. *See, e.g., Arbitral Tribunal on South China Sea Illegal, Ridiculous*, XINHUA, July 8, 2016.

60. CSIL Statement, *supra* note 20 ("As written by Rothwell and Stephens, both Australian international lawyers, '[t]he Part XV dispute settlement mechanisms . . . do not have jurisdiction over disputes arising under general international law'"; "As written by Klein, an Australian international lawyer, '[maritime entitlements] are rights of sovereignty . . .'"; "Ted L. McDorman, a Canadian international lawyer, wrote that, 'whether historic rights exist is not a matter regulated by UNCLOS. . . .'").

61. ROBERTS, *supra* note 2, ch. 5.

62. *See, e.g.,* Talmon, *supra* note 43; Stefan Talmon, *No Case to Answer for Beijing Before Arbitral Tribunal in South China Sea*, GLOBAL TIMES, May 20, 2013; Chris Whomersley, *Tribunal Proceedings on Manila's Claims Flawed*, CHINA DAILY, June 16, 2016.

63. Ku, *China's Ridiculously Weak Legal Argument, supra* note 43.

as its handmaids and surrounding itself with yes-men" because a "lack of diverse and dissenting voices may only lead to bad decisions."[64]

By writing in English and publishing in foreign outlets, Chinese scholars made a significant effort to present their and China's viewpoints to the Western world. This helped to enrich the English-language debates and allowed for greater consideration to be paid by Western scholars to the viewpoints of their Chinese counterparts. Yet, due to factors such as language barriers and explicit and implicit Chinese censorship, views critical of China's position were not generally available in Mandarin in Chinese outlets. In this way, the Chinese scholars facilitated outward, but not inward, diversity, strengthening the robustness and legitimacy of transnational debates but not necessarily domestic ones.

IV. INCENTIVE SYSTEMS AND SOCIALIZING EFFECTS

What should we make of the divisions within these debates? First, international law scholars from different states often end up taking positions that have a lot in common with those of their states and geopolitical alliances.

In the Crimean debates, the unity of views expressed by the Russian international lawyers, and the correlation between their positions and those of the Russian government, were particularly striking. Russian international lawyer Maria Issaeva explained that the positions espoused by Russian academics "generally reflect— occasionally with some improvisation, but often word-for-word—the official Russian line expressed by the Russian President and Ministry of Foreign Affairs, including at the UN Security Council."[65] Whatever evidence there was for pluralism in the approaches of Russian international lawyers after the demise of the Soviet Union,[66] Isaaeva concludes that the case of Crimea made it obvious that "Russian international legal doctrine continues to speak with unity of voice, and that voice continues to purport to be that of the Russian state."[67]

Although the Western scholars usually agreed that Russia's annexation of Crimea was illegal, there was room within their debates for criticism of the West's double standards and failure to adhere to international law in other circumstances, such as NATO's use of force in Kosovo. For instance, Swiss-based international lawyer Nico Krisch noted that: "it is ironical that [Russia's] claims have come into the realm

---

64. Cited in Shi Jiangtao, *Is Beijing Courting Disaster by Shunning South China Sea Tribunal?*, SOUTH CHINA MORNING POST, June 20, 2016.

65. MARIA ISSAEVA, QUARTER OF A CENTURY ON FROM THE SOVIET ERA: REFLECTIONS ON RUSSIAN DOCTRINAL RESPONSES TO THE ANNEXATION OF CRIMEA (forthcoming 2017).

66. Prior to Crimea, Russian specialist Lauri Mälksoo had tracked the way in which Russian international law scholarship had moved away from a monolithic "one and only state-approved" theory of international law that had been typical during the Soviet Union toward a more open, pluralist approach to a range of issues. *See* Lauri Mälksoo, *International Law in Russian Textbooks: What's in the Doctrinal Pluralism?*, 2 GÖTTINGEN J. INT'L L. 279, 281 (2009).

67. ISSAEVA, *supra* note 65.

of the arguable because traditional constraints in the law on the use of force and self-determination have been blurred by instances of liberal interventionism over the last two decades."[68] Likewise, UK-based international lawyer Marko Milanovic complained of the "rampant hypocrisy" on the part of all of the major players in the Crimean situation:

> Those same Western states that unlawfully invaded Iraq, and supported Kosovo's secession from Serbia while endlessly repeating that Kosovo was somehow a really super-special sui generis case, are now pontificating about the sanctity of the UN Charter and territorial integrity. On the other hand, that same Russia that fought two bloody wars in the 1990s to keep Chechnya within its fold, that same Russia that to this day refuses to accept the independence of Kosovo, has now rediscovered a principle of self-determination that apparently allows for the casual dismemberment of existing states.[69]

Such self-criticism was largely absent from the Russian debates,[70] even though it was warranted.[71] In Russian international law manuals predating Crimea, Russian scholars (like their government) routinely embraced the cardinal importance of the prohibition on the use of force and the principle of nonintervention, rejecting the notion of unilateral humanitarian intervention as a Western invention.[72] In Crimea, however, Russian scholars embraced the principles of self-determination and unilateral humanitarian intervention while remaining conspicuously silent about the importance of nonintervention and the nonuse of force. Instead of justifying their current positions by reference to their or Russia's previous statements, they relied on positions taken by Western states and scholars with respect to Kosovo. This allowed them to criticize the West for hypocrisy without interrogating their own or Russia's double standards.

Second, one potential explanation for these divisions of viewpoint is differences in incentives, particularly given that some of these academics come from states that do not offer robust levels of academic freedom.

In the context of the South China Sea arbitration, Ku noted that, other than Ling, scholars within the Chinese legal establishment seemed to have either expressed

---

68. Nico Krisch, *Crimea and the Limits of International Law*, EJIL: *Talk!*, Mar. 10, 2014.

69. Marko Milanovic, *Crimea, Kosovo, Hobgoblins and Hypocrisy*, EJIL: *Talk!*, Mar. 20, 2014.

70. Issaeva, *supra* note 65 (noting that, among nearly two dozen international legal articles published by Russian scholars on the annexation of Crimea, only two firmly take a critical stance in respect of popular Russian justifications for state actions). For an exception from a PhD candidate from Moscow State University, who formerly studied at Harvard Law School, see Grigory Vaypan, *(Un)Invited Guests: The Validity of Russia's Argument on Intervention by Invitation*, CAMBRIDGE INT'L L.J. BLOG, Mar. 5, 2014.

71. Lauri Mälksoo, *Crimea and (the Lack of) Continuity in Russian Approaches to International Law*, EJIL: *Talk!*, Mar. 28, 2014.

72. ROBERTS, *supra* note 2, ch. 4.

support for China's position or kept silent.[73] One explanation he offered was that Chinese academics might have been unwilling to dissent on an issue of importance to the government due to fears of censorship or soft retribution in the competitive domestic academic job market. According to Chinese specialist Jerome Cohen: "it requires an act of courage for any international law or foreign relations specialist within the government to contradict prevailing policy, although academic debate continues to be allowed."[74] But, some newspapers reported on Chinese scholars complaining (anonymously) about being shunned by the government if they expressed critical views on the case and about their dissenting views seldom making the headlines in China's state-controlled media.[75]

Lauri Mälksoo concluded that the failure of Russian international law scholars to criticize Russia's actions in Crimea provided good evidence that Russian academia was not entirely free, particularly on core issues of national interest such as Crimea.[76] Indeed, there were high profile examples of attacks on academic freedom of speech in relation to the Crimean issue. For example, Professor Andrey Zubov, a history professor at MGIMO, which is a feeder university for the Russian foreign ministry, was fired in March 2014 after publishing an article criticizing Russia's policy toward Ukraine and comparing Russia's action in Crimea to Hitler's annexation of Austria.[77] Although MGIMO was forced to reinstate him on a technicality, the administration noted that this did not in any way change the fact that Zubov had "violated the main principles of professional conduct."[78]

In Western states, levels of academic freedom are much higher. One would not expect to see examples of international law academics being fired or fearing for their jobs if they criticized the approach of the states in which they taught. Nonetheless, international law academics often end up working for—or aspiring to work for— their home states, which may have a chilling effect on the extent to which they are prepared to publicly criticize those states. Indeed, in discussing the phenomenon of *dédoublement fonctionnel*, Schachter noted that the mingling of scholarly and official roles in this way creates tensions as individuals move from one role to another,

---

73. Ku, *China's Ridiculously Weak Legal Argument, supra* note 43.

74. Jerome A. Cohen, *Forecasting the Aftermath of a Ruling on China's Nine-Dash Line*, FOREIGN POLICY, Apr. 20, 2016.

75. Shi Jiangtao, *Is Beijing Courting Disaster by Shunning South China Sea Tribunal?*, SOUTH CHINA MORNING POST, June 20, 2016 ("Speaking your mind at seminars organised by Beijing to discuss competing claims in the South China Sea won't see you invited back, something a leading mainland international law scholar discovered three months ago.").

76. LAURI MÄLKSOO, RUSSIAN APPROACHES TO INTERNATIONAL LAW 92 (2015).

77. Leonid Bershidsky, *Comparing Putin to Hitler Will Get You Fired*, BLOOMBERG VIEW, Mar. 25, 2014; Matthew Bodner, *Professor Says Sacked over Opinion Article*, MOSCOW TIMES, Mar. 5, 2014.

78. МГИМО уволило профессора "за критику действий государства" в связи с Украиной [MGIMO Fired a Professor "For his Criticisms of Government Policy" in Relations with Ukraine], UKRAINSKA PRAVDA, Mar. 24, 2014.

leading to questions about whether they are acting in the capacity of objective scientist and government advocate.[79] Similarly, James Crawford has explained that many international lawyers uncomfortably wear two hats as academic lawyers and professionals in active practice, which may raise questions about whether these individuals have given up their scholarly independence and become too caught up in pursuing the details of individual cases or the national interest.[80]

In some areas, such as the law of the sea, certain US international lawyers are very closely associated with their states. For instance, in observing how strongly Chinese international lawyers have propounded China's interests in the South China Sea arbitration, Peter Dutton noted that China has "mobilized its lawyers" and that China's "international-law specialists have become *adjunct soldiers* in China's legal campaign to challenge the dominant, access-oriented norms at sea, especially for military freedoms of navigation in the exclusive economic zone."[81] Albeit an insightful observation about the Chinese, the comment betrays a lack of insight into how the Chinese might view the US international lawyers. Indeed, three of the most frequent US international lawyers to write on disputes about the law of the sea are Dutton, Raul (Pete) Pedrozo, and James Kraska.[82] All three were career naval officers who went on to hold positions as civilian professors at the US Naval War College, which operates under the US Navy.[83] Their time in service likely helped to inform the robust approach that these scholars take to freedom of navigation, which includes being critical of their own state when they think that the United States is being weak or is vacillating on this point. One could well imagine China's viewing these US international lawyers as "adjunct soldiers" in America's legal campaign to

---

79. Schachter, *supra* note 1, at 218.

80. James Crawford, *International Law as Discipline and Profession*, 106 AM. SOC'Y INT'L L. PROC. 471, 480 (2012). *See also* Gillian Triggs, *The Public International Lawyer and the Practice of International Law*, 24 AUSTRALIAN Y.B. INT'L L. 201, 216 (2005).

81. Peter Dutton, *Introduction, in* MILITARY ACTIVITIES IN THE EEZ: A U.S.- CHINA DIALOGUE ON SECURITY AND INTERNATIONAL LAW IN THE MARITIME COMMONS 1, 3 (Peter Dutton ed., 2010) (emphasis added).

82. *See, e.g.,* Peter A. Dutton, *Caelum Liberam: Air Defense Identification Zones Outside Sovereign Airspace*, 103 AM. J. INT'L L. 9 (2009); Peter Dutton & John Garofano, *China Undermines Maritime Laws*, FAR EASTERN ECON. REV. 44 (2009); James Kraska, *Resources Rights and Environmental Protection in the Exclusive Economic Zone*, in note 81, at 75; Raul (Pete) Pedrozo, *Coastal State Jurisdiction over Marine Data Collection in the Exclusive Economic Zone: US Views, in* MILITARY ACTIVITIES IN THE EEZ: A U.S.- CHINA DIALOGUE ON SECURITY AND INTERNATIONAL LAW IN THE MARITIME COMMONS, *supra* note 81, at 23; Raul Pedrozo, *Military Activities in and over the Exclusive Economic Zone, in* FREEDOM OF SEAS, PASSAGE RIGHTS AND THE 1982 LAW OF THE SEA CONVENTION (M.H. Nordquist, Tommy Koh & John Norton Moore eds., 2009) 241; Raul Pedrozo, *Close Encounters at Sea, The USNS Impeccable Incident*, NAVAL WAR COLLEGE REVIEW 101 (2009); Raul Pedrozo, *Preserving Navigational Rights and Freedoms: The Right to Conduct Military Activities in China's Exclusive Economic Zone*, 9 CHIN. J. INT'L L. 9 (2010); James Kraska, *Commentary: Defend Freedom of Navigation*, DEFENSE NEWS, June 8, 2015.

83. See https://www.usnwc.edu/Academics/Faculty/Peter-Dutton.aspx; https://www.usnwc.edu/Departments---Colleges/International-Law/Who-We-Are/ILD-Faculty-Links/BIO---Pedrozo.aspx; https://www.usnwc.edu/Academics/Faculty/James-C--Kraska.aspx.

maintain the access-oriented norms at sea, especially for military freedom of navigation in the exclusive economic zone.

Third, another explanation is that these divergent viewpoints are held honestly, rather than strategically, as a result of differences in the way in which these international lawyers are socialized. One way of evidencing how people in a given state are socialized is to look at media reports in those states. One cannot assume that international lawyers from a given state or geopolitical grouping rely only on media from that state or grouping or that the views expressed in that media are identical to those held by international lawyers. But understanding the different facts that are reported, and the different narratives that are developed, in the media in different states can give some insights into the different doxas and opinions that exist in those societies.

How international law applies in a given case depends on the underlying facts, but international lawyers in different states sometimes rely on different media sources that present different representations of "reality." In the case of Crimea, the Western scholars typically relied upon the Western news reports and statements by Western states and organizations to develop their understanding of the facts, while the Russian scholars embraced the facts that the Russian government and Russian news reports presented. Both tended to assume that the other was being swayed by misinformation spread by their own state and media outlets. For instance, Russian international lawyer Kapustin detailed the deep connections between ethnic Russians in Ukraine and Russia based on their history, language, and culture, saying that one cannot "disregard these basic facts."[84] Despite this, he explained that the "US and the EU Mass Media, including reputable television broadcasting companies, ignore these facts and present the situation in such a manner that Ukraine has been allegedly invaded by 'pro-Russian separatists' that have set up authority over the local residents."[85] "Eventually," he concluded, "this fraud will be revealed."[86]

In reverse, German international lawyer Daniel Wisehart on the blog EJIL: *Talk!* explained that, although there were divergent views between Western and Russian media on what was currently happening to Russian nationals in Crimea, there were no reports clearly establishing that Russian nationals in Crimea or other parts of Ukraine had been threatened: "The Russian federation only generally asserts 'a real threat to the lives and health of Russian citizens' but fails to establish *in concreto* how Russian citizens are endangered by the governmental transition that has occurred in the Ukraine[.]"[87] Similarly, US international lawyer Ku on *Opinio Juris* concluded that much of the dispute was a factual one based on different media reports:

> Most scholars would accept the idea that self-determination is appropriate in certain exceptional circumstances, such as decolonization or when facing the

---

84. *Kapustin Letter to ILA, supra* note 15, pt. 3.

85. *Id.*

86. *Id.*

87. Wisehart, *supra* note 14.

threat of genocide or other mass killings. No one west of the Ukraine border seems to think Crimea qualifies (except the good folks at RT [the Russian government-funded television network]) because none of us think that the new Ukrainian government has threatened Crimea in any tangible way.[88]

It would be easy for Western scholars to conclude that their media is free and unbiased while Russian media is government-sponsored and full of propaganda. Certainly, there is a huge gulf between the freedom of the press in the West and in states like Russia and China. But the Western media isn't perfect. For instance, the 2003 Iraq war led to doubts about the reliability of the media on questioning, rather than reinforcing, government views, and commentators have raised concerns about bias in the Western media's portrayal of Russia and Putin.[89] Discourse analysis of media reporting in different states about Kosovo suggested that different publics received very different pictures of what was going on and that these were often sympathetic to their own government's position.[90] Taking too black-and-white an approach would lead to discounting all views in these non-Western media sources and failing to apply any critical lens to the Western media, both of which are problematic. But while the situation is more gray, the shades of gray differ radically.

Different media accounts may also reflect and reinforce different national narratives about international disputes and the virtue and vices of different states engaged in those disputes. For instance, news reports in China and the United States tended to present the story about the South China Sea arbitration and disputes differently in terms of focus (e.g., which issues were important and required explanation) and narrative (e.g., which states were aggressive and which were reactive, which states were violating the international rule of law, and which were upholding it). Both were also quick to discredit the other with accusations of censorship or bias.[91]

88. Julian Ku, *Is the Crimea Crisis a Factual or Legal Disagreement?*, OPINIO JURIS, Mar. 14, 2014.

89. *See, e.g., Is Western Media Coverage of the Ukraine Crisis Anti-Russian?*, GUARDIAN, Aug. 4, 2014; Antony Loewenstein, *Ukraine: Western Media Coverage's Bias Should Be Held into Account*, GUARDIAN, Mar. 12, 2014; Piers Robinson, *Russian News May Be Biased—But So Is Much Western Media*, GUARDIAN, Aug. 2, 2016. *See also* PIERS ROBINSON ET AL., POCKETS OF RESISTANCE: BRITISH NEWS MEDIA, WAR AND THEORY IN THE 2003 INVASION OF IRAQ (2010).

90. *See* Seth Ackerman & Jim Naureckas, *Following Washington's Script: The United States Media and Kosovo*, *in* DEGRADED CAPABILITY: THE MEDIA AND THE KOSOVO CRISIS 97 (Philip Hammond & Edward S. Herman eds., 2000); Philip Hammond, *Reporting "Humanitarian" Warfare: Propaganda, Moralism and NATO's Kosovo War*, 1 JOURNALISM STUDIES 365 (2000); Jin Yang, *Framing the NATO Air Strikes on Kosovo Across Countries Comparison of Chinese and US Newspaper Coverage*, 65 GAZETTE: INT'L J. COMM. STUDIES 231 (2003).

91. For example, the US publication *Foreign Affairs* reported on how the Chinese government used a combination of propaganda and censorship to discredit Western media as biased, particularly in its reporting of the South China Sea dispute. *See* Bethany Allen-Ebrahimian, *How China Won the War Against Western Media*, FOREIGN AFFAIRS, Mar. 4, 2016. For an example of such reporting, see, for example, *Truth about South China Sea Should Not Be Misrepresented by Western Media*, XINHUA, July 8, 2016. Wang Guan, the chief political correspondent at CCTV America, explained that the West may boast a free press, but that it was biased, as evidenced by the reporting on the South China Sea disputes. *See South China Sea: CCTV Reporter Debates with American Expert on the Arbitration Case*, July 22, 2016, https://www.youtube.com/watch?v=P51oELMTL1M (last visited Feb. 5, 2017).

In terms of focus, consider the editorials and news reports in the *New York Times*. In an early editorial, the *New York Times* noted that China objected to the tribunal's jurisdiction, but did not explain why.[92] After warning that China might ignore a negative decision, the Editorial Board concluded that China should participate in the process if it "wants to be recognized as a leader in a world that values the resolution of disputes within a legal framework."[93] When the tribunal took jurisdiction, the paper reported that the Philippines had won an important ruling in the case, without explaining China's objection.[94] Before the award on the merits, the Editorial Board explained that "China has been behaving in a bellicose fashion in the South China Sea for some time" and that this was part of a "sustained and increasingly dangerous effort to assert sovereignty over a vital waterway in which other nations also have claims."[95] It concluded that the "right response would be for China to accept the court's decision," though whether it would do so "remains to be seen."[96]

In terms of narrative, Western newspapers frequently situated the dispute in the context of China's rising global power, portrayed China as an aggressive bully in the region, and described China's reaction to the arbitration and award as a test case for whether China will comply with the international rule of law. For example, after the award was released, the Editorial Board of the *New York Times* framed the issue as: "How China reacts to the sweeping legal defeat over its claims to the South China Sea will tell the world a lot about its approach to international law, the use—measured or otherwise—of its enormous power, and its global ambitions."[97] The paper concluded that, so far, the signs were "troubling" because Beijing had "defiantly" rejected the court's jurisdiction over the case and insisted it would not accept the "path breaking" judgment.[98] The Editorial Board followed up with an article detailing "China's Defiance in the South China Sea," explaining that "China's activities in the South China Sea have increasingly persuaded more and more people that it is determined to . . . bully and dominate its coastal neighbors."[99]

Concerns about China's aggressive posture are typically bolstered by articles about how China is building up and militarizing disputed islands within the South China Sea and aggressively chasing away foreign vessels and aircraft.[100] By contrast,

---

92. Editorial Board, *The South China Sea, in Court*, N.Y. TIMES, July 17, 2015.

93. *Id.*

94. Jane Perlez, *In Victory for Philippines, Hague Court to Hear Dispute over South China Sea*, N.Y. TIMES, Oct. 30, 2015.

95. Editorial Board, *Playing Chicken in the South China Sea*, N.Y. TIMES, May 20, 2016.

96. *Id.*

97. Editorial Board, *Testing the Rule of Law in the South China Sea*, N.Y. TIMES, July 12, 2016 [hereinafter Editorial Board, *Testing*].

98. *Id.*

99. Editorial Board, *China's Defiance in the South China Sea*, N.Y. TIMES, Aug. 13, 2016 [hereinafter Editorial Board, *China's Defiance*].

100. *See, e.g.*, Chris Buckley, *China, Denying Close Encounter with American Plane, Points Finger at U.S.*, N.Y. TIMES, May 19, 2016; Joe Cochrane, *China's Coast Guard Rams Fishing Boat to Free It from*

the United States is presented as a neutral state that is seeking to uphold freedom of navigation and to encourage the disputing parties to uphold the international rule of law. For instance, the Editorial Board of the *New York Times* explained that:

> The United States, which is neutral on the various claims, can help ensure a peaceful, lawful path forward. The Obama administration has said that disputes should be resolved according to international law, a position it now reaffirms. It has built closer security relations with Asian nations and responded to China's assertiveness in the South China Sea with increased naval patrols. This combination of diplomacy and pressure is sound, but the hard part is getting the balance right.[101]

Likewise the Board explained in another piece that "The Obama administration has played an important restraining role. It has also demonstrated resolve in defending America's commitment to freedom of navigation by sending warships into the South China Sea."[102]

Unsurprisingly, the Chinese newspapers presented a very different picture of the arbitration and the United States' role in the region. Mirroring the language of Chinese government officials, many Chinese newspaper articles and editorials use emotive language that calls into question the legitimacy and validity of the tribunal and its award. For instance, they often refer to the arbitration as "unlawful" or a "farce" and to the decision as a "so-called" award that is "illegal" and "invalid."[103] Many of the articles explained in detail why the tribunal lacked jurisdiction. For instance, an op-ed in the *China Daily* by China's ambassador to the United Kingdom argued that the subject matter of the arbitration, and the intention of the Philippines in bringing the case, was to determine issues related to territorial sovereignty and maritime delimitation but that issues of territorial sovereignty are beyond the scope of

Indonesian Authorities, N.Y. TIMES, Mar. 21, 2016; Editorial Board, *China's Missile Provocation*, N.Y. TIMES, Feb. 18, 2016; Michael Forsythe, *Possible Radar Suggests Beijing Wants "Effective Control" in South China Sea*, N.Y. TIMES, Feb. 23, 2016; Jane Perlez, *China Building Airstrip on 3rd Artificial Island, Images Show*, N.Y. TIMES, Sept. 15, 2015; Michael S. Schmidt, *Chinese Aircraft Fly Within 50 Feet of U.S. Plane over South China Sea, Pentagon Says*, N.Y. TIMES, May 18, 2016; Michael D. Shear, *Obama Calls on Beijing to Stop Construction in South China Sea*, N.Y. TIMES, Nov. 18, 2015; Derek Watkins, *What China Has Been Building in the South China Sea*, N.Y. TIMES, Feb. 29, 2016; Derek Watkins, *What China Has Been Building in the South China Sea*, N.Y. TIMES, July 31, 2015.

101. Editorial Board, *Testing, supra* note 97.

102. Editorial Board, *China's Defiance, supra* note 99.

103. *See, e.g.,* Liu, *supra* note 25; *Op-ed II on the Philippines' South China Sea Arbitration Farce, China's Sovereignty over the South China Sea Islands Brooks No Denial*, PEOPLE'S DAILY, Dec. 15, 2015; *Op-ed I on the Philippines' South China Sea Arbitration Farce: Grandstanding Cannot Cover up Illegal Moves*, PEOPLE'S DAILY, Dec. 14, 2015; Shen Dingli, *Unlawful Arbitration Worsens Tensions in Disputed Fishing Waters*, GLOBAL TIMES, July 13, 2016; Su Xiaohui, *It's Time to Stop Political Farce in the South China Sea*, CHINA US FOCUS, July 25, 2016; Zhong Sheng, *Justice Is China's Best Ally in Sea Dispute*, CHINA DAILY USA, July 21, 2016; *Op-ed, Double Standards Applied in South China Sea Arbitration Profane International Law*, PEOPLE'S DAILY, July 16, 2016; *Unlawful Arbitration Cannot Negate China's Sovereignty over South China Sea*, PEOPLE'S DAILY, July 12, 2016.

UNCLOS and China excluded issues of maritime delimitation from its acceptance of dispute resolution under UNCLOS.[104]

The Chinese papers also repeatedly stressed the United States' double standards in calling for China to comply with UNCLOS and to abide by the tribunal's rulings.[105] For instance, an op-ed in the *People's Daily* criticized the United States for gaining benefits under UNCLOS while never having ratified it, and for refusing to accept the ICJ's jurisdiction and judgment in the *Nicaragua* case:

> Regarding the international rule of law, the US and some other countries can hardly qualify as a "teacher" to China. In addition, they should look back to their past mistakes, abandon their long-upheld hegemony, egoism, hypocrisy and double standard and implement the basic norms of the international law and international relations through practical actions.[106]

Similarly, an editorial in the *People's Daily* written under the pen name "Guo Jiping," which is used for editorials that are meant to outline China's stance and viewpoints on major international issues, stated that:

> The double standards adopted by the US have exposed its hypocrisy and deep-rooted "imperialistic mentality." That is to say, the US will only show strong support for international laws that are to its own benefit. Otherwise, no matter how legitimate a law may be, the US will pay it no attention.[107]

Far from being the aggressor or a bully, Chinese officials and media often invoke China's century of humiliation to cast the state as the victim of aggression by imperialist powers. China's century of humiliation lasted from the First Opium War in the 1840s to when the Communist Party took power in 1949. As an op-ed in the *China Daily* explained: "Unlike the US, whose history in the last 150 years has been seizing land and expanding territory, for China, it has been a bitter memory of that 'century of humiliation.'"[108] Chinese actors often draw on this humiliation narrative as a starting point for discussions about how China should interact with other states. It also provides helpful background for understanding why Chinese people

104. Liu, *supra* note 25.

105. *See, e.g.,* Chua Chin Leng, *The Hague's Theatrical Judgment on the South China Sea*, CHINA DAILY, June 29, 2016; Liu, *supra* note 25; *Spotlight: U.S. Refusal to Honor Court Ruling in Nicaragua Case Reflects Double Standards*, XINHUA, July 14, 2016; Zhang Junshe, *US Iraq Tricks Reused in Tribunal Award*, GLOBAL TIMES, July 12, 2016.

106. Op-ed, *Double Standards Applied in South China Sea Arbitration Profane International Law*, PEOPLE'S DAILY, July 16, 2016.

107. *Unlawful Arbitration Cannot Negate China's Sovereignty over South China Sea*, PEOPLE'S DAILY ONLINE, July 12, 2016.

108. Chen Weihua, *Century of Humiliation Still Cuts Deep into the Collective Psyche*, CHINA DAILY, Aug. 19, 2016.

are particularly sensitive to what they perceive as Western bullying or attempts to infringe upon China's sovereignty.[109] As an article in *Xinhua* explained:

> Though China is growing into a strong country, the painful memory of history is not long gone. The Chinese people have not forgotten that the country stumbled into the 20th century with its capital under the occupation of the imperialists' armies, and for over a century before and after, China suffered the humiliation of foreign invasion and aggression. That is why the Chinese people and government are very sensitive about anything that is related to territorial integrity and would never allow such recurrence even if it's just an inch of land.[110]

By contrast, the United States is portrayed as a state with inherently hegemonic desires and a proven track record of interfering in the business of other states. For instance, *Xinhua* asked "why does the United States want to poke its nose into the region?" before answering that "China's increasing say in the international rule-making process and growing influence on regional order establishment have made the United States uncomfortable, pricking its fragile ego as a hegemonic power."[111] According to the *China Daily*, the United States' "strategic rebalancing to Asia is widely perceived as a policy shift that [was] intended to contain China's rise" and, to that end, the United States had encouraged countries such as the Philippines and Vietnam to "stir up trouble" in the South China Sea.[112] Similarly, US freedom of navigation operations were portrayed as "very dangerous" actions, as a "muscle show," as an example of the US view that "might is right," and as "destabilizing regional peace and undermining coastal nations' security interests."[113]

---

109. *See, e.g.*, WANG ZHENG, NEVER FORGET NATIONAL HUMILIATION: HISTORICAL MEMORY IN CHINESE POLITICS AND FOREIGN RELATIONS 102 (2012); Luo Xi, *The South China Sea Case and China's New Nationalism*, THE DIPLOMAT, July 19, 2016.

110. Fu Ying & Wu Shicun, *South China Sea: How We Got to This Stage*, XINHUA, May 14, 2016. *See also* Eric Fish, *How Historical "Humiliation" Drives China's Maritime Claims*, ASIA SOCIETY, June 16, 2016; Emily Rauhala, *China Believes It Is the Real Victim in the South China Sea Dispute*, WASH. POST, July 11, 2016; Merriden Varrall, *How China's Worldviews Are Manifested in the South China Sea*, NAT'L INTEREST, Dec. 16, 2015.

111. *China Voice: Behind South China Sea Tensions, U.S. Tries to Maintain Domination over World Issue*, XINHUA, May 25, 2016.

112. Wang Hui, *US' Actions Are Steadily Eroding Bilateral Trust*, CHINA DAILY, Aug. 3, 2016.

113. *See* Leslie Fong, *Freedom of Navigation Ops: US Exercising Right or Might?*, PEOPLE'S DAILY, June 4, 2016; *Freedom of Navigation in South China Sea Not U.S. Vessels' "Muscle Show,"* PEOPLE'S DAILY, Feb. 23, 2016; *US Warships Abusing Freedom of Navigation Operations: PLA Newspaper*, XINHUA, May 12, 2016; *U.S. "Freedom of Navigation" Operations in South China Sea "Very Dangerous,"* XINHUA, Apr. 28, 2016; Zhang Junshe, *It Is the US That Is Militarizing the South China Sea*, PEOPLE'S DAILY, Feb. 25, 2016.

V. THE IMPORTANCE OF SEEING INTERNATIONAL LAW
THROUGH THE EYES OF OTHERS

It is not surprising that international lawyers in different states and geopolitical regional groupings might form different epistemic communities with their own doxas and opinions. In any given community, international lawyers are likely to have been subject to similar influences, such as where they have studied, what they have read, where they publish, and what professional experiences they have undertaken. These socializing factors and incentive structures frequently differ among states in ways that reflect and reinforce divisions within the divisible college of international lawyers.

The resulting relatively self-contained communities are most obvious with respect to Russia. Mälksoo has observed that international law scholars in Russia are often first and foremost *Russian* international law scholars in the sense that they tend to be "linguistically and network-wise relatively distinct and separated from international law scholars in the West."[114] To the extent that Russian international lawyers engaged in a relatively self-contained debate about Crimea, they did not expose themselves to diverse viewpoints that might have challenged their assumptions and arguments. They also limited their ability to effectively engage with and seek to influence those holding contrary views in the West. However, similar criticisms could be made of the Western international lawyers for largely engaging in a relatively self-contained Western debate.

Some commentators raised concern about the lack of engagement between these two scholarly communities and how this disconnect might skew understandings of the debate. For instance, in discussing Oxford University Press's Debate Map on Ukraine and blogs such as *Opinio Juris*, Boris Mamlyuk (a US international law professor who is a Russian specialist) lamented that these included little to no analysis of the international law arguments from the perspective of Russian jurists or policymakers even though the Russian blogosphere was alight with international law coverage of Crimea.[115] Ku acknowledged complaints about *Opinio Juris*'s "pro-Western bias," but explained that "[p]art of the problem is that there is a dearth of international law commentators writing in English in favor of the Russian legal position."[116]

Anne Peters has written about the phenomenon of international legal scholars often espousing positions that can be linked to prior education in their domestic legal system and that serve the national interest, which she refers to as "epistemic nationalism."[117] She does not argue that scholars should completely detach

---

114. MÄLKSOO, *supra* note 76, at 87.

115. Boris Mamlyuk, *Crisis in Ukraine: A Cascade of Many International Law Violations*, HUFFINGTON POST, Mar. 13, 2014 (last updated May 13, 2014).

116. Julian Ku, *Is the Crimea Crisis a Factual or Legal Disagreement?*, OPINIO JURIS, Mar. 14, 2014.

117. Anne Peters, *Die Zukunft der Völkerrechtswissenschaft: Wider den epistemischen Nationalismus* [*The Future of Public International Law Scholarship: Against Epistemic Nationalism*], 67 ZEITSCHRIFT FÜR AUSLÄNDISCHES ÖFFENTLICHES RECHT UND VÖLKERRECHT [Heidelberg J. Int'l L.] 721, 748, 771 (2007).

themselves from their educational and cultural context, which she concedes would be impossible and this would be unnecessary, but that they should make a conscious effort to internalize the perspectives of their "others."[118] Likewise, Anne van Aaken has advocated for the importance of trying to see international law and disputes through other eyes because becoming aware of the frames of others helps to relativize one's own frame.[119]

One should not expect that engaging in a common dialogue will necessarily result in agreement. The *Heidelberg Journal of International Law* symposium provides a good example of scholars from different traditions coming together in a common forum but being unable to find agreement. But these sorts of exchanges are still highly valuable because they enhance understanding of each other's positions and, in so doing, they can also encourage international lawyers to challenge and possibly reconsider some of their own views in a way that might not happen within their immediate communities. As Mamlyuk argues: "To start this dialogue across language barriers, professional jargon, and political commitments individual scholars will need space to collaborate, lest we return to Cold War postures where international law occupies an uneasy place alongside ideology and propaganda."[120]

International lawyers are unavoidably situated. No one can understand all aspects of the field from all viewpoints. The best that international lawyers can do is to become more conscious of some of the frames that shape their understandings of and approaches to the field and be aware of how these might be similar to and different from those of others. To this end, it is important to find connections with, and overcome disconnects among, different communities of international lawyers and to read about international law disputes from multiple and diverse media sources. The importance of seeing international law and international disputes from multiple perspectives is only going to increase as the era of Western-led international law gives way to a period of greater competition, and increased need for cooperation, among various Western and non-Western states.

---

118. *Id. See also* Marxsen et al., *supra* note 16, at 3 n.2.

119. Anne van Aaken, *Emerging from our Frames and Narratives: Understanding the World Through Altered Eyes*, EJIL: *Talk!*, Dec. 23, 2014 (book review).

120. Mamlyuk, *supra* note 115.

7

"*Shioki* (Control)," "*Fuyo* (Dependency)," and Sovereignty

The Status of the Ryukyu Kingdom in Early-Modern and Modern Times

MASAHARU YANAGIHARA

The status of the Ryukyu Kingdom[1] after 1609, when the islands were conquered by the Satsuma Clan from Japan, is profoundly puzzling and ambiguous, seen from a contemporary viewpoint.[2] The Ryukyu Kingdom continued to deliver tribute to China every two years, to have a Ryukyu house at Fuzhou in China, and to receive Chinese envoys of investiture at the coronation of new kings at Naha, the capital of Ryukyu. The Kingdom was at the same time under the supervision and control, "*shioki* (control)" or "*fuyo* (dependency)" called in Japanese, of the Satsuma Clan.

It should be especially emphasized that there appear to have been almost no serious issues concerning the status of Ryukyu among the countries concerned (Ryukyu, Japan, and China) at that time. A serious problem arose later, from the 1840s, as the result of encounters with Western countries such as Great Britain, France, and the United States, which rushed toward Ryukyu to request friendship and courtesy, and trade and missionary work too.

The purpose of this chapter is to closely investigate the status of the Ryukyu Kingdom in early-modern and modern times, not from a contemporary viewpoint, but from the perspectives of specific periods. The main goal is to compare the traditional status of the Kingdom, peculiar to the region at that time, namely "*shioki*" or "*fuyo*," to the idea of "sovereignty" or "independence" in modern European international law.

---

1. The Ryukyu Kingdom was established through unification of three local countries in 1429. The First Dynasty of "*Sho*" reigned until 1470, followed by the Second "*Sho*" Dynasty, which was a completely different family.

2. Robert K. Sakai, *The Ryukyu (Liu-ch'iu) Islands as a Fief of Satsuma*, in THE CHINESE WORLD ORDER: TRADITIONAL CHINA'S FOREIGN RELATIONS 112 (John King Fairbank ed., 1968).

Comparative International Law. Edited by Anthea Roberts et al. © Anthea Roberts, Paul B. Stephan, Pierre-Hugues Verdier, Mila Versteeg 2018. Published 2018 by Oxford University Press.

It is absolutely not my idea that historical precedents such as the status of the Ryukyu Kingdom can be directly relevant to current international law questions, such as the status of the Senkaku/Diaoyu islands. My point is rather that historical precedents, especially in countries or regions that followed different systems of modern European international law, for example in East Asia in early-modern and modern times, had their own unique concepts and ideas, which cannot be and should not be understood by an application of concepts and ideas of modern European international law. In other words, concepts and ideas unique to modern European international law are not directly effective retroactively to the non-European world in premodern and modern times. That leads to another idea that comparisons of concepts and ideas concerning "international law and international relations" across countries or regions is useful in illuminating the uniqueness of concepts and ideas in each region and each period, and furthermore in clarifying the process of how Asian countries thought of sovereignty in the nineteenth century and how these different conceptions affected their interactions with each other.

Section I deals with the period from 1609 to the 1830s, before Western people rushed suddenly toward Ryukyu, while Section 2 discusses the status of the Ryukyu Kingdom in the 1840s and the 1850s, in particular the nature of the Conventions concluded by the Kingdom with the United States, France, and the Netherlands respectively in 1854, 1855, and 1859. The final section deals with a series of administrative regulations from 1872 to 1879 by the New Meiji government bearing on the status of Ryukyu, which is known as the *"Ryukyu shobun* (Ryukyu Disposition)."

I. THE RYUKYU KINGDOM FROM 1609 TO THE 1830S

A. *"Shioki* (Control)" and *"fuyo* (Dependency)"

A letter of Ieyasu Tokugawa (1542–1616), the first Shogun of the Tokugawa government starting from 1603, addressed to Iehisa Shimazu, Daimyo of the Satsuma Clan, dated 7 July *Keicho* 14 (August 6, 1609), states:

> I am so much pleased to hear that you subjugated the whole country of Ryukyu with armed force. Hereby I decide as follows: Ryukyu is given to you and you are instructed to have *"shioki* (control)" there.[3]

The Satsuma Clan had sent about 3,000 soldiers to Ryukyu in April 1609, maintaining in particular that Ryukyu had not performed compulsory labor ordered by Hideyoshi Toyotomi (1537–1598) at the time of Japan's first invasion of Korea (1592–1593), had not sent an envoy to repay Ieyasu's rescue of Ryukyu's drifting ship, and had been impolite to Satsuma. It is often said that it was reasonably easy for Satsuma to gain mastery over that region, because it is highly probable that all weapons had been abolished in Ryukyu from the beginning of the sixteenth century. The

---

3. 3 NIHONSHI SHIRYO [MATERIALS OF JAPANESE HISTORY] 126 (Rekishigaku Kenkyukai ed., 2006).

reality is that 100 or 200 Satsuma soldiers were killed in the battle with the Ryukyu soldiers, who were equipped mainly with bows and arrows.[4] The king and some chief vassals of the Kingdom were taken as "prisoners of war" to Kagoshima, the capital of Satsuma. Satsuma got by the letter of Ieyasu an official approval from the Tokugawa government to have "*shioki*" there.

The term "*fuyo* (dependency)" was used in an exchange of letters between the Satsuma Clan and the Ryukyu Kingdom, such as a letter of Yoshihisa Shimazu addressed to the king of Ryukyu in February *Keicho* 9 (March 1604) and in written vows of the Kingdom addressed to the Magistrate of Satsuma dated 20 September *Keicho* 16 (October 25, 1611).[5]

The meaning of "*fuyo*" here is comparatively simple. Based mainly upon a 1592 license letter from Hideyoshi Toyotomi describing Ryukyu as "*yoriki*" of Satsuma [= person who stands by Satsuma under its command],[6] Satsuma regarded Ryukyu as its dependency. The issue is the meaning of "*shioki.*" "*Shioki*" in Japanese during the Warring States era (1467–1568) meant governmental control of a feudal lord: collection of annual land tax ["*nengu*"] was called "*shomu* (duty, business)," while other powers of a lord were "*shioki*" in a narrow sense. "*Shioki*" gradually changed its meaning during the Tokugawa era to signify mainly penalties and execution of a sentence, which were deemed the most important tasks among the powers of a lord.

The real content of "*shioki*" in the case of Ryukyu was mainly threefold: annual land tax, enforced written vows, and an ordered dispatch of envoys to Edo (Tokyo). A fief of the Kingdom was limited to the Ryukyu Islands, while the Satsunan Islands were regarded as a fief of the Satsuma Clan. And Ryukyu's stipend of 120,000 koku (18,000 metric tons) of rice, assessed in terms of rice production, was paid as an annual land tax to the Satsuma Clan.

In addition to paying tax, the Ryukyu Kingdom was forced to make a written vow comprising 15 articles. Critically important among them were the following three rules: a rule not to bring tribute to China except in the case of an order by Satsuma (Article 1), a rule not to allow Japanese merchants to go to Ryukyu without a permit from Satsuma (Article 6), and a rule to strictly prohibit the dispatch of Ryukyu merchant ships to Japan except for those approved by Satsuma (Article 13).[7] These rules mean that the Satsuma Clan had the tribute trade between China and the Ryukyu Kingdom under its absolute control, so that the Clan uniquely could obtain commercially valuable goods in Japan such as raw silk, silk fabrics, and pharmacopoeia. Both the Clan and the Kingdom endeavored to keep this rule secret from China, although it is not perfectly clear now if the Chinese government knew about it. Commissioners of the Clan were permanently stationed at Naha to keep watch

4. KIYOSHI NAKAMURA, HONNE DE KATARU OKINAWA SHI [HISTORY OF OKINAWA FROM AN HONEST PERSPECTIVE] 125–34 (2011).

5. 3 KYUKI ZATSUROKU KOHEN [MISCELLANEA OF AN OLD CHRONICLE, THE SECOND VOLUME] 927–28 (Kagoshimaken Ishinshiryo Hensanjo ed., 1983); 4 KYUKI ZATSUROKU KOHEN, *id.* at 345–49.

6. 3 NIHONSHI SHIRYO, *supra* note 3, at 46.

7. 4 KYUKI ZATSUROKU KOHEN, *supra* note 5, at 344–45.

on the observance of these written vows. Ryukyu's officials who violated them were sentenced to a severe punishment, as typically shown in the 1667 case of Chatan and Eso.[8]

The Ryukyu Kingdom was also ordered to send envoys, called "*Edo nobori* (go up to the Capital)" or "*Ryukyu shisetsu* (Ryukyu envoys)," to Edo at the coronation of new Ryukyu kings and Japanese Shoguns. Those envoys, sent 18 times from 1634 to 1850, were received with much courtesy, almost the same as with envoys of Korean kings sent to Edo, who were called "*Chosen tsushinshi* (Korean envoys)," sent 12 times from 1607 to 1811. Especially because Ryukyu envoys were costumed in a totally different way from ordinary Japanese and played totally different musical instruments, these encounters provided an excellent opportunity for the Satsuma Clan and the Tokugawa government respectively to show off the Clan that had control over "*ikoku* (alien countries)" and the government that received visitors from *ikoku*.

B. "*Tsushin no kuni* (Countries of Correspondence)" and "*tsusho no kuni* (Countries of Trade)"

The idea of "*tsushin no kuni* (countries of correspondence)" and "*tsusho no kuni* (countries of trade)"[9] is indispensable to understanding the status of the Ryukyu Kingdom in those days. This new idea was first developed by a Senior Councilor of the Tokugawa government, Sadanobu Matsudaira, when the Russian envoy, Adam Laxman, came to Hakodate in Ezo in 1793 to request trade with Japan. Matsudaira refused to accept a diplomatic message dispatched by the Russian Empress, because Russia was not *tsushin no kuni*, and therefore Japan was not able to have diplomatic relations with Russia. In the letter addressed to the Dutch minister in 1845 it was made fully explicit that the relations with Korea and Ryukyu were *tsushin*, including the exchange of diplomatic documents or envoys, and the relations with China and the Netherlands were *tsusho*, as these included trade and the traveling to Japan of merchants from those countries.[10]

The purpose of this concept is obvious: relations with the external world should be definitively limited to these four "countries." Thus Japan was not allowed to develop any kind of relations with other countries.[11] This idea was presumed to be ancestral law of Japan. Accordingly Ryukyu was considered to be "*tsushin no kuni*," together with Korea. Korea had been a typical "vassal country" of China for almost the entire period of its history, although it had insisted on its original conception of itself as a central empire, equal with China or next to China, in its relations with

8. 2 OKINAWA DAIHYAKKA ZITEN [OKINAWA ENCYCLOPEDIA] 771 (Okinawa Daihyakka Ziten Kanko Jimukyoku ed.,1983).

9. *See* Masaharu Yanagihara, *Significance of the History of the Law of Nations in Europe and East Asia*, 371 RECUEIL DES COURS 273, 364–66 (2014).

10. 20 ZOKU TSUSHINZENRAN [COMPLETE DOCUMENTS OF CORRESPONDENCE: THE SECOND SERIES] 665 (Gaimusho ed., 1985).

11. RONALD PAUL TOBY, SAKOKU TO IU GAIKO [THE POLITICS OF "SECLUSION"] 88–95 (2008).

neighboring countries such as Japan, Ryukyu, and Juchen, even though its relations with Japan had been fairly complex.

Tsushin with Ryukyu means simply that the Tokugawa government did not regard Ryukyu as being included into the proper domain of Japan, but rather *ikoku*, having the same status as Korea. *Tsushin* definitely connotes official "diplomatic" relations with *ikoku*.[12]

It was the fundamental policy of the Ryukyu Kingdom at that time to limit officially "foreign" relations to those with China and Japan. There were almost no practical relations between Korea and Ryukyu after 1609, although in the first years of the Joseon Dynasty in the fifteenth and sixteenth centuries the Korean government had been eager to accept Ryukyu subjects to carry out trade with them. Repatriation of castaways from Korea and Ryukyu continued to be made even after 1609, although in almost all cases the castaways were sent back to each country not directly between Korea and Ryukyu, but rather by way of Peking or Fujian in China.

While it is perfectly clear that the status of the Ryukyu Kingdom is embarrassing from a contemporary point of view, the far more important fact is that no serious incident concerning its status took place.

II. THE RYUKYU KINGDOM IN THE 1840S AND THE 1850S

A. Missionaries Who Resided in Ryukyu

The first instance of Western people arriving at Ryukyu occurred in 1816 and involved an English fleet, consisting of two ships, *Alceste* and *Lyra*. They stayed there only for 45 days to measure the depth of the neighboring sea and then took their leave.

The next visitor was a French warship, *L'Alcmène*, in 1844. Her captain, Commander Fornier-Duplan, requested friendship, trade, and missionary work, but departed from Naha without receiving any reply from the Kingdom, leaving a missionary, Augustin Forcade and a Chinese seminary student, Augustin Ko. They were obliged by the Kingdom to stay at a Japanese temple, cut off almost from the outside world, but tried to learn Ryukyuan and edited a Ryukyu-French dictionary later.

Two years later three more French warships, *Cléopâtre*, *Sabine*, and *Victorieuse*, with their admiral Cécille, came to Naha to request, this time with a strong hand, friendship, trade, and missionary work, but again in vain. In the same year an English merchant ship arrived at Naha to bring Bernard Jean Bettelheim, a doctor and a Protestant missionary, who stayed at Naha with his wife and children for eight years. During his stay at Ryukyu he translated the four Gospels into Ryukyuan and engaged in missionary work, converting just one Christian there.[13]

---

12. In this context the theory of four gates, especially the "Satsuma Gate" open to the Ryukyu Kingdom, is also highly intriguing. *See* Yanagihara, *supra* note 9, at 362–63.

13. JULES REVERTEGAT, UNE VISITE AUX ILES LOU-TCHOU 250–56 (Paris, Le Tour De Monde 1882); BÉNIGNE EUGÈNE FORNIER-DUPLAN, CAMPAGNE DE L'ALCMÈNE EN EXTRÊME-ORIENT (1843, 44, 45, et 46) 17–37 (1908); HENRI CORDIER, LES FRANÇAIS AUX ÎLES LIEOU K'IEOU 5–12 (1911).

When Matthew Calbraith Perry, commander in chief of the US Naval Forces, came to Naha in 1853 he employed Bettelheim, as Bettelheim had plenty of knowledge about Ryukyu. The Ryukyu government asked Perry to take on Bettelheim, saying that to look after him was a huge burden on Ryukyu as it was a small country. Bettelheim went to the United States by Perry's ship in 1854[14] and died there in 1870.

B. Conventions with Western Countries

As the French and English attempts in the 1840s to request friendship, trade, and missionary work were unsuccessful, Perry was the first Westerner to succeed in concluding a friendship convention with Ryukyu, as well as with Japan. A document, entitled "Rules for Replies to Aliens" drawn up by the Ryukyu government, probably in February *Kaei* 1 (March 1848), establishes the context of this agreement. It shows clearly that the Kingdom paid tribute to China and traded with the Tokara or Takara Islands, which meant substantially Satsuma, even though official relations with Satsuma were kept strictly confidential. It was the consistent and strict policy of the Kingdom to decline any kind of perpetual relationships with *ikoku* and to treat aliens as transient guests. To implement this policy the Kingdom created a meticulous system for receiving alien ships. This document is also extremely interesting with regard to detailing the "territory" of the Kingdom. It states that 36 islands of Ryukyu belong to the Ryukyu Kingdom and that none of them had ever been held by Japan.[15] This document, a set of possible questions for aliens and answers from the Kingdom, was a reliable manual for governmental officers in charge of aliens and alien ships that would come to Ryukyu.[16]

1. CONVENTION WITH THE UNITED STATES
When Perry came with four warships to Ryukyu for the first time in May 1853 on the way to Edo, he compelled the residents to supply living necessities, provide accommodations on land, and establish a coal bunker. He also strongly wanted to meet with the Ryukyu king himself in his Shuri Castle to negotiate. Without permission, he and his more-than-two-hundred crew marched into the Castle to meet the chief officers of the Kingdom. Ryukyu was forced to accept all of his demands in clear contravention of the above-mentioned "Rules for Replies to Aliens" and began building the demanded bunker. The following year, after the successful conclusion of the Treaty of Peace and Amity between Japan and the United States, signed in Japanese, English, Chinese, and Dutch on March 31, 1854 (3 March *Ansei* 1),[17] Perry

---

14. 7 RYUKYU OKOKU HYOJOSHO MONJO [DOCUMENTS OF THE EXECUTIVE OFFICE OF THE RYUKYU KINGDOM] No. 1505 at 603 (Ryukyu Okoku Hyojosho Monjo Hensan Iinkai ed., 1991).

15. 17 RYUKYU OKOKU HYOJOSHO MONJO, *id.*, No. 1921 at 322–33.

16. Kurakichi Takara, *Kaidai* [Bibliographical Introduction], *in* 3 OKINAWAKEN SHIRYO [DOCUMENTS CONCERNING THE OKINAWA PREFECTURE] 6, 7–9 (Okinawaken Okinawashiryo Henshujo ed., 1984).

17. Treaty of Kanagawa, U.S.-Japan, Mar. 31, 1854, 11 Stat. 597.

and his warships came again to Naha, arriving on July 1, 1854. Representatives of Ryukyu explained doggedly that their king was too young to decide extremely crucial political affairs and that instructions from China were needed, because Ryukyu had been "*Hankoku* (a fief)" of China since the Ming Dynasty. Throughout they stubbornly resisted putting their seal on any document. Perry, however, refused to listen to them, and successfully concluded a Convention in Chinese and English on July 11, 1854 (17 June *Ansei* 1),[18] almost three months after a treaty with the Tokugawa government. The latter treaty was the first international treaty under modern international law to which Japan was party.

After signing the Convention, the representatives of Ryukyu asked Perry to leave China uninformed of this Convention, and Perry graciously acceded.[19] Both Ryukyu and Japan were compelled under the military pressure of his black-hulled warships to accept these treaties. This acquiescence reflected Ryukyu's and Japan's lack of international law knowledge and especially their vast military inferiority.

The main points of the Convention between Ryukyu and the United States were the extension of friendship and courtesy to US citizens visiting Ryukyu (Article 1) and assistance to wrecked US ships "on Great Lew Chew or on islands under the jurisdiction of the Royal Government of Lew Chew" (Article 3).

This Convention was officially endorsed by the US president on March 9, 1855 and was considered in effect from that date.[20]

2. CONVENTION WITH FRANCE

One year later Ryukyu concluded a convention with France,[21] and then, one with the Netherlands.[22]

Guérin, an admiral of the French Navy, came to Naha on November 6, 1855, with three ships carrying a crew of 234 and left 22 days later. According to a document written by the Ryukyu government, the process leading to the conclusion of the Convention was remarkable. Representatives of the Kingdom had insisted on rejecting the proposed Convention, explaining that the Convention with the United States could be concluded because it was limited only to the supply of fuel and water and protection of wrecked ships, a courtesy that it had provided previously. Guérin replied that conclusion of a treaty was the command of the French

---

18. Compact with Lew Chew, U.S.-Japan, Jul. 11, 1854, 10 Stat. 1101.

19. 7 RYUKYU OKOKU HYOJOSHO MONJO, *supra* note 14, No. 1505 at 588–89, 594, 600–01, 606.

20. Compact with Lew Chew, *supra* note 18.

21. Convention entre la France et les Iles Liou-Tchou, Nov. 24, 1855 (15 October *Ansei* 2), *reproduced at* 3 RECUEIL DES TRAITÉS ET CONVENTIONS ENTRE LE JAPON ET LES PUISSANCES ÉTRANGÈRES 1854–1925 at 654 (Ministère des affaires étrangères ed., 1934). This Convention, together with the Convention with the Netherlands, is not collected in Parry's Consolidated Treaty Series, mainly because they were not ratified by France and the Netherlands, see *infra* text corresponding to note 31. *See* HENRI CORDIER, LE PREMIER TRAITÉ DE LA FRANCE AVEC LE JAPON (EDO, 9 OCTOBRE 1858) 205–90 (1912).

22. Traktaat tusschen Nederlanden en Lioe-Kioe, Jul. 6, 1859 (7 June *Ansei* 6), *reproduced at* 3 RECUEIL DES TRAITÉS, *id.* at 658.

emperor.[23] Ryukyu's representatives also protested that directions from China and Japan were necessary to conclude a treaty, because Ryukyu was a protectorate of China ("*Hanpei*") and had relations with Tokara, Japan.[24] A threat obliged the Ryukyu Kingdom to conclude the Convention. Drawing their swords, Guérin and his crew dragged the representatives of the Kingdom from the meeting room to the nearby garden during the fifth meeting on October 12, coercing them to sign and seal a Convention containing 11 articles.[25]

In a letter addressed to the Minister of the Navy dated December 6, 1855, Guérin tells a different story. He wrote that "Le point le plus sérieusement contesté a été l'article 2.... Les négociateurs Lou-Tchouans persistaient dans leurs refus.—Vous voulez donc être forcés leur dis-je alors d'un air menaçant et bien vous le serez: Ces paroles, les gestes qui les accompagnaient eurent l'effet que j'attendais d'eux."[26] He admitted to having threatened Ryukyu representatives with words, but not with violence.

The content of the French Convention covered more ground than did the Convention with the United States: Articles 2 (lending and borrowing of land, houses, and ships, and their inviolability), 9 (arrest of French and Ryukyu fugitive criminals), 10 (punishment of French and Ryukyu criminals), and 11 (restoration of wrecked ships) had no counterparts in the US Convention.

According to a "Commentary on the French-Japanese Convention" produced by the Ryukyu government on November 24, 1855, friendship between France and Ryukyu was not to be taken literally. This was the official interpretation of the Ryukyu government. The Commentary gave some examples: When people saw the French on the street, they were requested not to flee from them, but to make to them a salutation pertinent to the occasion; when the French came to a dwelling, tea and sweets should be served, but a very friendly manner should not be adopted.[27]

3. CONVENTION WITH THE NETHERLANDS

In contrast with the French Convention, the agreement between the Netherlands and Ryukyu was signed in an especially friendly manner. Captain J. van Capellen came to Naha by "Bali," with a crew of 120, on June 28, 1859. He declared that he acted at the command of the Dutch king. Representatives of Ryukyu insisted on concluding an agreement containing the same articles as that with the United States. The Convention as concluded contained nine articles, seven of which were the same as that with the United States. The major exception, article 8, dealt with most-favored-nation treatment. It was signed on July 6, 1859 (7 June *Ansei* 6) after 10 days of negotiation.[28] The explanation for the difference with the French encounter apparently lay in the traditional relationship of the Netherlands with Japan.

23. 11 RYUKYU OKOKU HYOJOSHO MONJO, *supra* note 14, No. 1535 at 187–88.

24. *Id.* at 207.

25. *Id.* at 215–17.

26. Service historique de la Défense (Vincennes, France), MV BB4 735, ff. 53–55.

27. 17 RYUKYU OKOKU HYOJOSHO MONJO, *supra* note 14, No. 1807 at 317.

28. 14 RYUKYU OKOKU HYOJOSHO MONJO, *supra* note 14, No. 1582 at 485–502.

In a document written by the Ryukyu government containing a series of potential questions by the Dutch and respective answers by Ryukyu, we find a statement that Ryukyu sells sugar, alcohol and so on in Kagoshima and buys tea, tobacco, and so on there, and that 12 or 15 of Kagoshima's ships come to Ryukyu for this trade. This fact was not disclosed to the Americans and French, but it was to the Dutch.[29]

While Perry's Convention was ratified by the United States, the Conventions with France and the Netherlands were not. A lack of cooperation between the Navy and the Foreign Ministry was clear in both cases. In each instance, the Navy had initiated the negotiations at its own discretion. According to a letter from the French minister at The Hague dated February 23, 1867, the Dutch foreign minister explained that the Netherlands had decided not to ratify the Convention with Ryukyu because they gained better information about the status of Ryukyu as a tribute country, and the Dutch government did not expect much in terms of commerce with Ryukyu.[30] The Dutch decision might have driven the French government not to ratify the Convention either.[31]

4. LEGAL QUESTIONS CONCERNING THESE CONVENTIONS

These Conventions of Ryukyu with the United States, France, and the Netherlands, even though the latter two ultimately were not ratified, give rise to two legal questions. The first is whether the Ryukyu Kingdom was a "sovereign and independent State" that had the ability to conclude treaties with Western countries.

In the negotiations between Perry and the Tokugawa government in March 1854, we find a remarkable statement by the government about the status of Ryukyu.[32] When Perry declared that he would be content with three ports to be opened to the American flag, Uraga or Kagoshima, Matsumae (Ezo) and Naha (Ryukyu), the commissioners of the government answered: "In regard to Lew Chew . . . as it was

---

29. 14 RYUKYU OKOKU HYOJOSHO MONJO, *supra* note 14, No. 1573 at 152. Nariakira Shimazu, Daimyo of the Satsuma Clan, with a far-reaching plan of trade with Western countries and China, had a policy of actively promoting conclusion of a treaty between Ryukyu and the Netherlands. *See id.* at 147–48.

30. Archives diplomatiques de France, Mémoires et documents, Japon, tome 1, 1854–1870, ff. 227–29.

31. Yoshinori Yokoyama, *Nihon no kaikoku to Ryukyu [The Opening of Japan and Ryukyu]*, in KOKKA TO TAIGAI KANKEI [STATES AND FOREIGN RELATIONS] 365, 411–12 (Yuji Sone & Naoya Kimura eds., 1996).

32. The Tokugawa government appears to have had a slightly different conception of the Ryukyu Kingdom in the 1840s. The position of the Tokugawa government and the Satsuma Clan in the 1840s, as described in a suggestive booklet by a Confucian scholar in Satsuma, was for Ryukyu to be sacrificed. *See* Hidetaka Godai, *Ryukyu Hisaku [Secret Policy for Ryukyu]*, in NANHEI KIKO [STUDY OF ACCOUNTS OF SOUTHERN MISSIONS] 104, 105–14 (Okinawa Rekishi Kenkyukai ed., 1966). One more example makes the point. When an English vessel in 1846 came to Ryukyu, the Tokugawa government allowed trade between the Westerners and the people in Ryukyu, so that the Westerners would not come to "Japan." 1 ISHIN SHIRYO KOYO [ELEMENTS OF HISTORICAL MATERIALS CONCERNING THE MEIJI RESTORATION] 20 (Ishin Shiryo Hensan Jimukyoku ed., 1937). It should be noted, however, that trade alone was allowed, and not official communication; nor was the Christian religion allowed to be practiced there.

a distant dependency, over which the Emperor of Japan had but limited control, they could entertain no proposition. And as for Matsmai [Matsumae, Ezo], that also stood in similar relation to the Japanese Government."[33] They said elsewhere that Ryukyu is "a very distant country, and a definite answer cannot be given," while Matsumae is "a very distant place, and belongs to a prince."[34] Although it is not clear whether the Tokugawa government made a strict distinction between "dependency" and "country,"[35] it was the consistent and express policy of the Tokugawa representatives that the opening of Naha port could not be discussed by the Tokugawa government.[36] It is also remarkable here that they did not use the theory of "*tsushin*" at this stage.

What about the policy of the Qing Dynasty regarding the Conventions between the Ryukyu Kingdom and Western countries in the 1850s? No official commitment from the Qing Dynasty has been found. The Qing Dynasty might have been utterly exhausted by its own politics.[37]

In the negotiation between Perry and the Ryukyu Kingdom, we find several interesting facts recorded in Perry's later account. What Bettelheim told Perry is truly remarkable: Bettelheim believed that "the country, though independent to a certain extent, (its ruler being permitted, for a good contribution to Peking, to assume the high-sounding title of king), yet is, to all ends and purposes, an integral part of Japan." He listed five reasons: there was a Japanese garrison quartered in Naha; Ryukyu's trade was entirely with Japan; the Japanese were numerous in Ryukyu; apparently Japanese inspectors controlled the Ryukyu officials; and the language, dress, customs, virtues, and vices of Ryukyu corresponded to those of Japan.[38]

33. Francis L. Hawks, Narrative of the Expedition of an American Squadron to the China Seas and Japan, Performed in the Years 1852, 1853, and 1854, Under the Command of Commodore M.C. Perry 364 (1856).

34. *Id.* at 365.

35. It was written in the Japanese document that Ryukyu is "*enkyo* (distant place, or distant boundary region)" and Matsumae "*henkyo* (frontier)." 5 Bakumatsu gaikoku kankei bunsho [Documents of Foreign Relations in the Closing Days of the Tokugawa Government] 249 (Tokyo Daigaku Shiryohensanjo ed., 1914).

36. Hawks, *supra* note 33, at 363. Perry's response to this statement was as follows: "As there can be no good reason why the Americans should not communicate freely with Lew Chew, this point is insisted on."
    The Satsuma Clan commanded the Ryukyu Kingdom on October 29, 1854, three months after the conclusion of the Convention with the United States, to revise a clause of direct trade between the United States and Ryukyu and not to conclude any more conventions with other Western countries. 1 Ishin shiryo koyo, *supra* note 32, at 648. The situation developed, however, totally differently from what the Satsuma Clan had hoped.

37. We find a historical document of November 1855 to the effect that the Ryukyu Kingdom was discussing a proposal to send a special envoy to the Qing Dynasty to explain the circumstances of why the Kingdom had decided to conclude the Convention with France. 2 Ishin shiryo koyo, *supra* note 32, at 146. Based upon the materials investigated, it is not clear whether such an envoy was dispatched.

38. Hawks, *supra* note 33, at 222–23.

Evidence of Perry's initial impression of the status of Ryukyu exists in his letter to the Secretary of the Navy on December 12, 1852, before he arrived at Ryukyu. He wrote: "The islands called the Lew Chew group are said to be dependencies of Japan, as conquered by that power centuries ago, but their actual sovereignty is disputed by the government of China. These islands come within the jurisdiction of the prince of Satsuma, the most powerful of the princes of the Empire."[39] Here Perry did not consider the Ryukyu Kingdom as an "independent State." The preamble of the original draft of the treaty expresses, however, a different position, one that departs from both Perry's initial view and that of Bettelheim's. A discussion concerning the preamble between representatives of Ryukyu and those of Perry on July 8, three days before finalization of the agreement, recognized Ryukyu as "an independent nation." Ryukyu "objected, saying that such an assessment on their parts would get them into trouble with China, to which country they owed allegiance . . . that it had better not bear on its face the assertion or appearance of their claiming absolute independence." The phrase "independent nation" was omitted in the final draft.[40]

One also might consider an explanation of the Convention entre l'Empire français et le Royaume des Ryûkyû (1855), found at the site of the Bibliothèque nationale de France. This states that "le royaume des Ryûkyû (aujourd'hui département d'Okinawa, alors supposé être un État indépendant et considéré comme une base-arrière utile aux abords du Japon."[41] This indicates that the French regard the Kingdom at that time as an "independent State."[42]

39. *Id.* at 85. In the same letter Perry wrote that "Now, it strikes me, that the occupation of the principal ports of those islands [Ryukyu] for the accommodation of our ships of war, and for the safe resort of merchant vessels of whatever nation, would be a measure not only justified by the strictest rules of moral law, but what is also to be considered, by the laws of stern necessity; and the argument may be further strengthened by the certain consequences of the amelioration of the condition of the natives, although the vices attendant upon civilization may be entailed upon them." Perry himself explained in detail later, during his fourth stay in Ryukyu from January to February 1854, his real intent concerning the possible "occupation" or "conquest" of the Ryukyu ports as follows: "It was not proposed by the Commodore to take Lew Chew, or claim it as a territory conquered by, and belonging to, the United States, nor to molest or interfere in any way with the authorities or people of the island, or to use any force, except in self-defense. In fact, there was not likely to be any occasion for violence, as the Americans already possessed all necessary influence in Lew Chew, which had been acquired by kindness and non-interference with the laws and customs of the island." *Id.* at 324.

40. *Id.* at 495. The same description is found in SAMUEL WELLS WILLIAMS, A JOURNAL OF THE PERRY EXPEDITION TO JAPAN (1853–1854) 240, 242 (1910) [Meetings on July 8 and July 10] as follows: "Fear of China was the only reason they assigned. It was a singular discussion; we desiring to have them sign this document on terms of equality as a sovereign State, and they debating every inch, preferring to own subjection to China and great inferiority to us." The discussion on July 8 is recorded also in the document of the Ryukyu Kingdom, but we don't find any similar description in it. 7 RYUKYU OKOKU HYOJOSHO MONJO, *supra* note 14, No. 1505 at 588–89.

41. Convention entre l'Empire français et le Royaume des Ryûkyû, Nov. 24, 1855, *available at* http://gallica.bnf.fr/html/und/asie/convention-et-traites (last visited Sept. 1, 2017).

42. Guérin's idea concerning the status of the Ryukyu Kingdom is totally different from the idea to regard the Kingdom as an "independent State." He wrote in his report as follows: "Je présume, Monsieur le Minister que Lieu-Tchou n'est qu'une province japonaise régie par un Proconsul envoyé

Whether the Ryukyu Kingdom could have been, or should have been, recognized as an independent or sovereign state is closely related to the general question of whether a "country" in the world order of East Asia, or in non-European areas, was able to be recognized as a sovereign state under contemporary Western international law. This is reminiscent of the category of "colonial and like treaties."[43] These include treaties between the United States and the Cherokee Nation between 1785 and 1819 (for example, Treaty between the U.S. and the Cherokee (North American Indians) on July 8, 1817),[44] the Treaty of Cession between Great Britain and New Zealand (Waitangi Treaty) on February 5/6, 1840,[45] or the Treaty between the German East African Company and the Sultan Fungo (Quafungo) of May 16, 1885.[46] The US Supreme Court under Chief Justice Marshall regarded the Cherokee tribes not as "sovereign and independent States" but as "domestic dependent nations,"[47] an extremely strange concept from the perspective of modern international law.

The concept of "State" is to be distinguished from polis, *civitas*, res publica, or *Imperium* in ancient Rome and medieval Europe. This concept of "State," or "*stato*," "*Staat*," "*État*," was invented in the sixteenth century, particularly by Niccolò Machiavelli (1469–1527). The origin of the word "State" is the Latin "*status*," which meant usually "a condition" or, in context, "a form of government." Machiavelli used the word "*stato*" mainly to signify "the body politic as organized for supreme civil rule and government." Another important aspect of the modern state is the concept of "*persona moralis*," according to which a political unity is regarded as an artificial or fictitious person, not as a physical person like real and living monarchs. Thomas Hobbes's idea of "Artificial Man (*homo artificialis*)" and Samuel Pufendorf's idea of "*entia moralia*" are representative of this concept.

The concept of "sovereignty (*summa potestas, summum imperium*)" was introduced in modern European thought by Jean Bodin (1530–1596). That concept is

d'Yedo. . . . Le Roi n'est qu'un enfant, et il est certain que l'ambassadeur Chinois n'est consulté que pour le forme et qu'il n'a nulle influence dans les affaires du Royaume." Service historique de la Défense, *supra* note 26, f. 55.

The minister of the Dutch Ministry of Colonization explained his idea about Ryukyu in his letter dated February 25, 1859, that the Netherlands should not conclude a treaty with Ryukyu, unless it is proven that Ryukyu is independent, but that a conclusion in the name of the Dutch Viceroy or the Representative Office in Japan would be approved even in that case. Cf. Yokoyama, *supra* note 31, at 397.

43. Special Chronological List: Special Chronologies, (A) Colonial and Like Treaties, (B) Postal and Telegraph etc. Agreements, 1648–1920 (Index-Guide to Treaties Based on the Consolidated Treaty Series) (Michael A. Meyer ed., 1984).

44. Treaty with the Cherokees, July 8, 1817, 7 Stat. 156.

45. Treaty of Cession between Great Britain and New Zealand, Feb. 5, 1840, 29 BSP 1111.

46. Treaty between the German East African Company and the Sultan Fungo (Quafungo), May 16, 1885, 77 BSP 14.

47. Cherokee Nation v. Georgia, 30 U.S. 1 (1831).

sharply distinguished from imperium or dominium in ancient Rome and medieval Europe. It is perfectly clear that the concept of sovereignty in its modern European form never existed in any previous periods.

It should be emphasized that it would be seriously misleading to apply directly, without any reservations, modern European ideas of sovereignty or territory to the East Asian World, including Ryukyu at that time, although certainly there existed an idea of possession or border peculiar to the area.

The second legal issue raised by those Conventions is the question of "treaty succession." Did the Conventions bind the Japanese Meiji government, which assumed power in 1868, after it virtually abolished the Ryukyu Kingdom by recognizing in its place the Ryukyu Clan on October 16, 1872?

In this connection some correspondence between Japan and the United States in 1872 is very intriguing. Charles De Long, Resident Minister of the United States at Tokyo, sent a letter to Taneomi Soejima, Minister of Foreign Affairs, dated October 20, 1872, asking if Japan would observe the Convention between Ryukyu and the United States with respect to all its provisions within the territorial limits of the former Kingdom.[48]

Soejima, in a reply dated November 5, 1872, stated: "The Lew Chew Islands (Ryukyu) have been dependencies (*"fuyo"*) of this empire (Japan) for hundreds of years, and to them the title of Han was recently given. As you say, the Lew Chew being an integral portion of the Japanese Empire it is natural that the provisions of a compact entered into between the Lew Chew and the United States on the 11th of July, 1854, will be observed by this government." Soejima makes clear in this letter that the Meiji government would abide by all provisions of that Convention.

A theoretically important issue here is whether the Meiji government could "succeed" to the Conventions concluded by the Ryukyu Kingdom. The official position of the Meiji government after October 1872 was that Ryukyu had been *"fuyo"* of Satsuma since 1609, and therefore that the Ryukyu Kingdom should be regarded not as an "independent State" having an official power to conclude treaties with foreign countries. This would lead to the conclusion that those Conventions concluded by the Ryukyu Kingdom without any official permission from the then Tokugawa government had to be by nature null and void and therefore not subject to succession by the Meiji government.

These Conventions cannot be put in the same theoretical category as those concluded by the Tokugawa government, the obligations of which the Meiji government assumed by succession. How then can we explain satisfactorily the fact that the Meiji government promised to "implement" those Conventions?

The Meiji government wrote in an 1879 Memorandum addressed to China that the foreign countries that concluded the Conventions with Ryukyu did not know that Ryukyu did not have any power to conclude treaties. It furthermore stated that the then Tokugawa government had governed in a purely feudal system, permitting local daimyos, including definitely the king of Ryukyu, to carry out services

---

48. 3 Recueil des traités et conventions entre le Japon et les puissances étrangères 1854–1925, *supra* note 21, at 662–63.

that could not have been allowed them in the contemporary centralized system.[49] Certainly this is a pathetically weak argument, taking in particular into considera- tion an interpretation of the Tokugawa government not to regard Ryukyu as being included in to the proper domain of Japan, but rather *ikoku*, when we see the idea of "*tsushin no kuni*." It is, however, closely connected to a radical view of the Meiji gov- ernment that did not regard the Ryukyu Kingdom as an "independent State" that had the power to conclude treaties with foreign countries.[50]

III. RYUKYU/OKINAWA IN THE MEIJI ERA

A. "*Fuyo* (Dependency)"

The policy of the Meiji government regarding Ryukyu in the beginning of the Meiji era in 1868 was deeply ambivalent. From around October 1872, however, it became clearer through the explicit denial of "dual subordination." Meiji authorities argued that Ryukyu belonged continuously to Japan from 1609 onward, when Ryukyu had been put under the supervision and control of the Satsuma Clan and obliged to pay an annual land tax, called "*nengu*." Ryukyu, while a fiefdom of Satsuma, had certainly sent envoys to the Qing Dynasty to pay tribute, but this was not regarded by the Meiji government as a tax. Here the payment of tax was viewed as play- ing an overwhelmingly important role in deciding to which country Ryukyu had belonged. That is definitely not a traditional Chinese rule, but an idea of modern European international law that the Meiji government accepted without any overt criticism.[51]

The Imperial Edict appointing the Ryukyu king as Chief of the Clan, dated October 16, 1872, provided:

> I maintain, in accordance with the great order, the status of a son of Heaven in an unbroken line, to have the four seas under my control and reign over the eight remote areas. Ryukyu is located now in the neighboring south area of Japan and Ryukyu people have the same personality with the Japanese and have no difference in the wording and spoken styles of a language. Ryukyu had been "*fuyo*" of Satsuma for generations, but you, Shotai, Ryukyu King, are

---

49. 12 NIHON GAIKO MONJO [DOCUMENTS ON JAPANESE FOREIGN POLICY] 192–93 (Gaimusho ed., 1879).

50. According to the instruction given by the Cabinet of Japan to the Ministry of Foreign Affairs dated October 30, 1872, "the treaties concluded formerly by the Ryukyu Clan with the countries should be subject to the jurisdiction of the Ministry." 5 NIHON GAIKO MONJO, *supra* note 49, at 392–93. It is noteworthy that it is written here that the treaties were concluded not by the Ryukyu Kingdom, but by the "Ryukyu Clan," which did start to exist, in fact, on October 2, 1872, definitely far after the conclusion of the treaties in the 1850s.

51. Michiyuki Matsuda, *Ryukyu shobun* [*The Ryukyu Disposition*] (1879), *in* 4 MEIJI BUNKA SHIRYO SOSHO GAIKOHEN [DOCUMENTS COLLECTION OF THE MEIJI CULTURE: DIPLOMACY] 94, 157, 214–15 (Fujio Shimomura ed., 1962).

formally requested to be devoted in the discharge of your duties for me, so that you are appointed as Chief of the Ryukyu Clan and raised to the peerage.[52]

It is perfectly clear here that the Ryukyu Kingdom is regarded as a Clan, namely, part of Japan, the same with other Clans such as Satsuma, Choshu, Aizu, and so on. The status of the Kingdom is explained as having been "*fuyo*" of Satsuma. A remarkable fact in the Edict is the use of "*fuyo*," not "*shioki*," as had been the case in the 1609 Ieyasu letter. The reason the Edict made use of "*fuyo*" instead of "*shioki*" appears to be a change of the meaning of "*shioki*" during the Tokugawa era. As of 1872 the primary meaning of "*shioki*" was punishment or an execution of a sentence, not "control" in a general sense.

B. "Ryukyu Disposition"

The Ryukyu Kingdom was abolished by recognizing in its place the Ryukyu Clan in October 1872; at the same time all communications between the Ryukyu Clan and foreign countries now came under the control of the Japanese Ministry of Foreign Affairs. After July 1875, the Meiji government expressly prohibited Ryukyu from paying tribute to China. Ultimately in March 1879 the Ryukyu Clan was abolished and replaced by the Okinawa Prefecture. Ryukyu/Okinawa then formally became a part of the centralized administration of the Meiji government.

It was made more explicit at that point that Ryukyu was continuously a territory in modern European international law of Japan. Ryukyu no longer was regarded as "*fuyo*" of Satsuma, as full sovereignty of Japan over Ryukyu/Okinawa had been formally established. In a "Proposal for a Disposition of the Ryukyu Clan" formulated in January or February 1879 by Michiyuki Matsuda, Chief Officer of the Ryukyu Disposition, we observe the following passage: Ryukyu should be regarded "not as a vassal State (*reizoku no kuni*) or half-sovereign State (*hanshu koku*) in international law, but as a region of a Clan purely located within Japan."[53]

The series of administrative regulations bearing on the status of Ryukyu is known as the "*Ryukyu shobun* (Ryukyu Disposition)." The basic nature of this Disposition is still discussed now, alternatively characterized as aggression, annexation, national unification, or internal reform ("*naisei no kaikaku*").[54]

Japan and China had heated and difficult negotiations over Ryukyu at that time. China proposed an arbitration process by the former US president, Ulysses S. Grant, who is said to have advanced a proposal of partition, dividing Ryukyu into three parts in 1879. According to the alleged Grant Proposal, two demarcation lines were identified- 27 degrees north latitude and 25 degrees north latitude. The northern

52. 4 NIHONSHI SHIRYO, *supra* note 3, at 98.

53. Matsuda, *supra* note 51, at 203.

54. RYUKYU, OKINAWA SHI NO SEKAI [WORLD OF THE HISTORY OF RYUKYU AND OKINAWA] 48–67 (Kazuyuki Tomiyama ed., 2003).

part would belong to Japan, and the southern part would go to China; the middle part was to become an independent Ryukyu Kingdom.[55]

Possibly taking the proposal into consideration, Japan offered to cede Miyako Islands and Yaeyama Islands, the southern part of Ryukyu that are completely south of 25 degrees north latitude, to China in 1880. Japan proposed simply to divide Ryukyu into two halves at the 25 degrees north latitude.[56] China rejected this proposal at the final stage of negotiations, saying that the whole of Ryukyu should belong to it. This dispute continued unresolved until China effectively abandoned its claim in 1895 during the Sino-Japanese War.[57]

An especially interesting story is associated with Gustave Emile Boissonade de Fontarabie's 1875 intervention, "*Ryukyu to mikomi an* (Proposal on a Possibility of Ryukyu Islands)."[58] He was one of the most famous *Oyatoi Gaikokujin* (employed foreign specialists) and had drawn up a draft of the Japanese Civil Code and Criminal Code. His draft for the Civil Code was discarded because of severe criticism contending that it would endanger the long and venerable tradition of Japan.

His opinion on Ryukyu was relatively moderate. He wrote that the Ryukyu Islands were now under the sovereignty of Japan, which fact the Chinese government acknowledged, because of the 1874 Sino-Japanese Treaty providing that people of Ryukyu were called "Japanese." He proposed that tribute from Ryukyu to China should be abolished, but that the Japanese government should seek to consult with the Chinese government first. As a practical matter, however, the Japanese government did not accept this proposal.

IV. CONCLUDING REMARKS

Two hotly contested issues concern Okinawa today: the planned relocation of US Marine Corps Air Station Futenma to Henoko within Okinawa Prefecture, and the territorial issue between Japan and China over the Senkaku/Diaoyu Islands. The main reasons many Okinawans, including the present Okinawa governor, strongly protest against the relocation are a feeling of having been victimized, especially during the Second World War and even after the reversion of Okinawa to Japan in 1972, as well as objecting to intolerable burdens tied to US military facilities on Okinawa. Some extremists in Okinawa are calling for secession from Japan and for Okinawa to become an independent state.

---

55. Kiko Nishizato, Shimmatsu chu ryu nichi kankei shi no kenkyu [A Study of Relations Between China, Ryukyu, and Japan in the Late Qing Period] 333 (2005). The Senkaku/Diaoyu Islands are located a little north of latitude 25 degrees north. In the negotiations between Japan and China, however, the Senkaku/Diaoyu question was never mentioned.

56. 13 Nihon gaiko monjo, *supra* note 49, at 369–88.

57. Nishizato, *supra* note 55, at 318–411.

58. Ito Hirobumi kankei monjo 1 [Documents Relating to Hirobumi Ito 1], No. 354, Kensei shiryo-shitsu [Modern Japanese Political History Materials Room], Kokuritsu kokkai toshokan [National Diet Library], Tokyo.

As for the second issue, the Japanese government insists that it made a Cabinet Decision on January 14, 1895, to erect a marker on the Islands to formally incorporate them, which had been terra nullius, into the territory of Japan and that since then they have been under the effective control of Japan as part of the Okinawa Prefecture. The Chinese government insists, to the contrary, that Japan's Cabinet Decision was made abruptly during the confusion of the Sino-Japanese War and that Diaoyudao and the other islands were effectively taken from China by the 1895 Peace Treaty. China argues that it possesses "historic, geographic and geological" evidence in support of its position.

When we examine the history of the Ryukyu Kingdom, it is perfectly clear that the present Senkaku Islands were not included at any time in the 36 islands of the Ryukyu Kingdom. In the negotiations between China and Japan from 1879 to 1881 concerning the status of Ryukyu no official document relating to the Senkaku Islands can be found.

This chapter does not advance immediate and practical solutions to these two issues. Rather, it demonstrates the importance of historical and comparative investigation concerning the status of the Ryukyu Kingdom. This can contribute to attacking these important issues from various points of view to achieve a real breakthrough in our understanding.

PART THREE

Comparative International Law and International Institutions

8

Comparative International Law Within, Not Against, International Law

Lessons from the International Law Commission

MATHIAS FORTEAU*

Public international law and comparative law have so far been regarded as largely distinct fields, with little to no overlap between them. The degree of separation between the two disciplines is rendered in particularly stark relief by the absence in practice or scholarship of any real inquiry into the relationship between comparative law on the one hand and customary international law and general principles of international law on the other.[1] Some eminent international lawyers go so far as to claim that it would be both unnecessary and unrealistic to have recourse to comparative law in the context of the identification of customary international law and general principles of law, pointing to the case law of the Permanent Court of International Justice and the International Court of Justice, which, according to them, "show[s] a clear disinclination towards the use of the comparative method."[2]

To some degree, this situation is a matter of curiosity since international law and comparative law share the same openness to the world and are both confronted by the diversity of domestic legal cultures and state practice. Given this state of

* The author is grateful for the research assistance of Umer Ali (NYU School of Law; Research Assistant at the UN International Law Commission during its 66th session [2014]). This chapter was first published in the *American Journal of International Law*, vol. 109, no. 3 (July 2015).

1. See Jaye Ellis, *General Principles and Comparative Law*, 22 Eur. J. Int'l L. 949, 949–50 (2011). *But see* Rudolph Schlesinger et al., Comparative Law 42–47 (1998). On comparative international law and general principles of law, see also Neha Jain, *Comparative International Law at the ICTY: The General Principles Experiment*, 109 Am. J. Int'l L. 486 (2015).

2. Alain Pellet, *Article 38, in* The Statute of the International Court of Justice: A Commentary 677, 769–72 (Andreas Zimmermann et al. eds., 2006).

affairs, initiatives aimed at bridging the gap between international law and comparative law (which is the purpose of "comparative international law") merit close attention.[3]

At the same time, however, the relevance and claimed novelty of such initiatives need to be approached with caution and viewed in proper context. It may be the case that the combination of both disciplines eventually proves more harmful than good to international law. Multiculturalism, which lies at the heart of the concept of "comparative international law" and conveys the idea that international law could be approached differently depending on the culture of each country, society, or peoples, is not a neutral approach. The mere concept of comparative international law could be seen as giving too much weight to the cultural aspect in international law by taking as given that there are differing approaches to international law (something that is not necessarily self-evident) and by putting more emphasis on cultural and national identities than on the more secular, ecumenical figure of the state (including the principle of sovereignty and its various expressions and reflections in concrete rules), which seems to remain more influential in the elaboration, interpretation, and application of today's international law.[4] More importantly, one may wonder whether the mere concept of comparative international law does not in fact entail a Catch-22: if one admits that there are different approaches to international law (i.e., a real *comparative* international law), is there still room for an "international law"?[5] It is one thing for international law to tolerate, as it does, multiculturalism in the domestic sphere[6] and quite a different thing for multiculturalism to have an impact on the international plane through the manifestation of different conceptions of international law.[7]

3. *See* Emmanuelle Jouannet, *Les Visions Française et Américaine du Droit International*, *in* DROIT INTERNATIONAL ET DIVERSITÉ DES CULTURES JURIDIQUES [INTERNATIONAL LAW AND DIVERSITY OF LEGAL CULTURES] 43, 88–89 (2008). For more detailed treatment, see Anthea Roberts, *Comparative International Law? The Role of National Courts in Creating and Enforcing International Law*, 60 INT'L & COMP. L.Q. 57, 73–92 (2011) (characterizing "comparative international law" as a "phenomenon . . . which loosely fuses international law substance with comparative law methodologies").

4. *See* Mohamed Bennouna, *Droit International et Diversité Culturelle*, *in* INTERNATIONAL LAW ON THE EVE OF THE TWENTY-FIRST CENTURY: VIEWS FROM THE INTERNATIONAL LAW COMMISSION 79, 81 (1997) [hereinafter INTERNATIONAL LAW], *available at* http://legal.un.org/docs/?path=../ilc/publications/pdfs/21stcentury.pdf&lang=E.

5. As Lauterpacht put it, the idea of international law presumes an inherently international, not domestic, nature. H. Lauterpacht, *Règles Générales du Droit de la Paix*, 62 RECUEIL DES COURS 95, 200 (1937 IV) ("En fait, il est difficile d'accepter comme logique toute conception nationale du droit international. La conception du droit international est par essence internationale.").

6. *See* Declaration on Principles of International Law Concerning Friendly Relations and Co-operation Among States in Accordance with the Charter of the United Nations, G.A. Res. 2625 (XXV), Annex (Oct. 24, 1970) ("Every State has an inalienable right to choose its political, economic, social and cultural systems. . . . ").

7. *See* Hanqin Xue, *Meaningful Dialogue Through a Common Discourse: Law and Values in a Multi-Polar World*, 1 ASIAN J. INT'L L. 13, 13 (2011) ("Although regional perceptions might contribute to a more

Admittedly, the risk of diluting international law by relying on comparative international law is not so great when comparative international law consists in academic studies that explore potential divergences among national conceptions of international law. But comparative law is not only an academic exercise; it is also used by practitioners, for practical purposes.[8] In international law, comparisons between domestic practices are particularly important for the identification and formation of customary international rules, which depend heavily on the assessment of existing state practice and *opinio juris*. To the extent that it can have a concrete effect on international law in force or *in statu nascendi*, the notion of "comparative international law" needs to be approached with caution. In practice, it is not an easy task to strike the right balance between the need for international rules and the imperative to avoid "negat[ing] cultural relevance in identifying common values."[9] The formation and development of international law presupposes the taking into account of existing approaches, however diverse they might be, *and* their encompassment by rules of international law that are both common and applicable to all states. Such a conciliation of diversity and unity is a challenging task, one which comparative international law also has to face.

Fortunately, such attempts are not wholly novel, and lessons can be learned from the past. Judge Owada has noted that in the encounter of Japan with the West in the mid-nineteenth century, Japanese intellectuals

> tried to identify this concept of "the law of nations" as one which should have its rational meaning as a concept of universal validity, and tried to understand it in the context of their own intellectual tradition. . . . They tried to comprehend the meaning of what was "specific" by identifying what was "universal" in that specificity. To borrow the words of Lévi-Strauss, a well-known social anthropologist who started the structuralist school of anthropology, the scientific approach of structuralism in anthropology should consist in the "quest for the invariant, or for the invariant elements among the superficial differences." It is my personal belief that this approach of "the quest for the invariant and universal elements among the superficial differences" should represent the essence of the process of Asia's approach to the "Community of Civilized Nations."[10]

nuanced understanding of global efforts in dealing with these challenges, the very idea of truly 'international' law renders the regional approach controversial."); *see also* Martti Koskenniemi, *The Case for Comparative International Law*, 20 FINNISH Y.B. INT'L L. 1, 3–4 (2009) (making similar observations).

8. This practical function of comparative law is sometimes neglected by comparative lawyers. *See, e.g.,* JOHN HENRY MERRYMAN, *Comparative Law and Scientific Explanation, in* THE LONELINESS OF THE COMPARATIVE LAWYER 478 (1999).

9. Xue, *supra* note 7, at 17.

10. Hishashi Owada, *Asia and International Law: The Inaugural Address of the First President of the Asian Society of International Law Singapore, 7 April 2007*, 1 ASIAN J. INT'L L. 3, 9 (2011) (footnote omitted); *see also* B.S. Chimni, *Is There an Asian Approach to International Law? Questions, Theses and Reflections*, 14 ASIAN Y.B. INT'L L. 249 (2008) (pointing to the necessity of taking due account of each country, region, or civilization's perspectives when identifying international law).

This approach provides a relevant blueprint for a successful combination of comparative law and international law.

Concrete examples are found in the work of international institutions over many decades of dealing with comparative international law (well before the expression was coined) in the process of identifying international law. This is the case with the International Law Commission (ILC), which was instituted in 1947 to assess the degree of uniformity of state practice and the extent to which it is possible to overcome such divergences.[11] As early as 1949, there was a clear view that "if the task of the International Law Commission were confined to fields with regard to which there is a full measure of agreement among States, the scope of its task would be reduced to a bare minimum."[12] In other words, the ILC's raison d'être lies in the existence of at least some degree of difference between states' practice, which needs to be overcome by codifying or progressively developing "one" international law. The ILC can, in that regard, be seen as a fruitful laboratory for assessing how comparative international law has operated *in practice* over the last 70 years. Accordingly, the present analysis will explore the extent to which the work of the ILC can provide useful insights about the benefits, drawbacks, and practical difficulties of resorting to comparative international law *within international law* (thus avoiding undermining it) in the process of establishing what international law is or should be.

In particular, I will show that there is a "vital necessity of maintaining the interplay of distinct legal cultures in the making of international law" and that such a process, which permits mutual tolerance and favors the acceptance and enforcement of international law, "may entail the salutary effect of assimilating or lessening the existing differences";[13] that this task requires reliance on representative international organs, which have to develop specific tools to formulate international rules in harmony with national or regional cultural approaches or concerns; and that this task may necessitate the formulation of international rules (at least universal ones) "in as general terms as possible," in order to guarantee sufficient flexibility.[14] The recourse to comparative international law within international law may accordingly eventually result in quite a subtle sharing of tasks and relationships between international law and domestic law. Section I of the present study will elaborate on these main observations by identifying the institutional ingredients that are required in order for comparative international law to obtain a sufficiently representative conception of international law. Section II will then explore the main tools used by the

11. The ILC was created by United Nations General Assembly Resolution 174 (II), dated November 21, 1947. G.A. Res. 174 (II) (Nov. 21, 1947).

12. U.N. Secretariat, Survey of International Law in Relation to the Work of Codification of the International Law Commission, Memorandum Submitted by the Secretary-General, ¶ 11, U.N. Doc. A/CN.4/1/Rev.1 (Feb. 10, 1949).

13. Sompong Sucharitkul, *Legal Multiculturalism and the International Law Commission*, in MULTICULTURALISM AND INTERNATIONAL LAW 301, 313–14 (Sienho Yee & Jacques-Yvan Morin eds., 2009); *see also* U.N. Secretariat, *supra* note 12, ¶ 111.

14. *See* James Crawford, *Chance, Order, Change: The Course of International Law: General Course on Public International Law*, 365 RECUEIL DES COURS 1, 251–52 (2013).

ILC on the substantive plane to draft common rules on the basis of existing and possibly divergent state practice or *opinio juris*. The focus will be placed in that regard on customary international law insofar as general principles of international law have for the most part never been considered by the ILC as a field to be explored on its own—presumably because both codification and progressive development of international law require the Commission to base its proposal at least on some emerging state practice, that is, on some customary law *in statu nascendi*, while general principles of international law are rather used as a measure of last resort when no other source can be relied on.

I. INSTITUTIONAL ASPECTS

According to Article 1, paragraph 1, of its Statute, the ILC "shall have for its object the promotion of the progressive development of international law and its codification."[15] The dual functions of the ILC are implicated in both the pre- and post-formation stages of international law. Codifying international law consists of identifying existing customary international rules. Progressive development of international law, on the other hand, entrusts the ILC with a quasi-legislative function, the expression being defined by the Statute of the Commission as "the preparation of draft conventions on subjects which have not yet been regulated by international law or in regard to which the law has not yet been sufficiently developed in the practice of States."[16] In other words, the ILC is charged with assessing state practice in order to identify what existing international law is or should be. It then participates in the universalization of international law by identifying possible differences in domestic approaches to interpreting, applying, or even determining the existence of customary international rules; by devising written formulae aimed at establishing a consensus regarding the manner in which the content of existing non-written rules can be expressed; and by proposing acceptable improvements to existing rules. Comparative law techniques are relevant to these ends, but their application requires well-designed institutions. The composition of the ILC and its methods of work (and their flaws) could provide interesting insights as regards the ways comparative international law should operate in practice, and are addressed in turn.

A. The Composition of the ILC

The codification of international law was viewed as a major tool in the second half of the twentieth century for overcoming tensions between old and newly independent states. Indeed, codification has been conceived of as an appropriate way for the

---

15. Statute of the International Law Commission, G.A. Res. 174 (II), Annex, art. 1 (Nov. 21, 1947) [hereinafter ILC Statute], *available at* http://legal.un.org/docs/?path=../ilc/texts/instruments/english/statute/statute.pdf&lang=EF, *amended by* G.A. Res. 485 (V) (Dec. 12, 1950); G.A. Res. 984 (X) (Dec. 3, 1955); G.A. Res. 985 (X) (Dec. 3, 1955); G.A. Res. 36/39 (Nov. 18, 1981).

16. *Id.* at art. 15.

initiation of a dialogue between Western states and former colonies that thought of international law as inspired by European conceptions and therefore unrepresentative of their own views.[17] When the ILC was created in 1947, the members of the United Nations attached great importance to its representativeness, at least in this dimension. According to Article 8 of its Statute, when UN Member States elect the members of the ILC, they "shall bear in mind that ... in the Commission as a whole representation of the main forms of civilization and of the principal legal systems of the world should be assured."[18] The 34 seats in the Commission are distributed among five regional groups inside the United Nations in order to promote the said representativeness.[19] The members of the ILC are then supposed to reflect, inside the Commission, the particular views of their region and/or country toward international law or, in other words, to act "as a kind of translator between the domestic and the alien legal orders."[20] Accordingly, the Secretary-General of the African-Asian Legal Consultative Organization (AALCO) pointed out in 2012 that "[g]iven that a large number of Commission members [are] from Asian and African States, several delegations [of AALCO] ha[ve] expressed the hope that their active participation in the Commission's work w[ill] help to reflect more prominently the views and aspirations of those States in the progressive development and codification of international law."[21] The fact that ILC members have to act as independent experts[22] and the collegial nature of the ILC are supposed to grant the overall process a sufficient degree of objectivity.

That being said, the representativeness of the ILC can be challenged on three grounds at least, which put into perspective the capacity of the ILC to constitute a relevant model for future comparative international lawyers.

First, on a theoretical plane, the ILC can be seen as "the 'priesthood' of orthodox Formalist legal thought."[23] In a time of deformalization in international law, in particular due to the increasing role of *soft law*, the ILC may be seen as symbolizing a too "old-fashioned" way of approaching international law, based mostly on an assessment of existing hard obligations and neglecting more flexible conceptions

17. *See* R. Ago, *La Codification du Droit International et les Problèmes de sa Réalisation, in* MÉLANGES GUGGENHEIM 93, 93–96 (1968).

18. ILC Statute, *supra* note 15, at art. 8. The 34 members of the ILC are elected by the General Assembly of the United Nations. *Id.* at art. 3.

19. *See id.* at art. 9.

20. Koskenniemi, *supra* note 7, at 7.

21. International Law Commission, Summary Records of the 3150th Meeting, 4, U.N. Doc. A/CN.4/SR.3150 (Aug. 17, 2012).

22. *See* U.N. Secretary-General, Regulations Governing the Status, Basic Rights and Duties of Officials other than Secretariat Officials, and Experts on Mission, Secretary-General's Bulletin, Regulation 1(b), U.N. Doc. ST/SGB/2002/9 (June 18, 2002).

23. The expression has been used to describe the American Law Institute's work on the Restatements on US law, which is, to some extent, similar to the work done by the ILC. *See* Kristen David Adams, *Blaming the Mirror: The Restatements and the Common Law*, 40 IND. L. REV. 205, 244 (2007).

of normativity. Actually, treaties and decisions of international courts or tribunals form the most significant part of the material that the ILC relies on to codify and even progressively develop international law. The truth is that the ILC is a subsidiary organ of the UN General Assembly and not a self-standing body of experts. From that perspective, the ILC operates in a specific context, driven mainly by orthodox attitudes toward international law. As a result, the recourse by the Commission to comparative law techniques is framed by a particular methodology that is essentially formalistic and that does not exhaust all the possible approaches to comparative international law.

Second, the specific composition of the ILC (with experts coming from all parts of the world and working together within the UN framework) may explain why the Commission is so deeply attached to a multilateral, universal approach to international law—which is obviously, on its own, a specific approach to international law as it tends to favor common, general values. As James Crawford observed, "the issue of regionalism is mostly not raised in the Commission's texts" and "the Commission's record reveals not merely an absence of reference to the issues of regionalism but even a deliberate attempt to eschew any such ideas—what I have described as a resolute universalism."[24] According to him, the Commission "has worked entirely on the assumption of universalism."[25] This approach runs contrary to other considerations that led the African Union some years ago to establish the African Union Commission on International Law (AUCIL), whose objectives are focused on "African international law."[26] During a discussion that took place in 2012 between the AUCIL and the ILC, some members of the ILC welcomed the creation of the AU Commission on the grounds that it "would encourage an 'African reading' of issues of international law" while other members of the ILC pointed out that they saw limited need for such a body as there already are eight African members in the ILC.[27] This example tends to show that, depending on the nature of the organ (whether universal or regional), the degree of openness to legal diversity can vary. Stated differently, the meaning or form of comparative international law can differ depending on the nature of the body or the official status of the persons involved in the comparative international law exercise. The functions of the organ resorting to comparative international law are also determinative, to some extent. With respect

24. James Crawford, *Universalism and Regionalism from the Perspective of the Work of the International Law Commission, in* INTERNATIONAL LAW, *supra* note 4, at 99, 103, 113.

25. *Id.* at 113.

26. *See* Statute of the African Union Commission on International Law, art. 4, A.U. Doc. EX.CL/478 (XIV) a (Feb. 4, 2009) (providing that the Commission will "undertake activities relating to codification and progressive development of international law in the African continent with particular attention to the laws of the Union as embodied in the treaties of the Union, in the decisions of the policy organs of the Union and in African customary international law arising from the practice of Member States"), *available at* http://www.jus.uio.no/english/services/library/treaties/14/14-03/au-african-ilc.xml; *see also id.* at art. 5(1), 6(1).

27. *See* International Law Commission, Summary Records of the 3146th Meeting, 6, 9, U.N. Doc. A/CN.4/SR.3146 (Aug. 13, 2012).

to the ILC, the fact that its particular function is the codification of international law yields such an impact because, as De Visscher puts it, "codification, even in its strictest sense, always implie[s] a certain legislative element, as it [is] aimed at achieving some uniformity and at reducing to a minimum the differences which exist[] between the various schools."[28]

Third, and on a more practical level, the representativeness of the Commission as a whole may be seen as not being sufficiently reflected in the selection and appointment of special rapporteurs by the Commission. It has been observed in particular that, to date, most special rapporteurs have been from the West.[29] In 2015, five special rapporteurs were from the West (Germany, Spain, Sweden, the United Kingdom, and the United States) and the Chairman of the Study Group on the Most Favored Nation clause was from Canada. Two special rapporteurs were from Central or South America (Colombia and Mexico), one was from Asia (Japan), and one was from Africa (South Africa). In the future, it will certainly be an important challenge for the ILC to overcome this certain lack of representativeness—which is somewhat compensated for by the efforts made by each special rapporteur to assess any relevant state practice over the world, sometimes with the help of the Secretariat, which prepares substantial memoranda on the relevant practice at the request of the Commission.[30] Presumably, this lack of representativeness will also affect comparative international law as a new academic field due to the disproportion in the academic resources of developed countries vis-à-vis other countries. This factor needs to be taken into due account to guarantee the legitimacy of comparative international law as a new branch of law. To a large extent, it is linked to the availability of a sufficiently representative sample of domestic practices, as explained below.

B. The Methods of Work of the ILC

The methods of work of the ILC are quite similar to those recommended by some proponents of comparative international law: that is, "comparative assessments of national court decisions . . . as a means of identifying and interpreting international law"[31] or cross-national comparisons of "how different legal systems interpret and apply substantive international norms in diverse ways."[32] In that regard, the work of the ILC, and in particular its extensive reviews of state practice (which is diffused through ILC documents in the six UN official languages), could be useful for comparative international lawyers when they are assessing, in a given field, whether states approach international law in a similar fashion. The compendium of state practices

28. *See* U.N. Secretariat, *supra* note 12, ¶ 5.

29. *See* Sucharitkul, *supra* note 13, at 310.

30. See, as the most significant example, the very detailed Memorandum on Expulsion of Aliens prepared by the Secretariat in 2006. U.N. Secretariat, Expulsion of Aliens, Memorandum by the Secretariat, Int'l Law Comm'n, U.N. Doc. A/CN.4/565 (July 10, 2006).

31. Roberts, *supra* note 3, at 81–91.

32. *Id.* at 60.

gathered by the Commission and assembled in a systemic, orderly way may even constitute today the most significant added value of the work of the Commission. However, in the course of its work, the ILC faces practical difficulties that are likely to mirror those confronting comparative international lawyers: namely, (1) a lack of availability of relevant material, and (2) linguistic difficulties.

With regard to the first point (the availability of state practice), the ILC Statute instructs the Commission to "consider ways and means for making the evidence of customary international law more readily available, such as the collection and publication of documents concerning State practice and of the decisions of national and international courts on questions of international law," and to "make a report to the General Assembly on this matter."[33] In 1950, the Commission adopted a final report on this issue, on the basis of substantial working papers prepared by the Secretariat and a member of the Commission.[34] These documents were at that time quite useful for comparative international law analyses because they provided clues as to where state practice related to international law could be found.

Unfortunately, the Commission has not updated these documents. This is particularly regrettable given the fact that since 1950 ways and means for establishing international law have changed dramatically—in particular in the Internet age. The "documentary landscape" is no longer comparable to the one existing in 1950, for various reasons (the most important evolutions include multipolarization, including in the academic community, the establishment since 1945 of many international organizations with a quasi-legislative function, and the creation of many new states following decolonization whose practice deserves to be widely disseminated). The need for a new assessment (and improvement) of ways and means for making the evidence of international law more readily accessible is particularly pressing for the purpose of the ILC's work, given the fact that the practice of many states and the academic literature of many countries are too often effectively ignored by the Commission, either because they are not readily accessible (due, among other things, to a lack of publication or a dearth of translations into a language accessible to the members of the Commission or the special rapporteurs) or because concerned states do not provide relevant examples of their practice when the Commission makes requests to that effect (the Commission does, perhaps too often, request from states a large amount of information on diverse topics that are quite difficult to collect).[35] In that respect, recent initiatives, such as the decision of the AUCIL to

33. ILC Statute, *supra* note 15, art. 24.

34. Rep. of the Int'l Law Comm'n, 2nd Sess., June 5–July 29, 1950, at 4, U.N. Doc. A/1316; GAOR, 5th Sess., Supp. No. 12 (1950). For related documents, see *Analytical Guide to the Work of the International Law Commission: Ways and Means for Making the Evidence of Customary International Law More Readily Available*, INTERNATIONAL LAW COMMISSION, at http://legal.un.org/ilc/guide/1_4.shtml (last updated July 15, 2015).

35. When the Commission adopts a text on first reading, states are invited to submit their written comments and observations. In practice, only a few of them do so. For instance, fewer than 30 states (among the 193 Member States of the United Nations) responded to the draft articles adopted on first reading in 2012 on the expulsion of aliens, even though they raise many issues of domestic law. In addition, the ILC frequently asks states to provide relevant information on more specific

prepare a digest of African practice of international law, need to be supported.[36] In addition, academic studies collecting and assessing a broad range of state practice, such as domestic practice on crimes against humanity or the protection of the environment in relation to armed conflicts, would be of inestimable value to the ILC.

The issue of the availability of state practice could be an element of the topic "Identification of Customary International Law," which has been in the Commission's program of work since 2012. In August 2014, the Commission provisionally adopted Draft Conclusion 7, according to which "[a]ccount is to be taken of all available practice of a particular State, which is to be assessed as a whole." The Chairman of the Drafting Committee gave the following explanations in connection with this conclusion: "The starting point in the assessment of a State's practice is that account is to be taken of all (relevant) available practice of a particular State. The assessment of State practice needs first to be exhaustive, within the limits of availability of the practice in question."[37] There is a need to determine more precisely which practice is to be deemed "available,"[38] what standard of representativeness applies, and, above all, to find appropriate ways (both through institutional and academic initiatives) to make state practice more easily available.[39] The more state practice that is available, the more comparative international law can be substantiated. There is likely to remain a serious inequality in the treatment of developed countries' practice, which is widely available, and other countries' practice, which can be difficult to access because of a lack of available resources, including in yearbooks of international law and information provided by the states themselves. The Internet provides still underutilized opportunities for improving accessibility

issues. This increasing practice is the source of many concerns. In 2014, it was observed in the Sixth Committee of the UN General Assembly "that the list of specific issues on which comments were requested from States by the Commission was excessively long, making it difficult for most States to comply within the time limits. Concerns were also voiced that only a minority of States provided comments to the Commission, which was due to disparities of resources among States rather than a lack of interest." International Law Commission, Topical Summary of the Discussion Held in the Sixth Committee of the General Assembly During its Sixty-Ninth Session, Prepared by the Secretariat, ¶ 88, U.N. Doc. A/CN.4/678 (Jan. 21, 2015).

36. See the Visit and Statement of the Chairman of the AUCIL, announcing that the African Commission is "preparing to publish a digest of the case law and practice of Member States, international legal texts regarding the regional economic communities, the case law of regional courts, the *travaux préparatoires* of African Union treaties and such diplomatic correspondence as could be made public." International Law Commission, Provisional Summary Record of the 3230th Meeting, at 3, U.N. Doc. A/CN.4/SR.3230 (Oct. 9, 2014).

37. International Law Commission, Identification of Customary International Law: Statement of the Chairman of the Drafting Committee, at 14 (Aug. 7, 2014), at http://legal.un.org/ilc/sessions/66/pdfs/english/dc_chairman_statement_identification_of_custom.pdf.

38. Compare to *Rules of Court*, INTERNATIONAL COURT OF JUSTICE, art. 50, at http://www.icj-cij.org/documents/index.php?p1=4&p2=3& (last visited Sept. 7, 2015) (distinguishing between documents that are published and "*readily* available" and other documents (emphasis added)).

39. See Rep. of the Int'l Law Comm'n, 66th Sess., May 5–June 6, July 7–Aug. 8, 2014, at 247, U.N. Doc. A/69/10; GAOR, 69th Sess., Supp. No. 10 (2014).

to treaties, unilateral declarations, judicial decisions, doctrine, and other practice, so that states participate on a more equal footing in influencing bodies concerned with development of international law, such as the ILC.[40] Comparative international law studies are especially helpful where they do not limit themselves to the (already well-known) practices of developed states.

The second practical difficulty concerns languages. International law is not only "English international law." International law is interpreted and applied in every national language of every state. According to Resolution 50/11 of the UN General Assembly, adopted on November 2, 1995, "the universality of the United Nations and its corollary, multilingualism, entail for each State Member of the Organization, irrespective of the official language in which it expresses itself, the right and the duty to make itself understood and to understand others."[41] So far as the ILC is concerned, Arabic, Chinese, English, French, Russian, and Spanish are all official and (at least in the Plenary) working languages. Of course, this linguistic diversity makes consensus more complicated to achieve.[42] But it is a prerequisite to faithfully taking account of a great variety of practice and a broad range of views representing different approaches not only to international law, but to law in general. Moreover, this reduces later difficulties in the enforcement of international law in domestic legal systems. To put it bluntly, multilingualism is a sine qua non for work on comparative international law.

II. SUBSTANTIVE TOOLS

The core function and methods of the work of the ILC clearly entail comparative international law in the narrow sense of comparisons between international rules or international practices. Both are concerned with identifying possible differences among state practices or *opinio juris* and, accordingly, expressing the minimum agreement among states on the content of existing international law. The work of the ILC could contribute to comparative international law techniques—at least as the identification, formation, and development of international law are concerned. In addition, the practice of the ILC itself may be illuminating regarding the real impact of multiculturalism in international law. In particular, analysis of the ILC's practice and experience since 1945 reveals that real different *approaches* to existing rules of international law are quite exceptional. State practice can vary or be inconsistent; this is the normal life of international law. On the other hand, the ILC does not frequently face, in its day-to-day work, cultural, "civilizational," or political opposition on what international law is or should be. While ILC members come from all continents, approaches such as Third-World Approaches to International Law do not receive nowadays much echo in ILC debates. It may in fact be that, so far

40. See, in particular, G.A. Res. 51/157, Annex ¶ 21 (Dec. 16, 1996).

41. G.A. Res. 50/11, pmbl. (Nov. 15, 1995).

42. This is particularly the case because the translation of precise concepts into six languages is not an easy task. *See* Denis Alland, *L'Interprétation du Droit International Public*, 362 RECUEIL DES COURS 41, 283 n.640 (2012).

as international law is concerned, differences in positive law are more relevant than differences affecting conceptions on law.

Differences in state practice or *opinio juris* regarding international law are managed by the ILC through two separate processes. When state practice is not sufficiently general, that is to say not "sufficiently widespread and representative, as well as consistent,"[43] or if there are too many discrepancies in state practice and/or *opinio juris*, the ILC is called on to make a legislative choice rather than accommodate diverging views. In such circumstances, it can (1) reject any codification or progressive development, (2) decide to codify anyway and give credit to the majority while considering other state practices as less relevant, or (3) opt for the progressive development of international law by expressing a normative preference for one state practice or *opinio juris* over another.

One example of the first situation (decision not to codify) is the decision to exclude any codification of the much-disputed "Calvo Clause" in the 2006 Draft Articles on Diplomatic Protection.[44] Examples of the second situation (codification even though there is no consensual state practice) include, among others, the Commission's 1991 decision to include "constituent units of a federal State" in the definition of "State" when adopting its Draft Articles on Jurisdictional Immunities of States and Their Property, even though the practice was not uniform on this point;[45] the decision in 2012 to adopt a "realistic approach" with regard to the procedural rights from which aliens unlawfully present on the territory of an expelling state can benefit, so as to accommodate the restrictive practice of "several" states (which was thereby given priority over more liberal state practices);[46] and Draft Article 3 of the Draft Articles on Immunity of State Officials from Foreign Criminal Jurisdiction adopted in 2013, which accords immunity *ratione personae* to heads of state, heads of government, and ministers of foreign affairs only, and does not enlarge this rule to cover other high-ranking officials despite some state practice going in that direction.[47] Examples of the third situation (progressive development

---

43. International Law Commission, *supra* note 37, at 19 (Draft Conclusion 8 on Identification of Customary International Law provisionally adopted by the Drafting Committee in 2014).

44. *See* Rep. of the Int'l Law Comm'n, 58th Sess., May 1–June 9, July 3–Aug. 11, 2006, at 73–74, U.N. Doc. A/61/10; GAOR, 61st Sess., Supp. No. 10 (2006) (paragraph 8 of the commentary to Draft Article 14).

45. *See* Rep. of the Int'l Law Comm'n, 43rd Sess., Apr. 29–July 19, 1991, at 18–20, U.N. Doc. A/46/10; GAOR, 46th Sess., Supp. No. 10 (1991) (paragraph 11 of the commentary to Draft Article 2).

46. *See* Rep. of the Int'l Law Comm'n, 64th Sess., May 7–June 1, July 2–Aug. 3, 2012, at 70, U.N. Doc. A/67/10; GAOR, 67th Sess., Supp. No. 10 (2012) (paragraph 11 of the commentary to Draft Article 26 of the Draft Articles on Expulsion of Aliens).

47. *See* Rep. of the Int'l Law Comm'n, 65th Sess., May 6–June 7, July 8–Aug. 9, at 63–65, UN Doc. A/68/10; GAOR, 68th Sess., Supp. No. 10 (2013) (paragraphs 10–12 of the commentary to Draft Article 3). In other situations, the Commission decided to disregard a specific state practice on the grounds that it was not compatible with the specific nature of the rule adopted by the Commission. For example, the Commission concluded that prosecutorial discretion to grant immunity, which is recognized in some legal systems, is not compatible with "the interests of the international community as a whole" in the case of genocide. *See* Rep. of the Int'l Law Comm'n, 48th Sess., May 6–July 26,

when codification is not possible due to the absence of consistent state practice) are the 2012 decision to extend the protection afforded by the 1951 Refugees Convention against expulsion, save on grounds of national security or public order, to any refugee unlawfully present in the territory of the state[48] and Draft Article 19 of the 2006 Draft Articles on Diplomatic Protection, which relies on the existence of a practice coming from a minority of states as a basis to formulate some recommendations regarding the exercise of diplomatic protection.[49] The Commission considered in this last case that since "there is some support in domestic legislation and judicial decisions for the view that there is some obligation, however limited, either under national law or international law, on the State to protect its nationals abroad when they have been subjected to serious violation of their human rights," it was appropriate to recommend that states "should . . . give due consideration to the possibility of exercising diplomatic protection, especially when a significant injury has occurred."[50]

In the instances described above (with the exception of the first), the Commission overrode pronounced divergences by taking a decision on the better policy regarding what international law should be in a given area.[51] More interesting for comparative international lawyers, however, are situations in which discrepancy of practice is less marked and can therefore be overcome by using "accommodating" tools, which permit a common agreement on the drafting of an international rule while simultaneously preserving the existing diversity. Three techniques have been used so far by the ILC to that end: recourse to linguistic tools, drafting general rules, and providing for normative flexibility.

A. Recourse to Linguistic Tools

In some instances, state practice does not reveal any real disagreement on the existence or meaning of the international rule; rather, it is the way in which the rule is to be worded in the six official languages of the United Nations (mainly English and French, as well as sometimes Spanish, which are, in practice, the working languages of the Drafting Committee that is entrusted with the task of formulating

---

1996, at 31, U.N. Doc. A/51/10; GAOR 51st Sess., Supp. No. 10 (1996) (paragraph 4 of the commentary to Draft Article 9).

48. *See* Rep. of the Int'l Law Comm'n, *supra* note 46, at 29–30 (paragraph 4 of the commentary to Draft Article 6).

49. *See* Rep. of the Int'l Law Comm'n, *supra* note 44, at 94–100 (Draft Article 19 and its commentary).

50. *Id.*

51. For another example where the difficulty was to decide whether a practice was worth being codified rather than assessing its "cultural" universality, see Rep. of the Int'l Law Comm'n, 41st Sess., May 2–July 21, 1989, at 292–95, U.N. Doc. A/44/10; GAOR 44th Sess., Supp. No. 10 (1989). Some members of the ILC felt that further clarification of the socialist "legal concept of a State enterprise with segregated State property" was needed, while at the same time considering that "the legal implications [of this concept] for developing countries would have to be carefully studied," and that it was not clear to what extent "the practice of socialist States could be applied to other States." *Id.*

the draft articles to be adopted by the Commission in the plenary), which proves difficult because the same idea cannot necessarily be expressed in a similar way in all domestic law systems. For instance, in 1989, in the context of its work on the law of state immunities, the Commission reported that "there was a need to examine in the Drafting Committee the use of such terms as 'interests' . . . and 'control' . . . since those terms were not clearly understood in certain legal systems."[52]

One option in such a case is to adopt different concepts in different languages to express the same idea, in order to stay consistent with the particularities of each legal system—something that is close to functional equivalence in comparative law.[53] When defining "The State" for the purpose of its 1991 Draft Articles on Jurisdictional Immunities, for instance,

> [t]he Commission discussed at length whether in the English text "sovereign authority" or "governmental authority" should be used and has come to the conclusion that "sovereign authority" seems to be in this case, the nearest equivalent to *prérogatives de la puissance publique.* Some members, on the other hand, expressed the view that the term "sovereign authority" was normally associated with the international personality of the State, in accordance with international law, which was not the subject of the paragraph. Consequently it was held that "governmental authority" was a better English translation of the French expression *la puissance publique.*[54]

The Commission adopted the same approach in 2014 for the definition of "State officials" ("représentants de l'Etat" in French and "funcionarios del Estado" in Spanish) for the purpose of its Draft Articles on Immunity of State Officials from Foreign Criminal Jurisdiction. The Commission pointed out that, although these terms "do not necessarily mean the same thing and are not interchangeable," the fact "that different terms are used in each of the language versions is of no semantic significance whatsoever. Rather, the various terms used in each of the language versions have the same meaning for the purposes of the present draft articles and have no bearing on the meaning that each term may have in domestic legal systems."[55]

In other cases, linguistic tools are used to override a disagreement on substance. In such cases, the Commission tends to rely on preexisting language incorporated in universal treaties (which is supposedly acceptable to the states concerned) to

---

52. *Id.* at 281.

53. On the continuing importance of functionality and functional equivalence in contemporary comparative scholarship, see generally THE METHOD AND CULTURE OF COMPARATIVE LAW: ESSAYS IN HONOUR OF MARK VAN HOECKE 8–9 (Maurice Adams & Dirk Heirbaut eds., 2014) [hereinafter METHOD AND CULTURE].

54. Rep. of the Int'l Law Comm'n, *supra* note 45, at 20–21 (paragraph 12 of the commentary to Draft Article 2).

55. Rep. of the Int'l Law Comm'n, *supra* note 39, at 236 (paragraph 16 of the commentary to Draft Article 2).

reach a consensual formulation to express customary international rules.[56] The reliance on predetermined formulae (in the context of treaties) for the purpose of drafting articles reflecting customary international law is quite frequent in the work of the ILC, whose members are cautious not to depart, so far as possible, from well-established phrasings, in order to maintain consistency between existing treaty rules and draft articles adopted by the ILC. In 2012, for instance, in the course of its work on Expulsion of Aliens, members of the ILC disagreed on the exact nature of the concept of human dignity. To accommodate varying views on the precise content of this notion (in particular whether it is a subjective or objective notion), the ILC used language from the 1966 International Covenant on Civil and Political Rights as a way of overcoming the disagreement.[57]

B. Drafting General Rules

Another different tool used by the Commission consists in drafting broad provisions whose general character permits the accommodation of different interpretations of the rule or different domestic practices related to the rule. To some extent, this technique is very similar to the notion of margin of appreciation as deployed before the European Court of Human Rights.[58] Beyond that, it shows that contemporary (at least universal) international law actually fits closely the medieval *ius commune*, which was based on *both* homogenization and pluralism and to which some comparative lawyers look today with great interest.[59] The core idea here is to maintain some room for international regulation without impairing domestic legal specificities and legal diversity.

One illustration is the ILC's 2006 determination that the precise content of the international obligation to exhaust local remedies before resorting to diplomatic protection varies from state to state depending on the state's particular legal (judicial) system. The Commission accordingly noted that "no codification can therefore succeed in providing an absolute rule governing all situations."[60] As a result, Article 14 of the 2006 Draft Articles on Diplomatic Protection only describes "in broad terms, the main kind of legal remedies that must be exhausted."[61] A similar approach was followed by the Commission with regard to Article 16 of the Draft Articles on

56. The relevant issue here is not to adopt a new rule but to find a way to express an existing (non-written) rule of international law in a way that is compatible with different approaches to said rule.

57. *See* Rep. of the Int'l Law Comm'n, *supra* note 46, at 42 (paragraph 3 of the commentary to Draft Article 14).

58. For an interesting analysis of techniques such as the margin of appreciation as a means of ensuring "sustainable diversity in law," see PATRICK GLENN, LEGAL TRADITIONS OF THE WORLD 379–81 (2010).

59. *See* Alain Wijffels, *"Ius Commune", Comparative Law and Public Governance, in* METHOD AND CULTURE, *supra* note 53, at 147, 151–53.

60. Rep. of the Int'l Law Comm'n, *supra* note 44, at 72 (paragraph 4 of the commentary to Draft Article 14).

61. *Id.*

Jurisdictional Immunities, which concerns the impermissibility for a state that owns or operates a ship to invoke immunity from jurisdiction when the ship was used, at the time the cause of action arose, "for other than government non-commercial purposes."[62] As the Commission pointed out, "the English language presupposes the employment of terms that may be in current usage in the terminology of common law but are unknown to and have no equivalents in other legal systems."[63] In particular, "the expressions 'suits in admiralty', 'libel *in rem*', 'maritime lien' and 'proceedings *in rem* against the ship', may have little or no meaning in the context of civil law or other non-common-law systems."[64] As a result, in Article 16, the Commission decided to use terms "intended for a more general application[,]"[65] such as the use in Article 16, paragraph 3, of the expression "any proceeding," which, according to the Commission, "refers to 'any type of proceeding', regardless of its nature, whether *in rem, in personam*, in admiralty or otherwise."[66] In 2001, the ILC relied on the same technique concerning the definition of the scope of "governmental authority" for purposes of attribution to a state of conduct of a person or entity that is not an organ of the state in the context of state responsibility. In that context, the Commission made the following observation, which reveals the complementarity between international and domestic law:

> Article 5 does not attempt to identify precisely the scope of "governmental authority" for the purpose of attribution of the conduct of an entity to the State. Beyond a certain limit, what is regarded as "governmental" depends on the particular society, its history and traditions. Of particular importance will be not just the content of the powers, but the way they are conferred on an entity, the purposes for which they are to be exercised and the extent to which the entity is accountable to government for their exercise. These are essentially questions of the application of a general standard to varied circumstances.[67]

A further solution for the Commission is to refrain from adopting any definition of a term used in the draft articles, including on key issues. This solution can be seen as the most extreme form of "generalization," in the sense that it is aimed at allowing the greatest flexibility in the concretization of the international rule. In 1991, for instance, the Commission indicated in the context of its Draft Articles on Jurisdictional Immunities of States and their Property that "[w]ith regard to the term 'judicial functions', it should be noted that such functions vary under different

---

62. Rep. of the Int'l Law Comm'n, *supra* note 45, at 50.

63. *Id.* at 51 (paragraph 3 of the commentary to Draft Article 16).

64. *Id.*

65. *Id.*

66. *Id.* at 53 (paragraph 13 of the commentary to Draft Article 16).

67. Rep. of the Int'l Law Comm'n, 53rd Sess., Apr. 23–June 1, July 2–Aug. 10, 2001, at 43, U.N. Doc. A/56/10; GAOR, 56th Sess., Supp. No. 10 (2001) (paragraph 6 of the commentary to Article 5 of the Articles on Responsibility of States for Internationally Wrongful Acts).

constitutional and legal systems. For this reason, [we] decided not to include a definition of the term 'judicial functions' in the present article."[68]

The broadening of the wording of a rule, or the refusal to give a precise definition, to accommodate varying domestic approaches eventually results in a more flexible, and thus less intrusive, international rule. It may also lead to the adoption of an ambiguous rule. At some point, actually, reliance on "the application of a general standard to varied circumstances" may lead to an empty rule.[69]

C. Providing for Normative Flexibility

In other circumstances, the ILC prefers to introduce some normative flexibility in order to preserve existing diversity in state practice. The Commission uses various methods to this end.

First, the Commission can adopt a permissive rather than a mandatory rule. For instance, the Commission can express the rule in a non-exhaustive way, which gives states some discretion in its application. For instance, Article 5(2) of the Draft Articles on Expulsion of Aliens adopted on second reading in 2014 provides that "A State may only expel an alien on a ground that is provided for by law."[70] In the commentary of Article 5, the Commission explains that

> It would be futile to search international law for a list of valid grounds of expulsion that would apply to aliens in general; it is for the internal law of each State to provide for and define the grounds for expulsion, subject to the reservation stated in paragraph 4 of the draft article, namely, that the grounds must not be contrary to the obligations of the State under international law. In this regard, internal laws may be found to provide for a rather wide variety of grounds for expulsion.[71]

In a similar vein, the Commission in 1991 examined the differing "nature" and "purpose" tests for determining whether a particular transaction is "commercial" and therefore exempt from state jurisdictional immunity. The Commission adopted Draft Article 2(2), according to which "[i]n determining whether a contract or transaction is a 'commercial transaction' under paragraph 1(c), reference should be made primarily to the nature of the contract or transaction, but its purpose should also be taken into account if, in the practice of the State which is a party to it, that purpose is relevant to determining the non-commercial character of the contract or

68. Rep. of the Int'l Law Comm'n, *supra* note 45, at 14 (paragraph 3 of the commentary to Article 2).

69. *See* U.N. Secretariat, *supra* note 12, ¶ 105 ("[I]n so far as the object of codification is to reconcile divergencies [*sic*] and remove causes of friction, that object can be achieved only imperfectly by drafts and conventions which may conceal continued disagreement behind the cloak of a vague and elastic statement of general principle.").

70. Rep. of the Int'l Law Comm'n, *supra* note 39, at 26.

71. *Id.* at 27–28 (paragraph 3 of the commentary).

transaction."[72] In the commentary to Article 2, the Commission gave useful insights on the interpretation to be given to this provision. In particular, it pointed out that "Paragraph 2 of article 2 is aimed at reducing unnecessary controversies arising from the application of a single test, such as the nature of the contract or transaction, which is initially a useful test, but not by any means a conclusive one in all cases."[73] According to the Commission, Article 2 is designed to provide "a supplementary standard" for determining whether a particular contract or transaction is "commercial" or "non-commercial," before relying, on this issue, on "the emerging trend in the judicial practice and legislation of some States."[74] In other words, a single rule—the one adopted by the Commission—is tailored so as to be applicable in different ways (through the inclusion of a "supplementary" standard) depending on the circumstances, to take into account the existence of different state practice on this matter.

The Commission can alternatively proceed by a renvoi to domestic law instead of adopting a uniform, international provision. This renvoi can be made subject to some minimal international conditions. In the 1996 Draft Code of Crimes, for instance, the Commission adopted Article 3, which provides for punishment in cases of international crimes. In the commentary, the Commission noted that "[t]he authors of the Code have not specified a penalty for each crime, since everything depends on the legal system adopted to try the persons who commit crimes against the peace and security of humanity."[75] At the same time, Article 3 provides that "the punishment shall be commensurate with the character and gravity of the crime."[76]

The renvoi to domestic rules can be accompanied by a renvoi to domestic authorities' adjudicating power. In the same 1996 Draft Code, Article 14 states that "the competent court shall determine the admissibility of defences in accordance with the general principles of law, in light of the character of each crime."[77] In the commentary to Article 14, the Commission points out that "[i]t would be for the competent court to decide whether the facts involved in a particular case constituted a defence under the article or extenuating circumstances under article 15 in the light of the jurisprudence of the Second World War as well as subsequent legal developments."[78] This means that the Commission may defer to the discretion of the relevant court, while guiding this discretion by referring to the relevant case law and general principles.

72. Rep. of the Int'l Law Comm'n, *supra* note 45, at 14.

73. *Id.* at 20 (paragraph 27 of the commentary).

74. *Id.*

75. Rep. of the Int'l Law Comm'n, 48th Sess., May 6–July 26, 1996, at 23, U.N. Doc. A/51/10; GAOR 51st Sess., Supp. No. 10 (1996) (paragraph 4 of the commentary to Article 3).

76. *Id.* at 22.

77. *Id.* at 39.

78. *Id.* at 40 (paragraph 6 of the commentary to Article 14).

III. CONCLUSION

The practice of the International Law Commission seems to suggest that there exist different ways to manage legal pluralism or different state practices or *opinio juris* in the international sphere. Between the solution consisting in opting for one practice instead of another and in tolerating states' discretion in handling an issue of international concern, there is a broad range of subtler, intermediate solutions. It eventually appears that in most cases diversity and unity are not conflicting, but rather complementary. From the viewpoint of the ILC, comparative international law operates mainly as a conduit between international law and domestic laws, thus echoing the views of comparative lawyers who see comparative law as an important means of "perceiv[ing] commonalities" and "form[ing] intercultural 'bridges,' enabling agreement across borders."[79] Enabling agreement is the very raison d'être of international law, and protecting cultural diversity is a core universal value.[80] In that sense, legal diversity and comparative international law can be seen as not threatening international law but as contributing to its refinement. However, this ecumenical conclusion depends heavily on the way diversity is approached. So far as diversity is assessed with the specific purpose of reaching a consensus on the definition of international, common rules, comparative international law harmoniously supplements international law. On the other hand, if comparative international law were to be designed as a way to claim the existence of specific approaches to international law, there is a risk that it would eventually lead to the disintegration of the core idea of international law as the common law of humankind.

---

79. BERNHARD GROSSFELD, CORE QUESTIONS OF COMPARATIVE LAW 12 (Vivian Grosswald Curran trans., 2005).

80. *See* Convention on the Protection and Promotion of the Diversity of Cultural Expressions, pmbl., Oct. 20, 2005, 2440 U.N.T.S. 311 ("Affirming that cultural diversity is a defining characteristic of humanity, Conscious that cultural diversity forms a common heritage of humanity and should be cherished and preserved for the benefit of all").

9

The Continuing Impact of French Legal Culture on the International Court of Justice

MATHILDE COHEN[*]

I. INTRODUCTION

This chapter proposes a reflection on comparative international *courts* rather than comparative international law more broadly understood. International courts are approached differently by various legal actors who may be influenced by their own national legal environments.[1] Though there is a long tradition of scholarly thinking about the role of particular national traditions in shaping international law, be it substantive or procedural law,[2] little attention has been paid to the influence of domestic legal cultures on the design and internal organization of international

[*] Thanks to Tomer Broude, Erin Delaney, Mark Janis, Richard Kay, Alexandra Lahav, Molly Lands, David Law, David Nanopoulos, and Julie Suk as well as to the organizers and participants in the Twenty-Eighth Sokol Colloquium on Private International Law who provided extremely helpful feedback on this project. For excellent research assistance, I thank Josh Perldeiner and for library assistance, Sarah Cox.

1. I take legal culture to refer to "the complex of beliefs, attitudes, cognitive ideas, values and modes of reasoning and perception which are typical of a particular society or social group." *See* ROGER COTTERRELL, THE SOCIOLOGY OF LAW: AN INTRODUCTION 25 (1984).

2. As early as 1931, International Court of Justice Judge Hersch Lauterpacht denied any such national bending. *See* Hersch Lauterpracht, *The So-Called Anglo-American and Continental Schools of Thought in International Law*, 2 BRIT. Y.B. INT'L L. 31 (1931). *See also* ANTHEA ROBERTS, IS INTERNATIONAL LAW INTERNATIONAL? (2017); Emmanuelle Jouannet, *French and American Perspectives on International Law: Legal Cultures and International Law*, 58 ME. L. REV. 292 (2006); Martii Koskenniemi, *Between Coordination and Constitution: International Law as a German Discipline*, 15 REDESCRIPTIONS 45 (2011); Francesco Messineo, *Is There an Italian Conception of International Law?*, 4 CAMBRIDGE J. INT'L & COMP. L. 681, 879 (2013); Colin Picker, *International Law's Mixed Heritage: A Common/Civil Law Jurisdiction*, 41 VAND. J. TRANSNAT'L. L. 1093 (2008).

courts.[3] Yet, is there such a thing as a specifically international way of designing and running courts tasked with resolving international disputes?

What would a truly *international* international court look like? Being international could mean that a court does not borrow at all from national judicial systems. Such a court would adopt novel, sui generis internal and external decision-making procedures: the judges and court personnel would devise their own deliberative and opinion-writing practices. Alternatively, being truly international could mean being a hybrid court, incorporating—and actively seeking influence from—several domestic judicial systems. Such a court could fashion its internationalness by blending multiple judicial traditions with an eye to representativeness of its member states. Many other options exist between these two poles. What is clear is that an international court dominated by a single domestic tradition would not be considered truly international.

This chapter aims to make the reach of domestic norms in the design and daily operation of international courts more salient. Building upon my earlier work on the French influence on the Court of Justice of the European Union, the European Court of Human Rights, and the International Court of Justice (ICJ),[4] this chapter focuses on the case of the ICJ and its predecessor court, the Permanent Court of International Justice (PCIJ).

The International Court of Justice is the United Nations' principal judicial organ. The adjective "international" is both descriptive and aspirational. It is descriptive in the sense that with the broadest membership of all international courts—the 193 UN Member States—the ICJ also endeavors to be the highest such court. Its bench is supposed to represent the "main forms of civilization" and the "principal legal systems of the world."[5] At the same time the label "international" is in large part aspirational given the court's Western roots. The very idea of resolving international disputes through third-party adjudication developed in the United States and Europe.[6] The old court, the PCIJ, created in the 1920s in The Hague in the heart of Europe, had a Eurocentric character. The new court established in 1945, the ICJ, is arguably still embedded within a European legal culture.

Just as there are different national understandings of international law, there are different national understandings of what an international court should be and do. These perspectives depend on those involved in a court's design and day-to-day life, whether they are judges, advocates, staff members, or litigants. When designing, working, or litigating at an international court, these various actors may be tempted

---

3. One notable exception is SARA MCLAUGHLIN MITCHELL & EMILIA JUSTYNA POWELL, DOMESTIC LAW GOES GLOBAL: LEGAL TRADITIONS AND INTERNATIONAL COURTS (2011).

4. *See* Mathilde Cohen, *The Linguistic Design of Multinational Courts. The French Capture*, 14 INT'L J. CONST. L. 498 (2016).

5. This language was introduced by the Statute of the Permanent Court of International Justice art. 9, Dec. 16, 1920, 6 L.N.T.S 390.

6. The origins of modern arbitration are often traced back to the 1794 Treaty of London, which settled hostilities between the United States and Great Britain. *See* SHABTAI ROSENNE, THE WORLD COURT: WHAT IT IS AND HOW IT WORKS 1–2 (2003) (tracing back the history of third-party settlement of international disputes to Hellenic culture).

to transpose, consciously or not, norms of decision-making that they have internalized at home or through their education. These norms pertain to such things as interactions between judges and between judges and the court's staff, modes of deliberation, and the content and style of judicial opinions. Due to path dependency, designers' plans for a court are likely to prove enduring in the long term. Designers come to the drafting table with a set of expectations colored by their domestic legal environment about what a court should be and how it should function. They may also hope to stabilize a set of power relationships via court rules and norms. One factor specific to international courts (as well as domestic courts in multilingual states), which epitomizes the dual importance of culture and politics in court design, is the choice of court language(s). Linguistic design has not only cultural and political significance, but it may also have long-lasting effects on a court's internal organization, drawing professionals with specific linguistic skills, cultural values, and expectations to work at the court.

French judicial culture has exerted a strong influence on the ICJ's design and still informs some of its daily operation. Ironically, I write at a time when the use of French and French law are declining internationally and when the French influence on the ICJ may be at its lowest.[7] Despite the Anglo-Americanization of law and adjudication around the globe,[8] including, perhaps of the ICJ,[9] French legal practices remain surprisingly salient in The Hague. The purpose of this study is to identify and describe these vestiges of French judicial culture and the mechanisms by which they remained in place for close to a century. To some extent, it is the civil law model and culture broadly conceived, and not merely French legal culture, which left a durable mark on the court. While the chapter specifically focuses on French civil law features, such as deliberative and opinion-writing styles, it is not always easy to distinguish neatly between what belongs to French law and to the civil law. Accordingly, some arguments about French influence could be reformulated as relating to the civil law.[10]

French judicial culture percolates at the international level in part through the continued use of French as a court language. In spite of its declining importance, French is still used at today's major international and regional courts, tribunals, and dispute-settlement bodies, which usually include it among their official languages.[11]

---

7. *See, e.g.,* Blandine Mallet-Bricout, *Libres propos sur l'efficacité des systèmes de droit civil,* 56 REVUE INTERNATIONALE DE DROIT COMPARÉ 865 (2004) (recognizing the decline in influence of the French civil law tradition in light of the growing popularity of the common law).

8. Wolfgang Wiegand, *Americanization of Law: Reception or Convergence?, in* LEGAL CULTURE AND THE LEGAL PROFESSION 137 (Lawrence M. Friedman & Harry N. Scheiber eds., 1996) (describing the Americanization of law in Europe). *See also,* Cesare Romano, *The Americanization of International Litigation,* 19 OHIO ST. J. DISP. RESOL. 89, 117–18 (2003).

9. *See infra,* Section IV.B.

10. For instance, the use of French as a court language permits the percolation of civil law models and culture, and not only French models and culture.

11. *See, e.g.,* African Court on Human and Peoples' Rights, RULES OF COURT, Rule 18 ("The official languages of the Court shall be the official languages of the African Union," which are Arabic,

This is not a Whorfian argument that language shapes thoughts, but rather a sociological and institutionalist one. French as a court language and French judicial culture as a source of influence for decision-making are two independent, yet interrelated features of the ICJ. They are independent in the sense that one could imagine that the status of French as an official language would have no repercussion on the court's internal organization and outputs. At international courts that merely use French ex post to translate finalized opinions that have been deliberated and drafted in English, this seems to be the case.[12] At the ICJ, the use of French intensifies the transmission of the French judicial model for two reasons. Historically, both the French language and the French judicial model were introduced in a common sweep at a time when French and French legal culture enjoyed a leading position internationally, French being (quite literally) a lingua franca, and French law, a donor system inspiring other countries. Over time the use of French as an official language reinforced the staying power of the French judicial model because the court strived to function truly bilingually, deliberating and drafting decisions in both French and English simultaneously. This bilingualism favored the recruitment as judges and staff lawyers of jurists trained in the French tradition defined broadly (either lawyers trained in France or lawyers acculturated into French legal culture, including those from Francophone countries). Collectively, these individuals contributed to maintaining aspects of the French judicial model that may have disappeared in an English-only working environment.

A word on methods: my methodology is mainly doctrinal and archival, though I supplement these approaches with semi-structured interviews conducted between 2010 and 2015 with judges and nonjudicial personnel at a number of international

---

English, French, Portuguese, Spanish, Kiswahili and any other African language); RULES OF THE COMMUNITY COURT OF JUSTICE OF THE ECONOMIC COMMUNITY OF WEST AFRICAN STATES (ECOWAS), art. 25 (providing that the official languages of the court shall be the languages of the community, which are French, English, and Portuguese); RULES OF PROCEDURE OF THE INTER-AMERICAN COURT OF HUMAN RIGHTS, art. 21 ("The official languages of the Court shall be those of the OAS, to wit, Spanish, English, Portuguese, and French."); International Tribunal for the Law of the Sea, RULES OF THE TRIBUNAL, art. 43 (providing that the official languages of the tribunal are English and French); Rome Statute of the International Criminal Court art. 50, Jul. 17, 1998, 2187 U.N.T.S. 3 ("1. The official languages of the Court shall be Arabic, Chinese, English, French, Russian and Spanish . . . 2. The working languages of the Court shall be English and French."); INTERNATIONAL CRIMINAL TRIBUNAL FOR THE FORMER YUGOSLAVIA, RULES OF PROCEDURE AND EVIDENCE, Rule 3 (providing that the working languages of the tribunal are English and French); International Criminal Tribunal for Rwanda, RULES OF PROCEDURE AND EVIDENCE, Rule 3 (same). In addition, the World Trade Organization's Appellate Body uses the three official languages of the WTO, English, French, and Spanish; and the Caribbean Court of Justice uses English, French, and Dutch. But see STATUTE OF THE COURT OF JUSTICE OF THE ANDEAN COMMUNITY, art. 34 (providing that Spanish is the language of the court); STATUTE OF THE SPECIAL COURT FOR SIERRA LEONE, art. 24 (providing that English is the language of the court).

12. One example is the WTO Appellate Body, where French is not an actual working language used among judges during deliberations and between judges and their support personnel during the preparation of cases. French is only an output language; once made, decisions are translated into French by professional translators removed from the decision-making process.

and French courts of last resort.[13] Given the paucity of law on the books and secondary literature on comparing the internal organization and decision-making of international courts and domestic courts, these interviews made it possible to obtain a better understanding of the ICJ's deliberative and opinion-writing practices compared to other courts. The point of the chapter is to emphasize the role of national legal culture on the ICJ's internal organization and drafting practices. Future research may shed light on how what I identify as the "French" characteristics of the court may affect substantive outcomes such as the propensity of states to accept the jurisdiction of the court and to actually use it, compliance with the decisions by their immediate addressees, and the perceived authoritativeness of the court's decisions on other actors such as national courts, other international courts, and member states' executive branches. For the purposes of this short chapter, however, I will not advance any empirical claim on the possible substantive implications of the French model.

The discussion proceeds in three sections. Section II retraces the historical origins of French language as an official ICJ language and its ongoing effects on the court's personnel. Section III examines present practices and claims that the French judicial model still influences the court's internal organization. Section IV discusses the various factors that limited the influence of the French judicial model both initially when the court was designed and throughout the years.

II. FRENCH LANGUAGE AT THE ICJ

A. History

Various historical and sociological-institutional reasons, which I analyze in turn, explain the ICJ's adoption of French along with English as an official language. Though the ICJ was set up in June 1945 under its present institutional structure as the principal judicial organ of the United Nations, the court derives from the Permanent Court of International Justice, established in 1922 and attached to the

---

13. More specifically, my study involved 28 interviews. The identity of the interviewees has been kept confidential: I occasionally quote directly from the interviews but without attribution to any named individual. The interviewees were two former Court of Justice of the European Union (CJEU) *référendaires*, two CJEU judges, one former CJEU administrator, two CJEU translators, four European Court of Human Rights (ECtHR) registry lawyers, four ECtHR judges, one ECtHR translator, one ECtHR administrator, two former legal officers for the ICJ, one current legal officer at the ICJ, a former ICJ university trainee, four French high court judges, one former legal officer for the WTO appellate body, one trial support staffer at the International Criminal Court, and one former legal officer for the ICTR and the Special Court for Sierra Leone. This is not in any sense a representative sample but a reflection of individual judges and court personnel whom I considered particularly interesting for this study and who made themselves available for interview. Beginning with a few contacts at the courts under study, I recruited research subjects through the contacts of previous interviewees (a practice known as "snowball sampling"). This method is necessary in the hard-to-access world of high courts, but subject to a number of biases. *See* Patrick Biernacki & Dan Waldorf, *Snowball Sampling: Problems and Techniques of Chain Referral Sampling*, 10 SOC. METHODS & RES. 141 (1981).

League of Nations. Three prominent French jurists were directly involved in the creation and design of the court, Albert de La Pradelle, who served on the expert Committee of Jurists appointed to draft the Statute of the court, Léon Bourgeois, who was elected as the League Council's first Chairman, and Henri Fromageot, who assisted Bourgeois and came to serve as a judge on the PCIJ.[14]

The Permanent Court used both English and French as its official languages. English was an afterthought, however. In the 1920s, French was still the language of diplomacy and international relations.[15] Had Lord Balfour not objected, the court would have used French as its sole official language.[16] In fact, during the first years of the court, French retained a dominant position. Looking at the PCIJ's 59 decisions (32 judgments on the merits and 27 orders) handed down between 1923 and 1940, only 5 indicate that the English version is the authentic one.[17] All the others either contain a phrase such as "done in English and French, the French version being authentic," or state that the parties themselves "agreed that the whole case should be conducted in French,"[18] or still do not indicate any language preference, but present the French text before the English text,[19] suggesting a hierarchy between

---

14. *See* GILBERT GUILLAUME, LA COUR INTERNATIONALE DE JUSTICE À L'AUBE DU XXÈME SIÈCLE: LE REGARD D'UN JUGE 48 (2003).

15. Until the seventeenth century, Latin was the language of international diplomacy, but the importance of French grew in the eighteenth and nineteenth centuries. *See generally* 1 OPPENHEIM'S INTERNATIONAL LAW 1054–55 (ROBERT JENNINGS & ARTHUR WATTS EDS., 9th ed. 1992); JAMES BROWN SCOTT, LE FRANÇAIS: LANGUE DIPLOMATIQUE MODERNE (1934); Anthony Leriche, *Les langues diplomatiques à l'Organisation des Nations Unies*, 31 REVUE DE DROIT INTERNATIONAL DE SCIENCES DIPLOMATIQUES ET POLITIQUES 45 (1953); Roland E. Vaughan Williams, *Les méthodes de travail de la diplomatie*, 4 REC. DES COURS 225, 262 (1924).

16. *See* Gleider I. Hernandez, *On Multilingualism and the International Legal Process*, *in* 2 SELECT PROCEEDINGS OF THE EUROPEAN SOCIETY OF INTERNATIONAL LAW 441–60 (Hélène Ruiz-Fabri, Ruediger Wolfrum & Jana Gogolin eds., 2010).

17. The Borchgrave Case (Belg./Spain), Judgment, 1937 P.C.I.J. (ser. A/B) No. 72 (Nov. 6); Consistency of Certain Danzig Legislative Decrees, Advisory Opinion, 1935 P.C.I.J. (ser. A/B) No. 65 (Dec. 4); Legal Status of Eastern Greenland (Den. v. Nor.), Judgment, 1933 P.C.I.J. (ser. A/B) No. 53 (Apr. 5); Interpretation of the Greco-Bulgarian Agreement of Dec. 9, 1927, Advisory Opinion, 1932 P.C.I.J. (ser. A/B) No. 45 (Mar. 8); Territorial Jurisdiction of the International Commission of the River Oder, Judgment, 1929 P.C.I.J. (ser. A) No. 23 (Sept. 10).

18. This latter formulation is found in: Electricity Company of Sofia and Bulgaria (Belg. v. Bulg.), Order, 1940 P.C.I.J. (ser. A/B) No. 80 (Feb. 26); Electricity Company of Sofia and Bulgaria (Interim Measures of Protection) (Belg. v. Bulg.), Order, 1939 P.C.I.J. (ser. A/B) No. 79 (Dec. 5); Electricity Company of Sofia and Bulgaria (Preliminary Objection) (Belg. v. Bulg.), Judgment, 1939 P.C.I.J. (ser. A/B) No. 77 (Apr. 4); Lighthouses in Crete and Samos (Fr./Greece), Judgment, 1937 P.C.I.J. (ser. A/B) No. 71 (Oct. 8); Diversion of Water from the Meuse (Neth. v. Belg.), Judgment, 1937 P.C.I.J. (ser. A/B) No. 70 (June 28).

19. The Borchgrave Case (Discontinuance) (Belg./Spain), Order, 1937 P.C.I.J. (ser. A/B) No. 73 (Apr. 30); The Losinger & Co. Case (Discontinuance) (Switz. v. Yugo), Order, 1936 P.C.I.J. (ser. A/B) No. 69 (Dec. 14); Pajzs, Czaky, Esterhazy (Preliminary Objection) (Hung. v. Yugo.), Order, 1936 P.C.I.J. (ser. A/B) No. 66 (May 23).

the two. Separate opinions, including dissents, provide a particularly reliable indication of language preferences given that in principle judges write them on their own,
with very limited help from the registry, in contrast to majority opinions, which are
drafted in both languages with heavy staff involvement. Among the 18 PCIJ judges
who wrote separate opinions during their tenure, 16 chose to write in French,
including, incredibly—from a contemporary perspective—the first US judge to sit
on the court, John Bassett Moore.

After the Second World War, with the transition from the Permanent Court to the
ICJ, the French delegates involved in the Committee of Jurists tasked with designing the new court—Jules Basdevant, Charles Chaumont, and Raoul Aglion—
pushed for continuity with the old court. The French contingent was adamant that
the court's Statute should remain as close as possible to the old Statute, in particular
when it came to defining the competence and selection of judges.[20] This position is
unsurprising given that the status quo was a sure way to ensure France's continuing
representation on the future court. The question also arose as to whether the new
court should change its language policy. Jules Basdevant demanded that French
remain a working language of the Committee of Jurists on the premise that the old
Statute, drafted in both French and English, would be the basis of the new Statute.[21]
He prevailed. Nowadays, as a former legal officer put it, "The two official languages
are French and English. Note I said *French* and English, *not* English and French."[22]
By emphasizing this order, the legal officer stressed the historical preeminence of
French over English.

There was a colonial quality to the choice of French and English at the old
Permanent Court and its continuation at the ICJ.[23] The spread of English and
French as international languages was due in great part to the linguistic imperial-
ism of Great Britain and France, the two leading imperial states. The old Permanent
Court overwhelmingly comprised Western European, North American, and Latin
American countries, where the local elite spoke English or French as a result of
earlier conquests or continuing cultural hegemony. For the longest time, the ICJ
was considered a "European" tribunal.[24] There were relatively few sovereign states
before World War II, and most of Asia and Africa were unrepresented at the PCIJ.
It was not until the late 1950s that the ICJ's composition began to diversify, mirroring decolonization and the United Nations' expanding membership. Yet this broadened base did not translate into a more inclusive language policy. While the UN set

20. *See* GUILLAUME, *supra* note 14, at 49.

21. 14 DOCUMENTS OF THE UNITED NATIONS CONFERENCE ON INTERNATIONAL ORGANIZATION
54 (1945).

22. Interview with former legal officer at the ICJ (2013) (my translation).

23. In fact several of the PCIJ judges had been colonial judges, such as Belgium Rolin-Jaequemyns
or Danish Didrik Nyholm.

24. *See* EDWARD MCWHINNEY, THE INTERNATIONAL COURT OF JUSTICE AND THE WESTERN
TRADITION OF INTERNATIONAL LAW 66–67 (1987).

out five official languages (later adding Russian as its sixth),[25] French and English remain the ICJ's sole languages.

The ICJ's commitment to bilingualism is an important factor in explaining the continued attachment to French. It is one of the few international courts that drafts its judgments and conducts its deliberations *simultaneously* in two languages.[26] Other courts usually conduct deliberations and draft their judgments in one language (typically English), using professional translators to translate the final product into the other official language(s). By contrast, ICJ judges debate both language versions of their judgments, which are published together in parallel (*"en regard."*) This requires the constant assistance of bilingual staff lawyers, translators, and interpreters. Even the most trivial comment added to a draft by a judge must be translated.

Unlike the PCIJ, the ICJ has issued a more or less equal number of decisions labeled as authentic in French as it has in English, reflecting a truly bilingual functioning. According to the legal officers I talked to, when it comes to publishing decisions, unless there is a specific reason to prefer one language version over the other, for example, because it is clearer on crucial aspects of the holding, the choice is quasi-arbitrary. The registry decides that one of the two language versions is to be declared "authentic" simply based on parity between the two languages. If the last few decisions were issued as authentic in French, English will be picked, and vice versa. This bilingualism, however, is increasingly the doing of the registry, rather than judges actually using both languages equally. Of the 109 judges who served on the ICJ since 1946, 56 wrote one or more separate opinions. 34 judges chose to write separately in English, 18 in French, and 4 alternated between French and English. These numbers testify to the rising prominence of English during the second half of the twentieth century, all the while suggesting the presence of quite a few French language holdouts on the court.

B. Effects on Court Personnel

To be truly international, international courts should represent diverse national legal professionals. They should draw judges, law clerks, staff lawyers, translators, and other personnel from a variety of jurisdictions and national educational training patterns.[27] In practice, however, some form of linguistic—and therefore often also cultural—screening takes place at the ICJ and other international courts that use French as a court language. In January 2006, 215 judges served on the bench

---

25. The official UN languages are: Arabic, Chinese, English, French, Russian, and Spanish.

26. Another example is the International Tribunal for the Law of the Sea, which also drafts its decisions in both French and English, as stated in the final paragraph of any order, judgment, or advisory opinion.

27. *See* Antoine Vauchez, *Communities of International Litigators*, in HANDBOOK OF INTERNATIONAL ADJUDICATION 656, 658 (Cesare Romano, Karen Alter & Yuval Shany eds., 2014) (noting that international courts "cannot count on the existence of a supranational judicial profession because there is no such thing as a supranational body competent for setting common educational requirement, nor is there an identified breeding ground from which international courts could select and recruit their members.").

of 13 major international courts and tribunals: 63 percent were from civil law countries, reflecting the large number of judges from continental Europe, including 7 French nationals.[28] Looking specifically at the PCIJ and ICJ, the screening effect of French is particularly striking, especially at the former. Of the 61 judges[29] who sat on the old court from 1922 to 1946, 27 (nearly half) were either French citizens or citizens of a francophone country, and/or lived in France, studied in France, or in a French-speaking educational institution.[30] Among the 109 judges who served full-time on the new court, 27 (nearly a quarter) have these types of connections to France and French legal culture.[31]

Language proficiency plays a particularly salient role in the hiring of nonjudicial personnel, that is, the registrar[32] and the deputy registrar, but also legal officers, law clerks, university trainees, administrative support staff, and obviously translators. When asked about the recruitment pool for legal officers and clerks, a current legal officer at the ICJ responded by pointing to the tension between the court's universalist aspirations and its language needs: "the principle, the same as at the United Nations, is the broadest possible diversity, but balanced against the linguistic requirements of the court, which can bias the statistics . . . This has favored the French and the British and people from countries using these two languages."[33] French's status as an official language, in particular, has led the court to screen for candidates for French proficiency in addition to technical competence—a practice that could be characterized as "adaptive" hiring.[34] Tellingly, a September 8,

28. See Daniel Terris, Cesare P.R. Romano & Leigh Swigart, The International Judge: An Introduction to the Men and Women Who Decide the World's Cases 17 (2007).

29. This figure includes full-time judges and deputy judges, as well as national judges.

30. I take these various ties to French and France as proxies for familiarity with French legal culture. This figure is based on an analysis of judges' biographies published in the PCIJ's Annual Reports, Series E.

31. This figure is based on an analysis of judges' biographies published in the ICJ's Yearbooks. It is conservative, as I counted only judges who lived and worked in France during their formative years, excluding cases such as Judge Lucio Manuel Moreno Quintana, who was born in France but later returned to his native Argentina, or Salvadorian judge Jose Gustavo Guerrero, who lived in France during the later part of his life, dying in Nice. I have excluded judges who lived in France on diplomatic missions, except for Egyptian judge Abdullah El Erian, who was an ambassador in France for a couple of years, on account of the fact that the Egyptian legal system is built on the combination of Islamic law and the Napoleonic Code. I included judges who were acculturated into French legal culture in addition to other legal cultures such as German Carl August Fleischhauer who studied in Grenoble and Paris, but also in Heidelberg, later serving as a Fulbright fellow at the University of Chicago.

32. The ICJ rules of court establish the knowledge of languages as a merit to be considered when electing the Registrar. See Rules of the Court, 2007 I.C.J. Acts & Docs. No. 6, art. 22(3).

33. Interview with ICJ legal officer (2015) (my translation).

34. Former ICJ translator James Brannan noted that there are more translators in French than English at the ICJ. See James C. Brannan, Translation at the World Court: The Weight of History, 33 ATA Chron. 38, 40 (2004).

2015, job advertisement for a legal officer position listed among its three required "qualifications and skills," "excellent knowledge of and drafting ability in French, *which will be the principal working language of the incumbent*; very good command of English."[35] In and of itself, the phrasing of this ad does not mean that there is always a preference for French speakers, but it shows that French proficiency remains a sought-after skill.

A former university trainee explained that to get hired, "you need to at least profess that you speak some French."[36] Similarly, a former legal officer confided, "I know that one of the essential reasons why I was hired in the face of competition was my capacity to write in the two [court] languages."[37] In contrast to the staffers, required to be fluent in both court languages, judges seem subject to more lenient requirements,[38] perhaps because these days it would be too difficult to find qualified candidates who are fluent in French. The rules governing the election of judges are silent on linguistic proficiency, but in practice judges are expected to have a working knowledge of *either* French or English.[39] As one of the legal officers quoted above recounts about his time in The Hague, "[l]et's say that the only people who didn't master the two languages were the judges. The only other exception I can think of were the drivers, perhaps."[40]

What is the effect of screening for French on the profile of the staff? French is no longer a lingua franca systematically used as a second language for communication between those who do not share a mother tongue. Qualified international lawyers who speak French tend to either come from francophone countries such as Belgium, Canada, France, Haiti, Luxembourg, Monaco, Switzerland, and francophone African countries, or to have spent a significant amount of time living, studying, or working in a francophone environment.[41] As cross-cultural psychologists have shown, people tend to travel with their training and worldviews, at least during the initial stages of their expatriation.[42] The worldwide decline of French as an international language exacerbates to some extent the French capture by increasing the likelihood that French proficiency will be the attribute of lawyers trained in French

35. The ad for a P-3 level legal officer position is available on the court's Website http://www.icj-cij. org/registry/index.php?v=146&p1=2&p2=5&p3=3.

36. Interview with former ICJ university trainee (2015).

37. Interview with former ICJ legal officer (2014) (my translation).

38. *See* TERRIS ET AL., *supra* note 28, at 29.

39. *See* 1 SHABTAI ROSENNE, THE LAW AND PRACTICE OF THE INTERNATIONAL COURT, 1920–2005, AT 166 (2006); Mariano Aznar-Gomez, *Article 2, in* THE STATUTE OF THE INTERNATIONAL COURT OF JUSTICE: A COMMENTARY 234 n.1 (Andreas Zimmermann et al. eds., 2012).

40. Interview with former ICJ legal officer (2014) (my translation).

41. *See* TERRIS, ET AL., *supra* note 28, at 18 (noting that in 2006, 11 alumni of Parisian universities served as judges on international courts).

42. *See, e.g.,* Kalervo Oberg, *Cultural Shock: Adjustment to New Cultural Environments,* 7 PRAC. ANTHROPOLOGY 177 (1960) (presenting a four-phase model of adjustment from a honeymoon stage to culture shock to recovery to adjustment).

or French-style legal systems. Thus, those most likely to know and embrace French judicial culture are also those most likely to end up on the court's rosters.

After having described the adoption of French as a court language and its enduring effects on court personnel, I turn to the influence of the French judicial model on the ICJ's internal organization and writing practices.

III. THE FRENCH JUDICIAL MODEL

This section focuses on the influence of the French judicial model on the ICJ's internal organizational culture and case law production. It argues that the French influence is most visible along two dimensions: the court's deliberative practices and its drafting conventions.

A. French Deliberations

In previous work on European, French, and Anglo-American courts of last resort, I argued that high courts follow one of two ideal types of decision-making, which I called the "ex ante" and the "ex post" models.[43] Neither model is all or nothing, as most courts can be characterized as falling along a continuum between these two poles. But each model has its paradigmatic cases. Is it possible to distinguish a distinctively "French" model from a broader "Civil Law" model? Yes and no. While continental courts in general follow a version of the ex ante model, it is, both historically and today, most typical of French high courts.

In the ex ante, French model, judges engage in what I refer to as "pre-deliberations" before convening for the court's (or the panel's) conference meeting. Typically, a court member assigns a case to a so-called "*juge rapporteur*" or reporting judge. The reporting judge's task is to propose a disposition and draft an opinion *before* the oral argument and formal conference meeting take place. The conference focuses not so much on how the court, as a collective entity, should decide the case, but rather on whether panel members will sign off to an already fully written opinion, which was previously circulated and discussed informally in small groups. A critical feature of this model is that it incentivizes debate among court members before the official deliberation takes place, for example, through pre-conference meetings, an advocate general, or teaming up the reporting judge with other judges or staff lawyers. Cases are justified before being decided, in the sense that the judgment's reasoning is already worked out before the outcome is officially reached.

The ex post model is typical of Anglo-American supreme courts, in particular the United States Supreme Court.[44] American justices engage in what I call

---

43. *See* Mathilde Cohen, *Ex Ante versus Ex Post Deliberations: Two Models of Judicial Deliberations in Courts of Last Resort*, 62 Am. J. Comp. L. 401 (2014).

44. Though historically the ex ante model is distinctly French, it has spread to numerous jurisdictions in the second half of the twentieth century for functionalist reasons. In an age of managerial judging and skyrocketing caseloads, the rapporteur system is appealing even in common law countries traditionally attached to the ex post model. Today a number of US and British courts seem to

"post-deliberations." They do most of the decision-making work *after* the conference meeting has taken place. In principle, for each case, all deciding justices receive briefs and have the opportunity to read and analyze them. Ex post courts usually employ a number of law clerks recruited by and assigned to individual court members. Judges tend to develop their thinking and do most of their debating within their chamber, with their clerks, rather than with other judges, and when they do debate with colleagues, it is often through the mediation of clerks. The conference discussion is said to be short. Its purpose is typically twofold: to quickly determine which outcome the majority favors and to assign the task of writing an opinion to one or several justices. It is to the opinion writers that conference participants allocate the authority and competence to instigate a conversation among justices and shape the court's reasoning. Cases are justified after being decided, in the sense that the reasoning of the judgment will only be worked out after the outcome has been officially designated during the conference meeting.

The ICJ presents us with a hybrid model of internal organization, combining ex ante and ex post traits. What separates the ICJ process from the typical ex ante court is that it does not appoint one of its members to act as the reporting judge for each case. In this respect, it follows the ex post model. The supreme courts of the United Kingdom and the United States, for example, remain attached to the idea that all deciding justices should inform themselves about the cases on equal terms, rather than pre-assigning them to one member. Likewise, after oral arguments are over in The Hague, all ICJ judges prepare their own "notes," that is, memos addressing the issues and questions of law raised by the case. The notes ensure that every judge has studied the case record independently.[45] They retain, however, an ex ante aspect in that they are anonymized prior to being circulated, a practice that surprises common lawyers used to judges taking ownership of their views. The notes are meant to spur discussions in a way that fosters debate over ideas, not a clash between personalities and judicial philosophies, as often happens in ex post courts. Of course, as court members begin to know one another, anonymity tends to become a pretense as judges' distinct styles and personalities can often be easily identified.

In nearly all other respects, the ICJ follows the French judicial model, particularly its method of drafting decisions through a series of group deliberations, alternating formal, plenary sessions with informal, small group gatherings. The court's

---

fit the ex ante model—be it at the appellate level for US federal courts and British courts, or at the appellate as well as the supreme court level for US state courts—in that they pre-assign the drafting of merits opinions to judges before cases are orally argued and discussed in conference meetings. *See, e.g.,* Daniel J. Bussel, *Opinions First—Argument Afterwards,* 61 UCLA L. Rev. 1194 (2014) (presenting the California Supreme Court's current decision-making process).

45. According to former ICJ judge Robert Jennings (who sat on the court from 1982 until 1995, serving as the court's president from 1991 to 1994), judges write their notes on their own. *See* Robert Yewdall Jennings, *The Internal Judicial Practice of the International Court of Justice,* 59 Brit. Y.B. Int'l L. 39 (1988). Practices seem to have evolved, however. According to two of the former legal officers I interviewed, judges increasingly rely on the nonjudicial personnel to help them prepare their notes, and in some instances they delegate the drafting altogether.

deliberation begins ex ante, before oral argument and formal conferencing take place. Informal meetings among small groups are organized for judges so inclined as soon as the pleadings and other procedural documents have been translated and circulated, according to Mohammed Bedjaoui, who served as a judge from 1982 to 2001, including as the court's president from 1994 to 1997.[46] This ex ante deliberative style is codified in the court's internal procedure. Article 1 of the Resolution concerning the Internal Judicial Practice of the Court thus states that:

> before the beginning of the oral proceedings, a deliberation is held at which the judges exchange views concerning the case, and bring to the notice of the Court any point in regard to which they consider it may be necessary to call for explanations during the course of the oral proceedings.[47]

Another similarity with the French model is the ICJ's mechanism for assigning the writing of advisory opinions and judgments: after judges have had the chance to circulate and debate each other's notes, the full court elects two of its members to serve on a "drafting committee," of which the court president is a member ex officio.[48] The committee resembles the French practice of deputizing judges to assist (or control) the reporting judge, for instance the trio known as the *"conférence"* at the *Cour de cassation*. The *conférence* is comprised of the reporting judge, the panel's most senior judge, and the panel's president. Both the ICJ's committee and the *Cour de cassation's conférence* are tasked with preparing the judgment *of the court*, taking into account "amendments" submitted by their colleagues. Following the French tradition, once a draft is ready in The Hague, the full court meets to finalize the text of the decision, reading it out loud and adopting its content paragraph by paragraph, similar to a legislative assembly voting on the final version of a statute, adopting and rejecting proposed amendments. This mode of collective decision-making is typical of French courts, which until the Revolution were called *Parlements* and had quasi-legislative functions as they could issue judgments of general applicability similar to statutes. In France as in The Hague, this modus operandi may explain why especially contentious decisions appear vague, much like multilateral treaties are vague when many parties must agree on one single text.[49] Traditionally, a number of ICJ judges have had a diplomatic background, reinforcing the practice of issuing compromise decisions combining precision with ambiguity—after all, diplomats are the masters in the art of finding formulations acceptable to all parties.[50]

---

46. *See* Mohammed Bedjaoui, *La "fabrication" des arrêts de la Cour internationale de justice, in* LE DROIT INTERNATIONAL AU SERVICE DE LA PAIX, DE LA JUSTICE ET DU DÉVELOPPEMENT. MÉLANGES MICHEL VIRALLY 87, 93 (1991).

47. *See* INTERNAL JUDICIAL PRACTICE OF THE COURT, 2007 I.C.J. Acts & Docs. No. 6, at 175.

48. *Id.* at 177.

49. Of course, many decisions of the court are detailed and at least as precise as domestic decisions in many countries.

50. *See generally* LANGUAGE AND DIPLOMACY (JOVAN KURBALIJA & HANNAH SLAVIK EDS., 2001).

This French-leaning mode of internal organization leads to the production of decisions that share a number of traits with French judicial opinions.

B. French Decisions

The ICJ issues three types of decisions: advisory opinions in non-contentious cases; judgments on the merits, and orders in contentious cases. The very idea of allowing a high court to issue advisory opinions violates the common law conception of judicial power, as epitomized by the US Constitution's case-or-controversy requirement.[51] By contrast, the practice is so entrenched into French judicial practice that the *Conseil d'État*, one of France's three courts of last resort, acts both as a legal adviser to the executive branch *and* as the supreme court for public law—hence its name, *Conseil d'État*, which is ordinarily translated "Council of State," but could also be translated as "*Counsel* of State."

Despite their distinctly non-common law flavor, the ICJ's advisory opinions, just like its judgments on the merits, have by and large followed the discursive model traditionally used in Anglo-American jurisdictions. They tend to be longer and more explanatory than the typical cryptic French judgment[52]—though French advisory opinions are usually more informative than judgments. This departure from the French model can be attributed in part to the court's enthusiasm for separate opinions, be they dissents or concurrences. Unlike French courts, which continue to prohibit public expressions of disagreement, the ICJ allows separate opinions. Since the first years of the court, judges have used dissents.[53] Of the 61 judges who sat on the old court, 18, nearly one-third, wrote one or more separate opinions. Notably, 16 of these dissenting judges wrote in French and came from civil law jurisdictions, suggesting an openness to adopting foreign judicial practices when presented with the opportunity—at the time, civil law jurisdictions did not allow separate opinions.[54]

Adherence to the formalist French style would have been difficult to reconcile with dissents and concurrences. French judgments do not leave room to respond to opposition as their quasi-deductive form denies the possibility of alternative holdings. Extralegal arguments borrowing from science, international relations, and policy are highly discouraged in judgments. Another departure from the French model is that unlike French appellate and supreme court judges who, akin to anonymous

---

51. U.S. CONST. ART. III, § 2 cl. 1. *See also* CHARLES HOWARD ELLIS, THE ORIGIN STRUCTURE & WORKING OF THE LEAGUE OF NATIONS 391 n.2 (2003).

52. *See* JUAN JOSÉ QUINTANA, LITIGATION AT THE INTERNATIONAL COURT OF JUSTICE: PRACTICE AND PROCEDURE 536 (2015) (pointing out that an ordinary judgment is between 50 and 150 pages long).

53. And since 1978, judges can also concur or dissent without opinion, a practice called "declaration." *See* Farrokh Jhabvala, *Individual Opinions Under the New Rules of Court*, 73 AM. J. INT'L L. 661 (1979).

54. On the spread of separate opinions in civil law jurisdictions, see John Alder, *Dissents in Courts of Last Resort: Tragic Choices?*, 20 OXFORD J. LEGAL STUD. 221, 237 (2000).

cogs in a judicial machine, are not personally responsible for an opinion, every ICJ judge's position (majority/dissent/concurrence) is recorded and publicly identified. That disclosure is a relatively recent development, however, instituted in 1978 when new court rules were adopted.[55] Though individual votes are now disclosed, to this day, those not privy to the deliberations do not know which judge is responsible for what aspect of the court's judgment. As Shabtai Rosenne noted in the 1960s, "[t]he opinion tends to be colourless and lack 'character.' "[56]

Despite these differences, notable aspects of the French opinion writing style remain visible. From the beginning, the ICJ delivered judgments in the name of the court, characterized by impersonal, collegiate, and sometimes formulaic prose. ICJ judgments are written in a detached style. They are not signed by individual judges. The judgment is written in the third person singular; "The Court" speaks, rather than individual judges. Much as French judges are acculturated into following templates rather than developing their own voice, ICJ judges are subject to what a former legal officer called a "socialization effect": "the more time one spends at the court, the more foreign one becomes toward one's own legal system. One thing is being a skilled international lawyer, quite another is to adapt oneself to the court's style."[57] Ironically, while this "court's style" may be foreign to a number of legal systems, in particular Anglo-American ones, it is very typical of the French judicial style.

Judgments on the merits follow a decisively discursive style, but orders remain surprisingly French-like, especially those pertaining to time limits. They are typically short documents running a couple pages, beginning by citations to the ICJ Statute, treaties, or any other relevant sources of law, for example, "Having regard to Article . . . of the Statute of the Court . . ." The text of the order then consists of short numbered paragraphs, each beginning with recitals—"Whereas" or "*Considérant*" clauses.[58] Phrases such as "it follows" or "consequently" connect the various

55. In 1920, when the Advisory Committee of Jurists met to discuss the creation of the PCIJ it was decided that though dissenters should be allowed to identify themselves and state their views by appending a statement of their individual opinion to the judgment, the anonymity of judges was crucial to the impartiality and authority of the court. *See* Jhabvala, *supra* note 53, at 662. In the first years of the court, "it became apparent that the court's protection was encouraging timorousness on the bench and that some judges were evading their responsibilities through the device of secret dissents, dissents included in the court's secret minutes but not published as part of the public record." *Id.* at 663. This led, four years after the court's creation, to the mandatory disclosure of dissenters' names, not without Dutch judge Bernard Loder and French judge André Weiss objecting that the court had been created in the "Continental" tradition to which public dissents were anathema. In 1946, the ICJ followed the PCIJ's approach, with the court rules then providing that "any judge may . . . attach his individual opinion to the judgment, whether he dissents from the majority or not, or a bare statement of his dissent."

56. *See* ROSENNE, *SUPRA NOTE* 6, AT 121 (1962).

57. Interview with former legal officer (2015) (my translation).

58. *See, e.g.*, Maritime Delimitation in the Indian Ocean (Som. v. Kenya), Order, 2014 I.C.J. 482 (Oct. 16).

paragraphs or sections to convey a sense of logical progression from major premises to minor premises to the formal holding.

With a pair of early exceptions,[59] the court has consistently avoided this syllogistic format for judgments on the merits, which nonetheless follow a script comprising a few basic elements. Judgments typically begin with the procedural history of the case, followed by a condensed presentation of the facts, and a discussion of jurisdictional and admissibility issues. The court then turns to the legal analysis, addressing the various claims and submissions made by the parties, before moving to a discussion of the merits, and concluding with the holding.[60] Judgments are presented in numbered paragraphs, which nowadays are labeled by section headings and subheadings and separated by typographical markers such as asterisks. There may be some interesting effects on ICJ practice associated with prominent individual judges. It is possible that during the ICJ presidency of French judge Gilbert Guillaume (2000–2003), judgments became shorter and more closely resembled French decisions.[61] In 2015, another French judge was elected as president, Ronny Abraham, who is "known for his three-line decisions"[62] during his first years on the ICJ and before that, at the *Conseil d'État*. Time will tell whether the court will become associated with more unscripted common law-style judgments or revert to the French approach.

By allowing separate opinions, the ICJ puts multiple perspectives on the table, leading to public disagreements among court members. Yet the court's "judgment" continues to take an unsigned and collegial form. Significantly, separate opinions are not part of the judgment, but "attached" to it.[63] Dissents and concurrences are available on the court's website as separate files; they are not included in the judgment or order's master file. In that respect, ICJ decisions depart from both the British and the American models of judicial opinions. Unlike the British tradition, the ICJ delivers a unitary judgment of the court rather than separate, seriatim judgments.[64] Unlike the American tradition, there is no "majority opinion" versus "minority opinions," but on the one hand, a judgment of the court, without indication of individual contributions to the drafting and, on the other hand, personalized separate opinions. In the United States, the majority frequently refers to separate opinions,

59. *See* Treaty of Neuilly, Article 179, Annex, Paragraph 4 (Interpretation), 1924 P.C.I.J. (ser. A) No. 3 (Sept. 12); Interpretation of Judgment No. 3, 1925 P.C.I.J. (ser. A) No. 4 (Mar. 26).

60. For recent examples, see Application of the Convention on the Prevention and Punishment of the Crime of Genocide (Croat. v. Serb.), Judgment, 2015 I.C.J. (Feb. 3); Obligation to Negotiate Access to the Pacific Ocean (Bol. v. Chile), Judgment, 2015 I.C.J. (Sept. 24).

61. *See infra* notes 98–100 and accompanying text.

62. Interview with former ICJ legal officer (2015) (my translation).

63. *See* RULES OF THE COURT, *supra* note 32, art. 95(2).

64. UK courts are evolving, however, increasingly adopting the American model. *See* Mads Andenas & Duncan Fairgrieve, *Simply a Matter of Style? Comparing Judicial Decisions*, 25 EUR. BUS. L. REV. 361 (2014).

thus integrating them in its argument, but the ICJ only referred three times to separate opinions in its judgments.[65]

These differences do not merely pertain to the outside presentation of the decisions, but also reflect internal organizational processes. ICJ judges, be they in the majority or in the minority, enjoy less freedom than their British or American counterparts. Both the court rules and the internal culture incentivize them, much like French judges, to take one another's position into account, minimizing external disagreements. Notably, *all* the judges sitting on the deciding panel, *including dissenters,* participate in drafting the court's judgment.[66] Whenever possible, their challenges and suggestions are considered.[67] This inclusive approach is typical of the French style and is hard to swallow for some common law judges. In France, judges who disagree with their brethren are not excluded from the panel's opinion-writing process. To the contrary, because disagreements cannot be channeled externally through separate opinions, they are resolved internally by the writing of compromise opinions incorporating (as much as possible) the objectors' concerns.[68] Similarly, at the ICJ, dissenters aren't totally free. Separate opinions escape their control to some extent, taking on composite features. As former ICJ judge and president Robert Jennings points out, the court "has the power, which is seldom exercised, to request deletions or changes in separate opinions."[69] Those writing separately must file with the court two successive drafts of their opinions not only to allow their colleagues to take into account their criticism, but also to facilitate efforts by the majority to persuade them.[70] In that scenario, the "majority" participates in the drafting of the "minority" opinion.

After having described elements of French influence that remain most salient at the ICJ, the next section explains why the ICJ has shunned the full French judicial model.

---

65. *See* GLEIDER I. HERNÁNDEZ, THE INTERNATIONAL COURT OF JUSTICE AND THE JUDICIAL FUNCTION 113 (2014).

66. Former British ICJ judge Jennings stresses this point: "even dissenting judges will continue, as members of the full Court, to work with the Court and its drafting committee on the Court's judgment (or opinion), not only throughout the first reading but also at the second reading and until the final vote ... The judges intending to dissent from the Court's decisions will continue till the final moment to work with their colleagues on the improvement and clarification of the Court's own draft." *See* Jennings, *supra* note 45, at 43.

67. *But see* Hugh Thirlway, *The Drafting of ICJ Decisions: Some Personal Recollections and Observations,* CHINESE J. INT'L L. 15, 28 (2006) (pointing out that the Drafting Committee, working on a tight timetable, does not always have the time to engage in a dialogue with dissenters.)

68. *See* Cohen, *supra* note 43, at 424–25.

69. Jennings, *supra* note 45, at 43.

70. QUINTANA, *supra* note 52, at 564.

IV. AN INTERSTATE COURT

Though the ICJ presents a number of characteristic French traits, at least four considerations explain why it has only partially adopted the French judicial model. Two of these played out ab initio when the court was first designed, leading to the exclusion of the rapporteur system. Two other considerations emerged over time, reinforcing both the rejection of the rapporteur and of certain conventions of French judicial writing.

A. Ab Initio Considerations

1. AN ARBITRAL JUSTICE MODEL

To understand the ICJ's current functioning, we need to go back in time again. The court went through several major transitions: from the Permanent Court of Arbitration (1899) to the Permanent Court of International Justice (1920), and only then to the current court (1946). Framers of the ICJ and its predecessor courts were not so much looking toward national high courts as their inspiration, but rather toward international arbitral tribunals. In 1920, the main question debated by the Advisory Committee of Jurists appointed by the League of Nations Council to draft a plan for a PCIJ was how to use international arbitration rules in an international court setting. This approach left little room for the French judicial model to dominate.

The composition of the Advisory Committee may explain this focus. The Dutch jurist Bernard Loder was the only member who had been a judge in his country prior to serving on the Committee. Other members were politicians or high-ranking civil servants.[71] Indeed, they disagreed as to whether much of a distinction "should be drawn between the new Court and the old Court of Arbitration," or whether their mission was to create "a new juridical body similar to the national courts of all countries."[72] Judicial experience proved to be more significant among the first judges appointed to the court. Six had been judges previously. Yet, their primary qualification remained international law: seven were prominent international arbitrators and the six former judges had substantial international experience.[73]

The ICJ's framers and early judges already constituted an epistemic community sharing a common international law background and an arbitral justice frame of reference.[74] The first judges on the PCIJ may have known or heard of one another—six

---

71. Jiří Malenovský, *Les opinions séparées et leurs répercussions sur l'indépendance du juge international,* in 3 ANUARIO COLUMBIANO DE DERECHO CONSTITUCIONAL 27, 42 (2010).

72. ADVISORY COMMITTEE OF JURISTS, PROCÈS-VERBAUX OF THE PROCEEDINGS OF THE COMMITTEE, June 16–July 24, P.C.I.J. 1920, at 177.

73. See RAPPORT ANNUEL DE LA COUR PERMANENTE DE JUSTICE INTERNATIONALE (1er janvier 1922–15 juin 1925), 1925 P.C.I.J. (ser. E) No. 1 [hereinafter RAPPORT ANNUEL].

74. On the emergence of an "international legal community" in the 1920s, see Guillaume Sacriste & Antoine Vauchez, *The Force of International Lawyers' Diplomacy on the International Scene in the 1920s,* 32 L. & SOC. INQUIRY 83 (2007).

of them had been arbitrators for the Permanent Court of Arbitration. They could rely on a shared domain of expertise such as international arbitration, being involved in a common professional network prior to their appointment. The sway of the arbitral model may account for the ICJ's main points of departure from ex ante courts, that is, the lack of a rapporteur system and the use of dissents. There was no reporting judge in international arbitrations, and arbitrators were accustomed to drafting dissenting opinions. At an arbitral tribunal, arbitrators were formally expected to be independent, but in practice they were presumed to represent the particular state that had appointed them. Until the early twentieth century, permanent agencies for arbitration were unheard of. Arbitral tribunals were created ad hoc to resolve particular disputes and ceased to function once that goal had been accomplished.[75] The idea of assigning the task of managing the case to one arbitrator or to prohibit dissents would have been completely out of place.

Once established in the 1920s, the Permanent Court several times considered and rejected the option of designating a reporting judge for each case.[76] The issue came up immediately in 1922 when the first judges discussed and adopted the Rules of Procedures. The draft Rules prepared by the Secretariat instituted a rapporteur system. The draft pointed out that "[t]he [Advisory] Committee . . . recognised the merits of the system whereby the Court would select a member, in each special case, to draft a judgment embodying the views of the majority, after the general discussion in private by the members of the Court."[77] During the meeting convened to discuss and adopt the new Rules, the British judge, Robert Finlay, disagreed with this interpretation of the Advisory Committee's intent. He assured his colleagues that the Committee had rejected the reporting judge model because:

> the system of appointing a *rapporteur* to study a given question and draft a judgment was not desirable for the Permanent Court of International Justice. It was necessary that each judge should make a complete study of every case, and that he should give his independent opinion . . . if the Court adopted the *rapporteur* system, *this would have a deplorable effect on opinion in legal circles in Anglo-Saxon countries.*[78]

Finlay's argument fostered early members' hope of preserving the appearance of a true "World" Court, which did not surrender to either dominant legal system at the time, the British and the French, but instead adopted neutral procedural rules in line with its arbitral origins. Finlay was successful at persuading his brethren to reject the reporting judge. It was decided that the complete dossier of each case would be sent to all judges so that they could "form a complete and independent opinion."[79]

75. *See* Manley O. Hudson, *The Permanent Court of Arbitration*, 27 AM. J. INT'L L. 440 (1933).

76. *See* MANLEY O. HUDSON, THE PERMANENT COURT OF INTERNATIONAL JUSTICE 512 (1934).

77. Preparation of the Rules of the Court, 1922 P.C.I.J. (ser. D) No. 2 at 305.

78. *Id.* at 78 (emphasis added).

79. *Id.*

Interestingly, the French model proved tenacious. The court designated a reporting judge at its first session after oral argument.[80] The practice soon gave away to the current system of electing a drafting committee and requiring that all judges write a note.

2. STATE REPRESENTATIVENESS

Another reason the ICJ turned down the rapporteur system and allowed separate opinions was a deep-seated sense among judges that it would be incompatible with the mission of an international court representing diverse legal systems for a state to go unrepresented on the court and for judges to be unable to voice their disagreements.[81] There is no "one state one judge" rule in place at the ICJ. Unlike regional courts such as the Court of Justice of the European Union and the European Court of Human Rights, where each member state is represented at all times by a national judge, the ICJ's 15 judges rotate among UN members, though the permanent members of the Security Council are de facto guaranteed a seat on the court. In 1920, the Advisory Committee explicitly rejected the thought that "judges ... [should] consider themselves representatives of their countries."[82] They are supposed to embody the "main forms of civilization and of the principal legal systems of the world."[83] The ICJ permits parties to a case who do not have a national sitting on the bench to appoint a judge ad hoc. This innovation nods toward arbitration practices, where it is typical for each disputing party to select at least one arbitrator. Despite this accommodation, there was from the beginning a sense of unease with the idea of assigning a case to a single reporting judge.[84] This anxiety is still alive today, as a former legal officer reports:

> The procedure must guarantee that no one representative of a given legal culture can dominate others. This leads to a number of consequences, the first of which is that one cannot entrust to a particular judge a different role from the others. And whatever the judge's position, ... one cannot exclude him/her from the decision process. This excludes the French or Strasbourg system of a reporting judge, which has enormous practical advantages.[85]

---

80. *See* RAPPORT ANNUEL, *supra* note 73, at 249.

81. *See, e.g.,* André Gros, *Observations sur le mode de délibération de la Cour de Justice, in* 14 COMUNICAZIONI E STUDI 377, 380 (1975) (referring to Preparation of the Rules of the Court, *supra* note 77, at 78, 223).

82. Advisory Committee of Jurists, *supra* note 72, at 363.

83. *See* Statute of the International Court of Justice, art. 9, June 26, 1945, 59 Stat. 1031.

84. For similar reasons, the vast majority of ICJ cases are decided in plenary sessions rather than smaller panels. In order to use panels, the ICJ must obtain the agreement of both states involved, which is rarely forthcoming given the uncertainty as to the panel's composition.

85. Interview with former ICJ legal officer (2014) (my translation).

The rapporteur system, therefore, was excluded early on not only because it was inconsistent with an arbitral justice frame of reference, but also because it conflicted with the court's worldly aspirations. The ICJ espoused a unitary and plenary modus operandi, combined with the possibility of writing separately, to make up for its lack of actual state representativeness.

The fact that the ICJ explicitly considered and rejected the reporting judge function supports the claim that the French judicial model has been, and continues to be, a force to be contended with. But diachronic factors may explain the court's continued resistance to greater French influence.

B. Diachronic Considerations

Over time, the decline of French law as an export legal system, compounded with the rise of English as one of the most spoken languages in the world and the Americanization of law, have contributed to confining the influence of the French judicial model on the ICJ. This, combined with two phenomena internal to the court, serves to explain the decreasing pull of the French model.

1. Caseloads

There may be a functionalist explanation for the continuing exclusion of reporting judges at the ICJ and the use of rather long, discursive judgments often accompanied by separate opinions. The rapporteur system, conjoined with the typical concise French judgment, represents a form of case management that makes particular sense in courts confronted with high volumes of cases. It functions as a division of labor: instead of each judge on a panel duplicating her colleagues' work by preparing the same case from scratch, a single member is assigned the task of writing the court's brief judgment, freeing up others' time for other cases. The rapporteur system does not shut out others from participation. All panel or court members get the opportunity to chime in at some point in the process. Yet, all but one are exempted from having to conduct their own exhaustive analysis of the record, write a memo, and draft a judgment.

It may well be that French high courts maintained this arrangement throughout the past centuries because of its resource-saving properties. French courts of last resort have very heavy caseloads. In 2013, the two French supreme courts, the *Cour de cassation* and the *Conseil d'État*, issued respectively 13,053 and 9,685 judgments on the merits.[86] That same year, the constitutional court, the *Conseil constitutionnel*, issued 357 decisions. Similarly, European courts, which have faced a looming docket crisis in the past decade—particularly the European Court of Human Rights—have been fervent espousers of the rapporteur system and shorter, boilerplate judgments for repetitive cases.[87] Despite relying on a large staff, it would be extremely difficult

---

86. *See* Cour de cassation, Statistiques (2013); Conseil d'État, Bilan d'activité 2 (2013).

87. In 2013, the Court of Justice of the European Union issued 635 decisions on the merits. This figure takes into account case joinders, but includes judgments as well as orders. *See* Court of

for the French and European courts of last resort to process their caseloads without a rapporteur system. In fact, the reporting judge model represents such an alluring case management strategy that a number of appellate and supreme courts in common law jurisdictions, undeterred by their attachment to the ex post tradition, have embraced it.[88]

Compared to its European counterparts, the ICJ does not have a caseload problem. Judges have ample time to work collectively on lengthy judgments and to undertake the solitary task of writing separately. There are only 193 Member States to the United Nations, that is, only 193 potential parties to disputes before the court. In addition to judgments, the ICJ delivers advisory opinions in response to questions submitted by UN bodies, but here too there are structural limits on the number of questions that can reach the court. At the time of writing the ICJ had 12 cases pending on its docket.[89] In 2013, it delivered 13 decisions (2 judgments and 11 orders), which, if anything, was an increase compared to the previous decades during which it issued an average of 7 decisions per year.[90] Of course, deciding the typical ICJ case is much more onerous than the average Court of Justice of the European Union or European Court of Human Rights case. ICJ cases can take several years to move through the different procedural phases. Incidental proceedings are frequent. Parties try to negotiate via diplomatic channels, which further slows down the process. In light of the complexity, length, and paucity of cases reaching the ICJ, committing cases to a reporting judge would make little organizational sense. Occasionally, it could lead to absurd results whereby in some years, some judges would not be assigned any new cases.

2. Clerks

A relatively recent development in the ICJ's support staff organization may contribute to further distance the court from the French judicial model. For the longest time, the ICJ followed the French usage of relying on a registry staffed with permanent employees recruited centrally by the court pursuant to a series of written and oral tests, rather than law clerks selected by individual judges.[91] The ICJ was designed as a bureaucratic court, resting on a permanent administrative department

---

JUSTICE OF THE EUROPEAN UNION, ANNUAL REPORT (2013). In 2013, the European Court of Human Rights issued 916 decisions on the merits. This figure takes into account case joinders. *See* EUROPEAN COURT OF HUMAN RIGHTS, ANALYSIS OF STATISTICS (2013).

88. *See* Bussel, *supra* note 44. And this is not only true of common law jurisdictions: the Brazilian Federal Supreme Court is known for its use of the rapporteur system (though it may be derived from the French model via the Portuguese influence during the colonization period).

89. *See* International Court of Justice, Pending Cases, http://www.icj-cij.org/docket/index. php?p1=3&p2=1 (last visited Oct. 22, 2016).

90. This figure includes all judgments, advisory opinions, and orders.

91. Both the German and the Italian constitutional courts use law clerks whose recruitment and job definition can be compared to that of American courts, but none of the three French courts of last resort uses them.

staffed by international functionaries enmeshed in a strict hierarchy.[92] The registry is headed by a Registrar, assisted by a Deputy Registrar, and the "Legal Matters" department, which works directly with judges, is staffed by a "principal secretary," "first secretaries," "secretaries," and "legal officers"—all ranked according to UN staff categories. Until the mid-2000s, there were no clerks in the Anglo-American sense of the term, that is, junior lawyers, typically straight out of law school, temporarily hired by and reporting to a particular judge. In 1991, former judge Bedjaoui could thus write that at the ICJ,

> the judge is a solitary background worker. No one is there to spoon feed him.... There are no "law clerks" like we know them for example at the Supreme Court of the United States, nor are there young lawyers directly serving under a judge as at the European Court in Luxembourg.[93]

When judges needed help with a particular case or project, they had to request it from one of the few legal officers. This situation presented a particularly heavy burden for the court president, who in addition to regular judicial work is tasked with representation and diplomatic missions such as yearly speeches before the UN Security Council, the General Assembly, and a host of other international organizations. According to a former legal officer, in the early 2000s, "New York University got wind of this situation and... offered the court to send five young lawyers, graduating students, who would be funded by NYU for an academic year, from September until June, to assist the court and the judges."[94] The "university trainee" program was born, opening up new opportunities abroad for American law schools in the context of a saturated domestic clerkship market, another symptom of the worldwide Americanization of law.[95]

With the university trainee program, ICJ judges came to appreciate the service of personal clerks and lobbied the UN for more stable personal assistants who would be full-time court employees rather than recent law graduates paid by their universities of origin for less than a year. These efforts were successful, with the result that the court now counts 15 clerks or "Associate Legal Officers"—one per judge— in addition to the university trainees provided by law schools around the world. Associate legal officers are specifically assigned to a judge for a term of two to four years—though they may also be required to provide legal assistance and support to a judge ad hoc participating in a particular case. This shift is likely to move the

---

92. On the bureaucratization of courts, see Mathilde Cohen, *Judges or Hostages? The Bureaucratization of the Court of Justice of the European Union and the European Court of Human Rights*, in EUROPEAN UNION LAW STORIES: CONTEXTUAL AND CRITICAL HISTORIES OF EUROPEAN JURISPRUDENCE 58 (Bill Davies & Fernanda Nicola eds., 2017).

93. *See* Bedjaoui, *supra* note 46, at 92–93 (my translation).

94. Interview with former ICJ legal officer (2014) (my translation).

95. The exportation of US-style clerkships has not been limited to international courts. Prompted by Ivy League law schools, foreign high courts have followed suit. For instance, the Supreme Court of India created clerkship positions at the instigation of Yale graduates.

court away from French norms of decision-making both in terms of deliberation and drafting. Instead of relying on the uniformizing force represented by the registry, judges now have the institutional capacity to develop, in relative isolation, their own routines and work habits.

A variety of factors, therefore, conspire to limit the sway of French judicial culture on the ICJ, despite the fact that common lawyers are and have always been the minority on the court. Both initially and throughout the years, the interstate character of the court has bestowed it with its hybrid character.

V. CONCLUSION

The ICJ presents an interesting case study for comparative international law: the principal international court and its decisions may have a differential impact across different countries because these countries may perceive the court's international character based on their own characteristics and experiences. As hinted at in the introduction, areas for further exploration include the question of whether the ICJ's French features impact the propensity of states to accept its jurisdiction and to actually use it, immediate addressees' compliance with its decisions, and other actors' perception of the authoritativeness of its decisions. Though the roster of states using the ICJ is growingly increasingly diverse, it remains dominated by a few countries. A court's audience cannot be reduced to its litigants, but it is striking to note that with the exception of India, the typical ICJ litigants are Northern and Western states, the top three being the United States, Britain, and France, closely followed by Belgium, Iran, India, Spain, Australia, and the Netherlands.[96] Could this have something to do with the court's French qualities?

Along the lines of Sara Mitchell and Emilia Powell's argument that characteristics of civil law, common law, and Islamic law influence states' willingness to create new international courts or join preexisting courts,[97] one could hypothesize that states with judicial traditions similar to the French might not only be more willing to accept the jurisdiction of the ICJ and use it, but also to perceive it as more trustworthy and predictable. By contrast, for states unfamiliar with the French judicial style, certain characteristics such as composite judgments integrating multiple judges' perspectives at the cost of clarity may hinder the authoritativeness of the court's decisions. Suffice it to consider the Israeli wall advisory opinion, in which the court unanimously upheld its jurisdiction to issue an opinion, concluding that Israel's construction of a wall in the Occupied Palestinian Territory violated several international obligations.[98] Though the opinion runs several dozen pages, the court disposed of Israel's alleged legal basis for the construction of the wall in a mere

---

96. See Eric Posner & Miguel de Figueiredo, *Is the International Court of Justice Biased?*, 34 J. LEGAL STUD. 599, 614 (2005).

97. See MITCHELL & POWELL, *supra* note 3, at 2.

98. Legal Consequences of the Construction of a Wall in the Occupied Palestinian Territory, Advisory Opinion, 2004 I.C.J. 136 (Jul. 9).

five sentences, via lapidary language on self-defense against nonstate actors.[99] Some commentators have pointed to the heavy hand in drafting of then ICJ president Gilbert Guillaume—a pure product of the French judicial system, having served on the *Conseil d'État* prior to his election to the ICJ.[100] This French-like reason-giving, short on detail in an area where much guidance was needed, could explain—at least in part—why the opinion was poorly received by the Anglo-American and Israeli legal community and seems increasingly marginalized in practice.

There may be other possibilities. The field of comparative international courts is in many ways in its infancy. Very little empirical work exists on the mechanisms through which international courts are both influenced by national legal cultures and themselves exert varying degrees of influence on domestic and international actors.

99. *Id.* at para. 139.

100. *See, e.g.,* Daphne Richemond, *Transnational Terrorist Organizations and the Use of Force,* 56 CATH. U. L. REV. 1001, 1010 n.42 (2007).

PART FOUR

Comparative International Law and Domestic Institutions

Legislatures and Executives

10

International Law in National Legal Systems

An Empirical Investigation

PIERRE-HUGUES VERDIER & MILA VERSTEEG[*]

I. INTRODUCTION

International legal scholars have long recognized the importance of the rules and processes by which states adhere to international legal obligations and "translate" them into their domestic legal systems.[1] Research by political scientists on specific issue areas likewise increasingly recognizes that domestic implementation is crucial to international law compliance and effectiveness.[2] Yet the lack of systematic data makes it difficult to assemble an overall picture of the relationship between international law and domestic law around the world, let alone to document its evolution over time. Recent qualitative surveys of state practice have begun to fill that gap, but provide only a snapshot in time and are limited to relatively few countries.[3] Some

[*] We would like to thank Benedict Kingsbury, Anthea Roberts, one anonymous reviewer, and participants in the 2014 Sokol Colloquium on Private International Law for helpful comments and suggestions. This chapter was first published in the *American Journal of International Law*, vol. 109, no. 3 (July 2015).

1. *See, e.g.,* Karen Knop, *Here and There: International Law in Domestic Courts*, 32 N.Y.U. J. INT'L L. & POL. 501 (2000); Harold Hongju Koh, *Why Do Nations Obey International Law?*, 106 YALE L.J. 2599 (1997).

2. *See, e.g.,* BETH A. SIMMONS, MOBILIZING FOR HUMAN RIGHTS: INTERNATIONAL LAW IN DOMESTIC POLITICS (2009); Yonatan Lupu, *Best Evidence: The Role of Information in Domestic Judicial Enforcement of International Human Rights Agreements*, 67 INT'L ORG. 469 (2013); Andrew Moravcsik, *Liberal Theories of International Law*, in INTERDISCIPLINARY PERSPECTIVES ON INTERNATIONAL LAW AND INTERNATIONAL RELATIONS: THE STATE OF THE ART 83, 96–100 (Jeffrey L. Dunoff & Mark A. Pollack eds., 2013).

3. *See, e.g.,* INTERNATIONAL LAW AND DOMESTIC LEGAL SYSTEMS: INCORPORATION, TRANSFORMATION, AND PERSUASION (Dinah Shelton ed., 2011); NATIONAL TREATY LAW AND PRACTICE (Duncan Hollis et al. eds., 2005).

quantitative projects cover more countries, but address only a limited number of questions based solely on the text of national constitutions.[4]

In this chapter, we draw upon a new dataset arising from a multi-year research project on international law in domestic legal systems. This dataset provides what we believe is uniquely systematic and comprehensive information on the relationship between international and national legal orders. The dataset captures numerous specific features of approaches in national legal systems to international law, including treaty-making procedures, the status of treaties in domestic law, and the reception of customary international law (CIL). It currently covers 101 countries for the period 1815–2013, thus expanding the scope of inquiry beyond well-known Western states to include numerous states in Africa, Asia, Latin America, and the former Soviet Union. It covers a longer period than existing data, thus allowing identification and analysis of historical trends. It incorporates information found not only in constitutions but also in statutes, case law, executive and administrative documents, and secondary sources. This data allows us to move beyond traditional monist-dualist classifications and provide a more nuanced exploration of how countries address international law in their domestic legal systems.

In the following sections, we describe salient features of the data, identify major trends in national approaches to international law, and discuss their implications for comparative international law. We find that, in aggregate, national approaches to treaty-making and implementation have changed considerably, and we suggest that the direction of change reflects simultaneous concern with securing effective implementation of a growing body of treaty law and addressing greater accountability and legitimacy concerns as more governance functions migrate to the international level. More specifically, we find that national legal systems have become more likely to give treaties direct effect and hierarchical superiority over domestic law, which is consistent with a desire to ensure effective implementation. At the same time, national legal systems have steadily expanded the categories of treaties whose ratification requires prior legislative approval, thus expanding the role of national legislatures in international lawmaking.

With respect to CIL, we find remarkable consistency across countries: the vast majority of national legal systems now recognize custom as directly applicable, at least in principle. At the same time, a growing portion of countries consider custom to be hierarchically inferior to domestic law, which limits the ability of courts to apply it directly in many circumstances and preserves the legislature's ability to displace customary rules. Thus, the reception regime for custom reflects both traditional ideas of automatic reception of the law of nations in the domestic legal order and contemporary suspicion of the custom formation process, including its lack of formal consent by domestic political institutions.

These trends in domestic legal orders' attitudes toward treaties and international custom hold important insights for comparative international law. For instance,

---

4. *See, e.g.,* Tom Ginsburg, et al., *Commitment and Diffusion: How and Why National Constitutions Incorporate International Law,* 2008 U. ILL. L. REV. 201; Oona A. Hathaway, *Treaties' End: The Past, Present, and Future of International Lawmaking in the United States,* 117 YALE L.J. 1236 (2008).

our data provides information on the respective roles of domestic political institutions, such as executives, legislatures, and courts, in engaging with international law, which can inform comparative analysis. Although we propose conjectures about how the trends we identify relate to broader phenomena—such as the changing nature of the international legal order and debates over the democratic deficit—the methods we use do not allow us to make any causal claims. Our sample of countries is too diverse and the number of confounding variables is too large for such claims to be made and substantiated within the framework of this chapter. Our primary purpose here is to document global patterns and trends and to propose hypotheses as to their potential causes and relationships that may be tested by future comparative international law scholarship.

II. A NEW DATASET ON INTERNATIONAL LAW IN DOMESTIC LEGAL SYSTEMS

Differences between countries in the relationship between international law and domestic legal systems are often accounted for in international law textbooks by reference to the monist-dualist distinction. According to this distinction, monist systems regard international law and national law as "two parts of a single system" in which "international law automatically passes into the state's legal system," so that "when the state ratifies a treaty, that treaty is automatically and fully incorporated into national law."[5] Indeed, in a "pure" monist system, "national law is seen as ultimately deriving its authority from international law, which stands higher in the hierarchy of legal norms."[6] By contrast, dualist systems regard international law and national law as "separate legal systems" wherein "[a] rule of international law binding upon the state does not automatically become a part of national law; it only does so when it has been transformed or incorporated into national law by an act at the national level, such as an implementing statute for a treaty."[7]

As our study makes clear, the monist-dualist distinction has fundamental limitations for the purpose of classifying national approaches to international law. First, because they derive from a theoretical debate about the nature of international law rather than an effort to classify actual legal systems, "neither theory offers an adequate account of the *practice* of international and national courts, whose role in articulating the positions of the various legal systems is crucial."[8] Second, national systems do not adopt a monolithic approach to international law; most of them combine aspects of the monist and dualist approaches. For example, in the United Kingdom treaties do not become part of domestic law unless implemented by

5. Lori Fisler Damrosch & Sean D. Murphy, International Law: Cases and Materials 621 (6th ed. 2014).

6. *Id.*

7. *Id.*

8. James Crawford, Brownlie's Principles of Public International Law 50 (8th ed. 2012).

Parliament, while courts may directly apply international custom. Finally, because the distinction is articulated at a high level of generality, scholars sometimes differ as to whether a particular country should properly be classified as "monist" or "dualist." For example, while many observers consider France to be a monist country, some leading French scholars maintain that, because the direct effect and superiority of treaties in France does not rest on their international validity but on the French constitution, the country is really "dualist."[9]

For these reasons, in assembling our dataset, we go beyond the monist-dualist distinction to provide a more detailed picture of state practice. In doing so, we also go substantially beyond existing research. Unlike existing qualitative surveys,[10] our dataset covers a broad range of countries from all regions of the world, systematically addresses a standard set of questions, and codes the answers in quantitative form to permit visual display and statistical analysis. Instead of providing a snapshot in time, our dataset covers the period 1815–2013, providing the first systematic picture of the evolution of national approaches to international law during that period. Another defining feature of our dataset is that it relies not only on national constitutions, but also on information found in ordinary legislation, case law, executive and administrative documents, and secondary sources. We follow this approach because constitutions usually only partially define a state's relationship with international law and, in some cases, are silent on the matter altogether. In that sense, our data differs from existing initiatives by Hathaway[11] and the Comparative Constitutions Project,[12] which assemble information on the domestic status of international law based on constitutions alone.

In collecting our data, a first step was to identify and define the substantive issues that define a state's relationship with international law. We identified about 50 issues under the categories of treaty-making, treaty reception, and CIL reception. For each country, we commissioned a written memorandum that provides a narrative answer to each of the questions and, where applicable, documents

9. *See, e.g.,* Alain Pellet, *Vous avez dit « monisme »? Quelques banalités de bon sens sur l'impossibilité du prétendu monisme constitutionnel à la française, in* L'ARCHITECTURE DU DROIT. MÉLANGES EN L'HONNEUR DE MICHEL TROPER 827 (Denys de Béchillon et al. eds., 2006). In this chapter, while we generally avoid using the terms "monist" and "dualist," it is sometimes necessary to do so to avoid repetition or describe how legal systems are conventionally classified. In such cases, we use the term "monist" to designate countries where treaties have direct effect upon ratification without further action by the legislature (even if legislative approval is required prior to ratification or if formal steps need to be taken by other branches to bring the treaty into effect) and "dualist" to designate countries where legislative action is required to incorporate a ratified treaty into domestic law. The monist-dualist distinction is much less salient for CIL, and we avoid its use in that context.

10. INTERNATIONAL LAW AND DOMESTIC LEGAL SYSTEMS, *supra* note 3; NATIONAL TREATY LAW AND PRACTICE, *supra* note 3; TREATY-MAKING—EXPRESSION OF CONSENT TO BE BOUND BY A TREATY (Council of Europe ed., 2001).

11. Hathaway, *supra* note 4.

12. Ginsburg et al., *supra* note 4.

how this answer has changed over time.[13] These memoranda were written by the principal investigators or by scholars, professors, and students who usually possessed substantial knowledge on the foreign legal system in question. Where multiple interpretations existed, we relied on the most authoritative source of that system to make a judgment call. The principal investigators conducted all of the coding.

Because our goal is to provide a comprehensive picture of international law in national legal systems, we include a wide range of countries: rich and poor, Western and non-Western, democratic and non-democratic. At first blush, this choice may raise questions as to the significance of the rules and procedures we identify across different regime types. For example, one might doubt that non-democratic states would require prior legislative approval of treaty ratification, and that if such provisions exist, they would have any meaningful impact.[14] Yet, a cursory exploration of the data reveals that, just as authoritarian regimes almost universally hold elections, establish constitutional courts, and adopt bills of rights, they also require legislatures to approve treaties.[15] The political science literature offers several explanations: some studies show that autocracies adopt seemingly democratic features merely because they are global symbols of statehood,[16] while others see them as concessions to popular pressure that may become real constraints.[17] Legislatures, constitutional courts, and other institutions may also represent the interests of powerful constituencies whose support the regime requires, imposing constraints upon leaders even in the absence of democratization. In this chapter, we do not purport to explain why individual countries choose specific approaches to international law or to measure their effects. But the fact that many features we describe appear across different regime types—and across other salient differences among states—justifies including a broad cross-section of the world in our dataset.

13. We thank the Comparative Constitutions Project for providing us access to their historical repository of constitutions.

14. Of the 101 countries in our sample, 30 percent are not currently "fully democratic." We define "fully democratic" as a score of 6 or higher on the Polity IV democracy scale that is commonly used in the political science literature.

15. Indeed, the correlation between democracy and legislative involvement in treaty-making is close to zero. *See infra* note 22 and accompanying text.

16. *See* David S. Law & Mila Versteeg, *Constitutional Variation Among Strains of Authoritarianism*, *in* CONSTITUTIONS IN AUTHORITARIAN REGIMES 165 (Tom Ginsburg & Alberto Simpser eds., 2013).

17. *See* STEVEN LEVITSKY & LUCAN A. WAY, COMPETITIVE AUTHORITARIANISM: HYBRID REGIMES AFTER THE COLD WAR (2010); RULE BY LAW: THE POLITICS OF COURTS IN AUTHORITARIAN REGIMES (Tom Ginsburg & Tamir Moustafa eds., 2008); Marc Morjé Howard & Philip G. Roessler, *Liberalizing Electoral Outcomes in Competitive Authoritarian Regimes*, 50 AM. J. POL. SCI. 365 (2006); Steven Levitsky & Lucan A. Way, *The Rise of Competitive Authoritarianism*, 13 J. DEMOCRACY 51 (2002).

III. TREATY-MAKING

The proliferation of treaties and the expansion of their substantive scope to matters previously regarded as domestic in nature—such as economic regulation, human rights, and environmental protection—have lent new urgency to concerns about the legitimacy and democratic accountability of international law.[18] From this perspective, participation by national legislatures in treaty-making plays an important role in conferring upon treaties the imprimatur of democratic legitimacy. In addition, such participation upholds the separation-of-powers principles central to many constitutional democracies, under which lawmaking should be the exclusive province of the legislature rather than the executive. More generally, the insistence on legislative involvement in treaty-making signals a commitment to national sovereignty and a desire to protect national political institutions from international encroachment.

In this respect, countries that require treaties to be implemented through domestic legislation (often referred to as "dualist" systems) are sometimes said to be more protective of sovereignty than countries where treaties become directly applicable upon ratification ("monist" systems). In the former, the executive usually possesses the power to conclude treaties, but these treaties do not become part of domestic law until implemented by legislative action. If the legislature is dissatisfied with a treaty, it can refrain from implementing it altogether, adopt legislation that alters its content, or circumscribe its application. This possibility provides the executive with strong incentives to anticipate potential legislative objections to the treaty and take them into account during the negotiation and drafting processes.[19] Thus, the "act of transformation serves as an important democratic check on the treaty-making process."[20] By contrast, systems where international law applies directly can be seen as more open to international law. Moreover, since these systems do not require treaties to be implemented through domestic legislation, they might allow the executive to create or modify domestic law through treaty-making without the consent of the legislature, potentially upsetting the separation of powers that formally characterizes most systems.[21]

Our data on legislative involvement in treaty-making reveals a more complicated picture than the one suggested by the traditional monist-dualist divide. First, our data shows that systems in which treaties apply directly almost universally require the executive to obtain legislative approval prior to ratification. Figure 10.1 shows the prevalence of such prior legislative approval requirements among "monist" systems (Panel A) and among "dualist" systems (Panel B), respectively.

18. *See* Mattias Kumm, *The Legitimacy of International Law: A Constitutionalist Framework of Analysis*, 15 EUR. J. INT'L L. 907 (2004).

19. Yoram Z. Haftel & Alexander Thompson, *Delayed Ratification: The Domestic Fate of Bilateral Investment Treaties*, 67 INT'L ORG. 355, 361 (2013).

20. John H. Jackson, *The Status of Treaties in Domestic Legal Systems: A Policy Analysis*, 86 AM. J. INT'L L. 310, 324 (1992).

21. *Id.* at 325.

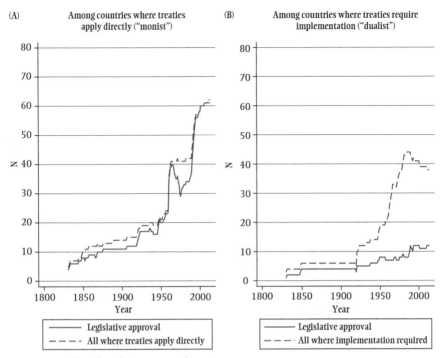

Figure 10.1 Prior legislative approval requirements.

Panel A reveals that, currently, every country where treaties apply directly requires prior legislative approval. It also shows that this practice has been common at least since the nineteenth century. Panel B shows that prior legislative approval is much less common in countries that require treaties to be implemented by domestic legislation.[22]

Second, not only do a growing number of states require legislative approval for treaty ratification, the list of treaties that require such approval has expanded considerably over time. Most notably, countries increasingly require legislative approval for treaties that fall within the traditional legislative domain.[23] As Figure 10.2, Panel A, shows, the percentage of states that require legislative approval for treaties that modify domestic law has increased. Likewise, the Figure shows an increase in legislative approval requirements for treaties that require domestic

22. As noted above, this requirement is found both in democracies and in non-democratic regimes. The correlation between democracy and whether a country requires prior legislative approval is 0.06, which means that the two features are almost entirely unrelated. Just as autocracies commonly hold elections, they require the legislature to approve treaty ratification, upholding a formal separation of power between the executive and legislative branches.

23. Specifically, in many civil law countries, the constitution distinguishes between legislative and regulatory domains. The legislative domain comprises of laws approved by parliament as a whole, while the regulatory domain consists of regulations adopted without parliamentary approval. In many cases, the constitution explicitly sets out which substantive issues fall within the legislative domain. Where treaties deal with the same issues that fall within the legislative domain, parliamentary approval is required.

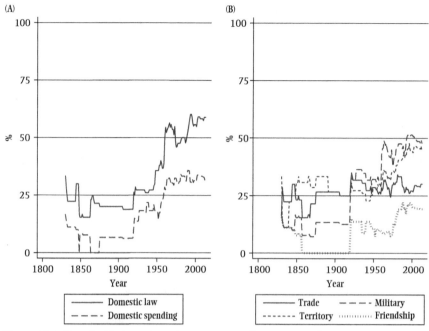

Figure 10.2 Prior legislative approval requirements (by treaty type).

spending, the monitoring of which is regarded as a core task of democratic legis-latures.[24] At the same time, as Panel B shows, legislative approval requirements for treaties that fall within the traditional realm of international relations (such as military treaties, friendship treaties, treaties that modify borders, or trade treaties) have remained more constant over time. Thus, as international treaties have prolif-erated, countries increasingly insist on legislative approval of those treaties that fall within the traditional legislative realm, thereby preserving the formal separation of powers among the different branches of government.[25] Notably, this trend appears both in democracies and non-democracies, which suggests that rather than a true democratization of international lawmaking, the trend may be a reaction to the increasing encroachment of treaties in areas traditionally regulated by national legislatures.[26]

24. In the words of Gladstone in an 1891 speech, "if the House of Commons can by any possibility lose the power of the control of the grants of public money, depend upon it your very liberty will be worth very little in comparison." 2 THE SPEECHES OF THE RIGHT HON. W. E. GLADSTONE 343 (A.W. Hutton & H.J. Cohen eds., 1902).

25. One might object that such formal treaty-making procedures are meaningless if the executive can bypass them by entering into international agreements through other means, such as executive agreements. However, in countries that require prior legislative approval of specific categories of treaties, the virtually uniform rule is that executive agreements may not constitutionally be used in these areas.

26. The correlation between democracy and legislative approval requirements for treaties that alter domestic law is −0.03, while the correlation between democracy and legislative approval require-ments for treaties that require domestic spending is −0.11.

Together, these two findings draw attention to the legislature as a critically important actor in treaty-making and implementation: legislatures commonly approve treaties prior to ratification and, in many cases, are also tasked with translating them into domestic law.[27] At the same time, these findings point to potentially important differences in the ways legislatures interact with international law in different systems. At first glance, one might expect that the legislature is able to alter domestic understandings of international law only in states where treaties require incorporation along traditional "dualist" lines. Legislative implementation offers numerous opportunities to clarify ambiguous language, insert new definitions and interpretations, and adapt the treaty to idiosyncratic domestic law concepts. Moreover, since legislatures are inherently political bodies,[28] they might attempt to strategically tailor the implementing legislation to the political preferences of their constituents.[29] In such systems, legislatures would play a central role in shaping the interpretation and application of international law rules. By contrast, one might expect that, in systems where treaties apply directly, courts would be the central actors in treaty application and interpretation. Unlike legislatures, courts may be presumed to be more faithful interpreters of international agreements, given their greater independence from electoral pressures and their participation in a broader worldwide community of judges.[30]

Our findings suggest that this picture, informed by the traditional monist-dualist distinction, might be somewhat misleading. Since virtually all "monist" systems require legislative approval prior to ratification, their legislatures also play a central role in the treaty-making process. However, important differences remain in the timing of legislative involvement: while "monist" systems require legislative approval prior to ratification, in "dualist" systems the legislature usually intervenes only after ratification. This raises the question whether ex ante or ex post legislative involvement is more protective of domestic accountability and sovereignty. One clue is that, as Figure 10.1, Panel B, shows, some countries in which treaties require incorporation have recently begun to adopt prior legislative approval requirements.[31] As a particularly salient example, the United Kingdom, long considered the epitome of the "dualist" model, adopted such a requirement in 2010.[32] The new British rule is unusual in that, rather than requiring affirmative approval of treaties by Parliament, it requires the government to lay proposed treaties before Parliament for 21 sitting days before ratifying them. During that period, either House may vote

---

27. Kevin L. Cope & Hooman Movassagh, *National Legislatures: The Foundations of Comparative International Law* (this volume).

28. *See generally* DAVID R. MAYHEW, CONGRESS: THE ELECTORAL CONNECTION (1974).

29. *See* Jackson, *supra* note 20, at 325.

30. *See generally* ANNE-MARIE SLAUGHTER, A NEW WORLD ORDER 65–103 (2004).

31. Here again, it is not necessarily the countries with the greatest democratic pedigree that have adopted this requirement: the correlation between democracy and ex ante democratic approval is close to zero in this subsample (0.12).

32. Constitutional Reform and Governance Act, 2010, c. 25, § 20 (U.K.).

against ratification, in which case the government normally cannot proceed.[33] The change was reportedly motivated by perceptions of a democratic deficit in the existing treaty approval process, despite the fact that treaties did not become part of domestic law without a subsequent Act of Parliament.[34] Other traditionally "dualist" countries such as Belize, Ireland, Ghana, Papua New Guinea, and Zimbabwe have also moved toward a greater parliamentary role in recent years by adopting prior approval requirements.

This development suggests that legislative implementation requirements are not necessarily seen as more effective than direct treaty application in protecting accountability and sovereignty. Specifically, ex post implementation may be seen as an insufficient democratic check on the government's ability to undertake burdensome international commitments. The most obvious benefit of involving the legislature prior to ratification in a "dualist" system is that ex post implementation is only required for those treaties that require incorporation in the domestic legal system in order to be effective. However, many treaties—such as those creating international organizations or military alliances, settling boundaries, or agreeing to international dispute settlement—do not typically require such implementation, even though they often create substantial commitments for a country and its citizens. Indeed, as Figure 10.2, Panel B, shows, prior legislative approval requirements often do cover such treaties, thereby giving the legislature a voice in a broader range of foreign policy matters. In this light, the nascent trend toward cumulating ex ante and ex post legislative intervention may be seen as a corrective to the insufficient coverage of ex post implementation alone.

More generally, this trend suggests that even for treaties that do modify domestic law, ex ante and ex post approval are not simply substitutes and that the policy implications of each mechanism should be explored in more detail. For example, legislatures that grant prior approval might be in a better position to require modifications or reservations to a treaty. The US Senate's frequent insistence on modifications and reservations illustrates this practice. In addition, parliamentary involvement prior to treaty ratification may signal to treaty partners that democratic institutions and major domestic constituencies support the treaty, thereby enhancing the credibility of the state's commitment. By contrast, legislatures in systems with ex post approval only will have to take the treaty as it is, but can tailor implementing legislation to the country's circumstances, potentially making implementation more efficient. Legislatures' ability to refrain from passing implementing legislation may also

33. The government may return the treaty to Parliament with a statement explaining why the treaty should nevertheless be ratified, triggering a new 21-day period during which only the House of Commons (not the House of Lords) may block ratification. *Id.* § 20(4)–(5). The Act goes further than the previously applicable Ponsonby Rule, under which Parliament could review treaties but not defeat ratification by the executive. *See* Arabella Thorp, Parliamentary Scrutiny of Treaties: Up to 2010, at 9 (2009), *available at* http://researchbriefings.files.parliament.uk/documents/SN04693/SN04693.pdf.

34. Lucinda Maer et al., House of Commons Library, Constitutional Reform and Governance Bill 21–22 (2009), *available at* http://researchbriefings.files.parliament.uk/documents/RP09-73/RP09-73.pdf.

enhance their bargaining position when treaty partners fail to uphold their commitments.[35] The existing literature has paid little attention to the design question whether the legislature should be involved ex ante or ex post. We believe that this is an important avenue for future research.

IV. TREATY RECEPTION

The second central feature of a national legal system's relationship to international law is the effect it gives to treaties once they are ratified. In some systems, treaties automatically become part of the domestic legal order and directly applicable in national courts without further legislative action. These states are traditionally referred to as "monist systems." However, several other aspects of national reception doctrine affect the domestic application of treaties and create variation among such systems. First, "monist" systems often distinguish between "self-executing" treaties, which are directly applicable, and "non-self-executing" treaties, which require implementing legislation. Second, the hierarchical status of treaties vis-à-vis domestic legislation varies across monist systems. Third, monist systems differ in the extent to which their courts apply interpretive canons to avoid conflicts between domestic laws and treaty obligations.[36] Such canons of interpretation are traditionally associated with dualist systems, where courts have long interpreted legislation in conformity with international agreements.

The choices a national system makes when adopting and applying each of these doctrines might have significant implications both for the effectiveness of treaties and for the democratic accountability and legitimacy of international law. On the one hand, choices that favor strong and unconditional reception of treaties—such as giving most or all treaties self-executing status, granting treaties hierarchical superiority over other sources of domestic law, and applying strong presumptions of conformity—may increase the credibility of a state's commitments and the effectiveness of the relevant international regime. On the other hand, the same features

---

35. *See* Eric A. Posner & Alan O. Sykes, Economic Foundations of International Law 141 (2013). Increasing domestic hurdles to treaty-making may also strengthen a state's bargaining position ex ante, as its counterparts will anticipate that an insufficiently favorable treaty may not gain domestic approval. *See* Robert D. Putnam, *Diplomacy and Domestic Politics: The Logic of Two-Level Games*, 42 Int'l Org. 427, 452–53 (1988). However, it is unclear whether ex ante approval or ex post implementation requirements should systematically be more effective in this respect—except of course for treaties that do not require domestic implementation for their effectiveness.

36. Importantly, these are not the only ways in which international law can enter national law. For example, in some well-known cases, national courts have considered a state's international legal obligations—albeit formally unincorporated—in circumscribing permissible administrative action. *See, e.g., Minister of State for Immigration and Ethnic Affairs v Teoh* (1995) 183 CLR 273 (Austl.). The degree of influence that international law can exert within a national legal system is ultimately a matter of degree. *See* Benedict Kingsbury, *The Concept of "Law" in Global Administrative Law*, 20 Eur. J. Int'l L. 23 (2009). In this contribution, we focus on those aspects of the relationship—including the formal applicability of ratified treaties by national courts and the explicit articulation of an interpretive presumption of conformity—that are well documented across many countries and therefore lend themselves to consistent coding.

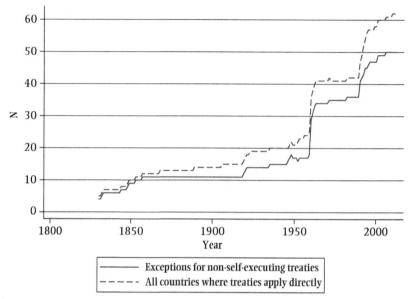

Figure 10.3 Exceptions for non-self-executing treaties (countries where treaties apply directly only).

reduce the ability of domestic institutions to serve as a check on international law and international institutions and to act as intermediaries in adapting treaties to the national legal order. Our data suggests how these doctrines have evolved over time as some of these concerns have become more salient.

First, while international lawyers have long recognized that the principle of direct application often comes with exceptions for non-self-executing treaties,[37] the prevalence of these exceptions is thus far unknown. Our data shows that the overwhelming majority of systems that, in principle, apply treaties directly recognize exceptions to this rule and grant courts substantial discretion in determining whether a treaty is self-executing. Figure 10.3 depicts the number of "monist" systems that allow for such exceptions. That number has grown steeply, even though the prevalence of such exceptions has remained relatively stable as a proportion of all "monist" countries. As of 2014, Belarus, Egypt, Estonia, Iran, Latvia, Morocco, Tajikistan, Turkey, Turkmenistan, and Ukraine are the only states for which we have found no evidence of a distinction between self-executing and non-self-executing treaties. The lack of such a doctrine might result from the fact that some of these countries have relatively weak judiciaries, which may discourage litigants from relying on treaties and explain why the question of self-execution rarely arises.[38] At the same time, many other countries with weak judiciaries do

---

37. *See, e.g.,* Thomas Buergenthal, *Self-Executing and Non-Self-Executing Treaties in National and International Law*, 235 RECUEIL DES COURS 303, 317 (1992).

38. In 2011, Belarus, Iran, Morocco, Tajikistan, Turkmenistan, and Ukraine were all rated as "not independent" by the CIRI human rights dataset (which rates judicial independence on a three-point scale: "not independent," "partially independent," and "generally independent"). *See* David L.

recognize this distinction. Indeed, the correlation between the existence of a non-self-executing treaty doctrine and judicial independence is fairly low.[39]

The near-universality of the distinction has several implications. First, it suggests that there is less at stake in the decision whether to apply treaties directly than is often suggested, because even those states that apply treaties directly in fact require legislative implementation for many treaties. This finding also points to the importance of self-executing treaties as an object of comparative international law, as a treaty that is deemed self-executing in one state may not be in another.[40] The distinction is notoriously imprecise, with the standards used by courts difficult to codify or even formulate, leaving substantial scope for judicial discretion that may be influenced by numerous legal and political factors. Thus, while few scholars believe that *Medellin v. Texas* adopted a presumption against self-execution, the US Supreme Court's emphasis on direct textual evidence of self-execution implies that the bar is quite high.[41] By contrast, Argentine courts have held some provisions of the International Covenant on Social, Economic and Cultural Rights to be directly applicable, a status denied by virtually all other national systems.[42] In civil law systems, different judicial orders within the same country have sometimes clashed over whether a particular treaty is self-executing.[43] The practice of national courts in designating some treaties as self-executing and others as non-self-executing is an important area of comparative international law research.

Cingranelli et al., *The CIRI Human Rights Dataset*, CIRI HUMAN RIGHTS DATA PROJECT (Apr. 4, 2014), at http://www.humanrightsdata.com/p/data-documentation.html. Egypt, Latvia, and Turkey were all rated "partially independent." *Id.* Only Estonia was rated as "independent." *Id.*

39. The correlation is 0.17. Of the 22 countries in our data that were rated as "not independent" by the CIRI dataset in 2011, 16 recognized a distinction between self-executing and non-self-executing treaties, while only 6 did not recognize such a distinction.

40. Buergenthal, *supra* note 37, at 317.

41. Medellín v. Texas, 552 U.S. 491, 506–20 (2008); *see* Curtis A. Bradley, *Intents, Presumptions and Non-Self-Executing Treaties*, 102 AM. J. INT'L L. 540 (2008); Carlos Manuel Vásquez, *Treaties as Law of the Land: The Supremacy Clause and the Judicial Enforcement of Treaties*, 122 HARV. L. REV. 599 (2008).

42. Cámara Federal de Apelaciones [CFed.] [Federal Court of Appeals], 2/6/1998, "Viceconte, Mariela c. Estado Nacional" / Acción de Amparo," La Ley [L.L.] (1998-F-305) (Arg.) (holding that the government's failure to manufacture a vaccine against Argentine hemorrhagic fever constituted a violation of Article 12 of the ICESCR); Corte Suprema de Justicia de la Nación [CSJN] [National Supreme Court of Justice], 24/10/2000, "Campodónico de Beviacqua, Ana Carina c. Ministerio de Salud y Acción Social / recurso de hecho," La Ley [L.L.] (2001-D-23) (Arg.) (finding that article 12 of the ICESCR required the government to continue providing a drug to a child who had an immunological condition). *See* Andrew Byrnes, *Second-Class Rights Yet Again? Economic, Social, and Cultural Rights in the Report of the National Human Rights Consultation*, 33 UNSW L.J. 193, 206–07 (2010); Iain Byrne, *Enforcing the Right to Health: Innovative Lessons from Domestic Courts*, *in* REALIZING THE RIGHT TO HEALTH 525, 527 n.15 (Andrew Clapham & Mary Robinson eds., 2009).

43. *See* PATRICK DAILLIER, MATHIAS FORTEAU & ALAIN PELLET, DROIT INTERNATIONAL PUBLIC 254–55 (8th ed. 2009).

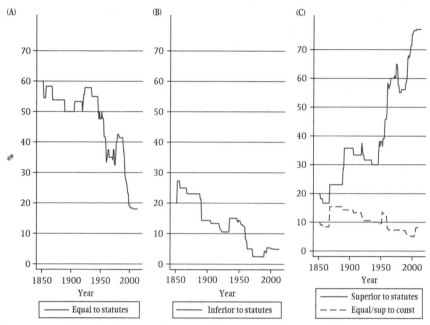

Figure 10.4 Hierarchical status of treaties vis-à-vis statutes (countries where treaties apply directly only).

A second finding that stands out from our data is that a growing number of states grant treaties greater domestic status than ordinary laws. Figure 10.4 depicts the percentage of systems that grant treaties equal status to domestic statutes (Panel A), those that consider treaties inferior to domestic statutes (Panel B), and those in which treaties trump domestic legislation (Panel C). In this Figure, our sample is limited to those countries that give direct effect to treaties. In the first century in our sample (from 1850 to 1950), most of those systems considered ratified treaties equal to statutes, so that domestic legislation could trump an earlier treaty. The number of "monist" systems that considered treaties superior to domestic legislation hovered between 25 and 40 percent. From the 1960s onward, however, this proportion has increased dramatically, with more than 70 percent now giving treaties hierarchical superiority. For the most part, this change has occurred through explicit constitutional revisions, although in some cases—such as Belgium—courts have affirmed the superiority of treaties over domestic statutes. A relatively small number of states give ratified treaties even higher status, treating them as equal or superior to the constitution.

The newly elevated status of treaties in monist systems may raise accountability and sovereignty concerns. As countries have granted higher status to treaties, they have effectively made it harder for legislatures to overturn treaty commitments through subsequent legislation. Instead, countries have empowered their courts to strike down legislation that contradicts international treaties. At the same time, these countries have steadily expanded the categories of treaties that require prior legislative approval for ratification. Thus, while insisting upon legislative involvement ex ante, they have marginalized the role of the legislature ex post. This choice may impose substantial constraints on national political institutions when the obligations imposed by a treaty turn out to impose greater costs or constraints on domestic policy autonomy than was anticipated at the time of ratification. This effect is likely to be particularly salient with respect to membership in international organizations that may make directly applicable, legally binding decisions.

Of course, making treaties superior to ordinary legislation may also bring benefits, such as by allowing states to signal that they are credible treaty partners.[44] The logic is the same as articulated by John Jay in the Federalist Papers, where he observed that "it would be impossible to find a nation who would make any bargain with us, which should be binding on them *absolutely*, but on us only so long and so far as we may think proper to be bound by it."[45] By making treaties trump domestic law, states effectively use their own courts as commitment mechanisms to tie their hands as to future treaty compliance. If this strategy works, other states may be more willing to engage in mutually beneficial treaty-based cooperation. This strategy may be particularly valuable to new states with a short record of international cooperation to demonstrate their reliability. If true, this gain in international credibility explains why countries are willing to sacrifice some degree of democratic involvement and future domestic policy flexibility.

From the perspective of comparative international law, differences in the hierarchical status of treaties across national legal systems may contribute to differences in interpretation and application. On the one hand, one might expect that countries where treaties enjoy supralegislative status will apply them more faithfully, as the legislature cannot—at least in principle—override treaties when countervailing political pressures arise. In many cases, national courts in such systems are empowered to displace national legislation that infringes treaties. In some cases, courts may even give certain treaties primacy over domestic law in the absence of express constitutional provisions to that effect, as the Nigerian Supreme Court did for the African Charter of Human and Peoples' Rights in a series of cases.[46] The effectiveness of this approach likely turns on a host of extralegal factors, such as the independence of courts and their willingness to enforce treaties against the will of the political branches.

On the other hand, hierarchical superiority of treaties may also lead to subtler effects on their interpretation and application. Because legislators know they will be unable to overturn the treaty by subsequent legislation, they may be more likely to condition their consent to ratification upon reservations or other modifications that reduce the domestic impact of the treaty. Once treaties are ratified, the impossibility of displacing them through the normal legislative process may increase the pressure on national courts to strategically reinterpret their provisions in order to avoid conflict with the executive or the legislature, satisfy powerful domestic constituencies, or advance their own policy preferences. Thus, giving treaties higher legal status may raise the stakes of domestic interpretive battles over treaty provisions, both in the treaty approval process and in litigation in national courts. As a result, the overall effect of treaty superiority on uniform interpretation and application of treaties

44. *See, e.g.*, Ginsburg et al., *supra* note 4.

45. The Federalist No. 64, at 362 (John Jay) (Clinton Rossiter ed., 1961).

46. *See* Frans Viljoen, International Human Rights Law in Africa 533–37 (2d ed. 2012).

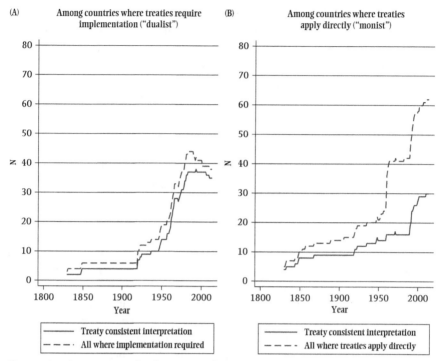

Figure 10.5 Interpretive rules favoring conformity.

may be more ambiguous than often suggested. If these conjectures are correct, the trend toward granting treaties higher domestic legal status may increase the prevalence of divergent national interpretations of treaties.[47]

One indication of how courts deal with the elevated status of international treaties is the growing prevalence of interpretive rules or presumptions similar to the well-known *Charming Betsy* doctrine, under which domestic law should, as far as possible, be interpreted to avoid conflict with international treaty obligations. Historically, such doctrines have been more salient in countries where treaties require domestic implementation because the lack of direct effect of treaties makes it more likely that potential conflicts will arise between domestic law and an unimplemented treaty. Indeed, as Figure 10.5, Panel A, shows, virtually all countries that require legislative implementation recognize such a doctrine, although the details of its application by courts may vary considerably across countries. By contrast, systems where treaties apply directly were historically less likely to rely on such doctrines, but Figure 10.5, Panel B, shows that an increasing number of these systems now recognize them as well. This convergence may be driven by the desire of courts in "monist" systems to give effect to some treaties—such as human rights conventions—without explicitly displacing inconsistent legislation. The trend thus suggests judicial caution in the face of a growing number of treaties that now trump domestic law.

47. As Anthea Roberts points out, courts as well as legislatures can be important fora for the "hybridization" of international and domestic norms. Anthea Roberts, *Comparative International Law? The Role of National Courts in Creating and Enforcing International Law*, 60 INT'L & COMP. L.Q. 57 (2011).

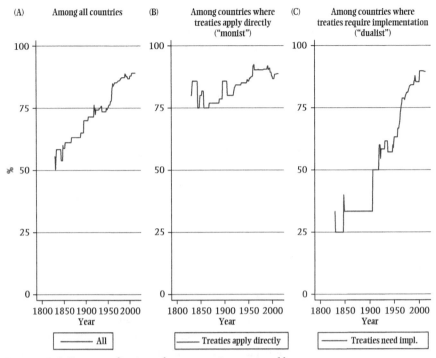

Figure 10.6 Direct application of customary international law.

V. CUSTOMARY INTERNATIONAL LAW

For international custom, one might expect concerns over accountability to be particularly salient. Unlike treaties, established CIL rules bind states that have not expressly consented to them. As a result, states could be more hesitant to empower domestic courts to identify CIL rules and apply them directly, especially since the existence and content of the rules are often controversial. The lack of explicit consent by a state to be bound by a CIL rule also means that the domestic procedural checks that often apply to treaty-making—such as prior legislative approval—are nonexistent. In addition, the legitimacy of CIL rules is often contested, notably because many of them were formed without the active participation of non-Western states. For these reasons, direct application of international custom may raise greater legitimacy concerns than for treaties. According to Posner and Sykes, "[p]eople who think that all law should have democratic pedigree are uncomfortable if customary international law can easily become domestic law."[48]

Yet, perhaps the most striking pattern that emerges from our data is that in virtually all states, CIL rules are in principle directly applicable without legislative implementation. Figure 10.6, Panel A, depicts the percentage of all countries in our sample that follow this approach (solid line). Panel B depicts the percentage, among states that apply treaties directly, that give direct effect to CIL. Panel C depicts the percentage of countries that require treaties to be incorporated but give direct effect to CIL. The Figure reveals that, while direct reception of CIL is somewhat more

---

48. POSNER & SYKES, *supra* note 35, at 143.

common among countries that also apply treaties directly (about 90 percent today), most countries that require treaty implementation do not apply the same rule to international custom, but rather apply it directly. For example, courts in the United Kingdom—often portrayed as the home of the "dualist" tradition—have long considered CIL to be directly applicable by courts. Thus, our data indicates that how domestic legal systems treat CIL is largely unrelated with their approaches toward treaties. It also suggests that the traditional monist-dualist distinction is inappropriate to classify national approaches toward CIL.

There are only a handful of countries that do not currently apply CIL directly in their domestic legal orders. These include countries such as Algeria, Iran, and Sri Lanka, which in the mid- to late twentieth century took strong anticolonial stances and actively resisted customary aspects of international economic law, such as limits on expropriation of foreign investments. As a result, they departed from the acceptance of international custom as a source of law that prevails in the vast majority of domestic legal systems. In 1966, the Algerian representative on the General Assembly's legal committee explained his country's resistance to custom, stating that "a distinction must be made between obligations voluntarily accepted and the general imposition of law made in another era by an exclusionary international community."[49] In some instances, these countries chose to substitute constitutional references to CIL—which were increasingly common in that period—with references to law made in international institutions that they considered more representative, such as the United Nations.

However, the almost universal acceptance of direct application of CIL does not mean that democratic accountability and legitimacy concerns are absent; instead, they appear to be channeled through other aspects of CIL reception doctrine. Most importantly, while ratified international treaties are increasingly given hierarchical superiority over statutes, the opposite is the case for international custom. Indeed, the proportion of states that consider CIL superior to ordinary legislation has decreased in recent decades. Figure 10.7 depicts the percentage of states that treat CIL as equal to domestic statutes (Panel A), inferior to domestic statutes (Panel B), and superior to domestic statutes (Panel C). The Figure reveals that from the 1950s onward, as a wave of new countries enters our sample, the percentage of countries that treat CIL as inferior has increased. Thus, around the same time that it became more common to make treaties superior to domestic law, it also became more common to make international custom inferior.

These findings have several implications for comparative international law. The dominant model for CIL reception is direct application coupled with hierarchical inferiority, a model that is uncommon for treaties. As a result, unlike for treaties, one might expect CIL compliance to be relatively fragile because a CIL rule can usually be displaced by legislation if it imposes excessive costs on the government or domestic interests. By the same token, while the relative imprecision of CIL rules may facilitate their strategic reinterpretation by national courts, there may be less pressure to engage in this indirect strategy because—unlike ratified treaties—burdensome CIL

---

49. ABDELMADJID DJEBBAR, LA POLITIQUE CONVENTIONNELLE DE L'ALGÉRIE (2000) (authors' translation).

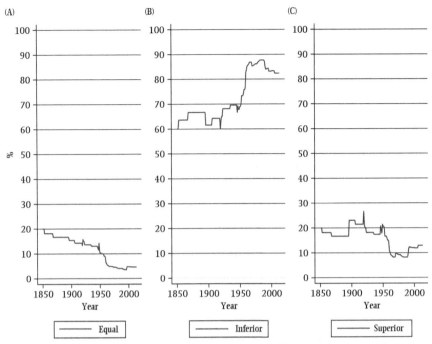

Figure 10.7 Hierarchical status of customary international law vis-à-vis statutes (countries that give direct effect to CIL only).

rules can simply be displaced by the legislature. In addition, despite the formal principle of direct application, courts sometimes carve out exceptions under which they refuse to apply CIL rules. For example, the UK House of Lords held that individuals could not be prosecuted criminally based on unimplemented CIL.[50] For these reasons, one might expect domestic litigants not to devote much effort to elaborating alternative interpretations of CIL rules, focusing rather on overriding it by legislative action or denying its applicability.

However, the stakes in domestic interpretation and application of CIL are often higher than suggested above. First, countries that wish to avoid inadvertently breaching CIL rules may—and often do—incorporate them by legislation, sometimes even giving them constitutional status. Thus, US law criminalizes "piracy as defined by the law of nations"[51] and allows civil actions for certain torts committed "in violation of the law of nations."[52] Likewise, national constitutions sometimes enshrine specific CIL rules such as those regarding human rights and international humanitarian law.[53] Second, domestic courts have invoked the *jus cogens* status of certain CIL rules to override domestic law, thus effectively giving these rules

50. R v. Jones, [2006] UKHL 16, [20]–[23] (appeal taken from Eng.).

51. 18 U.S.C. § 1651 (2012).

52. 28 U.S.C. § 1350 (2012).

53. *See, e.g.,* CONSTITUCIÓN POLÍTICA DE COLOMBIA [C.P.] art. 214.

supralegislative status. For example, the Chilean Supreme Court invoked the *jus cogens* CIL rule against torture to justify overturning a controversial amnesty law passed at the end of the Pinochet regime.[54] Finally, the very nature of CIL is that it can be altered or disappear when enough states change their practices.[55] As a result, the domestic interpretation given to CIL rules—especially by national courts, which play an important role in the recognition and development of CIL—is not a matter of indifference because it influences their evolution at the international level.

Just as is the case for treaties, domestic reinterpretation of CIL may occur in several ways. First, when lawmakers incorporate a CIL rule by legislation, they may interpret or modify the rule to provide additional detail and advance their preferred version of the rule. For example, when the United States and the United Kingdom codified foreign state immunity in the 1970s, they did not simply declare the CIL rule to be part of domestic law "as is" but adopted an extensive and detailed set of provisions, which turned out to be highly influential in subsequent applications of the rule both domestically and internationally.[56] Second, even though legislatures can in theory displace CIL rules, parties may still find it essential to devote substantial efforts to shaping interpretations of CIL rules by domestic courts. The US Congress could in theory repeal the Alien Tort Statute, but in practice high-stakes battles have been fought in US courts over the interpretation of both the provision itself and the CIL rules for which it provides a domestic remedy.[57] Finally, when states breach CIL rules, they may have incentives to dissimulate the breach by strategically reinterpreting the rules rather than simply overriding them by contrary legislation. The latter strategy would make the breach more obvious and lead to a greater likelihood of sanctions or reputational damage. On the other hand, proposing a new (and presumably more permissive) interpretation may create a precedent that undermines a rule that the state values.[58] An interesting question for comparative international law is to what extent national courts engage in strategic interpretation of CIL, as part of, or as opposed to, "good faith" interpretation based on prevailing practice and *opinio juris*.

---

54. *See* Marny A. Requa, *A Human Rights Triumph? Dictatorship-Era Crimes and the Chilean Supreme Court*, 12 HUM. RTS. L. REV. 79, 89–90 (2012).

55. Anthea Roberts, *Traditional and Modern Approaches to Customary International Law: A Reconciliation*, 95 AM. J. INT'L L. 757, 784–85 (2001); Pierre-Hugues Verdier & Erik Voeten, *Precedent, Compliance, and Change in Customary International Law: An Explanatory Theory*, 108 AM. J. INT'L L. 389 (2014).

56. Foreign Sovereign Immunities Act of 1976, 28 U.S.C. §§ 1330, 1332, 1391(f), 1441(d), 1602–1611 (1994); State Immunity Act 1978, 26 Eliz. 2, c. 33 (U.K.).

57. *See, e.g.*, Kiobel v. Royal Dutch Petroleum Co., 133 S. Ct. 1659 (2013); Sosa v. Alvarez-Machain, 542 U.S. 692 (2004); Filártiga v. Peña-Irala, 630 F.2d 876 (2d Cir. 1980), among dozens of appellate cases.

58. Pierre-Hugues Verdier & Erik Voeten, *How Does Customary International Law Change? The Case of State Immunity*, 59 INT'L STUD. Q. 209 (2015). Of course, this is a concern only when the state values the rule generally, but wishes to justify its defection in a particular instance. If the state dislikes the rule and actively wants to undermine it, then it should make the breach as "noisy" as possible.

VI. CONCLUSION

In this contribution, we have shown how national doctrines governing treaty-making and the status of treaties and CIL in the domestic legal order have changed over time. We have argued that these changes, which reflect a continuing effort to balance legitimacy and effectiveness, have important implications for the comparative international law project because these doctrines structure how apparently uniform international law is interpreted and applied across countries. Our findings also confirm that the traditional monist-dualist distinction, which originally arose out of theoretical debates on the nature of international law, has limited value for the purpose of classifying actual legal systems or examining their policy and normative implications. The canonical features of each model are less distinctive than traditionally suggested: "monist" systems often deny direct application to "non-self-executing" treaties, many such systems historically considered treaties equal—or even inferior—to legislation, and the dichotomy is largely irrelevant to explaining the domestic status of CIL. Thus, relying on a simple monist-dualist dichotomy may often obscure more than illuminate the relevant questions.

Our approach, albeit considerably more detailed than prior classifications, nevertheless has important limits. As Karen Knop notes, "the domestic interpretation of international law is not merely the transmittal of the international, but a process of translation from international to national."[59] By coding doctrine across many countries and long periods of time, we must inevitably set aside numerous subtle differences—legal but also economic, political, and cultural—in how national legal systems engage with international law. In addition, such data cannot directly capture the practical impact of international law, such as whether courts effectively enforce the rights and obligations created by a specific treaty in a specific national context. Yet, our approach also has important benefits, enabling a more comprehensive and precise picture to emerge and long-term trends to be identified and measured. This broader picture is meant to complement and situate, not substitute for, detailed scholarly efforts that focus on specific countries, regions, or areas of international law.

Our findings can inform the broader debate on the legitimacy of international law. We have suggested that one widespread long-term response to rising legitimacy concerns has been to require greater legislative participation in treaty-making. To be sure, this approach only partially addresses the issue. If countries lack the resources to participate effectively in treaty negotiations and cannot credibly refuse to join, formal legislative participation may seem illusory. Yet, political scientists have suggested that imposing constraints on domestic ratification may itself increase a country's leverage in international negotiations.[60] The effect may be compounded as more developing countries adopt such doctrines while their legislatures become more powerful and representative. Relatedly, one might doubt that formal rules giving domestic effect to international law will be effective where domestic courts are compromised by lack of resources, corruption, or

59. Knop, *supra* note 1, at 506.

60. Putnam, *supra* note 35, at 452–53.

political interference. Yet, national courts have sometimes been willing to take on alarming odds to implement international obligations. Formal doctrines such as constitutionally-entrenched superiority of treaties may contribute to the perceived legitimacy of such interventions.

While we do not pursue causal claims in this chapter, the dataset we assembled paves the way for quantitative exploration of the relationships between the trends we identify and, more broadly, of the causes and effects of international law reception doctrines. Why do certain countries opt for one model rather than the other? Are these choices driven by conscious concerns about effectiveness and legitimacy, or is an equal or greater role played by legal tradition, domestic political and economic factors, or historical contingencies? Do countries that grant their courts authority to apply treaties directly comply more consistently with their international commitments, disregarding domestic law if necessary? Are these countries more hesitant to ratify treaties in the first place? If the choices countries make as to the place of international law in their domestic legal order affect such outcomes, understanding these choices and their impact will be key to the success of comparative international law.

11

Objections to Treaty Reservations

A Comparative Approach to Decentralized Interpretation

TOM GINSBURG*

Treaty practice is a central activity of states in international law, yet there is relatively little scholarship on how states differ in their approaches to treaties.[1] This chapter examines a particular aspect of treaty practice, namely the use of objections to reservations, as an example of the comparative international law project described by the editors in their introduction to this volume.[2] The practice of objections, it argues, occurs when states have divergent interpretation of treaty requirements, but also illustrates the differential propensity of states to push their particular views of the object and purpose of treaties. Objecting states are providing a kind of collective good among the treaty parties, serving to help advance normative goals on behalf of the group.

Objections to reservations is a topic on which there is scarce case law, limited doctrinal work, and virtually no empirical work.[3] Basic questions, including the

* Thanks to Ashley Deeks, Katerina Linos, and the editors for comments. Thanks to Yao Yao for research assistance and Jessica Chow, MA, University of Chicago 2014, for her superb thesis on the ICCPR, from which some data has been drawn.

1. For a prominent exception, *see* Duncan B. Hollis, *A Comparative Approach to Treaty Law and Practice, in* NATIONAL TREATY LAW AND PRACTICE (Duncan B. Hollis et al. eds., 2005); *see also* INTERNATIONAL INVESTMENT LAW AND COMPARATIVE PUBLIC LAW (Stephan W. Schill ed., 2010).

2. Anthea Roberts, Paul B. Stephan, Pierre-Hugues Verdier & Mila Versteeg, *Conceptualizing Comparative International Law*, at 6 (this volume) (defining the practice of comparative international law as "identifying, analyzing, and explaining similarities and differences in how actors in different legal systems understand, interpret, apply, and approach international law").

3. Limited empirical work includes M. De Pauw, *Women's Rights: From Bad to Worse? Assessing the Evolution of Incompatible Reservations to the CEDAW Convention*, 77 MERKOURIOS 51 (2013). An important article covering some of the same terrain as this chapter is Ryan Goodman, *Human Rights Treaties, Invalid Reservations, and State Consent*, 96 AM. J. INT'L L. 531 (2002). *See also* Martin Scheinin, Reservations to the International Covenant on Civil and Political Rights and Its

legal effect of objections, remain unanswered. Simply put, we don't know what leads states to object to reservations, nor what the impacts of those objections are. This chapter starts to document the extent of the phenomenon in the context of human rights treaties. It focuses in particular on the International Covenant on Civil and Political Rights, one of the most prominent human rights treaties, and one that has a rich set of both reservations and objections.[4]

One methodological advantage of this focus on a single treaty is that it allows us to use a complete sample of a reservations and objections, providing leverage for understanding comparative treaty interpretation.[5] Another feature of this data is that it allows us to focus our comparative lens not on courts, but on national executives. Reservation practice is generally centered in the executive, although in some countries legislatures may play a role when they attach reservations, understandings, and declarations as a condition of ratification. Objections to reservations, on the other hand, are more narrowly concentrated in the executive, specifically in the legal departments of foreign ministries.[6] The objection is an interpretive act by executive officials, making assertions about the requirements of a treaty, typically about the incompatibility of a particular reservation.

The chapter first reviews the legal background on objections to reservations, and then provides a theory of which states are likely to engage in this form of bilateral activity within a multilateral scheme. It then provides descriptive and empirical analysis of objections to reservations to the International Covenant on Civil and Political Rights (ICCPR), along with some data on other prominent human rights treaties. Finally, the chapter speculates on doctrinal implications of the analysis. Treating objections to reservations as a form of decentralized interpretation has implications for monitoring and enforcement of treaty norms, as well as how we ought to structure the law of treaties. Objections are not simply expressive acts or one-off decisions, but should be encouraged as a way of making treaty regimes more robust.

I. WHY ARE OBJECTIONS NEEDED? LAW AND THEORY

Why do states object to reservations? To understand this, we must first understand reservations. We begin with a prototypical multilateral treaty negotiation. Several states get together to negotiate a treaty. One state wants to join the treaty, but has concerns about one particular provision—either because it does not think that it can get the treaty ratified at home, or because the provision would impose special

Optional Protocols—Reflections on State Practice (2004) (unpublished manuscript), http://www.nuigalway.ie/sites/eu-china-humanrights/seminars/ds0411i/martin%20scheinin-eng.doc.

4. International Covenant on Civil and Political Rights, *adopted* Dec. 16, 1966, 999 U.N.T.S. 171 (hereinafter ICCPR).

5. *See* Katerina Linos, *Methodological Guidance: How to Select and Develop Comparative International Law Case Studies* (this volume).

6. *See also* Ashley S. Deeks, *Intelligence Communities and International Law: A Comparative Approach* (this volume).

costs on the state. The other states would like that state to be inside the regime, but do not want to give in on the provision as a general matter. There are several options: (1) the other states could conclude the treaty among themselves, excluding the state in question; (2) they could allow an explicit carveout of the particular provision, making it explicitly inapplicable to the state in question; or (3) they could conclude the treaty, but allow states to make reservations of minor provisions.

The last option is the one that has been adopted in modern treaty law and practice, a decision that emphasizes breadth of participation over depth of obligation. Reservations are generally allowed so long as the treaty in question does not prohibit them, and the reservation is not "incompatible with the object and purpose of the treaty."[7] Reserving states must inform the other treaty parties of the reservation.[8] Reservations are then deposited along with the instrument of ratification with the depositary; this gives the other states parties the opportunity to object within one year of being informed.[9] An objection is an announcement by a state that it does not accept (fully or in part) a reservation made by another state; often they will be accompanied by a claim that the reservation violates the object and purpose of the treaty. As is evident, objections typically occur early in the formation of the treaty regime, after the instrument has been negotiated but during the process of ratification. [10] If no objection is lodged within the year, the state is deemed to have accepted the treaty reservation, and the reserving state is deemed to be a party to the treaty.

Before delving into objections, we should clarify why option 3 (allowing reservations) has been preferred over option 1 (multiple treaties among the treaty parties) or option 2 (an explicit carveout for one state). The answer in both cases is that it saves on transaction costs. Indeed, historically reservation practice evolved out of the classical scheme of unanimous consent over treaty provisions (option 1 above). Excluding a state, on the basis of a single provision it would not agree to, does not in any way preclude the formation of bilateral relations between that state and some of the others, absent the provision. So the excluded state could go to each of the various treaty parties, negotiate a treaty that is similar but without the single excluded provision. It would still get some of the treaty benefits, but with significant transaction costs in terms of multiple bilateral negotiations. The scheme of allowing a state to "reserve" was a way of avoiding these transaction costs, while shifting the burden onto states that did not accept the reservation.[11] Option 2, an ex ante carveout,

---

7. Vienna Convention on the Law of Treaties art. 19, *opened for signature* May 23, 1969, 1155 U.N.T.S. 331.

8. *Id.*, art. 23.

9. *Id.*, art. 20.5.

10. They may occur before or after the treaty actually enters into force, depending on the time of the reservation.

11. Swaine argues that the Pan-American system used this scheme. Edward Swaine, *Treaty Reservations, in* THE OXFORD GUIDE TO TREATIES 277, 282 (Duncan Hollis ed., 2012). *See also* Edward Swaine, *Reserving*, 31 YALE J. INT'L L. 307 (2006).

would also raise transaction costs in the context of complex multilateral schemes involving polycentric choices.

The scheme of allowing reservations was blessed by the International Court of Justice in the famous case *Reservations to the Convention on the Prevention and Punishment of the Crime of Genocide.*[12] The Court considered whether reservations to the Genocide Convention were allowable, given that the Convention was silent on the matter. The Court allowed the reservations on the theory that human rights treaties required broad consent, and that reservations were worth it to obtain the desired universality. The Court famously limited reservations, though, to those that did not conflict with object and purpose of the treaty, language that was later incorporated into the Vienna Convention.[13] In other words, minor reservations were allowed, but core obligations could not be avoided. This created a need for interpretation as to what exactly constitutes the object and purpose of a treaty.

What is to prevent a state from gratuitously reserving core obligations? In the absence of a court of general jurisdiction to act as an authoritative interpreter, the possibility of divergent views is great. The interpretive "enforcers" of the object and purpose requirement were to be other states, which could object if an incompatible reservation was issued. Objections thus originate as a decentralized mechanism of monitoring treaty obligations in a scheme designed to maximize breadth but not depth. As we will describe below, there is likely to be an undersupply of this monitoring.

The legal effect of the objection depends in the first instance on the objecting state. The basic rule is that, unless the objecting state asserts that the entire treaty is not in force as between the two states in question, only the limitations contained in the reservation will not apply. As Article 21(3) of the Vienna Convention on the Law of Treaties puts it, "the provisions to which the reservation relates do not apply as between the two States to the extent of the reservation." But this is odd: the result in many cases may be the same that would obtain if no objection were filed, since the standard effect of *accepted* reservations is that the provision does not apply![14] The objector can also assert that the treaty has no force at all between the two states.[15] But, in the human rights context in particular, this is a weak remedy. As human rights treaties are largely concerned with *others'* performance of an objective set of standards for treatment of their own populations,

---

12. Advisory Opinion, 1951 I.C.J. 15 (May 28). The reservation of the United States was particularly controversial. The second reservation read "[t]hat nothing in the Convention requires or authorizes legislation or other action by the United States of America prohibited by the Constitution of the United States as interpreted by the United States."

13. *See also* Vienna Convention on the Law of Treaties, *supra* note 7, art. 19(c).

14. *See* Curtis Bradley & Jack Goldsmith, *Treaties, Human Rights, and Conditional Consent*, 149 Pa. L. Rev. 399, 438 (2000); see also the discussion in Goodman, *supra* note 3, at 531–35. Admittedly, this is not quite accurate when a reservation simply modifies a provision. In that case, objecting removes the provision entirely, whereas non-objections would lead to the reserved version applying.

15. Vienna Convention on the Law of Treaties, *supra* note 7, art 21(3).

asserting that the treaty has no application does little good to advance the object and purpose of the treaty.[16]

In many cases, the objector simply claims that the reservation violates the object and purpose, that the reservation is generally invalid, or that it hopes that the reserving state will withdraw the reservation. These can be seen as "fire alarm" claims that seek to mobilize other states to follow the particular interpretation that has been advanced. Here the objecting state is taking action to note that another state is undermining the treaty regime, in some sense engaging in a kind of monitoring and enforcement action.

Some states, particularly Nordic countries, have asserted a right to object in a way that retains full effect of the treaty as originally negotiated, essentially saying the reservation is severable and void, and that the full treaty applies as between the two parties.[17] This approach is more consistent with the idea of objections as decentralized enforcement than is the standard approach, which essentially disincentivizes objections. That is, the objecting states' actions under severability will have the effect of maximizing the applicability of the treaty norms. But this approach is not accepted by all states.

As Swaine summarizes, the whole regime of the Vienna Convention is decentralized: "individual states propose reservations, individual states accept or object to reservations, and individual states determine what results from these exchanges, subject to the rules they have agreed to in the convention."[18] This scheme, codified in the Vienna Convention on the Law of Treaties, allows ample opportunities for strategic behavior. A state can negotiate the general provisions of a treaty in a way that maximizes its benefits, then reserve provisions that impose costs on it, while still gaining most of the benefits of the scheme of cooperation. Such a state will be able to do so absent a strong objection that asserts the reservation is incompatible with the object and purpose of the treaty; even this will have little concrete impact unless other states join the objection, and assert that the treaty still applies.

As mentioned above, the human rights context raises distinct difficulties for the general scheme. In, say, a multilateral trade treaty, objecting states might deny the reserving states the benefits under the treaty if they find that the reservation is invalid. But what precisely does this mean in a context in which the beneficiaries of the treaty are found wholly within the borders of the reserving state? For an objector to say that the reserving state is not a party to the treaty is to say the citizens of the reserver are not protected by the treaty's human rights provisions. It is this problem that the Nordic approach, asserting that the treaty is still in force, is designed to address.[19]

---

16. *See generally* Goodman, *supra* note 3. To be sure, if one adopts the "commitment" perspective as to why states adopt human rights treaties, there may be costs imposed on the reserving state by being excluded from the regime. *See* Andrew Moravcsik, *The Origins of International Human Rights Regimes: Democratic Delegation in Postwar Europe*, 54 INT'L ORG. 217 (2000).

17. Swaine, *Treaty Reservations, supra* note 11, at 294; *see also* Goodman, *supra* note 3, at 547.

18. Swaine, *Treaty Reservations, supra* note 11, at 298.

19. This is consistent with the idea that Nordic countries are norm entrepreneurs in the area of human rights. *See* Christine Ingebritsen, *Norm Entrepreneurs: Scandinavia's Role in World Politics*, 37 COOPERATION & CONFLICT 11 (2002).

One comes away from this analysis with the feeling that there is little incentive for states to bear the costs of objecting; indeed, the International Court of Justice (ICJ) itself, in the *Case concerning Armed Activities on the Territory of the Congo*, has asserted that states do not frequently object to others' reservations.[20] No wonder, perhaps, that multilateral treaties are relatively weak instruments, and why the most recent schemes of global cooperation are moving away from this form. The Rome Statute famously deviates from the standard model by disallowing reservations; more broadly, multilateral treaties in general may be a thing of the past.[21] If reservations law favors breadth over depth, then proponents of deeper obligations may be trying to find alternative modalities of cooperation.

It is interesting to note that regimes with centralized interpretive bodies tend to prefer to minimize reservations, instead of relying on the decentralized mechanism of objections. The Human Rights Committee, the centralized monitor of the ICCPR, takes the view that human rights treaties do not allow incompatible reservations, and that they are severable, leaving the treaty intact even as to the reserving party.[22] The International Law Commission approach seems to follow this logic in that it presumes that reserving states desire to be subject to the treaty, even if the reservation is objected to, unless the state expressed otherwise.[23] The Human Rights Committee has also asserted that it has competence to evaluate whether a reservation was incompatible with the object and purpose of the treaty. These assertions drew sharp rebuke from powerful states. Whatever one thinks of the Human Rights Committee, its proposal makes sense from the perspective of incentivizing enforcement. Centralized enforcement of the object and purpose requirement has a distinct advantage over decentralized enforcement.

Another scheme with centralized enforcement is the European Convention on Human Rights. In one prominent case, the European Court of Human Rights (ECtHR) found that reservations were severable. When Switzerland sought to enter into the Convention while reserving Article 6 (which provides for a right to a fair trial), the ECHR rejected the reservation by Switzerland as invalid and found that the country remained bound by the treaty, even though no state had objected to the reservation at the time that it was made.[24] As with the position of the Human

---

20. 2006 I.C.J. 31, 65–71 (Feb. 3) (joint separate opinion of Judges Higgins, Kooijmans, Eleraby, Owada, and Simma).

21. *See* AJIL Unbound, *The End of Treaties? An Online Agora*, http://www.asil.org/blogs/ajil-unbound.

22. Hum. Rts. Comm., General Comment No. 24 (52), U.N. Doc. CCPR/C/21/Rev.1/Add.6 (Nov. 11, 1994).

23. The Guide to Practice on Reservations to Treaties was finalized by the International Law Commission in 2011. U.N. Doc. A/66/10/Add. 1. Guideline 4.5.3 says that "The status of the author of an invalid reservation in relation to a treaty depends on the intention expressed by the reserving State or international organization on whether it intends to be bound by the treaty without the benefit of the reservation or whether it considers that it is not bound by the treaty."

24. Belilos v. Switzerland, 132 Eur. Ct. H.R. (ser. A), at para. 47 (1987) ("The [Swiss] Government derived an additional argument from the fact that there had been no reaction from the Secretary

Rights Committee, it was the centralized interpreter that played the role of ensuring the validity of reservations.

Conversely, this suggests that when there is no centralized interpreter, it will be the decentralized community of states parties, with their potentially diverse approaches to interpreting the treaty document, that play the major role in policing overly broad reservations from the treaty obligations. This creates a collective action problem among the states parties.

II. WHY OBJECT?

What might lead a state to bear the costs of advancing the goals of human rights treaties by objecting to incompatible reservations? Consider three sets of factors: those related to the objecting state itself, those related to the relationship between the reserving state and the potential objector, and those characteristics of the particular reservation.

We begin with state-level factors. An initial point is that objecting may be politically costlier than reserving. Reserving increases a state's degrees of freedom, and so has concentrated benefits, whereas the costs of the state's reduced obligations are diffused broadly onto other treaty parties. Crafting a reservation takes some effort, possibly in the form of coordination between an executive and a legislature. But it remains the case that the state as a whole may benefit from the reservation.

In contrast, objecting has concentrated costs, but diffused benefits, if indeed it is conceptualized as a means of enhancing compliance with the purpose of the regime. The concentrated costs of objections come in several forms. First, objecting states must spend resources to monitor reservations. Second, there may be political costs. The reserving state is likely to be frustrated with the objection and may contest the objector's interpretation of the treaty; in extreme cases it may even retaliate in some form. This might lead states to be reluctant to object.[25]

If objecting is costly, we might expect it to be a characteristic of richer states, as well as those with large legal departments in the foreign ministry.[26] It will also be more desirable for states and governments that can obtain domestic political benefits from enforcement. In the human rights context, richer, democratic states are likelier to have a policy of promoting human rights abroad, and thus bear the costs of objecting. The countries for which this is especially true are those that specifically seek to use human rights *law* as opposed to other policy tools (such as military intervention or economic pressure) to advance human rights.

General of the Council of Europe or from the States Parties to the Convention. . . . The Swiss Government inferred that it could in good faith take the declaration as having been tacitly accepted for the purposes of Article 64. The Court does not agree with that analysis. The silence of the depositary and the Contracting States does not deprive the Convention institutions of the power to make their own assessment . . . "). *Compare* Temeltasch v. Switzerland, App. No. 9116/80, 31 Eur. Comm'n H.R. Dec. & Rep. 120 (1982) (upholding reservations).

25. Goodman, *supra* note 3, at 537.

26. *Id.*

The decision to object is also likely to depend on the relationship between the reserver and potential objector. If the reservation generates negative externalities toward particular other states, we would expect those states to be likelier to object. On the other hand, this source of pressure may be mitigated if the states have dense relations. After all, an objection can be seen as a challenge to a particular state, potentially generating counterattacks. One might expect neighbors, for example, to be more vulnerable and so therefore prefer to free-ride on enforcement activity of other states, if the objection would be perceived as a challenge by the reserver.

In the human rights context, we have already stipulated that there are few negative externalities produced by reservation, in the sense that reduced protection in the reserving state doesn't really harm others' citizens. So no particular state is especially likely to be willing to pay the costs of objecting unless it itself gets some domestic political benefits from doing so. However, we can predict that some states will be particularly *unlikely* to enforce. Those states with denser interactions with the reserver will be more vulnerable to counterattacks, and so less likely to bear the costs of objecting. We might think that geographic and cultural distance between two states will be positively correlated with objections, and that close links will be negatively correlated.

It is also quite likely that the decision to object depends very much on the nature of the reservation. Reservations that are seen as narrowly tailored, good faith efforts to participate in the treaty regime are probably less likely to generate objections than are those that are broadly formulated, and seen to be pretextual. We predict that broader reservations designed to escape obligation will more frequently generate objections than narrower ones.

III. CHARACTERISTICS OF OBJECTIONS: THE ICCPR AS A CASE STUDY

This section provides some descriptive data on objections, focusing initially on the ICCPR as a way of getting a handle on the underlying dynamics. An objection is obviously conditional on the prior existence of a reservation, and we are fortunate that some good recent work has been done on reservations. Eric Neumayer shows that reservations are more common in human rights law than in other areas of law, and are more likely to be adopted by democracies than autocracies.[27] However, in her study of human rights, Beth Simmons finds that democracies are *less* likely to enter reservations.[28] She finds that Muslim countries, common law countries, and those that have the rule of law tend to submit more reservations, likely for diverse reasons. Examining reservations to the ICCPR, Daniel Hill argues that reservations are more likely when (1) domestic legal constraints are significant, and (2) domestic

---

27. Eric Neumayer, *Qualified Ratification: Explaining Reservations to International Human Rights Treaties*, 36 J. LEGAL STUD. 397 (2007); *see also* JACK GOLDSMITH & ERIC POSNER, THE LIMITS OF INTERNATIONAL LAW 127–29 (2005) (showing reservations to the ICCPR).

28. BETH A. SIMMONS, MOBILIZING FOR HUMAN RIGHTS 98–103 (2009).

standards are lax compared with the international agreement, so that international law implies a larger adjustment in behavior.[29] Reservations are thus tied to domestic enforcement.

There is also some suggestion in the literature that states object to reservations less often in the human rights context than in others, though this has not been thoroughly tested.[30] Simmons asserts that objections to human rights treaties are rare.[31] Leblanc, writing on the Convention of the Rights of the Child, concurs "Few states are inclined to object to reservations made by others, even when they seriously undermine the integrity of the convention's provisions."[32] And as noted above, some judges of the ICJ have asserted that objections were rare.[33]

To explore objections practice, we first examine data from the ICCPR. The ICCPR, adopted in 1966 and in force from 1976, has 168 states parties at this writing, and the ratification process has generated numerous reservations. Indeed, a cursory examination of the ICCPR belies the claim that reservations are rare. Out of 168 state parties, some 42 (more than 25 percent) have reserved one or more provisions, with an average of 2.9 articles reserved. A total of 116 individual reservations have been filed, to which 47 different objections have been filed by 29 countries. This suggests that some are willing to bear the costs, and that objecting is more common than heretofore recognized.

Note that the ICCPR is hardly exceptional in this regard. We also analyze the six other major human rights treaties with broadest participation: the Conventions on Discrimination against Women (CEDAW), the Rights of the Child (CRC), the Elimination of Racial Discrimination (CERD), Torture (CAT), Disabilities, and the International Covenant on Economic, Social and Cultural Rights (ICESCR). As Appendix B shows, the other major human rights treaties all have significant numbers of states parties making reservations, ranging from 54 for CEDAW and the CRC, to 41 for the CERD, 29 for the CAT, and 27 each for the ICESCR and the Disabilities Convention. While not every reservation generated objections, each of the treaties had objections by more than a dozen different states parties. These ranged from 26 objections for the CAT, 20 for CEDAW, 18 for the CERD, 16 for the Disabilities Convention, 12 for the ICESCR, and 10 for the CRC. Objecting is clearly not rare behavior.

---

29. Daniel W. Hill, Jr., *Avoiding Obligation: Reservations to Human Rights Treaties*, 60 J. CONFLICT RES. 1129 (2016).

30. Swaine, *Treaty Reservations, supra* note 11, at 297.

31. SIMMONS, *supra* note 28, at 98 ("a very small number of countries take on this policing role").

32. Lawrence J. Leblanc, *Reservations to the Convention on the Rights of the Child*, 4 INT'L J. CHILDREN'S RIGHTS 357, 379 (1996).

33. *Case Concerning Armed Activities on the Territory of the Congo*, 2006 I.C.J. 31, 65–71 (Feb. 3) (joint separate opinion of Judges Higgins, Kooijmans, Eleraby, Owada, and Simma).

A. What Do States Reserve?

In theory, states can reserve for a variety of reasons. Some states might reserve because they have a sincere desire to comply with the treaty, but face significant capacity constraints in implementing it. Obviously some rights provisions are easier to implement than others. Delivering on a right to universal public education requires a massive bureaucratic effort and significant expense; delivering on a right to free speech, on the other hand, simply requires the government to refrain from passing censorship laws. Appendix A lists the ICCPR articles most reserved. By far the most common articles referred to are those concerning the judicial process, which might be seen as recognition that punishment practices vary, but also that reform of the criminal justice process is complex.

Another reason that states may reserve is because of a desire to avoid large portions of the treaty in the event of conflict. Certain states, including the United States and many Muslim countries, put aspects of their domestic legal order above international obligations. Muslim countries frequently make reservations related to sharia and Islamic law, and the United States often objects to treaties on the grounds that it not be required to undertake any behavior incompatible with its own Constitution. In the ICCPR context, the United States has reserved the right to allow freedom of speech that violates Article 20's prohibition against hate speech, and to apply punishments consistent with its own Constitution, even if these violate the ICCPR. Both of these types of reservations, based on sharia law and the domestic constitution, seem to be motivated by a desire to avoid additional legal constraints beyond what is required by the domestic legal order.

Appendix B, column 1 lists the 42 states that have filed reservations to the ICCPR, as of 2013, and the propensity of reserving states to generate objections. (Appendix B also provides a fuller list for all seven human rights treaties examined here.) Table 11.1 lists the bases that states give for their objections. Even a cursory glance shows that the reservations that are presumably grounded in avoiding obligation are far more likely to generate objections than others. The reserving states that have generated the most objections are all Muslim countries: Pakistan, the Maldives, Mauritania, and Bahrain. Other than these countries, only the US reservations have generated double digit objections. Pakistan's ICCPR reservation was in some sense the perfect storm: it asserts "that the provisions of Articles 3, 6, 7, 18 and 19 shall be so applied to the extent that they are not repugnant to the Provisions of the Constitution of Pakistan and the sharia laws."[34] As Table 11.1 shows, the most controversial reservations, likeliest to provoke objections, are those based on sharia law or the domestic constitution.

Sometimes, reservations are clustered by region. For example, the Nordic countries of Denmark, Finland, Iceland, Norway, and Sweden all submitted similar reservations to articles 10 (rights regarding persons in detention), 14 (rights regarding the judicial process) and 20 (prohibiting propaganda for war or racial/religious hatred).

---

34. Reservation of Pakistan. The reservations and objections to the ICCPR cited in this chapter may be found on its treaty status page on the UN Treaty Collection website, http://treaties.un.org.

Table 11.1. BASES OF RESERVATION TO ICCPR

Basis	#	# objected to	p*objection
Domestic Constitution	27	18	.67
Domestic Practices	67	19	.28
Sharia	8	8	1.00
Implementation Problems	7	1	.14
Others	7	1	.14
TOTAL	116	47	.41

Table 11.2. RANK ORDERING OF TOP TEN OBJECTING COUNTRIES: ICCPR AND ALL TREATIES

Rank	Objecting country	ICCPR objections	Objecting country	Total for seven treaty regimes
1	Netherlands	13	Netherlands	63
2	Sweden	9	Sweden	52
3	Germany	9	Germany	48
4	Finland	7	Finland	40
5	Portugal	7	Norway	35
6	France	6	Portugal	30
7	Ireland	5	Austria	23
8	Italy	4	France	19
9	Portugal	4	Ireland	17
10	Austria	3	Denmark	15
10	Denmark	3	Italy	15

B. Who Objects and Why?

Our core concern is to understand the characteristics of the countries that choose to bear the costs of enforcement of the ICCPR regime, through making objections. We can get some leverage by placing the ICCPR objections in the context of other treaty regimes, and so produce an indicator of the total number of objections issued across the seven major human rights treaty regimes listed earlier (including the ICCPR). The ICCPR objections are correlated with the total for the other six at a level of .86, so objecting in one regime seems to predict objecting to another.

As Table 11.2 demonstrates, the top objectors tend to be a small set of European countries, with the four Nordic countries and the Netherlands playing a major role. Outside of North America and Australia, the only non-European countries to ever object to a reservation for any treaty are Mexico, Mongolia, Pakistan, and Uruguay, each of which filed one objection to an ICCPR reservation.[35]

States that frequently object have invested in capacity for monitoring and enforcement. One indicator is the institutionalization of the foreign affairs department. Objecting countries with a separate human rights division in their foreign ministries have objected to an average of 4.5 reservations; those which do not have a separate division objected to an average of 1.3.[36] While causality is uncertain, the correlation seems consistent with our view that objection is costly, and that it is a practice centered in legal departments, rather than the legislature or some other location in the state.

States differ in the form of their objections. Some seem to offer alternative interpretations of the reservation, perhaps allowing the objecting state to try to constrain the implementation of the reservation down the road. Germany seems to be particularly likely to use objections in this way, as four out of its nine objections fit the bill. As mentioned earlier, the Nordic countries consistently declare that the reserving country "does not benefit from the reservation," while the Netherlands consistently declares that the reservation is "inadmissible," or "shall not be permitted."[37] Sweden declares some reservations to be "null and void." It is most common to use the "object and purpose" formulation when making an objection, but sometimes states use the opportunity to make other points about the reservation. Other states simply file objections without elaboration. Mexico's objection to Bahrain's reservation fits this bill. Table 11.3 lists some of the bases of objection in the context of the ICCPR.[38]

We thus have some indication of the factors that seem to predict objection: wealth, democracy, and most likely some capacity in the foreign ministry. Let us look at the other end of the equation: What states' reservations have generated the most objections? Is there anything about the relationship among the reserving and objecting countries that predicts objection? Table 11.4, on the next page, provides a list of the countries whose reservations have generated the most objections, both for the ICCPR and the entire set of seven treaties. Most of the countries in both lists are majority Muslim countries, and many of the most controversial reservations implicate Islam.

---

35. Mexico objected to Bahrain's reservation that "The Government of the Kingdom of Bahrain interprets the Provisions of Article 3, (18) and (23) as not affecting in any way the prescriptions of the Islamic Shariah." Pakistan objected to India's reservation to Article 9(5) (right to compensation for victims of unlawful arrest or detention). Mongolia objected to the Khmer Rouge government's assertion of authority to sign the ICCPR. Uruguay objected to Pakistan's assertion that the Human Rights Committee could not request information from it. While the other countries listed had only one total objection, Mexico was a prolific objector in the CEDAW regime in addition to its ICCPR objections.

36. Jessica Chow, Why Object? An Analysis of the Practice of Objections-to-Reservations in the International Covenant on Civil and Political Rights (ICCPR) (2014) (unpublished master's thesis, University of Chicago).

37. Id.

38. Id.

Table 11.3. RANK ORDERING OF THE BASIS OF OBJECTIONS IN THE ICCPR

Basis of Objection	Total # of times this reason has been utilized (out of 116 objections)
Violates object and purpose of treaty	92
Reservation is unclear and does not clarify the extent to which the state considers itself bound by treaty obligations/therefore reassess doubt about the country's commitment	87
Convention specifically prohibits derogation (from specific articles)	31
International treaty law prohibits invoking of domestic law for failure to comply with treaty	30
Reservations were submitted to essential articles which are of great importance to the ICCPR	7
Behavior may constitute a precedent that might have considerable effects at the international level	2

Table 11.4. RANK ORDERING OF COUNTRIES WITH MOST OBJECTED-TO RESERVATIONS

Rank	ICCPR objections received		Total objections over seven treaties	
	Country	ICCPR Objections	Country	Total Objections
1	Pakistan	26	Pakistan	59
2	Maldives	18	UAE	28
3	Bahrain	14	Bahrain	23
4	USA	11	Saudi Arabia	23
5	Mauritania	10	Thailand	23
6	Botswana	9	Turkey	21
7	Laos	6	Syria	20
8	Turkey	6	Mauritania	19
9	Kuwait	4	Laos	18
10	Korea, South	3	Maldives	18
11	Algeria	2	Iran	16
11	Trinidad and Tobago	2	Malaysia	16
			Qatar	16

This is especially true when one moves from the ICCPR context to the treaties that touch most heavily on family law: CRC and CEDAW. Appendix B shows just how controversial these treaties are, in the sense of generating a good deal of reservations and objections thereto.

Combined with the earlier findings, we can say that there seems to be something relational going on that predicts objection. Reserving states that emphasize sovereign particularity, such as the United States, trigger objections, but it also seems that much of objections practice is part of an intense contest between two universalisms: international human rights law and Islam. In carving out limits to general treaties on the basis of Islam, reserving states have induced European countries to reassert the universality of human rights law. This contest, while taking place in the terrain of international treaty practice, reflects much deeper comparative divergence in the understanding of the purposes of international law.

IV. CONCLUSION

Far from being rare, objections to treaty reservations are very common, at least in the human rights treaties examined here. We have argued that the intensive activity among states in making reservations and issuing objections reflects different approaches to treaty interpretation, particularly over how broadly to read the object and purpose of human rights treaties. Given the background legal limitations on reservations, reserving states are implicitly interpreting human rights treaties to require less of states parties, whereas objecting states are reading the object and purpose requirement broadly.

Objections may also reflect very different ideas as to the purpose of treaties: one country could be using treaties to signal to a domestic audience, while others seek genuine constraint at the international level. These divergent purposes may inform different treaty practices.

It has often been asserted that international human rights law, as embodied in the ICCPR, involves cheap talk among states.[39] Yet, as a matter of comparative international law, this is too broad a statement. We have argued that objecting to treaty reservations is costly, and we thus expect states to free-ride. Yet, there are a small number of states that do repeatedly object to treaty reservations. Repeat objectors are all found in Europe, and concentrated in the northern latitudes. This reflects a different approach to international law than, say, majority Muslim countries that make sharia law-based objections. The objecting states have helped overcome a free-riding problem that might lead to a kind of race to the bottom in terms of obligation, with each state maximizing its degree of interpretive freedom at the expense of the regime as a whole. Their behavior is designed, it seems, to police the "cheap talk" quality of international human rights law.

---

39. ERIC POSNER, THE TWILIGHT OF HUMAN RIGHTS LAW (2015); GOLDSMITH & POSNER, *supra* note 27.

APPENDIX A

RANK ORDERING OF ICCPR ARTICLES, BY NUMBER OF RESERVATIONS SUBMITTED[40]

	Articles	Total reservations	No. of reservations that received at least 1 objection
Art 14	Rights regarding how a person must be treated by the judicial process	25	4
Art 10	Rights regarding judicial process	15	3
Art 20	Prohibits propaganda for war or racial/religious hatred	13	2
Art 12	Rights for movement into, out of, and within a state	7	3
Art 25	Right to political participation	6	2
Art 19	Freedom of expression	5	1
Art 22	Freedom of association	5	2
Art 9	Right to liberty and physical security	4	2
Art 13	Rights regarding movement out of a state	4	1
Art 3	Universality of rights	3	3
Art 7	Freedom from torture	3	3
Art 23	Rights pertaining to marriage	3	2
Art 26	Equality of persons before the law	3	1
Art 4	Provisions pertaining to derogation	2	1
Art 6	Protection of life	2	2
Art 11	Rights regarding imprisonment	2	1
Art 18	Freedom of religion	2	2
Art 21	Right to peaceful assembly	2	1
Art 1	Right to self-determination	1	1
Art 2	Universality of rights	1	1
Art 15	Prohibits retrospective criminal punishment	1	1
Art 17	Right to privacy	1	0
Art 24	Rights pertaining to children	1	0
Art 27	Group rights protecting a community of individuals	1	1

40. Chow, *supra* note 36.

APPENDIX B

OBJECTIONS RECEIVED TO RESERVATIONS

KEY: 0 indicates a reservation without objections; * indicates that reservation was withdrawn after objection.

Reserving Country	ICCPR	ICESCR	CEDAW	CRC	CAT	CERD	Conv. on Disabilities	TOTAL
Pakistan	26	4	6		23			59
Afghanistan				0	0	0		0
Algeria	2	2	3	0				7
Andorra				1				1
Antigua Barbuda						0		0
Argentina				0				0
Australia	1		0	0		0	0	1
Austria	0		0	0	0	0		0
Azerbaijan							1	1
Bahamas	0	0	0	0	0	0		0
Bahrain	14	0	9		0	0		23
Bangladesh	0	3	4	2	4			13
Barbados	0	0				0		0
Belgium	0	0		0		0	0	0
Belize	0							0
Botswana	9			3	3			15
Brazil			0*					0
Brunei			0	7				7

Bulgaria				0		0
Canada			0		0	0
Chile	3		0	0		0
China			0	0		3
Colombia			0			0
Congo	1					1
Cook Islands			0			0
Croatia			0			0
Cuba	0		0	0		0
Cyprus			0		0	0
Denmark	0	0	0			0
Ecuador		0	0			0
Egypt	0	4		0	0	4
El Salvador	0	0	0	0	7	7
Equatorial Guinea			0			0
Ethiopia		0				0
Finland	0					0
France	0	0	0	0	0	0
Gambia	0					0
Germany		0	0			0
Greece					0	0
Grenada				1		1

(Continued)

Reserving Country	ICCPR	ICESCR	CEDAW	CRC	CAT	CERD	Conv. on Disabilities	TOTAL
Guyana	0					0		0
Hungary						0		0
Iceland	0			0				0
India	1	4	1	0		0		6
Indonesia			0		0	0		0
Iran				7			9	16
Iraq			4	0				4
Ireland	0	0	0			0		0
Israel	0		0		0	0	0	0
Italy						0		0
Jamaica			0*	0		0		0
Japan		0		0		0	0	0
Jordan			1	2				3
Kiribati				3				3
Korea, North			9					9
Korea, South	3		7			0	1	11
Kuwait	4	6	4			0	0	14
Laos	6				12			18
Lebanon			3			0		3
Lesotho			2					2
Libya			6			0		6
Liechtenstein	0			1				1
Lithuania							0	0

248

Country							
Luxembourg	0		2				2
Madagascar		0			0		0
Malaysia		8				8	16
Maldives	18	0					18
Mali		0					0
Malta	0				0	0	0
Mauritania	10	0	9	0			19
Mauritius			0*				0
Mexico	0		0				0
Micronesia			3			0	3
Monaco	0	0	0	0	0	0	0
Mongolia					0		0
Morocco		0	1	0	0		1
Mozambique					0		0
Nepal					0		0
Netherlands	0	0	0	0		0	0
New Zealand	0	0	0	0		0	0
Niger			4				4
Norway	0					0	0
Oman		5	0		0		5
Papua New Guinea							0
Poland		0			0	0	0

(Continued)

Reserving Country	ICCPR	ICESCR	CEDAW	CRC	CAT	CERD	Conv. on Disabilities	TOTAL
Qatar				7	9			16
Samoa				0				0
Saudi Arabia			9	6	0	8		23
Singapore			3	7			1	11
Spain			0	0				0
Sweden	0	0						0
Switzerland	0		0					0
Syria			14	6	0		0	20
Thailand	1	0	4	1	9	4	4	23
Trinidad and Tobago	2	0	0					2
Tunisia				0	0			0
Turkey	6	6	3	3	0	3		21
UAE			14	2	12			28
United Kingdom	0	0	0	0			0	0
Uruguay				0				0
USA	11				3			14
Venezuela	0		0	0			0	0
Vietnam			0		0			0
Yemen			0			13		13
TREATY TOTAL	116	27	54	54	29	41	27	478

Intelligence Communities and International Law

A Comparative Approach

ASHLEY S. DEEKS[*]

I. INTRODUCTION

How must states' intelligence communities (ICs) approach their international law obligations? From the perspective of international law itself, there is a fairly clear answer: like all substate entities, ICs must comply with those international obligations that their states have assumed.[1] International law does not allow certain substate actors to invoke their domestic laws and structures as an excuse for ignoring international law.[2]

And yet intelligence activities—recruiting foreign assets, conducting electronic surveillance on foreign leaders, and undertaking covert actions[3] to influence political and economic conditions in other states—look very different from traditional statecraft. Espionage and covert action frequently take place inside the territory of

[*] Thanks to Jack Goldsmith, Rebecca Ingber, Marty Lederman, and Matthew Waxman for helpful comments.

1. *See generally* Human Rights Council, Compilation of Good Practices on Legal and Institutional Frameworks and Measures That Ensure Respect for Human Rights by Intelligence Agencies While Countering Terrorism, Including on Their Oversight, A/HRC/14/46, ¶ 6 (May 17, 2010).

2. Vienna Convention on the Law of Treaties art. 27, *opened for signature* May 23, 1969, 1155 U.N.T.S. 331.

3. By "covert action," I mean an act undertaken to achieve military, economic, or political goals, with the expectation that the state taking the action will decline to acknowledge its participation in that act. *See, e.g.,* 50 U.S.C. § 3093 (2012). Whether any particular covert action is consistent with applicable international law depends on the nature of that action. Alexandra H. Perina, *Black Holes and Open Secrets: The Impact of Covert Action on International Law*, 53 COLUM. J. TRANSNAT'L L. 507 (2015); Michael Reisman, *Covert Action*, 20 YALE J. INT'L L. 419, 420 (1995).

Comparative International Law. Edited by Anthea Roberts et al. © Anthea Roberts, Paul B. Stephan, Pierre-Hugues Verdier, Mila Versteeg 2018. Published 2018 by Oxford University Press.

other states in secret, using techniques intended to be undetectable. These acts often appear, at least at first glance, to be in tension with international law constraints. Moreover, states rarely articulate their views about the relationship between intelligence activities and international law. These factors render state-to-state conversations about these activities extremely fraught. Most states neither proclaim the legality nor concede the illegality of their intelligence activities under international law, seeming to prefer the ambiguity of the status quo.

This lack of certainty about the precise status of various intelligence activities in international law fosters conditions under which states can choose—and have chosen—different paths through the thicket. This chapter compares how certain states' ICs approach their international law obligations. Its unit of analysis is executive practice, because the executive in most legal systems plays a dominant role in developing and executing intelligence activities. The United Kingdom asserts that its IC's activities comply with international law. The United States is far more circumspect about whether its IC uniformly complies with international law. The United States even acknowledges that its domestic law authorizes some violations of international law, but employs various compensatory techniques to minimize overt international law violations. These two contrasting approaches—which have come to light in the wake of Edward Snowden's leaks about foreign electronic surveillance programs—offer lessons about the capacity of international law to constrain core national security activities.

The competing approaches reveal distinct domestic legal regimes, interpretive mechanisms, policy rationales, and effects on the contents of international legal norms. Given the difficulty in reconciling some IC activity with certain substantive international law commitments, the UK approach—which apparently requires absolute compliance with human rights law and international humanitarian law, and likely compliance with all of the United Kingdom's international law obligations—creates incentives to contort existing interpretations of particular international rules that arguably could apply to IC activity. This, in turn, may affect that state's interpretation of these international laws in other, more "normalized" areas. The United States, in contrast, concededly contemplates the possibility that certain IC actions may violate international law, though it avoids specific public statements about whether and when such deviations occur. The United States also avers that at least some IC actions, such as foreign surveillance, fall outside the purview of international regulation (a conclusion that attracts criticism from several quarters), implying that those actions are lawful, even under international law. This approach may result in more cases in which international law is inapplicable or is violated, but it may also protect international law in its "ordinary" contexts. For those seeking to preserve the overall integrity and viability of particular international rules, these divergent approaches each pose problems and offer benefits.

Methodologically, this chapter adopts an approach to comparative international law that draws from the analysis of two "most similar systems."[4] One might expect

---

4. Katerina Linos, *Methodological Guidance: How to Select and Develop Comparative International Law Case Studies*, at 45 (this volume). Of course, the United States and United Kingdom are not similar in every way. As a result, this chapter does not posit the precise cause of the differences in their

the United Kingdom and United States—wealthy, democratic, internationally-engaged states with extensive intelligence capabilities—to approach the issues similarly; the fact that they do not allows us to begin to identify factors that account for those differences.[5]

II. INTELLIGENCE AND INTERNATIONAL LAW: THE TRADITION

Before examining the approaches of various states to IC compliance with international law, it is important to note that in at least one important area of IC activities—espionage—the application and scope of international law restraints is itself deeply uncertain.[6] International law traditionally has had little to say about how, when, and where governments may spy on other states and foreign citizens. Historically, spying was heavily driven by states' efforts to collect intelligence about foreign government decision-making. Most states that were able to spy did so, seeing it as a key national security and foreign policy tool. States faced little pressure from each other or from the public to regulate their intelligence activities and sensibly concluded that the benefits to unregulated spying were high and the corresponding costs were few.

Specifically, spying has proven hard to regulate for five reasons.[7] First, spying implicates a state's core national security interests in anticipating hostile actions by states and terrorist groups and countering strategic threats.[8] States therefore have been loath to reduce their own flexibility to protect themselves by any means that are not obviously unlawful. Second, espionage is intended to occur without detection; the secrecy that attaches to such acts would make it difficult for one state to detect violations of an agreement that reciprocally limits spying. As a result, a state

respective approaches to international law; instead, it identifies explanations for those differences that warrant further exploration.

5. *Id.* Indeed, British and US intelligence have cooperated very closely since World War II, which gives their distinct approaches even greater salience.

6. Espionage is not the only intelligence activity that may operate outside the reach of international law constraints. Some argue that international law does not purport to regulate various forms of covert action either. *See* Michael Adams, *Jus Extra Bellum: Reconstructing the Ordinary, Realistic Conditions of Peace,* 5 HARV. NAT'L SECURITY J. 377, 402–03 (2014) ("Of particular relevance . . . is international law's silence on countless low-visibility national security activities, including forms of intelligence collection, clandestine activities, covert action, and low visibility operations."); Robert D. Williams, *(Spy) Game Change: Cyber Networks, Intelligence Collection, and Covert Action,* 79 GEO. WASH. L. REV. 1162, 1165, 1178 (2011) ("The status of covert actions under transnational legal regimes is a subject of some debate, but there are no treaties or customary norms that explicitly proscribe the practice. . . . The status of covert action under international law is at least as uncertain as the status of espionage."). *But see* Perina, *supra* note 3, at 535 (arguing that international law applies to covert actions). The rest of this section emphasizes espionage, but many of the same arguments apply to non-forcible covert actions such as distribution of propaganda and payments to foreign officials.

7. *See* Ashley S. Deeks, *An International Legal Framework for Surveillance,* 55 VA. J. INT'L L. 291 (2015).

8. Loch K. Johnson, *Spies,* FOREIGN POL'Y (Sept. 2000).

will be less likely to enter into such a commitment. Third, states closely guard their spying capacities. It is difficult for states seriously to discuss ways to limit spying on other states without revealing certain information about those capabilities. Fourth, states with high levels of expertise have incentives to resist excessive regulation. Finally, because much spying historically was quite costly, states rarely directed their focus against nonstate actors. As a result, public pressure to regulate spying previously was minimal, because spying rarely affected the average citizen.

In the face of these incentives not to regulate espionage, there was until recently significant consensus about international law's relation to espionage. With a few exceptions discussed below, most scholars agreed that international law either failed to regulate spying or affirmatively permitted it. One group, drawing on the *Lotus* case in the Permanent Court of International Justice, invoked the proposition that, in the absence of a positive rule, states are free to act as they see fit.[9] Another group interpreted the widespread state practice of espionage as indicating that states affirmatively recognize a right to engage in that conduct under international law.[10]

Notwithstanding this general historical consensus, the Snowden leaks have begun to foster a transformation in thinking, at least among human rights and civil liberties groups and certain states. These groups have identified various bodies of international law that could be read to regulate spying, though some of those bodies lack precise content and have not been read consistently by states to inhibit either human intelligence collection or foreign surveillance. One source of law is the International Covenant on Civil and Political Rights (ICCPR).[11] Article 17(1) states, "No one shall be subjected to arbitrary or unlawful interference with his privacy, family, home or correspondence, nor to unlawful attacks on his honour and reputation." Human rights groups argue that various types of foreign surveillance constitute an unlawful interference with privacy, even though few courts, treaty bodies, or states to date have viewed that treaty as extending to purely foreign intelligence collection. States may begin to interpret the right to privacy in this way, but the application and nature of that right is nascent.[12]

9. *See, e.g.*, DEP'T OF DEF. OFFICE OF GEN. COUNSEL, AN ASSESSMENT OF INTERNATIONAL LEGAL ISSUES IN INFORMATION OPERATIONS 6 (2d ed. 1999); Gary Brown, *The Wrong Questions About Cyberspace*, 217 MIL. L. REV. 214 (2013); Nigel Inkster, *The Snowden Revelations: Myths and Misapprehensions*, SURVIVAL (Nov. 15, 2013).

10. *See, e.g.*, Myres S. McDougal, Harold D. Lasswell & W. Michael Reisman, *The Intelligence Function and World Public Order*, 46 TEMP. L.Q. 365, 394 (1973); Jeffrey H. Smith, *State Intelligence Gathering and International Law*, 28 MICH. J. INT'L L. 543, 544 (2007). For recent examples of states spying on each other, see David Sanger, *In Spy Uproar, "Everyone Does It" Just Won't Do*, N.Y. TIMES, Oct. 25, 2013.

11. International Covenant on Civil and Political Rights art. 17(1), *adopted* Dec. 16, 1966, 999 U.N.T.S. 171. For states parties to the Council of Europe, the European Convention on Human Rights provides another potentially relevant international obligation. Article 8 establishes a right to respect for privacy and correspondence, subject to limited interference.

12. Current and former state leaders and human rights groups effectively concede as much. *See* Ryan Gallagher, *After Snowden Leaks, Countries Want Digital Privacy Enshrined in Human Rights*

Another potential source of international regulation is the Vienna Convention on Diplomatic Relations (VCDR), which requires all persons receiving diplomatic immunity to "respect the laws and regulations of the receiving State."[13] Likewise, the treaty requires receiving states to treat foreign missions and archives as inviolable.[14] One could interpret these provisions as an agreement that diplomats and receiving states will not spy on each other. However, recent (and historical) news reports are rife with descriptions of spying conducted from within and against diplomatic posts.[15] In view of this practice, it would be a notable change for states to interpret the VCDR to prohibit such activities.[16]

Third, some scholars and advocates urge states to interpret the customary international law (CIL) principles of sovereignty[17] and territorial integrity as regulating espionage and other intelligence activities. Though widely treated as foundational concepts in international law, the substantive content of these broad principles remains nebulous. One might argue that surveillance interferes indirectly with the internal affairs of another state by detecting communications related to those affairs.[18] One also might argue that the principle of territorial integrity "negates the general permissibility of strategic observation in foreign territory."[19] But the widespread and long-standing practice of (human or electronic) spying by many states during time periods that both precede and postdate the norms' development complicates arguments that these CIL principles were intended to prohibit espionage. Yet it is not hard to see how such provisions have *some* relevance to physical

---

Treaty, SLATE, Sept. 26, 2013 (describing Germany's efforts to clarify that the ICCPR applied to electronic privacy); *Jagland: International Spy Laws Necessary After Snowden Leaks*, UPI, Nov. 20, 2013 (former Norwegian prime minister arguing for new international laws applicable to new surveillance technologies); Laura Pitter, Comments of Human Rights Watch, Privacy and Civil Liberties Oversight Board Hearing on the Surveillance Program Operated Pursuant to Section 702 of the Foreign Intelligence Surveillance Act, Mar. 19, 2014, at 8.

13. Vienna Convention on Diplomatic Relations art. 41, 18 April, 1961, 500 U.N.T.S. 95. The domestic laws of many states criminalize espionage.

14. *Id.*, arts. 22, 24.

15. Jens Glusing, Laura Poitras, Marcel Rosenbach & Holger Stark, *NSA Accessed Mexican President's Email*, DER SPIEGEL, Oct. 20, 2013; Spiegel Staff, *How NSA Spied on Merkel Cell Phone from Berlin Embassy*, DER SPIEGEL, Oct. 27, 2013; George Roberts, *Indonesia Summons Australian Ambassador to Jakarta Greg Moriarty over Spying Reports*, ABC, Nov. 1, 2013.

16. *See* Smith, *supra* note 10, at 544 (stating that he could recall no instance in which a state accused another state of violating international law when the latter allowed its intelligence officers to operate under diplomatic cover).

17. James Crawford has defined "sovereignty" to mean "the collection of rights held by a state, first in its capacity as the entity entitled to exercise control over its territory and second in its capacity to act on the international plane, representing that territory and its people." JAMES CRAWFORD, BROWNLIE'S PRINCIPLES OF PUBLIC INTERNATIONAL LAW 448 (8th ed. 2010).

18. Quincy Wright, *Espionage and the Doctrine of Non-intervention in Internal Affairs*, *in* ESSAYS ON ESPIONAGE AND INTERNATIONAL LAW 1, 12 (Wright et al. eds., 1962).

19. JOHN KISH, INTERNATIONAL LAW AND ESPIONAGE 84 (1995).

intrusions into one state by another to gather intelligence or conduct certain non-forcible covert actions.

Finally, for intelligence activities that take place in the context of armed conflict, the laws of armed conflict are relevant to those activities.[20] The greater quantity of activities undertaken by intelligence services during armed conflict is a relatively new development, attributable to changes in the actors posing threats to states and the globalization of those networks.[21]

In short, the status of espionage and certain other intelligence activities in international law is unsettled. This gives states the opportunity to take different legal approaches to these activities. Until recently, states have largely remained reticent about their positions, preferring to keep intelligence activities in the shadows. But the Snowden revelations shined a new light on a major subcategory of spying, forcing the discussion about electronic surveillance onto the international stage and creating occasions for states to take more public positions on the relationship between ICs and international law. The next section considers and compares two of those divergent positions.

III. INTERNATIONAL LAW COMPLIANCE BY INTELLIGENCE COMMUNITIES: DIVERGENT APPROACHES

Snowden's revelations and other recent debates, such as those about targeted killings, have flushed out a long-running but under-analyzed issue: assuming a state's international law obligations apply to its IC's activities, how do states reconcile those obligations with the actions of their ICs? One set of states expressly accepts that its ICs must comply with international law, but then must engage in strained readings of that law's substance. Another state is far more circumspect about whether and how its IC complies with international law, but employs various compensatory techniques to minimize overt acknowledgment of international law violations, and to minimize actual violations as well. This section dissects and analyzes the competing approaches, identifying trade-offs between preserving the integrity of international law generally and the meaning of discrete international rules in particular.

A. Methodology

I selected the United Kingdom and United States as representative of these contrasting approaches for two reasons: first, because they represent "most similar

---

20. *See* Venice Comm'n, Opinion on the International Legal Obligations of Council of Europe Member States in Respect of Secret Detention Facilities and Inter-State Transport of Prisoners, CDL-AD(2006)009 (Mar. 17, 2006).

21. *See* Richard Aldrich, *International Intelligence Cooperation in Practice, in* INTERNATIONAL INTELLIGENCE COOPERATION AND ACCOUNTABILITY 20 (Hans Born et al. eds., 2011) (describing intelligence operations today as "more kinetic and more controversial"); The Report of the Detainee Inquiry 5.7, Dec. 2013 [hereinafter Detainee Inquiry] (Before 2001, UK SIS lacked experience in interviewing detainees in the field because of lack of operational need.).

systems,"[22] such that their different approaches to IC compliance with international law is striking; and second, because we know the most about the practices of these states. Because UK and US surveillance activities have come under extensive scrutiny recently, those two states have had a greater number of occasions than other states to discuss the relationship between intelligence activities and international law. Given the inherently secret nature of intelligence activities, few other states have set forth clearly whether, how, and to what extent their ICs' actions are consistent with international law. Yet a comparison between the United States and United Kingdom alone offers a fruitful window into how states conceive of the relationship between international law and intelligence activities.

In addition, these two states serve as salient case studies because neither of them takes an extreme approach to IC international law compliance (or noncompliance). States that conduct few or no intelligence activities have incentives to condemn all of those activities as inconsistent with international law, because doing so costs them little. States that conduct significant amounts of espionage and covert action but lack genuinely democratic political systems, a robust press, or self-conceptions that emphasize government openness and law-compliance may care little about potentially applicable international law when engaged in intelligence activities.[23] Assuming that many states have political systems and intelligence capabilities that fall somewhere between those two extremes, it is useful to evaluate the divergent approaches of two states whose practice lies in the middle of the range.

Unlike much comparative international legal analysis, which focuses on judicial decisions or legislation, this chapter examines executive practice. In most states, the executive is responsible for carrying out intelligence activities because it can better ensure the necessary secrecy and is structured to carry out overseas activities. This raises certain challenges for a comparative analysis, particularly because states generally attempt to conceal much of their activity in this area. As a result, it is hard to obtain extensive examples of state practice, either on the macro level (how do states view their ICs' relationship with international law?), or on the micro level (do states interpret a particular intelligence activity as consistent with a particular rule of international law?). Nevertheless, executive branches play a critical role in applying and developing international law; understanding their activities in the intelligence area is indispensable to evaluating how international law has penetrated those activities.

B. Asserted Compliance: The United Kingdom

1. MECHANISMS

The United Kingdom has clearly stated that its IC's activities, including those of the Government Communications Headquarters (GCHQ), the NSA's equivalent, comply with the United Kingdom's international law obligations, including human

---

22. Linos, *supra* note 4, at 12.

23. *See, e.g.*, Daniel Wagner & John Margeson, *The Globalization of Covert Action*, THE WORLD POST, Sept. 9, 2012 (describing Russian industrial sabotage and political assassinations of foreign officials).

rights treaties.[24] GCHQ's own website states that "GCHQ is subject to rigorous legal oversight, and complies with the European Convention on Human Rights."[25] Shortly after Snowden's first leaks, UK Foreign Secretary William Hague testified, "I [] have nothing but praise for the professionalism, dedication and integrity of the men and women of GCHQ. I know from my work with them how seriously they take their obligations under UK and international law."[26]

Foreign surveillance is not the only intelligence activity for which the United Kingdom claims unequivocal international law compliance. In consolidated guidance to intelligence and military officials regarding detention, the UK government stated, "When we work with countries whose practice raises questions about their compliance with international legal obligations, we ensure that our co-operation accords with our own international and domestic obligations."[27] The UK's Secret Intelligence Service (SIS) believes that it must comply with international human rights laws.[28] Indeed, the UK Parliamentary Committee that oversees intelligence activities has stated that "the observance of human rights is an important part of" the training of SIS and the Security Service.[29] Finally, a 2005 SIS policy made clear that SIS staff is bound by the provisions of the Geneva Conventions, the ICCPR, and the Convention Against Torture (CAT).[30]

24. Although this section uses the United Kingdom as the model, several other states follow this general approach. South Africa's constitution states that its security services must act in accordance with CIL and treaties binding on South Africa. Constit. of the Repub. of S. Africa, No. 108 of 1996, arts. 198–99. Most Council of Europe member states, which are bound by the European Convention on Human Rights (ECHR), likely take an approach similar to the United Kingdom's. *See* Aldrich, *supra* note 21, at 35 ("In the 1990s, the European intelligence services went through a regulatory revolution during which many services were given a legal identity and in some cases the European Convention on Human Rights was written into their core guidance.").

25. GCHQ, *GCH-Who?*, Gchq.gov.uk/Pages/GCH-Who.aspx (last visited Apr. 11, 2016).

26. UK Foreign Secretary William Hague, Statement to the House of Commons, June 10, 2013.

27. Cabinet Office, Consolidated Guidance to Intelligence Officers and Service Personnel on the Detention and Interviewing of Detainees Overseas, ¶ 7 (July 2010), https://www.gov.uk/government/uploads/system/uploads/attachment_data/file/62632/Consolidated_Guidance_November_2011.pdf.

28. Duncan Gardham, *Does MI6 Have a License to Kill?*, Telegraph (UK), Dec. 3, 2012 (quoting MI6's chief as stating that the service is prepared to let terrorist activity proceed in order to stay within UK and international law). *See also* UK Government Response to the Intelligence and Security Committee's Report on Rendition, July 2007, ¶ K, https://www.gov.uk/government/uploads/system/uploads/attachment_data/file/224655/rendition-govt-response.pdf.

29. Intelligence and Security Committee, Report on the Handling of Detainees by UK Intelligence Personnel in Afghanistan, Guantanamo and Iraq, Mar. 1, 2005, ¶ 38. *See also* UK Cabinet Member Kenneth Clarke, Statement to Parliament, Dec. 19, 2013 (noting that the UK expects "there to be strict oversight of those [intelligence] operations to ensure that at all times they respect the human rights that are a cornerstone of this country's values").

30. Detainee Inquiry, *supra* note 21, at 5.60.

These statements likely reflect the fact that the United Kingdom has incorporated the European Convention on Human Rights (ECHR) into its domestic law through the Human Rights Act.[31] Thus, the United Kingdom (including its IC) is bound as a matter of domestic law to comply with the provisions of the ECHR. The United Kingdom, through the International Criminal Court Act 2001, also has criminalized war crimes in its domestic law, using the definitions contained in the Rome Statute.[32] Further, as the result of a 2000 judicial decision, UK ICs may not engage in renditions.[33] It is not clear whether the UK believes that categories of international law other than human rights law and international humanitarian law apply to and constrain its intelligence activities. For instance, as discussed in Section II *supra*, the UK, like some other states, may believe that customary rules such as territorial integrity and respect for other states' sovereignty contain an implicit carveout for human intelligence collection and certain covert actions.[34] At the very least, though, the UK regards international human rights law and international humanitarian law as binding on its IC, including as a matter of domestic law.

Yet assertions that its intelligence activities comply with UK international legal obligations (including the ECHR) appear to compel the UK to take aggressive legal interpretations of international law itself, so as to cabin its scope in a way that is compatible with the imperatives of its IC. For example, by adopting the position that its electronic surveillance activities comply with the ECHR, the UK must argue that Tempora, a program that reportedly intercepts massive amounts of Internet (and maybe telephonic) content and metadata from some 200 fiber-optic cables passing into and out of the UK, constitutes "necessary and proportionate" interference with the right to privacy.[35]

Some have challenged that interpretation. The Interception of Communications Commissioner's report raises questions about whether particular aspects of UK surveillance meet ECHR requirements.[36] Outside groups have argued strongly that Tempora is unlawful (because the program's rules are not clearly prescribed by law) and arbitrary (because the program collects and monitors the communications of millions of people, few of whom are legitimate targets for interception).[37] GCHQ itself reportedly was concerned about legal justifications for some of its electronic

---

31. Human Rights Act 1998, ch. 42 (Eng.).

32. International Criminal Court Act 2001, arts. 50–51 and Schedule 8.

33. R v. Mullen [2000] QB 520.

34. It is not clear from the United Kingdom's public statements whether it believes that its human intelligence collection on foreign soil is consistent with the norm of territorial integrity. It seems more likely that the UK interprets the territorial integrity norm as inapplicable to (or possibly containing a carveout for) intelligence activities such as this.

35. Ewen MacAskill, *GCHQ Taps Fibre-Optic Cables for Secret Access to World's Communications*, GUARDIAN (UK), June 21, 2013.

36. INTERCEPTION OF COMMUNICATIONS COMMISSIONER REPORT ANNUAL 2013, sec. 6.5.49.

37. Privacy Int'l v. Sec'y of State for the Foreign and Commonw. Office, Statement of Grounds, July 8, 2013.

activities. One UK official quoted in a leaked NSA document noted that "continued GCHQ involvement" in a technique used against a foreign telecom provider "may be in jeopardy due to British legal/policy restrictions."[38] Even in the context of defending against current litigation about GCHQ's surveillance, UK counsel said he believed the process was compliant with the ECHR but sought time for further clarification.[39] The UK's Investigatory Powers Tribunal (which oversees UK IC activities) recently concluded that GCHQ's surveillance activities are consistent with the ECHR,[40] though litigants have appealed to the European Court of Human Rights (ECtHR).[41]

Similarly, the United Kingdom's detention guidance states, "In no circumstance will UK personnel ever take action amounting to torture or [cruel, inhuman, or degrading treatment (or CIDT)]." At the same time, the guidance notes that "there is no agreed or exhaustive definition of what constitutes CIDT," and that although CIDT "cover[s] a wide spectrum of conduct," different considerations and legal principles may apply depending on the facts and circumstances of each case.[42] This approach, which suggests flexibility in legal interpretation, prompted the UN Committee Against Torture, in its Concluding Observations on the UK submission, to urge the UK to reword that guidance "to avoid any ambiguity or possible misinterpretation."[43] Specifically, the Committee was concerned that the UK was prepared to accept assurances from foreign intelligence services even in cases in which there was a serious risk of torture or CIDT.[44] The UK has established a robust process by which to obtain and evaluate diplomatic assurances,[45] but its assurances policy remains controversial and has faced court challenges.

The UK faces at least one set of countervailing pressures that limits the extent to which it will take overly aggressive interpretations of international law. If the UK suspects that a particular IC activity will come to light, whether through leaks, litigation, or parliamentary oversight, the UK has incentives to be cautious in its interpretation of relevant provisions of international law, because UK courts and the

38. Kim Zetter, *ISPs File Legal Complaint in Europe over Spying*, WIRED, July 2, 2014.

39. Owen Bowcott, *Government Defends Mass Interception of Online Data at Tribunal*, GUARDIAN (UK), July 14, 2014.

40. Liberty v. Sec'y of State, [2014] UKIPTrib 13_77-H, Dec. 5, 2014.

41. Andrew Griffin, *UK Surveillance on Citizens Is Legal, Rules Spying Authority*, INDEPENDENT (UK), Dec. 5, 2014.

42. Consolidated Guidance, *supra* note 27, ¶¶ 5–7.

43. Committee Against Torture, Concluding Observations on the Fifth Periodic Report of the United Kingdom of Great Britain and Northern Ireland, CAT/C/GBR/CO/5, ¶ 11 (June 24, 2013).

44. *Id.*

45. Fifth Periodic Report of the United Kingdom of Great Britain and Northern Ireland, CAT/C/GBR/5, ¶¶ 43–60 (May 21, 2012).

ECtHR have evidenced some appetite for entertaining claims and holding against the UK IC and military.[46]

2. ANALYSIS

The UK presumably has adopted this approach to international law compliance for two related reasons. First, even if UK domestic law or practice might allow the government to authorize its IC to violate international law in certain limited circumstances,[47] the UK may be loath to hint publicly that any part of its state actions violate international law. Few states choose to declare openly that they have decided to violate a particular rule of international law, but this is particularly true in Europe, where international law is deeply integrated into domestic law.[48] Second, the UK is keenly aware that, if revealed, many of its intelligence actions could face judicial review, including both in UK domestic tribunals and the ECtHR. Even if the UK would prefer to obfuscate its position on international law compliance, it obtains little benefit from failing to claim that its IC complies with UK international legal obligations, given that it almost certainly will have to take that position in litigation anyway. Controversial intelligence policies that come to light in the UK frequently find their way into the ECtHR. This means those policies will be subject to supranational legal assessments by an institution whose mandate is to enforce compliance with international human rights norms. It therefore is unsurprising that, when pressed, the UK claims that its IC complies with international law.

This approach has several implications. First, it seems likely that the UK's need to strictly comply with human rights law and international humanitarian law means that its interpretation of the potentially relevant international norms (such as the right to privacy and the prohibition on cruel, inhuman, and degrading treatment discussed above) will be colored by the activities of its IC. It therefore may find itself adopting certain legal interpretations that may be quite controversial, given the particular circumstances and requirements of intelligence activity. Doing so risks importing those interpretations back into more "normal" governmental activities.[49] Where the IC-related interpretation takes a narrower view of a particular right, that "backwash" could have important implications for the robustness of the right in its more common guises. One analogy is to the trend, seen in some domestic systems, toward reinterpreting (and weakening) criminal procedural safeguards in terrorism

---

46. *See* Ashley Deeks, *Intelligence Communities, Peer Constraints, and the Law*, 7 HARV. NAT'L SECURITY J. 1 (2016).

47. Perina, *supra* note 3, at 536–37 (stating that section 7 of the Intelligence Services Act of 1994 has been viewed as creating a legal framework that allows the government to authorize individuals to engage in conduct that would otherwise violate the law). It is not clear whether section 7 envisions authorizations of domestic or international law violations.

48. Jed Rubenfeld, *Unilateralism and Constitutionalism*, 79 N.Y.U. L. REV. 1971, 1986 (2004).

49. *See* Perina, *supra* note 3, at 556 (noting that secret legal theories within a government may pollinate a government's internal legal thinking as applied to non-secret situations).

trials to address the particular challenges raised by terrorism prosecutions.[50] Though pragmatic and possibly necessary, this phenomenon raises concerns that relaxing certain rules in one set of criminal trials could bleed over into otherwise "normal" trials, depriving the average criminal defendant of the more robust protections he currently receives.[51]

Adopting a strained interpretation of an existing, relatively specific international norm also may undercut the interpreting state's credibility as a legal actor. Observers who view the state's interpretation as opportunistic potentially will treat other state claims about international law and the IC with increased skepticism. Additionally, when the UK adopts a position on the content of an international legal rule relevant to IC activity and that position becomes public, the UK creates a precedent that potentially feeds back into how other states understand that rule. These UK interpretations could have unwelcome implications if other states later use the precedent to justify actions of which the UK disapproves.

Of course, if the UK determines that a particular IC activity cannot be reconciled with any reading of an international legal commitment, the UK presumably would decline to conduct that activity. From the perspective of those who worry about the effect of IC activities on individual citizens, aspects of the UK approach appear more rights-protective than the US approach described in the next section.

C. Textual Escape Hatches: The United States

1. MECHANISMS

The US approach differs from the United Kingdom's.[52] The United States has shaped the interface between international law and its IC using four tools. First, the United States interprets narrowly the geographic scope of some potentially applicable human rights treaties that would otherwise arguably impinge upon common US IC practices. Second, the United States has indicated that the president may have authority *as a matter of domestic law* to disregard CIL and "non-self-executing"

---

50. *See, e.g.*, Robert Chesney & Jack Goldsmith, *Terrorism and the Convergence of Criminal and Military Detention Models*, 60 STAN. L. REV. 1079, 1108 (2008).

51. *See generally* Oren Gross, *Chaos and Rules: Should Responses to Violent Crises Always Be Constitutional?*, 112 YALE L.J. 1011, 1022–23 (2003) (describing how "models of accommodation" during states of emergency can create a slippery slope toward excessive government infringement on individual rights in times of normalcy).

52. This section focuses only on the United States, but Canada has recently introduced a "textual escape hatch" into its domestic law as well. In Bill C-44, the Canadian parliament amended the Canadian Security Intelligence Service Act to clarify that a judge may issue a warrant to authorize activities by CSIS outside Canada to "enable the Service to investigate a threat to the security of Canada," without regard to any other law, including foreign law (and presumably also international law). *See* Craig Forcese, *The Ugly Canadian? International Law and Canada's New Covert National Security Vision* (May 28, 2015 6:45 PM), http://craigforcese.squarespace.com/national-security-law-blog/2015/5/28/the-ugly-canadian-international-law-and-canadas-new-covert-n.html. Thus, Canada's domestic law envisions that domestic courts may authorize CSIS to violate international law.

treaty provisions, and has suggested that Congress has authorized the president to direct covert actions that violate treaties more broadly. Third, as a result, the United States has declined to make sweeping public statements about whether its IC—and the US executive branch more broadly—always complies with international law. Finally, notwithstanding that, the government has frequently announced *policies* of compliance with international law, intended to narrow perceived compliance gaps. To be clear, the United States does not claim publicly that international law simply does not apply to IC activity. Instead, the US approach jurisdictionally narrows the reach of international norms that might conceivably apply to IC activity and often tries to ensure that it conducts IC activities in a manner consistent with well-established international rules.

a. Narrow interpretations of geographic scope
One aspect of the US approach is to limit the set of international laws that might apply to IC activity abroad by interpreting the geographic reach of those laws narrowly. For example, the United States asserts that the ICCPR generally only applies to activities that take place on US territory and fall under its jurisdiction.[53] It applies this approach in all contexts: this is not a position driven by IC concerns alone. Nevertheless, this means that there are fewer occasions in which those US treaty obligations conceivably might reach IC activity, which generally take place outside US territory.

b. Domestic legal authorization to disregard international law
Second, in certain circumstances, the executive branch has authority under US domestic law to violate international law. For example, pursuant to the "last-in-time" rule, Congress may by statute authorize the executive to violate a treaty or CIL.[54] Further, US law appears to authorize the president to violate CIL when he is exercising his constitutional authorities, at least where statutes do not require him to act otherwise.[55] The executive has suggested that when the president acts under his constitutional authorities—and perhaps even under statutes—he is not required to comply with non-self-executing treaty provisions.[56]

Finally, Congress has arguably authorized *covert* actions that violate CIL and, perhaps, treaties. For example, in the National Security Act of 1947, as amended, Congress required the president to make particular findings before authorizing a covert action, and forbade the president from authorizing action that "would violate

53. Human Rights Committee, Concluding Observations on the Fourth Periodic Report of the United States of America, CCPR/C/USA/CO/4, Apr. 23, 2014 (ICCPR); Conclusions and Recommendations of the Committee Against Torture: United States, May 18, 2006, para. 20.

54. The *Charming Betsy* canon, by which US courts should construe later-in-time statutes in a manner consistent with international law where possible, affords a strong presumption against the idea that Congress intends to override existing international rules. Murray v. Schooner Charming Betsy, 6 U.S. 64 (1804).

55. The Paquete Habana, 175 U.S. 677 (1900).

56. Ashley Deeks, *Covert Action and International Law Compliance*, LAWFARE, Dec. 18, 2013.

the Constitution or any statute of the United States."[57] The statutory language notably fails to prohibit the president from authorizing treaty violations. In recent testimony by Caroline Krass, the then-nominee for the CIA General Counsel position, she noted, "By this language, Congress did not prohibit the President from authorizing a covert action that would violate a non-self-executing treaty or customary international law."[58]

Another example is found in 50 U.S.C. § 3231, which states:

> No Federal law enacted on or after December 27, 2000, that implements a treaty or other international agreement shall be construed as making unlawful an otherwise lawful and authorized intelligence activity of the United States Government or its employees . . . , unless such Federal law specifically addresses such intelligence activity.[59]

The statute implicitly appears to authorize the executive not to implement fully the US treaty obligations, in order to allow domestically lawful IC activity to continue. Finally, in enacting the Foreign Intelligence Surveillance Act, which authorizes various forms of foreign electronic surveillance and the acquisition of technical intelligence from property under the control of foreign powers, Congress made clear that the Act would trump the VCDR as a matter of domestic law.[60] To be clear, none of this means that, as a matter of international law, the United States may invoke its domestic laws to overcome its international obligations. It merely suggests that the US IC, and other components of the executive branch, may have flexibility under domestic law to violate those obligations in an uncertain category of cases—something that other states such as the United Kingdom and South Africa either cannot or do not do.

c. Limited or ambiguous statements about compliance

Unlike the United Kingdom's public statements about IC compliance with international law, the United States tends to use carefully crafted but ambiguous language when discussing international law relevant to its IC, and sometimes declines to discuss the matter. For instance, in her nomination hearing to become CIA General Counsel, Caroline Krass stated, "As a general matter, and including with respect to the use of force, the United States respects international law and complies with it to the extent possible in the execution of covert action activities."[61] Similarly, a May 2013

---

57. 50 U.S.C. § 3093(a)(5) (2012).

58. S. Select Comm. on Intel., Additional Prehearing Questions for Ms. Caroline D. Krass upon Her Nomination to Be the General Counsel of the Central Intelligence Agency, http://fas.org/irp/congress/2013_hr/121713krass-preh.pdf.

59. 50 U.S.C. § 3231(a) (2012).

60. See H.R. Rep. No. 1283, Pt. I, 95th Cong, 2d Sess., 1978 U.S.C.C.A.N. 4048, at 70 (June 8, 1978).

61. Krass, supra note 58 (emphasis added). See also Stephen Preston, Speech, CIA and the Rule of Law, 6 J. Nat'l Security L. & Pol'y 1 (2012) (describing "how an Agency program involving the use of lethal force would be structured so as to ensure that it satisfies applicable U.S. and international law").

document that laid out US use-of-force policies in counterterrorism operations stated, "Capture operations are conducted only against suspects who may lawfully be captured or otherwise taken into custody by the United States and only when the operation can be conducted *in accordance with all applicable law* and consistent with our obligations to other sovereign states."[62] These statements are carefully drafted to avoid stating what international law may be applicable, while identifying the importance the United States places on having its IC comply with international law where possible. These carefully lawyered, precisely imprecise statements decline to specify what law applies in a given context, leaving unresolved the extent to which the United States views international law as governing or limiting any particular intelligence action.

In the surveillance context, the United States has not publicly set forth its views on whether or how its international human rights obligations extend to domestic or foreign surveillance. A former Department of Justice official has stated that most of the internal legal assessments related to surveillance would take the form of a constitutional analysis, not one that expressly takes into account the language of applicable human rights treaties.[63] Whether for that reason or because the United States has concluded internally that international law (including human rights law) does not regulate foreign surveillance, the US position remains obscured from public view.

d. Policy commitments to comply

Notwithstanding—indeed, perhaps because of—the ways it employs those first three tools, the United States has adopted policies requiring the IC to act in a manner consistent with international law in a number of circumstances, even if that compliance is not legally compelled as a matter of domestic law. In 2009, President Obama signed an executive order requiring all elements of the US government to comply with Common Article 3 of the Geneva Conventions when holding detainees.[64] Various US officials have described IC compliance with law-of-war targeting rules. Former CIA general counsel Stephen Preston stated, for instance, that the CIA uses force "in a manner consistent with the four basic principles in the law of armed conflict governing the use of force: Necessity, Distinction, Proportionality, and Humanity. Great care would be taken in the planning and execution of actions to satisfy these four principles. . . . "[65] Even with regard to international law governing the resort to force, the United States has declared that, away from "hot battlefields," it will only undertake targeted killings of individuals or groups that pose a

---

62. The White House Office of the Press Secretary, *Fact Sheet: U.S. Policy Standards and Procedures for the Use of Force in Counterterrorism Operations Outside the United States and Areas of Active Hostilities*, May 23, 2013 (emphasis added) [hereinafter Targeted Killings Fact Sheet].

63. HUMAN RIGHTS WATCH, WITH LIBERTY TO MONITOR ALL 68 (2014), available at https://www.hrw.org/sites/default/files/reports/usnsa0714_ForUPload_0.pdf.

64. Exec. Order No. 13,491, § 3(a) (2009).

65. Preston, *supra* note 61.

"continuing, imminent threat to U.S. persons," a standard generally consistent with the UN Charter.[66]

Some of these US policy commitments are rendered particularly credible by the fact that the international laws at issue have been incorporated into US law via implementing statutes. For instance, like the United Kingdom has done for its nationals, the United States has criminalized the commission of various war crimes by US nationals.[67] Therefore, because the IC must comply with US statutes, it finds itself in compliance with the international laws that those statutes implement. Nevertheless, in myriad policy statements, the United States has articulated a conceptual commitment to certain precepts of international law as such, even when conducting intelligence activities.

2. ANALYSIS

Why has the United States chosen this approach to IC international law compliance, rather than an approach like the United Kingdom's? First, although the audience for US policies and speeches is both domestic and international, the United States faces less domestic pressure than the United Kingdom to be unequivocal about whether its intelligence activities comply with international law. Most US citizens are concerned about whether the executive complies with domestic legal constraints, and presumably are less aware of the existence of international rules that may regulate spying and other intelligence actions.[68] There is therefore less political pressure to comply with those rules. (In contrast, UK domestic law itself is infused with international human rights law via the Human Rights Act.) Second, even if the US public supports compliance with international law, it gives priority to fighting terrorism over strengthening international law.[69] Third, the United States seems to be concerned about offering a stable legal framework to those in its IC. Because its IC is heavily regulated domestically (unlike many other ICs), the United States perhaps is worried that new treaty rules inadvertently will complicate or confuse these regulated activities.[70] Fourth, the United States faces a reduced risk of litigation on the merits about whether its IC activities comply with international law. The state secrets privilege, political question, and standing doctrines, and the concept of non-self-executing treaties all erect

---

66. Targeted Killings Fact Sheet, *supra* note 62. This policy arguably even meets international human rights law standards for the use of lethal force against individuals, depending on what one considers an "imminent" threat.

67. 18 U.S.C. § 2441 (2012). The United States has incorporated fewer war crimes than the United Kingdom, because it is party to fewer law-of-war treaties than the UK and is not a party to the International Criminal Court.

68. ERIC POSNER, THE PERILS OF GLOBAL LEGALISM 58 (2009) ("[I]t seems unlikely that [Americans] care enough about international law to punish governments that violate international law in order to advance other goals—security, national wealth—that citizens care about.").

69. *Id.* at 57.

70. *See* S. REP. No. 106-279 (2000) (stating rationale for 50 U.S.C. § 3231(a) (2012)).

hurdles that make it difficult for a particular plaintiff to challenge an IC program that might appear to violate international law.[71]

The US approach to international law and intelligence actions affects the US relationship with international law in several ways. First, it presumably alters the standard US interagency process. As illustrated supra, the IC likely feels less pressure to understand and analyze international law than many other US government agencies.[72] In "standard" US interagency policymaking, international legal questions are considered as a matter of course. If one establishes a different interagency process that focuses on domestic legal constraints, those officials who must focus on (and are most conversant with) international law likely will have limited input into policymaking.[73] Adopting a US-type approach therefore could alter the process by which government policy-setting occurs, limiting the executive's focus on possible international legal requirements ex ante, before crafting intelligence policies. For instance, Human Rights Watch recently reported that the United States did not design its electronic surveillance programs with human rights law in mind.[74] On the other hand, if, during negotiations for new international rules, US negotiators do not tend to have in mind the activities of the US IC, the positions they adopt and the rules to which they agree may produce "normal" rules that are, from the perspective of human rights advocates, normatively superior.

Second, the US approach creates a "zone of excludability," in which some intelligence actions may transpire without attention to identifiable international law-based limits. For those concerned about international law's integrity and functionality, the US approach holds benefits and perils. On one hand, the United States faces fewer situations in which it must undertake strained substantive interpretations of international norms. It therefore does not risk "tainting" the right to privacy, say, by insisting that all of its foreign surveillance activities are consistent with that right. It also avoids specifically asserting that certain actions are permitted as a matter of international law, unlike the United Kingdom. On the other hand, the US approach implicitly admits that a "zone of excludability" exists for international law

71. Al-Aulaqi v. Obama, 727 F. Supp. 2d 1 (D.D.C. 2010); Mohamed v. Jeppesen Dataplan, 614 F.2d 1070 (9th Cir. 2010) (en banc).

72. I do not assume that the IC affirmatively seeks to violate international law. Rather, I assume that IC members may be less familiar with potentially applicable international law and may be unable to introduce an international law perspective into the discussion.

73. Cf. MICHAEL REISMAN & JAMES BAKER, REGULATING COVERT ACTION 14–15 (1992) (discussing secrecy's distortive effects on decision-making). The United States has stated that, when reviewing covert action activities, the CIA general counsel works with lawyers from other agencies, including the Justice, State, and Defense Departments. Thus, in the case of covert action discussions, at least part of the standard interagency process for considering legal issues remains intact. Caroline Krass, Questions for the Record, https://www.intelligence.senate.gov/sites/default/files/hearings/krasspost.pdf (last visited July 25, 2017). It is not clear the extent to which the executive considers possible international law constraints when policymakers are assessing other intelligence activities.

74. See Human Rights Watch, supra note 63, at 67–68.

compliance, the location, parameters, and depth of which are unclear. One may anal-
ogize to "extra-constitutional" activities by the executive in times of crisis. Arthur
Schlesinger wrote that the Founding Fathers contemplated the possibility that "crisis might require the Executive to act outside the Constitution," but did not intend
to confer constitutional legitimacy on such acts.[75] He believed, however, that the
"legal order would be better preserved if departures from it were frankly identified
as such than if they were anointed with a factitious legality and thereby enabled to
serve as constitutional precedents for future action."[76] Given the IC's commitment
to secrecy, departures from international law are unlikely to be "frankly identified."
The US approach preserves the integrity of the "ordinary rules" of international law,
but at the expense of suggesting that certain areas of action remain unregulated by
that law, and without clearly identifying those areas.

IV. IMPLICATIONS FOR INTERNATIONAL LAW

Parsing two dominant ways in which states currently view their ICs' relationship
with international law brings into sharp relief a recurring question in international
law about the trade-offs between under-compliance—or even noncompliance—
with applicable law and, alternatively, interpretive exertions that alter the traditional
meaning of that law. Analyzing the implications of each approach leads to the conclusion that the US approach may be preferable when dealing with a certain set of
international norms (CIL norms related to sovereignty and territorial integrity), but
that the UK approach has greater merit in relation to a different set of norms (well-
defined, treaty-based norms that implicate individual rights).

The two competing approaches discussed in Section III pose the following
conundrum. Assume that it frequently will be difficult to reconcile many state IC
activities with existing international rules, which states almost always craft during
public or quasi-public negotiations (or, for CIL, while engaged in detectable state
practice) with overt actions on their minds. Is it better for a state to aver—explicitly
or implicitly—that existing international laws that *might* be read to apply to some
IC activities simply do not reach these particular intelligence contexts or may be
ignored, where violations are likely to be relatively small-scale and may never come
to light? Or is it better for a state overtly to purport to comply with international legal
rules, sometimes in contexts well beyond what the drafters had in mind, but then
expand or contract the meaning of those rules, potentially altering the underlying
rule itself? States with advanced intelligence capabilities often face this Scylla-or-
Charybdis dilemma. The former offers a perverse form of respect for international
law, recognizing the importance of international legal regulations under ordinary
circumstances and acknowledging that it is wrong to violate them. This approach
also places a value on ensuring that international law retains its pragmatism and utility, rather than embodying norms that simply do not fit the circumstances. But the

75. Arthur Schlesinger, Jr., The Imperial Presidency 8 (1973).

76. *Id.*

assertion of a "zone of excludability" can be deeply threatening when it is not clear whether those actions are constrained by any other norms or what types of situations fall within that zone. And surely some international rules, such as the *jus cogens* prohibition on torture, cannot be altered, even for activities within the zone.[77]

The latter course offers its own perversities. If states interpret the right to privacy to mean the same thing in the context of IC activity against foreign leaders and in domestic law enforcement investigations against their own citizens, that right would begin to look far less potent—and less appealing—in most contexts in which it arises. All state activities technically would be covered by whatever international legal rules exist, such that states would not purport to locate their activity beyond the reach of international law, but this would occur at the risk of legal discoloration. Some will fight the implicit premise of this chapter, arguing that there are never circumstances in which states may step outside international law, and that existing legal rules must be read to regulate IC activity. After all, the argument goes, states most need to be bound by law when they are under pressure to act wholly in their own self-interest, and those who operate most in the shadows need rules the most. This approach is not always realistic, however.[78] Often, states must make a choice between noncompliance and reinterpretation.

Each approach challenges the integrity of the international legal system—the first on a higher plane, and the second on the level of the content of particular rules. But unless one is prepared to boldly proclaim either that international law in toto is simply irrelevant to intelligence activities or that states should interpret all rules that might possibly apply to IC activity to in fact do so, one must pick one's poison.

One possible way to navigate the dilemma is to view IC compliance with international law as existing on a continuum. In this model, ICs must comply rigorously with those norms that are both specific and intended to protect individual rights (including rules such as those on torture, inhumane treatment, and targeting and detention, which are regulated by human rights law, the laws of armed conflict, or both). These norms usually will derive from treaty obligations. As the norms move away from affecting individual rights toward norms such as those related to bribery and trade and investment practices, and/or as the norms become increasingly intangible (sovereignty, territorial integrity), the expectations of IC compliance would wane. Putting this in terms of the US and UK approaches, states would recognize that ICs may operate more or less "extra-constitutionally" with regard to the more nebulous CIL sovereignty norms, but should operate pursuant to the UK model with regard to norms mandating treatment protections and international humanitarian law compliance. Professor Thomas Franck's argument that more determinative rules exert greater "compliance pull" than less determinative rules supports the

---

77. *Cf.* Bruce Ackerman, *The Emergency Constitution*, 113 YALE L.J. 1029, 1058–59 (2004) (arguing that even if one accepts a different set of constitutional rules for an emergency, one must deny the US government the authority to torture, censor, or revise basic laws organizing the structure of government).

78. Gross, *supra* note 51, at 1043–44 (critiquing as naïve the view that the Constitution applies equally in times of emergency and peace).

idea that states will (and perhaps should) take more seriously their compliance with the quite specific human rights norms that affect individuals than they do the less sculpted norms of sovereignty and territorial integrity.[79] This approach runs the risk of potentially problematic interpretations of some human rights rules, but that cost seems acceptable in the face of the alternative, which is to allow those activities to occur without perceptible international law constraints.

79. THOMAS FRANCK, THE POWER OF LEGITIMACY AMONG NATIONS 28 (1990).

13

National Legislatures

The Foundations of Comparative International Law

KEVIN L. COPE & HOOMAN MOVASSAGH*

One critique of some common-law legal scholarship is its intensively "court-centric" focus,[1] which, some believe, "marginalize[s]" the role of the legislative branch.[2] The same may be said of the extant comparative international law literature: most of it concerns the interpretive approaches of national courts.[3] In fact, one of the field's seminal pieces defines comparative international law as the process of "seeking to identify and interpret international law" by comparing "various domestic court decisions."[4] So it is not surprising that nearly all of this volume's contributions deal mostly or exclusively with courts and judicial decisions.[5] We agree with the other contributors that courts can play a significant part in diversifying international law

* The authors thank the volume editors for their comments and observations on an earlier draft of this chapter.

1. See Elizabeth Garrett, *Teaching Law and Politics*, 7 N.Y.U. J. Legis. & Pub. Pol'y 11, 11 (2003) (observing a "court-centric" bias in US law schools); *accord* Ethan J. Leib, *Adding Legislation Courses to the First-Year Curriculum*, 58 J. Legal Educ. 166, 170 (2008) (noting that in the United States, "the first-year slate of courses tends to be dominated by a judge-centered perspective on the law, in which all legal questions are answered by people in black robes.... That neither reflects reality, nor approximates how lawyers need to perceive the workings of the law.").

2. Michael E. Libonati, *State Constitutions and Legislative Process: The Road Not Taken*, 89 B.U. L. Rev. 863, 863 (2009) (noting that "the comparative study of state and federal legislatures ... is doubly marginalized in the legal academy," in part because "it has to do with the legislative branch of government."); *accord* Leib, *supra* note 1.

3. See, e.g., Anthea Roberts, *Comparative International Law? The Role of National Courts in Creating and Enforcing International Law*, 60 Int'l & Comp. L.Q. 57, 57 (2011).

4. *Id.*

5. See Anthea Roberts, Paul Stephan, Pierre-Hugues Verdier & Mila Versteeg, *Conceptualizing Comparative International Law* (this volume).

across different systems, but we contend that the foundation of the comparative international law project lies elsewhere. We argue that among the most important and underappreciated interpretative acts—and therefore, those currently most needing study—are the international law interpretations of national legislatures.

As we elaborate below, two distinguishing characteristics of national legislatures make them especially relevant to comparative international law. First, legislators have great incentives to confer benefits on their national, subnational, or party interest groups. They have relatively little political motivation to enact policies that achieve or maintain cross-country international law consistency. This inward focus may reinforce (and be reinforced by) legislators' relative lack of engagement with transnational legal networks. Second, legislatures as a whole have gradually gained a greater say in treaty-making, empowering them to promote disuniformity in how international law is received in their respective systems.[6] Although heads of state or government have historically dominated foreign relations, a "constitutional revolution" over the past 20 years has given legislatures in many states unprecedented power over treaty-making and international engagement.[7] Our own review of national constitutions reveals that the number of constitutions that expressly provide a role for legislatures in respect of treaties now stands at 159.[8] Another recent study found that required legislative participation in treaty-making increased significantly through the late nineteenth and early twentieth centuries, and shot up dramatically in the second half of the twentieth century.[9] Legislatures' adjustments to and interpretations of international law therefore increasingly influence how rules apply to and in their respective states. In making these decisions, legislatures limit the range of interpretative choices later available to other branches. In essence, legislatures act as the primary gatekeepers for international law, determining if and how it will enter their respective states.

I. THE INCENTIVES OF NATIONAL LEGISLATORS

National courts have traditionally been seen as loyal agents of international law. Comparativists and international law scholars generally believe that, among the

---

6. CAMPBELL MCLACHLAN, FOREIGN RELATIONS LAW 149–50 (2014) (citing Mai Chen, *A Constitutional Revolution? The Role of the New Zealand Parliament in Treaty-Making*, 19 N.Z.U. L. REV. 448 (2001)) (addressing this trend in Anglo-Commonwealth systems).

7. *Id* at 150.

8. *See* Kevin L. Cope & Hooman Movassagh, *National Legislatures: The Foundations of Comparative International Law* App'x, *at* http://papers.ssrn.com/sol3/papers.cfm?abstract_id=2790507 (June 5, 2016). This figure does not include states such as the United Kingdom and Australia, which do not have express constitutional provisions on the role of legislatures regarding treaties, but which nevertheless involve the legislature in practice or by virtue of a legislative act. As such, the actual number of national legislatures involved in states' treaty-making process is somewhat higher.

9. Pierre-Hugues Verdier & Mila Versteeg, *International Law in National Legal Systems: An Empirical Investigation*, 109 AM. J. INT'L L. 514, 519 (2015); *see also* BETH A. SIMMONS, MOBILIZING FOR HUMAN RIGHTS: INTERNATIONAL LAW IN DOMESTIC POLITICS App'x 3.2 (2009), *available at* http://scholar.harvard.edu/files/bsimmons/files/APP_3.2_Ratification_rules.pdf.

three branches of governments, courts most faithfully interpret international rules. In the early twentieth century, Hersch Lauterpacht characterized national courts as "the trusted mouthpieces of international law," which operated as "local divisions of the great High Court of Nations."[10] To him, international law was "the only branch of law containing identical rules administered as such by the courts of all nations."[11] As Olga Frishman and Eyal Benvenisti note, there is a long-standing normative tradition (which they criticize) of scholars' implying that courts *should* be applying international law uniformly.[12]

Many adherents of this perspective subscribe to the "convergence" or "uniformity" thesis of international law, in which any given international rule should mean the same thing in every system.[13] These adherents tend to identify courts as the main instruments of this convergence.[14] There is some empirical support for this normative view. In analyzing an original data set of national court interpretations of CEDAW, Christopher McCrudden notes "a remarkable absence of divergence across jurisdictions as to the [treaty's] substantive meaning."[15] Notably, McCrudden finds "significant differences between jurisdictions" in how CEDAW "is received into the national legal and judicial systems," "in the techniques of interpretation applied," and "in the legal status of CEDAW at the national level," but finds that those differences have fairly little impact on the treaty's substantive interpretation.[16] He concludes that, although courts interpreting CEDAW pursue strategic institutional goals, by and large they do not appear to "see themselves as agents of a domestic community" who tailor their interpretive approaches to their own domestic system.[17] On the other hand, a core premise of this volume is that courts are not always the faithful interpreters that commentators have long thought—or

10. Hersch Lauterpacht, *Decisions of Municipal Courts as a Source of International Law*, 10 Brit. Y.B. Int'l L. 65, 93 (1929) (citing Thomas Alfred Walker, The Science of International Law 49 (1893)).

11. *Id.* at 95.

12. Olga Frishman & Eyal Benvenisti, *National Courts and Interpretative Approaches to International Law: The Case Against Convergence*, *in* Interpretation of International Law by Domestic Courts: Uniformity, Diversity, Convergence 317–18 (Helmut Philip Aust & Georg Nolte eds., 2016).

13. *See id.* at 318.

14. *Id.; see also* Daniel Abebe & Eric Posner, *The Flaws of Foreign Affairs Legalism*, 51 Va. J. Int'l L. 507 (2011) (discussing and criticizing the related view that US courts should enforce universalist notions of international law against congressional and presidential encroachment).

15. Christopher McCrudden, *Why Do National Court Judges Refer to Human Rights Treaties? A Comparative International Law Analysis of CEDAW*, 109 Am. J. Int'l L. 534, 535 (2015) ("[A]lthough there are prominent examples of cases in which national courts adopt substantively different interpretations of CEDAW, the evidence from [my] dataset shows a remarkable absence of divergence across jurisdictions as to the substantive meaning of CEDAW.").

16. *Id.*

17. *Id.* at 536.

urged—them to be. As several contributions and other studies illustrate, court interpretations of international law do sometimes differ in meaningful ways.[18]

Regardless of whether courts act as state (rather than international) agents, and regardless of how much they contribute to international disuniformity, we should expect legislatures to do so more. Legislatures are a foundation for comparative international law in part because they have relatively little motive to harmonize their interpretations with those of foreign and international institutions. They should therefore be even less likely than courts to serve as faithful agents of the international legal order. This is true for two main reasons: (1) legislators tend to be less connected to the global networks that disseminate international law norms, and (2) legislators face greater political incentives to diverge.

A. Global Networks

First, most legislators (at least in non-EU national parliaments) are less likely to engage with global professional networks. They generally have no universal requirement for particular education or professional training; professionally, they are a diverse group.[19] Political office-seekers receive a bigger payoff from local networks than from international ones, so foreign education and experience represent an opportunity cost—or perhaps an actual cost—if those activities allow legislators to be branded as outsiders.[20] It is little surprise, then, that the socioeconomic background of parliamentarians tend to more closely match those of their local or national constituents. As Donald Matthews observes, "[w]hile legislators as a group enjoy high social status, they tend to be less atypical in their social backgrounds than chief executives, top-level civil servants, or economic elites."[21]

Compare this dynamic to that of judges. Judges receive comparatively standardized training and education, which typically (especially outside the United States, United Kingdom, and Japan) includes substantial training in international law.[22]

---

18. See, e.g., Helmut Philipp Aust, Alejandro Rodiles & Peter Staubach, *Unity or Uniformity? Domestic Courts and Treaty Interpretation*, 27 Leiden J. Int'l L. 75, 111 (2014); Martti Koskenniemi, *The Case for Comparative International Law*, 20 Finn. Y.B. Int'l L. 1 (2009); Boris N. Mamlyuk & Ugo Mattei, *Comparative International Law*, 36 Brook. J. Int'l L. 385, 389 (2011); Roberts, *supra* note 3.

19. Greg Power, Global Parliamentary Report: The Changing Nature of Parliamentary Representation 109 (2012), at http://www.ipu.org/pdf/publications/gpr2012-full-e.pdf. For detailed data, *see* Global Parliamentary Rep., data on age, gender, and profession of parliamentarians, at http://www.ipu.org/gpr/gpr/downloads/index.htm (last visited Aug. 5, 2016).

20. See Michael Hill, *Arrogant Posh Boys? The Social Composition of the Parliamentary Conservative Party and the Effect of Cameron's "A" List*, 84 Pol. Q. 1 (2013).

21. Donald R. Matthews, *Legislative Recruitment and Legislative Careers*, 9 Legis. Stud. Q. 547 (1984); *see* Grant Reeher, Narratives of Justice: Legislators' Beliefs About Distributive Fairness 6 (1996).

22. See Anthea Roberts, Is International Law International? 149–51 (2017); Ryan Scoville & Milan Markovic, *How Cosmopolitan Are International Law Professors?*, 38 Mich. J. Int'l L.

National judges often go abroad for extended legal education and subsequent training and networking. Anne-Marie Slaughter writes that, over the last couple of decades, judges have created a "global community of courts."[23] Their decisions might therefore reflect an emerging international consensus of this global network of judges, which has formed as judges embrace a transnational judicial dialogue through Internet-based correspondence, international conferences, and legal training abroad.[24] Indeed, according to former ICJ president Rosalyn Higgins, national courts are increasingly engaged with international law because they want to become "part of the international mainstream."[25]

The transnational networks for domestic legislators are nowhere near as robust. Granted, advances in communication technology and globalization generally have allowed corporate and government officials increasingly to work with their counterparts across national borders, and some legislators have done so.[26] But the lack of uniform educational and professional requirements across parliamentary electoral systems, together with the fact that such overseas education or professional experience tends to have less salience for their constituencies, means that these international interactions translate less readily into international-oriented policy.

B. Political Incentives

The second reason we expect legislatures to embrace a less internationally consistent policy is that legislative policymaking is more closely tied to domestic constituents and interest groups[27] than judicial decision-making. The desire to obtain re-election is thought to be the primary driver of legislators' behavior.[28] Legislators depend on

119 (2016); PILMap, *at* http://pilmap.org (last visited Sept. 14, 2017) (showing the United States, United Kingdom, and Japan among the outliers in rates of compulsory law school public international law training, with less than 5 percent of schools in those countries so requiring).

23. Anne-Marie Slaughter, *A Global Community of Courts*, 44 HARV. INT'L L.J. 191 (2003) [hereinafter *A Global Community of Courts*]; *see* Christopher McCrudden, *A Common Law of Human Rights? Transnational Judicial Conversations on Constitutional Rights*, 20 OXFORD J. LEGAL STUD. 499 (2000); Anne-Marie Slaughter, *A Brave New Judicial World*, *in* AMERICAN EXCEPTIONALISM AND HUMAN RIGHTS 278 (Michael Ignatieff ed., 2005).

24. *A Global Community of Courts, supra* note 23.

25. Eyal Benvenisti & George W. Downs, *National Courts, Domestic Democracy, and the Evolution of International Law: A Rejoinder to Nikolaos Lavranos, Jacob Katz Cogan and Tom Ginsburg*, 20 EUR. J. INT'L L. 1027, 1028 (2009) (quoting Judge Higgins).

26. ANNE-MARIE SLAUGHTER, A NEW WORLD ORDER 119–27 (2004) (discussing regional legislative networks).

27. CECIL C. CRABBJR. ET AL., CONGRESS AND THE FOREIGN POLICY PROCESS: MODES OF LEGISLATIVE BEHAVIOR 137–57 (2000).

28. *See generally* DAVID R. MAYHEW, CONGRESS: THE ELECTORAL CONNECTION (1974); Roger Congleton, *The Median Voter Model*, *in* THE ENCYCLOPEDIA OF PUBLIC CHOICE (2002) (explaining the median voter theory of legislative motivation); LEGISLATIVE BEHAVIOR: A READER IN THEORY AND RESEARCH (John C. Wahlke & Heinz Eulau eds., 1959).

domestic actors to keep their jobs and therefore have a powerful incentive to provide goods and other benefits—both public and private—to these actors.[29] They
are not directly accountable to foreign or international interests, and they have little
incentive to prioritize those interests over domestic ones. Several studies show that
because the public "is rarely informed enough to hold leaders accountable"[30] for
their foreign policy positions, those positions are fairly disconnected from electoral
success.[31] We might therefore expect legislators to oppose policies that promote
international cooperation or coordination (and which may yield broad or long-term
utility) but are thought to harm local interests. Prominent examples include stricter
factory emissions standards, open immigration rules, and some trade liberalization.

In some electoral systems, legislators answer electorally not even to the nation
as a whole, but to the provincial or sectarian interests of their respective districts,
interest groups, or political parties. Compared with judges, "legislators reflect more
of the diversity of opinion found in any given geographic area."[32] As Anne-Marie
Slaughter has observed,

> Legislators are most directly tied to territorially defined policies. In this sense,
> it could be said that remaining resolutely "national," or even parochial, is their
> job. Even when they focus on international issues, it is generally through the
> prism of domestic interests rather than through an independent interest in
> foreign policy, much less global governance.... To the vast majority of these
> constituencies, international cooperation usually takes a low priority.[33]

Indeed, a 2011 study of Canadian foreign policy finds that "[m]ost parliamentarians tend to have a parochial outlook that keeps their gaze fixed on domestic issues,"
which "makes it difficult for ordinary parliamentarians to usurp the longstanding
prerogatives of the executives in the shaping of external policy."[34] In fact, some
have argued that perceived provincialism of directly elected legislators made the
American founders reluctant to give the treaty powers to the whole Congress.[35] The

---

29. See BRUCE BUENO DE MESQUITA ET AL., THE LOGIC OF POLITICAL SURVIVAL (2005), for a
theory of how variations in the distribution of political power affect to what extent leaders provide
constituents with public versus private goods (i.e., "selectorate theory").

30. Elizabeth N. Saunders, War and the Inner Circle: Democratic Elites and the Politics of Using Force,
24 SECURITY STUD. 466, 471–72 (2015).

31. OLE R. HOLSTI, PUBLIC OPINION AND AMERICAN FOREIGN POLICY (2004); Philip B.K. Potter
& Matthew A. Baum, Looking for Audience Costs in All the Wrong Places: Electoral Institutions, Media
Access, and Democratic Constraint, 76 J. POL. 167, 169 (2014) ("[T]he prevailing evidence suggests
that the public's attention to matters of foreign policy is generally quite low.").

32. REEHER, supra note 21, at 6.

33. SLAUGHTER, supra note 26, at 105.

34. KIM RICHARD NOSSAL ET AL., INTERNATIONAL POLICY AND POLITICS IN CANADA (2011).

35. See David M. Golove & Daniel J. Hulsebosch, A Civilized Nation: The Early American Constitution,
the Law of Nations, and the Pursuit of International Recognition, 85 N.Y.U. L. REV. 932, 939–40 (2010)

founders ultimately entrusted this task only to the smaller, more elite Senate, which at the time was not popularly elected.

These domestically driven policy preferences of legislatures play out in a number of international issues areas. For instance, though international trade liberalization creates winners and losers in the short term, most economists accept that it benefits most societies in the long run.[36] Yet the American voting public and legislature (like those in many other developed countries) have historically preferred protectionist policies that insulate vulnerable domestic industries,[37] a dynamic present in the debate over the North American Free Trade Agreement (NAFTA). Since the 1970s, leaders in the Democratic coalition, especially organized labor groups, have opposed free trade generally and NAFTA specifically.[38] Many faced heavy pressure from constituents and interest groups to retain protectionist trade barriers. In contrast, presidents of both parties are more isolated from public opinion, better positioning them to "focus on the big picture," and "think more globally."[39] The internal debate over NAFTA's ratification showcased these phenomena; Democratic president Bill Clinton defied his party leadership's protectionist positions in aggressively lobbying Congress to support the agreement. Similar tensions between internally focused legislators and more globally oriented heads of state have occurred in other countries across a variety of international cooperation issues.[40]

High-court judges are somewhat like executives in this sense. Compared with legislators, they are generally more insulated from domestic electoral politics, their average standard terms are longer, and they are unlikely to face popular election or re-election.[41] Their career paths are less likely to depend on the electorate, and more on senior judges or executive officials.[42] As a result, judges are politically freer to

---

(noting the framers' view that "representative institutions could not always be relied upon to uphold international obligations, especially when their members were drawn from small districts and were subject to frequent elections").

36. *See, e.g.,* L. Alan Winters et al., *Trade Liberalization and Poverty: The Evidence so Far,* 42 J. ECON. LIT. 72, 72 (2004).

37. Sharyn O'Halloran, *Congress and Foreign Trade Policy, in* CONGRESS RESURGENT: FOREIGN AND DEFENSE POLICY ON CAPITOL HILL 283 (Randall B. Ripley & James M. Lindsay eds., 1993)); Eric M. Uslaner, *Let the Chits Fall Where They May? Executive and Constituency Influences on Congressional Voting on NAFTA,* 23 LEGIS. STUD. Q. 347, 347 (1998) (citing William Schneider, *The Old Politics and the New World Order, in* EAGLE IN A NEW WORLD: AMERICAN GRAND STRATEGY IN THE POST-COLD WAR ERA (Kenneth A. Oye et al. eds., 1992)).

38. Uslaner, *supra* note 37, at 347.

39. *Id.* at 348.

40. *See generally, e.g.,* Nathan Leites & Christian de la Malene, *Paris from EDC to WEU,* 9 WORLD POL. 193 (1957) (analyzing the French Parliament's domestic political reasons, including sovereignty concerns, for rejecting the European Defense Community treaty in 1954).

41. *See generally* EVAN HAYNES, THE SELECTION AND TENURE OF JUDGES (2005).

42. *See generally* RULE BY LAW: THE POLITICS OF COURTS IN AUTHORITARIAN REGIMES (Tom Ginsburg ed., 2008); J. Mark Ramseyer & Eric B. Rasmusen, *Why Are Japanese Judges So Conservative in Politically Charged Cases?,* 95 AM. POL. SCI. REV. 331 (2001).

align their interpretations with prevailing or emerging international law norms. This
is not to say that judges are untouched by domestic politics; considerations such as
institutional preservation and legitimacy can and do affect judicial decision-making,
including on international issues.[43] In fact, Eyal Benvenisti argues that strategic
considerations—that is, protecting national and institutional interests—motivate
courts to conform their decisions to international norms, thereby signaling fidelity
to existing international law and preempting encroachment by international institutions. [44] Nonetheless, compared with legislatures, national courts facing international issues are more oriented toward international legal norms than toward
particular domestic policy considerations. At least where doing so is in tension with
achieving short-term domestic goals, legislators' relative provincialism coupled
with their political incentives give them little reason to achieve or maintain global
international law uniformity. As a result, we would expect that legislatures are most
likely to adopt domestic-oriented—rather than international-oriented—stances on
international legal issues, thereby diversifying states' international legal approaches.

II. LEGISLATIVE ADJUSTMENTS TO TREATIES
THROUGH RESERVATIONS

With these motivations in mind, we consider how the constitutional powers of legislatures equip them to act on their incentives. Despite legislators' comparatively
provincial orientation, national constitutions and/or custom generally give them
authority over how international law binds their states, including the power to
accept or reject treaties. Whether or not they are well-suited to take positions on
international cooperation issues, legislators are forced to do so. In fact, formal legislative influence over international engagement in many systems has increased in
recent decades.[45] For instance, the United Kingdom enacted statutory reforms in
2010 that, for the first time, gave its House of Commons formal power to block
treaty ratification.[46]

43. See generally LEE EPSTEIN & JACK KNIGHT, THE CHOICES JUSTICES MAKE (1998) (espousing a strategic theory of judicial decision-making); Martin Shapiro, Stability and Change in Judicial
Decision-Making: Incrementalism or Stare Decisis?, 2 L. TRANSITION Q. 134 (1965).

44. Eyal Benvenisti, Reclaiming Democracy: The Strategic Uses of Foreign and International Law by
National Courts, 102 AM. J. INT'L L. 241, 251, 268–70 (2008).

45. See MCLACHLAN, supra note 6, at 149–50.

46. House of Commons Library, Parliament's New Statutory Role in Ratifying Treaties (2011), available at http://www.parliament.uk/briefing-papers/sn05855.pdf. Granted, some have observed an
"erosion" or "waning" of foreign affairs legislative oversight in the United States and some other
states, though the opposite trend appears to be more influential. See, e.g., LINDA L. FOWLER,
WATCHDOGS ON THE HILL: THE DECLINE OF CONGRESSIONAL OVERSIGHT OF U.S. FOREIGN
RELATIONS (2015); LEE H. HAMILTON & JORDAN TAMA, A CREATIVE TENSION: THE FOREIGN
POLICY ROLES OF THE PRESIDENT AND CONGRESS 65 (2002); PARLIAMENTARY CONTROL OVER
FOREIGN POLICY (Antonio Cassesse ed., 1980).

In 2000, an Inter-Parliamentary Union-organized conference produced a declaration titled, "The Parliamentary Vision for International Cooperation at the Dawn of the Third Millennium."[47] Among other things, it outlined the main ways that parliaments work in international affairs.[48] Adapting and modifying that typology for our purposes, we focus on three ways in which legislatures are constitutionally empowered to affect international law: (1) by issuing reservations to treaties, which alter the country's international law obligations, including bargaining with executive officials over these reservations; (2) by expressing their understanding of treaties' meaning during pre-ratification deliberations, which narrows the range of interpretative choices available to domestic courts; and (3) by deciding, consistent with their policy preferences, how to transform international law into domestic law, thereby defining the country's international law conduct,[49] which can in turn partially shape both custom and future treaty meaning.[50] The rest of this chapter shows how these duties empower legislatures to shape the diversity of international law across systems.

A legislature's ability to force a treaty *reservation* changes the meaning of international law for that state alone. With some multilateral treaties,[51] especially human rights and security/disarmament treaties, states exempt themselves from certain provisions through reservations. [52] For human rights treaties, these reservations often provide that the state's obligation regarding a provision (or the treaty as a whole) will not exceed the standards of some other national institution.[53] This other institution is expressly mentioned in the text of the reservations and may consist of the reserving state's constitution, national law, or state religion. Across all issue areas, seeking exemption from monitoring mechanisms or jurisdictional immunity is also a common basis for reservations. Whatever its form, reservations alter the respective obligations of states regarding the treaty, which changes the substance of international law.[54]

---

47. CONFERENCE OF PRESIDING OFFICERS OF NATIONAL PARLIAMENTS, THE PARLIAMENTARY VISION FOR INTERNATIONAL COOPERATION AT THE DAWN OF THE THIRD MILLENNIUM, *available at* http://www.ipu.org/splz-e/sp-dclr.htm (last visited Sept. 14, 2017).

48. *Id.* (stating that parliaments affect international cooperation by: "(i) Influencing their respective countries' policy on matters dealt with in the United Nations and other international negotiating forums; (ii) Keeping themselves informed of the progress and outcome of these negotiations; (iii) Deciding on ratification, where the Constitution so foresees, of texts and treaties signed by governments; and (iv) Contributing actively to the subsequent implementation process").

49. *Cf.* Kevin L. Cope, *Congress's International Legal Discourse*, 113 MICH. L. REV. 1115, 1128–30 (2015).

50. Roberts, *supra* note 3.

51. Reservations generally apply only to multilateral treaties, as disagreements over specific terms of bilateral treaties are typically resolved through continued negotiation rather than reservations. *See* ANTHONY AUST, NATIONAL TREATY LAW AND PRACTICE 119 (2014).

52. BARBARA KOREMENOS, THE CONTINENT OF INTERNATIONAL LAW 163 tbl.6.3 (2016).

53. *See* Eric Neumayer, *Qualified Ratification: Explaining Reservations to International Human Rights Treaties*, 36 J. LEGAL STUD. 397, 407 (2007).

54. *See* IAN BROWNLIE, PRINCIPLES OF PUBLIC INTERNATIONAL LAW 612–15 (7th ed. 2008).

The division of domestic power for entering reservations differs by country, but in many systems, the legislature has some authority either to enter reservations unilaterally or to condition consent to ratification on the entry of reservations it prefers. In Iran, the parliament can demand reservations by including reservations in the domestic version of the treaty during the process of ratification. Parliament did so for Iran's reservations to the Convention on the Rights of the Child, the Organisation of the Islamic Conference Convention to Combat Terrorism, and the Convention on the Rights of Persons with Disabilities.[55] Indeed, Iran's parliament has enough sway over ratification that the Guardian Council (whose appointments are split between the parliament and Supreme Leader) effectively barred Iran's accession to the CEDAW, despite the executive's attempts at ratification. Upon ratifying the Convention on the Rights of the Child, Iran reserved "the right not to apply any provisions or articles of the Convention that are incompatible with Islamic Laws and the international legislation [sic] in effect."[56] As with other reservations required by Iran's parliament, this was included in the act passed by Iran's parliament, whereby the executive was "permitted" to accede to the CRC with the condition that it enter the reservation. Many other states also give legislatures power over reservations. To give just a few examples, under the Dutch system, the approval of the Staten-Generaal is required for all almost all types of treaties,[57] and the lower chamber is empowered to add reservations itself.[58] In South Africa, parliamentary committees can also demand reservations.[59] And in Chile, the Congress may "suggest" the formulation of reservations and interpretative declarations to international treaties.[60]

Even without formal power to add or request reservations unilaterally, legislatures can still affect their entry into force. A study by Beth Simmons shows that in the majority of national constitutions, the executive needs formal legislative approval to ratify at least some types of treaties.[61] Nearly 61 percent of the 177 surveyed states require legislative consent for treaty ratification (with 49 percent requiring a majority of one body for treaty approval and 12 percent requiring either a supermajority in one body or a majority in two bodies).[62] An additional 7 percent have a "rule or

---

55. For the text of these laws in Farsi, see CRC, at http://dastour.ir/brows/?lid=271250, OIC Convention, at http://dastour.ir/brows/?lid=320173, and CRPD, at http://dastour.ir/brows/?lid=320173.

56. Convention on the Rights of the Child, Sept. 2, 1990, 1577 UNTS 3. The actual enactment of Iran's parliament requires a "national legislation" exemption.

57. A few narrow classes of treaties do not need the approval of the Dutch parliament, mainly short or unimportant ones. Pieter van Dijk & Bahiyyih G. Tahzib, *Parliamentary Participation in the Treaty-Making Process of the Netherlands*, 67 CHI.-KENT L. REV. 413, 422–23 (1991).

58. *Id.* at 432.

59. N.J. Botha, *National Treaty Law and Practice: South Africa*, *in* NATIONAL TREATY LAW AND PRACTICE (Duncan B. Hollis et al. eds., 2005).

60. CONSTITUCIÓN POLÍTICA DE LA REPÚBLICA DE CHILE [C.P.] art. 54(1).

61. Verdier & Versteeg, *supra* note 9, at 514–33.

62. SIMMONS, *supra* note 9.

tradition" of informing and consulting the legislature about potential treaties, and perhaps, receiving informal guidance.[63]

Thus, whether or not they have formal power to make reservations, legislators may leverage their veto power over treaties to negotiate their reservations of choice.[64] As Helen Milner and Peter Rosendorff observe, "legislative rejection of international agreements ... indicates a failure of the legislature to exercise influence over the executive, rather than a successful influence attempt."[65] In any treaty submitted to the parliament, the executive must gain support from at least the median legislator. Unless the executive's party holds a majority of the body, this often requires enlisting members outside the executive's party. This is even more difficult in systems that require a supermajority for ratification. As such, legislative leaders may engage in behind-the-scenes, inter-branch bargaining with executive treaty negotiators.[66] Even in the 39 percent of countries that have no formal rule or tradition of parliamentary involvement in ratification,[67] the legislature may still be able to exert influence over treaty content. A significant fraction of that group constitutes Commonwealth or ex-Commonwealth countries with dualist approaches to international law. Approved treaties in those systems need parliamentary approval before taking domestic effect, so parliamentarians may be able to leverage that power during the treaty negotiation and ratification stages.

The off-the-record nature of inter-branch bargaining makes it difficult to know how often it happens or how it affects the substance of treaties globally. But it appears to occur to some extent in a significant number of systems. In Sweden, for instance, for treaties whose compliance requires passage or amendment to a domestic statute or which is otherwise within the purview of the parliament, the Riksdag can condition the ratification of a treaty both on entering certain reservations and on objecting to other states' reservations.[68] Likewise, in the United States, the Senate has long exercised the power to condition its "resolution of advice and consent" (which authorizes the president to ratify a treaty) on the entry of certain reservations.[69] In Iran, the executive must assess the value of entering a reservation to a treaty and report its findings to parliament.[70] The parliament may request modifications to a

---

63. *Id.*

64. Cope, *supra* note 49, at 1170–71.

65. Helen V. Milner & B. Peter Rosendorff, *Democratic Politics and International Trade Negotiations: Elections and Divided Government as Constraints on Trade Liberalization*, 41 J. CONFLICT RESOL. 117, 118 (1997).

66. *See* Cope, *supra* note 49, at 1170–72.

67. *See supra* text accompanying note 62.

68. *See* Iain Cameron, *Swedish Parliamentary Participation in the Making and Implementation of Treaties*, 74 NORDIC J. INT'L L. 429, 452–53 (2005).

69. LOUIS HENKIN, FOREIGN AFFAIRS AND THE U.S. CONSTITUTION 180 (2d ed. 1996).

70. Article 177(2) of the Law on the Internal Rules of Procedure of the Islamic Consultative Assembly [Majlis] of 13 June 1982 as later amended and article 8 of the Bylaw on Method of Drafting and Conclusion of International Agreements of 30 May 1992.

treaty submitted to it for ratification,[71] in which case, the executive effectively must renegotiate the terms based on parliament's requirements.

III. LEGISLATIVE INTERPRETATION OF TREATIES THROUGH UNDERSTANDINGS

Even where legislative action does not formally alter a state's treaty obligations in a way sanctioned by the Vienna Convention, legislatures promote cross-country variation by entering respective *understandings* of treaty terms. Unlike reservations, understandings do not exclude treaty obligations. Rather, they constitute the state party's interpretations of vague or ambiguous provisions, including how they will apply in the state's domestic order. By changing how legislatures' own domestic courts and other officials interpret the treaty, understandings bolster differences in how governments view a given international law provision.

The US system offers a fine example of legislative power to interpret treaty obligations for the state. There are different schools of thought on the extent of that power. The majority view, implied in the most recent restatement of US foreign relations[72] and advocated by Louis Henkin, holds that "if the Senate makes its understanding [of a treaty provision] explicit, that understanding is binding" on domestic court interpretations.[73] Thus, while US courts make treaties' language the starting point of their analysis and consider drafter intent,[74] the interpretation of the legislature often prevails.[75] In fact, the US Supreme Court in *United States v. Stuart* implied in dicta that even understandings conveyed during pre-ratification Senate debate constitute strong evidence of a treaty's meaning.[76] Some judges and authors believe that such intent carries more authority even than the treaty's negotiating history.[77]

Legislative understandings can also affect a state's international legal behavior indirectly. For instance, in the US Supreme Court's 2008 *Medellin v. Texas* decision, the Court held that neither the UN Charter nor the Optional Protocol to the Vienna Convention on Consular Relations (VCCR) were

---

71. Article 177(2) of the Law on the Internal Rules of Procedure of the Islamic Consultative Assembly [Majlis] of 13 June 1982 as later amended.

72. RESTATEMENT (THIRD) OF THE LAW OF FOREIGN RELATIONS § 314 cmt. d (Am. Law Inst. 1987).

73. *The ABM Treaty and the Constitution: Joint Hearings Before the Committees on Foreign Relations and Judiciary*, 100th Cong. 90 (1987) (statement of Louis Henkin, University Professor, Columbia Law School).

74. *See, e.g.,* Sumitomo Shoji Am., Inc. v. Avagliano, 457 U.S. 176, 185 (1982).

75. *See generally* David A. Koplow, *Constitutional Bait and Switch: Executive Reinterpretation of Arms Control Treaties*, 137 U. PA. L. REV. 1353, 1406 (1989).

76. United States v. Stuart, 489 U.S. 353, 368 n.7 (1989); *see also* Detlev F. Vagts, *Senate Research Materials and Treaty Interpretation: Some Research Hints for the Supreme Court*, 83 AM. J. INT'L L. 546 (1989) (arguing that legislative materials are pertinent to treaty interpretations).

77. *Stuart*, 489 U.S. at 368 n.7; *see* Koplow, *supra* note 75, at 1420.

self-executing.[78] The majority concluded that the lack of a "clear statement" of self-execution in the treaty text or ratification materials suggested it was not intended to be self-executing. The United States had violated the VCCR when Texas state officials did not give then-murder suspect Jose Medellin consular access and, after his conviction and appeal, refused the ICJ-ordered relief of "review and reconsideration of the convictions and sentences."[79] These events spurred the Senate to take greater responsibility for treaties' domestic operation. Shortly after *Medellin*, the US Senate Committee on Foreign Relations started a practice of adding to its articles of advice and consent the Court's suggested "clear statement." These statements clarified whether the body considers the treaty to be self-executing,[80] thereby bolstering legislative control over how treaties are internally enforced.

Because Congress's understandings of treaty provisions can directly impact how the state performs its obligations, they can also carry international legal effect.[81] Relying on congressional expressed or implied understandings of meaning, domestic courts sometimes interpret a treaty differently from how a tribunal relying on plain treaty language or negotiation history would. When doing so, those courts rarely mean to enforce domestic law over international law, thereby violating the latter, as when enacted legislation contradicts a prior binding international law. Rather, they are taking the view of their national legislature as the persuasive or controlling authority on what international law means. In this sense, the legislative understandings of a given international law norm are transformed into judicial interpretations of that norm. And because domestic judicial interpretations of international law are one source of authority for international courts and other bodies,[82] these decisions can in turn affect the broader formation of that norm.[83] Although this phenomenon has been more closely examined in the context of US law, its logic applies to any national system in which domestic courts give deference

---

78. Medellin v. Texas, 128 S. Ct. 1346 (2008). *See* Ilya Shapiro, *Medellin v. Texas and the Ultimate Law School Exam*, 2008 CATO SUP. CT. REV. 63, for an excellent background of *Medellin* and the legal issues it presented.

79. Avena and Other Mexican Nationals (Mex. v. U.S.), Judgment, 2004 I.C.J. Rep. 12, ¶ 97 (Mar. 31).

80. S. EXEC. REP. NO. 110-12, at 9–10 (2008). That practice appears to have ended when the Republican Party regained a Senate majority in 2014.

81. *See* Stefan A. Riesenfeld & Frederick M. Abbott, *The Scope of U.S. Senate Control over the Conclusion and Operation of Treaties, in* PARLIAMENTARY PARTICIPATION IN THE MAKING AND OPERATION OF TREATIES: A COMPARATIVE STUDY 613–15 (1994) (criticizing this approach).

82. *See, e.g.,* Statute of the International Court of Justice art. 38(1)(d), June 26, 1945, 33 U.N.T.S. 993 (listing "judicial decisions . . . of the various nations, as subsidiary means for the determination of rules of law"); Roberts, *supra* note 3, at 58 ("In explicating international law, textbooks and articles habitually draw on domestic judgments, . . . The same is true of international courts like the (ICJ) and the (ICTY).").

83. Roberts, *supra* note 3, at 59.

to legislative interpretations of enacted treaties. In this way, legislatures can shape domestic courts' interpretation of international law, leading to divergent practices between states in the short term but more universal norms in the long term.

IV. LEGISLATIVE DOMESTICATION OF INTERNATIONAL LAW

In addition to affecting international law at the creation stage, legislatures diversify state conceptions of a single international norm by *implementing* or *domesticating* it. Legislatures play an active role in interpreting international law by passing laws that give treaties life in national jurisdictions. That is, particularly in dualist systems[84] (though also in monist ones), legislatures define how a state will respond to international law by translating non-self-executing treaty law into domestic law through a process that is variously known as incorporation, domestication, or implementation. Legislatures also decide whether and how to take international rules into account when enacting or repealing related domestic legislation. These decisions matter for how a given law norm operates within a state and often prevail over the corresponding treaty terms themselves.[85] They also affect the content of customary international law, by enacting laws pertaining to the international relations of the state, and by codifying existing or emerging customary law into statute. This is particularly important in civil law systems, where courts are generally bound by the enactments of their national legislatures as to both treaties and customary law.[86]

A. Deciding How to Domesticate Treaties

Legislatures can often use an implementing statute both to clarify ambiguities and to stipulate the legislature's policy preferences, particularly where those preferences diverge from the plain meaning of the international norm being domesticated.[87] This act of international-to-domestic transformation can frame other state organs' view of the treaty's requirements. This, in turn, can shape the state's compliance. In the United Kingdom, the power to legislate pursuant to treaties (even before the 2010 reforms)[88] "provided Parliament with an important means to check the Crown's power in foreign affairs, one that it gradually used to seize an influential

---

84. *See* Verdier & Versteeg, *supra* note 9, at 523 (noting that almost all monist systems recognize exceptions for non-self-executing treaties).

85. BROWNLIE, *supra* note 54, at 45–49.

86. For instance, Iranian courts may apply custom only in cases expressly indicated by law or where written law is lacking or ambiguous. QANUNI ASSASSI JUMHURII ISLAMAI IRAN [CONSTITUTION OF THE ISLAMIC REPUBLIC OF IRAN] 1358 [1980], arts. 166–67; AINI DADRASSII MADANI [CIVIL PROCEDURE CODE] Tehran 1379 (2000) art. 3 (Iran).

87. John H. Jackson, *Status of Treaties in Domestic Legal Systems: A Policy Analysis,* 86 AM. J. INT'L L. 310, 324–25 (1992).

88. *See supra* text accompanying note 46.

role in the setting of national policy."[89] Indeed, the implementing statutory framework often binds national courts who might have preferred a different approach. As one Indian author put it, even where a treaty has been ratified, national courts of India "cannot say yes if Parliament has said no to" whether or how a treaty should be received domestically.[90] Likewise, the US Congress has power to determine the state's response to international obligations. Though statutory interpretation principles require courts where possible to conform statutes to binding international law, Congress can pre-empt such constructions—perhaps triggering an international law violation—by clearly expressing that intent.[91] Though there are important variations, the parliaments of most dualist systems hold similar authority.[92] In essence, legislatures as a whole hold considerable power over whether and how states follow their treaty obligations.

In monist systems (which coincide strongly with countries featuring civil law traditions), legislatures' role in transforming most treaty law into domestic law is relatively small. Instead, that transformation occurs automatically with the treaty's ratification. Yet a non-trivial number of treaties requires even monist systems to take additional steps for the treaty to have full effect. For instance, the 1993 Chemical Weapons Convention requires state parties to prohibit their subjects from using chemical weapons, with "chemical weapons" defined quite broadly.[93] The Convention leaves to the state party's discretion both the legal apparatus for this prohibition and the punishment for violation. How precisely to comply with these treaty requirements therefore depends largely on a national legislative process, even in monist systems. The same is true of all treaties on international and transnational crimes. These treaties invariably depend on national legislatures to provide the teeth for the crimes enumerated in the treaties and to enact specific laws for the prevention and punishment of the relevant crime within their jurisdictions.

Moreover, even in systems where treaties can have direct domestic effect, courts and administrative agencies may take cues from the legislature on whether and how to respond to ratified treaties. For instance, in deciding how to weigh a treaty's provisions, courts may look to whether the legislature has acted specifically to implement the treaty through legislation. Where it has been silent or implied that no legislation is necessary, courts and agencies may be reluctant to apply the terms of even a self-executing treaty. As one author notes about Sweden, "in cases where a

---

89. Melissa Waters, *Creeping Monism: The Judicial Trend Toward Interpretive Incorporation of Human Rights Treaties*, 107 COLUM. L. REV. 628 (2007) (citing John C. Yoo, *Globalism and the Constitution: Treaties, Non-Self-Execution, and the Original Understanding*, 99 COLUM. L. REV. 1955, 2004 (1999)). These statements were made before the 2010 reforms mentioned above, which gave Parliament formal power to block treaty ratification. *See supra* text accompanying note 46.

90. Nihal Jayawickrama, *India, in* THE ROLE OF DOMESTIC COURTS IN TREATY ENFORCEMENT: A COMPARATIVE STUDY (David Sloss ed., 2009).

91. Murray v. Schooner Charming Betsy, 6 U.S. (2 Cranch) 64 (1804).

92. Verdier & Versteeg, *supra* note 9.

93. Kevin L. Cope, *Lost in Translation: The Accidental Origins of* Bond v. United States, 112 MICH. L. REV. First Impressions 133, 135–36 (2014).

treaty has been approved but not converted to Swedish law, administrative agencies which should take account of the treaty, have, at least, on occasion, not felt any pressure to do so [particularly] if the parliament has stated its opinion that Swedish law fully complies with the demands of the treaty."[94]

To illustrate how legislative implementation can contribute to comparative international law, consider the implementation of the Rome Statute of the International Criminal Court (ICC).[95] As one of us has noted elsewhere,[96] the Rome Statute's implementation shows how legislation can cause the ostensibly uniform ICC scheme to operate differently in different systems.[97] Under the Rome Statute, the ICC has "complementary" jurisdiction over certain international crimes: states are the preferred venue for prosecutions, and the ICC can take jurisdiction only if the domestic system of the alleged perpetrator is "genuinely unwilling or unable" to prosecute the accused. Where a state lacks adequate prosecutorial, judicial, or statutory mechanisms, the ICC is therefore likely to assume jurisdiction. To function effectively as partner jurisdictions, states parties must therefore criminalize those things that the Rome Statute criminalizes: war crimes, crimes against humanity, genocide, and (as of 2017) the crime of aggression. Despite following the same Rome Statute blueprint, national legislatures implementing the Rome Statute crimes have used substantially different approaches.

For instance, the United Kingdom, Australia, and South Africa are a few of the states parties that match the Rome Statute crimes precisely; the British statute simply attaches several key articles verbatim to the implementing legislation.[98] The Netherlands and Germany include two of the articles verbatim. [99] In contrast, several states have adopted narrower definitions of prohibited conduct or provided no definitions. This is meaningful, because if the alleged criminal conduct does not meet the elements of the domestic definition (or if there is no domestic definition), a state cannot prosecute the offense. France, for example, did not enact a law specifically implementing the Rome Statute. For genocide, it maintained its existing, pre-ICC definition requiring that the crime be carried out as part of a "coordinated plan," which is not an element of the crime in the ICC's definition.[100] This approach has consequences for how the ICC operates with regard to these states,

---

94. *See* Cameron, *supra* note 68, at 454.

95. *See generally* W.N. FERDINANDUSSE, DIRECT APPLICATION OF INTERNATIONAL CRIMINAL LAW BY NATIONAL COURTS (2006).

96. Kevin L. Cope, *Treaty Law and National Legislative Politics, in* RESEARCH HANDBOOK ON THE POLITICS OF INTERNATIONAL LAW (Wayne Sandholtz & Christopher Whytock eds., 2017).

97. Wayne Sandholtz, Implementing the International Criminal Court (Aug. 15, 2014) (unpublished manuscript), *at* http://ssrn.com/abstract=2454824.

98. *See* Julio Bacio Terracino, *National Implementation of ICC Crimes Impact on National Jurisdictions and the ICC*, 5 J. INT'L CRIM. JUSTICE 421, 423–24 (2007).

99. Goran Sluiter, *Implementation of the ICC Statute in the Dutch Legal Order*, 2 J. INT'L CRIM. JUSTICE 158 (2004).

100. Terracino, *supra* note 98, at 426–27.

as the ICC is more likely to take jurisdiction because of those states' "inability to prosecute." Still other parties, such as Venezuela, Mexico, and Colombia, define few or no ICC crimes at all. The Venezuelan legislature has defined only the crimes of torture and forced disappearance of persons.[101] Venezuela could therefore also face the inability-to-prosecute scenario for the other crimes,[102] giving the ICC jurisdiction over potential defendants in that country. This diversity of responses to a single international law norm means that the ICC mechanism might handle Rome Statute-related conduct occurring in South Africa or Australia differently from how it would handle the very same conduct occurring in Venezuela or Columbia.

There are undoubtedly many reasons for these varying approaches to implementation. One theory is that the political climate of certain states explains some of it; the political will to hold officials liable for crimes such as genocide, crimes against humanity, and war crimes has "rarely existed in the states of [the Latin American] region."[103] This lack of political will was expressed most effectively by many of the states parties' national legislatures' reluctance to adopt fully the ICC scheme. The result is the development of not one, but a patchwork of Rome Statute cooperation regimes.

Although the examples above mostly illustrate international law divergence, legislative treaty implementation can also foster convergence. Though domestic interpretations of international law formally bind only that state, they can influence international law externally.[104] The VCLT makes the subsequent practice of states relevant to treaty interpretation by other bodies.[105] The substance of implementing legislation can constitute a key aspect of this subsequent practice. If a sufficient number of states enacts legislation adopting a particular interpretation of a treaty provision, that same interpretation is more likely to gain acceptance elsewhere, thereby fostering convergence.

B. Codifying Customary International Law

In addition to implementing treaties, legislatures sometimes codify existing or emerging customary law into domestic code. Though courts often recognize and apply custom themselves, the norms are sometimes complex enough that a detailed statutory framework is more appropriate. For example, both the United Kingdom (State Immunities Act of 1978) and United States (Foreign Sovereign Immunities

---

101. Hugo Relva, *The Implementation of the Rome Statute in Latin American States*, 16 Leiden J. Int'l L. 331, 364 (2003).

102. Terracino, *supra* note 98, at 428.

103. Relva, *supra* note 101, at 366.

104. Jackson, *supra* note 87, at 325 (citing Vienna Convention on the Law of Treaties art. 31, *opened for signature* May 23, 1969, 1155 U.N.T.S. 331); Roberts, *supra* note 3.

105. *See* Vienna Convention on the Law of Treaties, *supra* note 104; Anthea Roberts, *Power and Persuasion in Investment Treaty Interpretation: The Dual Role of States*, 104 Am. J. Int'l L. 179, 179 (2010).

Act of 1976) codified the customary law of foreign state immunity. These statutes developed specific statutory regimes that were largely in line with the existing "restrictive approach" to foreign sovereign immunity, under which states are not immune for commercial-like conduct.[106] In 1972, the Council of Europe states had also enacted a state immunity treaty, the European Convention on State Immunity. Other states, including Argentina, Australia, Canada, Malaysia, Pakistan, Singapore, and South Africa codified the restrictive approach in their own statutes in the years following.[107] Though each was modeled after the same CIL norm, their approaches differ in important ways. For example, the European Convention adopts a presumption of non-immunity and enumerates conditions in which states are immune, while the UK and US acts begin with a presumption of immunity and list criteria for stripping that immunity.[108] These different legislative approaches to the same international rule mean that a state might receive state immunity in the United States for a given transaction but no immunity in a European state for a similar transaction.

As with treaties, national legislative codifications of customary international law can also foster convergence. Legislative actions constitute state practice and *opinio juris* for the purpose of developing evidence of customary international law. [109] The ICJ recognized as much in a 1955 decision. Having stated that nationality laws are an exercise of domestic jurisdiction, the *Nottebohm* court further stated that certain principles were deducible from such national legislation that could be applied on the international plane.[110] In determining the customary international law on jurisdictional immunities, the ICJ also recognized the diversity of national legislation on the issue. It conducted a comparative analysis of national legislation on the question of a "territorial tort exception" to immunity regarding acts of state causing death, personal injury, or damage to property.[111]

---

106. Pierre-Hugues Verdier & Erik Voeten, *How Does Customary International Law Change? The Case of State Immunity*, 59 INT'L STUD. Q. 209, 214 (2015).

107. David Gaukrodger, *Foreign State Immunity and Foreign Government Controlled Investors*, OECD Working Papers on Int'l Inv. 2010/02 (2010), *at* http://dx.doi.org/10.1787/5km91p0ksqs7-en (citing State Immunity Act 1978, 26 Eliz. 2, c. 33 (UK); State Immunity Act, R.S.C. 1985, c S-18 (Can.); *Foreign States Immunities Act 1985* (Cth) (Austl.); Immunities and Privileges Act 1984 (Malay.); State Immunity Ordinance, No. 6 of 1981, PAK. CODE (Pak.); State Immunity Act 1979 (Sing.); Foreign States Immunities Act No. 87, 1981 (S. Afr.); Law No. 24488, May 31, 1995 [28173] B.O. 1 (Arg.)).

108. Georges R. Delaume, *The State Immunity Act of the United Kingdom*, 73 AM. J. INT'L L. 185, 186–87 (1979).

109. *See Statement of Principles Applicable to the Formation of General Customary International Law*, International Law Association London Conference, 17–18 (2000), *at* http://www.ila-hq.org/download.cfm/docid/A709CDEB-92D6-4CFA-A61C4CA30217F376.

110. Nottebohm Case (second phase) (Liech. v. Guat.), Judgment, 1955 I.C.J. Rep. 4, 20–23 (Apr. 6).

111. Jurisdictional Immunities of the State (Ger. v. It.: Greece intervening), Judgment, 2012 I.C.J. Rep. 99, ¶¶ 62 *et seq.* (Feb. 3).

If we return to the state immunity example, both the UK and US approaches have influenced the development of foreign sovereign immunity in national legislatures and courts, as well as the customary international law itself.[112] For instance, the United Nations adopted a convention in 2004 using the restrictive approach, which was partly inspired by the US and UK models.[113]

C. Legislative Opposition and Structure

Finally, the diverse preferences of legislatures, as well as the constitutional rules governing foreign relations, can determine how a state complies with international law. Legislatures are not monoliths, and a given body can comprise a wide range of views about its state's ideal relationship with the international legal system. This distribution typically exceeds that of a state's executive officials, who are likely appointed by a single head-of-state seeking like-minded actors to carry out her agenda.

Distribution of legislative preferences can affect how a state responds to international law even after it is created. For example, divided government and more rigorous lawmaking processes both can frustrate attempts to implement any law that would implement some prior commitment. Legislative systems with greater structural barriers to enacting legislation may make compliance with international law more difficult in some cases, but easier in others. For instance, Yonatan Lupu finds that the more legislative "veto players" a state has (i.e., independent political actors empowered to block a state action), the more costly it is for executives to violate human rights treaties.[114] He finds that although more veto players makes ratification more difficult, opposition groups in legislatures can raise the costs of enacting legislation that would violate the treaty post-ratification. Although authoritarian leaders can bypass the legislature, it is costly to do so; cloaking repression in the rule of law via democratic mechanisms is preferable. As a result, states that empower opposition parties with legislative veto powers, Lupu concludes, experience less repression and other rights abuses.[115] In a similar vein, Lisa Martin argues that institutional struggles between domestic branches legitimize state commitments and strengthen international cooperation.[116] And Kenneth Schultz finds that domestic competition from opposition parties can in some cases make a government's threats to use force stronger and more credible.[117]

---

112. Verdier & Voeten, *supra* note 106, at 214.

113. *Id.* The Convention had not yet entered into force as of September 2016, though it had acquired 28 signatures and 21 of the 30 ratifications needed.

114. Yonatan Lupu, *Legislative Veto Players and the Effects of International Human Rights Agreements*, 59 Am. J. Pol. Sci. 578 (2015).

115. *Id.*

116. *See generally* Lisa L. Martin, Democratic Commitments: Legislatures and International Cooperation (2000).

117. Kenneth A. Schultz, Democracy and Coercive Diplomacy 9 (2001).

Such mechanisms and opposition veto players can also complicate international law compliance. That is, they can empower opposition parties to block measures intended to uphold prior commitments. For instance, in 2005, after the ICJ's *Avena* decision but before the Supreme Court decided *Medellín*, Republican president George W. Bush intervened in the matter, issuing a memorandum to the US attorney general. The memo purported to direct Texas courts to fulfill the United States' international legal obligations by complying with *Avena* and by reconsidering Medellín's and the other 50 Mexican nationals' cases.[118] In 2008, a few months before the Supreme Court decided *Medellín*, two Democratic members of Congress introduced a bill in the US House of Representatives, the *Avena Case Implementation Act of 2008*, to address the impasse.[119] The bill created a cause of action for foreign nationals who, like the *Avena* petitioners, had been convicted of crimes but had not received their Vienna Convention consular notification rights. One might have expected it to receive bipartisan support: it was largely consistent with President Bush's position on the issue, and it might have spared the United States further international embarrassment. Yet the House Committee on the Judiciary never acted on the bill.[120] The legislative history provides no insight into the reason. But we can assume that few legislators were eager to support retrials for foreigners convicted of violent felonies, especially on the basis of esoteric international-law procedural errors!

V. CONCLUDING THOUGHTS

To explain how a state's behavior relates to international norms and why that behavior differs from that of other states, it is important to examine more than just judicial decisions. We also need to look at what happens before a court receives the case: at how that law was received in the national legal system. In the case of treaties, this can be a lengthy, multistage process, involving the national legislature, civil society, executive officials, administrative agencies, courts, and, sometimes, branches of subnational and local governments.[121] In this sequence, the first significant domestic point-of-entry for these agreements often involves the national parliament. Legislatures serve this role through the several dynamics discussed above. Parliament-demanded reservations, legislative understandings, executive-legislature bargaining, and minority parties' leveraging concessions can all help or hinder a state's attempts at coordination.

---

118. Memorandum from President George W. Bush to Attorney Gen. U.S. (Feb. 28, 2005), *available at* https://georgewbush-whitehouse.archives.gov/news/releases/2005/02/20050228-18.html.

119. Avena Case Implementation Act of 2008, H.R. 6481, 110th Cong. (2008).

120. Legislative History of H.R. 6481 Avena Case Implementation Act of 2008, *available at* https://www.govtrack.us/congress/bills/110/hr6481 (last visited Sept. 14, 2017).

121. *See* Kevin L. Cope & Cosette D. Creamer, *Disaggregating the Human Rights Treaty Regime*, 56 VA. J. INT'L L. 459 (2016).

Those decisions about the treaty's place in the state's legal system also shape later decisions by other governmental and nongovernmental actors. And even before an issue reaches the courts, these interpretations can help to diversify an ostensibly uniform international rule. National legislatures and legislation should therefore form the presumptive starting point for most comparative international law analyses. Studies that try to explain international law variations across systems, but that overlook this process, risk missing a big part of the comparative international law story.

PART FIVE

Comparative International Law and Domestic Institutions

National Courts

14

International Law in Chinese Courts during the Rise of China

CONGYAN CAI*

I. INTRODUCTION

The number of countries in which domestic courts are actively engaged with major public affairs has increased markedly since the early 1990s. In many transitional states, in particular, domestic courts have ruled on great constitutional controversies, which influence the national political process.[1] They have also taken an active role in the application of international law—especially human rights treaties—and at times treat such treaties as a "New Standard of Civilization."[2] In particular, domestic courts have at times invoked international law in becoming more aggressive toward the executive branch.[3] This trend has been one normative element inspiring some theorists to propose a new field known as comparative international law.[4] This chapter highlights a different set of elements that become manifest in assessing the rapid overall rise in references to, and application of, international law by courts in China in recent years.

---

* This chapter was first published in the *American Journal of International Law*, vol. 110, no. 2 (Apr. 2016).

1. See generally, CONSEQUENTIAL COURTS: JUDICIAL ROLES IN GLOBAL PERSPECTIVE (Diana Kapiszewski, Gordon Silverstein & Robert A. Kagan eds., 2013).

2. See Jack Donnelly, *Human Rights: A New Standard of Civilization?*, 74 INT'L AFF. 1 (1998).

3. See THE ROLE OF DOMESTIC COURTS IN TREATY ENFORCEMENT (David Sloss ed., 2009); SHARON WEILL, THE ROLE OF NATIONAL COURTS IN APPLYING INTERNATIONAL HUMANITARIAN LAW (2014).

4. See Symposium, *Exploring Comparative International Law*, 109 AM. J. INT'L L. 467–550 (2015); Anthea Roberts, *Comparative International Law? The Role of National Courts in Creating and Enforcing International Law*, 60 INT'L & COMP. L.Q. 57 (2011).

While human rights treaties, a frequent focus of Western international law-yers when assessing practices of national courts, have hardly been applied by Chinese courts (which leads Nollkaemper to place Chinese courts and the courts of Afghanistan, Cuba, Iran, and North Korea in a group that he derides as playing "no role whatsoever in fulfilling" the protection of the international rule of law[5]), Chinese courts have significantly increased their application of international law over the past three decades, a trend that can be expected to accelerate. In contrast to existing research on the application of international law by Chinese courts, which focuses on purely textual analysis or case description and, more importantly, fails to explore the public policy underlying the courts' structural application of international law,[6] this chapter puts this trend in the context of the rise of China, which is believed to significantly shape world order in the twenty-first century. This new perspective would lead to a very different understanding of international law in Chinese courts, even though they apply international law in a same or similar manner in many respects as courts do in other states.

This chapter seeks to theorize Chinese judicial policy toward international law, without discussing this policy's legitimacy. My core argument is that China's 30-year pursuit of great power status has been a significant causal and explanatory factor in the particularities of approach, methodology, and structure in judicial application of international law by Chinese courts. Section II presents and dis-cusses the Chinese legal system's pathways for giving effect to international law. Section III reviews Chinese courts' sensitivity to differences among the various categories of relationships governed by specific international rules, and explores their connection with, and implications for, the economic and geopolitical rise of China.

---

5. ANDRÉ NOLLKAEMPER, NATIONAL COURTS AND THE INTERNATIONAL RULE OF LAW 13, 55 (2011).

6. *See* Dai Ruijun (戴瑞君), GUOJI RENQUAN TIAOYUE DE GUONEI SHIYONG YANJIU: QUANQIU SHIYE (国际人权条约的国内适用研究:全球视野) [DOMESTIC IMPLEMENTATION OF INTERNATIONAL HUMAN RIGHTS TREATIES: GLOBAL PERSPECTIVE] 254–95 (2013); Gong Renren, *Implementing International Human Rights Treaties in China, in* BRIDGING THE GLOBAL DIVIDE ON HUMAN RIGHTS: A CANADA-CHINA DIALOGUE 99 (Errol P. Mendes & Anik Lalonde-Roussy eds., 2003); Zhaojie Li (James Li), *The Role of Domestic Courts in the Adjudication of International Human Rights: A Survey of the Practice and Problems in China, in* ENFORCING INTERNATIONAL HUMAN RIGHTS IN DOMESTIC COURTS 329 (Benedetto Conforti & Francesco Francioni eds., 1997); Zheng Sophia Tang, *International Treaties in Chinese Private International Law,* 42 HONG KONG L.J. 311 (2012); Sanzhuan Guo, *Implementation of Human Rights Treaties by Chinese Courts: Problems and Prospects,* 8 CHINESE J. INT'L L.161 (2009); Jie Huang, *Direct Application of International Commercial Law in Chinese Courts: Intellectual Property, Trade, and International Transportation,* 5 MANCHESTER J. INT'L ECON. L. 105 (2008); Xiao Yongping & Long Weidi, *Selected Topics on the Application of the CISG in China,* 20 PACE INT'L L. REV. 61 (2008); WANG GUANXIAN (王光贤), JINZHI KUXING DE LILUN YU SHIJIAN (禁止酷刑的理论与实践) [THEORY AND PRACTICE AGAINST TORTURE] 270–77 (2007).

II. JUDICIAL POLICY AND PATHWAYS FOR THE APPLICATION OF INTERNATIONAL LAW

A. Historical Context

There are two main explanatory variables for modern China's judicial policy toward international law: socialism, and the rise of China. As to the socialist institutional system, Deng Xiaoping, the "chief architect" of China's economic reforms and opening-up policy, once argued that:

> The greatest advantage of the socialist system is that when the central leadership makes a decision, it is promptly implemented without interference from any other quarters. . . . We don't have to go through a lot of discussion and consultation, with one branch of government holding up another and decisions being made but not carried out. From this point of view, our system is very efficient. . . . We should keep it—we should retain the advantages of the socialist system.[7]

Deng's words reflect the institutional environment in which Chinese courts administer justice. Under the current Constitution of 1982, the Chinese Communist Party (CCP) is the sole ruling party.[8] Through its Party Committees at different levels, the CCP controls the operation of legislative, executive, and judicial organs. As Professor Zhu Suli observes, "the CCP's influence and control is ubiquitous; it penetrates every aspect of society," meaning that "there is no such thing as government policy independent from the CCP."[9] All state organs, especially executive bodies, pursue public policy set by the CCP. However, the extent of executive authority directly correlates with the risk that the executive branch will abuse its power and thereby threaten the rule of law. It is well recognized that executive bodies frequently interfere in the administration of justice, seriously damaging judicial independence.[10]

The other variable is the rise of China. In the late 1970s, after 10 years of "Cultural Revolution" (1966–1976), China was at the edge of economic collapse, political paralysis, and further social turmoil. Given this context, it is remarkable that China developed into a great power over the ensuing 40 years. The ideological approach for China's rise, sometimes dubbed the Beijing Consensus,[11] has two core elements: (1) a focus on economic growth over political democracy and social justice, which echoes Kennedy's argument that economic power is fundamental to the rise

---

7. 3 DENG XIAOPING, SELECTED WORKS OF DENG XIAOPING 187–88 (1994).

8. XIANFA (宪法) [CONSTITUTION] pmbl. (2004) (China).

9. Zhu Suli, *Political Parties in China's Judiciary*, 17 DUKE J. COMP. & INT'L L. 533, 535, 538 (2006).

10. RANDALL PEERENBOOM, CHINA'S LONG MARCH TOWARD RULE OF LAW 302–09 (2002).

11. *See* Bradley Klein, *Democracy Optional: China and the Developing World's Challenge to the Washington Consensus*, 22 UCLA PAC. BASIN L.J. 89 (2004).

of great powers;[12] and (2) an authoritarian regime with an executive branch that can pursue public policies, especially economic growth, as efficiently as possible, even though they are often in potential conflict with rule of law or legitimacy. For instance, as examined below, the executive branch often enjoys shields under the Administrative Procedure Law (APL) of 1990 too much.[13]

These two elements tend to encourage shielding executive authority from systematic challenge, which is a key element of Chinese judicial policy as a whole. This issue has been the subject of much debate among scholars of Chinese law. For instance, the APL (1990), a law adjudicating disputes between private entities and executive bodies including their agents, and the State Compensation Law (SCL) of 1994[14]—two key laws intended to control the abuse of executive power—have been identified as being poorly written and under-enforced. The APL (prior to amendment in 2014) sought to "support" rather than "supervise" the executive branch,[15] and remedies available to victims of executive misconduct are significantly limited under the SCL.[16] Furthermore, Chinese courts often convince themselves that they are required to respect, coordinate with, and assist executive bodies in the pursuit of their economic and social policies,[17] enhancing the "Chinese Dream of great rejuvenation of the Chinese nation."[18]

As waves of governmental scandals are uncovered, social stability deteriorates and the public loses its confidence in the quiescent judiciary,[19] China has responded by adjusting its traditional strategy of national development to focus on closer scrutiny of public authority.[20] In October 2014, the CCP adopted its first decision focusing

---

12. PAUL KENNEDY, THE RISE AND FALL OF THE GREAT POWERS xv, xxii (1989).

13. Xingzheng Susong Fa (行政诉讼法) [Administrative Procedure Law] [APL] (promulgated by the Nat'l People's Cong., Apr. 4, 1989, effective Oct. 1, 1990) (China).

14. Guojia Peichang Fa (国家赔偿法) [State Compensation Law] (promulgated by the Standing Comm. Nat'l People's Cong., May 12, 1994, effective Jan. 1, 1995) (China), translated in 6 P.R.C. LAWS 39.

15. Ji Weidong, The Judicial Reform in China: The Status Quo and Future Directions, 20 IND. J. GLOBAL LEGAL STUD. 185, 196 (2013).

16. See Ying Songnian & Yang Xiaojun (应松年、杨小君), Guojia Peichang Ruogan Lilun yu Shijian Wenti (国家赔偿若干理论与实践问题) [Some Theoretical and Practical Issues on State Compensation Law] 1 CHINESE LEGAL SC. 3, 3 (2005) (China).

17. HOU MENG (侯猛), ZHONGGUO ZUIGAO RENMIN FAYUAN YANJIU (中国最高人民法院研究) [A STUDY ON THE SUPREME PEOPLE'S COURT OF CHINA] 67–71 (2007) (China).

18. See, e.g., Zhou Qiang, Report on the Work of the Supreme People's Court: Delivered at the Second Session of the Twelfth National People's Congress on March 10, 2014, XINHUANET (May 9, 2014), at http://news.xinhuanet.com/legal/2014-05/09/c_126481178.htm.

19. See Ji Weidong, supra note 15, at 208–09.

20. See Zhonggong Zhongyang Guanyu Quanmian Shenhua Gaige Ruogan Zhongda Wenti de Jueding (中共中央关于全面深化改革若干重大问题的决定) [CCP Central Committee Decision on Major Issues Concerning Comprehensively Deepening Reforms], XINHUANET (Nov. 16, 2013), at http://www.sn.xinhuanet.com/2013-11/16/c_118166672.htm (parts IX and X).

on the promotion of the rule of law.[21] Then, in November 2014, the CCP amended the APL to ensure the people's courts *supervise* the exercise of the executive powers in accordance with law.[22] The amended version of the APL also includes a provision that forbids administrative organs from interfering with or obstructing the courts in accepting and hearing administrative cases.[23] Whether the positive trend extends to China's judicial policy toward international law will be examined later.

It is against this background that the Chinese legal system's approach to international law needs to be analyzed.

B. China's Constitutional Silence on International Law

In many domestic legal systems, the constitution determines international law's status in the domestic legal system. The Chinese Constitution, however, is silent about international law.

Two straightforward explanations exist for China's silence regarding international law in its Constitution. The first is the influence of Soviet international legal theory and practice. The Soviet states once claimed that a handful of Western states controlled international law. As a result, they never mentioned international law in their constitutions. China's decision to model its 1954 Constitution on the Soviet Constitution of 1936 may thus partly explain the absence of any mention of international law. The second explanation lies within China's history. After the First Opium War (1839–1842), Western powers and Japan forced China to conclude many "unequal" treaties under duress. This experience, known in China as the "Century of Humiliation," led China to treat international law with hostility well into the twentieth century.[24]

China's constitutional silence regarding international law contributes to the fragmentation and unpredictability that characterizes its domestic application. Almost all Chinese international lawyers agree that this issue should be clarified at the constitutional level,[25] but the government has yet to include such a clarification in its

---

21. *See Zhonggong Zhongyang Guanyu Quanmian Tuijin Yifa Zhiguo Ruogan Zhongda Wenti de Jueding* (中共中央关于全面推进依法治国若干重大问题的决定) [*CCP Central Committee Decision on Major Issues Concerning Promoting the Rule of Law*], Xinhuanet (Oct. 28, 2014), http://news.xinhuanet.com/2014-10/28/c_1113015330.htm; Xi Jinping (习近平), *Guanyu "Zhonggong Zhongyang Guanyu Quanmian Tuijin Yifa Zhiguo Ruogan Zhongda Wenti de Juiding"* ("关于《中共中央关于全面推进依法治国若干重大问题的决定》的说明")[Notes on *CCP Central Committee Decision on Major Issues Concerning Promoting the Rule of Law*], Xinhuanet (Oct. 28, 2014) (China), http://news.xinhuanet.com/politics/2014-10/28/c_1113015372.htm.

22. Administrative Procedure Law [APL of 2014], Art. 1 (amended by the Standing Comm. Nat'l People's Cong., Nov. 11, 2014 effective May 1, 2015) (China).

23. *Id.* art. 3.

24. Wang Tieya, *International Law in China: Historical and Contemporary Perspectives*, 221 Recueil des Cours 195, 250–62 (1990).

25. *See* Guoji Tiaoyue yu Guonei Fa de Guanxi (国际条约与国内法的关系) [Relations between International Treaties and Domestic Law] 17, 40, 159 (Zhu Xiaoqing (朱晓青), Huang Lie (黄列) eds., 2000).

agenda. In 2014, during debates on the amendment of the Legislation Law, some members of the Standing Committee of the National People's Congress (NPC) suggested that the amended Legislation Law should include provisions clarifying the status of treaties in the domestic legal system.[26] Other NPC members, however, maintained that inclusions of these provisions might be inappropriate.[27] The final version of the law, promulgated in March 2015, does not include any provisions clarifying the status of treaties in the Chinese domestic legal system.[28]

Examined from another angle, I would like to highlight that fragmentation and unpredictability also imply flexibility. For a state such as China, which is in the midst of rising within a rapidly changing world, flexibility is more important than formal commitment-stability. Flexibility grants China a greater margin to pursue public policy. Also, in a sense, China's approach to the domestic application of international law accords with the recent trend toward the incorporation of international law in domestic legal systems in a flexible manner in order to balance concerns regarding the effectiveness of international law with beliefs in the greater legitimacy and normative priority of domestic governance.[29]

C. Automatic Incorporation

Automatic incorporation empowers courts to give effect to international law in the absence of implementing legislation.[30] More than one hundred provisions in nearly 80 laws passed between 1978 and 2004 embrace automatic incorporation to varying extents.[31]

This flexibility regarding the usage of automatic incorporation, when mandated by specific legislation rather than a constitutional provision, makes sense in the context of the rise of China. For example, the maintenance of executive authority, a core element of the Beijing Consensus, tends not to support the use of automatic incorporation of international law. But, since automatic incorporation can have little effect on executive authority in cases where the international legal rules govern

---

26. Chen Liping (陈丽平), *Mingque Guoji Tiaoyue zai Woguo de Shiyong* (明确国际条约在我国的适用) [*The Application of Treaties in China Should Be Clarified*], LEGALDAILY (Nov. 24, 2014), *available at* http://www.npc.gov.cn/npc/cwhhy/12jcwh/2014-11/24/content_1886934.htm.

27. *Id.*

28. Lifa Fa (立法法) [Law on Legislation] (promulgated by the Nat'l People's Cong., Mar. 15, 2000, effective July 1, 2000, amended by the Standing Comm. Nat'l People's Cong., Mar. 13, 2015) (China).

29. *See* Pierre-Hugues Verdier & Mila Versteeg, *International Law in National Legal Systems: An Empirical Investigation*, 109 AM. J. INT'L L. 514 (2015).

30. NOLLKAEMPER, *supra* note 5, at 73.

31. WANG YONG (王勇), TIAOYUE ZAI ZHONGGUO SHIYONG ZHI JIBEN LILUN WENTI YANJIU (条约在中国适用之基本理论问题研究) [FUNDAMENTAL THEORY OF THE APPLICATION OF TREATIES IN CHINA] 146 (2007).

solely the legal relations between private parties, no relative authority concerns arise in these contexts, and automatic incorporation is accordingly sometimes used.[32]

In this regard, a good example is Article 142 of the General Principles of Civil Law (GPCL). Article 142 provides:

> If any international treaty concluded or acceded to by the People's Republic of China contains provisions differing from those in the civil laws of the People's Republic of China, the provisions of the international treaty shall apply, unless the provisions are ones on which the People's Republic of China has announced reservations.[33]

The GPCL serves to regulate civil and commercial affairs between private entities, which have little to do with executive authority. The significance of this provision lies in its reference to the plural "civil laws" as opposed to the singular "civil law." In such context, it should be interpreted to apply not only to the GPCL itself, but also to all laws classified as "civil laws."[34]

Interestingly, Article 72 of the APL of 1990 also provided that "If an international treaty concluded or acceded to by the People's Republic of China contains provisions different from those found in this law, the provisions of the international treaty shall apply, unless the provisions are ones on which the People's Republic of China has announced reservations."[35] This version of Article 72 of the APL embraced automatic incorporation, which means Chinese courts should not be prevented from giving direct effect to international legal commitments, such as the International Covenant on Economic, Social and Cultural Rights of 1966 (ICESCR). Indeed, this version of Article 72 was an important legal basis for the statement of the Chinese representative to the International Convention Against Torture and Other Cruel, Inhuman or Degrading Treatment or Punishment (CAT) Committee that the convention is directly applicable by Chinese courts.[36]

However, the NPC repealed Article 72 as a legal basis for automatic incorporation in the 2014 amendments to the APL,[37] which was the first time China repealed provisions regarding international law from its domestic laws. The NPC provided no explanation for this repeal in the Report by the Legal Committee of National

---

32. *See infra* Section III.D.

33. Minfa Tongze (民法通则) [General Principles of Civil Law] [GPCL] (promulgated by the Nat'l People's Cong., Apr. 12, 1986, effective Jan. 1, 1987) 37 FAGUI HUIBIAN 1 (China). Unless otherwise indicated, translations of Chinese law provisions are not official translations.

34. Wang Tieya, *supra* note 24, at 332.

35. APL of 1990, *supra* note 13, Art. 72.

36. Convention Against Torture and Other Cruel, Inhuman or Degrading Treatment or Punishment, Dec. 10, 1984, 1465 U.N.T.S. 85, *at* https://treaties.un.org/doc/Publication/MTDSG/Volume%20I/Chapter%20IV/iv-9.en.pdf. The 1990 statement in quotes in the text accompanying note 97, *infra*.

37. *See* ALP of 2014, *supra* note 22.

People's Congress on the Amendment of Administrative Procedural Law.[38] According to the amended APL, Chinese courts must exclusively apply national laws to decide claims against executive organs and can only utilize international law for interpretative purposes.[39] This repeal has a number of negative consequences. While it is too early to argue that China has returned to its former hostile treatment of international law, the repeal is consistent with a conservative judicial policy toward international law as a constraint on public authority. Furthermore, the repeal makes it more difficult for China to honor its treaty obligations. For instance, all Chinese investment treaties allow foreign investors to bring claims against the Chinese government,[40] but the amended APL prevents Chinese courts from deciding disputes based on those treaties.

There are three likely reasons for the repeal of Article 72 from the APL. First, the NPC may have eliminated Article 72 because it is rarely invoked in practice, which makes it unnecessary. Second, the former Article 72 of the APL had not in practice been intended to mean that China would be willing to put its executive authority under systematic and close surveillance by reference to international law, in particular. Thus, the NPC may have eliminated Article 72 to align the legal text with the long-prevailing intention. The main consideration, however, may be that the NPC intended to shield China's executive authority from potentially increasing judicial challenges. China might have grown increasingly concerned with the potential that judicial reform, combined with China's ratification of a growing number of multilateral treaties, will empower the courts to contain executive authority by applying international law. Repealing Article 72 responds to these concerns regarding implication of any growth in judicial independence. This explanation suggests that increasing judicial independence, combined with the conclusion of more treaties that grant rights to individuals vis-à-vis the state, could prompt further constraints on the direct application of such treaties by Chinese courts.

D. Transformation

Transformation requires legislatures to act in relation to each specific international commitment before courts can enforce that specific international law.[41] While China continues to have many laws that adopt automatic incorporation, transformation

---

38. *See* Quanguo Renmin Daibiao Dahui Falu Weiyuanhui guanyu "Zhonghua Renmin Gongheguo Xingzheng Susong Fa Xiuzheng An (Cao'an)" Xiugai Qingkuang de Huibao (全国人民代表大会法律委员会关于《中华人民共和国行政诉讼法修正案（草案）》修改情况的汇报) [Report by the Legal Committee of National People's Congress on the Amendment of Administrative Procedural Law (draft)], NPC (Aug. 31, 2014) (China), *at* http://www.npc.gov.cn/npc/lfzt/2014/2014-08/31/content_1876868.htm.

39. *See* ALP of 2014, *supra* note 22, Art. 63.

40. *See* WENHUA SHAN, THE LEGAL FRAMEWORK OF EU-CHINA INVESTMENT RELATIONS: A CRITICAL APPRAISAL 210 (2005).

41. *Id.* at 77.

is the most common way for the country to implement its treaty obligations.[42] However, transformation as a systematic technique only began to be taken seriously upon China's accession to the World Trade Organization (WTO) in 2001. At that time, most Chinese lawyers proposed that Chinese courts could directly apply at least some WTO rules.[43] In 2002, the Supreme People's Court (SPC) effectively rejected these proposals with the promulgation of its Regulations on Issues Concerning the Trial of Administrative Cases Relating to International Trade (Trade Case Regulations).[44] Judge Li Guoguang, the SPC's Deputy President at that time, clarified that WTO rules could not be directly applied in disputes between private parties and executive organs.[45] This means that private parties cannot invoke WTO rules before courts and courts cannot directly use WTO rules as the basis for adjudication,[46] which, of course, is a rule for other WTO members. In the *Shenzhen Chengjie'er Trade Co., Ltd. Case*, the respondent, Tianjin Customs District, detained the imported goods of the plaintiff, Chengjie'er.[47] The plaintiff argued that the prolonged detention breached Article 55 of the Agreement on Trade-Related Aspects of Intellectual Property Right (TRIPS).[48] A Tianjin court decided that, according to the Trade Case Regulations, Chinese laws should be applied, rather than the TRIPS Agreement.[49] In *Longines Co. v. Trademark Review & Adjudication Board*, a Beijing court affirmed that the defendant was justified in not relying directly in its decision upon the TRIPS Agreement because its provisions were "included in the current Trademark Law."[50]

42. Xue Hanqin & Jin Qian, *International Treaties in the Chinese Domestic Legal System*, 8 CHINESE J. INT'L L. 299, 308 (2009).

43. *See* CAI CONGYAN (蔡从燕), SIREN JIEGOUXING CANYU DUOBIAN MAOYI TIZHI (私人结构性参与多边贸易体制) [PRIVATE STRUCTURAL PARTICIPATION IN THE MULTILATERAL TRADE SYSTEM] 265–68 (2007).

44. Zuigao Renmin Fayuan Guanyu Shenli Guoji Maoyi Xingzheng Anjian Ruogan Wenti de Guiding (最高人民法院关于审理国际贸易行政案件若干问题的规定) [Regulations of the Supreme People's Court on Issues Concerning the Trial of Administrative Cases Relating to International Trade] (promulgated by the Sup. People's Ct., Aug. 27, 2002, effective Oct. 1, 2002) SUP. PEOPLE'S CT. GAZ. 165 (China).

45. *See* Li Guoguang (李国光), "Guanyu Shenli Guoji Maoyi Xingzheng Anjian Ruogan Wenti de Guiding" Xinwen Fabu Hui Shang de Jianghua (《关于审理国际贸易行政案件若干问题的规定》新闻发布会上的讲话) [Regulations of the Supreme People's Court on Issues Concerning the Trial of Administrative Cases Relating to International Trade] (Aug. 29, 2002) (China), *at* http://www.lawxp.com/statute/s898388.html.

46. *Id.*

47. RENMIN FAYUAN ANLI XUAN (人民法院案例选) [Selected Collection of People's Court Cases] 365–68 (Shen Deyong(沈德咏) eds., 2013) (China).

48. *Id.* at 366.

49. *Id.* at 368.

50. Langqinbiao Youxian Gongsi Su Guojia Gongshang Xingzheng Guanli Zongju Shangbiao Pingshen Weiyuanhui (浪琴表有限公司诉国家工商行政管理总局商标评审委员会)

Generally, transformation allows China to deal with treaty commitments on a case-by-case basis and to water down those commitments which may grant rights to individuals vis-à-vis the state.[51]

E. Consistent Interpretation

Even in the absence of legislative action, judiciaries in practice can apply international law by interpreting national law in conformity with an international obligation (the principle of consistent interpretation).[52] The Chinese courts sometimes employ the principle of consistent interpretation when considering domestic laws that do not explicitly provide for it. For instance, in *Nanning XX Service LLC v. Nanning XX Bureau*, there was disagreement regarding the meaning of "workplace."[53] China's Work Injury Insurance Regulations of 2010 fail to provide a definition.[54] The court decided that the Regulations should be interpreted in conformity with Article 3(c) of the Convention Concerning Occupational Safety and Health and the Working Environment (to which China is a contracting party), which provides that "the term workplace covers all places where workers need to be or to go by reason of their work and which are under the direct or indirect control of the employer."[55]

Consistent interpretation might be used in a subtler manner as well. Searches on Pkulaw.cn (北大法宝), a leading legal database in China, reveal that international law is often mentioned in case reviews written by judges who generally are colleagues of judges hearing the cases. Therefore, it might be assumed that, while the principle of seeking to make an interpretation that is consistent with international law does not appear so much in judgments, it is employed in judicial reasoning.

Most directly, the principle of consistent interpretation has been used in relation to China's WTO commitments. While excluding the direct effect of WTO rules, the Trade Case Regulations, already discussed above, utilize the principle of consistent interpretation. While most states do not provide an explicit mandate for the principle in their domestic law,[56] China is one of the few that does. According to Article 9 of the Trade Case Regulations, "[i]f there are two or more

[Longqinbiao Co. Ltd. v. Trademark Review & Adjudication Bd.] (Beijing Interm. People's Ct. Aug. 14, 2012) (China), *at* http://www.pkulaw.cn/case/pfnl_118497741.html?match=Exact.

51. Admittedly, the existing surveillance mechanisms of many, if not most, treaties are not effective enough to prompt states parties to incorporate treaties into their domestic legal systems.

52. NOLLKAEMPER, *supra* note 5, at 73–81.

53. Nanning XX Fuwu Youxian Zeren Gongsi Su Nanning Shi XX Ju (南宁XX服务有限责任公司诉南宁市XX局) [Nanning XX Serv. LLC. v. Nanning XX Bureau] (Nanning Dist. People's Ct., Jan. 10, 2012) (China), *at* http://www.pkulaw.cn/case/pfnl_118505863.html.

54. *Id.*

55. *Id.*

56. NOLLKAEMPER, *supra* note 5, at 147.

reasonable interpretations for a provision of the law or administrative regulation applied by a people's court in the hearing of an international trade administrative case, and among which one interpretation is consistent with the relevant provisions of the international treaty that the PRC concluded or entered into, such interpretation shall be chosen, unless China has made reservation to the provisions."[57] In *Chongqing Zhengtong Pharmaceutical Co. Ltd. v. Trademark Review & Adjudication Board*, the SPC referred to Article 9 for the first time.[58] It held that the "agent" in Article 15 of China's Trademark Law could be interpreted in accordance with "agent" and "representative" in Article 6(7) of the 1883 Paris Convention for the Protection of Industrial Property.[59] The Trade Case Regulations stand alone as the only Chinese law to explicitly mandate the principle of consistent interpretation. This shows that China views the WTO regime as sufficiently important to establish this sophisticated judicial policy.

III. CHINESE DOMESTIC COURTS' RELATIONSHIP-SENSITIVE APPROACH TO INTERNATIONAL LAW

Chinese domestic courts' approach toward international law is sensitive to the relationship that the international legal rule seeks to govern. For present purposes, four different categories of these relationships may be highlighted (although this is not of course an exhaustive or even a standard categorization). First are rules of immunity, which govern the relationship between domestic individuals and foreign states and their agents. Second are international-law-based grants of rights to individuals vis-à-vis states, most prominently through human rights treaties. A third category of rules are those in which international law extends states' jurisdictional authority over a new or expanded class of subjects or situations, for example through rules of universal jurisdiction in the case of piracy. Last are international law rules governing relations between individuals (i.e., relations in which the state is not directly involved at all). This categorization aids in exploring why Chinese domestic courts embrace certain kinds of international legal rules and are reluctant to apply others.

A. Rules of Immunity

Rules of immunity touch directly upon traditional foreign relations between states. As foreign relations are "much less capable to be directed by antecedent, standing,

---

57. Regulations of the Supreme People's Court on Issues Concerning the Trial of Administrative Cases Relating to International Trade, *supra* note 47, at Art. 9.

58. Chongqing Zhengtong Yaoye Youxian Gongsi, Guojia Gongshang Xingzheng Guanli Zongju Shangbiao Pingshen Weiyuanhui yu Sichuan Huashu Dongwu Yaoye Youxian Gongsi (重庆正通药业有限公司、国家工商行政管理总局商标评审委员会与四川华蜀动物药业有限公司) [Chongqing Zhengtong Pharm. Co., Ltd. & Trademark Review & Adjudication Bd. of the State Admin. for Indus. & Commerce v. Sichuan Huashu Veterinary Pharm. Co., Ltd.] (China), *at* http://www.pkulaw.cn/case/PFnl_117526660.html.

59. *Id.*

positive laws" than domestic affairs, the power to conduct foreign affairs, defined by Locke as the Federative Power, should be left to the executive branch: "the Prudence and Wisdom of those hands it is in, to be managed for the publick good."[60] In dealing with international politics, domestic courts traditionally deferred to executive authority (the deference approach).[61] However, the adoption of the State Immunity Convention in 2004 indicates that there is a global consensus that domestic courts may play a larger role in foreign relations. Several national courts have challenged the traditional policy of deference even further. For example, in the *Grundlagenvertrag* case, a Greek court of first instance decided that Germany could not invoke immunity for the killing and rape committed by German SS in a Greek village in 1944 because they violated a *jus cogens* norm.[62] The Areios Pagos, the supreme court of Greece, affirmed the lower court's decision.[63] Upon the initiation of enforcement proceedings, however, the Greek minister of justice refused to seize German property.[64] The Greek Special Highest Court, which is empowered to settle issues of international law, held that Germany's immunity extended to tort suits in all Greek civil courts.[65] Some Greek claimants initiated enforcement proceedings in Italy. Later, Germany sued Italy at the International Court of Justice. The Court held that Italy violated Germany's sovereign immunity under international law.[66] Similar controversies have arisen in other jurisdictions (e.g., Spain[67]). In short, while there is a trend that domestic courts rule more aggressively than before in relation to state immunity, substantial disagreements remain. Therefore, it seems advisable that domestic courts should not go too far.

Absolute state immunity has long been China's policy. Chinese courts have neither exercised jurisdiction over acts of foreign states nor enforced any decisions involving foreign states.[68] China has also effectively relied upon state immunity to

---

60. JOHN LOCKE, TWO TREATISES OF GOVERNMENT 365–66 (Peter Laslett ed., 1988).

61. Eyal Benvenisti, *Reclaiming Democracy: The Strategic Uses of Foreign and International Law by Domestic Courts*, 102 AM. J. INT'L L. 241, 245 (2008).

62. *See* Kerstin Bartsch & Björn Elberling, *Jus Cogens vs. State Immunity, Round Two: The Decision of the European Court of Human Rights in the* Kalogeropoulou et al. v. Greece and Germany *Decision*, 4 GERMAN L.J. 477, 478–79 (2003). *Jus cogens* norms are peremptory norms from which no derogation is permissible. *See* ALEXANDER ORAKHELASHVILI, PEREMPTORY NORMS IN INTERNATIONAL LAW 8 (2006).

63. Bartsch & Elberling, *supra* note 62, at 480.

64. *Id.*

65. *Id.* at 481.

66. Jurisdictional Immunities of the State (Ger. v It.; Greece Intervening), 2012 ICJ REP. 37, 39 (Feb. 3).

67. Mugambi Jouet, *Spain's Expanded Universal Jurisdiction to Prosecute Human Rights Abuses in Latin America, China, and Beyond*, 35 GA. J. INT'L & COMP. L. 495 (2007).

68. Xue Hanqin, *Chinese Contemporary Perspectives on International Law: History, Culture and International Law* 355 RECUEIL DES COURS 41, 100–01 (2011).

avoid the exercise of jurisdiction in foreign courts, such as in the famous case of *Jackson v. People's Republic of China*.[69]

On September 14, 2005, China signed the State Immunity Convention,[70] signaling that the country would shift its policy from absolute immunity to relative immunity. Under the new relative immunity policy, Chinese courts apply international law to determine the extent of a state's immunity. As China has not ratified the Convention thus far, it still strategically uses its traditional policy of absolute state immunity when it finds itself being sued in foreign courts (e.g., *Morris v. People's Republic of China*[71]) or finds the issue raised in courts such as those of Hong Kong (e.g., *Democratic Republic of the Congo v. FH Hemisphere Associates*[72]).

Furthermore, factors such as doubts regarding the professional capability of judges and the lack of enabling law may lead Chinese courts to continue for a time to apply absolute state immunity.[73] However, Chinese courts will almost certainly hear claims against foreign states sooner or later. Chinese private parties have tremendously expanded their engagements with foreign states as China rises as a great power. Chinese private parties increasingly invest abroad, trade with foreign entities, and are employed by (or contract with) foreign diplomatic bodies. Many reports show that the officials of host governments often misuse authority and infringe upon the rights of Chinese living and working abroad.[74] In 2014, China declared a new state strategy of "protecting the legal rights and interests of Chinese nationals and corporations abroad in accordance with the law."[75] This policy has two features. First, it attaches more importance to increasingly expanding private interests, which constitute an indispensable component of China's rise. Second, it puts a greater emphasis on legal rather than diplomatic means, which is aimed at depoliticizing relations between Chinese individuals and foreign states.

In China, a contentious issue regarding state immunity is whether a foreign state could be sued in domestic courts for activities that infringe upon *jus cogens*

---

69. *Id.* at 101–02; Jackson v. People's Republic of China, 794 F.2d 1490 (11th Cir. 1986); *see also* Jill A. Sgro, *China's Stance on Sovereign Immunity*, 22 COLUM. J. TRANSNAT'L L. 101 (1983).

70. United Nations Convention on Jurisdictional Immunities of States and Their Property, Dec. 2, 2004, U.N. Doc. A/59/508, *at* https://treaties.un.org/doc/Publication/MTDSG/Volume%20I/Chapter%20III/III-13.en.pdf.

71. *See* Reply Mem. of Law in Further Supp. of China's Mot. to Dismiss, Morris v. People's Republic of China, 478 F. Supp. 2d 561 (S.D.N.Y. 2007), 2006 WL 2581974.

72. Democratic Republic of the Congo v. FG Hemisphere Associates, [2011] 14 H.K.C.F.A.R. 95 (C.F.A.).

73. Dahai Qi, *State Immunity, China and Its Shifting Position*, 7 CHINESE J. INT'L L. 307 (2008).

74. *Zhongguoren Zai Haiwai Weihe Pingshou Qinghai* (中国人在海外为何频受侵害) [*Why Are Chinese Infringed Abroad?*], JFDAILY.COM (China), *at* http://newspaper.jfdaily.com/jfrb/html/2014-05/22/content_1169309.htm.

75. *See CCP Central Committee Decision on Major Issues Concerning Promoting the Rule of Law, supra* note 21, Part VII, Art. 7.

norms. A number of Chinese international lawyers have suggested that if Chinese courts were to sue Japan for its violations of *jus cogens* norms during World War II, such as the use of lethal bacteria and indiscriminate bombing, Japan could not invoke state immunity.[76] Chinese individuals have initiated several such lawsuits against Japan. For example, in September 2012, some Chinese victims of the Chongqing Grand Bombing, the bombing operations conducted by Japan during World War II, brought claims against Japan before the Chongqing High People's Court.[77] Similarly, in March 2014, a group of forced laborers and their descendants filed cases against Japan and several Japanese companies before the Tangshan Intermediate People's Court.[78] In Memorials,[79] plaintiffs in both cases argue that Japan cannot invoke state immunity because its actions violated *jus cogens* norms. Neither court has ruled on the exercise of jurisdiction yet—both cases remain pending.

In March 2014, however, the Beijing First Intermediate People's Court registered a case filed by 37 Chinese forced laborers and their descendants against two Japanese companies alleging their involvement, and consequent liability, in Japan's

---

76. *See, e.g.,* Xiao Mingqing (肖明清), *"Guojia Huomianquan" Zai Xijunzhan Susongan Zhong Shifou Shiyong* (《国家豁免权》在细菌战诉讼案中是否适用) [*Are "National Immunity" Rights Applicable to Bacteria War Lawsuits?*], 1 J. HUNAN U. ARTS & SCI. 23, 25–26 (2005) (China).

77. *"Chongqing Dahongzha" Shouhaizhe Zhengshi Qisu Riben, Zuigao Baqian Wan* ("重庆大轰炸"受害者正式起诉日本 最高八千万) [*Victims of "Chongqing Grand Bombing" Bring Lawsuit Against Japan and the Biggest Claim Reaches 80 Million Yuan*], BEIJINGNEWS (Sept. 11, 2012) (China), *available at* http://www.scopsr.gov.cn/shgj/shkx/201209/t20120911_181769.html.

78. *Erzhan Zhongguo Laogong Tangshan Zaisu Riqi* (二战中国劳工唐山再诉日企) [*Following up Lawsuits Brought by Chinese Laborers Against Japanese Government and Enterprises*], NIKKEI (Mar. 27, 2014) (China), *at* http://cn.nikkei.com/politicsaeconomy/politicsasociety/8622-20140327.html.

79. Tang Guangqin & Tang Guangrong Su Ribenguo Zhengfu Minshi Qisushu (唐光琴、唐光荣诉日本国政府民事起诉书) [Complaint from Tang Guangqin & Tang Guangrong to the Japanese government] (2012) (on file with author) (China); Huang Daihui Su Riben Zhengfu Minshi Qisushu (黄代蕙诉日本政府民事起诉书) [Complaint from Huang Daihui to the Japanese government]; Zhang Shan Den Deng Su Riben Zhengfu Minshi Qisushu (张山等诉日本国政府民事起诉书) [Complaint from Zhang Shan et al. to the Japanese government] (2012) (on file with author) (China); Dong Zhi Deng Su Riben Zhengfu Ji Riben Sanleng Zonghe Cailiao Zhushi Huishe (Yuan Sanleng Kuangye Zhushi Huishe) Minshi Qisushu (董志等等诉日本政府及日本三菱综合材料株式会社(原三菱矿业株式会社)民事起诉书) [Complaint from Dong Zhi et al. to the Japanese government & Mitsubishi Materials Co.] (Mar. 24, 2014) (on file with author) (China); Yan Zizhen Deng Su Riben Zhengfu Ji Riben Jiaotan Gongye Zhushi Huishe (Yuan Sanjing Kuangshan Zhushi Huishe) Minshi Qisushu (阎子珍等诉日本政府及日本焦炭工业株式会社(原三井矿山株式会社)民事起诉书) [Complaint from Yan Zizhen et al. to the Japanese government & Japanese Coke Industry Joint-Stock Co.] (Mar. 24, 2014) (on file with author) (China); Chongqing Dahongzha Minjian Duiri Suopei Zhuanjia Falu Yijian (重庆大轰炸民间对日索赔专家法律意见) [Expert Legal Opinion Letter on Compensation Requested by Chinese Victims to Japan regarding the Chongqing Grand Bombing] (July 21, 2012) (on file with author) (China).

forced labor programs during World War II.[80] This case marks the first time that Chinese courts have exercised jurisdiction over disputes regarding Japan's treatment of the Chinese during the war.[81]

At first glance, this case appears to be similar to other private transnational disputes. However, it concerns the application of the 1972 Joint Communiqué of the Government of Japan and the Government of the People's Republic of China,[82] which contains a provision regarding war reparations for Japan's actions during the war—a key issue in nearly all claims brought by Chinese victims against Japan and Japanese nationals. According to Paragraph 5 of the Joint Communiqué, "[t]he Government of the People's Republic of China declares that in the interest of the friendship between the Chinese and the Japanese peoples, it renounces its demand for war reparation from Japan."[83]

In the mid-1990s, some Chinese war survivors and their descendants began to file lawsuits in Japan. The Chinese plaintiffs claimed that Japan and certain Japanese companies should be held liable for the crimes they committed in World War II, such as forced labor and sexual slavery ("comfort women"). The Japanese government and, sometimes, its courts rejected all of these claims based primarily on the argument that China had relinquished its right and the right of its nationals to claim compensation for war crimes in the 1972 Joint Communiqué.[84] Of all the cases, the *Nishimatsu Construction* and *Second Chinese "Comfort Women"* cases were the most decisive.[85] In two judgments rendered together on April 27, 2007,

---

80. *Court Accepts Chinese WWII Forced Labors Lawsuit*, CHINA RADIO INT'L (Mar. 19, 2014), *at* http://english.cri.cn/6909/2014/03/19/3521s818167.htm.

81. *Id.*

82. Joint Communiqué of the Government of Japan and the Government of the People's Republic of China, China-Japan, Sept. 29, 1972, *at* http://www.mofa.go.jp/region/asia-paci/china/joint72.html.

83. *Id.* para. 5.

84. GUANG JIANQIANG (管建强), GONGPING, ZHENGYI, ZUNYAN—ZHONGGUO MINJIAN ZHANZHENG SHOUHAIZHE DUIRI SUOCHANG FALU JICHU (公平、正义、尊严—— 中国民间战争受害者对日索偿法律基础) [EQUITY, JUSTICE, AND DIGNITY—LEGAL FOUNDATION OF CLAIMS AGAINST JAPAN BY CHINESE WAR VICTIMS] 174–75 (2006); Zhang Xingjun (张新军), *Minjian Duiri Suopei Susong Shang De Bianqian He Zhongguo Zhengfu de Huiying—Jianlun Buganshe Yuanze* (民间对日索赔诉讼上的变迁和中国政府的回应—— 兼论不干涉原则) [*War Reparation Lawsuits and Judgments in Japan and the Reactions of the Chinese Government—Some Reflections on the Principle of Non-intervention*], 4 TSINGHUA L.J. 96 (2007) (China); Xing Aifeng & Li Tianzhi (邢爱芬、李天志), *Zhanzheng Peichang yu Minjian Peichang—Jianlun Rijun Yihua Huaxue Wuqi Susong An Jiqi Qianjing* (战争赔偿与民间赔偿—— 兼论日军遗华化学武器诉讼案及其前景) [*War Reparation and Civil Compensation—On the Lawsuits for Civil Compensation by Chinese Victims of the Chemical Weapons Abandoned by the Japanese Army*], 9 INT'L F. 57, 57 (2007) (China).

85. For a review of both cases, *see* Masahiko Asada & Trevor Ryan, *Post-war Reparations Between Japan and China and the Waiver of Individual Claims: Japan's Supreme Court Judgments in the Nishimatsu Construction Case and the Second Chinese "Comfort Women" Case*, 19 ITALIAN Y.B. INT'L L. 205 (2009).

the Supreme Court of Japan (SCJ), held that "[i]t should be out of doubt that all claims arising from the war, including the claims by private individuals, are abandoned mutually."[86] The SCJ had not previously reached such a definite conclusion, which effectively closed the window for Chinese victims to seek justice in Japan. Immediately, the spokesman for China's Ministry of Foreign Affairs (MFA) condemned the SCJ's interpretation as "void" and "invalid" and asserted that the MFA had demanded that the Japanese government "take Chinese concerns seriously and properly resolve this issue."[87]

China and Japan disagree about the meaning of paragraph 5 of the Joint Communiqué. Chinese leaders contend that the Communiqué only waives the right of the Chinese government to bring war reparations claims, which means that Chinese nationals are free to bring such claims.[88] However, China has not supported this interpretation with any significant legal actions. China limited its response to the SCJ's judgments in 2007 to oral protest; it took no further action (e.g., explicitly allowing Chinese victims to bring claims in Chinese courts).

In recent years, relations between China and Japan have deteriorated. For instance, in September 2012, Japan claimed that it had purchased the Diaoyu Islands from a Japanese family that, under Japanese law, owned the land.[89] The Diaoyu Islands, known as the Senkaku Islands in Japan, are the subject of an ongoing territorial dispute between China and Japan. China responded to Japan's action with several measures, including the issuance of a white paper on the Diaoyu Islands[90] and the establishment of the East China Sea Air Defense Identification Zone (ADIZ).[91] China, a new great power, and Japan, an old great power, have fallen into strategic confrontations.

The utility of the pending case at the Beijing First Intermediate People's Court is evident. First, the two Japanese defendants will likely invoke the SCJ's 2007 decisions to defend themselves. The Beijing First Intermediate People's Court

---

86. Saikō Saibansho [Sup. Ct.] Apr. 24, 2007, 224 SAIKŌ SAIBANSHO MINJI HANREISHŪ [MINSHŪ] 325, at http://www.courts.go.jp/app/files/hanrei_jp/591/034591_hanrei.pdf (Japan).

87. *Zhongfang Fandui Ri Zuigaofa Renyi Jieshi "Zhongri Lianhe Shengming" Xiangguan Tiaokuan* (中方反对日最高法任意解释《中日联合声明》相关条款) [*China Opposes Japan's Supreme Court's Arbitrary Interpretation of the Relevant Provisions of China-Japan Communiqué*], XINHUANET (Apr. 28, 2007, 10:49 AM) (China), at http://news.xinhuanet.com/mrdx/2007-04/28/content_6039307.htm.

88. *See Experts Advise Chinese WWII Laborers to File Class Action*, PEOPLE'S DAILY ONLINE, (Jan. 15, 2002), at http://en.people.cn/200201/15/eng20020115_88683.shtml; Xing Aifeng & Li Tianzhi, *supra* note 84, at 60.

89. Wu Gufeng (吴谷丰), *Riben Zhengfu Jiang Yi 20.5 Yi Riyuan "Goumai" Diaoyudao* (日本政府将以20.5億日元"购买"钓鱼岛) [*The Government of Japan Will "Purchase" the Diaoyu Islands for 2.05 Billion Yen*] (Sept. 5, 2012, 11:03 AM 2012) (China), at http://news.qq.com/a/20120905/001233.htm.

90. State Council Information Office, *Diaoyu Dao, an Inherent Territory of China*, CHINA DAILY (Sept. 25, 2012), at http://www.chinadaily.com.cn/china/2012-09/25/content_15782158.htm.

91. *Defense Ministry Spokesman on China's Air Defense Identification Zone*, XINHUANET (Dec. 3, 2013), at http://news.xinhuanet.com/english/china/2013-12/03/c_132938762.htm.

thus has an opportunity to clarify the meaning of paragraph 5 of the 1972 Joint Communiqué. It must affirm the established position of China's executive branch and refute the SCJ's position. Second, in contrast with the lawsuits in Tangshan and Chongqing, the plaintiffs in the Beijing case did not list Japan as a defendant. Listing only Japanese companies as the defendants significantly reduces the risk that the case will lead to further diplomatic confrontations between China and Japan. The Beijing First Intermediate People's Court cannot hear the case without the SPC's consent and the MFA's support according to an instrument jointly issued by the MFA, the Chinese Ministry of Public Security (MPS), the Ministry of State Security, the Ministry of Justice, the SPC, and the Supreme People's Procuratorate.[92] The Beijing case thus demonstrates that the Chinese judiciary is subtly becoming involved in foreign relations through the application of international law.

While domestic courts such as those in the United States have at times gone very far in the exercise of jurisdiction over matters involving other states,[93] Chinese courts remain at the other extreme. They have no say in foreign affairs. In this context, it is hardly surprising that the Chinese courts have been reluctant to exercise jurisdiction in lawsuits brought by Chinese individuals for the actions of Japan in World War II. In some other countries, for instance, the United States, domestic courts, which were once aggressive in traditional foreign relations, appear to have recently shifted from judicial activism to judicial passivism.[94]

As China continues to rise as a great power, Chinese courts will inevitably increase their role in foreign relations. Wang E'xiang, former vice president of the SPC, has argued that the role of Chinese courts in foreign relations should be expanded, which would include empowering them to decide whether a treaty is self-executing or non-self-executing.[95] Although it seems unlikely that Chinese courts will become as involved in foreign relations as American courts, an increase in the involvement of Chinese courts in foreign affairs is probable.

With regard to the long reluctance of Chinese courts to apply international law in relation to state immunity cases, this reflects more than just China's judicial policy toward international law. Rather, many developing states and former socialist states share this reluctance and, in general, support absolute sovereignty. China has become more powerful during its rise and, as a result, it has begun to take seriously

92. Guanyu Chuli Shewai Anjian Ruogan Wenti de Guiding (关于处理涉外案件若干问题的规定) [Rules Concerning the Resolution of Foreign-Related Cases] (promulgated by the Ministry of Foreign Affairs et al., June 20, 1995, effective June 20, 1995) (China), at http://www.chinalawedu.com/news/1200/22598/22604/22717/2006/3/ga316316535413136002199936-0.htm.

93. *See generally* Anne-Marie Slaughter & David Bosco, *Plaintiff's Diplomacy*, 79 FOREIGN AFF. 102 (2000); JOHN NORTON MOORE, FOREIGN AFFAIRS LITIGATION IN UNITED STATES COURTS (2013); Curtis A. Bradley, *Supreme Court Holds That Alien Tort Statute Does Not Apply to Conduct in Foreign Countries*, ASIL INSIGHTS (Apr. 18, 2013).

94. *See, e.g.,* Chimène I. Keitner, *The Reargument Order in Kiobel v. Royal Dutch Petroleum and Its Potential Implications for Transnational Human Rights Cases*, ASIL INSIGHTS (Mar. 21, 2012).

95. GUOJIFA YU GUONEI FA GUANXI YANJIU (国际法与国内法的关系研究) [A STUDY ON THE RELATIONSHIP BETWEEN INTERNATIONAL LAW AND NATIONAL LAW] 476–81 (Wan E'xiang ed., 2011) (China).

the protection of Chinese private interests against foreign states. China's decision to sign the State Immunity Convention indicates that it has begun to refine its traditional conception of sovereignty. In time, Chinese courts will begin to hear disputes between Chinese nationals and foreign states.

B. Rules Granting Rights to Individuals vis-à-vis the State

A second category of cases where Chinese courts engage with international law are those where treaties grant rights to individuals vis-à-vis states. A search using Pkulaw.cn reveals that Chinese courts have occasionally applied international law in such cases, for instance, *Longines Co. v. Trademark Review & Adjudication Board* mentioned above. However, the search did not reveal any cases in which Chinese courts gave direct effect to human rights treaties, which constitute the core of this kind of legal relationship and are crucial to enhancing the rule of law, especially in transitional states.

China has ratified many human rights treaties, including most of the core conventions, such as the CAT[96] and the ICESCR.[97] At a minimum, China itself has expressed its intention to grant direct effect to the CAT. In 1990, China's representative to the Committee Against Torture stated that:

> [O]ffences under the Convention were also regarded as offences under Chinese domestic law. When China acceded to any convention, it became binding as soon as it entered into force. China then fulfilled all its obligations, and it was not necessary to draft special laws to ensure conformity. If an international instrument was inconsistent with domestic law, the latter was brought into line with the former. Where subtle difference remained, international instruments took precedence over domestic law.[98]

This statement was widely regarded as important evidence that treaties are automatically incorporated in China.[99] In 2000, China's representative to the Committee Against Torture stated more explicitly that the Torture Convention "could be invoked before the Chinese courts."[100] Unfortunately, China's criminal law does not include torture as a crime, despite reports of widespread use of torture.[101] In addition,

96. Convention Against Torture, *supra* note 36.

97. International Covenant on Economic, Social and Cultural Rights, Dec. 16, 1966, 993 U.N.T.S. 3, *at* https://treaties.un.org/doc/Publication/MTDSG/Volume%20I/Chapter%20IV/IV-3.en.pdf (last visited Aug. 12, 2015).

98. Committee Against Torture, Summary Record of the 51st Meeting, para. 2, U.N. Doc. CAT/C/SR.51, (May 4, 1990).

99. *See, e.g.,* Li Zhaojie, *supra* note 6, at 341; Sanzhuan Guo, *supra* note 6, at 165.

100. Committee Against Torture, Summary Record of the 419th Meeting, para. 9, U.N. Doc. CAT/C/SR.419 (May 12, 2000).

101. *See* Committee Against Torture, Concluding Observations of the Committee Against Torture: China, para. 11, U.N. Doc. CAT/C/CHN/CO/4, (Dec. 12, 2008); Wang Guanxian, *supra* note 6, at 273–74; Dai Ruijun, *supra* note 6, at 273.

Chinese courts have thus far ignored the Chinese representatives' statements that they can directly apply the CAT. Interestingly, however, the MPS has ordered, at least rhetorically, that its local branches "strictly abide" by the provisions of the CAT.[102] This demonstrates that the executive branch recognizes that the executive power should be contained. However, it prefers to rely on its own internal executive mechanism rather than external judicial mechanism. The major reason seems clear: more discretion would be protected under the former mechanism than the latter one.

In recent years, China has attempted to distance itself from its earlier statements regarding the Torture Convention. It has sought to clarify that its courts would not directly apply human rights conventions. For instance, in its second periodic report to the Committee on Economic, Social and Cultural Rights, China claimed that human rights treaties "do not directly function as the legal basis for the trial of cases in Chinese courts, and human rights treaties are no exception; rather, they are applied after being transformed into domestic law through legislative procedures."[103] In response, the Committee recommended that China should "guarantee the direct applicability of all rights" under the ICESCR.[104] China's statement in its periodic report is not totally convincing for two reasons. First, as indicated above, China previously recognized the direct effect of the CAT at the international level, which remains unchanged. Second, as discussed above, the NPC repealed Article 72 of the APL of 1990 as a legal basis for automatic incorporation in the 2014 amendments to the APL.[105] From the perspective of Chinese courts, Article 72 of the APL of 1990 had justified incorporating China's CAT obligations into its legal system.

The application of international legal commitments granting rights to individuals vis-à-vis the state is characterized by a critical distinction. On the one hand, China is a state party to many instruments, including human rights treaties, which help to contain executive authority. It is well known that, since the late 1980s (especially since the Tiananmen Square incident in 1989), China and the West have fiercely sparred over human rights affairs, and China has been accused of systematic violations of human rights.[106] China's increasing acceptance of human rights treaties

102. Ministry of Public Security (公安部), *Gong'an Bu Guanyu Yange Lüxing Guoji Gongyue Zhong yu Gong'an Gongzuo Youguan de Guiding de Tongzhi* (公安部关于严格履行国际公约中与公安工作有关的规定的通知) [*Ministry of Public Security Note on Strictly Implementing Provisions in International Conventions Related to Public Security*] (promulgated by the Ministry of Public Security, Mar. 24, 1989, effective Mar. 24, 1989) (China), *at* http://www.chinala-wedu.com/news/1200/22598/22604/22717/2006/3/ga826618292513136000212124-0.htm.

103. Committee on Economic, Social and Cultural Rights, Second Periodic Report Submitted by States Parties Under Articles 16 and 17 of the Covenant: China, U.N. Doc. E/C.12/CHN/2, at 9 (July 6, 2012).

104. Committee on Economic, Social and Cultural Rights, Concluding Observations on the Second Periodic Report of China, para. 9, U.N. Doc. E/C.12/CHN/CO/2 (June 13, 2014).

105. *See* the accompanying text of note 38.

106. *See generally* Rosemary Foot, Rights Beyond Borders: The Global Community and the Struggle over Human Rights in China (2000).

has helped it to better integrate into the international community. An acceptance of human rights is indispensable for a state in the process of rising as a great power in the era of human rights. On the other hand, China seeks to insulate its executive authority from international pressure by neutralizing the application of human rights treaties in the judiciary. In practice, China disallows the automatic incorporation of treaties under which executive authority might be seriously challenged. As a result, China's executive branch can take advantage of the supposed socialist "efficiency" advantage. The 2014 amendment of the APL demonstrates that China remains reluctant to allow the application of international law in its domestic courts.

C. Rules-Based Extensions to States' Authority

A third category of rules concerns international law extending states' authority over a new class of subjects, for example through rules of universal jurisdiction in the case of piracy. Private actors, such as pirates and terrorists, currently pose serious challenges and threaten peace and security, which makes this category one of growing importance for domestic courts, which will increasingly need to address such threats.[107]

Until the 1980s, China had no law relating to the exercise of jurisdiction for cases where international law, rather than national law, permitted jurisdiction. In 1987, China enacted a law requiring courts to exercise criminal jurisdiction over crimes prescribed in treaties to which it acceded or is a state party.[108] The NPC later incorporated this law in the 1997 amendments to China's criminal law.[109]

---

107. M.D. Saiful Karim, *Prosecution of Maritime Pirates: The National Court Is Dead—Long Live the National Court?*, 32 WIS. INT'L L.J. 37 (2014).

108. Quanguo Renmin Daibiao Dahui Changwu Weiyuanhui Guanyu Dui Zhonghua Renmin Gongheguo Dijie Huozhe Canjia de Guoji Tiaoyue Suo Guiding de Zuixing Xingshi Xingshi Guanxiaquan de Jueding (全国人民代表大会常务委员会关于对中华人民共和国缔结或者参加的国际条约所规定的罪行行使刑事管辖权的决定) [Decision of the Standing Committee of the National People's Congress Regarding Exercising Criminal Jurisdiction over the Crimes Proscribed in the International Treaties to Which the People's Republic of China Is a Party or Has Acceded] (promulgated by the Standing Comm. Nat'l People's Cong., June 23, 1987) (China), *at* http://www.npc.gov.cn/wxzl/gongbao/2001-02/06/content_5004485.htm. China is a party or has acceded to such conventions as, among others, the Convention for the Suppression of Unlawful Seizure of Aircraft, the Convention for the Suppression of Unlawful Acts against the Safety of Civil Aviation, the Convention on Psychotropic Substances, and the Single Convention on Narcotic Drugs. *See* Convention for the Suppression of Unlawful Seizure of Aircraft, Dec. 16, 1970, 860 U.N.T.S. 105, *at* https://treaties.un.org/doc/db/Terrorism/Conv2-english.pdf; Convention for the Suppression of Unlawful Acts Against the Safety of Civil Aviation, Sept. 23, 1971, 974 U.N.T.S. 177, *at* https://treaties.un.org/doc/db/Terrorism/Conv3-english.pdf; Convention on Psychotropic Substances, Feb. 21, 1971, 1019 U.N.T.S. 175, *at* https://treaties.un.org/doc/Publication/MTDSG/Volume%20I/Chapter%20VI/VI-16.en.pdf; Single Convention on Narcotic Drugs, Dec. 13, 1964, 520 U.N.T.S. 151, *at* https://treaties.un.org/doc/Publication/MTDSG/Volume%20I/Chapter%20VI/VI-18.en.pdf.

109. Xing Fa (刑法) [Criminal Law of the People's Republic of China] (promulgated by the Nat'l People's Cong., July 1, 1979) 1979 STANDING COMM. NAT'L PEOPLE'S CONG. GAZ. 83, Art. 9 (amended 1997).

On some occasions Chinese authorities should have exercised jurisdiction but failed to do so. This may result from a lack of knowledge of international law, which is indicated from the SPC's requirement of strengthening the knowledge of international law to lower courts.[110] For example, in 1998, Indonesian pirates in the South China Sea hijacked the *M.V. Petro Ranger*, a Malaysian flagged cargo ship.[111] The pirates renamed it the *M.V. Wilby* and reflagged it as a Honduran ship.[112] Later, when the ship arrived in China, the local authorities detained the ship and arrested all non-crew personnel on board for smuggling.[113] However, the Chinese authorities decided not to prosecute the arrestees because they determined there was a lack of convincing evidence, a decision criticized by the International Maritime Bureau (IMB).[114]

On other occasions, however, Chinese courts have exercised jurisdiction. For instance, in June 1999, 10 pirates hijacked the *Siamxanxai*, a Thai flagged oil tanker, in Malaysian territorial waters.[115] Later, the tanker entered Chinese territorial waters and the local authorities arrested the hijackers.[116] The Shantou City Intermediate People's Court held that these pirates violated treaties to which China is a party, including the United Nations Convention on the Law of the Sea and the Navigation Safety Convention of 1988.[117] As China's criminal law does not proscribe piracy, the court held that the defendants committed robbery instead.[118]

While Chinese courts are sometimes reluctant to exercise their jurisdiction when international law permits, or even requires it, they are becoming more willing to do so. China's increasing engagement in economic globalization has led to threats to its economic and security interests, such as piracy, transnational organized crime, and international terrorism. In response to these threats, China has opened a window

---

110. On several occasions, the SPC has urged that local judges increase their knowledge of international law. *See, e.g.,* Guanyu Shenli He Zhixing Shewai Min Shangshi Anjian Yingdang Zhuyi de Ji Ge Wenti de Tongzhi (关于审理和执行涉外民商事案件应当注意的几个问题的通知) [Notice of the Supreme People's Court on Several Issues Concerning the Trial and Enforcement of Foreign-Related Civil and Commercial Cases] (promulgated by the Sup. People's Ct., Apr. 17, 2000, effective on Apr. 17, 2000) (China), *at* http://www.tpan.cn/html/5196.htm.

111. *See* TONG WEIHUA (童伟华), HAISHANG KONGBU ZHUYI FANZUI JI HAIDAO FANZUI DE XINGSHI GUIZHI. (海上恐怖主义犯罪及海盗犯罪的刑事规制) [TERRORIST CRIMES AT SEA AND CRIMINAL REGULATION ON THE CRIME OF PIRACY] 8–9 (2013) (China).

112. *Id.*

113. *Id.*

114. *Id.*

115. ATAN NAIM Deng Qiangjiean (阿丹·奈姆等抢劫案。) [ATAN NAIM et al., Robbery] [2003] (Shantou Municipal Interm. People's Ct. Jan. 15, 2003) (China), *at* http://www.pkulaw.cn/Case/payz_117675567.html?match=Exact.

116. *Id.*

117. *Id.*

118. *Id.*

for its courts to exercise jurisdiction. For example, Huang Huikang, a former director general of the MFA, has argued that there is no legal hindrance for Chinese courts to exercise universal jurisdiction over Somali pirates.[119]

D. Rules Governing Relations between Private Individuals

For Chinese courts, a fourth relationship often governed by international law is that between private parties, predominantly in the business context. Disputes between private parties have little to do with public authority and the subject area is widely treated as transnational private law rather than public international law. Thus, international lawyers focused on public law concerns rarely publish works on the United Nations Convention on Contracts for the International Sale of Goods (CISG), even though it is a treaty.

Chinese courts apply international law regulating relations between individuals more frequently than any other category of international law. In this category, scholars have conducted case studies on the application of the CISG, the Convention on the Recognition and Enforcement of Foreign Arbitral Awards (New York Convention), the Paris Convention for the Protection of Industrial Property (Paris Convention), the Berne Convention for the Protection of Literary and Artistic Works (Berne Convention), and the International Convention on Civil Liability for Oil Pollution Damage (CLC).[120] For the purposes of this chapter, it is not necessary to introduce more cases here. Rather, it suffices to provide several figures. A search on Pkulaw.cn reveals that the CISG has been applied in 198 cases, the New York Convention has been applied in 66 cases, the Paris Convention has been applied in 381 cases, the Berne Convention has been applied in 622 cases, and the CLC has been applied in 16 cases as of January 18, 2016. Although there are some drawbacks in the application of these treaties,[121] the SPC firmly supports the position that they should be applied in good faith. It has established reporting and reviewing mechanisms to guide and supervise the application of treaties by local courts.[122] According to one empirical study, these mechanisms effectively remedy the legal errors that occur in local courts.[123]

---

119. Huang Huikang (黄惠康), *Junjian Huhang Daji Suomali Haidao: Falu Yiju He Sifa Chengxu Anpai* (军舰护航打击索马里海盗：法律依据和司法程序安排) [*Fighting Somali Pirates by Naval Escort: Legal Basis and Judicial Procedure*], 2011 ANN. CHINA MARITIME L. 1, 5 (China).

120. *See* Tang, *supra* note 6; Huang, *supra* note 6; Yongping & Weidi, *supra* note 6.

121. Yongping & Weidi, *supra* note 6, at 101–02.

122. *See* Zuigao Renmin Fayuan Guanyu Renmin Fayuan Chuli yu Shewai Zhongcai ji Waiguo Zhongcai Shixiang Youguan Wenti de Tongzhi (最高人民法院关于人民法院处理与涉外仲裁及外国仲裁事项有关问题的通知) [Supreme People's Court Notice Concerning Issues Regarding Foreign-Related Arbitration and Foreign Arbitration by People's Courts] (promulgated by the Sup. People's Ct., Aug. 28, 1995, effective Aug. 28, 1995) (China), *at* http://www.chinalawedu.com/news/1300/12/21727/2006/3/zl04194055531236002106500-0.htm.

123. Yang Honglei (杨弘磊), *Renmin Fayuan Shewai Zhongcai Sifa Shencha Qingkuang de Diaoyan Baogao* (人民法院涉外仲裁司法审查情况的调研报告) [*Report on the Judicial Review of International Arbitration in Chinese Courts*] 9 WUHAN U. INT'L L. REV. 304, 311 (2009) (China).

Interestingly, treaties that clearly regulate relations between states parties are sometimes used to adjudicate disputes arising between private parties. A prominent example is the TRIPS Agreement. As indicated by Pkulaw.cn, the TRIPS Agreement has been applied in dozens of cases between private parties. In *Beijing Tianyu Tongsheng Information Technology Co. v. Shenyang Yanxitang Food & Beverage Service Co.*, for instance, the plaintiff obtained an exclusive license from HIM International Music, a company in Taiwan, to distribute MTV products in mainland China.[124] The plaintiff argued that the defendant's use of these products infringed upon its exclusive license.[125] The court noted that both Taiwan and mainland China are parties to the TRIPS Agreement, which, according to its national treatment obligation, required mainland China to apply its copyright law to HIM.[126] However, the fact is that the WTO national treatment obligation is not imposed upon private parties. Therefore, infringements can occur between a private party and a WTO member state, but not between two private parties.

How can the prominence of this set of international legal rules in Chinese domestic law be explained? One of China's primary strategies arising from the economic collapse that followed the Cultural Revolution (1966–1976) was to attract capital and technology from Western states. China's command economy discouraged international investors and traders who operated in market economies, and it could not create a legal regime to support a fully fledged market economy in a short period of time. Therefore, it became expedient for China to incorporate international regimes (e.g., the CISG and the Paris Convention) into its domestic legal system, which increased foreign confidence in investment and trade without seriously challenging executive authority. This increased investment and trade confidence allowed massive amounts of foreign capital and technology to flow into China, which accelerated the country's prodigious economic growth.

IV. CONCLUSION

There is a close relationship between the economic and geopolitical rise of China and the categories of international law applied by Chinese courts. Initially, in pursuit of economic development, China strongly stressed the application of international laws governing commercial relationships between private parties, but attached little importance to international law extensions of its jurisdiction, and disallowed the application of rules infringing on the principle of absolute state sovereignty. Now, as China rises, it has begun to adjust its traditional judicial policy in order to protect its expanding overseas interests and exhibit its growing status as a power. Under the new judicial policy,

---

124. Beijing Tianyu Tongsheng Xinxi Jishu Youxian Gongsi Su Shenyang Yanxitang Canyin Fuwu Youxian Gongsi (北京天语同声信息技术有限公司诉沈阳燕喜堂餐饮服务有限公司) [Beijing Tianyu Tongsheng Information Technology Co. Ltd. v. Shenyang Yanxitang Food & Beverage Service Co. Ltd.] (Shenyang City Interm. People's Ct. Nov. 16, 2011) (China), *at* http://law1.chinalawinfo.com/case/display.asp?Gid=118262020.

125. *Id.*

126. *Id.*

Chinese courts have begun to exercise jurisdiction on the basis of international law permissions and have the opportunity to exercise jurisdiction due to international-law-based relaxations of absolute state immunity. By contrast, the new judicial policy still provides little room for the application of rules granting substantive rights to individuals vis-à-vis the state in general, and human rights treaties in particular. As indicated by the amended APL of 2104, little progress can be expected in the near future. China continues to support the position that a strong executive authority is necessary for its rise. Therefore, China's ratification of future treaties, including those governing the relationship between individuals and the state, will likely be accompanied by measures to neutralize the judicialization of such treaties.

A state's judicial policy toward international law is often inseparable from its public policy pursuits. In order to evaluate a state's judicial policy, therefore, an understanding of its public policy pursuits is necessary. Over the last three decades, the fundamental public policy of China has consistently been to rise as a great power. The basic approach to achieving this policy goal is the Beijing Consensus, which has two core elements: an emphasis on economic growth over political freedom and social justice; and the maintenance of an authoritarian regime with unfettered executive authority. The Beijing Consensus and the pursuit of China's rise guide the methodology and relationship-sensitive approach of Chinese judicial policy toward international law. China thus illustrates how a state reorients its judicial policy toward international law as it changes its identity.

China deals with its constitutional silence on the status of international law in its legal system on a case-by-case basis. On the one hand, this leads to fragmentation and reduces the predictability of the application of international law. On the other hand, this allows for significant flexibility when deciding whether to apply international law. The constitutional silence makes it easier for China to decide which methodology to use in the application of a particular treaty—automatic incorporation or transformation.

The international law actually applied by Chinese courts in the past three decades—namely, no application of relaxed immunity rules, limited application of rules granting rights to individuals vis-à-vis the state (especially human rights treaties), rare application of international law extending jurisdiction, and frequent application of rules governing private relationships—makes sense within the context of China's rise. As China rises, Chinese courts are likely to become more involved in foreign affairs, possibly leading to greater participation in the application of context sensitive and possibly relaxed immunity rules and use of international law permitting the extension of sovereignty. The resulting body of case law would be of great interest to comparative international law scholars.

This trend, however, comes with an important caveat. Recent developments at international and national levels demonstrate that Chinese courts' greater involvement in foreign affairs is likely to remain limited by China's desire to maintain its authoritarian regime and shield its executive authority. Therefore, while China is increasingly applying international law granting rights to individuals in relation to public authorities, the Chinese judicial policy toward these rights appears rather conservative. In other words, China's rise has produced a judicial policy that is open to the application of international law, but only when it poses little threat to executive authority.

15

The Democratizing Force of International Law

Human Rights Adjudication by the Indian Supreme Court

NEHA JAIN

I. INTRODUCTION

Do domestic courts applying international legal norms act as agents of international law? Does extensive citation to international law in national court decisions imply increased acceptance of international law in the municipal system? Intuitively, the answer to both questions is in the affirmative, and most academic commentary on the relationship between international law and domestic courts presumes as much.[1] The Indian Supreme Court's relationship to international law challenges these assumptions. It gestures toward the need to expand the range of state practice, particularly that of states which have traditionally been at the periphery of international law discourses, which has served as the reference point for the formulation of theories about the interpretation and enforcement of international legal norms by domestic actors.[2]

The Indian Supreme Court is frequently referred to as one of the most powerful apex courts in the world.[3] While the court rarely invoked international law in the

---

1. See, e.g., ANDRE NOLLKAEMPER, NATIONAL COURTS AND THE RULE OF INTERNATIONAL LAW 8–10 (2010); Richard B. Lillich, *The Proper Role of Domestic Courts in the International Legal Order*, 10 VA. J. INT'L L. 1, 12 (1970–1971); Symposium, *Domestic Courts as Agents of Development of International Law*, 26 LEIDEN J. INT'L L. 531 (2013). For an exception to this general trend, see Eyal Benvenisti, *Reclaiming Democracy: The Strategic Uses of Foreign and International Law by National Courts*, 102 AM. J. INT'L. L. 241 (2008); Eyal Benvenisti & George W. Downs, *National Courts, Domestic Democracy, and the Evolution of International Law*, 20 EUR. J. INT'L L. 59 (2009).

2. See also Congyan Cai, *International Law in Chinese Courts During the Rise of China* (this volume).

3. Robert Moog, *Judicial Activism in the Cause of Judicial Independence: The Indian Supreme Court in the 1990s*, 85 JUDICATURE 268, 270 (2002); Katie Cella, *The World's Most Meddlesome Supreme Courts*, FOREIGN POL'Y (June 25, 2012), http://www.foreignpolicy.com/articles/2012/06/25/

first few decades of its existence, and only then in limited areas such as territorial and boundary disputes, the situation changed dramatically in the period following the 1980s.[4] The most controversial recourse to international legal principles has been in the realm of fundamental rights and environmental protection. The Supreme Court's innovative uses of international law have, however, invited remarkably little scrutiny. The Indian professoriate has contributed primarily descriptive accounts of the Supreme Court's jurisprudence,[5] the court's pronouncements have not resulted in any significant backlash from the other branches of government, and the Indian Supreme Court is rarely discussed in international law circles or analyzed by international law academics outside India.[6]

This chapter argues that international law has served as a useful tool for the Indian Supreme Court in fulfilling aims that have little to do with the court's purported status as an organ of the international community. On the contrary, the Supreme Court has appropriated international legal norms to pursue primarily domestic goals and to champion the rights of individuals and groups that have been unrepresented or under-represented in Indian democracy[7] in a bid to secure popular support and bolster its position vis-à-vis other state organs. However, this exercise in using international law to expand the scope of domestic rights and protections has been eclectic and, at times, even reactionary.[8] The court's attitude toward international law thus serves as an important marker in the broader debate on differences and similarities in state and substate approaches to international law and how these are influenced and mediated by domestic legal, political, and social structures.

This chapter proceeds as follows. Section II gives a brief overview of the status of international law in the Indian constitutional scheme. Section III analyzes the creative uses of international law by the Indian Supreme Court to fill in and add to the content of constitutional rights and guarantees, enabling its encroachment into domains that are normally the prerogative of the legislature and the executive. Section IV puts

---

the_world_s_most_meddlesome_supreme_courts; Amol Sharma, *In India, The Supreme Court Takes an Activist Role*, WALL ST. J. (May 15, 2011), http://online.wsj.com/news/articles/SB10001 424052748703509104576325660087117274?mg=reno64-wsj&url=http%3A%2F%2Fonline.wsj. com%2Farticle%2FSB10001424052748703509104576325660087117274.html.

4. V.G. Hegde, *Indian Courts and International Law*, 23 LEIDEN J. INT'L L. 53, 55–56 (2010).

5. This is a curious shortcoming, as Indian international law scholars have been in the forefront of the TWAIL movement and contributed sophisticated treatments of other areas of international law. *See, e.g.,* B.S. Chimni, *Towards a Radical Third World Approach to Contemporary International Law*, 5 INT'L CENTRE FOR COMP. L. & POL'Y REV. 14 (2002); B.S. Chimni, *International Law Scholarship in Post-colonial India: Coping with Dualism*, 23 LEIDEN J. INT'L L. 23 (2010) (and references therein).

6. For rare exceptions, see Reem Bahdi, *Globalization of Judgment: Transjudicialism and the Five Faces of International Law in Domestic Courts*, 34 GEO. WASH. INT'L L. REV. 555, 562–64, 569, 574–75, 585, 593 (2002); Benvenisti, *Reclaiming Democracy, supra* note 1, at 258–62.

7. *See* Justice K.G. Balakrishnan, *The Role of Foreign Precedents in a Country's Legal System*, Lecture at Northwestern University (Oct. 28, 2008).

8. Upendra Baxi, *Preface* to S.P. SATHE, JUDICIAL ACTIVISM IN INDIA, xiii n. 2 (2002) (discussing different kinds of judicial activism as eclectic, opportunistic, progressive, and reactionary).

forward a possible explanation for this appropriation of international legal norms and suggests that international law has performed a legitimizing function in the Supreme Court's articulation of its vision of the state. It advances the thesis that increased citation to international law by a domestic court may have little connection with how friendly or open the organ is to international law and institutions as such, or with the court's willingness to engage in a trans-judicial dialogue.[9] Instead, the strategic appeal to international law might serve entirely domestic goals and purposes.

II. THE CONSTITUTIONAL STATUS OF INTERNATIONAL LAW

The Indian Constitution does not specify the precise status of international law in the Indian legal system. Article 51 of the Constitution, which is part of the nonjudicially enforceable Directive Principles of State Policy, refers to the state's obligation to promote international peace and security. The state must thus endeavor to "foster respect for international law and treaty obligations in the dealings of organized peoples with one another," "maintain just and honorable relations between nations," and encourage arbitration as a means of international dispute settlement.[10] The Article is widely considered to be inspired by the text of the International Labor Organization's Havana Declaration of November 30, 1939.[11] The inclusion of respect for international law under the umbrella heading of promotion of international peace and security appears to subsume the state's legal posture toward international obligations under the foreign policy goal of maintaining peaceful and secure international relations.[12] The ambit of the term "international law" as distinguished from "treaty obligations" in Article 51 is also unclear. Some commentators suggest that the former refers to customary international law principles.[13]

The Constitution vests the Parliament with the authority to make laws governing the entry into and implementation of treaties.[14] However, Parliament has yet to enact any laws regulating this area,[15] resulting in the adoption of the British and

---

9. *See, e.g.,* Anne-Marie Slaughter, *Judicial Globalization,* 40 VA. J. INT'L L. 1103 (2000) (describing the various ways in which national courts and judges are engaged in a common global adjudicative enterprise).

10. INDIA CONST. art. 51.

11. P. CHANDRASEKHARA RAO, THE INDIAN CONSTITUTION AND INTERNATIONAL LAW 4 (1993); Hegde, *supra* note 4, at 57–58.

12. Mani interprets Article 51 slightly differently as including a mixture of foreign policy and international law elements. *See* V.S. Mani, *Effectuation of International Law in the Municipal Legal Order: The Law and Practice in India,* 5 ASIAN Y.B. INT'L L. 145, 157 (1995).

13. Mahendra Pal Singh, *India, in* THE PRIVILEGES AND IMMUNITIES OF INTERNATIONAL ORGANIZATIONS IN DOMESTIC COURTS 141 n.3 (August Reinisch ed., 2013); C.H. Alexandrowicz, *International Law in India,* 1 INT'L & COMP. L.Q. 289, 291 (1952).

14. INDIA CONST. art. 246 read with Seventh Sch., List I, Entry 14.

15. Nat'l Comm'n to Review the Working of the Constitution, *A Consultation Paper on Treaty-Making Power under Our Constitution* (Jan. 8, 2001) paras. 5, 10.

Commonwealth practice with respect to treaty-making and implementation.[16] Thus, the executive has the prerogative to enter into and ratify treaties,[17] and may also decide the manner of the treaty's implementation unless the nature of the treaty compels implementing legislation by Parliament.[18]

While the executive has the power to enter into treaties, these treaties do not automatically become part of the domestic legal system upon ratification, but must be incorporated into it.[19] Certain treaties require constitutional amendment or legislation by the Parliament to take effect in domestic law. No comprehensive list of such treaties can be found either in the Constitution or in judicial pronouncements, but they include treaties that affect the private rights of individuals, involve cession of territory, and alter existing law.[20]

The Constitution is also vague when it comes to the status of customary international law in the Indian legal system, and commentators posit that the Indian practice in this respect mirrors the British model.[21] Article 51 of the Constitution's exhortation to the state to foster respect for international law is considered to include customary international law. Additionally, customary international law principles that were recognized as such in pre-1950 English common law, and were incorporated in the (Indian) common law or statute law prior to the commencement of the Indian Constitution, continue to be part of Indian law unless they are altered or repealed by the legislature or deemed to be inconsistent with the Constitution.[22]

III. INTERNATIONAL LAW IN THE INDIAN SUPREME COURT

While international law does not feature prominently in the Indian constitutional scheme, it has come to occupy an important place in the legal system through an unexpected ally: the Indian Supreme Court. In a series of decisions beginning in the 1970s, the court has elevated international law to an additional source of law that is nearly as powerful as domestic sources, and in some cases, as the only source that it can wield effectively against the other organs of government. The court has adopted various techniques, both homegrown and borrowed, in this process.

---

16. For a succinct discussion of the constitutional position, *see* Thomas M. Franck & Arun K. Thiruvengadam, *International Law and Constitution-Making*, 2 CHINESE J. INT'L L. 467, 484–85 (2003).

17. INDIA CONST. arts. 73, 246, 253 read with Seventh Sch., List I, Entry 14; Robert B. Looper, *The Treaty Power in India*, 32 BRITISH Y.B. INT'L L. 300, 304–05 (1955-56).

18. Nat'l Comm'n, *supra* note 15, at para 5.

19. Jolly Jeorge v. Bank of Cochin, (1980) 2 SCC 360, para. 6.

20. RAO, *supra* note 11, at 137–48; *see also* Maganbhai Ishwarbhai Patel v. Union of India, (1970) 3 SCC 400, para. 80.

21. Franck & Thiruvengadam, *supra* note 16, at 499.

22. INDIA CONST. art. 273; Mani, *supra* note 12, at 153–55.

A. Creative Interpretative Techniques

Since international treaties that affect private rights or alter existing law do not ipso facto become part of domestic law in the absence of implementing legislation, Parliament can in principle delay the transformation of international obligations into domestic law for as long as it wishes. There is nothing in the constitutional scheme that enables the courts to question the Parliament's authority in this respect. The Supreme Court has, however, effectively circumvented these limitations by holding that even though international conventions may not be directly enforceable in Indian courts, they can be used to interpret and fill in gaps in domestic law, as long as there is no inconsistency with domestic law.[23] This interpretative posture is not confined to statutes or subordinate legislation, but extends to provisions of the Constitution where the court has stated that "[a]ny international convention not inconsistent with the fundamental rights and in harmony with its spirit must be read into these provisions to enlarge the meaning and content thereof, to promote the object of the constitutional guarantee."[24] It also explicitly permits international legal sources to be read into constitutional rights to "enlarge" their content, thus acknowledging that the constitutional right would be much more limited in the absence of the international norm.

The court also has an inordinately expansive view of the categories of international norms that can be used to expand the content of constitutional rights: it does not always distinguish between treaties that India has ratified on the one hand, and other international conventions and international legal sources on the other.[25] The court has consistently held that customary international law rules that are not contrary to domestic Indian law are deemed to be incorporated into municipal law.[26] However, it has mostly failed to clarify the basis on which specific rules may be considered part of customary international law.

Vellore Citizens' Welfare Forum[27] illustrates vividly the court's indifference toward the steps required to establish the customary international law status of a rule before importing it into domestic law. In this case, the court introduced into domestic jurisprudence the concept of sustainable development.[28] The concept was pioneered by the Stockholm Declaration 1972 and championed in the 1987 Brundtland Report of the World Commission on Environment and Development, and was subsequently endorsed by various international bodies including the World Conservation Union, the United Nations Environment Programme, and the Worldwide Fund for Nature,

---

23. Nat'l Legal Services Authority v. Union of India, (2014) 5 SCC 438, paras. 54–59.

24. Vishaka v. State of Rajasthan, (1997) 6 SCC 241, para. 7. *See also* Apparel Exp. Promotion Council v. A.K. Chopra, (1999) 1 SCC 759, para. 27.

25. Additional Dist. Magistrate, Jabalpur v. Shivakant Shukla, (1976) 2 SCC 521, para. 542.

26. *See, e.g.,* People's Union for Civil Liberties v. Union of India, (1997) 1 SCC 301, paras. 21–22; Vellore Citizens' Welfare Forum v. Union of India, (1996) 5 SCC 647, para. 15.

27. Vellore Citizens' Welfare Forum, (1996) 5 SCC at para. 15.

28. *Id.* at para. 9.

and in various international conferences and fora. The court concluded that sustain-able development was thus part of customary international law, "even though its salient features ha[d] yet to be finalised by the international law jurists."[29]

According to the court, sustainable development encompassed several environ-mental principles, including the "polluter pays principle," which had been recog-nized in the previous jurisprudence of the court, and the "precautionary principle," both of which were accepted as part of the law of the land.[30] Thus, in light of the various statutory and constitutional instruments recognizing the need for environ-mental protection, both the "polluter pays principle" and the "precautionary princi-ple" could be deemed part of Indian law.[31] Even otherwise, as these were customary international law principles, in the absence of any domestic law to the contrary, they were considered to be incorporated into municipal law and could be followed by Indian courts.[32]

The methodology used by the court to arrive at the concepts of "polluter pays," "precautionary principle," and "sustainable development" as part of customary inter-national law betrays a lack of understanding of the process of formation of custom-ary international law norms.[33] The court seems to take their repeated endorsement by a large number of governments in international fora as evidence of customary international law.[34] In the same breath, it refers to the "writings of jurists" as a legit-imate source for their refinement.

The court has not always been this careless. In another case dealing with the pro-cedure for allocation of licenses/radio spectrum for 2G services by the Ministry of Telecommunications and Information Technology, the court framed the issue as a matter of the state's responsibilities in the allocation of natural resources.[35] The court drew upon various international legal sources, citing the endorsement of the principle of permanent sovereignty of peoples and nations over their natural resources by the 17th session of the UN General Assembly, and added that it had been affirmed as a norm of customary international law by the International Court of Justice in the case of *Democratic Republic of Congo v Uganda*.[36] It also noted the position of the state as a custodian of natural resources for the benefit of the people in various national constitutions and in the common law.[37]

This use of customary international law is notably different from the one in *Vellore Citizens' Welfare Forum*. The court does not attempt to compile a list of international

---

29. *Id.* at para. 9.

30. *Id.* at paras. 11–13.

31. *Id.* at paras. 13–14.

32. *Id.* at para. 15.

33. Hegde, *supra* note 4, at 69.

34. *See* Benvenisti, *Reclaiming Democracy, supra* note 1, at 261.

35. Centre for Public Interest Litigation v. Union of India, (2012) 3 SCC 1, paras. 74–75.

36. *Id.* at para. 76.

37. *Id.* at para. 76.

instruments or cite writings to demonstrate whether a principle is part of customary international law. Instead, it relies on a prior decision of the International Court of Justice confirming its status. The court also cites the customary-international-law basis of the principle in the same vein as other legal sources; there is no mention of the obligatory nature of customary international law. Indeed, one suspects that the court treats this source in much the same manner as any other non-binding persuasive source of authority. This might in fact be a more sensible interpretation of the court's citation to "soft law" international instruments (which it mistakenly categorizes as customary international law in *Vellore Citizens' Welfare Forum*), which it invokes generously in a number of cases and which seem to function primarily as persuasive authority.

A more extreme example of this use of soft international law sources can be seen in one of the most recent decisions of the court. In *National Legal Services Authority v. Union of India*,[38] the court considered whether non-recognition of transgender identity as a third gender by the state violated the right to equality under Article 14 and the right to life and liberty under Article 21. The court approached the issue in terms of the rights to gender identity and sexual orientation as fundamental aspects of human life.[39] It referred to a wide range of international legal sources including the Universal Declaration on Human Rights, the International Covenant on Civil and Political Rights, the set of principles developed by the International Commission of Jurists and the International Service for Human Rights,[40] the Yogyakarta Principles on the Application of Human Rights in Relation to Sexual Orientation and Gender Identity framed by a group of human rights experts,[41] and General Comments and Reports by UN Human Rights Treaty Bodies.[42] Additionally, it cited judgments and legislation recognizing transgender rights from numerous countries and the decisions of the European Court of Human Rights[43] and various instruments under European Union law recognizing the right against discrimination arising out of transgender identity.[44]

The court seemed to place international conventions that have been ratified by India, other "non-binding" international law instruments, and decisions of international and foreign courts on the same level with respect to their relevance to domestic law interpretation.[45] This extensive citation to non-domestic sources was,

---

38. Nat'l Legal Services Authority v. Union of India, (2014) 5 SCC 438.

39. *Id.* at paras. 21-22.

40. *Id.* at para. 23.

41. *Id.* at paras. 24–26.

42. *Id.* at paras. 26–27.

43. *Id.* at paras. 35–36.

44. *Id.* at paras. 41–42.

45. The Delhi High Court, in the landmark decision of Naz Foundation v. Government of NCT of Delhi, 160 DLT 277 (2009), similarly does not distinguish between the different kinds of foreign law sources. *See* Madhav Khosla, *Inclusive Constitutional Comparison: Reflections on India's Sodomy Decision*, 59 Am. J. Comp. L. 909 (2011).

however, oddly divorced from its noticeably sparse discussion of the constitutional provisions applicable to the case.[46] What could account for this curious disconnect? One possible explanation is that the detailed recitation of international sources signals the court's efforts to enter into a dialogue with the international community and demonstrate both its respect for it, as well as to claim membership in it.[47] Relatedly, the inclusion of a wide range of foreign sources in service of a progressive judgment might have been motivated by the court's awareness that the world was watching and evaluating its decision and a desire to project a positive image on the world stage.[48]

One can, however, account for this respect accorded to international legal sources in other ways that have less to do with the Court's attempts to reach out to the world community, and are more oriented toward persuading domestic constituencies and pressure groups. For instance, in referring to the endorsement of these rights in national and international instruments and fora, the court might have sought to establish the transcendental nature of these values, which may then be used to interpret the open-textured guarantees of equality, dignity, and non-discrimination in domestic constitutional law.[49] The universal recognition of these values could assist the court in fending off potential criticism from other organs of the state, especially in light of the fact that this declaration of rights in *National Legal Services Authority* was accompanied by a comprehensive set of instructions to the executive for their implementation.[50]

In the majority of cases where the court has cited international sources, it would have been perfectly possible for the court to adjudicate the matter by referring solely to constitutional provisions.[51] One could interpret the court's tacking on of non-binding international legal norms as supplemental sources that add heft to a

46. Nat'l Legal Services Authority, (2014) 5 SCC at paras. 81–83.

47. Khosla proffers this as a possible explanation for the Delhi High Court's references to international and comparative law sources in *Naz Foundation*. *See* Khosla, *supra* note 45, at 915–16.

48. *See* Khosla, *supra* note 45, at 926 (on *Naz Foundation*). Bahdi terms this attitude "globalized self-awareness." *See* Bahdi, *supra* note 6, at 590–93. *See also* Cai, *supra* note 2, at 317–18 (suggesting that Chinese courts may be moving in the same direction with a view to increasing China's soft power internationally).

49. Similar arguments have been made by scholars evaluating the use of comparative and international law by other courts around the world. *See* Bahdi, *supra* note 6, at 568–75. Compare Chris McCrudden's thesis on why domestic courts might be able to draw on international human rights law. *See* Christopher McCrudden, *CEDAW in National Courts: A Case Study in Operationalizing Comparative International Law Analysis in a Human Rights Context* (this volume).

50. Nat'l Legal Services Authority, (2014) 5 SCC at para. 135.

51. This pattern can be seen even in cases that are concerned with other legal issues such as maritime law (Aban Loyd Chiles Offshore Ltd. v. Union of India, (2008) 11 SCC 439); criminal law (Ankush Shiwaji Gaikwad v. State of Maharashtra, (2013) 6 SCC 770); and the rights of noncitizens (Chairman, Railway Bd. v. Chandrima Das, (2000) 2 SCC 465).

primarily domestic law analysis.[52] A more radical explanation of the weight given to soft law international law instruments may lie in a lingering dissatisfaction with the manner in which international law norms achieve binding status. Thus, by failing to adhere to the distinction between hard and soft law, the court is indirectly challenging both the hierarchy and categorization of international law norms, and the manner in which they percolate into domestic legal systems.

B. Going beyond Interpretation

As the above decisions reveal, the court's excursions into using international law for gap-filling purposes has led to the enunciation of rights and constitutional guarantees that are either not contained explicitly in the constitutional text, or which considerably expand the scope and content of the constitutional guarantee. In some instances, these decisions come close to an amendment of the content of the constitutional rights, while in others they alter the relationship between the organs of the state.

This role of the court is most evident in the environmental context, where the court has read soft law instruments proclaiming concepts such as sustainable development, polluter pays, and the doctrine of public trust, into constitutional provisions that do not directly support these as mandatory and justiciable state obligations. For instance, in *A.P. Pollution Control Board v. Prof. M.V. Nayudu*,[53] the court relied on a wide range of non-binding international law principles to conclude that the state is obligated to provide adequate judicial and scientific inputs in the adjudication of environmental cases that involve highly complicated scientific and technical facts, and cannot simply leave these to be decided by adjudicatory bodies with officers drawn from the executive.[54] The court derived this duty from the precautionary principle, which had been accepted as customary international law in its earlier decision in *Vellore Citizens' Welfare Forum*,[55] and had also been recommended by the UNEP Governing Council in 1989 and by the Bamako Convention.[56] Citing the Special Rapporteur for the International Law Commission's (ILC) Report on "Prevention of Transboundary Damage from Hazardous Activities" on the status of the precautionary principle, the court held that the principle reversed the burden of proof such that the person proposing the environmental activity had to demonstrate that it would not be harmful.[57]

---

52. Waters labels this use of international law as "gilding the domestic lily." *See* Melissa A. Waters, *Creeping Monism: The Judicial Trend Towards Interpretive Incorporation of Human Rights Treaties*, 107 COLUM. L. REV. 628, 654–57 (2007).

53. A.P. Pollution Control Bd. v. Prof. M.V. Nayudu, (1999) 2 SCC 718.

54. *Id.* at para. 42.

55. *Id.* at paras. 31–32.

56. *Id.* at paras. 33–35.

57. *Id.* at para. 38.

The court then examined deficiencies in the Indian judicial and appellate system for adjudicating technical and scientific environmental issues in light of these environmental principles.[58] It referred to the components of good governance set out in the Reports of the UN Secretary General on the Work of the Organisation and of the Working Group of the ILC that required the state to take measures to prevent environmental harm.[59] The court concluded that the government of India must, therefore, introduce amendments to the existing laws to ensure that in all environmental courts, tribunals, and appellate authorities, there is always a judge of the rank of a High Court Judge or a Supreme Court Judge and a scientist or group of scientists to help proper adjudication of disputes relating to pollution and the environment.[60] It also recommended that there should be a right to a regular appeal to the Supreme Court from decisions issued by appellate authorities and that the government should consider introducing legislation or amending notifications to this effect.[61]

The judgment in *M.V. Nayudu* is remarkable for a near complete absence of any references to domestic law provisions supporting the court's directive to the legislature and the executive to implement far-reaching changes to the composition and working of environmental adjudicatory bodies. Nor is there any attempt to justify its reliance on an eclectic range of soft law international sources for principles ranging from good governance to environmental conservation. Based almost entirely on these soft law international sources, the court is able to arrogate to itself the authority to intervene in what would normally be a legislative or executive prerogative.

The court has indeed gone further in championing the cause of good governance by usurping the executive's power to define the extent of its commitment to binding international obligations under international treaties. For instance, the court has nullified the effect of reservations to treaties specified by the executive at the time of ratification. In *C. Masilamani Mudaliar v. Idol of Sri Swaminathanswami*,[62] the court was concerned with a widow's right to maintenance under Section 14(1) of the Hindu Succession Act, 1956 and whether the widow had acquired only a limited estate in terms of the testator's will or whether her rights had blossomed into an absolute estate. The court referred to the constitutional affirmation of the right to dignity and equality in the Preamble, the Fundamental Rights, and the Directive Principles of State Policy and stated that this included the right to non-discrimination on grounds of gender.[63] It then cited the United Nations General Assembly Declaration on the "Development of the Right to Development" in which India had played a major role, which affirmed the status of the right to development as an inalienable human right and obligated the state to take steps to secure

58. *Id.* at para. 40.

59. *Id.* at para. 42.

60. *Id.* at para. 47.

61. *Id.* at para. 72.

62. C. Masilamani Mudaliar v. Idol of Sri Swaminathanswami, (1996) 8 SCC 525.

63. *Id.* at para. 15.

its realization.[64] In addition, the state had to enact measures to promote equality and to eliminate discrimination on grounds of gender under the Universal Declaration of Human Rights[65] and the Convention on the Elimination of All Forms of Discrimination against Women (CEDAW), which India had ratified.[66]

According to the court, even though India had made a reservation to Article 5(a) of CEDAW concerning the elimination of social and cultural practices based on the idea of the superiority of men, the effect of this reservation had been nullified by virtue of Article 2(f) of the Convention, which enjoined the state to "take all appropriate measures, including legislation, to modify or abolish existing laws, regulations, customs and practices which constitute discrimination against women." CEDAW and the Declaration on Development added teeth and urgency to the constitutional imperative under the fundamental rights and directive principles to immediately implement measures for the elimination of discrimination and the promotion of gender equality.[67] The court also referred to its previous decision in the case of *Valsamma Paul v. Cochin University*,[68] holding that the reservations India had made to various provisions of CEDAW were of little consequence in light of the prohibition of non-discrimination on grounds of gender in Articles 15(1) and 15(3) and the right to life and liberty under Article 21.[69]

The court's reference to CEDAW is not only unnecessary for the decision in this case, which could have been rendered solely with reference to constitutional provisions, but also mistaken in its construction of the practice of reservations to treaties. If one follows the court's interpretation of Article 2(f) of CEDAW as nullifying the effect of reservations made by the executive to all other Convention provisions, this means that the state is effectively barred from making any reservations under CEDAW.

Relatedly, in *D.K. Basu v. State of West Bengal*,[70] the court was faced with the violent treatment, torture, and death of inmates in Indian prisons and considered whether monetary compensation should be awarded for the violation of their fundamental rights to life and liberty under Articles 20 and 21 of the Constitution. The court held that a mere declaration of illegality would be an insufficient remedy and that it must go further and give compensatory relief for the breach of the state's duty to safeguard the fundamental rights of its citizens.[71] The court acknowledged

---

64. *Id.* at paras. 16–17.

65. *Id.* at para. 18.

66. *Id.* at para. 19.

67. *Id.* at paras. 21–23. This form of referencing CEDAW seems to conform to the practice of courts applying and interpreting in most jurisdictions. *See* McCrudden, *supra* note 49, at 482.

68. Valsamma Paul v. Cochin University, (1996) 3 SCC 545.

69. Masilamani Mudaliar, (1996) 8 SCC at para 25.

70. D.K. Basu v. State of West Bengal, (1997) 1 SCC 416.

71. *Id.* at para. 41.

that India had made an express reservation to Article 9(5) of the ICCPR, which provided individuals who had been subject to unlawful arrest or detention with an enforceable right to compensation. However, this reservation had lost its relevance in light of a series of previous decisions in which the court had awarded compensation for the violation of the right to life. This right to compensation had, therefore, evolved through court jurisprudence in spite of the fact that the Indian constitution did not explicitly guarantee it.[72] The court also cited a number of cases in other jurisdictions in support of the right to compensation from the state for violation of an established fundamental right.[73]

This rewriting of treaty obligations undertaken by the executive is a remarkable usurpation of the role of the executive by the court. The less charitable explanation for this unprecedented judicial maneuver is that the court simply does not comprehend the function and effect of reservations to treaties.[74] The court may, however, be acting with the full consciousness that it is amending the express decision of the executive by judicial fiat.

C. Exercising Quasi-legislative Powers

The Supreme Court has deployed international law to assist its metamorphosis from an entity that is responsible primarily for resolving disputes between the parties before it, to one that acts in an administrative and legislative capacity where it issues detailed directives to state organs and at times continues to be seized of the matter to oversee the administration of the relief granted in the dispute.

One of the earliest and most striking instances of this use of international law was in the case of *Vishaka v. State of Rajasthan*,[75] where the court dealt with the enforcement of the right to equality as it related to promoting gender equality and combating sexual harassment of women at the workplace. The court noted the lack of any legislation on this issue and stated that in light of this legislative and executive vacuum, it was the responsibility of the court to lay down some guidelines for the protection of these rights.[76]

The court held that it could rely on international conventions and norms to interpret the right to gender equality and the right to work with dignity contained in the fundamental rights and the implicit guarantee against sexual harassment found within them.[77] The court thus cited Article 32 of the Constitution on the enforcement of fundamental rights, alongside the Beijing Statement of Principles of the

---

72. *Id.* at para. 42.

73. *Id.* at paras. 46–53.

74. The Indian judges' lack of expertise in international law had been lamented as far back as 1962. *See* S.K. Agrawala, *Law of Nations as Interpreted and Applied by Indian Courts and Legislature*, 2 INDIAN J. INT'L L. 431, 477 (1962).

75. Vishaka v. State of Rajasthan, (1997) 6 SCC 241.

76. *Id.* at para. 3.

77. *Id.* at para. 7.

Independence of the Judiciary in the LAWASIA Region that were accepted by the chief justices of the courts of the Asia and Pacific Region in 1995, to emphasize the judiciary's obligation to promote the observance of human rights.[78] It referred to Article 11 of CEDAW on the states' obligation to eliminate discrimination against women in employment and noted the general recommendations of CEDAW on Article 11, which singled out workplace sexual harassment as a serious obstacle to gender equality at the workplace.[79] The court noted that India had ratified CEDAW and made an official commitment at the Fourth World Conference on Women in Beijing to formulate policies and set up mechanisms to safeguard women's rights. The court concluded that it had "no hesitation in placing reliance on the above for the purpose of construing the nature and ambit of the constitutional guarantee of gender equality in our Constitution."[80]

The court went on to formulate a detailed set of binding guidelines and norms to combat sexual harassment at work until suitable legislation was enacted to address the issue.[81] These dealt with the definition of sexual harassment and the duties of employers to prevent and deter its commission by taking various steps, including creating secure working conditions and instituting various mechanisms of redress such as criminal proceedings, disciplinary rules, and complaint procedures. The court also requested the Central and state governments to consider adopting measures, including legislation, to facilitate the observance of the guidelines in the judgment by private employers.[82]

The court has repeated this practice in a number of cases. In *Vellore Citizens' Welfare Forum*, the court directed the Central government to constitute an authority under Section 3(3) of the Environment Protection Act, 1986 that would implement the polluter pays and precautionary principles to deal with the pollution and damage to the environment caused by the tanneries. It issued a comprehensive set of directions on the composition, functions, and duties of this authority and on the duties to be performed by various governmental authorities to achieve an end to the environmental degradation in the area, and measures for stopping pollution by industries.[83] The court also imposed a pollution fine on the tanneries in the area that had to be collected by the district magistrate of the respective district by a certain date, and directed that the failure to do so will result in their closure. Additionally, it mandated the setting up of individual pollution control devices by all the tanneries in the affected districts.[84] Finally, the court provided for a monitoring mechanism to supervise the implementation of these directives by requesting the chief justice of

78. *Id.* at para. 11.

79. *Id.* at paras. 12–13.

80. *Id.* at para. 13.

81. *Id.* at paras. 16–18.

82. *Id.* at para. 17.

83. Vellore Citizens' Welfare Forum v. Union of India, (1996) 5 SCC 647, para. 25.

84. *Id.* at para. 25.

the Madras High Court to constitute a "green bench" that would deal with this case and other environmental matters.[85]

Again, in *National Legal Services Authority*, the court directed the Central and state governments to grant legal recognition to the gender identity of the members of the transgender community who had the right to decide their self-identified third gender. In addition, it directed the Central and state governments to undertake a host of measures aimed at securing the health, well-being, and social welfare of members of the transgender community.[86] The court also noted with approval the government's establishment of an expert committee to recommend measures to ameliorate the problems faced by the transgender community, and directed that these recommendations be examined on the basis of the court's directions and implemented by the government within six months.[87]

These cases showcase the court's embrace of a particular vision of a state that is duty-bound to secure basic and decent human conditions of life for its citizens. To translate this vision into reality, the court uses international law as an instrument to encroach upon the legislative and executive spheres in order to rectify government failures and to promote government accountability.[88]

IV. THE RATIONALE FOR RELIANCE ON INTERNATIONAL LAW

A. The Bid for Legitimacy

What may be the explanation for the extraordinary ways in which international law has become embedded in the Supreme Court's rights jurisprudence? One could trace the trajectory of the court's embrace of international law within the context of the court's larger bid for political and moral legitimacy within the Indian political landscape.[89] Indian scholars have argued persuasively that in the period following the declaration of a nationwide emergency by then-Prime Minister Indira Gandhi (1975–1977), the Supreme Court deliberately took steps to transform itself into a liberal political institution.[90] The emergency period and the years leading up to it represented a nadir in the image of the Supreme Court, where it found itself locked in a constant battle with the executive and when it was deemed an elitist institution

---

85. *Id.* at para. 26.

86. Nat'l Legal Services Authority v. Union of India, (2014) 5 SCC 438, para. 135.

87. *Id.* at para. 135.

88. This is remarkably different from the posture that Chinese courts adopt toward the executive in the pursuit of a common vision of the aims and goals of the State. *See* Cai, *supra* note 2, at 298, 318.

89. For a similar attempt to situate the use of foreign legal sources (mostly comparative law) by the court within its political history, see Adam M. Smith, *Making Itself at Home—Understanding Foreign Law in Domestic Jurisprudence: The Indian Case*, 24 BERKELEY J. INT'L L. 218 (2006).

90. Upendra Baxi, *Taking Suffering Seriously: Social Action Litigation in the Supreme Court of India*, in JUDGES AND THE JUDICIAL POWER 289, 294 (Rajeev Dhavan et al. eds., 1985); Smith, *supra* note 89, at 252.

that was out of touch with the concerns of the vast majority of the populace. The post-Emergency period signaled the court's emergence as an institution that was conscious of the need to repair its tarnished image, not least so that it would be able to withstand any future attempts by the executive to encroach on the court's domain.[91] The court thus sought to establish a "popular" legitimacy by setting itself firmly on the side of "the people," especially those who had been ignored by the democratic institutions of government.[92] This period thus saw the court adopting an expansive construction of first-order and second-order fundamental rights.[93]

The most innovative step in this direction was the institution of "Public Interest Litigation" or "Social Action Litigation" whereby the court relaxed the rules of standing and pleading before the court. Thus, any public-spirited individual or entity could bring a case before the court for the enforcement of a fundamental right. In addition, the court dispensed with the procedural formalities required to bring a petition, and converted all sorts of instruments (including letters written to the judges, postcards addressed to the court, and newspaper articles highlighting rights violations) to writ petitions. The court also expanded its own powers to develop a range of remedies that at times involved taking control over the activities of other agencies.[94]

The introduction of liberal rules of standing encouraged a partnership between the court and civil society movements that had been fueled by loss of confidence in the state and the distrust of market forces. A vast number of petitions were filed in the 1970s and 1980s by social action groups and by individual lawyers and social activists on behalf of the underprivileged and unrepresented sections of Indian society.[95] The court's engagement with broader social movements that used, among other strategies, international law norms to push forward their claims may be contrasted with the apathy of Indian international law scholars to do the same. As Chimni notes, the dominant international law scholarship in the post-Emergency era largely failed to take up issues that were relevant to the marginalized sections of Indian society, leaving this task to NGOs and individual crusaders.[96]

B. The Use of International Law as a Tool

The turn to international law sources by the Supreme Court may be considered a strategic move in its pursuit for rehabilitation in the Indian political structure, where the court has become a high-profile public institution that has contrived to

---

91. Baxi, *supra* note 90, at 292, 294; S.P. Sathe, *Judicial Activism: The Indian Experience*, 6 J.L. & POL'Y 29, 50 (2001).

92. Baxi, *supra* note 90, at 296; Sathe, *supra* note 91, at 50–51.

93. Smith, *supra* note 89, at 256–57.

94. Baxi, *supra* note 90, at 292, 294; Sathe, *supra* note 91, at 72–73, 75; Smith, *supra* note 89, at 252–53.

95. Baxi, *supra* note 90, at 296; Sathe, *supra* note 91, at 79.

96. Chimni, *International Law Scholarship*, *supra* note 5, at 48.

serve as the last hope for the stigmatized and the underprivileged who have long been excluded from full participation in society and ignored or doubly disadvantaged by political structures that seek to maintain the status quo. While the court could undoubtedly have relied on domestic law and techniques of constitutional interpretation alone in at least some of the cases where it referenced international legal sources, by citing international law it has been able to invoke authoritative or quasi-authoritative norms that are not expressly present in the municipal legal system. This has lent its decisions an aura of legitimacy and facilitated an expansive interpretation of rights and the reading of new (enforceable) rights into the Constitution. The aggressive invocation of international law has also enabled the court to fashion new remedies for legislative inaction by labeling them as a form of sanction for Parliament's non-implementation of treaty obligations into domestic law. The court in *Vishaka* does not hesitate to remind its audience that India has ratified CEDAW and made an express commitment in an international forum to secure the rights of women. The individual thus becomes an appropriate subject of direct rights and obligations under international law—even though these might be mediated through the act of treaty ratification by the state—with the domestic court acting as the domestic enforcer of these rights and obligations. The court has appropriated international law as a vehicle through which it can legitimately chastise the other organs of the state for having failed to fulfill their duties toward their citizens. This usurpation of the executive and legislative role, with the court casting itself in the position of a monitor and supervisor to ensure the implementation of its directives, needs every possible source of justification. International law, with its claims of universality, slips neatly into this justificatory role, which the court can assert while affecting a nonpartisan posture.

C. Arbitrariness

Lest this portrait of the Supreme Court appear too salutary, it is worth noting that the court has been far from consistent in the causes it has chosen to champion. For instance, in *Sarbananda Sonowal v. Union of India*,[97] the petitioners challenged the constitutional validity of the Illegal Migrants (Determination by) Tribunals Act, 1983 (IMDT) and Rules made thereunder that extended solely to the state of Assam, and only in respect of the detection and determination of illegal migrants who had entered India after a certain date. The court noted that the state's primary duty was the protection of the state's borders and the safety and security of its citizens, and referred to Article 355 of the Indian Constitution, which mandated the state to protect itself against external aggression and internal interference.[98] In construing the term "aggression," the court cited debates on the meaning of acts of aggression in Article 1 in the UN Charter and the attempts to formulate a comprehensive definition of aggression at the international level. The court noted the position taken by India's representative to the Sixth Committee of the General Assembly on the

---

97. Sarbananda Sonowal v. Union of India, (2005) 5 SCC 665.

98. *Id.* at para. 51.

Definition of Aggression in 1971, which defined the influx of large numbers of individuals from a state into a neighboring state as indirect aggression.[99] The court also referred to pronouncements by US and English authorities deeming the influx of large numbers of people into their borders as "aggression" or invasion."[100]

The court concluded that the term "aggression" included a wide variety of acts, and its meaning could not be restricted to the definition endorsed by the General Assembly in Resolution No. 3314 (XXIX), which was geared solely toward situations when the UN could intervene in the case of an act of aggression by one state against another.[101] It held that the state of Assam was facing "external aggression and internal disturbance" due to the widespread illegal migration of Bangladeshi nationals into its borders, and the Union of India was thus mandated under Article 355 to protect the state from such aggression. The IMDT Act and its provisions were wholly contrary to this mandate and were unconstitutional.[102]

One can interpret this unorthodox use of the international definition of "aggression" to clarify and distinguish the constitutional meaning of the term as yet another attempt by the court to garner popular support amongst its citizenry: affected Assamese residents versus poor Bangladeshi foreign migrants who lack voice. The court has, however, been accused of picking and choosing even among domestic causes, such as favoring environmental protection but not labor rights, or supporting urban developers over urban slum dwellers.[103]

In the context of the broader debate on the use of public interest litigation, scholars have posited that the lack of any attempt at principled decision-making is a deliberate strategy by the court to avoid serious conflict with the other organs of the state. The court has taken up the causes of the oppressed and the voiceless, but always with an eye to its own political aspirations and authority.[104] Thus, its decisions "seek to provide a workable *modus vivendi* rather than to articulate high values."[105] The court has cultivated an image of itself as an organ for establishing government accountability while embracing political accommodation. It has carefully avoided upsetting any major political players, and concentrated on political issues that are unlikely to directly threaten their interests.[106]

What is true of the Supreme Court's interventions in public interest causes more generally may also be an accurate interpretation of the selective instances where it has used international law to do so. Far from acting as a neutral interpreter of a

99. *Id.* at paras. 53–56.

100. *Id.* at paras. 57–60.

101. *Id.* at para. 61.

102. *Id.* at paras. 63–65.

103. *See* Benvenisti, *Reclaiming Democracy, supra* note 1, at 259 and references therein.

104. Baxi, *supra* note 90, at 302, 304; Pratap Bhanu Mehta, *The Rise of Judicial Sovereignty,* 18 J. DEMOCRACY 70, 76 (2007).

105. Mehta, *supra* note 104, at 75.

106. Baxi, *supra* note 90, at 302, 304; Mehta, *supra* note 104, at 76.

doctrinally pure international law, the court has consciously avoided articulating a public philosophy on the legitimate uses of international law norms in the Indian legal system and has pursued a policy of implicit accommodation with powerful structural and political interests.

V. CONCLUSION

This survey of the Supreme Court's jurisprudence on international law as a tool to interpret and expand constitutional rights gives rise to the intriguing possibility that there is no necessary or positive relationship between a domestic court's citation to international law and its willingness to embrace a global, cosmopolitan vision. In the absence of any coherent principle or philosophy guiding its decisions, it is difficult to discern the motivations for the court's extensive citation to all varieties of international law norms to resolve a range of legal disputes. This chapter has suggested that the court's innovative invocations of international law for myriad purposes—gap filling, interpretation, enlargement of the content of rights, chastisement of the other organs of government, supervision and monitoring of executive and legislative functions—may be inspired by distinctively domestic, and not entirely benevolent, aims. This thesis should serve as a cautionary tale for those who would consider increased reference to international law by domestic courts as an indication of a true openness to the international community or to greater respect for the rules of international law.

It should also make advocates of the unity of international law, who view municipal courts as mere agents of a universal international law, wary. The Indian Supreme Court has expended little effort in explaining its judicial philosophy or the logic behind controversial uses of international law. Moreover, its pronouncements on the nature and derivation of customary international norms and on the effect of reservations to treaties betray a worrying incomprehension of international legal sources. There is thus a tension between the image of the court as a champion of international law and its approach to the status of substantive international rules and principles and to international law's understanding of the hierarchy and status of norms. This could be interpreted either as an act of resistance to the dominant international law tradition, or simply as an opportunistic appropriation of international law for reasons of domestic law and policy.

16

Case Law in Russian Approaches to International Law

LAURI MÄLKSOO*

I. INTRODUCTION

In her comparative study on the use of case law in international law textbooks, Anthea Roberts demonstrates a number of structural differences between textbooks in different countries.[1] For example, international law textbooks in the United Kingdom and the United States include many references to case law as do, although to a somewhat lesser extent, textbooks in Germany and France. At the same time, textbooks in these Western countries vary in terms of the proportion of case law coming from international, domestic, and foreign courts. Although there can also be substantive differences between different textbooks in the same country, generally US textbooks tend to emphasize national cases related to international law and foreign relations law, while such domestic cases receive less attention in the textbooks used in other Western countries. In contrast, international law textbooks in China and Russia refer altogether much less frequently to case law in general. For example, in Chinese textbooks, domestic cases are essentially missing when international law is presented.[2]

Prima facie, Roberts's finding about the lack of emphasis on case law in Russian international legal materials seems to be corroborated by Russian international

* Research and writing of this chapter has been supported by a research grant No IUT20-50 of the Estonian Research Council.

1. Anthea Roberts, Is International Law International? ch. 1 (2017).

2. *Id.* at 135–38.

jurists. For example, Vladislav Tolstykh of Novosibirsk State University has observed about Russian legal education:

> The practice of international courts has so far not become a mandatory element in the educational process [in Russia]. In international law textbooks the emphasis is put on treaty provisions to the detriment of material related to the application of law.[3]

But why is this so and what difference does it make? In this chapter, I will further explore the Russian situation and ask whether Roberts's comparative findings regarding Russian international law textbooks reflect the dominant approach in Russian international law scholarship, and whether they also reflect a distinct approach in Russian state practice. I will then discuss what might explain both Russian scholarly and governmental approaches and, finally, what international lawyers can learn from this practice in the context of comparative international law. My main argument is that cautiousness about case law and international courts has historically been characteristic of the Russian approach to international law. In my view, this cautiousness reflects Russia's semi-peripheral status in the making and application of international law.

The main method used in this chapter is a historical one, because only the history of international law and its ideas can teach us how concrete legal-political circumstances in a country have come into being. It is also my conviction that academic projects in comparative international law should take history into account as much as possible as an explanatory factor. However, it is crucial to realize—although this may sound trivial—that the history of international law has not necessarily been one and the same everywhere. In addition to historically oriented "constructivism," I also use some realist arguments about how international law plays out in practice.

II. CASE LAW IN RUSSIAN INTERNATIONAL LAW SCHOLARSHIP

Further study of Russian international law scholarship demonstrates cautiousness about and distance from the practice of international courts, which supports Roberts's findings. For Russian scholars, international law is first and foremost what the executive branch does, not what the courts do. In addition, Russian scholarship tends to be theoretically and dogmatically oriented, rather than focused on the practice of national or international courts.[4]

The starting point for examining the contemporary Russian approach to international law is inevitably the Soviet period, because all of today's international law scholars were educated during that time or—in the case of younger scholars—educated by scholars trained during the Soviet era. Soviet legal theory evinced considerable skepticism regarding the value of judgments of the International Court

---

3. Vladislav Tolstykh, Mezhdunarodnye sudy i ikh praktika 138 (2015).

4. *See* Lauri Mälksoo, Russian Approaches to International Law 77–97 (2015).

of Justice (ICJ) and other international courts, as well as those of national courts on international law. In his main theoretical treatise, the leading international law scholar of the late Soviet period, Grigory Tunkin (1905–1993), argued against leading British international law jurists, such as Lauterpacht and Fitzmaurice, on the proper place of ICJ judgments in the hierarchy of sources of international law. Tunkin's main point was that ICJ judgments could not themselves be precedents like in a common law system. To argue otherwise, as he believed British scholars had done, was ultra vires in terms of the ICJ Statute.[5] Tunkin also argued that national court judgments, even when they concerned international law or international relations, could be important only in the context of the national law of a particular state, not international law more generally.[6]

During perestroika, this very cautious attitude regarding the possibility of international law being applied by both international and domestic courts was considered ripe for substantive revision in Russian international legal scholarship. Mark Entin of MGIMO University in Moscow published an article in which he suggested that the new, democratically oriented Russia should adopt a much more open attitude toward the ICJ.[7] After the collapse of the USSR, Igor Lukashuk (1926–2007) of the Institute of State and Law of the Russian Academy of Sciences published a monograph entitled "International Law in Domestic Courts" in which he carried out an important act of transferring knowledge from the West to Russia by examining at length the existing literature and court practice in English and other Western languages. He strongly endorsed the idea of applying international law more extensively in domestic courts.[8] The two-volume textbook of international law authored by Lukashuk was also written in the "Western style," incorporating dozens of detailed references to cases from the ICJ, Permanent Court of International Justice (PCIJ), and European Court of Justice, as well as national cases from countries as diverse as the United States, Japan, Austria, Germany, and Poland—and a few from the new post-Soviet Russia.[9]

More recently, some—typically younger—Russian international law scholars are paying significant attention to international court practice. Vladislav Tolstykh of Novosibirsk State University has recently authored and edited specialized monographs on international courts and their respective practice.[10] Aleksandr Vylegzhanin of MGIMO University has focused specifically on international cases

---

5. Grigory Tunkin, Teoria mezhdunarodnogo prava 159–63 (1970).

6. Id. at 164.

7. Mark L. Entin, Sovetskaya doktrina mezhdunarodnogo prava o sudebnykh sredstvakh razreshenia mezhdunarodnykh sporov, 1989-90-91 Sovetskii Ezhegodnik Mezhdunarodnogo Prava [Soviet Y.B. Int'l L.] 100.

8. Igor Lukashuk, Mezhdunarodnoe pravo v sudakh gosudarstv (1993).

9. 1 & 2 Igor Lukashuk, Mezhdunarodnoe pravo (2d ed. 2001).

10. Tolstykh, supra note 3; Instituty mezhdunarodnogo pravosudia (Vladslav Tolstykh ed., 2014).

in the law-of-the sea context.[11] As far as the use of international law by domestic courts is concerned, most academic attention has predictably been paid to the application of the European Convention on Human Rights in Russian courts.[12] Perhaps most notably, the relatively recent Russian international law journal *Mezhdunarodnoe pravosudie* ("International Justice") has attempted a minor revolution in the Russian literature by focusing specifically on the jurisprudence of the European Court of Human Rights (ECtHR), ICJ, and other international courts.[13] However, it is yet difficult to estimate how much individual monographs and new journal publication efforts "count," that is, what weight they carry in shaping the perception of international law among the country's internationalist elites. So far, the direction of the international law journal *Mezhdunarodnoe pravosudie* seems to be an act of counterculture in Russia.

At the same time, a number of leading Russian international law scholars remain skeptical about what they see as an exaggeration of the importance of case law in Western—and especially Anglo-Saxon—approaches to international law. A number of the arguments in this context repeat what Tunkin said in his time. One such argument is that unlike in common law countries, there is no rule of precedent in international law. For example, Anatoly Kapustin, the president of the Russian Association of International Law, emphasizes that "[t]he principle of *stare decisis* that is characteristic of the English law of precedent, is not applied by the ICJ, which is why many of its judgments present only limited interest."[14] According to Kapustin, while some ICJ judgments are more important than others, in the end no ICJ judgment is by itself a source of international law. It has that authority only if it reflects "positive norms of international law," which must be established separately.[15]

The prestigious MGIMO University textbook also reflects skepticism about the use of national court judgments, emphasizing that such judgments cannot be sources of *international* law:

> What Western international lawyers do, namely singling out specific countries (United Kingdom, United States, etc.) in which judgments of national courts are then supposed to be sources of international law, is without justification. First of all, the Statute of the ICJ does not give grounds for such differentiated approach among states. Secondly, in each country judges may have different

11. Alexander Vylegzhanin, *Vklad Mezhdunarodnoga Suda OON v progressivnoe razvitie morskogo prava (1949–1990), in* Mezhdunarodnoe morskoe pravo: Stat'i pamiati Anatoly Kolodkina 40 (2013); Reshenia Mezhdunarodnoga Suda OON po sporam o razgranichenii morkikh prostranstv (R.A. Kolodkin & S.M. Punzhin eds., 2004).

12. *See* Anton L. Burkov, Konventsia o zashchite prav cheloveka v sudakh rossii (2010); Olga A. Egorova & Yuri F. Bespalov, Evropeiskaya konventsia o zashtshite prav cheloveka i osnovnykh svobod v sudebnoi praktike (2015).

13. The journal's website is: http://www.ilpp.ru/en/journal/mp/.

14. Mezhdunarodnoe pravo 84 (Anatoly Ya. Kapustin ed., 2008).

15. *Id.*

qualifications and moral qualities, and court judgments may also differ based on their reasoning.[16]

Essentially the same view is shared by Stanislav Chernichenko, the leading theoretician of international law formerly at the Diplomatic Academy of the Russian Ministry of Foreign Affairs (MFA) and currently at the Institute of State and Law of the Russian Academy of Sciences.[17]

At the same time, in the international law textbook of the Diplomatic Academy one can find separate and lengthy sections on international law as it is applied by the Russian Constitutional Court, Russian courts of general jurisdiction, and the so-called *arbitrazh* courts, as well as on the practice of the ECtHR regarding Russia.[18] Similarly, the textbook edited by Ignatenko and Tiunov discusses quite extensively the application of international law by the Constitutional Court of the Russian Federation, the Supreme Court, the Higher Arbitrazh Court (now defunct), and other courts of the Russian Federation.[19]

Thus, unlike in China, at least some leading Russian textbooks discuss extensively the nation's domestic cases relating to international law, particularly on the question of international law's position in the constitutional system. It is quite possible that by doing so such textbooks imitate the US international law tradition to some extent. After all, the United States, along with Western Europe, has been a central point of reference for post-World War II Russia (and particularly for the post-Soviet generation of international lawyers.) The US "great power" approach to international law, primarily approaching it through one's own Constitution, seems to be attractive for at least some Russian scholars. In this sense, extensive attention to domestic court practice in some Russian textbooks can be interpreted as a way to "catch up" with the United States, and as an attempt to construct international law proceeding primarily from one's own constitutional order.

III. HOW TRENDS IN RUSSIAN SCHOLARSHIP REFLECT STATE PRACTICE

A certain cautiousness and minimalism regarding case law in the Russian international law scholarship makes sense. It is realistic, because Russia's engagement with international courts has historically been cautious and has recently again

16. MEZHDUNARODNOE PRAVO 96 (A.N. Vylegzhanin ed., 2009).

17. STANISLAV V. CHERNICHENKO, KONTURY MEZHDUNARODNOGO PRAVA 169 (2014).

18. Bakhtiyar R. Tuzmukhamedov, *Mezhdunarodnoe pravo v deyatel'nosti Konstitutsionnogo Suda Rossiiskoi Federatsii, in* MEZHDUNARODNOE PRAVO 128 (Sergei A. Egorov ed., 5th ed. 2013); Bakhtiyar R. Tuzmukhamedov, *Realizatsia norm mezhdunarodnogo prava sudami obshtshei iurisdiktsii i arbitrazhnymi sudami Rossiiskoi Federatsii, in* MEZHDUNARODNOE PRAVO, *id.,* 142; Anatoly I. Kovler, *Deyatel'nost' Evropeiskogo suda po pravam cheloveka i pravovaia sistema Rossiiskoi Federatsii, in* MEZHDUNARODNOE PRAVO, *id.,* 417.

19. MEZHDUNARODNOE PRAVO 212–61, but also 107, 143, 543 (G.V. Ignatenko & O.I. Tiunov eds., 6th ed. 2013).

experienced new backlashes since the initial thaw of the perestroika period and the 1990s. It is important to take into account that this cautiousness did not first arise from the Soviet tradition in Russia, but to some extent can be traced back as far as the late Tsarist period.

With pride, contemporary Russian scholars have suggested that Russia's leading nineteenth century international law experts, especially Fedor Martens (1845–1909) of St. Petersburg University[20] and Leonid Kamarovskii (1846–1912) of Moscow University, were worldwide forerunners in propagating the idea of establishing a permanent international court.[21] When President Putin held a speech at the festive anniversary gathering in the ICJ in November 2005, he claimed the honor of conceiving of the ICJ for the Russian internationalist tradition: "This innovative idea was born in our country and it was self-denyingly propagated by progressive representatives of the Russian legal science."[22]

"Self-denyingly" is an appropriate word, because there was indeed a gap between the ideas propagated by imperial Russian international law scholars and the government's actual practice in international adjudication. For example, when Count Kamarovskii predicted and advocated the establishment of an international court, he supported his prediction by reference to legal and political developments in *Western* Europe. Indeed, he explicitly made the point that in actual state practice, Tsarist Russia had stood apart from these progressive developments, mainly because of its severe limits to political freedom.[23] However, Count Kamarovskii also argued against the English philosopher John Stuart Mill (1806–1873) regarding the importance of the US Supreme Court's practice in the evolution of international law. He disagreed with Mill's view that the US Supreme Court constituted "the first example of real international jurisdiction which the contemporary civilized society needs so much."[24] Thus, different approaches in different "civilized" countries—the Anglo-Saxon countries and Tsarist Russia—regarding the importance of case law and domestic courts were already articulated in the international legal literature.

Another Russian international law scholar, Nikolai Korkunov (1853–1904), observed that by 1884, the United States had participated in 30 arbitrations and

20. *See* Aleksandr M. Solntsev, *Vklad Rossiskikh uchenykh kontsa XIX-nachala XX v. v utverzhdenie i razvitie idei mezhdunarodnogo pravosudia, in* INSTITUTY MEZHDUNARODNOGO PRAVOSUDIA 116 (Vladislav Tolstykh ed., 2015).

21. *See* LEONID A. KAMAROVSKII, O MEZHDUNARODNOM SUDE (2015). *See also* ASLAN KH. ABASHIDZE, ALEKSANDR M. SOLNTSEV & KONSTANTIN V. AGEICHENKO, MIRNOE RAZRESH-ENIE MEZHDUNARODNYKH SPOROV: SOVREMENNIE PROBLEMI 120 (2011); MEZHDUNARODNOE PRAVO, *supra* note 16, at 484–85.

22. Vladimir Putin, President, Russ, Vystuplenie na zasedanii Mezhdunarodnogo Suda Organizatsii Ob'edinennykh Natsii (Jan. 11, 2005) *available at* http://www.kremlin.ru/events/president/transcripts/23247/audios.

23. KAMAROVSKII, *supra* note 21, at 375. Translation in French: LEONID KAMAROVSKY, LE TRIBU-NAL INTERNATIONAL (Serge de Westman trans., Paris, G. Pedone-Lauriel 1887).

24. *Id.* at 332.

England in 21, but that Russia, Germany, Austria, Sweden, Denmark, Belgium, Greece, Serbia, Romania, Chernogoria (Montenegro), and Turkey had participated in none.[25] Nevertheless, before World War I, one arbitration involving the Russian Empire was carried out before the Permanent Court of Arbitration (PCA), concerning Ottoman debts to Russia. [26] A decade before that, in 1902, Dutch arbiter Tobias Asser issued judgments in cases arising from the arrest of US fishing vessels near the Russian coast in the Far East.[27]

If Tsarist Russia had not been as active in international arbitrations as the United States and the United Kingdom, its practice was not much different from that of other continental European Empires, such as Germany and Austro-Hungary. A major break happened only when the Soviets come to power in Russia in 1917. Soviet Russia was outright isolationist and hostile toward international adjudication. The USSR recognized neither the jurisdiction of the PCIJ nor that of the PCA. The same situation continued after the ICJ was created in 1945. While the USSR, as a permanent Security Council member, was effectively guaranteed a judge on the ICJ, Moscow did not regard the court as a judicial body where it would actually be willing to settle its own international legal disputes. In his autobiographical note, Fedor Kozhevnikov (1893–1998), the Soviet judge on the ICJ from 1953 to 1961—and an influential international law professor of Moscow during the two immediate post-World War II decades—explained that the majority of the ICJ's bench could not be trusted ideologically because of its Western and bourgeois identity. He confessed that his own role there sometimes had been to "look in the eyes of the adversary."[28] The USSR managed to avoid the ICJ, turning down some US suggestions for solving their mutual disputes there in an ad hoc manner.[29]

Writing in 2002, the then Russian judge in the ICJ, Vladlen Vereshchetin, concluded that although no particular love for the ICJ could be detected on the American side, the United States had nevertheless been a plaintiff or defendant 20 times, Britain 13, France 10, and Germany 6. By contrast, Russia (and the former USSR) had never been.[30] This difference is surprisingly high, even though the

---

25. Nikolai M. Korkunov, *Lektsii po mezhdunarodnomu pravu, chitannye v Voenno-Yuridicheskoi Akademii v 1883–1884 g.*, 1 ZOLOTOI FOND ROSSIISKOI NAUKI MEZHDUNARODNOGO PRAVA 361 (2007).

26. Russ. Claim for Interest on Indemnities (Russ. v. Turk.), 11 R.I.A.A. 421 (Perm. Ct. Arb. 1912).

27. *See* Tolstykh, *supra* note 3, at 121–23 (discussing Cape Horn Pigeon (U.S. v. Russ.), 9 R.I.A.A. 51 (Perm. Ct. Arb. 1902)).

28. Fedor F. Kozhevnikov, *Iz zapisok diplomata*, *in* ROSSIA I MEZHDUNARODNOE PRAVO. MATERIALY MEZHDUNARODNOI KONFERENTSII, POSVYASHTSHENNOI 100-LETIU F.I. KOZHEVNIKOVA 27, 30 (Aleksandr N. Vylegzhanin & Yuri M. Kolosov eds., 2006).

29. Vladislav Tolstykh, Mezhdunarodnyi Sud Organizatsii Obedinennykh Natsii, *in* INSTITUTY MEZHDUNARODNOGO PRAVOSUDIA, *supra* note 10, at 142.

30. *See* Vladlen S. Vereshchetin, *Mezhdunarodnyi Sud OON na novom etape*, *in* 2002 ROSSIISKII EZHEGODNIK MEZHDUNARODNOGO PRAVA [RUSSIAN Y.B. INT'L L.] 25.

United States had abandoned its heavily qualified acceptance of the ICJ's compulsory jurisdiction after the *Nicaragua* case.[31]

Neither the USSR nor Russia accepted the ICJ's compulsory jurisdiction under the "optional clause" of Article 36 of the ICJ Statute.[32] Only in August 2008 did the Russian Federation experience its first case in the ICJ—although in a manner that, as two international lawyers from the Russian MFA disappointedly put it, "none of us imagined the premiere to be."[33] During the war between Russia and Georgia, Georgia filed suit at the ICJ against the Russian Federation, trying to take advantage of the window of opportunity created in 1989 when the USSR denounced its former reservations to six UN human rights treaties.[34] The human rights treaty at issue was the UN Convention against Racial Discrimination,[35] which, Georgia claimed, Moscow had violated by expelling Georgians en masse based on their citizenship. However, as the Convention foresaw specific procedures in the case of a dispute between parties, which Georgia had not followed, the ICJ case did not proceed beyond the jurisdiction phase.[36]

Russian popular attitudes toward the ICJ are also fascinating. In 2009, World Public Opinion researchers asked respondents in 21 countries whether they believed that, if a case were initiated against their country at the ICJ, the judgment would be just and impartial. The "yes" and "no" responses came out in the following way: in the United States, 57 percent to 42 percent; in Germany, 74 percent to 21 percent; in Poland, 73 percent to 16 percent; in France, 69 percent to 25 percent; in Great Britain, 68 percent to 30 percent; and in Russia, 25 percent to 49 percent.[37] Although the outcome in Russia may have been influenced by unfavorable Russian

---

31. Military and Paramilitary Activities in and Against Nicaragua (Nicar. v. U.S.), Judgment, 1986 I.C.J. 14 (June 27).

32. Statute of the International Court of Justice art. 36(2), June 26, 1945, 33 U.N.T.S. 993.

33. I.A. Volodin & D.S. Taratukhina, *Rossiisko-gruzin'skoe razbiratel'stvo v Mezhdunarodnom Sude,* 2008 ROSSIISKII EZHEGODNIK MEZHDUNARODNOGO PRAVA [RUSSIAN Y.B. INT'L L.] 28.

34. Ukaz Prezidiuma VVS SSSR ot 10 fevralya 1989.g No. 10125-XI O sniatii sdelannykh ranee ogovorok SSSR o nepriznanii obyazatel'noi iurisdiktsii Mezhdunarodnogo Suda OON po sporam o tolkovanii i primenenii riada mezhdunarodnykh dogovorov, VEDOMOSTI VERKHOVNOGO SOVETA SSSR [VVS SSSR] [Bulletin of the USSR Supreme Council] 1989, No. 10125-XI O, at 79.

35. International Convention on the Elimination of All Forms of Racial Discrimination, Mar. 7, 1966, 660 U.N.T.S. 195.

36. Application of International Convention on Elimination of All Forms of Racial Discrimination (Geor. v. Russ.), Judgment, 2011 I.C.J. 70 (Apr. 1). *See* Phoebe Okowa, *The International Court of Justice and the Georgia/Russia Dispute,* 11 HUM. RTS. L. REV. 739 (2011).

37. INSTITUTY MEZHADUNARODNOGO PRAVOSUDIA, *supra* note 20, at 143. The data has been taken from Levada-Center, *Mirovoe obstshestvennoe mnenie o mezhdunarodnykh zakonakh i Mezhdunarodnom Sude* (Nov. 10, 2009), http://www.levada.ru/old/10-11-2009/mirovoe-obshchestvennoe-mnenie-o-mezhdunarodnykh-zakonakh-i-mezhdunarodnom-sude, *translated in* World Public Opinion, *People in 17 of 21 Nations Say Governments Should Put International Law Ahead of National Interest* (Nov. 2, 2009), http://www.worldpublicopinion.org/pipa/articles/btjusticehuman_rightsra/643.php.

news coverage of the Georgia-Russia case and of Western criticism of the war more generally, it nevertheless clearly sets Russian attitudes apart, especially from other European nations.

Russia is a historical latecomer in the context of international adjudication. Post-Soviet Russia's practice in international courts and tribunals other than the ICJ is not abundant either, with the major exception of the ECtHR. Russia ratified the European Convention on Human Rights in 1998 and, since then, the ECtHR has become the most relevant international court for Russia. However, Russia's relationship with the ECtHR has been quite tense and the Russian government complied with Strasbourg judgments somewhat selectively.[38] Moreover, on July 14, 2015, the Constitutional Court of the Russian Federation issued a judgment in which it reserved itself the right not to authorize the implementation of a judgment of the ECtHR if the latter was deemed not compatible with the Russian Constitution.[39]

Another interesting set of cases concerns foreign investor-state arbitration. According to the predominant view in the Russian doctrine of international economic law, foreign investor-state arbitration is not part of "international law" proper,[40] and therefore, Russian academic works on public international law tend to say relatively little on international investment law. In state practice too, Russia has recently become much more cautious about foreign investor-state arbitration, and it has not recognized the 2014 PCA award in the Yukos arbitration.[41]

In the context of international trade law, Russia only joined the WTO in 2012 and soon thereafter, in 2014, due to Russia's annexation of Crimea and events in Eastern Ukraine, Western sanctions were imposed on certain Russian officials, individuals, and companies, followed by Russian counter-sanctions on Western agricultural products. At the time of completing this chapter, Russia has lost its first cases in the WTO's dispute settlement system.[42] It remains to be seen how diligently Russia will comply with WTO dispute settlement reports.

---

38. *See* COURTNEY HILLEBRECHT, DOMESTIC POLITICS AND INTERNATIONAL HUMAN RIGHTS TRIBUNALS: THE PROBLEM OF COMPLIANCE 120 (2014).

39. Postanovlenie Konstitutsionnogo Suda Rossiiskoi Federatsii [Konst. Sud RF] ot 14 iuliya 2015 g. No. 21-P [Ruling of the Russian Federation Constitutional Court of July 14, 2015], ROSSIISKAIA GAZETA [ROS. GAZ.] July 27, 2015. *See also* Lauri Mälksoo, *Russia's Constitutional Court Defies the European Court of Human Rights*, 12 EUR. CONST. L. REV. 377 (2016).

40. *See, e.g.,* MEZHDUNARODNOE PRAVO 28, 32 (E.T. Usenko & Galina Shinkaretskaya eds., 2005); MEZHDUNARORDNOE PRAVO 91–92 (Aleksandr A. Kovalev & Stanislav V. Chernichenko eds., 3d ed. 2008).

41. *See* Hulley Enter. Ltd. v. Russ. (Cyprus v. Russ.), PCA Case No. AA 226, Final Award (Perm. Ct. Arb. 2014); Veteran Petroleum Ltd. v. Russ. (Cyprus v. Russ.), PCA Case No. AA 228, Final Award (Perm. Ct. Arb. 2014); Yukos Universal Ltd. v. Russ. (Isle of Man v. Russ.), PCA Case No. AA 227, Final Award (Perm. Ct. Arb. 2014).

42. Panel Report, Russian Federation—Measures on the Importation of Live Pigs, Pork and Other Pig Products from the European Union, WTO Doc. WT/DS475/R (adopted Aug. 19, 2016); Panel Report, Russia—Tariff Treatment of Certain Agricultural and Manufacturing Products, WTO Doc. WT/DS485/R (adopted Aug. 12, 2016).

In terms of the practice of domestic courts, one again needs to keep in mind the Soviet legacy. In the Soviet system, domestic courts were not major players in the application of international law. Sergei Marochkin of Tyumen State University has pointed out that in the USSR, the relatively few court cases in which references to international law were made concerned bilateral treaties on family matters, adoption, transportation issues, etc.[43]—in other words, only the less political realm of private or public international law. Mostly, international law textbooks did not even bother to discuss such subjects due to their relative technicality, usually "private" character, and political insignificance. Thus, the fact that the Constitutional Court, the Supreme Court, and other high courts have started to deal more extensively with international law symbolizes a considerable shift in the Russian domestic practice after the collapse of the USSR in 1991. As pointed out before, this shift in practice is reflected in at least some leading Russian international law textbooks.

The significance of Russia's domestic transformation after 1991 lends itself to competing interpretations. William E. Butler from the United States offers an enthusiastic picture of the use of international law in domestic courts in contemporary Russia:

> The role of Russian domestic courts has been veritably revolutionary [in terms of the use of international treaties] during the past fifteen years. Individuals and juridical persons may invoke treaty rights directly in Russian courts pursuant to Article 15 (4) of the Russian Constitution. Judges are encouraged as part of their training to draw on international legal acts when appropriate (and are not necessarily dependent on counsel directing their attention to them).[44]

Butler points out that the Constitutional Court has cited various UN documents "in more than fifty cases."[45] Yet the examples Butler cites from Russian court practice are not necessarily groundbreaking in terms of political relevance, concerning topics such as the taxation of a foreign national or the non-publication of a treaty.[46] By contrast, in March 2014 the Constitutional Court of the Russian Federation did not see any constitutional problems with the annexation of Crimea and approved of it almost immediately.[47] Therefore, it is doubtful that these court cases are "veritably

43. SERGEY Y. MAROCHKIN, DEISTVIE I REALIZATSIA NORM MEZHDUNARODNOGO PRAVA V PRA-VOVOI SISTEME ROSSIISKOI FEDERATSII 14 (2011).

44. William Butler, *Russian Federation*, *in* THE ROLE OF DOMESTIC COURTS IN TREATY ENFORCEMENT: A COMPARATIVE STUDY 410, 410 (David Sloss ed., 2009).

45. *Id.* at 414.

46. *See id.* at 415, 422, 436–37.

47. Postanovlenie Konstitutsionnogo Suda Rossiiskoi Federatsii [KS RF] ot 19 marta 2014 g. No. 6-P [Ruling of the Russian Federation Constitutional Court of Mar. 19, 2014 No. 6-P] Sobranie Zakonodatel'stva Rossiiskoi Federatsii [SZ RF] [Russian Federation Collection of Legislation] 2014, No. 13, Item 1527.

revolutionary" developments in Russian courts' application of international law. David Sloss also suggests that we should approach such cases with caution:

> ...if domestic courts in Russia consistently enforced the [European Convention on Human Rights] in cases where private parties alleged human rights violations by the government, there would not be so many cases against Russia in the European Court, and Russia would have a better win-loss record in those cases. Therefore, Russia's record before the European Court demonstrates that Russian courts have not been enforcing treaty-based human rights constraints on government actors.[48]

Along the same lines, Anton Burkov of the University of Humanities in Yekaterinburg has regretted that in practice, the interest of Russian courts (and often, even practicing lawyers) in applying the European Convention on Human Rights has remained relatively low.[49] Of course, this is often also the result of educational practices at the universities—something that might change in the future. As already pointed out, the focus of international law studies at Russian universities has been on general norms and principles—as in studying a domestic law code—rather than on how these norms and principles have been applied in international or domestic courts. However, with efforts being made to expose students to international court practice, such as participation in the Jessup International Law Moot Court, which has become a significant competitive event in Russia, educational approaches and attitudes in this regard may be changing.

Although Russian courts are more likely to refer to international law than Soviet courts were, they have rarely if ever gone seriously against the "vertical of power"— a specific Russian notion that the governmental power is (and must be) hierarchical and that all power below must refer to the top of the pyramid, that is, the Kremlin. In politically important cases, especially in foreign affairs, Russian courts and judges do not seem to claim the role of counterweight to the executive and the legislative powers. The authority of the judiciary has been recently used to support the political decisions made by the executive, not to challenge them.[50] In Congyan Cai's terms, the "deference approach" rather than the "check approach" clearly continues to dominate in contemporary Russian courts.[51]

48. David Sloss, *Treaty Enforcement in Domestic Courts: A Comparative Analysis, in* THE ROLE OF DOMESTIC COURTS IN TREATY ENFORCEMENT, *supra* note 44, 1 at 42–43.

49. ANTON L. BURKOV, KONVENTSIA O ZASTSHITE PRAV CHELOVEKA V SUDAKH ROSSII 270 (2010).

50. *See, e.g.,* Valery Zorkin, *Pravo—i tol'ko pravo,* ROSSIISKAIA GAZETA (Mar. 23, 2015).

51. *See* Congyan Cai, *International Law in Chinese Courts During the Rise of China,* 110 AM. J. INT'L L. 269 (2016).

IV. EXPLAINING RUSSIAN ATTITUDES TOWARDS CASE LAW: RUSSIA'S SEMI-PERIPHERAL STATUS IN THE INTERNATIONAL SYSTEM

Russian attitudes toward case law and courts in the context of international law—both in scholarship and in state practice—can best be explained by reference to the country's semi-peripheral status in the international system. This is a paradox of sorts: while it does not belong to the Western core of the international community, Russia continues to be a Great Power in international affairs. The country's interaction with international law (or historically, rather *jus publicum europaeum*) has been unique. It became part of the "civilized states" in the early eighteenth century, and then again opposed them since the early twentieth century. This unique Russian history with international law has also left its marks on the country's attitudes to international adjudication. For example, Messianic traits in the Orthodox Christianity practiced by Muscovy, as well as the country's sheer size after it was enlarged enormously in the sixteenth to twentieth centuries, may have made it hard to accept other nations as truly equal in terms of international law. Yet international adjudication presumes the acceptance of a certain basic idea of ontological equality.

Of course, there are other historical factors explaining Russia's cautious attitudes toward international law adjudication, such as the country's belonging to the civil law rather than common law tradition. Martens, in his late nineteenth century Russian textbook of international law, already criticized the international law tradition in Anglo-Saxon countries for opposing the "progressive tendencies" in continental Europe, revealing certain cultural and political tensions between civil and common law countries.[52] However, these are altogether less significant factors compared to the country's historical semi-peripheral status in the international system.

The idea that Russia's position in the international system is semi-peripheral has recently been expressed in the Russian political theory and political science (IR) literature.[53] Russia does not belong to "the West" and it constantly perceives that international legal processes continue to be dominated by "the West." At the same time, as a historical Great Power, Russia has definitely not lost its appetite to challenge "the West" ideologically and geopolitically, or defend itself from it. In Russia's understanding and perhaps also experience, international and Western court cases are, at least partly, a form and expression of Western dominance in international law.

Russia has never in recent history been subjugated by foreign powers, but neither has it played a prominent role in the ideational construction or practical application of international law—especially not in courts. Western states, such as the United Kingdom, France, and post-World War II Germany, have been intellectually much closer to institutions such as the ICJ than Russia, as they always were closer to The Hague and Geneva geographically.

---

52. 1 Fedor F. Martens, Sovremennoe mezhdunarodnoe pravo tsivilizovannykh narodov 135 (Moscow, Yuridicheskii kolledzh MGU, 1996) (1882).

53. *See, e.g.*, Boris Yu. Kagarlitski, Periferiinaya imperia: Rossiya i mirosistema (3d ed. 2012); Viatcheslav Morozov, Russia's Postcolonial Identity: A Subaltern Empire in a Eurocentric World (2015).

For example, this semi-peripheral status of Russia affects the choice of language. Russian is a language not only with official status in the UN but also widespread enough to support a relatively strong native and regional culture of international law scholarship. At the same time, Russia is not central enough in order to make its discourse, "dialect," and "way of thinking" about international law dominant globally. Yet it is strong enough to hold up to one's own traditional discourse, however noncompetitive it might be globally. As a consequence, some Russian international law scholars point out that a significant number of their colleagues are not even proficient in English or French. As a result, large parts of international and foreign case law remain outside their attention, not necessarily for any deep-rooted ideological reasons but simply because such scholars are unable to access these materials.[54]

This situation reflects a center-periphery dynamic in the practice of international law, which impacts the country's actual practice in international adjudication. Thus, according to Tolstykh, "[t]he interests of Russia in international courts are sometimes represented by foreign lawyers, which testifies to the lack of qualified native specialists."[55] However, I would argue that it does not demonstrate only that; it also demonstrates the fact that the language of international law—and of international courts—is one that is easier to speak the closer one is to the Western core, culturally and geographically. It seems only logical that after 70 years of self-isolation imposed by the Soviets, Russian international lawyers would not yet be the top "linguists" of international law and courts.[56]

Studying international court cases, as Tolstykh and his colleagues propose, then mostly amounts to studying the practice of other nations.[57] Emphasizing such court judgments further highlights Russia's semi-peripheral situation in the practice of international law and reveals that control over the creation of international law is located to a considerable extent outside of Russia. Perhaps this is another reason it has not been done too extensively. Paradoxically then, ignoring the case law of international courts—and especially Western courts—can also be understood as Russia's attempt at intellectual resistance against the Western core.

The international court in which the core-periphery relationship is most salient is the one that post-Soviet Russia has trusted the most by accepting its jurisdiction: the ECtHR. However, as already pointed out, the honeymoon between Strasbourg and Russia remained relatively brief and a tense reality kicked in in which both sides have criticized the other, inter alia ontologically.[58] The rhetoric

54. *Cf.* Vladislav Tolstykh, *Iazik i mezhdunarodnoe pravo*, 2 ROSSIISKII YURIDICHESKII ZHURNAL 44, 61 (2013); VLADISLAV TOLSTYKH, MEZHDUNARODNIE SUDY I IKH PRAKTIKA 138 (2015); A.V. Dolzhikov, *Keis-metod v prepodovanii mezhdunarodnogo prava i analiz reshenii mezhdunarodnykh sudov, in* INSTITUTY MEZHDUNARODNOGO PRAVOSUDIIA, *supra* note 10, at 478.

55. TOLSTYKH, *supra* note 54, at 138.

56. *See* Anna Dolidze, *The Non-native Speakers of International Law: The Case of Russia*, 15 BALTIC Y.B. INT'L L. 77 (2015).

57. *See* TOLSTYKH, *supra* note 54.

58. *See* RUSSIA AND EUROPEAN HUMAN RIGHTS LAW: THE RISE OF THE CIVILIZATIONAL ARGUMENT (Lauri Mälksoo ed., 2014).

used in this context has many traits of the West European liberal core trying to "civ-ilize" the sovereignty-oriented periphery, and the Russian periphery increasingly resisting such attempts and challenging the core's way of thinking. Therefore, it is unsurprising that Russia's own practice in the ECtHR has not yet significantly found its way into major Russian international law textbooks. Who knows, perhaps soon the political power in Russia will declare that the entire experiment with Strasbourg has come to an impasse.

My main point is that Great Powers differ from each other in the international community. For example, if in many contexts the United States and post-Soviet Russia are reluctant participants in international courts, the reasons they are so may sometimes be quite different. It is important to understand such cultural and geopo-litical differences and nuances. The semi-peripheral empire of Russia is too strong to be subjugated by the Western core, and yet it is also too weak to dominate interna-tional legal processes. What results is often a "splendid isolation" from international courts, and therefore also from the possibility of observing what *others* are doing in international courts and arbitrations.

Can the theory of Russia's semi-peripheral status in the international system also broadly explain the use of domestic case law in the country's international law discourse? I believe it can, at least partly. Elites in semi-peripheral Great Powers, in order to resist the dominance of the global (Western) core think that they need to stay united and alert. They tend to see dangers rather than opportu-nities in fragmented sovereignty.[59] In their view, sovereignty must remain one and indivisible, which is why domestic courts should not challenge the executive in foreign affairs.

Russia's centralized and often authoritarian practice of governance has a lot to do with its semi-peripheral status in the world. Many Russians seem to believe that because of its vast territory and cold climate, the country needs a "strong hand" in order to stay together and not lose out to competing powers. Among considerable parts of the Russian people, the fear of the country breaking apart, losing its sover-eignty and being "subjugated" (at least in terms of ideas) to the West looms so large that many would prefer to have fewer rights, less democracy, and less court-based accountability than to risk these outcomes.[60] Based on this approach, international law does not need multiple speakers in the country, and if such speakers—such as highest courts—emerge, at least they should not contradict each other.

V. CONCLUSION

In conclusion, Russia's approach to international courts and case law reflects its historical mistrust, and semi-peripheral status, vis-à-vis the Western core. Much

---

59. ALEKSEI A. MOISEEV, SUVERENITET GOSUDARSTVA V MEZHDUNARODNOM PRAVE (2009).

60. Compare the cultural analysis of the 2015 Nobel literature prize winner Swetlana Alexijewitsch from Belarus, who examines the mentalities in Russia, Ukraine, and Belarus and even comes to the conclusion that "the Russian people cannot bear freedom." Swetlana Alexijewitsch, *Die Russen ertra-gen keine Freiheit*, FRANKFURTER ALLGEMEINE ZEITUNG (Nov. 30, 2015).

has been written on international law as historically mainly a Western construct. Apparently, this phenomenon also has repercussions in international adjudication. For example, Onuma Yasuaki of Meiji University in Tokyo has criticized the "'domestic model (of Western society) approach' in international legal studies, represented by excessive judiciary-centrism."[61]

Without taking Russia's historical cautiousness vis-à-vis international adjudication into account, one cannot really understand how international law works and plays out in the country. One can also be excessively sanguine that different countries will inevitably follow the Western or Anglo-Saxon path, according to which adjudication and arbitration are essential in public international law. One of the lessons to be learned is also that the "judicialization" of international relations[62] is not a perspective shared with equal enthusiasm in all regions of the world.

The conservative bulk of the contemporary Russian academic discussion of international law does not fundamentally differ from that of the late nineteenth century, when Martens compiled his impressive collection of imperial Russia's treaties and supplemented it with his own historical-legal commentaries.[63] The international law that emerges based on reading Martens's treaty collection is one of emperors and ambassadors, foreign ministers, and struggles for the balance of power among the Great Powers. The main characters in this version of international law are sovereigns—not the disaggregated state, and certainly not courts. In its ideal world, a sovereign can almost always decide what it wishes to do, whereas international courts would be less predictable because a single sovereign cannot control the outcome there. These kinds of considerations are even more relevant for powers that feel insufficiently represented—culturally and politically—in the international community and its institutions (even though Russia has been able to count on a semi-automatic seat in the ICJ, even after the annexation of Crimea).

International court and arbitral cases are a key part of the reality of contemporary international law, but we must be aware of *which countries* have participated in these cases and which countries have, in fact, stood apart. If there is little real risk of international courts making adverse decisions toward a semi-peripheral Great Power, the Western core cannot use international law decisively against the perceived interests of that power. Moreover, without strong international courts making binding judgments, semi-peripheral Great Powers can ensure that in cases of conflict in their own geopolitical backyards, their power will prevail. International law without strong courts will remain an "indeterminate" language that can be used with some rhetorical or propagandistic success by all sides of the conflict. Thus, we should not be naive and assume that "more international adjudication is progressive" will be

61. Yasuaki Onuma, A Transcivilizational Perspective on International Law 245 (2010).

62. *See, e.g.,* Anne-Marie Slaughter, A New World Order (2005) (emphasizing the role of international courts and transnational networks of judges).

63. F. Martens, Sobranie traktatov i konventsii, zakliuchennykh Rossieyu s inostrannimi derzhavami (1874–1909).

a call perceived to be in everyone's interests in the international community. Of course, these points and findings should be further corroborated with evidence from other Western and non-Western major states in the international community. Comparative international law is the most suitable and promising method for exploring the actual role of judiciaries—and of international law generally—in different parts of the globe.

17

Doing Away with Capital Punishment in Russia

International Law and the Pursuit of Domestic Constitutional Goals

BAKHTIYAR TUZMUKHAMEDOV

I. INTRODUCTION

The Russian Constitution protects the right to life. At the same time, it states that "capital punishment until its complete abolition may be established by federal law as an exclusive form of punishment for particularly grave crimes against life," but only on the condition that an accused in a capital case shall be entitled to a trial by a court comprising professional judges and a lay jury (Article 20 (2)).[1] Russia is not a party to either Protocols 6 and 13 to the European Convention for the Protection of Human Rights and Fundamental Freedoms (ECHR),[2] or to the Second Optional

---

1. Konstitutsiia Rossiiskoi Federatsii [Konst. RF] [Constitution] art. 20(2) (Russ.). An authoritative translation of the Constitution, inclusive of all amendments, may be found on the website of the Constitutional Court of the Russian Federation at http://www.ksrf.ru/en/INFO/ LEGALBASES/CONSTITUTIONRF/Pages/default.aspx. However, this author tends to disagree with the use of the term "exclusive" for the Russian *isklyuchitelnaya* in the cited excerpt and would rather suggest using the term "extraordinary" or "exceptional."

2. Protocol No. 6 to the Convention for the Protection of Human Rights and Fundamental Freedoms concerning the Abolition of the Death Penalty, Apr. 28, 1983, ETS No. 114. Protocol 6 became effective on March 1, 1985. In 2002, the Council of Europe adopted Protocol 13, which removed the exceptions stipulated in Article 2 of Protocol 6 and abolished the death penalty in all circumstances. Protocol No. 13 to the Convention for the Protection of Human Rights and Fundamental Freedoms, concerning the Abolition of the Death Penalty in All Circumstances, May 3, 2002, ETS No. 187. It entered into force on July 1, 2003. As of the time of this writing, Russia remains the only member state of the Council of Europe, out of 47, that has not acceded to Protocol 6, and one of three nonparties to Protocol 13, the others being Armenia and Azerbaijan.

Comparative International Law. Edited by Anthea Roberts et al. © Anthea Roberts, Paul B. Stephan, Pierre-Hugues Verdier, Mila Versteeg 2018. Published 2018 by Oxford University Press.

Protocol to the International Covenant on Civil and Political Rights (ICCPR),[3] all three of which require abolition of the death penalty, either with certain caveats (Protocol 6 and the Second Optional Protocol) or unconditionally (Protocol 13). Although Russia signed Protocol 6 in 1997, soon after becoming a member of the Council of Europe, and pledged to ratify it in an expedited manner, this has yet to happen.

The period that followed the signing of the Protocol witnessed rather erratic actions by branches of the government, including sentencing practices of courts of general jurisdiction that, in the opinion of this author, may have brought Russia to the brink of a violation of its fundamental obligation under the Vienna Convention on the Law of Treaties (VCLT) to "refrain from acts which would defeat the object and purpose of a treaty."[4] Ultimately, it was not the political branches of government, but rather the judiciary, that resolved both the constitutional and, at least in a palliative manner, the international legal issues.

The Constitutional Court of the Russian Federation first broached the issue of capital punishment in rulings[5] of minor prominence in 1997. The seminal judgment was handed down in 1999, when the Court decided that no one could be sentenced to death until collegia of jury had been introduced in all constituent entities of the Federation. Conspicuously, it made no reference to Protocol 6 or any other international instrument. As the date when that requirement was supposed to have been met came closer, the Supreme Court petitioned the Constitutional Court requesting clarification as to whether the 1999 judgment implied that upon nationwide introduction of jury courts to try capital cases, these bodies could resume imposition of death penalties. This time, the Constitutional Court's unequivocal negative response contained abundant references to various international sources.

However, in the opinion of this author, the Court was concerned primarily with legal uncertainty in the domestic context, which it resolved by means of a consolidated constitutional and international legal argument. This time the Court, unlike in several other instances when it referred to international sources, was cautious enough not to assume the existence of *de lege ferenda*, or the clear establishment of *de lege lata* in the form of a universal, as opposed to regional European,[6] international rule binding states to abolish capital punishment. At the same time the judicial branch, or more precisely the more superior department thereof, ameliorated a rather

---

3. Second Optional Protocol to the International Covenant on Civil and Political Rights, aiming at the abolition of the death penalty, Dec. 15, 1989, 1642 U.N.T.S. 414.

4. Vienna Convention on the Law of Treaties art. 18, May 23, 1969, 1155 U.N.T.S. 331.

5. The Constitutional Court, when deciding a case on its merits, will issue a "judgment" (*postanovlenie*). When it rules that a petition is inadmissible or shall not be decided on its merits for other reasons, it will issue a "ruling" (*opredelenie*). Some of the latter may be rather brief and merely state, for example, that a petitioner does not have standing. Others may carry more substance and express an argumentative position of the court on a matter of law, or expound a legal position that the court formulated earlier.

6. Belarus is the only European state that is not a member of the Council of Europe and that has kept capital punishment both in codified law and in practice.

precarious quandary in which Russia has placed itself vis-à-vis the Council of Europe. In two major leaps, with smaller steps in-between, the Constitutional Court initially restrained the courts of general jurisdiction, temporarily barring them from handing down death sentences, and then implicitly bypassed the political branches of power that may have been reluctant or hesitant to ratify Protocol 6 to declare that abolition of the death penalty was "an essential element of regulation of the right to life."[7]

This chapter will describe the uneasy relationship of Russia with the death penalty, both domestically and internationally. It will speculate whether the Constitutional Court applied international law as a common denominator to interpret the Constitution, or instead turned to international sources as an auxiliary means to support its own understanding of constitutional goals.

II. CONSTITUTIONAL APPROACHES TO CAPITAL PUNISHMENT

An explicit right to life, though restricted by capital punishment, was unknown to Soviet constitutions until a late version of the Constitution of the Russian Soviet Federal Socialist Republic (RSFSR), an instrument first adopted in 1978 that survived the formal dissolution of the Soviet Union in December 1991, by which time the original constitutional text had become a patchwork of amendments that had changed it almost beyond recognition. One of the most dramatic single amendments was the incorporation into the constitutional text of the Declaration of Human and Citizen's Rights, which the RSFSR Supreme Soviet adopted on November 22, 1991. Article 7 of the amended Constitution stated:

> Everyone has the right to life. No one shall be deprived of life arbitrarily. The State strives to attain complete abolition of death penalty.[8] Until its abolition the death penalty may be applied as an exceptional punishment for particularly grave crimes under a sentence handed down by a court with the participation of a jury.[9]

7. Konst. Sud RF [Russian Federation Constitutional Court] Ruling No. 1344-O-R, ¶ 4.3, Nov. 19, 2009. "O-R" following the digit in designation of the ruling stands for "*opredelenie raz'yasnyayushcheye*"—"explanatory ruling"—namely a ruling that explains an earlier decision by the Court, if so requested by a proper party. All decisions of the Constitutional Court in Russian are available on its official website at: http://www.ksrf.ru/ru/Decision/Pages/default.aspx. Texts and resumes of selected judgments in English, further grouped by year, may be found at http://www.ksrf.ru/en/Decision/Judgments/Pages/default.aspx.

8. The modality of Russian wording "*gosudarstvo stremitsya k polnoi otmene smertnoi kazni*" does not necessarily imply a binding commitment of the state. It is rather a declaration of intent.

9. VEDOMOSTI S'EZDA NARODNYKH DEPUTATOV RSFSR I VERKHOVNOGO SOVETA RSFSR [VED. RSFSR] [Bulletin of the Congress of People's Deputies and of the Russian Soviet Federal Socialist Republic and Supreme Council of the RSFSR] 1991, No. 52, Item 1865. A homonymous Declaration adopted by the Congress of People's Deputies of the USSR on September 5, 1991, did not foresee an abolition of the death penalty and stated only that "the right to life is an inalienable right of every human. No one shall be deprived of life arbitrarily." VEDOMOSTI S'EZDA NARODNYKH DEPUTATOV SSSR I VERKHOVNOGO SOVETA SSSR [Bulletin of the Congress of People's Deputies of the USSR and Supreme Council of the USSR] [VED. SSSR] 1991, No. 37, Item 1083.

On April 21, 1992, this language was imported almost verbatim into Article 38 of the re-amended Constitution as part of a completely rewritten Chapter 5 entitled "Human and Citizens' Rights."[10] However, the text of this amendment did not refer to the right to have a jury participate in a capital trial.

The current Constitution, adopted on December 12, 1993, further developed that language. Article 20 now states:

1. Everyone shall have the right to life.
2. Capital punishment until its complete abolition may be established by federal law as an exclusive[11] form of punishment for particularly grave crimes against life, and the accused shall be granted the right to have his case examined by a court with the participation of a jury.

Similarities between the two texts are apparent, and so are the differences. First, the right to be tried with participation of the jury was reinstated as an option available to a defendant in a capital case. Second, while the amended 1978 Constitution provided for the "application" of the death penalty, its successor allows the "establishment by federal law" of that punishment.

Both wordings provide for an extraordinary and temporary ("until abolition") option of the death penalty. Moreover, under the 1993 Constitution the death penalty could not be handed down until three conditions had been met cumulatively: first, the existence of a federal law in effect providing for capital punishment (which is the current Criminal Code of 1996); second, the limitation of such a sentence to particularly grave crimes against life; and, third, the existence of a right of defendant in a capital case to be tried by a jury.[12]

Some commentators went even further. Professor Tamara Morshchakova, former judge and vice president of the Russian Constitutional Court, posited that "sentences providing for such punishment became a violation of the Constitution [of 1993] from the moment of its adoption,"[13] because the state at that time could not provide jury trials in all the constituent entities of the Russian Federation. As plausible as that interpretation may be, even after the adoption of the new Constitution courts in Russia continued to hand down death sentences, some of which were carried out. Morshchakova admitted that Article 20 proceeded from an

---

10. Federal'nyi Zakon RF o Popravkakh i Dopolneniakh k Konstitutsii (Osnovnoi Zakon) Rossiiskoi Sovetskoi Federativnoi Sotsialisticheskoi Respubliki [Law of the Russian Federation on Amendments and Additions to the Constitution (Basic Law) of the Russian Soviet Federal Socialist Republic], VED. RSFSR 1992, No. 20, Item 1084.

11. See supra text accompanying note 1 regarding the use of the term "exclusive."

12. See Petr Kondratov, Stat'ya 20 [Article 20], in KOMMENTARII K KONSTITUTSII ROSSIISKOI FEDERATSII [COMMENTARY TO THE CONSTITUTION OF THE RUSSIAN FEDERATION] 139 (V.D. Karpovich ed., 2d ed., 2002).

13. Tamara Morshchakova, Stat'ya 20 [Article 20], in KOMMENTARII K KONSTITUTSII ROSSIISKOI FEDERATSII [COMMENTARY TO THE CONSTITUTION OF THE RUSSIAN FEDERATION] 205 (V.D. Zorkin ed., 3d ed., 2013).

assumption that "such measure of punishment could be established only for a limited period of time, that is, until its mandatory abolition. Hence, the legislator was set to focus on a prospective elimination of death penalty from law and practice."[14]

As the death penalty "may be established by federal law," by the same token it should be abolished by a federal law, which would remove it from the inventory of punishments. The most straightforward approach would seem to be the introduction of amendments to relevant legislation that would delete provisions describing acts punishable by death, and establishing sentencing procedures, the carrying out of sentences, and the legal consequences of such sentences. The legislation to be amended should have included the criminal, criminal procedural, and penal codes, as well as laws on burial and funeral matters and on civil registry. Another possible—and seemingly expeditious—approach would be accession, by way of federal law, to an international instrument banning capital punishment, with the concurrent or subsequent amendment of relevant legislation. Either approach—amendment of legislation or accession to an international instrument—would result in the conclusion of the limited period ("until abolition") of restrictive application of the right to life, as prescribed by Article 20(2) of the Constitution. The end of that limited, or transitional, period would not require amendment of the Constitution, because legislative abolition of the death penalty would attain an objective set by the Constitution itself.

The Constitution gives no indication as to the duration of that transitional period. Apparently it may not continue ad infinitum, otherwise there would be a risk of a temporary measure becoming habitually permanent. Some guidance may be found in the jurisprudence of the Constitutional Court. The Court ruled on February 2, 1999, that the legislator had ample time—over five years since adoption of the Constitution—to implement the requirement of "Concluding and Interim Provisions" of the Constitution regarding the bringing into effect a federal law regulating hearing of cases by courts with participation of the jury.[15] The Court applied the same benchmark in a less notable decision delivered on April 19, 2001, where it stated that a period of over seven years should have sufficed for the passage of legislation regulating the arrest, remand, and detention of persons suspected of crimes.[16] The Court assumed that any further procrastination on the part of the legislator would infringe upon rights protected by the Constitution that had direct effect.[17]

---

14. *Id.*

15. Konst. Sud RF Judgment No. 3-P, ¶ 6, Feb. 2, 1999. "P" following the digit in the designation of the Judgment stands for "*postanovlenie,*" *see supra* text accompanying note 5.

16. Konst. Sud RF Ruling No. 101-O, ¶ 4, Apr. 19, 2001. "O" following the digit in the designation of the Ruling stands for "*opredelenie,*" *see supra* text accompanying note 5.

17. Compare with the approach taken by the Supreme Court of the United States in Garcia v. Texas, 564 U.S. 940, 942 (2011), in which it denied a stay of execution of the applicant, a Mexican citizen, and ruled, in the wake of Avena and Other Mexican Nationals (Mex. v. U.S.), 2004 I.C.J. 12 (Mar. 31), that "[i]f a statute implementing *Avena* had genuinely been a priority for the political branches, it would have been enacted by now." *Avena* was delivered on March 31, 2004, more than seven years before *Garcia*. However, the Supreme Court referred to an earlier denial of a stay of execution of another Mexican, José Medellin, Medellin v. Texas, 554 U.S. 759 (2008), when it opined that four

III. EXTERNAL INFLUENCES AND DOMESTIC RESPONSES

Apparently the single most persistent external source of influence exerted on Russia to compel it to abolish the death penalty has been the Council of Europe.

Russia formally expressed its wish to be invited to become a member of the Council on May 6, 1992,[18] but it was not until February 8, 1996, that the Committee of Ministers extended an invitation "in the light of the commitments entered into and the assurances for their fulfillment given by the Russian Government."[19] An Opinion of the Parliamentary Assembly of the Council of Europe earlier had presented a rather extensive list of Russia's commitments and understandings, including a statement of the intention "to sign within one year and ratify within three years from the time of accession Protocol No. 6 to the European Convention on Human Rights on the abolition of the death penalty in time of peace, and to put into place a moratorium on executions with effect from the day of accession."[20] Under Article 1 of that Protocol, "the death penalty shall be abolished. No one shall be condemned to such penalty or executed." However, Article 2 provides an exception:

> A State may make provision in its law for the death penalty in respect of acts committed in time of war or of imminent threat of war; such penalty shall be applied only in the instances laid down in the law and in accordance with its provisions. The State shall communicate to the Secretary General of the Council of Europe the relevant provisions of that law.

Russia became a member of the Council of Europe as of February 28, 1996. Under the terms of its commitment, no death sentence that may have been handed down before that date, or after it, could be carried out. It should be underscored that the moratorium applied to executions, rather than to judicial decisions in capital cases. In other words, courts could, and in fact, did continue to hand down death sentences. However, it has been reported that quite a few of those sentences were carried out after February 28, 1996,[21] the last one on September 2, 1996.[22]

---

years could suffice for the legislature to progress beyond the bare introduction of a bill prompted by *Avena.*

18. COUNCIL EUR. COMM. MIN. RES. (92)27 (Jun. 25, 1992).

19. COUNCIL EUR. COMM. MIN. RES. (96)2 (Feb. 8, 1996).

20. Eur. Parl. Ass., *Opinion 193, Application by Russia for Membership of the Council of Europe* (1996).

21. According to Anatoly Pristavkin, the then chairman of the Presidential Commission on the Matters of Pardoning, an advisory body now defunct, 62 death penalties were carried out in 1996, after Russia became a member of the Council of Europe. Pristavkin was quoted in Igor Vandenko, *62 cheloveka kazneni posle prinyatiya Rossiiv Sovet Evropi* [62 Persons Executed after Russia's Admission to the Council of Europe], IZVESTIIA (Jan. 25, 1997).

22. A popular Russian weekly reported that the executed person was a serial killer whose victims were minors. Yelena Slobodian, *Komu v Rossii grozit smertnaya kazn, esli na neyo otmenyat moratoriy* [Who in Russia Will Come Under Threat of Execution, Should the Moratorium be Repealed], ARGUMENTI I FACTI (May 30, 2014).

As to legislation, the new Criminal Code that the State Duma[23] adopted on May 24, 1996, that the president signed into law on June 13 and that became effective as of January 1, 1997, stipulated that the death penalty was an optional punishment for five criminal acts. While this was a significant reduction as compared to the previous 1960 RSFSR Criminal Code, which provided for the death penalty as punishment for 14 criminal acts,[24] a zealous pedant might question the propriety of the very inclusion of capital offenses into the prospective Code in the wake of Russia's commitment to the Council of Europe "to put into place a moratorium on executions." Presumably the wording of the Resolution of the Council's Committee of Ministers implied that Russia's commitments and assurances were inherently linked to the invitation to become a member of the Council. Professor Vadim Sobakin convincingly argued that "legislatively formalized acceptance by the Russian Federation of the invitation extended on certain conditions signified that those conditions were binding rather than advisory."[25] By "legislatively formalized acceptance," Sobakin apparently referred to the federal laws on ratification of the Statute and the General Agreement on Privileges and Immunities of the Council of Europe, both signed by the president on February 23, 1996,[26] followed by the deposit of instruments of accession five days later.

It may be assumed that Russia was not in compliance with its commitment regarding the moratorium on executions during the period from February 28 to September 2, 1996. Until early 1997 this noncompliance did not provoke any strong response from the Council of Europe, other than a letter that the then president of the Parliamentary Assembly of the Council of Europe reportedly sent to the Russian president sometime in March 1996 expressing concerns over continued executions and reminding him of the moratorium commitment.[27] However, on January 29, 1997, the Parliamentary Assembly passed a strongly worded resolution that condemned Russia "for having violated her commitment to put into place a moratorium on executions, and deplore[d] the executions that have taken place," warning the Russian authorities that "should any more executions be carried out following the adoption of this resolution, the Assembly may consider the

23. The State Duma is the legislative chamber of the bicameral parliament, the Federal Assembly.

24. On May 16, 1996, the president promulgated Decree 724 "On the Gradual Reduction of Application of the Death Penalty in Connection with Russia's Accession to the Council of Europe." The president "recommended to chambers of the Federal Assembly to . . . consider, while deliberating the draft of the Criminal Code of the Russian Federation, an issue of reduction of criminal acts which may be punishable by death." SOBRANIE ZAKONODATEL'STVA ROSSIISKOI FEDERATSII [SZ RF] [Russian Federation Collection of Legislation] 1996, No. 21, Item 2468.

25. Vadim Sobakin, Pravovie aspekti vneseniia na ratifikatsiu mnogostoronnikh mezhdunarodnykh dogovorov [Legal Aspects of the Introduction for Ratification of Multilateral International Treaties], 3 MOSCOW J. INT'L L. 7, 7–8 (1997).

26. SZ RF 1996, No. 9, Item 774.

27. As reported in Vandenko, supra note 21.

non-ratification of the credentials of the Russian parliamentary delegation at its next session."[28]

As to the capital offenses in the newly adopted Criminal Code, again, it may be assumed that neither the president, who requested that the number of crimes punishable by death be reduced, rather than eliminated, nor the legislators who complied with that request, were entirely convinced that the prospective introduction of Protocol 6 to the State Duma would result in its prompt and painless ratification. Finally, it may also be assumed that both branches of government were well aware that abolition of the death penalty has been a controversial and divisive issue in Russian society.[29]

Neither did Russia abide by its commitment to sign within one year Protocol 6. Only on February 27, 1997, did the president sign an order instructing the Ministry of Foreign Affairs to sign that treaty,[30] which it carried out on April 16, 1997. That signature has not been followed either by ratification or any explicit declaration not to become a party of the treaty. However, Russia remains subject to its obligations under Article 18 of the VCLT. According to that Article:

A State is obliged to refrain from acts which would defeat the object and purpose of a treaty when:

> (a) It has signed the treaty or has exchanged instruments constituting the treaty subject to ratification, acceptance or approval, until it shall have made its intention clear not to become a party to the treaty; or
> (b) It has expressed its consent to be bound by the treaty, pending the entry into force of the treaty and provided that such entry into force is not unduly delayed.[31]

Apparently paragraph "b" does not apply, as the Protocol has been in force as of March 1, 1985, but paragraph "a" does. Even if the Protocol itself did not provide for ratification, Russia would have been bound to do so by its own Federal Law

---

28. Eur. Parl. Ass. Res. 1111 (Jan. 29, 1997). The Assembly referred to 53, rather than 62, executions carried out after Russia's accession to the Council of Europe, and to August 2, rather than September 2, 1996, as the day of the last execution.

29. Polls conducted by the All-Russian Center of Public Opinion Research in 1994 and 1999 (national sampling) showed that, respectively, 37 and 36 percent of respondents favored retention of the death penalty, 24 and 23 percent would rather its application were broadened, 15 percent in both polls preferred its gradual abolition, and 5 percent responded in favor of its prompt abolition. Boris Dubin, Rossiiyane o smertnoi kazni [Russians on the Death Penalty], http://www.index.org. ru/turma/sk/ro/020506-1.htm (last visited July 27, 2017). But polls conducted by another prominent organization, Levada-Center, in September 1997 brought somewhat different results: the breakup of responses to the same questions was 44, 16, 23, and 10 percent. Levada-Center, Praktika naznachenie smertnoi kazni [The Practice of Imposing the Death Penalty], https://www.levada.ru/ 2014/07/14/praktika-naznacheniya-smertnoj-kazni (last visited July 27, 2017).

30. SZ RF 1997, No. 9, Item 1092.

31. Vienna Convention on the Law of Treaties art. 18, May 23, 1969, 1155 U.N.T.S. 331.

"On International Treaties of the Russian Federation." Article 15(1) of this statute provides:

> Subject to ratification shall be international treaties of the Russian Federation: (a) the execution of which requires an amendment of effective or adoption of new federal laws, as well as those that set rules different from the ones established by a law; (b) the object of which are fundamental human and citizen's rights.[32]

The fundamental obligation under the Protocol is the abolition of the death penalty, including deletion from legislation of that penalty except "in respect of acts committed in time of war or of imminent threat of war." Hence as of April 16, 1997, Russian courts could neither hand down death sentences, nor could such sentences be carried out. The binding obligations undertaken by Russia with respect to Protocol 6 under Article 18 of the VCLT reinforced the commitments and undertakings regarding non-execution of death sentences given to the Council of Europe at accession to that organization.

That Russia has not ratified Protocol 6 despite its commitment to do so does not mean that no attempt was ever made. In August 1999 the president introduced in the State Duma a draft law on ratification along with an explanatory note, and appointed deputy ministers of justice and of foreign affairs as his official representatives at the hearings.[33] However, the draft law never left the Council of the State Duma and thus was not submitted to the plenary session. It may be plausibly speculated that had it been submitted to the plenary session, it would have been, in all likelihood, voted down. On February 15, 2002, the State Duma adopted an Appeal to the president that asserted the ratification of Protocol 6 was untimely, citing, in particular, "the impermissibility of ignoring the will of the people who do not accept the abolition of the death penalty, only to accommodate foreign policy interests."[34] This action prompted a painful reaction from the Parliamentary Assembly of the Council of Europe, which was:

> shocked by the vote in the State Duma on 15 February 2002, asking President Putin to re-introduce the death penalty. Whilst recognising that the official moratorium on executions introduced by President Yeltsin on 2 August 1996

---

32. Federalniy Zakon o mezhdunarodnykh dogovorakh Rossiyskoy Federtsii [Federal Law on International Treaties of the Russian Federation], originally published in SZ RF 1995, No. 29, Item 2757. Subsequent amendments did not affect the provision cited here.

33. Official representatives were first appointed in November 1999 in anticipation of expected hearings. In time they had to be reappointed, as the original representatives had moved on or retired. The currently effective Order of August 28, 2001, No. 462-rp lists as official representatives persons who, too, no longer hold senior positions at the Ministry of Justice and Ministry of Foreign Affairs. SZ RF 2001, No. 36, Item 3555.

34. SZ RF 2002, No. 8, Item 799.

is respected, the Assembly nevertheless urges the Russian authorities to abolish the death penalty de jure and to conclude the ratification of Protocol 6.[35]

In spite of the Appeal, the president did not withdraw the draft law, which thus remains before the State Duma. Had the legislature voted down the draft law, that action in and of itself would not have relieved Russia of its obligation under Article 18 of the VCLT not to "defeat the object and purpose of a treaty." In that case the State Duma would have notified the president of its decision not to pass the law, giving him grounds, should need be, to notify the depositary of the treaty to make Russia's "intention clear not to become a party to the treaty." And yet, even a notification to that effect would not reverse the obligation to maintain the moratorium on carrying out of death penalties, which would remain in force until and unless Russia were to withdraw from the Council of Europe.

The pacta sunt servanda obligation with respect to an effective treaty applies to any state organ. The International Law Commission stated in the draft articles on Responsibility of States for Internationally Wrongful Acts that:

> The conduct of any State organ shall be considered an act of that State under international law, whether the organ exercises legislative, executive, judicial or any other functions, whatever position it holds in the organization of the State, and whatever its character as an organ of the central government or of a territorial unit of the State.[36]

In its Commentary to that draft article, the ILC cited international jurisprudence, including that of the International Court of Justice, to demonstrate that the rule embodied in that Article has acquired a "customary character."[37] As to a signed treaty pending its ratification, the obligation to refrain from acts that would defeat its object and purpose is vested in a state as a whole, rather than in any particular branch of government. If a branch were to deviate from the obligation, it would be for other branches to correct such behavior to keep the behavior of the state as a whole within the bounds of Article 18 of the VCLT.

Despite the moratorium on executions that should have been in effect for Russia as of February 28, 1996, a number of death penalties were carried out during that year until August 2—according to the Council of Europe, or September 2—according to Russian sources. Moreover, Russian courts continued to hand down death penalties both after February 28, 1996, and even after April 16, 1997, the day when Russia signed Protocol 6. While data illustrating the dynamics of death sentences and the exact numbers are not available to this author, there is circumstantial

---

35. EUR. PARL. ASS. RES. 1111 (Jan. 29, 1997). A reference to a "moratorium introduced on 2 August 1996" is perplexing, as no records of such an official action are available to this author.

36. G.A. Res. 56/83, art. 4(1) (Jan. 28, 2002).

37. Rep. of the Int'l Law Comm'n, 53rd Sess., Apr. 23–June 1, July 2–Aug. 10, 2001, at 40, U.N. Doc. A/56/10.

evidence based on petitions filed with the Constitutional Court by persons sentenced to that penalty. Rulings on those petitions refer to dates when death sentences had been handed down going from March 4, 1997, to December 24, 1998.[38] While these references do not disclose the total number of death sentences handed down during the relevant period, it is safe to assume that they go into double digits. This practice may be explained by the ignorance of judges of lower courts of general jurisdiction about international law and international affairs. But another explanation lies in the deeply-rooted tradition of lower courts accepting as binding instructions the occasional resolutions passed by Plenary Sessions of the Supreme Court that summarize judicial practices on particular matters and offer guidelines. In particular, one such Resolution issued on October 31, 1995, directed courts to seek legal guidance from international treaties in force, without referring to an intermediate period between the signing of a treaty pending its ratification and its actual entry into force, or clarifying the legal consequences of such a signature.[39] As to death sentences, the Resolution of the Supreme Court Plenary Session specifically dealing with cases of criminal homicide, issued on January 27, 1999, explicitly stated that "the death penalty as an extraordinary measure of punishment may be applied for commission of a particularly grave crime against life."[40] Not only did the Supreme Court ignore the commitment to the Council of Europe, let alone the fact that Russia had signed Protocol 6, it also misinterpreted the language of the Constitution ("capital punishment . . . may be established") as if it guided courts to continue handing down death sentences with a view to application of the penalty. Moreover, this author is aware of at least one appeal case in which the Supreme Court rejected as "unfounded" an argument of an appellant that a moratorium on executions had been in effect "since the end of 1996."[41] Adding to the confusion, the president of the Supreme Court Vyacheslav Lebedev was reported by a national TV channel "Rossiya" as stating on March 10, 2006, that the Supreme Court would "continue abiding by the moratorium on executions . . . that has been in effect since

38. Konst. Sud RF Ruling No. 620-O-O, May 26, 2011; Konst. Sud RF Ruling No. 284-O-O, Apr. 15, 2008; Konst. Sud RF Ruling No. 54-O-O, Jan. 24, 2008; Konst. Sud RF Ruling No. 52-O-O, Jan. 24, 2008; Konst. Sud RF Ruling No. 692-O-O, Oct. 16, 2007; Konst. Sud RF Ruling No. 380-O-O, May 15, 2007; Konst. Sud RF Ruling No. 943-O-O, Dec. 18, 2007.

39. Postanovlenie Plenuma Verkhovnogo Suda Rossiyskoy Federatsii o nekotorykh voprosakh primeneniya Konstitutsii Rossiyskoy Federatsii pri osushchestvlenii pravosudiya [Resolution of the Plenary meeting of the Supreme Court of the Russian Federation On Certain Matters of Application of the Constitution of the Russian Federation in the Administration of Justice], ROSSIISKAIA GAZETA [ROS. GAZ.], No. 247, Dec. 28, 1995.

40. Postanovlenie Plenuma Verkhovnogo Suda Rossiyskoy Federatsii o sudebnoy praktike po delam ob ubiystve [Resolution of the Plenary meeting of the Supreme Court of the Russian Federation On Judicial Practice in Homicide Cases], ROS. GAZ., No. 24, Feb. 9, 1999, ¶ 20. Subsequent amendments to the Resolution introduced on February 6, 2007, and April 3, 2008, did not alter that particular provision, which was repealed only on December 3, 2009.

41. Verkhovnyi Sud Rossiiskoi Federatsii [Verkh. Sud RF], Delo No. GKPI07-355, Reshenie, 27 aprelya 2007 goda [Russian Federation Supreme Court], Case No. GKPI07-355, Decision, Apr.

1998 [sic], hence courts of general jurisdiction were barred from handing down death sentences."[42]

Finally, as of early 2008 the Supreme Court assumed the position—to which it subsequently adhered—that the moratorium had been introduced from February 2, 1999,[43] citing as the point of reference a seminal Judgment of the Constitutional Court in which it ruled that courts could not hand down death sentences until collegia of jury were established in all constituent entities of the Russian Federation. That Judgment will be discussed below.

Death sentences handed down by Russian courts, let alone executions, would have amounted to a violation of Russia's obligations under Article 18 of the VCLT, the object of those violations being prospective obligations under Protocol 6. However, the negligence of courts of general jurisdiction were remedied by presidential commutations that grew in number and became standard practice after the last reported execution in 1996. The president did not interfere with authority of the judiciary, but corrected their blunders by the constitutional means available to his office, that is, by commuting sentences. As a result, internationally erroneous domestic judicial actions did not bear irreversible consequences, and the state as a whole did not end up violating its international obligations.

IV. POWERS OF THE CONSTITUTIONAL COURT

To facilitate a better understanding of the procedural actions and legal positions taken by the Constitutional Court as it broached the issue of capital punishment in Russia, an overview of the Court's jurisdiction may be helpful. The first reference to the Constitutional Court of the Russian Federation, then the RSFSR and part of the Soviet Union, appeared in amendments to the RSFSR Constitution passed in 1990. Its precursor was the Soviet Union's Committee of Constitutional Control, a prototype judicial body with limited powers. As the Russian Constitutional Court was conceived amid intensifying strife between Russian and the Union (federal) governments, it had authority to review, albeit in a limited manner, the compatibility of Soviet Union statutes with the Constitution of the Republic. However, the Court was not established until the end of 1991, shortly before the Soviet Union ceased to exist. The sources of its authority were the RSFSR Constitution, which, with its patchwork of amendments, hardly resembled the original text of 1978, and the Law on the Constitutional Court of the RSFSR of 1991. The Court decided its

27, 2007, available on the official website of the Russian Federation Supreme Court at http://www. supcourt.ru/stor_pdf.php?id=168606.

42. Mikhail Antonov (anchor), "Vesti" ["Messages", TV news program], aired on March 10, 2006, at 5:00 PM, cited excerpt available on the official website of the Russian Federation Supreme Court at http://www.supcourt.ru/print_page.php?id=4226.

43. Verkhovnyi Sud Rossiiskoi Federatsii [Verkh. Sud RF], Delo No. KAS07-713, Opredeleniye, 15 yanvarya 2008 goda [Russian Federation Supreme Court], Case No. KAS07-713, Ruling, Jan. 15, 2008, available on the official website of the Russian Federation Supreme Court at http://www. supcourt.ru/stor_pdf.php?id=190192.

first case in January 1992. It failed to stay clear of the power struggle between the president and the Parliament that reached its violent climax in the fall of 1993, and as a consequence was suspended until February 1995.

Currently, the Constitutional Court derives its powers from the 1993 Constitution and its latest governing statute—the 1994 Federal Constitutional Law "On the Constitutional Court of the Russian Federation" (the Law on the Constitutional Court).[44] It is part of a two-tier judicial system.[45] But unlike the Supreme Court, which sits at the apex of the pyramid of courts of general jurisdiction and courts of arbitration, the Constitutional Court does not rest on a foundation of lower courts.[46]

Article 125 of the Constitution and Article 3 of the Law on the Constitutional Court give a general description of particular cases that may be decided by the Constitutional Court. The first category involves legislative acts passed by public authorities, whether federal or regional, and only public authorities may petition the Court. These cases need not arise from any ongoing dispute. A party with due authority may request an abstract review of a statute. This authority is vested in the president of the Russian Federation, the Council of Federation, the State Duma, one-fifth of the members of the Council of Federation or of the deputies of the State Duma, the Government of the Russian Federation, the Supreme Court of the Russian Federation, and bodies of legislative and executive power of constituent entities of the Russian Federation. When confronted with such petitions, the Court shall rule on the constitutionality of federal laws and normative acts issued by the president, either chamber of Parliament, or the Russian government. It also may rule on the constitutionality of constitutions, charters, and laws of the constituent entities of the Russian Federation, as well as on treaties concluded by those entities with the federal authorities and between those entities. Finally, the Court may decide on the conformity with the Constitution of international treaties that have not yet come into force.

The second category comprises cases about jurisdictional disputes between federal authorities, or between federal and regional authorities, or between regional authorities. More specifically, those could be disputes (1) between federal state government bodies, (2) between state government bodies of the Russian Federation

---

44. Federal'nyi Konstitutsionnyi Zakon o Konstitutsionnom Sude Rissiyskoi Federatsii [Federal Constitutional Law on the Constitutional Court of the Russian Federation], original version published in SZ RF 1994, No. 13, Item 1447. Current consolidated version available on the official website of the Constitutional Court at http://www.ksrf.ru/ru/Info/LegalBases/FCL/Pages/default.aspx. Consolidated English version available at http://www.ksrf.ru/en/Info/LegalBases/FCL/Pages/default.aspx although at last visit (August 31, 2017) it did not include recent amendments that are not pertinent to the subject matter of this chapter.

45. Prior to judicial reform of 2014 the system was three-tiered, the third entity being the Higher Court of Arbitration.

46. The constitutional and charter courts that have been established in 17 constituent entities of the Russian Federation (14 and 3, respectively) review the conformity of local laws and regulation only with constitutions and charters of those entities.

and state government bodies of constituent entities of the Russian Federation, or (c) between higher state government bodies of constituent entities of the Russian Federation.

The third category consists of cases in which private persons or their associations petition the Constitutional Court, or courts request a constitutional review of a law that, respectively, has been applied or ought to be applied in a particular case. A decision of the Constitutional Court in cases in this category becomes a class action that will affect a group of people with some common characteristics, even though that group may be rather small.

The fourth category, based on the most recent amendments to the Federal Constitutional Law on the Constitutional Court, are cases arising from petitions filed by a duly authorized department of the executive branch of the government (which is, by implication, the Ministry of Justice), to review the practicability of execution of decisions rendered by international bodies for the protection of human rights and freedoms.[47]

Finally, the Council of the Federation may request the Constitutional Court to deliver an opinion on the prescribed procedure for impeachment of the president.

It is only natural to expect the supreme judicial body for constitutional review to interpret the Constitution; however, unlike the US Supreme Court, the Russian Constitutional Court may deal with it as an abstract question. Such an interpretation may be requested by the president of the Russian Federation, the Council of Federation, the State Duma, the Government of the Russian Federation, and legislative authorities of constituent entities of the Russian Federation. It should be noted that there have been very few requests and even fewer judgments in which the Court offered such an interpretation of the Constitution in isolation from a specific dispute.

Legislation that regulates more specific areas modified the jurisdiction of the Constitutional Court by adding the Human Rights Commissioner[48] and the General Prosecutor[49] to the nomenclature of parties that may petition the Court to initiate cases in the third category, and vesting in the Court the authority to review the constitutionality of a motion to hold a referendum.[50]

47. For further discussion of precursors for those amendments, see Bakhtiyar Tuzmukhamedov, *The Russian Constitutional Court in International Legal Dialogues, in* JUDGES AS GUARDIANS OF CONSTITUTIONALISM AND HUMAN RIGHTS 224 (Martin Scheinin et al. eds., 2016).

48. Federal'nyi Konstitutsionnyi Zakon RF ob upolnomochene po pravam cheloveka v Rossiiskoi Federatsii [Federal Constitutional Law of the Russian Federation on the Human Rights Commissioner in the Russian Federation], art. 29(1)(5), original version published in SZ RF 1997, No. 9, Item 1011. Current consolidated version *available at* http://www.ksrf.ru/ru/Info/LegalBases/RepRights/Pages/default.aspx.

49. Federal'nyi Zakon RF o prokurature Rossiiskoi Federatsii [Federal Law of the Russian Federation on the Prosecutor's Office in the Russian Federation], art. 35(5), original version published in VED. RSFSR 1992, No. 8, Art. 366. Current consolidated version *available at* http://www.ksrf.ru/ru/Info/LegalBases/PublicProsecutor/Pages/default.aspx.

50. Federal'nyi Konstitutsionnyi Zakon RF o referendume Rossiiskoi Federatsii [Federal Constitutional Law of the Russian Federation on the Referendum of the Russian Federation],

Neither the Constitution nor the Law on the Constitutional Court directs the Court to apply any other sources of law than the Constitution. However, since its early days the Constitutional Court has looked for arguments in international sources in support of a conclusion based on the Constitution. Eventually, it went farther than making mere references to provisions of international sources that were consonant with the Court's own conclusions, and developed an approach to certain principles and norms of international law, sources thereof, and their interpretation by international judicial bodies that would describe them as "corresponding to"[51] or, less often, as "correlating with"[52] the Constitution or the legal positions of the Court itself. That would appear to be more than implicit "domestication" of particular norms and principles of international law and amount to extension of their coverage by Article 15(4) of the Constitution.

As to the international judiciary, the Constitutional Court has become a conduit for interpretations of treaty-based rights and freedoms offered by the European Court of Human Rights (ECtHR) established under the ECHR. By discovering a confluence of constitutional and conventional rights and freedoms when the latter "correspond to" or "correlate with" the former, the Constitutional Court, by virtue of the binding nature of its decisions, whether judgments or rulings, imposes a combined constitutional and international understanding of rights and freedoms on the national executive, legislative, and judicial authorities.

Moreover, the Court may turn to international law to expound a constitutional provision. In March 2000 the Court ruled on a petition in which several citizens alleged that their right to free elections was violated by several provisions of a local law. They looked for sources of that right in respective provisions of the Constitution, as well as in Article 25(b) of the ICCPR. Not only did the Court recognize that argument in its judgment, it also dissected the right to free elections as stipulated by the ICCPR into its component parts or principles (the right to elect and to be elected; the right and the duty to conduct periodic, genuine, free elections by secret ballot). It went even further and stated that "it is only such mechanisms of the organization and conduct of elections that guarantees the observance of those democratic principles that may be considered as being constitutional."[53] Thus the Court used the Covenant to interpret a rather terse wording of the Constitution.

Of the variety of ways to address international sources that the Constitutional Court has entertained, several may seem of particular relevance for this discussion. It would not be totally unusual for the Court to seek authority in an international

art. 23(1)–(3), original version published in SZ RF 2004, No. 27, Item 2710. Current consolidated version *available at* http://www.ksrf.ru/ru/INFO/LEGALBASES/REFERENDUM/Pages/default.aspx.

51. In its earlier decisions the Court stated that provisions of the Constitution "corresponded to norms of international law" (*see, e.g.,* Konst. Sud Judgment RF 8-P, ¶ 6, Mar. 11, 1998), but soon it reversed the argument (*see, e.g.,* Konst. Sud RF Judgment No. 26-P, ¶¶ 3, 8, Nov. 17, 1998).

52. Konst. Sud RF Judgment No. 4-P, ¶ 2.2, Mar. 22, 2005.

53. Konst. Sud RF Judgment No. 4-P, ¶ 3, Mar. 23, 2000.

treaty to which Russia has not become a party, at least not yet. In a judgment rendered in March 1998, by which time Russia had already signed the ECHR, but prior to its ratification later that same year, the Court referred to its provisions, along with those of the ICCPR, as belonging to "generally recognized norms and principles of international law,"[54] as if it were unaware of the Convention not yet falling within the ambit of Article 15(4) of the Constitution. When dealing with the issue of capital punishment, the Court discussed Protocol 6 quite extensively, though this time it constructed a legal framework that allowed the non-ratified treaty to acquire legal weight in the domestic legal system.

On several occasions the Constitutional Court demonstrated conspicuous indifference to the hierarchy of international sources and, moreover, to their affiliation with hard or soft law. It could supplement a constitutional provision with that of a United Nations General Assembly (UN GA) resolution and then reinforce the latter with a reference to international legal sources.[55] Or it could pack into a single paragraph UN GA resolutions and a treaty, and then summarily and indiscriminately describe them as "international legal acts."[56] However, in the ruling on capital punishment it cautiously described UN GA resolutions calling for a moratorium on execution of death penalties as "evidence of a global tendency," rather than an international legal fait accompli.

The Law on the Constitutional Court authorizes the Constitutional Court to "take legislative initiative on matters pertaining to its jurisdiction,"[57] first and foremost to propose amendments to that very statute. Otherwise, unless the Court upholds a challenged law, the outcome of a review of a particular provision can be described as negative, that is, a provision is struck down as unconstitutional. Aside from those two outcomes explicitly provided for by the governing statute, the Court has developed ways and means of arriving at other results, including what this author may describe as "legislative hint,"[58] "legislative prompt," and "legislative instruction," the last gravitating toward the legislative initiative. Some of those steps were initiated by the Court as part of its reliance on international sources, specifically on the interpretative jurisprudence of the ECtHR. Thus the Court prompted the legislator to amend the Code of Arbitration Procedure and the Code of Civil Procedure to respond to a ECtHR judgment in favor of a petitioner whose case had been previously decided by a national court, so that the judgment could serve as a

---

54. Konst. Sud RF Judgment No. 9-P, ¶ 4, Mar. 19, 1998.

55. Konst. Sud RF Judgment No. 1-P, ¶ 3, Jan. 15, 1999 (citing G.A. Res. 40/34, Declaration of Basic Principles of Justice for Victims of Crime and Abuse of Power (Nov. 29, 1985)).

56. Konst. Sud RF Judgment No. 20-P, ¶ 5, July 1, 2014 (referring repeatedly to G.A. Res. 3447 (XXX), Declaration on the Rights of Disabled Persons (Dec. 9, 1975); G.A. Res. 48/96, Standard Rules on the Equalization of Opportunities for Persons with Disabilities (Dec. 20, 1993); and G.A. Res. 61/106, Convention on the Rights of Persons with Disabilities (Dec. 13, 2006)).

57. *See* Federal Constitutional Law on the Constitutional Court of the Russian Federation, *supra* note 44, art. 3(6).

58. Bakhtiyar Tuzmukhamedov, *The Role of the Russian Constitutional Court in Protecting the Rights of Active Duty and Retired Servicemen*, 52 A.F. L. Rev. 81, 87, 89 (2002) (discussing "legislative hint.").

"newly discovered circumstance" and therefore grounds for a reconsideration of the case.[59]

The Court was more resolute and intrusive into the powers of other branches of government when it effectively withdrew the reservations that Russia made at the time of ratification of, and accession to the ECHR. The reservations related to the terms and duration of placing criminal suspects into custody,[60] which were more stringent than those envisaged by the Convention. The Court held that provisions of the then effective Code of Criminal Procedure that provided for detention of a suspect for more than 48 hours and the remanding of a suspect in custody as a measure of restraint without a court order were not in conformity with the Constitution and could not be applied after the deadline set by the Court.[61] Although the Court did not explicitly say so, the treaty reservations were to lose their force as of the same date.

As will be shown below, the Constitutional Court applied several of those methods when it dealt with the issue of capital punishment.

V. CONSTITUTIONAL COURT AND CAPITAL PUNISHMENT
   (GUTTA CAVAT LAPIDEM)

Early references to the death penalty may be found in several rulings that the Constitutional Court issued in 1997 on petitions by individuals.[62] The Court denied consideration on the merits either because the issue had been resolved by the legislator[63] or due to petitioner's lack of standing, because he was not affected by the law or court sentence that provided for such penalty.[64]

On February 2, 1999, the Constitutional Court pronounced a judgment on petitions filed by several persons who had received death sentences that were not carried out due to commutation or acquittal, and by a municipal court that had to adjourn proceedings in a capital case as it could not grant defendants' requests to be tried by jury, which had not been formed in that particular constituent entity of the Federation. Under the then current laws the jury was to be introduced throughout the Federation by 2007. The Court made an explicit caveat that as the petitioners did not "challenge the constitutionality of imposing this exceptional measure of punishment by the federal legislator," that issue would "not be the subject matter of the present proceedings."[65] This statement may also be interpreted as an abstention

---

59. Konst. Sud RF Judgment 27-P, Dec. 6, 2013; Konst. Sud RF Judgment No. 1-P, Jan. 21, 2010.

60. Council of Europe, Reservations and Declarations for Treaty No.005—Convention for the Protections of Human Rights and Fundamental Freedoms, http://www.conventions.coe.int/Treaty/Commun/ListeDeclarations.asp?NT=005&CM=8&DF=04/02/2015&CL=ENG&VL=1.

61. Konst. Sud RF Judgment No. 6-P, ¶ 1, Mar. 14, 2002.

62. The phrase *gutta cavat lapidem* ("A drop of water hollows a stone") is attributed to Ovid.

63. Konst. Sud RF Ruling No. 5-O, Feb. 4, 1997.

64. Konst. Sud RF Ruling No. 104-O, Oct. 1, 1997.

65. Konst. Sud RF Judgment No. 3-P, Feb. 2, 1999.

of the Court from proprio motu delving into the interpretation of the constitutional right to life in view of retention of capital punishment.

The Court ruled that any defendant in a capital case must enjoy a guaranteed right to have his case tried by a court with participation of the jury and it urged the legislator to expeditiously amend the legislation to ensure that right throughout the Federation. In the meantime,

> From the moment of entry into force of the present Judgment until the entry into force of the respective federal law guaranteeing each person accused of committing a crime punishable by death with the right to be tried by a jury in the whole territory of the Russian Federation, punishment in the form of a death penalty shall not be imposed regardless of whether the case was considered by a jury, a panel of three professional judges, or a judge and two lay judges.[66]

What the Court did not do, apart from not analyzing the right to life, was to refer to any international sources to substantiate its conclusions based on the application and interpretation of the Constitution. Since its early decisions, specifically, the second judgment rendered in February 1992, the Court has consistently sought authority in international sources—treaties, documents of international organizations, judicial decisions, though almost exclusively those of the ECtHR—to augment its constitutional argument. In this judgment the Court referred only to the right to fair trial as envisaged by the ICCPR (Article 14) and the ECHR (Article 6(1)). It did not make any reference to Protocol 6, although judges could not have been unaware of Russia's accession to the Council of Europe and the signing of that treaty.

This author can only speculate that the Court did not consider the right to be tried by jury as having a foundation in international legal sources. Besides, as indicated above, the Court chose not to interpret the right to life without being asked to do so. Also, judges, being aware of the deadline for the ratification of Protocol 6 and assuming that the president and the Federal Assembly intended to meet it, did not want to interfere in the political process. Finally, judges could not but be sensitive to the prevailing mood in society, the majority of which was unwilling to accept the abolition of death penalty. It should be underscored that these are mere speculations, and that later the Court gave different reasons for its silence.

The ultimate outcome of the judgment was a temporary moratorium on the exercise by courts of their authority to hand down death sentences, pending the establishment of collegia of jury in all constituent entities of the Russian Federation. However, combined with the moratorium on executions effective since the accession to the Council of Europe, that amounted to a temporary abolition of the death penalty, even though the Constitutional Court did not consider the legal weight of the signature under Protocol 6 in light of Article 18 of the VCLT.

66. *Id.* ¶ 5.

In several subsequent decisions the Court, while referring to the Judgment of February 2, 1999, underscored the temporary nature of the moratorium on handing down death sentences, which was to expire upon entry into force of a federal law.[67] It even suggested that the judgment "did not exclude death penalty from the inventory of punishments envisaged by the criminal law."[68] At the same time, the Court did not hasten the legislator. In what sounded like a deviation from the rather stern language of that judgment regarding sufficient time that the Federal Assembly had to pass the law, a judgment delivered on April 6, 2006, said:

> The fact that, notwithstanding a considerable period of time after the Constitution of the Russian Federation entered into force, the creation of a jury trial in the Russian Federation is not completed yet may not be in itself considered a violation of the requirements of the Constitution of the Russian Federation.[69]

Has the Court mellowed? Or was it acutely aware that the prospect of having juries before the 2007 deadline in the last remaining constituent entity lacking such was chimerical, that entity being the Chechen Republic? Incidentally, the Judgment of April 6, 2006, was delivered in a case brought to the Constitutional Court by the president of that Republic.

On October 17, 2006, in a rather inconspicuous and very brief ruling denying consideration on the merits of a petition that was filed by a person who had received a death sentence on June 5, 1997, which then was commuted to life imprisonment by a presidential decree, the Constitutional Court made a reference to Protocol 6.[70] A sophisticated petitioner (or his lawyer) argued that he could not have been sentenced to death after April 16, 1997, the day when Russia signed the Protocol. The Constitutional Court chose to acknowledge that argument in the ruling, though it was not obliged to do so, but did not offer any comments.

The Court went further in another ruling, also very brief and denying consideration on the merits of a petition, though this time the three petitioners, all sentenced to death after April 16, 1997, with their sentences commuted to life imprisonment by the president, referred to Protocol 6 viewed in light of Article 18 of the VCLT. The Court commented that the Protocol:

> was signed by the Russian Federation but as of now has not yet been submitted for ratification. As to the obligation not to apply executions undertaken in connection with accession to the Council of Europe, it is currently fulfilled by other means—by pardons and in accordance with the Judgment of the

---

67. Konst. Sud RF Ruling No. 306-O, July 15, 2003; Konst. Sud RF Ruling No. 81-O, Feb. 19, 2003; Konst. Sud RF Ruling No. 68-O, Mar. 6, 2001; Konst. Sud RF Ruling No. 86-O, Mar. 4. 1999.

68. Konst. Sud RF Ruling No. 568, Dec. 21, 2006.

69. Konst. Sud RF Judgment No. 3-P, Apr. 6, 2006.

70. Konst. Sud RF Ruling No. 434-O, ¶ 1, Oct. 17, 2006.

Constitutional Court No. 3-P of February 2, 1999. . . . Thus the legal situation, as it stands now, does not breach the obligations of the Russian Federation under international law.[71]

The Court did not discuss Article 18 of the VLCT, but was unambiguous in describing the moratorium on executions as an obligation in effect as of February 28, 1996.

The Court reproduced that same argument one month later,[72] but soon conspicuously modified it when it stated in several brief rulings denying consideration of a petition on its merits that:

> in view of the signing by the Russian Federation on April 16, 1997 of Protocol No. 6 ... and the delivery by the Constitutional Court of the Russian Federation of Judgment No. 3-P of February 2, 1999 ... that punishment currently may not be applied in the territory of the Russian Federation. Thus the established legal situation does not contradict the meaning of either constitutional or international legal obligations of the Russian Federation.[73]

The Court chose not to reiterate its legal position regarding the moratorium, once having stated it would be valid until and unless amended or repealed by the Court itself. Instead the Court identified a link between an international treaty and domestic judicial decision that together and in a complementary mode abolished the death penalty including both sentencing and executions.

As far-reaching as it may seem, the refined approach of the Constitutional Court did not resolve the issue of the provisional nature of an almost comprehensive ban on the death penalty. The deadline for the establishment of collegia of jury in the Chechen Republic had been extended till January 1, 2010,[74] following which date the requirement that the Constitutional Court stipulated in the Judgment of February 2, 1999, would be fulfilled. After that the provisional ban would have hinged on the moratorium on executions and Article 18 of the VLCT with respect to Protocol 6.

In theory, the legislator could resume the ratification procedures. After all, the State Duma had not voted down the draft law on ratification of Protocol 6, nor had the president withdrawn the draft. Even if that happened and the president

---

71. Konst. Sud RF Ruling No. 380-O-O, ¶ 2, May 15, 2007. For some time the Court had been adding an extra "O" in designation of rulings, which stood for *"otkaznoe"*—"denying," implying denial of consideration on the merits without extensive argumentation.

72. Konst. Sud RF N Ruling o. 592-O-O, ¶ 2.1, June 19, 2007.

73. Konst. Sud RF Rulings 682-O-O to 684-O-O, 686-O-O to 689-O-O, 692-O-O, 712-O-O, Oct. 16, 2007. That legal position was reiterated in Konst. Sud RF Rulings 935-O-O, 943-O-O, Dec. 18, 2007.

74. Federalnyi Zakon o vnesenii izmeneniya v stat'yu 8 Federalnogo Zakona o vvedenii v deystviye Ugolovno-Protsessual'nogo Kodeksa Rossiyskoy Federatsii [Federal Law on an Amendment to Article 8 of the Federal Law on Enactment of the Criminal Procedural Code of the Russian Federation], art. 4, SZ RF 2007, No. 1 (Part 1).

instructed the Ministry of Foreign Affairs to notify the Secretary General of the Council of Europe of Russia's non-intention to become a party of the Protocol, Russia would still be bound by its commitment to impose a moratorium on executions. To waive the latter, Russia would have had to withdraw from the Council of Europe. While these scenarios were highly unlikely, the imminent removal of the constitutional constraint—as interpreted by the Constitutional Court—on death sentences could have led to a situation of legal uncertainty in which courts of general jurisdiction might be confronted with an uneasy choice of either handing down death sentences guided by a literal and isolated reading of the Judgment of February 2, 1999, or not doing so because of international legal obligations. As noted above, the Supreme Court in the Plenary Session Resolution of October 31, 1995, failed to offer to lower courts any guidance regarding the status of signed international treaties pending their ratification. Neither did it offer any clarifications to that effect in a later resolution, that one being specifically dedicated to application of international law by courts, though again it instructed the courts to apply only treaties that were in force for Russia.[75]

In retrospect it may seem that a looming problem could have been resolved preemptively, had the Supreme Court addressed the issue of treaties falling under Article 18 of the VCLT in a Plenary Session resolution, whether dealing generally with application and applicability of international treaties or specifically focused on the death penalty. Instead, the Supreme Court chose to petition the Constitutional Court requesting an official explanation of Paragraph 5 of the Disposition of the Judgment of February 2, 1999, to avoid confronting courts of general jurisdiction with legal uncertainty.

The explanatory Ruling rendered by the Constitutional Court is remarkable both procedurally and in substance. First, it was written and delivered in a most expeditious manner. The application was filed on October 29, 2009, and the Ruling appeared on November 9, 11 days later. Apparently the Court considered the matter to be urgent in light of the January 1, 2010, deadline for the introduction of juries in the Chechen Republic, and heard it out of normal order. Second, in a rather unusual move the Court decided to hold public hearing, which rarely, if at all, happens when a petition is not expected to culminate in a judgment, as applications for explanation never do.

The Ruling[76] is noteworthy in what it says, including in hindsight, and as well as in what it does not say. The Court reaffirmed that its Judgment of February 2, 1999, was based on the assumption that punishment by death was a provisional and extraordinary measure and, by virtue of Article 20(2) of the Constitution, courts

---

75. Postanovleniye Plenuma Verkhovnogo Suda Rossiyskoy Federatsii o primenenii sudami obshchey yurisdiktsii obshchepriznannykh printsipov i norm mezhdunarodnogo prava [Resolution of the Plenary of the Supreme Court of the Russian Federation No. 5, Oct. 10, 2003 on the Application by Courts of General Jurisdiction of Generally Recognized Norms and Principles of International Law and International Treaties of the Russian Federation], Ros. Gaz., Dec. 2, 2003.

76. Konst. Sud RF Ruling No. 1344-O-R Nov. 19, 2009. "R" in the designation of the ruling stands for "*razyasnyayushcheye*"—"explanatory."

could not sentence anyone absent a jury throughout the Federation. In doing so, the Court claimed that it had grounds to presume that the matter of abolition of the death penalty could be resolved in a reasonable time, not exceeding the time needed to complete formation of collegia of jury—something that the Court had not explicitly stated in the earlier judgment. The Court also claimed that as it developed its legal positions expressed in the judgment, it was cognizant of "generally recognized principles and norms of international law and international treaties of the Russian Federation" that could not be ignored in interpretation of the constitutional rights to be tried by jury in capital cases.[77] That would seem to be an overstatement, at least with respect to principles and norms of international law, because there is hardly anything approaching a universal consensus regarding either trial by jury or the death penalty, let alone the two combined. And yet again, that statement cannot be found in the text of the earlier judgment. It only can be assumed that both arguments figured in the in camera deliberations of the judges.

The Court then created a link between its interpretation of the Constitution and the international legal environment by referring to a "sustained tendency in international norm-making towards the abolition of death penalty,"[78] citing Protocols 6 and 13 to the ECHR, the Second Optional Protocol to the ICCPR, and the Protocol to the American Convention on Human Rights to Abolish the Death Penalty, as well as resolutions of the UN GA calling on Member States progressively to restrict the use of the death penalty, to reduce the number of offenses for which it may be imposed, and to establish a moratorium on executions with a view to abolishing the death penalty. That argument was augmented by a reference to commitments undertaken upon Russia's accession to the Council of Europe and the signing of Protocol 6 with ensuing obligations under Article 18 of the VCLT.

The Court's ultimate conclusion was that there existed a long-standing complex and comprehensive moratorium on the death penalty, comprising domestic and international legal norms and practices, resulting in an "irreversible process directed at the abolition of death penalty."[79] The Disposition was quite explicit in that "the introduction of trials by jury throughout the territory of Russian Federation will not reopen the possibility of application of death penalty."[80]

The Court may have gone too far in attributing to Protocol 6 the quality of an "essential element of legal regulation of the right to life"[81] in Russia. That statement, in the opinion of this author, should not create a general rule applicable to other treaties that were, or would be, signed pending their ratification. The "essential element" quality in that case was recognized exclusively because the Protocol happened to be a component of an aggregate of national and international measures

77. *Id.* ¶ 4.

78. *Id.* ¶ 4.1.

79. *Id.* ¶ 7.

80. *Id.* ¶ 1 of the Disposition.

81. *Id.* ¶ 4.3.

directed at the attainment of the constitutional goal of removal of the death penalty from the inventory of punishments.

The Constitutional Court eliminated the legal uncertainty that appeared as a result of insufficient activity of some branches of government, or passivity of others, or even erroneous action by some, including even the Supreme Court. The Constitutional Court effectively transformed a provisional abstention from the death penalty into a permanent one, though making this a ban on the death penalty would require legislative action.

VI. CONCLUSION

It would seem that the Constitutional Court was aware of the non-existence of a universal norm banning capital punishment, despite the "sustained tendency" toward abolition. It may be argued that it selected international sources that could fit its argument based on its own perception of constitutional goals, even though some lacked universal adherence either globally (Second Optional Protocol to the ICCPR), or regionally (Protocol to the American Convention on Human Rights),[82] or were not binding.[83]

The Court was not asked to interpret the right to life either by individual petitioners, or by the Supreme Court, and deliberately refrained from proprio motu constitutional interpretation. It combined selected international sources, recalled that Russia by virtue of its signature under Protocol 6 and prior to ratification is bound by Article 18 of the VCLT ("not to defeat the object and purpose of a treaty"), and then used this combination to supplement the argument that there exist unalterable guarantees of the right not to be subjected to the death penalty.

Although the Constitutional Court referred to generally recognized principles and norms of international law, it stopped short of asserting that any such norms applied to abolition of the death penalty. International legal argument appeared to be quite prominent in the Ruling of November 19, 2009, and yet it was assigned an auxiliary role only as support for the Court's understanding of a national constitutional goal. Moreover, that understanding was not necessarily shared by broad public opinion. As the President of the Constitutional Court admitted, the Court's decisions regarding capital punishment represented "a compromise between domestic public opinion and international legal undertakings of the State."[84] That may have been the reason why the Court, while acknowledging the delay in ratification,

82. As of the time of rendering the ruling the Second Optional Protocol had 79 ratifications; the Protocol to the American Convention had 11 ratifications.

83. The voting record for the two UN General Assembly resolutions cited by the Court was as follows: G.A. Res. 62/149 (Dec. 18, 2007), 104 in favor, 54 against, 29 abstentions; G.A. Res. 63/168 (Dec. 18, 2008), 106 in favor, 46 against, 34 abstentions.

84. V.D. Zorkin, Keynote Lecture at the Third International Legal Forum, St. Petersburg (May 16, 2013), *available at* http://www.ksrf.ru/ru/News/Speech/Pages/ViewItem.aspx?ParamId=61.

clearly stated that it did not interfere with the "prerogatives of the Federal Assembly regarding the ratification of Protocol 6."[85]

The fate of Protocol 6 with respect to Russia is yet unclear. The escalation of tensions between Russia and the Council of Europe in 2014 and 2015, most vivid in repeated suspensions of voting rights of Russian delegates at the Parliamentary Assembly, prompted the delegates to suspend their participation in the activities of that body. This has led to renewed speculations about Russia's possible withdrawal from the Council and its legal instruments, including the ECHR, as well as termination of Russia's commitments, undertaken as part of accession to the Council. Several prominent deputies of the State Duma, including its vice-chair, stated that, should Russia leave the Council, the Duma or the president "will be entitled to terminate the moratorium and to reinstate the death penalty in our legal field."[86] However, he was promptly corrected by the Duma's Chair who, in a nationally televised interview, said that Russia would be faithful to its humanitarian principles and would not apply capital punishment even if it had to quit the Council of Europe.[87] Alas, the debate was largely devoid of sound legal argument, except for a contribution made by the president's adviser on human rights who reminded the legislators that "the issue of the death penalty in our country had been decided by the Constitutional Court, rather than by the Council of Europe. Perchance it should be recalled that no one, not even deputies, can repeal or review a decision of the Constitutional Court."[88]

Assuming the Protocol is not ratified in the foreseeable future, and even if Russia withdraws from the Council of Europe and would consider itself no longer bound by moratorium commitment, the ban on capital punishment will hinge on the jurisprudence of the Constitutional Court and its conclusion that the grace period offered to the legislature by the Constitution to codify the prospective abolition has expired. That conclusion amounts to a binding interpretation of the Constitution. The only way to reinstate capital punishment would seem to be the adoption of a new Constitution with a clear provision for that type of penalty.

85. Konst. Sud RF Ruling No. 1344-O-R, ¶ 7, Nov. 19, 2009.

86. Interview by Govorit Moskva [Moscow Speaks] with Igor Lebedev, Vice-Chairman, State Duma (Jan. 29, 2015), http://govoritmoskva.ru/news/27286/ (in Russian).

87. Interview by Sergey Brilev with Sergey Naryshkin, Chairman, State Duma (Jan. 31, 2015), http://newsru.com/russia/31jan2015/naryshkin_kazn.html (in Russian).

88. Interview by RIA Novosti with Mikhail Fedotov, Chairman, Presidential Council for Civil Soc'y & Human Rights (Jan. 30, 2015), http://rapsinews.ru/incident_news/20150130/273067580.html (in Russian).

PART SIX

Comparative International Law and Human Rights

18

Comparative Views on the Right to Vote in International Law

The Case of Prisoners' Disenfranchisement

SHAI DOTHAN*

I. INTRODUCTION

The right to vote in democratic elections is one of the most basic rights recognized by international law. This right is enshrined in the Universal Declaration of Human Rights and the International Covenant on Civil and Political Rights (ICCPR), as well as in many regional treaties, such as the European Convention on Human Rights. Yet for all this consensus about the right to vote itself, there is widespread disagreement about who may exercise it.[1]

The disagreement about the breadth of the right to vote can be seen in the various ways states treat the voting rights of prisoners. Some states allow all prisoners to vote, while others disenfranchise all their prisoners. In many countries, the right to vote can be taken away from prisoners only under certain conditions.

This chapter explores the interpretations of the right to vote under international law in the courts of several democratic countries. While policies on the issue are ultimately determined by the legislature, not by courts, the analysis of judgments provides a unique opportunity to observe the underlying theories behind competing conceptions of the right to vote. This analysis highlights the fact that these courts not only opt for different regimes; rather they adhere to fundamentally different

* I thank Patrick Barry, Or Bassok, Lisa Bernstein, Eszter Bodnár, Olga Frishman, Christopher McCrudden, and Mila Versteeg for many instructive conversations and comments. I gratefully acknowledge the financial support of the Global Trust Research Project directed by Professor Eyal Benvenisti and funded by an ERC Advanced Grant.

1. *See, e.g.*, Rainer Bauböck, *Expansive Citizenship: Voting Beyond Territory and Membership* 38 POL. SCI. & POL. 683, 683–85 (2005) (describing different regimes regarding the voting rights of noncitizens who are residents or citizens who live abroad).

conceptions of the right to vote. Some courts view the right to vote as an inherent part of citizenship—a right that cannot be revoked—while others view it more as a privilege that is used to facilitate the democratic process. Several courts view suffrage as a conditional right, a right that can be taken away under certain conditions.

The diversity of views among the states about the nature of their international obligations feeds back into international law as it is applied by international courts, such as the European Court of Human Rights (ECtHR). Because the policies adopted by the states stem from fundamentally different theories of citizenship, simply following the majority of the states and setting their policies as a rule for the rest of Europe—as the court regularly does under the so-called Emerging Consensus doctrine—risks undermining the rationale that justifies this doctrine. Yet other mechanisms still exist to bridge the gap between differing state interpretations of the right to vote and to set minimum standards with which all states must comply.

Section II describes the right to vote in international law. Section III briefly surveys, as a case study, the legal regimes in Europe regarding the rights of prisoners to vote. Section IV analyzes the way judgments of several democratic countries treat the right of prisoners to vote and demonstrates that these countries adopt divergent views of the right to vote in international law. Section V explores the effect that this divergence has on the development of international law by the ECtHR. It shows the link between comparative international law and the doctrine set by international tribunals. Section VI concludes by highlighting the processes that can minimize the differences between national interpretations.

II. THE RIGHT TO VOTE IN INTERNATIONAL LAW

In 1948, the United Nations adopted the Universal Declaration of Human Rights.[2] While this document isn't legally binding, it outlines the most basic human rights obligations of states under international law. In fact, many scholars view at least parts of the declaration as constituting customary international law.[3] This declaration foreshadows many human rights commitments later undertaken by states in binding treaties. Article 21 of the Declaration enshrines the right of everyone to take part in the government of her country and determines that the will of the people, as expressed in elections with universal and equal suffrage, shall be the basis for the authority of government.[4]

---

2. G.A. Res. 217 (III) A, Universal Declaration of Human Rights (Dec. 10, 1948).

3. *See* Hurst Hannum, *The Status of the Universal Declaration of Human Rights in National and International Law*, 25 GA. J. INT'L & COMP. L. 287, 340, 348 (1995) (arguing that although some scholars point to an emerging right to democracy in customary international law, many states did not accept the right to participate in political life guaranteed in Article 21 of the declaration).

4. "1. Everyone has the right to take part in the government of his country, directly or through freely chosen representatives. 2. Everyone has the right to equal access to public service in his country. 3. The will of the people shall be the basis of the authority of government; this will shall be expressed in periodic and genuine elections which shall be by universal and equal suffrage and shall be held by secret vote or by equivalent free voting procedures."

The right to vote was later included in the ICCPR, a binding international treaty with 168 state parties.[5] Article 25 of the treaty enshrines the right to vote in periodic elections that are universal, equal, and held by a secret ballot.[6] The Human Rights Committee issued a general comment—an official document interpreting this right—which includes a specific reference to prisoners' disenfranchisement. The committee stated that any deprivation of the right to vote should be based on reasons that are objective and reasonable, and that the period of suspension of voting rights for convicts should be proportionate to the offense and the sentence.[7]

Regional human rights conventions, which are binding on states in the region that joined them, also protect the right to vote. For example, the right to free elections is enshrined in Article 3 of Protocol 1 of the European Convention on Human Rights.[8] The ECtHR has issued several important judgments that interpret this provision as protecting the rights of prisoners to vote under certain conditions. These judgments are discussed in Section V.

Similar provisions on the right to vote appear in the American Convention on Human Rights[9] and in the African Charter on Human and Peoples' Rights,[10] as well as in numerous other treaties and international instruments.[11] Some authors argue that the commitment of most countries to protect the right to vote from the more extreme forms of prisoners' disenfranchisement grants prisoners a binding right under customary international law.[12]

---

5. International Covenant on Civil and Political Rights, Dec. 16, 1966, 999 U.N.T.S. 171.

6. "Every citizen shall have the right and the opportunity, without any of the distinctions mentioned in Article 2 and without unreasonable restrictions: (a) To take part in the conduct of public affairs, directly or through freely chosen representatives; (b) To vote and to be elected at genuine periodic elections which shall be by universal and equal suffrage and shall be held by secret ballot, guaranteeing the free expression of the will of the electors; (c) To have access, on general terms of equality, to public service in his country."

7. "The grounds for such deprivation [of the right to vote] should be objective and reasonable. If conviction for an offence is a basis for suspending the right to vote, the period of such suspension should be proportionate to the offence and the sentence. Persons who are deprived of liberty but who have not been convicted should not be excluded from exercising the right to vote." Hum. Rts. Comm., General Comment No. 25, ¶ 14, U.N. Doc. CCPR/C/21/Rev.1/Add.7 (Aug. 27, 1996).

8. "The High Contracting Parties undertake to hold free elections at reasonable intervals by secret ballot, under conditions which will ensure the free expression of the opinion of the people in the choice of the legislature." Protocol to the Convention for the Protection of Human Rights and Fundamental Freedoms art. 3, Mar. 20, 1952, 213 U.N.T.S. 262.

9. American Convention on Human Rights art. 23, Nov. 22, 1969, 1144 U.N.T.S 143.

10. African Charter on Human and Peoples' Rights art. 13(1), June 27, 1981, 21 I.L.M 58 (1982).

11. See Scott Ferguson, Study Guide: The Right to Vote, http://www1.umn.edu/humanrts/edumat/studyguides/votingrights.html (last visited July 12, 2016), for a comprehensive survey of these documents.

12. See Robin L. Nunn, Lock Them up and Throw away the Vote, 5 Chi. J. Int'l L. 763, 779–81 (2005).

III. THE RIGHT OF PRISONERS TO VOTE IN EUROPEAN
STATES: A CASE STUDY

Despite the multitude of abstract international commitments to the right to vote, states greatly diverge in how they apply this right to prisoners. Some states unequivocally retain the right to vote for all prisoners; others deny this right from all prisoners for the duration of their sentence. There are also many states that fall somewhere in the middle: they remove voting rights only from prisoners sentenced for long imprisonments or from prisoners who committed certain crimes that are especially severe or bear some connection to the mechanisms of democratic government. Some states let judges decide whether prisoners should be allowed to vote, and some let judges withhold the right to vote even after a prisoner is released, sometimes permanently.

The next section of the chapter analyzes the underlying interpretations of international law by several national courts. But first, this section provides some general information on the regimes concerning prisoners' disenfranchisement adopted by countries in the Council of Europe. This brief overview provides some idea of the diversity of legal regimes adopted by democracies that share the same region and the same commitment to the right to vote enshrined in the European Convention on Human Rights.[13] This case study can show how states that share the same international commitments may nevertheless adopt widely divergent regimes.

Out of a total of 47 European states, only 18 allow all prisoners to vote in national elections. Even in these states, there are sometimes limitations on how prisoners can participate in politics. Ukraine, for example, allows prisoners to vote in presidential and parliamentary elections, but because prisoners are not part of any recognized municipality while in prison, they cannot vote in local elections.

Nine states prevent all prisoners from voting for the duration of their sentence. Andorra is unique in this respect; its laws do not prevent prisoners from voting, but there are no procedures to allow them to vote in practice. However, this country has a very small prison population, and most of its prisoners are foreigners who never had the right to vote in Andorra to begin with.

Several countries remove the right to vote only from prisoners who committed crimes of special severity, usually determined by the duration of their sentence. In Romania, for example, prisoners are not allowed to vote if they were sentenced to at least two years in prison or if the court specifically disenfranchises them. Prisoners who are detained pending a judicial decision can vote. In Italy, sentences of between one and five years lead to temporary disenfranchisement, while sentences of more than five years lead to permanent disenfranchisement. In Austria, prisoners who committed premeditated acts and are sentenced to more than a year in prison

---

13. The data is from Isobel White, Prisoners' Voting Rights (2012), *available at* http://www.procon.org/sourcefiles/UK-report-eu-felon-voting.pdf. See Nat'l Ass'n of Crim. Def. Law., Restoration of Rights Project: Jurisdiction Profiles, http://www.nacdl.org/ResourceCenter.aspx?id=25091 (last visited July 12, 2016), for a similar overview of the legal situation in different US states.

cannot vote until six months after their sentence is served.[14] In Luxembourg, prisoners sentenced to more than 10 years lose their vote for life. Judges have the discretion to prevent prisoners who received sentences of between 5 to 10 years from voting, either for the duration of their sentence or for longer periods, even for life.

Other countries do not consider simply the severity of the crime and the sentence. They find a connection between disenfranchisement and a certain quality of the crime that renders it contrary to the very ethos of voting and democratic government. For example, in Germany only prisoners convicted of crimes that target the state's integrity or the democratic order lose their right to vote until they serve their sentence. In Portugal, prisoners can vote unless the court convicts them of a crime against the state or a crime related to elections or public office and decides to take away their political rights as part of the sentence. In some countries, the power to withdraw the right to vote for crimes that target the very essence of democracy seems mainly declarative and is rarely used in practice. In the Netherlands, for example, judges can revoke the right to vote of prisoners sentenced to one year or more in prison if their crimes contradict the foundations of the state, such as trying to forge the ballot or assaulting the monarch. But this power has not been used recently. Similarly, in Norway, judges can revoke the right to vote in cases of treason, electoral fraud, or national security, but there is no record of this power ever being used. Bosnia and Herzegovina, due to its long history of bloody conflict, is unique: it disenfranchises only prisoners convicted of humanitarian law violations.

Some countries vest the discretion to disenfranchise prisoners entirely in the hands of judges. For example, prisoners in Cyprus can usually vote, but their rights can be taken away by the sentencing court. In Monaco too, prisoners can vote as a rule, but this right can be denied in individual cases by the court. Some countries give judges discretion but guide their decision either by setting a default or by conditioning disenfranchisement on certain requirements. In France, for example, courts can add disenfranchisement as an additional penalty. For some offenses such an additional penalty is the default, but judges can decide not to use it. In Belgium, courts have discretion to disenfranchise prisoners, but the more severe the offense, the longer the possible period of disenfranchisement. This period can exceed the prison time and even be permanent. In Poland, if offenders committed a crime with intent and were sentenced to more than three years in prison, they can be disenfranchised at the judge's discretion. The period of disenfranchisement will only start counting when the prisoner is released.

All states in the Council of Europe are subject to the jurisdiction of the ECtHR. In 2005, the ECtHR issued a judgment in the *Hirst* case deciding that the United Kingdom's policy of banning all prisoners from voting violates the European Convention on Human Rights.[15] Usually, the ECtHR condemns policies as violating the Convention if they contradict the policies of the majority of states in

---

14. *See* in this respect the discussion of the ECtHR *Frodl v. Austria* case, *infra* note 40 and accompanying text. In this case this policy was condemned as violating the convention, but the later *Scoppola* case retreated from some of the legal requirements set in this judgment.

15. Hirst v. United Kingdom (No. 2), 2005-IX Eur. Ct. H.R. 187.

Europe, a doctrine called "Emerging Consensus."[16] In the *Hirst* case the ECtHR noted that while only a minority of states in Europe indiscriminately prevent all prisoners from voting—like the United Kingdom whose practices were discussed in this case—there are many states that prevent prisoners from voting under certain conditions, sometimes permanently. Despite the fact that a clear majority could not be discerned, the ECtHR found the United Kingdom in violation. The judgment stressed that even if there is no European consensus on the issue, the policy of the United Kingdom violates the Convention as it constitutes "a general, automatic and indiscriminate restriction on a vitally important Convention right."[17] Following this judgment, a series of other cases—some of which will be discussed later in the chapter—refined the doctrine adopted by the ECtHR.

The *Hirst* case led to severe criticism in the United Kingdom, which failed to comply with it. Yet some other states tried to conform to this judgment and changed their laws to allow more prisoners to vote. Specifically, prisoners in Ireland can vote today only because the law was changed in 2006. Prior to that change, prisoners could not vote. Parties who lobbied for this change cited the *Hirst* case as a reason the law should be changed. Similarly, in Latvia today all prisoners can vote. They were first granted this right in legislation passed in 2008.

Table 18.1 below summarizes the legal regimes regarding voting rights in the Council of Europe.

Table 18.1. RIGHTS OF PRISONERS TO VOTE IN COUNCIL OF EUROPE COUNTRIES

	Complete ban on prisoners' right to vote	Some prisoners cannot vote for life	Partial ban on prisoners' right to vote	No ban on prisoners' right to vote, but they cannot vote de facto	All prisoners can vote
Albania					X
Andorra				X	
Armenia	X				
Austria			X		
Azerbaijan					X
Belgium		X	X		
Bosnia and Herzegovina			X		

(*Continued*)

16. *See* Laurence R. Helfer & Erik Voeten, *International Courts as Agents of Legal Change: Evidence from LGBT Rights in Europe*, 68 INT'L ORG. 77, 106 (2014) (showing that the ECtHR requires states to protect LGBT rights when the majority of states grant these protections); Laurence R. Helfer, *Consensus, Coherence and the European Convention on Human Rights*, 26 CORNELL INT'L L. J. 133, 139 (1993) (discussing three possible interpretations of the Emerging Consensus doctrine: following the laws of European states, following the consensus of experts, and following a consensus in European public opinion).

17. *Hirst* (No. 2), 2005-IX Eur. Ct. H.R. 187, at para. 82.

Table 18.1. (CONTINUED)

	Complete ban on prisoners' right to vote	Some prisoners cannot vote for life	Partial ban on prisoners' right to vote	No ban on prisoners' right to vote, but they cannot vote de facto	All prisoners can vote
Bulgaria	X				
Croatia					X
Cyprus			X		
Czech Republic					X
Denmark					X
Estonia	X				
Finland					X
France			X		
Georgia	X				
Germany			X		
Greece			X		
Hungary	X				
Iceland			X		
Ireland					X
Italy		X	X		
Latvia					X
Liechtenstein	X				
Lithuania					X
Luxembourg		X	X		
Malta			X		
Republic of Moldova					X
Monaco			X		
Montenegro					X
Netherlands			X		
Norway			X		
Poland			X		
Portugal			X		
Romania			X		
Russian Federation	X				
San Marino	X				

(*Continued*)

Table 18.1. (CONTINUED)

	Complete ban on prisoners' right to vote	Some prisoners cannot vote for life	Partial ban on prisoners' right to vote	No ban on prisoners' right to vote, but they cannot vote de facto	All prisoners can vote
Serbia					X
Slovak Republic			X		
Slovenia					X
Spain					X
Sweden					X
Switzerland					X
The former Yugoslav Republic of Macedonia					X
Turkey			X		
Ukraine					X
United Kingdom	X				
Total:	9	3	19	1	18

IV. COMPARATIVE VIEWS ON THE INTERNATIONAL RIGHT OF PRISONERS TO VOTE

As the previous section shows, democracies that are committed to the right to vote under international law nevertheless adopt very different regimes when it comes to the right of prisoners to vote. The doctrines on prisoners' disenfranchisement reflect fundamentally different conceptions of the essence of the right to vote. To unveil these conceptions, this section analyzes judgments of several national courts. The great advantage of judgments is that they are reasoned and allow a glimpse of the conceptions behind policy choices. The theoretical conceptions voiced by the judges in this section do not necessarily reflect the theories that their states adhere to when they choose their policies. Nevertheless, exploring the reasons put forth by these judges can outline possible reasoned views on the issue of prisoners' right to vote and highlight the differences between these views.

Different conceptions adopted by courts often derive from a different reading of the state's constitutional or other domestic legal obligations. Yet judgments of national courts that develop these conceptions sometimes rely on divergent interpretations of obligations under international law. The following subsections analyze judgments of several courts in democratic countries. They try to tease out, specifically, the divergent interpretations of international law that motivate the different policies these courts adopt on the issue of prisoners' disenfranchisement.

A. Enfranchisement as an Inalienable Right

While many democracies prevent at least some of their prisoners from voting, some democracies are committed to the idea that no prisoner should be denied his full rights to participate in elections. Often the protection of this right is based on an interpretation of the constitutional protections granted within the state. A prominent example is South Africa. In the *August* case, the Constitutional Court of South Africa stressed that universal suffrage is a uniquely fundamental value of that country's constitutional order. This universal right protects the dignity of every citizen and ensures that everyone within a country plagued by many disparities will still be full members of the nation, which means that every legal provision must be interpreted in favor of enfranchisement.[18] As a result, the court ruled that, unless Parliament makes an explicit decision to disenfranchise citizens, they maintain their right to vote.[19] As such a provision didn't exist, the court ordered the electoral commission to make all the arrangements necessary to allow prisoners to vote.

Israel is another country that always enfranchised all of its prisoners, at least in theory. Until the 1980s polling stations were not placed in prisons. Because voters in Israel have to vote in their assigned station near their home address, prisoners could not practically use their right. Prisoners would sometimes submit applications a short time before the elections demanding to use their right to vote. These applications were usually formally rejected on the grounds that they were delayed, that is, they were unjustifiably filed too late to allow the court to issue any useful remedy.[20] In the 1984 *Hokama* case, five justices of the Israeli Supreme Court wrote concurring opinions, all of them stressing that prisoners maintain their constitutional voting right, but that the court cannot grant them practical use of this right for a variety of technical reasons. The justices called on the Israeli Parliament to intervene and grant a practical opportunity for prisoners to use their voting rights.[21] In 1986, Parliament complied with this request and changed the law, requiring that polling stations be placed in all prisons to allow prisoners to exercise their rights.[22]

On November 4, 1995, the prime minister of Israel, Yitzhak Rabin, was assassinated by a Jewish Israeli citizen, Yigal Amir. After Amir's trial and conviction, applicants wanted to revoke his right to vote in national elections. Their attempt to ask the Israeli Supreme Court to take away Amir's voting rights was legally doomed to failure. Article 5 of the Basic Law: The Knesset grants the right to vote to every Israeli citizen over 18 years of age unless the court denied him this right *according to law*. But Parliament made no law that allows the denial of voting rights. Consequently, their application on this ground was denied as totally unfounded.[23]

---

18. August v. Electoral Comm'n, 1999 (3) SA 1 (CC) at para. 17 (S. Afr.).

19. *Id.* at para. 31.

20. *See* HCJ 378/81 Amsalem v. Chairman of the Election Committee 35(3) PD 673 [1981] (Isr.)

21. *See* HCJ 337/84 Hokama v. the Interior Minister 38(2) PD 826 [1984] (Isr.).

22. *See* Knesset Election Law, 1969, SH 556, Article 116B(2).

23. *See* HCJ 2757/96 Alrei v. Minister of Interior 50(2) PD 18, 25–26 [1996] (Isr.)

Yet the applicants found another route that was intended to reach the same result. They argued that the Interior Minister is authorized by law to revoke the citizenship of a person that committed an act that violated his loyalty to the state of Israel. They further argued that the minister must exercise this authority in this case due to the severity of the circumstances. Importantly for our context, the minister argued that he denied the request to revoke Amir's citizenship because citizenship is a fundamental right under international law. It is a right protected in Article 15 of the Universal Declaration of Human Rights and in Article 8 of the 1961 Convention on the Reduction of Statelessness, as well as in the constitutional law of many countries.[24] Due to the fundamental nature of the right to citizenship, the Interior Minister views taking away this right as an extreme and drastic measure that it would usually avoid. Justice Zamir, who wrote the court's opinion in this case, agreed with the Interior Minister that taking away citizenship is an extreme measure specifically *because* the right to citizenship protects the right to vote. This makes the right to citizenship, which is not granted a formal constitutional status in Israel, a fundamental right in Israeli law.[25] Zamir therefore concluded that the Interior Minister was authorized to make the reasonable decision not to take away Amir's citizenship, leading to a rejection of the application.[26]

Apparently, the Israeli court provides the right to citizenship under international law with a special protection because it guarantees the right to vote. But the unconditional guarantee of the right to vote—even when it can be indirectly taken away by other means that are not formally excluded by the letter of the law—already involves an interpretation of this right as an inalienable right. It involves a complete rejection of the possibility that the right to vote is a privilege that can be denied from convicts if formal means to do so are available in domestic law. Because Israeli law gives the Interior Minister an explicit authority to revoke citizenship, the court cannot make a formalist decision that revocation is ungrounded in law and must instead make explicit its view of the nature of the right to vote as inalienable. It is the inalienable nature of the right to vote that gives special strength to the right to citizenship under international law and leads the court to find the minister's decision not to revoke Amir's citizenship reasonable.

B. Enfranchisement as a Privilege

Many countries allow the broad disenfranchisement of prisoners. A prime example is the United States, where most states disenfranchise prisoners for the duration of their sentence or more. Yet in the United States, the main challenge to this policy is on grounds of constitutionality, not on grounds of international law. Thus, in the *Richardson v. Ramirez* case the US Supreme Court ruled that prisoners' disenfranchisement is constitutional as it is sanctioned, albeit incidentally, by section 2 of the Fourteenth Amendment to the Constitution.[27] The position of the United

---

24. *Id.* at 22.

25. *Id.* at 22, 24.

26. *Id.* at 25.

27. Richardson v. Ramirez, 418 U.S. 24, 54–55 (1974).

Kingdom is different though. It is bound by the European Convention on Human Rights to protect voting rights and hence its courts found it necessary to circumscribe the scope of this international obligation.

Article 3 Protocol 1 of the European Convention on Human Rights requires the signatory states to hold free elections "under conditions which will ensure the free expression of the opinion of the people in the choice of the legislature." This obligation can be interpreted in different ways: either as only requiring states to provide the necessary procedures for a functioning democracy or as granting citizens an individual right to vote. In the *Mathieu-Mohin* case, the ECtHR clearly adopted the latter interpretation. While the judgment decided that the right to vote is not absolute and that states should be granted a margin of appreciation in protecting this right, it determined that the ECtHR will not allow a violation of the essence or the effectiveness of the individual's right to vote.[28]

The *Pearson* case issued by the High Court of England and Wales adopts a far more restrictive interpretation of the right to vote than the one adopted by the ECtHR. The judgment acknowledges that preventing a prisoner from voting certainly impairs the very essence of his right to vote. But the court immediately moves on to say that the convention is really concerned with the general question of universal suffrage and the free expression of the people's opinion, not with the rights of individual prisoners.[29]

Therefore, in the *Pearson* case the right to vote is dethroned from its position as a right of every citizen and relegated to the status of a privilege used in the service of the democratic process. Once this interpretive choice is made, denying the vote from prisoners becomes much easier. While the exact aim of disenfranchising prisoners isn't clearly defined, the court in the *Pearson* case contents itself with leaving the multiple potential grounds for this policy to the discussions of philosophers. Similarly, the proportionality of the measure is left to the discretion of the legislature.[30] The application against the general disenfranchisement of prisoners is consequently dismissed.

C. Voting Rights as Revocable Rights

As Section III demonstrates, many states require an additional condition besides conviction and imprisonment to disenfranchise a prisoner. These conditions can be learned from domestic law and must concur with the constitution. Countries may diverge as to the propriety of conditions for prisoners' disenfranchisement based on their own laws and judicial history. For example, in the *Sauvé* case, the Canadian Supreme Court decided that denying the right to vote of convicts who were sentenced to two years in prison or more is unconstitutional.[31] In contrast, in the *Roach* case the High Court of Australia decided that, while preventing all prisoners from voting is unconstitutional, disenfranchising only prisoners with a three-year

28. Mathieu-Mohin v. Belgium, 113 Eur. Ct. H.R. (Ser. A) at paras. 51–52 (1987).

29. R (Pearson) v. Sec'y of State for the Home Dep't [2001] EWHC (Admin) 239 at para. 40 (Eng.).

30. *Id.* at paras. 40–41.

31. Sauvé v. Canada (Chief Electoral Officer), [2002] 3 S.C.R. 519 (Can.).

sentence is legal as it legitimately distinguishes between prisoners according to the seriousness of their crimes.[32] This analysis reflects differences in constitutional provisions and constitutional history.

Yet two justices who wrote opinions in these cases specifically addressed the compatibility of limited disenfranchisement of prisoners with international standards. Dissenting Canadian Justice Charles Gonthier and Australian Justice Kenneth Hayne, who decided against the majority not to grant relief in these cases, have a similar take on the issue of international obligations to grant voting rights to prisoners. Justice Gonthier concludes his presentation of comparative views on the issue with reference to the ICCPR provision and to its interpretation by the United Nations Human Rights Committee that allows restrictions on the right to vote provided that they are objective and reasonable. His final conclusion from this analysis is that there are many legitimate legal regimes on the issue.[33] Justice Hayne similarly rejects the argument that there is a generally accepted international standard on the issue by calling attention to the substantive differences between states' laws.[34]

The view presented by Justices Gonthier and Hayne certainly differs from the conception of voting as an inalienable right, as they both agree that prisoners can be disenfranchised. Yet they do not accept the view that voting is a privilege meant only to serve society either. For them, voting is a right that can be taken away for a reason. But what constitutes a sufficient reason? Their view is that differences between state policies are simply too great to provide a definitive answer to that according to international law.

This view leads to outcomes that form a middle ground solution between the two views described above. But the three different views do not just form gradations of protection to the right to vote. Rather, they are theoretically distinct ways to think about voting rights in international law.

V. THE EFFECT OF COMPARATIVE LAW
ON INTERNATIONAL LAW

As the preceding sections suggest, different states interpret their international obligations to protect the right to vote differently and form several competing international law regimes. Yet these domestic interpretations and the domestic practices that stem from them in turn affect the content of international law itself.

State practice shapes customary international law and the so-called "general principles of law recognized by civilized nations," both traditional sources of international law.[35] In fact, Justice Gonthier and Justice Hayne, who were mentioned in the previous section, argue that the differences between state practices on the issue

---

32. *Roach v Electoral Comm'r* [2007] HCA 43 at para. 102 (Austl.).

33. *Sauvé*, [2002] 3 S.C.R. at 593–94.

34. *Roach* [2007] HCA 43 at 165–66.

35. Statute of the International Court of Justice art. 38(1), June 26, 1945, 59 Stat. 1055, 33 U.N.T.S. 993.

of voting rights prevent a general international standard from developing and limit states' obligations to a commonly accepted minimum.

In recent years, the judgments of international courts have played a growing role in shaping international law as well. The ECtHR, for example, interprets the obligations of states under the European Convention on Human Rights. The court developed the doctrine of Emerging Consensus, which gives national interpretations another way to feed back into international law. This doctrine is often used to require states to comply with human rights standards accepted by the majority of the states in the Council of Europe.[36]

In the *Hirst* case, the ECtHR makes it clear that a blanket ban on prisoners' voting rights violates the Convention because it indiscriminately denies a vital Convention right, even if there is no common European approach on the issue. At the same time, however, the court's majority opinion does note that only a minority of the states keep such a blanket ban.[37] This side note is severely criticized by five dissenting judges who argue that a substantial number of states restrict prisoners' voting rights, partially or completely, even in their constitutional provisions.[38] This indicates that although the court does not apply the doctrine of Emerging Consensus, the doctrine lurks in the background and may have affected the ruling.

The *Hirst* case is not fully explicit about the conditions that can allow the disenfranchisement of prisoners. This fact as well is subject to criticism by dissenting judges who argue that many countries would have trouble discerning whether their rules comply with this judgment.[39] However, in the later *Frodl* case, the court ruled that applying the legal test used in the *Hirst* case implies that the decision of disenfranchisement must be taken by a judge based on particular circumstances and on a link between the offense and the process of democratic elections.[40]

This judgment is reversed in the later *Scoppola* case. There, the court stresses that the *Hirst* case doesn't imply that a decision by a judge is an essential condition for a legitimate disenfranchisement[41] and rules that states should be allowed the discretion to set their own conditions for disenfranchising prisoners. The *Scoppola* case further notes that of the 24 states examined that have some restrictions on prisoners voting rights, only 11 require a specific judicial decision to disenfranchise a prisoner.[42] Again, therefore, the attempt to set standards that are widely accepted in Europe surfaces in the court's reasoning.

---

36. *See supra* note 16.

37. Hirst v. United Kingdom (No. 2), 2005-IX Eur. Ct. H.R. 187 at para. 81.

38. *Id.* at para. 6 (Wildhaber, Costa, Lorenzen, Kovler, & Jebens, JJ., dissenting).

39. *Id.*

40. Frodl v. Austria, App. No. 20201/04, 52 Eur. H.R. Rep. 267, para. 34 (2010).

41. *See* Scoppola v. Italy (No. 3), App. No. 126/05, 56 Eur. H.R. Rep. 663, (2012) (Björgvinsson, J., dissenting), for a critique of this argument.

42. *Id.* at paras. 97–102 (majority opinion).

The ECtHR resists applying Emerging Consensus to prisoners' voting rights, but at the same time it tries to set rules that would be accepted by most European states. The attempt of the ECtHR to set international standards that concur with the policy of the majority of the states in Europe leads to the adoption of a middle-ground solution. States are not allowed to disenfranchise all prisoners, but neither are they required to allow all prisoners to vote. The court seems to adhere to the third view of suffrage—namely, that it is a right that can be revoked under certain conditions. Faced with the variety of policies requiring different conditions for disenfranchisement, the court leaves the states some room to maneuver while at the same time excluding certain policies as illegitimate.

The ECtHR has repeatedly stressed that states' policies on voting rights deserve a wide margin of appreciation. The underlying reason for this wide margin of deference to the states is that there are many alternative ways to maintain a functioning democracy.[43] For that reason, the ECtHR only creates a "floor"—a set of minimum standards that is required of all states, while at the same time permitting states to adopt regimes that are even more progressive.[44] In contrast, states that don't live up to this minimum standard are easily found in violation. Such a violation was found in the policies of Turkey in the *Söyler* case, where the court repeatedly stressed that more lenient rules on disenfranchisement than the ones used by Turkey were already found in violation in previous judgments.[45]

This method allows the ECtHR to use the majority of the states in Europe as a tool to actively push forward human rights, without at the same time pulling back states that adopt regimes that are better than the minimum.[46] Empirical research suggests that European states regularly improve their human rights standards to

---

43. *See id.* at para. 83; Söyler v. Turkey, App. No. 29411/07, para. 33 (Eur. Ct. H.R. Sept. 17 2013); Mathieu-Mohin v. Belgium, 113 Eur. Ct. H.R. (Ser. A) at para. 52 (1987). Normatively speaking, this choice could be criticized: prisoners' disenfranchisement excludes a part of society from the democratic process in the most direct way. This implies that the state cannot hide behind claims of greater democratic legitimacy than the unelected ECtHR and should be granted a narrow margin of appreciation. *See* Eyal Benvenisti, *Margin of Appreciation, Consensus and Universal Standards*, 31 N.Y.U. J. INT'L L. POL. 843, 849 (1999) (arguing that the ECtHR should not grant a margin of appreciation in issues that involve the rights of minorities who may not be properly represented by the political process); Shai Dothan, *In Defense of Expansive Interpretation in the ECHR*, 3 CAMBRIDGE J. INT'L & COMP. L. 508, 521 (2014) (arguing that if prisoners are excluded from voting, states do not represent their prisoners and therefore the ECtHR may expand the states' obligations under the Convention by means of interpretation).

44. *See* FEDERICO FABBRINI, FUNDAMENTAL RIGHTS IN EUROPE: CHALLENGES AND TRANSFORMATIONS IN A COMPARATIVE PERSPECTIVE 38–39 (2014).

45. *See Söyler*, App. No. 29411/07, at paras. 38, 43.

46. *Cf.* Alec Knight, *An Asymmetric Comparative International Law Approach to Treaty Interpretation: The CEDAW Committee's Tolerance of the Scandinavian States' Progressive Deviation* (this volume) (arguing that the CEDAW committee also sets a minimum standard for the states. States that deviate from the standard in the progressive direction receive a margin of appreciation and are not criticized. In contrast, states that deviate in the conservative direction are criticized by the committee).

conform to the minimum standards set by the ECtHR judgments, even judgments issued against another state.[47] In this way, the intervention of an international court promotes progressive interpretations of rights across Europe.

VI. CONCLUSION

In the *Hirst* case, the majority opinion abandons the attempt to establish a genuine European consensus on prisoners' voting rights because the United Kingdom is joined by a sizeable minority of other states who disenfranchise prisoners. Some of these states actually have more extreme disenfranchisement policies than the United Kingdom. Yet the fact that there are several other states that maintain similar policies to those of the state under scrutiny should not deter the ECtHR from establishing an Emerging Consensus and has not deterred it from doing so in the past. In fact, empirical research suggests that the court establishes an Emerging Consensus once the *majority* of states provide certain protections, even if many other states act otherwise.[48]

The problem that prevents the court from finding an Emerging Consensus is not that states are not unanimously opposed to disenfranchising prisoners. It is that states are committed to fundamentally different conceptions of the right to vote. These different conceptions prevent the court from finding a true majority solution. Even if a large group of states end up sharing a similar policy—such as not allowing the disenfranchisement of all prisoners—they may do so for different reasons and therefore their decisions shouldn't be aggregated to form a majority opinion that constitutes an Emerging Consensus.[49] The court's decision in *Hirst* not to rely

---

47. *See* Helfer & Voeten, *supra* note 16, at 80. The legislative amendments in Ireland and Latvia to conform to the standards set by the ECtHR in the *Hirst* case, which are discussed in Section III *supra*, are examples of such a tendency with regard to prisoners' voting rights.

48. *See id.* at 106.

49. The policy of following the majority of states without waiting for a unanimous decision is theoretically justifiable by reference to the Condorcet Jury Theorem. This mathematical theorem postulates that when a group of sophisticated decision-makers has to choose between two options, the majority's decision is more likely to be correct than the decision of every individual decision-maker. *See* Shai Dothan, *The Optimal Use of Comparative Law*, 43 Denv. J. Int'l L. & Pol'y. 21 (2014) [hereinafter Dothan, 2014]; *see also* Eric Posner & Cass Sunstein, *The Law of Other States*, 59 Stan. L. Rev. 131 (2006) (arguing that states should use comparative law to learn from the experience of other states by utilizing the same Jury Theorem logic).

The reason Emerging Consensus is not a useful tool on this question is that states are not divided between two potential answers to one policy question. Instead, states are divided among three fundamentally different conceptions of the right to vote. The choice among these conceptions cannot be a reduced to a simple preference of A over B. Such problems cannot be solved by the Jury Theorem. Problems that involve multiple considerations can lead to several potential solutions that decision-makers would rate differently if they had to choose. It is impossible to establish a majority view in such situations, because the preferences of the group lack transitivity. This problem was acknowledged by Condorcet as an exception to his Jury Theorem.

A simple example can demonstrate the problems that may occur with the transitivity of states' preferences on prisoners' voting rights. While states may have very different ratings of preferences

exclusively on the presumed majority of the states and instead to rely on normative arguments—such as resisting indiscriminate measures that infringe important convention rights[50]—is therefore justified.

More generally speaking, international courts can and should use interpretive mechanisms to determine the proper boundaries of the right to vote under international law. This chapter only cautions against using the Emerging Consensus doctrine to assist with setting the boundaries of this right, because of the different existing conceptions of the right to vote.

from the hypothetical case mentioned here, it presents one *possible* set of preferences for states with the various conceptions of the right to vote described in the last part. Let A signify a policy of letting all prisoners vote, B a policy of disenfranchising only some prisoners under certain conditions, and C a policy of disenfranchising all prisoners. States that view voting as an inalienable right would opt for policy A. Their second best policy is difficult to guess, but if they want to let as many prisoners participate in politics as possible they would prefer B over C. The order of preferences for states who view voting as an inalienable right would therefore be A > B > C. States that view voting as a privilege and are committed to the view that prisoners violated the social contract and therefore are subject to civic death and should be excluded from politics would opt for policy C. *See* Susan Easton, *The Prisoner's Right to Vote and Civic Responsibility: Reaffirming the Social Contract?*, 56 PROBATION J. 224, 227–28 (2009) (presenting and criticizing the concept of "civic death"). Their second best policy is uncertain. It is plausible that they would prefer letting all prisoners vote to letting some of them vote. In their view, the declaration that all prisoners are *equally* unworthy of the vote is what matters. They may resist setting conditions that would allow some prisoners an equal part in the political game. They would therefore prefer A over B. The order of preferences for states who view voting as a privilege would therefore be C > A > B. Finally, states that view voting as a right that can—and should—be taken away from prisoners under certain conditions would clearly prefer policy B. Given a choice, they may prefer C over A. Their resistance to allowing certain types of prisoners to vote, combined with their readiness to disenfranchise on normative grounds, overcomes their preference for letting some prisoners maintain their political rights. The order of preferences for states who view voting as a revocable right would therefore be B > C > A.

In this hypothetical example two states prefer A over B, two states prefer B over C, and two states prefer C over A. If A > B > C > A, the preferences of the group are intransitive and a true majority view is impossible to establish. This simple mathematical illustration demonstrates a larger principle: when states support different conceptions that by their nature involve a host of competing considerations, establishing a majority for a certain policy choice may be meaningless. The majority would depend on the way the question is phrased. If the court starts by asking if states prefer partial disenfranchisement to universal suffrage, it will reach a different result than if it asks whether states prefer universal suffrage to complete disenfranchisement. As a result, when states are divided among fundamentally different conceptions, the issue isn't amenable to the use of the Emerging Consensus doctrine.

A similar problem may have arisen in A. v. Ireland, 2010-VI Eur. Ct. H.R. 185 where the court in paragraph 237 says that although many states in Europe allow access to abortion, they did not reach a consensus on whether the fetus is a person, and therefore the European majority cannot determine whether Ireland balanced correctly between the rights of the mother and the fetus. Other judges on the panel criticized the way the issue in question was delimited, suggesting that sometimes it is difficult to define the question about which Emerging Consensus has to be established. *See* Shai Dothan, *Judicial Deference Allows European Consensus to Emerge*, 18 CHI. J. INT'L. L. (forthcoming 2017).

50. Hirst v. United Kingdom (No. 2), 2005-IX Eur. Ct. H.R. 187 at para. 82.

The tensions between the different interpretations states give to the right to vote surface when states adopt contrasting policies regarding prisoners' suffrage. Maintaining these contesting interpretations of international law is challenged by the transnational dialogue between foreign courts. Courts are clearly aware of policies adopted in other jurisdictions and contend with their competing arguments as they form their national policies.[51] This process may, over time, erode the differences between national interpretations of international law.

The same note of caution applied to the use of Emerging Consensus in this area also applies to any national court that may consider looking to interpretations of the right to vote in other countries when it determines its own interpretation. If such courts attempt to follow the policies adopted by the majority of the states without acknowledging the underlying theories that support their interpretations of this international human right, they may opt for policies most states would actually view as contradictory to their conceptions of the right to vote.[52]

Besides international courts' intervention and transnational dialogue, the differences between the interpretations of states to the right to vote can also be eroded by new international instruments, such as treaties, United Nations resolutions, or international declarations. These international sources may fill gaps in the content of states' international obligations and exclude certain interpretations of international voting rights as no longer acceptable.[53]

51. See Eyal Benvenisti, Reclaiming Democracy: The Strategic Uses of Foreign and International Law by National Courts, 102 AM. J. INT'L L. 241, 255–56 (2008) (describing the growing phenomenon of national courts citing each other and learning from each other).

52. When national courts try to follow the policies of the majority of the states in the world, another problem may arise—courts may follow states who did not make their policies independently, but rather followed other states in turn, forming a so-called "informational cascade." This problem is acknowledged by Posner and Sunstein who advocate the use of comparative law. See Posner & Sunstein, supra note 49, at 162–63. Elsewhere, I argued that when the ECtHR uses Emerging Consensus it can resolve this problem by letting each state decide independently and then setting policy according to the majority of the independent choices made by the states. See Dothan, 2014, supra note 49.

53. See Reuven Ziegler, Legal Outlier, Again? U.S. Felon Suffrage, Comparative and International Human Rights Perspectives, 29 B.U. INT'L L. J. 197, 253 (2011) (arguing that such developments in international law already make blanket bans on the voting of convicts and disenfranchisement of ex-convicts incompatible with international obligations).

19

When Law Migrates

Refugees in Comparative International Law

JILL I. GOLDENZIEL[*]

I. INTRODUCTION

Record numbers of migrants and refugees have crossed the high seas to reach Europe, Australia, and elsewhere in the 2010s. Europe is now facing its worst displacement crisis since World War II, largely as a result of migration by sea. In response, the European Union (EU), its member states, and Australia have launched programs to interdict migrants at sea. This practice of migrant interdiction has been particularly controversial. In this law enforcement activity, states' military or police vehicles halt irregular migrants before they reach land and return them to their country of departure.[1] Wealthy states have employed interdiction at sea to avoid their own stringent immigration rules and processes. States may also use this practice to circumvent their international legal obligations to asylum seekers and refugees.[2]

The primary international legal issue implicated by interdiction at sea is whether it violates the principle of non-refoulement, or not returning a refugee back to a place where his or her life would be endangered. Non-refoulement lies at the core of the 1951 Convention Relating to the Status of Refugees and its 1967 Protocol ("Convention"), to which the United States, Australia, and nearly all European states are parties.[3] Most commentators consider non-refoulement to be a *jus cogens*

* Thanks to Sarah Bidinger, Noah Feldman, Michael Pine, Anthea Roberts, Kevin Rudd, Mila Versteeg, and participants in the 2014 Sokol Colloquium in International Law at the University of Virginia.

1. Anja Klug & Tim Howe, *The Concept of State Jurisdiction and the Applicability of the Non-refoulement Principle to Extraterritorial Interception Measure*, in EXTRATERRITORIAL IMMIGRATION CONTROL: LEGAL CHALLENGES, 69, 69–70 (Bernard Ryan & Valsamis Mitsilegas, eds., 2010).

2. *See id.*

3. Convention Relating to the Status of Refugees art. 33, July 28, 1951, 189 U.N.T.S. 137 [hereinafter "Convention"]; 1967 Protocol Relating to the Status of Refugees, Jan. 31, 1967, 606 U.N.T.S. 267

norm.[4] The Convention exempts states from the obligation of non-refoulement only when individual refugees present threats to national security or public order, or when an asylum seeker has been involved in war crimes or criminal acts.[5] International refugee law thus conflicts with the right of a sovereign state to expel aliens, and demands that states give certain protections to non-citizens.

Faced with tremendous numbers of people wishing to enter, wealthier states have increasingly restricted their borders to protect national security. The challenge of balancing national security interests with international human rights commitments has fallen to courts. Cases involving interdiction at sea and non-refoulement have reached the highest courts of the United States, Australia, and the European Court of Human Rights (ECtHR).[6] Each court has interpreted international refugee law differently in its jurisprudence, creating a discrepancy as to what non-refoulement actually requires. A major contrast has emerged between the US and Australian approach and the European approach to interdiction at sea. The US and Australian courts have determined that their practices of interdiction at sea did not violate non-refoulement or their own domestic laws involving refugee protection. More recently, the ECtHR determined that Italy's practices of interdiction at sea violated the principle of non-refoulement, causing Italy and the EU to change their policies. International refugee law, and these courts' interpretations of it, continuously plays a major role in shaping the refugee and asylum law of nation-states. As states increasingly develop creative solutions to manage migration, domestic courts will play a greater role in interpreting international refugee law.

This chapter will analyze how the concept of non-refoulement has been treated in domestic courts. Drawing on cases from the United States, Australia, and the ECtHR, this chapter will compare how the Convention has been interpreted across countries and over time. Its object is to compare when and how courts creatively avoid non-refoulement and when courts uphold a stricter interpretation of the principle. Comparing state jurisprudence on this topic helps determine what international refugee law actually requires of states.[7] More broadly, this analysis sheds light on the question of what extraterritorial obligations human rights law demands.

This chapter employs the techniques of comparative law to illuminate our understanding of what international refugee law, although ostensibly uniform, means when applied in various jurisdictions. These country cases were selected because

---

[hereinafter "1967 Protocol"]. The United States is a party to the 1967 Protocol, which incorporates the Convention.

4. *See* Jean Allain, *The Jus Cogens Nature of Non-refoulement*, 13 INT'L J. REFUGEE L. 533 (2001).

5. Convention, *supra* note 3, at arts. 1(F)(a)–(b).

6. Sale v. Haitian Centers Council, 509 U.S. 155 (1993) [hereinafter, "HCC"]; Ruddock v. Vadarlis (2001) FCA 1329 (Austl.); Hirsi Jamaa and Others v. Italy, App. No. 27765/09 (Feb. 23, 2012) (Eur. Ct. H.R.); M.S.S. v. Belgium and Greece, App. No. 30696/09 (Jan. 21, 2011) (Eur. Ct. H.R.).

7. While executive or legislative interpretations of the Convention, or national legislation implementing it, may also exist, discussion of these important units of analysis for comparative international law lies beyond the scope of this chapter.

they are common asylum destinations for migrants traveling by sea.[8] Moreover, their state practice has been influential in the development of international law, particularly refugee law, and the cases' fact patterns present similar circumstances that enable useful cross-jurisdictional comparison.

This chapter will proceed in three sections. Section II will discuss the tensions between the principle of non-refoulement and practices of interdiction at sea. Section III will review major cases on interdiction at sea that have reached high courts in the United States, Australia, and Europe. Section IV will analyze the problems that differing interpretations of non-refoulement create within the international human rights regime, and conclude with the implications of these cases for understanding the extraterritorial reach of human rights law.

II. THE OBLIGATION OF NON-REFOULEMENT IN INTERNATIONAL LAW

The *jus cogens* norm of non-refoulement binds states not to return anyone who meets the Convention's definition of refugee, or any asylum-seeker awaiting refugee status determination, to his country of origin. Non-refoulement does not require states to allow asylum-seekers to enter; it only requires that refugees not be returned to a place where they would be endangered. Most state practice has supported the idea that non-refoulement means non-return and non-rejection at the border.[9] However, where exactly those borders begin is unclear when migrants are interdicted at sea.

In the modern environment of mass migration, compliance with non-refoulement and the Refugee Convention creates a tremendous burden for states. The requirement of protection while claims are being processed has overwhelmed legal infrastructures, even in the most developed nations. The United States, Europe, and Australia, for example, have built massive systems of detention centers to house migrants. States have also adopted creative measures to comply with the letter of non-refoulement. For example, to curtail migration, Western states have employed restrictive visa requirements, carrier sanctions, safe third country designations, readmission agreements, safe zones inside conflict areas, and programs of interdiction at sea.[10] Many of these policies have been criticized by UNHCR, the Office of the United Nations High Commissioner on Refugees, for amounting to violations of human rights or non-refoulement.

To analyze the obligation of non-refoulement, courts must confront the contested issue of when a state's human rights commitments under international law apply extraterritorially. States engaged in interdiction at sea first encounter refugees in offshore locations. The question arises as to whether states are bound by

---

8. *See* Katerina Linos, *Methodological Guidance: How to Select and Develop Comparative International Law Case Studies* (this volume).

9. Guy Goodwin-Gill & Jane McAdam, The Refugee in International Law 208 (3d ed., 2007).

10. Deborah Anker, Joan Fitzpatrick & Andrew Shacknove, *Crisis and Cure: A Reply to Hathaway/Neve and Schuck*, 11 Harv. Hum. Rts. J. 295, 297 (1998).

non-refoulement when they are technically operating outside their own territory. Cases involving refugee rights, then, have important implications for states' extra-territorial obligations under other human rights instruments.

III. CASES INVOLVING NON-REFOULEMENT

A. United States: *Sale v. Haitian Centers Council*

The 1993 case of *Sale v. Haitian Centers Council* is the only one that has brought the principle of non-refoulement before the US Supreme Court.[11] In the 1980s and 1990s, pro-democracy Haitians involved with the Convention for Democratic Unity movement (KID) worked to put Jean-Bertrand Aristide in power by advocating for democratic elections in Haiti. In September 1981, the US and Haitian governments signed a bilateral agreement creating a cooperative inter-diction program.[12] The US Coast Guard began interdicting Haitian vessels and interviewing the migrants aboard to determine whether they had credible fears of political persecution, and were therefore eligible for refugee status. The Coast Guard brought to the United States those who were "screened-in" and returned all others to Haiti.

In 1990, following UN-supervised elections, Aristide became president. But democracy was short-lived. Aristide was ousted in a brutal coup on September 29–30, 1991. In its immediate aftermath, hundreds of KID supporters were killed, kid-napped, jailed, tortured, illegally detained, attacked with machetes, beaten, or had their property destroyed.[13] Thousands of democracy supporters fled and sought refuge in Cuba or the United States. Their flight was further fueled by a severe economic downturn after the Organization of American States instituted a trade embargo against Haiti to protest the coup.[14]

During the six months following October 1991, the US Coast Guard interdicted 34,000 Haitians.[15] Initially, the Coast Guard conducted informal exclusion hearings for the Haitians aboard US cutters, pursuant to the 1981 agreement.[16] But the sheer number of fleeing Haitians soon made screenings at sea impossible. After failed attempts to send Haitians to other Caribbean countries, the United States set up a makeshift camp at Guantanamo Bay to house Haitians while it conducted exclusion hearings.[17] However, the facilities at Guantanamo could only accommodate 12,500

---

11. *HCC*, 509 U.S. at 155.

12. Haiti-United States: Agreement to Stop Clandestine Migration of Residents of Haiti to the United States, U.S.-Haiti, Sept. 23, 1981, 20 I.L.M. 1198; implemented by Exec. Order No. 12,324, 46 Fed. Reg. 48,109 (Sept. 29, 1981).

13. BRANDT GOLDSTEIN, STORMING THE COURT 12 (2005).

14. *See id.*

15. *HCC*, 509 U.S. at 163.

16. *See id.*

17. *Id.* at 163.

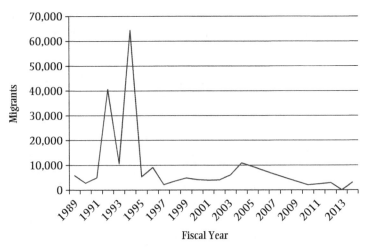

Figure 19.1 US migrant sea interdiction 1989–2014.

persons, and soon became overcrowded. On May 22, 1992, President George H.W. Bush issued Executive Order 12807, authorizing the Coast Guard to summarily repatriate Haitians without screening. Figure 19.1 shows the overall number of migrants interdicted at sea by the United States for each year during the relevant period.

A group of these Haitians, represented by a team from Yale Law School led by Professor Harold Koh, sued the US government. They claimed the United States had violated its own domestic immigration laws and the Convention by forcibly refouling them without individualized processing.[18] At the heart of the litigation was section 243(h) of the Immigration and Nationality Act (INA), which states:

> [t]he Attorney General shall not deport or return any alien ... to a country
> if the Attorney General determines that such alien's life or freedom would be
> threatened in such country on account of race, religion, nationality, member-
> ship in a particular social group, or political opinion.[19]

This provision was intentionally drafted to mirror the non-refoulement obligations in the Convention.

The Haitians prevailed in the Second Circuit, and the government appealed the case to the Supreme Court. Meanwhile, the Haitian crisis became a major issue in the presidential campaign between Bill Clinton and George H.W. Bush. While a candidate, Clinton criticized the interdiction program and vowed to overturn it.

---

18. *See* Harold H. Koh & Michael J. Wishnie, *The Story of* Sale v. Haitian Centers Council: *Guantanamo and Refoulement, in* HUMAN RIGHTS ADVOCACY STORIES (Deena Hurwitz et al. eds., 2009).

19. 8 U.S.C. § 1253(h)(1) (1988 Supp. IV).

Once elected, upon news that Haitians were building boats in preparation for his inauguration, Clinton reversed course and endorsed the interdiction program.[20]

1. The Decision

In an 8-1 opinion, the Supreme Court held that neither section 243(h) of the INA nor Article 33 of the Convention barred the United States' program of interdiction at sea. Writing for the Court, Justice Stevens first determined that section 243(h) limits the actions of the attorney general only, and does not apply to the president or the Coast Guard.[21] Second, the Court held that the INA applies "only to aliens who reside in or have arrived at the border of the U.S.," and not extraterritorially.[22] The Court cited the presumption against extraterritoriality in American law and the fact that the INA itself makes no reference to extraterritorial application.[23] The Court explained that Congress's choice to use both the words "return" and "deport" together in the 1980 Amendment demonstrates that the statute is not meant to apply extraterritorially, as the use of two words refers to both deportation and exclusion proceedings.[24]

Turning to the Convention, the Court held that the United States did not incur an extraterritorial obligation by acceding to the 1967 Protocol. The Court found that neither Congress nor the executive branch explicitly mentioned assuming any extraterritorial obligations when the United States acceded to the Protocol, and therefore, the United States could not have intended to do so.[25] First, the Court noted that Article 33.2 of the Convention contains an "explicit reference ... to the country in which the alien is located."[26] If the prohibition against refoulement applied on the high seas, "no nation could invoke the second paragraph's exception

---

20. *See* David Martin, *YLS Sale Symposium: Interdiction of Asylum Seekers—The Realms of Policy and Law in Refugee Protection*, OPINIO JURIS (Mar. 15, 2014), http://opiniojuris.org/2014/03/15/yls-sale-symposium-interdiction-asylum-seekers-realms-policy-law-refugee-protection/; reversal discussed in Koh & Wishnie, *supra* note 18, at 398.

21. HCC, 509 U.S. 155, 171–74 (1993).

22. *Id.* at 160.

23. *See id.* at 173.

24. *See id.* at 174–75.

25. *Id.* at 178.

26. *Id.* at 179. Article 33, section 1 of the Convention reads:

> No Contracting State shall expel or return ("refouler") a refugee in any manner whatsoever to the frontiers of territories where his life or freedom would be threatened on account of his race, religion, nationality, membership of a particular social group or political opinion.

Article 33, section 2 of the Convention reads:

> The benefit of the present provision may not, however, be claimed by a refugee whom there are reasonable grounds for regarding as a danger to the security of the country in which he is, or who, having been convicted by a final judgment of a particularly serious crime, constitutes a danger to the community of that country.

with respect to an alien there."[27] In the Court's view, extraterritorial application of Article 33.1 would "create an absurd abnormality: dangerous aliens on the high seas would be entitled to the benefits of [the prohibition against refoulement in Article 33.1] while those residing in the country that sought to expel them would not."[28] The Court thus read a geographic limitation into the prohibition against refoulement in Article 33.1 based on the language in Article 33.2. They decided that if the exception to the rule of non-refoulement is geographically limited to the territory of the country that the refugees are in, the rule must have that limitation as well.

The Court also reasoned that Article 33.1 uses both "expel" and "return ("refouler"),'' and that "refouler" has a legal meaning narrower than its common meaning.[29] "Refouler" better translates to "repulse," "repel," "drive back," or "expel," implying that "return," as used in the Convention, "means a defensive act of resistance or exclusion at a border rather than an act of transporting someone to a particular destination."[30] Thus, it concludes that the Protocol was not intended to apply extraterritorially. After interpreting the text of the INA and the Convention, the Court further supported its argument by looking to the Convention's *travaux préparatoires*. Three non-US drafters had stated that they did not intend Article 33 to apply extraterritorially.[31] While nothing suggests that other signatories agreed with these delegates, the Court adopted their position.[32]

2. Justice Blackmun's Lone Dissent

Justice Blackmun issued a blistering dissent rejecting the majority's interpretation of both section 243(h) of the INA and especially the Convention's prohibition against refoulement. Blackmun noted that the Refugee Act of 1980 indisputably was amended to align US immigration law with the Convention.[33] The plain language of Article 33.1 does not include any geographical limitations. In Blackmun's view, "The terms are unambiguous. Vulnerable refugees shall not be returned. The language is clear, and the command is straightforward; that should be the end of the inquiry."[34] Until this litigation, he said, "the Government consistently acknowledged that the Convention applied on the high seas."[35] The prohibition against refoulement, however translated, clearly "prohibits the Government's actions."[36] He

---

27. *HCC*, 509 U.S. at 179–80.

28. *Id.* at 179–80.

29. *See id.* at 180.

30. *Id.* at 182.

31. *See id.* at 183–87.

32. *See id.* at 187.

33. *See id.* at 190.

34. *Id.* at 190.

35. *Id.*

36. *Id.* at 192–93.

noted that the statements of the Convention's drafters are "not entitled to deference, were never voted on or adopted, probably represent a minority view, and . . . do not address the issue in this case."[37]

Similarly, Justice Blackmun found section 243(h) of the INA to be unambiguous.[38] He found that the Coast Guard is obviously an agent of the attorney general, who is bound not to return refugees.[39] Moreover, by deleting the words "within the United States" from the pre-1980 version of section 243(h), Congress clearly meant for it to apply extraterritorially.[40] He stated that rather than the presumption against extraterritoriality, the Court should have relied on the *Charming Betsy* canon, the idea that a congressional act should never be construed to violate the law of nations if any alternative construction is possible.[41] Invoking the Convention's enactment in response to the refoulement of Jewish refugees during World War II, Blackmun ended on a cautionary note:

> The refugees attempting to escape from Haiti do not claim a right of admission to this country. They do not even argue that the Government has no right to intercept their boats. They demand only that the United States, land of refugees and guardian of freedom, cease forcibly driving them back to detention, abuse, and death. That is a modest plea, vindicated by the treaty and the statute. We should not close our ears to it.[42]

These words would later inspire European justices to adopt his conclusion.

3. Impact

The *Sale* decision permits US presidents to utilize interdiction at sea whenever it is convenient for restricting migration. In December 1993, President Clinton agreed to change the direct return policy after intensive lobbying by human rights organizations. The Inter-American Commission of Human Rights and UNHCR condemned the US interdiction program.[43] Despite this, after Aristide's second removal from power, President George W. Bush reinstated the program.

The US interdiction at sea program is said to have inspired similar policies in Australia and Europe. However, Australian and European courts have interpreted non-refoulement to expand it beyond what the US Supreme Court requires. The ECtHR explicitly criticized the *Sale* decision in its own opinion on non-refoulement.

---

37. *Id.* at 198.

38. *See id.* at 199.

39. *See id.* at 200–01.

40. *Id.* at 202.

41. *See id.* at 207.

42. *Id.* at 207.

43. *See* Inter-Am. Comm'n H.R., Report No 51/96, ¶ 171 (1997); Brief for UNHCR as Amici Curiae Supporting Respondents, Sale v. Haitian Centers Council, 509 U.S. 155 (1993) (No. 92-344).

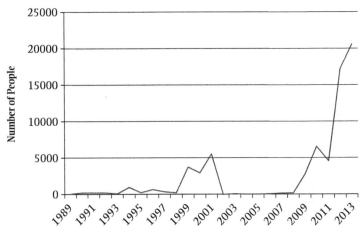

Figure 19.2 Australia asylum-seekers arriving by boat 1989–2013.

B. Australia: The *Tampa* Case

Australian courts have sought to avoid reaching Australia's commitments under the Convention. Their controversial human rights decisions take place against the backdrop of heated political debate. Australian policy toward "boat people" has been a major issue in national politics in recent decades. The proximity of its outlying islands to Southeast Asia makes it a convenient destination for migrants and human smugglers. A favorite landing spot is Christmas Island, an Australian external territory that lies only 360 kilometers south of Java and 2,600 kilometers northwest of Perth. Figure 19.2 shows the overall number of asylum-seekers arriving by sea for each year between 1989 and 2013.

In 2001, a very controversial case reached the Federal Court of Australia, the highest federal court of appeals before the High Court. On August 26, 2001, the *MV Tampa*, a Norwegian commercial ship, rescued 433 people from a sinking craft in international waters near Christmas Island. The passengers on the shoddy, overcrowded boat were mostly Afghans and Iraqi asylum-seekers who had been smuggled to Australia via Indonesia. The *Tampa*'s captain determined that some of the migrants needed urgent medical attention and sought help from Australian authorities.

When no assistance arrived, the *Tampa* initially headed toward Indonesia, but turned for Christmas Island when five passengers threatened suicide. One hundred thirty-six boats sailing from Indonesia had been allowed to enter Australia in the preceding 12 months, but the government refused to allow the *Tampa* to land.[44] Commentators have speculated that the Liberal government was reluctant to allow

---

44. Susan Kneebone, *Controlling Migration by Sea: The Australian Case, in* 21 EXTRATERRITORIAL IMMIGRATION CONTROL, *supra* note 1, at 357.

additional asylum-seekers to enter in a highly visible way so close to an election.[45] As one cartoonist noted, the 433 people on the *Tampa* represented millions of votes.[46] In the ensuing litigation, the government did not explain why it singled out the *Tampa*, but admitted that it did not want the passengers to enter Australia's migration zone, where they could claim protection under the Convention.[47]

The Australian Secretary of the Department of Immigration and Multicultural Affairs determined that Indonesia and Norway were responsible for the passengers, and so refused to allow the ship to land. Instead, 45 Australian Special Armed Services troops (SAS) stormed the ship as the public watched. The passengers expressed their desire to seek peaceful asylum. The SAS forces responded by controlling the *Tampa* for more than a week, refusing to allow it on Australian soil, and even closing the harbor and cutting off communication with the passengers. By this time, the case had attracted international attention. UNHCR called the governments of Australia, Norway, and Indonesia to Geneva to try to broker a solution.

When talks broke down, Australia arranged for the rescuees (as the Australian courts would come to call them) to be transferred to Nauru. No one explained this plan to the passengers in their native language, and no processing system was established in Nauru. On September 3, the passengers were transferred to an Australian ship. At this point, an Australian NGO filed a lawsuit on behalf of the passengers in Australian Federal Court, arguing that they had been unlawfully detained aboard the *Tampa* and petitioning for their right to enter Australia.

1. THE DECISION

In what became known as the "*Tampa* Case," the Federal Court avoided the issue of non-refoulement. The court held that the government must release the rescuees onto mainland Australia if they refused to go to Nauru or New Zealand, which had by then agreed to take some of the passengers. The court held that the removal of aliens is governed entirely by statute, namely the Migration Act of 1958, leaving no room for the exercise of prerogative power to remove particular aliens. Although it could easily have done so, the court did not address the issue of refoulement, the asylum claims of the rescuees, or the potential refugee claims among them. The Convention was not mentioned, and the plaintiffs were referred to as "rescuees" throughout the decision, a peculiar term that suggests the court wished to avoid the terms "asylum-seeker" or "refugee."

The decision was quickly appealed to the full Federal Court and became titled *Ruddock v. Vadarlis.*[48] In the meantime, hours after the Federal Court's initial decision, two airplanes struck the twin towers of the World Trade Center in New York, changing both public opinion and immigration policies on the entry of Afghans and

45. *See id.*

46. *See id.*

47. *See id.*

48. Ruddock v. Vadarlis (2001) FCA 1329 (Austl.).

Iraqis. With an election looming, the Liberal Government needed to curry votes by appearing tough on refugees.[49]

On September 18, 2001, the full Federal Court reversed the panel decision. It held that the Australian Minister of Immigration Affairs acted within his executive power under section 61 of the Australian Constitution by preventing the rescuees from landing on the mainland. The Migration Act of 1958 did not abrogate this power. In the court's view, Australian authorities did not restrict the rescuees' freedom, as they were free to go to a third country. Therefore, the refugees were not detained by Australia, but actually had been detained by the captain of the *Tampa*. The odd term "rescuee" was again used throughout the decision. The rescuees' asylum claims and the question of whether Australia had violated its obligations under the Convention were never mentioned. Petitioners' appeal to the High Court of Australia was subsequently denied. Implicitly criticizing the decision, UNHCR awarded the *Tampa's* captain its Nansen Refugee Award for outstanding work on behalf of the forcibly displaced.

2. IMPACT

After "The *Tampa* Affair," the Howard government responded by adopting the ominously named "Pacific Solution." Commentators have speculated that the US-Caribbean interdiction program and the *Sale* decision inspired this plan for interdiction of migrants at sea.[50] Seven new parliamentary acts restricted the entry of aliens into Australia and validated all actions taken in the wake of the *Tampa* Affair.[51] They developed a new category of territory, the "excise offshore place," which included territories outside of the mainland such as Christmas Island. An unlawful alien entering via an excise offshore place would now be identified as an "offshore entry person" and prohibited from submitting a valid visa application unless the Minister of Immigration deems it in the public interest. Authorized by the legislature, the Australian Defense Forces introduced Operation Reflex to interdict boats carrying potential asylum-seekers before they reached Australian territory.

The acts also allowed Australia to identify third countries where they could redirect offshore entry persons. Sending asylum-seekers to a safe third country does not violate the principle of non-refoulement if the third country is safe for them and no danger of refoulement exists there. Australia has identified Nauru, Papua New Guinea, and Cambodia as places to send asylum-seekers, despite protests from human rights groups that conditions there are unsatisfactory. Once in these third countries, Australia's Migration Act no longer applies, so aliens could submit a valid

---

49. Penelope Mathew, *Australian Refugee Protection in the Wake of the* Tampa, 96 AM. J. INT'L L. 661, 662 (2002).

50. *See id.* at 666.

51. *Border Protection (Validation and Enforcement Powers) Act 2001* (Cth) (Austl.); *Migration Amendment (Excision from Migration Zone) Act 2001* (Cth); *Migration Amendment (Excision from Migration Zone) (Consequential Provisions) Act 2001* (Cth); Migration Legislation Amendment Act (No. 1) 2001 (Cth); *Migration Legislation Amendment Act* (No. 5) 2001 (Cth); *Migration Legislation Amendment Act* (No. 6) 2001 (Cth).

visa application. However, these aliens would be limited to certain visa categories and unable to apply for protection visas. In other words, asylum-seekers directed to third countries would never receive refugee status in Australia.

After the 2008 election, Prime Minister Kevin Rudd's Labor government suspended the Pacific Solution, although migration had dropped dramatically during the years it had been in effect, per the figures in the chart above.[52] While the policy was suspended, the High Court of Australia clarified the rights of asylum-seekers under the Pacific Solution. In the *M61 Case*, the Court held that asylum-seekers detained in excised offshore places are individuals to whom Australia owes protection, and therefore are entitled to procedural fairness and access to courts.[53] In *M70*, the High Court held that two offshore entry persons who claimed to be refugees under the Convention could not be released to Malaysia without processing of their refugee claims in Australia.[54] The Court reasoned that the Minister of Immigration did not have the power to enter into an agreement with Malaysia to release asylum-seekers there, as Australia could not ensure that Malaysia would give adequate and fair protection to asylum-seekers. Therefore, sending asylum-seekers to Malaysia would potentially violate Australia's non-refoulement obligations.

In the wake of an influx of boat people and a number of publicized deaths at sea, the succeeding Labor government reinstated the Pacific Solution, reopening the Nauru and Manus Island detention centers for offshore processing of asylum-seekers, striking a new agreement with Papua New Guinea for third-country processing, and giving unauthorized maritime arrivals no possibility of obtaining Australian residency. Prime Minister Tony Abbott defeated Kevin Rudd in 2014 on a campaign promise to "stop the boats."

So far, the High Court has largely upheld Abbott's policies regarding asylum-seekers, although they have come under fire domestically and internationally. In January 2015, the High Court upheld Australia's interdiction of 157 Sri Lankan asylum-seekers, holding them on a windowless boat for a month, and subsequently transferring them to Nauru.[55] The court held that interdiction at sea and third country-processing were legal under the Maritime Powers Act, but that Australia was bound to ensure the asylum-seekers' safety in any country to which they were transferred. The court declined to reach the question of Australia's non-refoulement obligations, but several justices raised concerns about the practice of summary return. The court also left open the question of whether the Australian government has the power to turn back the boats. UNHCR promptly criticized the decision.[56]

52. *See* Ariane Rummery, *Australia's "Pacific Solution" Draws to a Close*, UNHCR, (Feb. 11, 2008) http://www.unhcr.org/cgi-bin/texis/vtx/search?page=search&docid=47b04d074&query=australia.

53. Plaintiff M61/2010E v. Commonwealth of Australia & ORS; Plaintiff M69 of 2010 v. Commonwealth of Australia & ORS (2010) HCA 41 (Austl.).

54. Plaintiff M70/2011 v. Minister for Immigration and Citizenship (2011) HCA 32 (Austl.).

55. CPCF v. Minister for Immigration and Border Protection & ANOR (2015) HCA 1 (Austl.).

56. UNHCR, UNHCR Legal Position, Feb. 4, 2015, http://www.unhcr.org/54d1e4ac9.html.

Thus, in the wake of *Ruddock v. Vadarlis*, Australia has continued to experiment with migration-control policies involving interdiction at sea and extraterritorial processing by third countries. Its High Court has repeatedly held that Australia's non-refoulement obligations extend to ensuring that third countries will not subject asylum-seekers to ill treatment and will not refoule them. However, *Ruddock* still stands, and despite repeated opportunities to do so, neither the Australian Federal nor High Court has addressed whether Australia's interdiction at sea practices conflict with its non-refoulement obligations. On October 7, 2015, the Court heard arguments on the constitutionality of the Australian government's agreement for third-country processing in Papua New Guinea. If successful, this case could end Australia's entire offshore processing program, and would have implications for Australia's practices of interdiction at sea.[57]

C. European Court of Human Rights: *Hirsi Jamaa*

Faced with a massive influx of asylum-seekers crossing the Mediterranean, many European states have sought to restrict their borders. In 2003, the EU enacted the Dublin Agreement, designed to discourage migration by sending asylum-seekers back to their country of entry within Europe for processing.[58] In 2004, the EU also created an extensive border patrol agency called Frontex.[59] NGOs have repeatedly accused Frontex of refoulement for its interdiction and return of migrants at sea.[60] Southern European states, particularly Italy and Greece, are the most frequent points of entry for migrants. Both have built massive detention centers to house asylum-seekers while they await processing. UNHCR and NGOs have criticized Greece, in particular, for lengthy processing times and unsafe conditions for asylum-seekers. Cases against Italy and Greece involving improper treatment of asylum-seekers have come before the ECtHR.

The ECtHR interprets non-refoulement more liberally than courts in the United States and Australia. The ECtHR cannot consider violations of the non-refoulement provision in the Convention directly. However, Article 3 of the European Convention on Human Rights (ECHR) prohibits the related practices of

---

57. Madeleine Morris, *Asylum Seekers Launch High Court Challenge to Legality of Offshore Detention System*, May 14, 2015, http://www.abc.net.au/news/2015-05-14/asylum-seekers-launch-high-court-challenge/6471376. As of this writing, Australia has agreed to close the Manus Island detention center following the Papua New Guinea Supreme Court's ruling that the detention program there was illegal. It is unclear what will happen to this suit as a result. *See* Brett Cole, *Australia Will Close Detention Center on Manus Island but Still Won't Accept Asylum-Seekers*, N.Y. TIMES (Aug. 17, 2016).

58. *See* Council Regulation 343/2003, 2003 O.J. (L/50/1), sometimes known as "Dublin II."

59. Council Regulation (EC) 2007/2004, 2004 O.J. (L 349/1) authorized Frontex, which became operational on October 3, 2005.

60. *See, e.g.*, 41st Meeting of the UNHCR ExCom Standing Committee, March 4–6, 2008, NGO Statement on International Protection: The High Commissioner's Dialogue on Protection Challenges.

torture and inhuman or degrading treatment or punishment. In 2011, the ECtHR issued a decision similar to the *M70* decision of the Australian High Court in *M.S.S. v. Belgium and Greece*.[61] Belgium had sent an asylum-seeker back to Greece, his point of first entry to Europe, without ensuring that Greece would adequately protect him, process his claims, and not put him at risk for refoulement. The ECtHR held that both Belgium and Greece were responsible for violations under Article 3 of the ECHR. In doing so, the ECtHR effectively held that Article 3 of the ECHR prohibits refoulement.

In 2012, *Hirsi Jamaa and Others v. Italy* became the first ECtHR case to address migrant interdiction at sea.[62] Italy and Libya had signed a Treaty of Friendship, Partnership and Cooperation in 2008 that included provisions for mutual assistance in fighting irregular migration.[63] Italy and Libya agreed to joint operations in the Mediterranean to interdict and return boats carrying illegal migrants.[64] Data from Italian immigration officials show that the number of irregular migrants arriving from North Africa decreased since this Treaty was adopted.[65]

Human rights organizations decried Italy's interdiction practices.[66] NGOs argued that the policy subjected returned migrants to ill treatment in Libya, amounting to a violation of ECHR Article 3.[67] Further, Italian authorities openly acknowledged that they do not engage in formal identification and processing of migrants intercepted at sea, even though Article 4 of the ECHR's Protocol No. 4 bans collective expulsion of aliens.[68]

In 2009, 11 Somali nationals and 13 Eritrean nationals brought suit before the ECtHR alleging violation of these two articles of the ECHR. The migrants had been among 200 individuals aboard three vessels crossing the Mediterranean from Libya.[69] On May 6, 2009, the Italian police and coast guard intercepted them in

---

61. M.S.S. v. Belgium and Greece, *supra* note 6.

62. *See Hirsi Jamaa, supra* note 6.

63. *See id.* at § 19–20.

64. By July 30, 2009, Italy had pushed back 602 migrants to Libya and 23 to Algeria. *European Committee for the Prevention of Torture and Inhuman or Degrading Treatment or Punishment Report to the Italian Government on the July 27–31, 2009 Visit to Italy*, CPT (Apr. 28, 2010) [hereinafter "CPT Report"].

65. *See* Violeta Moreno-Lax, *Seeking Asylum in the Mediterranean: Against a Fragmentary Reading of EU Member States' Obligations Accruing at Sea*, 23 INT'L J. REFUGEE L. 174, 184 (2011).

66. *See, e.g.,* UNHCR, Press Release: UNHCR Deeply Concerned over Returns from Italy to Libya (May 7, 2009); *Italy/Libya: Migrants Describe Forced Returns, Abuse: EU Should Press Italy to Halt Illegal Forced Returns to Libya*, HUMAN RIGHTS WATCH (Sept. 21, 2009) http://www.hrw.org/news/2009/09/17/italylibya-migrants-describe-forced-returns-abuse); CPT Report, *supra* note 64.

67. *See* Moreno-Lax, *supra* note 65, at 207; *see* Convention for the Protection of Human Rights and Fundamental Freedoms art. 3, Apr. 11, 1950, E.T.S 5 [hereinafter "ECHR"].

68. *See* CPT Report, *supra* note 64, at ¶ 13.

69. *See Hirsi Jamaa, supra* note 6, at §9.

international waters approximately 35 nautical miles south of Lampedusa. The forces transferred them to military ships, where their personal effects and identity documents were confiscated. Ten hours later, the Italian forces turned the migrants over to the Libyan authorities in the Port of Tripoli.[70] Aboard the ship, Italian officials did not attempt to identify, interview, or process the migrants, nor did they inform them of their destination before returning them to Libya.[71]

Two of the applicants later died in unknown circumstances. Fourteen others were granted refugee status by UNHCR offices in Tripoli, and brought suit before the ECtHR. The applicants argued that Article 3 of the ECHR and Article 4 of Protocol No. 4 required Italy to allow them to make a claim for asylum and to review their claims on an individual basis, and prohibited Italy from returning them to a state where they might be subject to mistreatment.[72] The applicants further argued that they were arbitrarily refouled, and had been denied the opportunity to challenge their refoulement or seek refugee protection under international law.

1. THE DECISION

The applicants first had to prove that they had standing before the ECtHR because they were interdicted on the high seas. They brought suit under Article 34 of the ECHR, which permits "applications from any person, non-governmental organization or group of individuals claiming to be the victim of a violation by one of the High Contracting Parties." Italy argued that its actions were not subject to the ECHR because they occurred outside of Italian territory and because Italy did not exert absolute and excessive control over the applicants as the Italian forces did not use force.[73] Moreover, they did not involve a "maritime police action" because they were simply rendering the humanitarian aid required by the United Nations Convention on the Law of the Sea (UNCLOS) and the Convention on Maritime Search and Rescue (SAR).[74]

The Court held that it had jurisdiction and the migrants had standing. Relying on a standard developed in other cases involving extraterritoriality, the Court held that Italy had exerted "effective control" over the migrants and their craft when they took them aboard the military vessel flying the Italian flag.[75] The alleged violations took place entirely aboard the Italian ships. Thus, the fact that they were intercepted on the high seas did not remove them from jurisdiction.[76] Regarding Italy's UNCLOS and SAR arguments, the Court pointedly stated that Italy could not "circumvent

---

70. *See id.* at §§ 10–12.

71. *See id.* at § 11.

72. *See id.* at §§ 84–88.

73. *See id.* at § 64.

74. U.N. Convention on the Law of the Sea art. 98, Dec. 10, 1982, 1833 U.N.T.S. 3.

75. *Hirsi Jamaa, supra* note 6, at § 64.

76. *See id.* at §§ 76–82.

its 'jurisdiction' under the Convention by describing the events at issue as rescue operations. . . . "[77]

Moving to the merits, the Court found that Italy violated Article 3 and Article 13 of the ECHR and Article 4 of the Protocol. The Court found Italy violated Article 3 by returning the migrants to Libya, where they were at risk of inhuman and degrading treatment. Moreover, in Libya they would be exposed to the risk of repatriation to Somalia and Eritrea, where they would likely be subjected to maltreatment.[78] The Court stressed that "expulsion, extradition or any other measure to remove an alien may give rise to an issue under Article 3, and hence engage the responsibility of the expelling state under the Convention." It affirmed the "absolute character" of the prohibition against torture and inhuman and degrading treatment under Article 3. The Court concluded that, given numerous reports by international organizations, states, and NGOs regarding the lack of safety in Libya, Italy "knew or should have known" that the migrants could be exposed to maltreatment, which violated Article 3. The Court further held that Italy violated Article 4 of Protocol No. 4 by not allowing the migrants to make asylum claims or receive individual consideration, which constituted an illegal collective expulsion of aliens.[79] Finally, the court held that Italy violated Article 13 of the Convention, as the applicants did not have an effective remedy or procedural process that they could pursue after the incident occurred. The migrants were denied the protections of Article 13 because they were offered no processing aboard the Italian ships, and were not informed of their destination before they were returned to Libya.

The concurring opinion, issued by Justice Pinto de Albuquerque, directly discussed the principle of non-refoulement in relation to the ECHR. He argued that neither migrants nor refugees should be subject to refoulement. The justice stated that the prohibition against refoulement was "an absolute obligation of all states" and a *jus cogens* norm. Moreover, he argued "de jure refugees" deserved the same protection as "de facto refugees," as all share equivalent needs for international protection.[80] Any difference of treatment between these two groups of refugees, or between refugees arriving individually or as part of a mass influx, would create a second class of refugees, subject to a discriminatory regime.

The majority opinion noted Justice Blackmun's "powerful" dissent in *Sale v. Haitian Centers Council*.[81] In his concurrence, Justice Pinto de Albuquerque elaborated:

> The words of Justice Blackmun are so inspiring that they should not be forgotten. Refugees attempting to escape Africa do not claim a right of admission to Europe. They demand only that Europe, the cradle of human rights idealism

77. *See id.* at § 64.

78. *See id.* at §§ 138, 158.

79. *See id.* at § 186.

80. *See id.* at 62.

81. *See id.* at 67, n.1.

and the birthplace of the rule of law, cease closing its doors to people in despair who have fled from arbitrariness and brutality. That is a very modest plea, vindicated by the European Convention on Human Rights. "We should not close our ears to it."[82]

With that, the ECtHR issued a landmark decision in human rights law.

2. Impact

Hirsi represents a landmark ruling in at least two respects. By holding that interdictions at sea fall within a state's jurisdiction, the Court effectively outlawed many contemporary European migrant interdiction practices. Interdiction at sea might still be possible in cases permitted by the law of the sea, but states may no longer refuse to process migrants, summarily repatriate them to a third country without ensuring their safety, or hide behind claims of impossibility due to mass influx. Also, migrants must now be able to challenge the decision to transfer them to another state.

The second notable outcome of the Court's holding was its pronouncement that Italy could not circumvent its ECHR obligations by arguing that it was only acting pursuant to obligations imposed on it by UNCLOS and SAR. It also prohibits states from claiming they are engaging in humanitarian "rescue-at-sea" missions when in reality they are intercepting and turning back migrants. Italy is now also foreclosed from using its bilateral migration agreement with Libya as a legal shield from its ECHR commitments. More broadly, this holding forecloses future reliance by European states on multilateral agreements or bilateral treaties to circumvent their obligations to incoming migrants. To comply with their obligations under the ECHR, member states must offer individual processing to migrants intercepted at sea.

Moreover, the decision implies that the obligation of non-refoulement applies to migrants and not just to de jure refugees.[83] The decision refers to "persons," "applicants," or "migrants"; nothing in it suggests that its prohibitions should not apply to all persons equally. The opinion implies that a state cannot apply a lower human rights standard to migrants, regardless of the reason for their flight.[84]

While the ECtHR decision is technically only binding on Italy, the European Parliament responded with legislation affecting all EU members. The new legislation explicitly added the protection against refoulement and the protection of fundamental rights to its rules governing maritime surveillance operations by Frontex.[85] It states that no one can be "disembarked in, forced to enter, conducted to

---

82. *See id.*, Separate Opinion, at 79.

83. See Irini Papanicolopulu, *Hirsi Jamaa v. Italy, Application No. 27765/09*, in International Decisions, 107 Am. J. Int'l L. 396, 417, 421–22 (2013).

84. *See id.* at 422.

85. *See* Steve Peers, *New EU Rules on Maritime Surveillance: Will They Stop the Deaths and Push-Backs in the Mediterranean?*, Statewatch (Feb. 2014), http://www.statewatch.org/analyses/no-237-maritime-surveillance.pdf.

or otherwise handed over to" an unsafe country where he or she would be at risk of the death penalty, torture, persecution, or other inhuman or degrading treatment, or where "the migrant's life or freedom would be threatened" on Convention grounds, as well as sexual orientation.[86] The regulation also banned "chain refoulement": a migrant cannot be handed over to a third country if that country itself would put the migrant at risk for refoulement. Reflecting the judgment in *M.S.S. v. Belgium and Greece*, the regulation says that the member state must consider the situation in the third country regarding safety for migrants and the risk of chain refoulement before deciding whether to send a migrant there. The regulation also grants the migrants certain procedural rights, stating that before any return to a third state the member states must "use all means" to identify the migrants, assess their circumstances, inform them of their destination, and give them an opportunity to object and assert the non-refoulement rule.

The *Hirsi* decision has made interdiction at sea difficult, but not impossible. Processing a boat of hundreds of migrants at sea, or even screening out economic migrants from those with plausible asylum claims, would be complicated. If, for example, screening interviews take approximately half an hour, processing a boat of 300 migrants would take 19 8-hour workdays. Migrants would need to be fed and cared for during that time. Many of them would arrive in need of medical treatment after a harsh voyage or suffering maltreatment abroad; some would need to be airlifted to shore. Even if the EU could screen out economic migrants, it would need to find a safe country to which it could return them and ensure that they would not face maltreatment. Given these requirements, migrants could not be returned to Libya, the most common embarkation point for migrants coming to Italy, or many of their countries of origin. Interdiction at sea would still be possible if the EU or European countries could find a safe third country to take screened-out migrants, or on which to process migrants, a proposal under discussion by EU ministers as of this writing. As mentioned above, the Australian High Court recently upheld the legality of holding 157 migrants for a month on a windowless boat off of the Australian coast pending a decision on what to do with them. Although human rights groups condemned the decision, the EU could legally try a more humane version of a similar program.

After *Hirsi* and the resulting legislation, the case also may have affected migrants' decisions to risk the journey at sea. Migrants would know that they could no longer be interdicted and summarily returned. The *Hirsi* case, and the difficulty of screening migrants at sea, therefore increased the probability that migrants could reach Europe. While human desperation, not the ECtHR, is responsible for the current flood of migrants in Europe, and the journey across the Mediterranean remains perilous, the *Hirsi* decision may have made migration by sea a more attractive option of escape.

---

86. *Commission Proposal for a Regulation of the European Parliament and of the Council Establishing Rules for the Surveillance of the External Sea Borders in the Context of Operational Cooperation Coordinated by the European Agency for the Management of Operational Cooperation at the External Borders of the Member States of the European Union*, COM (2013) 197 final (Feb. 12, 2014).

It is unclear whether *M.S.S. v. Belgium and Greece, Hirsi,* and the ensuing leg-islation have been followed by all states.[87] Still, in principle, these two landmark judgments could serve as guidance for other states to revise their enforcement of domestic migration laws to comply with international legal principles.

IV. CONCLUSION

International refugee law is meant to be universally applicable, and its protection against refoulement absolute. However, the requirement of non-refoulement has been interpreted differently in different courts, making it unclear what the princi-ple actually means. A human rights regime cannot be universal if it means differ-ent things in different places. When people migrate, they deserve the same human rights protections wherever they may go. But when law migrates, it may not be the same.

As the analysis above shows, courts in the United States, Europe, and Australia do not agree on what the obligation of non-refoulement means. The ECtHR and the Australian High Court say that non-refoulement requires the state of entry to ensure that moving an asylum-seeker to a third country will not put him in danger of per-secution, maltreatment, or refoulement in that country. Nothing in US law contra-dicts this principle, although the issue has not come before the US Supreme Court. However, the US Supreme Court (explicitly) and the Australian High and Federal Courts (implicitly) have allowed the summary return of refugees interdicted at sea. The ECtHR, meanwhile, has struck down the practice of summary returns.

What explains the divergence in these three opinions? The political context surrounding the decisions may provide some explanation for the courts' different interpretations of non-refoulement. In the United States and Australia, public opin-ion was either neutral or against the entry of large numbers of boat people. Europe, on the other hand, was under major criticism for its treatment of migrants at the time of the *Hirsi* decision. Recent upheavals in the Middle East have led to large influxes of migrants approaching Europe by sea. Many highly visible cases in which migrants have drowned crossing the Mediterranean have caused backlash in pub-lic opinion. While right-wing parties in Europe gained popularity on anti-migrant platforms, elites began to advocate for humanitarian protection for migrants. The ECtHR, an elite institution and not a popular one, decided *Hirsi* in this context. In doing so, the Court broadened the interpretation of non-refoulement and required greater human rights protections for migrants.

The ECtHR's more expansive interpretation of non-refoulement can also be explained by its unique position as a human rights tribunal. Unlike any courts in the United States and Australia, the ECtHR is explicitly charged with enforcing and implementing a human rights convention. Ignoring the Convention, an instrument of human rights law, would have severe consequences for the Court's legitimacy. Its

---

87. See Italy: *Summary Returns to Greece Violate Rights: Unaccompanied Children, Asylum Seekers Should Not Be Turned Away,* HUMAN RIGHTS WATCH (Jan. 22, 2013), http://www.hrw.org/news/ 2013/01/22/italy-summary-returns-greece-violate-rights.

explicit mission to protect human rights would also weigh on the side of expanding human rights protections.

Because it is a supranational court, the ECtHR is also insulated from the political pressures in any single country. As an apolitical entity, the ECtHR can make decisions that the governments of most states cannot. Governments could experience social, economic, and political costs from deciding to relax or restrict their human rights laws for migrants. The ECtHR is free to make its decisions in a political vacuum. Technically, its decisions are only binding on the state against which the application is filed, not other signatories of the ECHR. The Committee of Ministers of the Council of Europe will work with the country concerned to ensure compliance with any ECtHR decision, and will ensure that the state pays any monetary damages. But unless the ministers decide to act, the penalty for violating a decision is merely that the Court may deliver new judgments against the state. The ECtHR can therefore make its decisions without regard for whether they are politically feasible or whether the ministers will choose to enforce them, and without concern of any backlash against the Court.

Although opinions in these three jurisdictions differ, analyzing these cases together reveals a strengthening of the international legal norm of non-refoulement. First, states cannot ignore non-refoulement, as they do with other areas of international law. Although the *Sale* and *Tampa* decisions appear to narrow or ignore the concept of non-refoulement, the actions of these states reveal how influential the concept has been. If states felt they could simply disregard international refugee law, they would not need to adopt expensive and complicated practices to avoid it. Moreover, the ECtHR cases and the Australian *M70* case show that, in the years since *Sale v. Haitian Centers Council*, the prohibition against refoulement has been increasingly recognized as an international legal obligation. *Sale* makes the United States an outlier for permitting summary return of migrants without screening to determine whether they have a bona fide refugee claim. *Sale* has not been overruled, but given the emerging norm against summary returns and domestic and international criticism of *Sale*, another SCOTUS opinion explicitly permitting summary return of refugees seems unlikely. The Australian High Court may soon hear a direct challenge to its program of interdiction at sea, which was modeled on the US program at issue in *Sale*. If the High Court strikes down the program, the United States will become still more of an outlier in its human rights practices, and it and other countries employing summary returns will face increased pressure to stop.

But how far does the obligation of non-refoulement extend? Future court cases will need to clarify this. Overextension of non-refoulement may conflict with other national security and human rights concerns. Under the broadest interpretation of non-refoulement, practically anyone on a boat interdicted at sea could claim asylum to receive at least temporary international protection. Anti-piracy programs have already been restrained because states fear that non-refoulement obligations will require them to protect pirates against return to their home countries.[88] Given

---

88. *See* David Martin, *Human Rights and Migration Management: Of Complexity, Balance, and Nuance,* 106 Am. Soc'y Int'l L. Proc. 69, 71 (2012).

such quandaries involving the appropriate balance between non-refoulement and national security, David Martin has argued that governments need discretion to adjust to rapidly changing circumstances and balance human rights protections with manageable migration policies.[89] Future decisions must clarify states' non-refoulement obligations and guide them in striking an appropriate balance.

Beyond the non-refoulement context, cases involving interdiction at sea add to our understanding of the extraterritorial application of human rights trea-ties.[90] The question of the extraterritorial application of human rights treaties and domestic human rights guarantees has been an important and controversial issue in recent years. The EU has been called upon to provide human rights guarantees for both refugees and migrants arriving by sea, and the *Hirsi* decision makes clear that ECHR signatories must not refoule individuals in either category. Faced with an overwhelming number of migration and asylum applications, states will likely continue to adopt creative policies to circumvent their non-refoulement obliga-tions, including extraterritorial processing. UNHCR and human rights organ-izations strongly prefer processing of asylum-seekers within the territory of the intercepting state to extraterritorial processing.[91] However, extraterritorial screen-ing or processing of asylum-seekers may be permissible, particularly when part of a burden-sharing arrangement to distribute the responsibilities of refugee protec-tion. Third-state processing, out-of-country processing, regional processing, and processing involving maritime vessels may all be permissible if they comply with the norm of non-refoulement and ensure that any third countries involved comply with generally accepted international human rights standards.

The decisions in the ECtHR and Australian cases suggest that the "effective con-trol" standard announced by the ECtHR may apply to migration control or other extraterritorial operations involving potential human rights violations. UNHCR views the "effective control" standard as a generally recognized norm in refugee law, and it is viewed as a standard in human rights cases more generally, with the United States being an outlier.[92] Cases involving whether states comply with these human rights norms are likely to continue to come before high courts, including in the United States, which can be said to have "effective control" over many areas in which its military operates, on the high seas and elsewhere. If these cases are used

---

89. *See id.*

90. On the relationship between refugee law and human rights law, see Jill I. Goldenziel, *The Curse of the Nation-State: Refugees, Migration, and Security in International Law*, 48 Ariz. St. L.J. 579 (2016).

91. *See* UNHCR Division of International Protection, *Protection Policy Paper: Maritime Interception Operations and the Processing of International Protection Claims: Legal Standards and Policy Considerations with Respect to Extraterritorial Processing*, in 2 Rescue at Sea, Stowaways and Maritime Interception: Selected Reference Materials 97 (Dec. 2011), http://www.unhcr.se/fileadmin/user_upload/PDFdocuments/Rescue_at_Sea__Stowaways_and_Maritime_Interception.pdf.

92. *See* UNHCR Division of International Protection, *supra* note 91, at 115; Oona Hathaway et al., *Human Rights Abroad: When Do Human Rights Obligations Apply Extraterritorially?*, 43 Ariz. St. L.J. 339 (2011).

as precedent in cases involving US military operations, the United States will be required to apply international human rights standards extraterritorially.

States increasingly conduct activities beyond their borders, from migration controls to targeted killings and activities involving military occupation or humanitarian intervention. The European and Australian judgments come at a time when domestic courts are looking to ensure accountability under domestic law for the extraterritorial actions of states, as evidenced in the recent *Al-Skeini* judgment in Europe[93] and in constitutional judgments in the United States holding that international legal obligations and procedural rights guaranteed under the Constitution apply to the United States' extraterritorial actions.[94] The above cases suggest that international human rights guarantees extend beyond state borders to areas where states have effective control, and apply to non-citizens. The reach of these holdings, therefore, may soon migrate to other areas of human rights law.

93. *See* Al-Skeini v. United Kingdom, 2011 Eur. Ct. H.R. 99 (July 7, 2011) (holding that the United Kingdom's human rights obligations under ECHR applied extraterritorially to actions in Iraq).

94. *See* Boumediene v. Bush, 553 U.S. 723 (2008); Rasul v. Bush, 542 U.S. 466 (2004).

20

An Asymmetric Comparative International Law Approach to Treaty Interpretation

The CEDAW Committee's Tolerance of the Scandinavian States' Progressive Deviation

ALEC KNIGHT*

I. INTRODUCTION

The Convention on the Elimination of All Forms of Discrimination Against Women (CEDAW) is perhaps an odd choice to illustrate the utility of a comparative perspective in international law. CEDAW is one of the nine core United Nations human rights treaties that embrace universalism, that is, that there are "minimum standards of human dignity that must be protected in all societies."[1] States parties to CEDAW must abide by its provisions, irrespective of their sociocultural differences.[2] Moreover, the CEDAW Committee, which oversees the implementation of the Convention, has a mandate to apply the provisions to all states parties equally.[3] Even among UN human rights treaties, CEDAW is especially universalist in orientation. The Convention casts culture as a potential barrier to the goal of ending discrimination against women.[4] Article 5(a) of the Convention requires that states parties take all appropriate measures to modify "social and cultural patterns

* I thank Suzie McCarthy, Anthea Roberts, Paul Stephan, Pierre-Hugues Verdier, and Mila Versteeg for their helpful comments and criticism.

1. Sally Engle Merry, *Gender Justice and CEDAW: Convention on the Elimination of All Forms of Discrimination Against Women*, 9 J. WOMEN MIDDLE E. & ISLAMIC WORLD 49, 53 (2011).

2. *See id.* at 54.

3. *Id.*

4. *See* Berta E. Hernández-Truyol, *Glocalizing Law and Culture: Towards a Cross-Constitutive Paradigm*, 67 ALB. L. REV. 617, 618 (2003).

Comparative International Law. Edited by Anthea Roberts et al. © Anthea Roberts, Paul B. Stephan, Pierre-Hugues Verdier, Mila Versteeg 2018. Published 2018 by Oxford University Press.

of conduct to eliminate prejudices and stereotypes."[5] CEDAW is the only human rights treaty with this kind of provision.[6]

However, CEDAW's universalist orientation does not mean that the interpretation of the treaty is uniform. The Committee does not insist on identical interpretations and implementations of CEDAW across all states parties. Instead, the Committee allows for a margin of appreciation in the interpretation of the Convention's provisions. During constructive dialogue and concluding observations, the CEDAW Committee often "calibrates" the Convention's obligations to the particular context of the state party under consideration.[7]

Yet the Committee's flexibility does not extend equally to all states parties and all interpretations. The Committee allows, if not encourages, Scandinavian state feminist[8] countries to adopt interpretations of CEDAW that go beyond the margin of appreciation in a politically progressive direction. By contrast, the Committee regularly criticizes predominantly Muslim states for their deviations from the text, which would bend the Convention in a politically conservative direction. The Committee's negative view of these deviations from CEDAW is well recognized.[9] The Committee consistently and emphatically calls for the removal of reservations, understandings, and declarations (RUDs) that reference Islamic law.

This chapter shifts the focus to a less acknowledged trend, the adoption by Scandinavian countries of deviant and progressive interpretations of CEDAW. Norway, Sweden, and Denmark have interpreted Articles 4(1) and 5 to address men and masculinities and to adopt affirmative action measures that benefit men. The CEDAW Committee's disinterest in curtailing this Scandinavian approach creates a regional community of interpretation. The interpretation could eventually become a part of CEDAW, whether through Committee practice, a general recommendation (GR), or an optional protocol. Yet, the incorporation of the Scandinavian interpretation remains far from certain.

As the Scandinavian approach to CEDAW fits within the broader ambit of gender equality, it would be misleading to characterize it as the same as Muslim RUDs. However, neither fits comfortably within the meaning of the Convention as

---

5. Convention on the Elimination of All Forms of Discrimination Against Women art. 28, Dec. 18, 1979, 1249 U.N.T.S. 13 (entered into force Sept. 3, 1981) [hereinafter CEDAW].

6. Philip Alston & Ryan Goodman, International Human Rights: The Successor to International Human Rights in Context 180 (2013).

7. Judith Resnik, *Comparative (In)equalities: CEDAW, the Jurisdiction of Gender, and the Heterogeneity of Transnational Law Production*, 10 Int'l J. Const. L. 531, 545 (2012).

8. Helga M. Hernes, Welfare State and Woman Power: Essays in State Feminism 153 (1987) (defining state feminism as "feminism from above in the form of gender equality and social policies and the feminization of welfare state relevant professions."). Under Hernes's definition, all Scandinavian countries exhibit state feminism, though Sweden is the most institutionalized example. *See* Anette Borchorst & Birte Siim, *Woman-Friendly Policies and State Feminism: Theorizing Scandinavian Gender Equality*, 9 Feminist Theory 207, 210–11 (2008).

9. *See, e.g.,* Yvonne Donders, *Cultural Pluralism in International Human Rights Law: The Role of Reservations, in* The Cultural Dimension of Human Rights (Ana Vrdoljak ed., 2014).

interpreted by the Committee. Either interpretation requires a significant change to the Convention's object and purpose. The space granted to the Scandinavian countries to develop a minority community of interpretation indicates a much greater willingness on the part of the Committee to allow for progressive deviation as opposed to regressive deviation.

This chapter illustrates these dynamics by examining the interactions between the CEDAW Committee and states parties, with a focus on the "constructive dialogue" that occurs as part of the reporting process of the Convention. Section II discusses how the Committee's asymmetric approach to treaty interpretation fits within a comparative international law project. Section III provides an introduction to the CEDAW Committee, with a focus on its interpretative tools and its use of calibrated obligations. Section IV illustrates the CEDAW Committee's inflexible treatment of Muslim states parties' regressive deviations from the Convention. Section V analyzes the Committee's permissive treatment of the Scandinavian approach to CEDAW. Section VI explores how the asymmetric approach allows states to develop interpretations of treaties. Section VII concludes and describes potential future avenues of research into the asymmetric comparative international law approach to treaty interpretation.

II. THE ASYMMETRIC COMPARATIVE INTERNATIONAL LAW APPROACH TO TREATY INTERPRETATION

The CEDAW reporting process may initially appear to be somewhat outside the scope of the project that brings a comparative perspective to international law because of the prominent position of the treaty body, which serves as the arbiter with the authoritative voice on the meaning of the treaty's provisions.[10] This differentiates human rights law from other areas of international law, where supervisory bodies with interpretative powers are atypical.[11]

However, states submitting reports to the CEDAW Committee do play a role in the interpretation of human rights treaties.[12] They put forward their own interpretations of the Convention, which sometimes differ from the interpretation of the treaty body. When this occurs, the treaty body mediates these interpretations in constructive dialogue sessions. The treaty body can make recommendations, but it cannot enforce its views that certain interpretations violate the Convention. In addition, states communicate their ideas with one another regarding interpretations of the Convention, whether by adopting or objecting to another state's interpretations. State practice that exhibits a high level of concordance can indicate agreement regarding an interpretation.[13] Seen in this light, the relationship between states parties and the treaty body is more triangular than vertical.

---

10. *See* Kerstin Mechlem, *Treaty Bodies and the Interpretation of Human Rights*, 42 VAND. J. TRANSNAT'L L. 905, 919 (2009).

11. *Id.*

12. *Id.* at 920.

13. *Id.*

This relationship is characteristic of human rights law. States that come before the European Court of Human Rights (ECtHR) justify their practices as valid interpretations of the European Convention on Human Rights. For example, Jill Goldenziel describes in this volume the claims put forward in *Hirsi Jamaa and Others v. Italy*.[14] The Italian government claimed that its interdiction policy fell outside the Court's purview because, inter alia, its seizures were extraterritorial. The Court rejected this claim and barred Italy from continuing its policy. *Hirsi Jamaa* is a useful case for comparison not just because it reveals the ECtHR's liberal approach to non-refoulement but also because it demonstrates that the Italian government shares a common interpretation with the United States regarding extraterritorial interdictions and non-refoulement.

These triangular relationships are crucial to understanding comparative international human rights law. Case law is becoming more common at the national level,[15] but the reporting process and the case law of international courts remain the primary fora in which human rights law is interpreted. States that come before international arbiters present their interpretations of the treaty in question, which may be compared with other interpretations presented to the same international arbiter, different international arbiters, or domestic courts.

The reporting process is particularly useful for examining comparative international human rights law because it offers a window into executive views regarding human rights and illustrates interpretations of rights that are often seen as nonjusticiable, such as socioeconomic rights. Courts are less likely to consider socioeconomic rights because courts lack the capacity to deal with questions of social and economy policy.[16] Regardless of whether socioeconomic rights are justiciable, treaty bodies play a different role than courts and can directly address socioeconomic policies. Treaty bodies often make recommendations that governments implement a particular policy. Indeed, the main interpretations considered in this chapter concern a socioeconomic provision. Under Article 4(1), the CEDAW Committee recommends affirmative action policies for states. Focusing solely on court cases would underemphasize socioeconomic rights and interpretations of them.

From a comparativist perspective, it might also seem curious to compare the practices of the Scandinavian states with those of predominantly Muslim countries. As Katerina Linos notes in this volume, comparative scholars typically select two countries that are similar to one another in all aspects save for the aspect under examination, which allows scholars to support the claim that effects are traceable to the dissimilar aspect.[17] The Scandinavian states and predominantly Muslim states

14. Jill I. Goldenziel, *When Law Migrates: Refugees in Comparative International Law*, at 401–13 (this volume).

15. *See generally* Gábor Halmai, *Domestic Courts and International Human Rights*, *in* THE SAGE HANDBOOK OF HUMAN RIGHTS 749–67 (Anja Mihr & Mark Gibney eds., 2014).

16. U.N. OFFICE OF THE HIGH COMM'R OF HUM. RTS., ECONOMIC, SOCIAL, AND CULTURAL RIGHTS, at 86, U.N. Doc. HR/P/PT/12, U.N. Sales No. E.04.XIV.8 (2005).

17. Katerina Linos, *Methodological Guidance: How to Select and Develop Comparative International Law Case Studies*, at 45 (this volume).

stand apart in many ways, including the metric of women's rights. According to the Global Gender Gap Report, which measures the gaps between women and men in health, education, economy, and politics, the Scandinavian countries have the smallest gender gaps of all countries.[18] With the exception of Bangladesh, all of the predominantly Muslim countries with RUDs to CEDAW rank in the bottom third of the index.[19]

Yet, the same Millian comparative logic need not be limited to comparing similar states. Scholars can utilize this method in cases of similar actions and divergent effects. When states take actions that are similar in all aspects except one and a neutral arbiter treats those actions dissimilarly, the difference in response likely stems from the differing aspect. This claim is particularly apt in human rights law, where differences between the states are ostensibly of minimal importance. This variant of comparative logic supports the claim that the CEDAW Committee's asymmetric responses to similarly deviant interpretations of the Convention stem from the political leaning of those interpretations. The Committee permits progressive interpretations and prohibits regressive interpretations. There is a floor, but not a ceiling, for interpretations.

The asymmetric approach likely extends beyond the CEDAW Committee. Other human rights regimes likely respond to deviant interpretations asymmetrically because they share a living instrument approach and the margin of appreciation. Human rights treaties are viewed as living instruments, with interpretations that evolve over time.[20] Treaty bodies frequently argue that human rights treaties should address "changing social realities."[21] The ECtHR and the Inter-American Court of Human Rights (IACHR) both utilize a living instrument doctrine, which holds that their conventions evolve through interpretation and must acknowledge present-day conditions.[22] In addition, much like the ECtHR's "margin of appreciation" doctrine,[23] human rights law generally grants states discretion to select the means of implementation.[24] The IACHR has cited the doctrine with

---

18. World Econ. Forum, The Global Gender Gap Report 2014, 7 (2014).

19. *Id.* at 8–9.

20. Julian Arato, *Accounting for Difference in Treaty Interpretation over Time, in* Interpretation in International Law 205, 206 (Andrea Bianchi et al. eds., 2015).

21. Birgit Schlütter, *Aspects of Human Rights Interpretation by the UN Treaty Bodies, in* UN Human Rights Treaty Bodies: Law and Legitimacy 261, 265 (Helen Keller & Geir Ulfstein eds., 2012).

22. Laurence Burgorgue-Larsen & Amaya Ubeda de Torres, The Inter-American Court of Human Rights: Case Law and Commentary 62 (Rosalind Greenstein trans., 2011); Luzius Wildhaber, *The European Court of Human Rights in Action,* 21 Ritsumeikan L. Rev. 83, 84 (2004).

23. Yuval Shany, *Toward a General Margin of Appreciation Doctrine in International Law?,* 16 Eur. J. Int'l L. 907, 909–10 (2005).

24. Rebecca Cook, *Obligations to Adopt Temporary Special Measures Under the Convention on the Elimination of All Forms of Discrimination Against Women, in* Temporary Special Measures: Accelerating de Facto Equality of Women Under Article 4(1) UN Convention on the Elimination of All Forms of Discrimination Against Women 119, 132 (Ineke Boerefijn ed., 2003).

approval,[25] and other human rights bodies have issued decisions consistent with the doctrine.[26]

The scope of the unidirectional approach may even extend beyond human rights. The living instrument approach has also been applied to treaties on environmental law, humanitarian law, and territorial law,[27] and the International Court of Justice and European Court of Justice have used the margin of appreciation.[28] Additional research is necessary to determine whether the unidirectional approach extends to other treaty regimes. Bodies such as the CEDAW Committee, which utilize the living instrument approach and grant a margin of appreciation, are likely candidates.

III. THE CEDAW COMMITTEE

The CEDAW Committee is the chief enforcer of the Convention.[29] It is one of the 10 treaty bodies that function as a panel of independent experts that monitor the implementation of the United Nations human rights treaties.[30] Unlike a court, the treaty bodies cannot make legally binding interpretations.[31] However, this does not indicate that states are on an equal footing with the treaty bodies in the interpretation of the treaties. The treaty bodies were created to fill an independent supervisory role.[32] They have the primary responsibility for determining appropriate interpretations.[33] The treaty bodies "assume to a large extent . . . the interpretative role that is normally played by states."[34] Their views are "more or less authoritative statements of interpretation" of the human rights treaties.[35] States do play a role in treaty interpretation, but only substantial shared practice can establish

25. Shany, *supra* note 23, at 929.

26. *Id.*

27. Arato, *supra* note 20.

28. Shany, *supra* note 23, at 926–29.

29. Neil A. Englehart & Melissa K. Miller, *The CEDAW Effect: International Law's Impact on Women's Rights*, 13 J. Hum. Rts. 22, 24 (2014).

30. Office of the High Commission of Human Rights, *Monitoring the Core International Human Rights Treaties*, http://www.ohchr.org/EN/HRBodies/Pages/TreatyBodies.aspx (last visited Sept. 6, 2016).

31. Christine Chinkin & Marsha Freeman, *Introduction, in* THE UN CONVENTION ON THE ELIMINATION OF ALL FORMS OF DISCRIMINATION AGAINST WOMEN: A COMMENTARY 1, 24 (Marsha A. Freeman et al. eds., 2012).

32. Mechlem, *supra* note 10.

33. *Id.*

34. *Id.*

35. Chinkin & Freeman, *supra* note 31 (citing HENRY STEINER ET AL., INTERNATIONAL HUMAN RIGHTS IN CONTEXT: LAW, POLITICS, MORALS (3d ed. 2007)).

authoritative interpretations.[36] Thus, minority interpretations that flout the treaty body's interpretations can be considered deviant.

A. Tools of Interpretation

The CEDAW Committee's primary interpretative tool is the consideration of periodic reports submitted by states parties.[37] In accordance with Article 18 of the Convention, every four years states parties must submit reports on their implementation of the Convention.[38] When the Committee receives a report, it requests that representatives from the state appear for two sessions of "constructive dialogue."[39] During these sessions, the Committee meets with a delegation from the state, commonly including a senior minister for women's affairs.[40] The delegation introduces its report and then the Committee asks questions.[41] The dialogue between the delegation and the Committee can be confrontational at times.[42] The Committee then develops concluding observations,[43] which include sections on positive developments, areas of concern, and recommendations to address those concerns.[44] Within two years of their adoption, states must inform the Committee about steps taken to address the concluding observations.[45]

The CEDAW Committee supplements its jurisprudence through other tools, the most important of which is the general recommendation. GRs allow the Committee to formally state the nature of states parties' responsibilities under CEDAW.[46] The elaboration of GRs is "based on the examination of reports and information received from the States Parties."[47] GRs describe substantive measures required under the provisions of the Convention.[48] For example, GR 19 brought violence against women under the ambit of the Convention.[49]

---

36. Mechlem, *supra* note 10, at 920.

37. Andrew Byrnes, *The Committee on the Elimination of Discrimination Against Women, in* WOMEN'S HUMAN RIGHTS: CEDAW IN INTERNATIONAL, REGIONAL AND NATIONAL LAW 27, 27 (Anne Hellum & Henriette Sindig Aasen eds., 2013).

38. CEDAW, *supra* note 5, art. 18(1).

39. Englehart & Miller, *supra* note 29.

40. Merry, *supra* note 1, at 63.

41. Byrnes, *supra* note 37, at 36.

42. Merry, *supra* note 1, at 51.

43. *Id.* at 66.

44. Byrnes, *supra* note 37, at 36.

45. Englehart & Miller, *supra* note 29, at 25.

46. Elizabeth Evatt, *Finding a Voice for Women's Rights: The Early Days of CEDAW*, 34 GEO. WASH. INT'L L. REV. 515, 535 (2003).

47. CEDAW, *supra* note 5, art. 21(1).

48. Byrnes, *supra* note 37, at 39.

49. *Id.*

B. Calibrated Obligations

The reporting process also allows the Committee to tailor its recommendations to the report and baseline conditions of each state party.[50] Judith Resnik describes this as the creation of "calibrated obligations," treating differently situated states differently in accordance with conditions such as wealth, legal traditions, and cultural practices.[51] Constructive dialogue sessions are well suited for this, as they allow Committee members with diverse backgrounds to compare their belief systems with those of the state's delegation.[52] The Committee recommends certain measures as "transnationally" necessary, but it makes recommendations that recognize the diversity of the states parties.[53]

Calibrated obligations are not formal elements of human rights law, but they are comparable to the margin of appreciation doctrine.[54] The margin of appreciation, developed by the ECtHR, grants states parties to the European Convention some discretion in the methods used to implement the Convention[55] and allows judges to consider the "cultural, historical and philosophical difference between Strasbourg and the nation in question."[56] The margin of appreciation is smallest when states parties share common domestic practices and greatest when states parties exhibit a diversity of practices.[57]

Calibrated obligations do not grant states limitless discretion in the interpretation of CEDAW's provisions. If the Committee were to accept any interpretations of the Convention on the basis of wealth, legal traditions, or cultural practices, it would effectively cede its authority to the states parties. Instead, the Committee polices the border between acceptable measures and deviant measures. The Committee takes an absolutist approach regarding the creation and maintenance of reservations, understandings, and declarations that purport to bind predominantly Muslim states parties to CEDAW's provisions only to the extent that they do not conflict with Islamic law.

50. Resnik, *supra* note 7, at 545.

51. *Id.*

52. *See id.* at 545.

53. *See id.* at 544.

54. *See id.* at 547.

55. Oren Gross & Fionnuala Ní Aoláin, *From Discretion to Scrutiny: Revisiting the Application of the Margin of Appreciation Doctrine in the Context of Article 15 of the European Convention on Human Rights*, 23 Hum. Rts. Q. 625, 626 (2001).

56. Sabine Gless & Jeannine Martin, *The Comparative Method in European Courts: A Comparison Between the CJEU and ECtHR?*, 1 Bergen J. Crim. L. & Crim. Just. 36, 40 (2013).

57. *Id.* at 40.

IV. THE CEDAW COMMITTEE'S PROHIBITION OF DEVIATION BY PREDOMINANTLY MUSLIM STATES PARTIES

Reservations allow for formally recognized differences in states parties' interpretations of their treaty obligations.[58] They offer "affiliations recognizing (sometimes disquieting) distinctions among polities that nonetheless agree to share legal relatedness."[59] While CEDAW is widely ratified with 189 states parties,[60] it is also subject to a higher number of reservations than any other human rights treaty.[61]

Predominantly Muslim states parties' objections to potential conflicts with Islamic law constitute a substantial share of reservations to CEDAW.[62] Currently, 15 states parties have reservations that explicitly refer to potential conflicts with sharia or Islam.[63] Among these states, nearly two-thirds have reservations that address Article 16's provisions on marriage and family life and Article 2's non-discrimination provisions.[64]

The CEDAW Committee objects to these reservations because it views them as incompatible with the "object and purpose" of the Convention.[65] The Committee generally recommends that states parties "modify, narrow, or withdraw" these reservations.[66] This tactic derives from the Committee's desire to keep states parties within the CEDAW regime in order to press for reform in future constructive dialogue sessions.[67] The Committee sometimes challenges the substance of these reservations by asking states parties to specify the discrepancies and explain why they cannot revoke or amend their reservations despite the success of other predominantly Muslim countries in ratifying CEDAW without reservations.[68]

---

58. *See* Daniel N. Hylton, *Default Breakdown: The Vienna Convention on the Law of Treaties: Inadequate Framework on Reservations*, 27 VAND. J. TRANSNAT'L L. 419, 422 (1994).

59. Resnik, *supra* note 7, at 549.

60. United Nations Treaty Series status page for CEDAW, https://treaties.un.org/ (last visited Sept. 6, 2016).

61. Linda M. Keller, *The Impact of States Parties' Reservations to the Convention on the Elimination of All Forms of Discrimination Against Women*, 2014 MICH. ST. L. REV. 309, 311 (2014) (noting, however, that the Convention on the Rights of the Child has more "substantive reservations" than CEDAW).

62. Jennifer Riddle, *Making CEDAW Universal: A Critique of CEDAW's Reservation Regime Under Article 28 and the Effectiveness of the Reporting Process*, 34 GEO. WASH. INT'L L. REV. 605, 627 (2003).

63. UN Women, *Declarations, Reservations and Objections to CEDAW*, http://www.un.org/womenwatch/daw/cedaw/reservations-country.htm (last visited Sept. 6, 2016).

64. *Id.*

65. Byrnes, *supra* note 37, at 57.

66. Donders, *supra* note 9, at 234.

67. Byrnes, *supra* note 37, at 57.

68. *Id.*

A. Libya's Reservations

The Committee's review of Libya's most recent periodic report is illustrative of its prohibitive approach regarding reservations to Articles 16 and 2 purportedly based on sharia. Libya has a reservation to Article 2 that states that the country will apply its provisions "with due regard to the definitive provisions of the Islamic Shariah, concerning the determination of the share of the heirs to the estate of a deceased person, male or female."[69] Libya also has a reservation to Article 16(c) and (d), which states that the country will apply those provisions "without prejudice to any rights guaranteed to women by the Islamic Shariah."[70] Libya's second, third, fourth, and fifth combined periodic reports contain statements that the country's accession to CEDAW occurred in "full harmony" with the Convention."[71] In response to the Committee's request that Libya consider "amending the Shariah," the report states, "Islamic Shariah is valid for all time and place and capable of keeping pace with development in all areas . . . "[72]

During the constructive dialogue, the Committee's first comments addressed reservations. Committee member Jaising stated that Libya's reservations were "incompatible with the object and purpose of the Convention."[73] Committee member Flinterman reminded the representatives that Libya had no reservations to the International Covenant on Civil and Political Rights's non-discrimination clauses.[74] Representative Amer responded that it was "wrong to judge all peoples and all cultures by the same yardstick, particularly when international human rights instruments specifically affirmed peoples' right to retain their cultural characteristics."[75] Representative Anbar then claimed that non-Muslims falsely assumed that male heirs consistently received more than female heirs.[76] In addition, she asserted that Islamic law's placement of the burden of financial support on men "should be viewed not as discrimination against women, but as evidence of the respect with which women were regarded."[77] In its concluding observations, the Committee urged Libya to take "all necessary steps" toward withdrawing its reservations to CEDAW.[78]

---

69. UN Women, *supra* note 63.

70. *Id.*

71. Committee on the Elimination of Discrimination Against Women [hereinafter CEDAW Committee], Combined Second, Third, Fourth and Fifth Periodic Reports of States Parties: Libyan Arab Jamahiriya, at 11–12, U.N. Doc. CEDAW/C/LBY/5 (Dec. 4, 2008).

72. *Id.* at 13.

73. CEDAW Committee, Combined Second, Third, Fourth and Fifth Periodic Reports of States Parties: Libyan Arab Jamahiriya, ¶ 16, U.N. Doc. CEDAW/C/SR.878 (May 29, 2009).

74. *Id.* ¶ 18.

75. *Id.* ¶ 23.

76. *Id.* ¶ 26.

77. *Id.*

78. CEDAW Committee, Concluding Observations of the Committee on the Elimination of Discrimination Against Women, ¶ 14, U.N. Doc. CEDAW/C/LBY/CO/5 (Feb. 6, 2009).

B. Statements and General Recommendations on RUDs

The CEDAW Committee has also adopted GRs and statements that call for the withdrawal of reservations. GR 21 "note[s] with alarm" the reservations to Article 16 based on "cultural or religious beliefs or on the country's economic or political status."[79] The Committee's Statement on Reservations to the Convention states that Articles 2 and 16 are "core provisions of the Convention" and that reservations based on "perceived conflict between article 2 and the Islamic shariah law" pose an "acute problem for the implementation of the Convention."[80]

The CEDAW Committee's critical response to predominantly Muslim states parties' RUDs reflects its desire to prevent regressive interpretations from receiving its implicit approval. The Committee argues that reservations to Articles 2 and 16 run contrary to CEDAW. Moreover, the Committee posits that, as a number of predominantly Muslim countries have ratified or acceded to the treaty without reservations, there is no reason for other predominantly Muslim countries to maintain their reservations. As long as a state party maintains its religious reservations on these articles, the Committee has little patience for any explanations regarding their compatibility with Islamic law.

Yet, not all deviations from CEDAW receive the same treatment. When state parties' deviations are politically progressive, such as the Scandinavian approach to Articles 4(1) and 5(a), the Committee does not attempt to suppress them.

V. THE SCANDINAVIAN APPROACH TO ARTICLES 4(1) AND 5(A)

Article 4(1) of CEDAW allows states parties to take temporary special measures (TSM) that treat men and women differently as long as they accelerate de facto equality between men and women.[81] TSM, known as affirmative action in the United States and positive action in Europe,[82] include well-known examples such as preferential treatment of candidates, targeted recruitment, and quotas.[83] Article 4(1) gives states parties the latitude to take any executive, legislative, administrative, or regulatory action in any field of human activity[84] as long as that action is a non-permanent means to accelerate de facto equality between men and women.

---

79. CEDAW Committee, General Recommendation No 21 on Equality in Marriage and Family Relations, ¶ 41, U.N. Doc. A/49/38 (2004).

80. CEDAW Committee, Statement on Reservations to the Convention, ¶¶ 6, 10, U.N. Doc. A/53/38/Rev.1 (1998).

81. CEDAW, *supra* note 5, art. 4(1).

82. Cook, *supra* note 24, at 119–20.

83. Lisa Waddington & Laura Visser, *Temporary Special Measures Under the Women's Convention and Positive Action Under EU Law: Mutually Compatible or Irreconcilable, in* THE WOMEN'S CONVENTION TURNED 30: ACHIEVEMENTS, SETBACKS, AND PROSPECTS 95, 100 (Ingrid Westendorp ed., 2012).

84. Frances Raday, *Systematizing the Application of Different Types of Temporary Special Measures Under Article 4 of CEDAW, in* TEMPORARY SPECIAL MEASURES: ACCELERATING DE FACTO

Article 5(a) of the Convention requires that states parties take measures to "modify the social and cultural patterns of conduct of men and women" in order to eliminate "prejudices and customary and all other practices which are based on the idea of the inferiority or the superiority of either of the sexes or on stereotyped roles for men and women."[85] Article 5(a) provides little guidance to states parties for its implementation.[86] Common measures to implement Article 5(a) include education initiatives and affirmative action programs.[87] The following subsections describe the Scandinavian approach, which utilizes a combined reading of Articles 4(1) and 5(a) to allow TSM that benefit men.

A. Norway's Use of the Scandinavian Approach

Norway began to develop the Scandinavian approach in its Third and Fourth periodic reports in 1991 and 1994. In 1991, Norway reported that any quota measures in favor of men could only come under consideration for fields in which men were underrepresented in number and influence.[88] In 1994, Norway reported that preferential treatment of women was pertinent when the Gender Equality Act (GEA) was passed in 1978, but that 15 years of progress toward the goal of gender equality meant that future action "must focus on the fact that equality also applies to men and requires changes in male roles."[89] In accordance with this goal, the report announces the government's intention to amend the GEA to allow for "the preferential treatment of men" applying for jobs in "caring professions" traditionally dominated by women.[90] Also in accordance with this policy, the report announces the creation of the "father's quota," a measure that sets aside paid parental leave exclusively for fathers.[91]

During the continuing dialogue corresponding to Norway's 1991 and 1994 periodic reports, the representatives from Norway discussed both the father quota and the proposed change to the GEA.[92] Members of the CEDAW Committee

---

EQUALITY OF WOMEN UNDER ARTICLE 4(1) UN CONVENTION ON THE ELIMINATION OF ALL FORMS OF DISCRIMINATION AGAINST WOMEN 35, 35 (Ineke Boerefijn ed., 2003).

85. CEDAW, *supra* note 5, art. 5(a).

86. Elizabeth Sepper, *Confronting the "Sacred and Unchangeable": The Obligation to Modify Cultural Patterns Under the Women's Discrimination Treaty*, 30 U. PA. J. INT'L L. 585, 589 (2008).

87. *Id.* at 613–17.

88. CEDAW Committee, Third Periodic Report of States Parties: Norway, at 4, U.N. Doc. CEDAW/C/NOR/3 (May 6, 1991).

89. CEDAW Committee, Fourth Periodic Report of States Parties: Norway, at 7, U.N. Doc. CEDAW/C/NOR/4 (Sept. 22, 1994).

90. *Id.*

91. *Id.* at 27.

92. CEDAW Committee, Third and Fourth Period Reports of Norway, ¶¶ 4, 9, U.N. Doc. CEDAW/C/SR.277 (Feb. 17, 1995).

responded positively to these measures. The Committee members praised the country's approach as "enlightening"[93] and welcomed the father quota as a "model to be emulated by other countries."[94]

In its Fifth and Sixth periodic reports to the CEDAW Committee in 2000 and 2002, Norway re-established its commitment to the idea of TSM for men as a way to work toward de facto equality between women and men. In its Fifth report, under Article 4(1), Norway stated that it amended the GEA in 1995 to allow "preferential treatment of men."[95] The new GEA allows preferential treatment for men in teaching and childcare professions.[96] In 2002, Norway clarified that quota systems could be utilized toward this end.[97]

In its Seventh periodic report, Norway cited "forms of positive differential treatment in favour of men" in teaching and caring professions among its measures to implement Article 4(1)[98] and included an extended section regarding the basis for such measures under Article 5.[99] In the section, Norway contends that changes among men are "essential" to promote gender equality.[100] The section draws a connection between hegemonic masculinity, "the male type that dominates and culturally defines how a man should be in our society," and the prevalence of violence against women.[101] The section further stresses that hegemonic masculinity has negative consequences for men, including the sacrifice of family for career and increased susceptibility to violent crime.[102]

The CEDAW Committee did not address Norway's TSM targeting men during the continuing dialogue in 2000 and 2002,[103] but Norway's 2007 report drew a mixed reaction. Committee member Coker-Appiah lauded Norway's "innovative measures" to address gender roles.[104] By contrast, Chairperson Dairiam expressed

93. *Id.* ¶ 39.

94. *Id.* ¶ 43.

95. CEDAW Committee, Fifth Periodic Report of States Parties: Norway, ¶ 29, U.N. Doc. CEDAW/C/NOR/5 (Mar. 29, 2000).

96. *Id.*

97. CEDAW Committee, Sixth Periodic Report of States Parties: Norway, at 14, U.N. Doc. CEDAW/C/NOR/6 (June 5, 2002).

98. CEDAW Committee, Seventh Periodic Report of States Parties: Norway, at 24, U.N. Doc. CEDAW/C/NOR/7 (Mar. 26, 2007).

99. *Id.* at 26–28.

100. *Id.* at 26.

101. *Id.* at 27–28.

102. *Id.* at 27.

103. *See* CEDAW Committee, Fifth and Sixth Periodic Reports of Norway, U.N. Doc. CEDAW/C/SR.597 (Feb. 6, 2003); CEDAW Committee, Fifth and Sixth Periodic Reports of Norway, U.N. Doc. CEDAW/C/SR.598 (Feb. 6, 2003).

104. CEDAW Committee, Seventh Periodic Report of Norway, ¶¶ 31–32, U.N. Doc. CEDAW/C/SR.803(B) (Sept. 20, 2007).

her concerns that "privileges accorded to men" could lead to "feelings of superiority among the male population."[105] She asked why the report discussed discrimination against men and argued it "should have focused on women . . . "[106] However, discrimination against men did not appear in the Committee's Concluding Observations.[107]

B. Denmark's Use of the Scandinavian Approach

Denmark was an early adopter of the Scandinavian approach to Articles 4(1) and 5. A 1976 draft of Article 4(1) explicitly permitted only TSM for women.[108] Denmark unsuccessfully proposed to alter the provision to explicitly allow TSM for men.[109] Denmark again discussed TSM targeting men in its 1997 periodic report. Under Article 4(1), the report states that the Danish Equal Status Council created a "think tank on men" to launch a discussion on the development of "men's roles in society, of making their position visible in the gender equality work, and of formulating their interests in and proposals for the future equal status policy."[110] In its Fifth periodic report, Denmark reports a burgeoning interest in addressing "the special problems faced by men."[111] The report states that the Equal Status Council published a book to begin a discussion on men's roles as fathers, spouses, divorced fathers, and employees with family responsibilities as well as on "if the dominance of female values makes it difficult to be a man at 'the bottom of society.' "[112] Denmark's Sixth periodic report expresses its intention to address the "gender equality problems" that men face in the job market, the family, and lifestyle.[113] In its Seventh periodic report, Denmark reports the creation of "junior social educator positions targeted at adolescent boys" as TSM.[114] Denmark's Eighth periodic report from 2013 lists a project intended to address the "increasing drop-out of

---

105. *Id.* ¶ 34.

106. *Id.*

107. *See* CEDAW Committee, Concluding Comments of the Committee on the Elimination of Discrimination Against Women: Norway, U.N. Doc. CEDAW/C/NOR/CO/7 (Aug. 10, 2007).

108. Commission on the Status of Women, Draft Convention on the Elimination of All Forms of Discrimination Against Women, at 112, U.N. Doc. E/CN.6/591 (June 21, 1976).

109. *Id.* at 56.

110. CEDAW Committee, Fourth Periodic Reports of States Parties: Denmark, at 9, U.N. Doc. CEDAW/C/DEN/4 (Feb. 10, 1997).

111. CEDAW Committee, Fifth Periodic Reports of States Parties: Denmark, at 13, U.N. Doc. CEDAW/C/DEN/5 (July 3, 2000).

112. *Id.* at 34.

113. CEDAW Committee, Sixth Periodic Reports of States Parties: Denmark, at 19, U.N. Doc. CEDAW/C/DEN/6 (Oct. 4, 2004).

114. CEDAW Committee, Seventh Periodic Reports of States Parties: Denmark, at 19, U.N. Doc. CEDAW/C/DEN/7 (July 21, 2008).

boys from the educational system" and reports the creation of a website, changejob. dk, which provides information on how to recruit unemployed men into tradition- ally female-dominated careers.[115]

C. Sweden's Use of the Scandinavian Approach

Sweden also began to utilize the Scandinavian approach before Norway. In 1987, Sweden's Second periodic report states that TSM for men and women were "essen- tial if equality is to be achieved," but that most measures thus far were "oriented to women for obvious reasons."[116] The report describes a pilot program that cre- ated a 15 percent quota system for men to gain admission to a preschool teacher- training course.[117] Sweden's Third periodic report specifies that a significant "point of departure" for Swedish policy is that TSM for men and women are necessary for the achievement of equality.[118] Sweden's Fourth periodic report contains several measures directed toward men under Article 5, such as the adoption of a father quota and projects to teach fathers about childbirth and childcare.[119] Sweden's two most recent periodic reports in 2000[120] and 2006[121] both contain sections on men and gender equality under Article 5. The 2000 report states that the Swedish gov- ernment disbursed funding for projects aimed at increasing the number of men in childcare and schools.[122]

D. The Scandinavian Approach and the Committee's Interpretation of CEDAW

While some aspects of the Scandinavian approach fit with the Committee's inter- pretations, others deviate from it. The simplest way to distinguish between the two is to identify whether the measure *targets* or *benefits* men. Measures that target men but primarily benefit women, such as programs to educate men about domestic

115. CEDAW Committee, Eighth Periodic Reports of States Parties: Denmark, at 10–11, U.N. Doc. CEDAW/C/DNK/8 (Sept. 11, 2013).

116. CEDAW Committee, Second Periodic Reports of States Parties: Sweden, at 43, U.N. Doc. CEDAW/C/13/Add.6 (Mar. 26, 1987).

117. *Id.* ¶ 45.

118. CEDAW Committee, Third Periodic Reports of States Parties: Sweden, ¶ 59, U.N. Doc. CEDAW/C/18/Add.1 (Apr. 10, 1991).

119. CEDAW Committee, Fourth Periodic Reports of States Parties: Sweden, at 22–30, U.N. Doc. CEDAW/C/SWE/4 (Apr. 10, 1991).

120. CEDAW Committee, Fifth Periodic Reports of States Parties: Sweden, at 20, U.N. Doc. CEDAW/C/SWE/5 (Dec. 18, 2000).

121. CEDAW Committee, Combined Sixth and Seventh Periodic Reports of States Parties: Sweden, at 21–22, U.N. Doc. CEDAW/C/SWE/7 (Sept. 14, 2006).

122. CEDAW Committee, *supra* note 120.

violence, do not deviate. By contrast, measures that primarily benefit men, such as quotas for men in childcare professions, deviate from the treaty. Measures that explicitly address discrimination against men deviate the furthest. Although a strictly textualist reading of Articles 4(1) and 5(a) indicate that these measures constitute permissible readings of the treaty, the Committee's GRs indicate that TSM cannot benefit men.

Article 4(1) does not specify whether TSM can benefit men. It allows measures "aimed at accelerating de facto equality between men and women . . . "[123] Similarly, Article 5 requires states parties to take all appropriate measures to "modify the social and cultural patterns of conduct of men and women" to eliminate prejudice and practices "based on the idea of the inferiority or the superiority of either of the sexes or on stereotyped roles for men and women."[124] When read together, measures that set aside quotas for men to enter female-dominated fields appear to be permissible measures.

However, the CEDAW Committee's views on Article 4(1) clarify that TSM that benefit men are impermissible. The Committee's GRs on Article 4(1) limit it to measures that benefit women. The early GRs on Article 4(1) indicated the Committee's assumption that TSM measures were meant only to benefit women. GR 5 encourages states parties to utilize TSM "to advance *women's* integration into education, the economy, politics and employment."[125] Similarly, GR 8 recommends that states parties adopt TSM "to ensure women . . . the opportunities to represent their Government at the international level and to participate in the work of international organizations."[126]

GR 25 states that TSM are limited to measures that benefit women. According to the GR, the meaning of Article 4(1) must be defined "in the context of the overall purpose and scope of the Convention, which is to eliminate all forms of discrimination against women . . . "[127] The GR further distinguishes Article 4(1) from neutral affirmative action laws. According to the GR, CEDAW's concept of discrimination is unlike "many national and international legal standards and norms."[128] Whereas other laws "prohibit discrimination on the grounds of sex and protect both men and women from treatment based on arbitrary, unfair and/or unjustifiable distinctions," CEDAW "focuses on discrimination against women, emphasizing that women have suffered, and continue to suffer from various forms of discrimination because they

123. CEDAW, *supra* note 5, art. 4(1).

124. *Id.*, art. 5(a).

125. CEDAW Committee, General Recommendations Made by the Committee on the Elimination of Discrimination Against Women, http://www.un.org/womenwatch/daw/cedaw/recommendations/recomm.htm#recom1 (last visited Sept. 6, 2016).

126. *Id.*

127. CEDAW Committee, General Recommendation No 25 on Article 4, Paragraph 1, of the Convention on the Elimination of All Forms of Discrimination Against Women, ¶ 4, U.N. Doc. A/59/38 (2004).

128. *Id.* ¶ 5.

are women."[129] The recommendation states that the purpose of Article 4(1) is to achieve women's de facto equality with men, correct discrimination, and provide compensation for past discrimination.[130]

According to the CEDAW Committee, a reading of Article 4(1) in light of the purpose of the treaty, which is manifestly the elimination of discrimination against *women*, must yield only TSM that benefit women. As the CEDAW Committee's views in GRs constitute authoritative interpretations, the Scandinavian states cannot appeal to the strict textualist reading to defend TSM that benefit men.

The measures that benefit men under the Scandinavian approach deviate from the treaty because they are based on a more radical ideology with more radical goals. CEDAW uses a framework of anti-discrimination that positions women as victims.[131] By contrast, the Scandinavian approach aims to bring about, as Norway's 2007 report states, "radical change in the gender hierarchy and gender relations."[132] The Scandinavian approach uses a model of gender equality that aims to fundamentally transform gender roles. While CEDAW Committee members may be sympathetic to the Scandinavian approach, the tension between the framing of the treaty and the approach is demonstrable.

E. The Debate over CEDAW's Future

The tension identified above relates to an emergent scholarly discussion regarding CEDAW's future. This debate centers on whether the Convention's scope, which is explicitly limited to discrimination against *women*, should be redefined. Darren Rosenblum, one of the progenitors of the debate, contends that CEDAW cannot successfully create gender equality if it maintains its exclusive focus on women.[133] Rosenblum argues that CEDAW operates under the premise that women are victims and men are the perpetrators of discrimination, a "binarist construction of gender" that excludes men from the "diagnosis of, and the remedy to gender oppression."[134] According to Rosenblum, the solution to this problem would be to "unsex" CEDAW by replacing the term "women" with "gender," which would allow human rights law to move beyond "essentialist notions of womanhood" and "reach more deeply into the inequalities that plague humanity."[135]

Similarly, Lara Stemple criticizes the CEDAW Committee's conflation of the terms "gender" and "women" in GR 19, which defines "gender based violence" as

---

129. *Id.*

130. *Id.* ¶ 15.

131. Darren Rosenblum, *Unsex CEDAW, or What's Wrong with Women's Rights*, 20 COLUM. J. GENDER & L. 98, 158 (2011).

132. CEDAW Committee, *supra* note 98, at 26.

133. Rosenblum, *supra* note 131, at 100.

134. *Id.* at 166.

135. *Id.* at 193.

"violence that is directed against a woman, because she is a woman, or that affects women disproportionately."[136] Stemple argues that this conflation "prohibits the application of law to situations that do not follow traditional gender scripts," such as male rape.[137]

Berta Hernández-Truyol, while agreeing with Rosenblum that CEDAW ought to protect against discrimination based on gender, argues that women remain a necessary "organizing category" in human rights law.[138] Hernández-Truyol points to the ubiquity of women's inequality "across continents, cultures, religions, social classes, and nations" as evidence of the continuing significance of "women" as a category.[139] She concludes that the answer to Rosenblum's concerns would be to "super-sex" CEDAW by adding discrimination on the basis of sexuality, gender, and gender identity along with discrimination against women.[140]

The Scandinavian approach partially responds to the concerns raised by Rosenblum, Stemple, and Hernández-Truyol. Indeed, Rosenblum suggests that, short of redrafting CEDAW, one way to unsex the treaty would be to reinterpret Article 5(a) as the "dominant method of interpreting CEDAW's Articles."[141] The Scandinavian construal of the text could be a step toward such an interpretation.

Assuming that a redrafting of CEDAW or the adoption of another optional protocol remains unlikely, the Scandinavian approach will remain a deviant interpretation of the treaty unless the Committee formally recognizes it. The Committee could legitimize the Scandinavian approach through a GR or Statement. The Committee's lack of action to this point suggests that, for now, it prefers to remain neutral regarding the Scandinavian approach. The Committee may wish to wait until the approach receives support from a larger portion of states parties. The use of TSM for men is a distinctly minority interpretation of the Scandinavian states.[142]

VI. THE DEVELOPMENT OF HUMAN RIGHTS LAW THROUGH MINORITY INTERPRETATIONS

The asymmetric approach to treaty interpretation is functionally similar to the relationship between general and special customary international law. General

---

136. Lara Stemple, *Human Rights, Sex, and Gender: Limits in Theory and Practice*, 31 PACE L. REV. 824, 827 (2011) (quoting Committee on the Elimination of Discrimination Against Women, General Recommendation 19: Violence Against Women, U.N. Doc. A/47/38 (Jan. 29, 1992)).

137. *Id.* at 828.

138. Berta Esperanza Hernández-Truyol, *Unsex CEDAW? No! Super-Sex It!*, 20 COLUM. J. GENDER & L. 195, 197 (2011).

139. *Id.* at 205.

140. *Id.* at 221.

141. Rosenblum, *supra* note 131, at 194.

142. In a search of reports dating back to June 2009, I found only nine that mentioned men under Article 4(1).

customary international law applies to all states equally and special customary international law applies only to non-generalizable topics or to countries of a specific region.[143] Once established, no state can unilaterally withdraw from a general custom.[144] However, a group of states may establish a special custom, which binds only those states that consent to it.[145] These special customs may even contradict general customs, though they cannot violate *jus cogens* norms.[146] Special customs sometimes become general customs or a part of treaty law. For example, the 12 nautical mile limit for the span of the territorial sea was initially a special custom among Middle Eastern countries before its widespread adoption.[147]

Similarly, the asymmetric approach to treaty interpretation allows states to promote a more demanding interpretation of a treaty, which can then be adopted by like-minded states but not imposed on other states in the absence of consent. Unlike in special customary international law, states cannot promote a lower standard in human rights treaties because this would violate their obligations to nonstate actors. Yet permissiveness for progressive minority interpretations creates opportunities to develop human rights law in a decentralized manner. States that promote minority interpretations essentially serve as "laboratories" and other states or a treaty monitoring body may adopt their innovations.

Not every innovation will become a majority interpretation. Some will remain local or specialized interpretations. If most minority interpretations were never to become majority interpretations, the approach would tend to fragment international law. In the context of human rights law, which rests upon an ideology of universalism, this could be concerning.

However, more demanding interpretations can exist in parallel with majority interpretations in a way that regressive interpretations cannot. The Scandinavian approach does not directly undermine CEDAW like the RUDs of the predominantly Muslim states. The Scandinavian states implement both TSM that fit within the majority interpretation and TSM that do not. Moreover, the possibility of adoption by the majority persists as long as the relevant supervisory body remains permissive regarding the interpretation. The Scandinavian approach began to develop in the late 1980s and has since co-existed alongside the majority approach with little criticism by the CEDAW Committee.

---

143. Anthony D'Amato, *The Concept of Special Custom in International Law*, 63 Am. J. Int'l L. 211, 212–13 (1969).

144. The "persistent objector" rule allows objecting states to opt out of a general custom as it emerges. Michael P. Scharf, *Accelerated Formation of Customary International Law*, 20 ILSA J. Int'l Comp. L. 305, 317 (2014).

145. *See* D'Amato, *supra* note 143, at 215.

146. Farhad Talaie, *The Importance of Custom and the Process of Its Formation in Modern International Law*, 5 James Cook U. L. Rev. 27, 40–41 (1998).

147. *Id.* at 41.

VII. CONCLUSION

Neither the Muslim RUDs nor the Scandinavian approach fit within the confines of CEDAW and the jurisprudence of the CEDAW Committee. The Committee's use of calibrated obligations is not sufficiently capacious to accept either form of deviation. The Muslim RUDs go against the core obligations of the states parties, as defined by the Committee and its Statement on Reservations to the Convention. The quotas afforded to men under the Scandinavian approach fall outside of the scope of Article 4(1) as defined by GR 25.

The CEDAW Committee could restrict both deviations, but instead it grants latitude to the Scandinavian countries to utilize their own interpretation. While the Committee vigorously calls upon the predominantly Muslim states parties to withdraw their reservations, it permits the Scandinavian approach to develop. The Committee is more willing to allow deviation in a progressive direction than in a conservative deviation, such that the law is more malleable for progressive states than for conservative states.

Under this asymmetric approach to treaty interpretation, human rights treaties are only living instruments for states that wish to develop innovative and progressive interpretations. States can include these interpretations in their periodic reports with little fear of criticism. Their interpretations can evolve into minority interpretations shared among like-minded progressive states. These communities of interpretation may eventually achieve majority status through the agreement of the bulk of states parties, the official approval of the treaty body, or even the establishment of a separate treaty. The history of human rights treaties at the United Nations is one of increasing specialization. Each new human rights treaty deals with another subset of rights, issues, and identities. The asymmetric approach may allow for the development of the seeds of these treaties.

The future of CEDAW is not yet written and only the passage of time will reveal whether the Scandinavian approach remains a minority approach, gains acceptance under the CEDAW treaty regime, or becomes the subject of another treaty regime entirely. In the interim, additional research on the asymmetric comparative international law approach to treaty interpretation is necessary to determine the extent of the phenomenon in both human rights and other subfields of international law.

21

Comparative International Law
and Human Rights

A Value-Added Approach

CHRISTOPHER McCRUDDEN*

I. INTRODUCTION

The principal issue that effectively defines the idea of comparative international human rights law scholarship is whether the interpretation of international human rights law at the *domestic* level has resulted in similarities or differences between jurisdictions that require explanation. By "interpretation" I mean to include within that term what the editors of this volume have described more accurately as "the way in which international law is understood, interpreted, applied, and approached."[1] If striking similarities of interpretation, thus defined, are apparent at the domestic level when we might expect differences, or significant differences are found when we might expect similarities, the primary question is why these similarities and differences have emerged, and what these tell us about the use to which international human rights law is put at the domestic level. It is this question that raises the most interesting scholarly puzzles, not least because, ultimately, it may help us understand better what international human rights law *is*.

Discrete approaches within international law, and within comparative law, suggest some, already well-known, answers to why similarities and differences exist at the domestic level: some *international* law scholarship suggests that differences can

* This chapter was written whilst I was a Fellow of the *Wissenschaftskolleg zu Berlin* (2014–2015). I would like to thank Veronika Fikak, Benedict Kingsbury, Christoph Möllers, Brendan O'Leary, Daniel Peat, Steve Ratner, Anthea Roberts, Mila Versteeg, participants of the Sokol Colloquium on Comparative International Law, participants at a seminar at Humboldt University, and several anonymous referees, for helpful comments and suggestions on earlier drafts.

1. See Anthea Roberts, Paul B. Stephan, Pierre-Hugues Verdier & Mila Versteeg, *Conceptualizing Comparative International Law* (this volume).

be explained by the fragmentation of international law at the level of the relevant *international* institutions (domestic jurisdictions simply reflect these differences); some comparative *constitutional* law scholarship suggests that broad *institutional* differences between national jurisdictions explain substantive differences in interpretation (domestic jurisdictions differ no more in interpreting international human rights law than they do in interpreting human or constitutional rights more generally, and for the same reasons).

This chapter suggests that previous explanations either from comparative constitutional law or from international law are not exhaustive in explaining similarities and differences, and that the field of comparative international law usefully draws attention to additional factors. The field of comparative international law shares with comparative constitutional law a focus on the operation of domestic bodies rather than international bodies, and a focus on comparing how these domestic bodies operate. The field differs from comparative constitutional law in focusing primarily on the interpretation of international norms, rather than domestic constitutional norms. The field shares with the "fragmentation" literature a focus on the differences in the interpretation of international law, but differs from it in focusing on the way these differences in interpretation arise at the domestic level rather than the international level.

My argument is, however, that within the field of comparative international law, there is an additional element that needs to be taken into account. My hypothesis is that what similarities and differences are observable in the pattern of domestic implementation of international human rights law result, at least in part, from the different functions that *international human rights law*, as such, fulfills in different domestic contexts.

For example, in a recently published article in the *American Journal of International Law* concerning the domestic interpretation of the Convention on the Elimination of all Forms of Discrimination Against Women (CEDAW), I argued that the observable patterns of references to CEDAW in national level courts may result, to a significant degree, from the combination of four elements that, taken together, are unique to international human rights law: that it is international law; that it concerns human rights; that it is law; and that it is being applied domestically.[2] The first three elements combined offer domestic courts a set of norms that is consensus-based ("international") and purportedly universal ("human rights"), which courts and legal advocates are able to draw on ("law"), to help address domestic concerns, or escape from otherwise troublesome "domestic" constraints.

Courts and advocates in different jurisdictions draw on such norms to address similar or different domestic constraints, and similarities or differences may therefore emerge between these different jurisdictions as to the meaning and scope of the human right in question. The similar or different functions played in different jurisdictions by this set of four elements contribute to an explanation of similarities or differences in substantive interpretation at the national level that

---

2. Christopher McCrudden, *Why Do National Court Judges Refer to Human Rights Treaties? A Comparative International Law Analysis of CEDAW*, 109 Am. J. Int'l L. 534 (2015).

neither previous international law literature taken by itself, nor the scholarship of comparative human rights taken by itself, delivers. I suggested that the study highlighted a role for domestic judicial use of international human rights standards that differs from orthodox interpretations, demonstrating the utility of a comparative international human rights analysis.

In this chapter, I hope to offer a more sustained justification for separating comparative international human rights law from other related scholarly approaches. CEDAW will be used as a running example throughout. The chapter proceeds as follows. In Section II, I attempt to isolate the field of comparative international law from other connected fields, distinguishing it from, but showing its links to, comparative constitutional law and general international law scholarship. Section III, drawing on this analysis, sets out conceptually what I understand to be necessary and sufficient elements that define the field of "comparative international *human rights* law." In my view, to qualify as "comparative international human rights" each of the following three elements must be present: (1) an element of *international human rights law*, (2) *domestic* legal "use" of this international human rights law, and (3) a *comparison* between two or more of these domestic legal uses of international human rights law. The implications of this definition for what is included and what is excluded are identified and considered.

In Section IV, I consider differences between the approach I suggest and the broader approach adopted by the editors in their introduction to this volume, and I suggest that such differences as exist may be due to the fact that I am primarily concerned with human rights, and that comparative international *human rights* law has features that distinguish it from comparative international legal scholarship more generally. This has important implications for future research, and I then turn to consider some fundamental issues. I suggest some of the practical questions that arise when one is attempting to undertake a comparative international *human rights* legal analysis, including the type of issues that might best form the basis for such an analysis. In particular, I develop the functional hypothesis for why it is important to separate the role of international human rights law at the domestic level from other domestic level systems of rights, I suggest a broad defense of the modestly functionalist approach suggested against possible criticisms, and I consider some possible implications of a comparative international human rights law analysis if this hypothesis is correct, returning at the end to the issue of how far it matters that I am dealing with human rights. Section V concludes.

II. DEFINING THE FIELD

A. Human Rights and Comparative Constitutional Law

The phenomenon of "human rights law" (the definition of which will be considered further below) has contributed to at least three particular sets of scholarship that are of immediate importance for a comparative international human rights law approach. It is necessary to identify these with some particularity to clarify what added value a fourth set of scholarship ("comparative international human rights law") brings.

The first is the growth of comparative constitutional law, much of which is primarily concerned in practice with comparing how the courts of domestic jurisdictions have interpreted provisions in their domestic Bills of Rights in similar or contrasting ways, although it often purports to be broader than this, investigating structural and institutional issues, such as federalism and the separation of powers. The roots of comparative constitutional law are in comparative law and in constitutional law, rather than in international law, and those engaging in comparative constitutional law have largely ignored international law, seeing it as a separate discipline.[3]

International human rights law is of some interest to comparative constitutional law, but principally in two respects. First, different domestic legal systems have different constitutional relationships with international law, and this is regarded as a topic suitable for comparative study in itself.[4] So, for example, whether a state is monist or dualist (or somewhere in-between) is largely a matter of domestic constitutional law, and is a topic that generates comparative scrutiny. International human rights law, in this field of study, tends to be considered largely from this constitutional perspective, analyzing the who, what, where, when, and why of the relationship between the domestic constitutional law of different states and the body of international human rights law. How far, for example, do domestic courts directly apply international human rights law as part of their domestic legal system, and is it hierarchically superior or inferior to other legal norms in that system?

In this context, the primary interest of constitutional law comparativists is, understandably, in the structural and institutional implications of international human rights law for domestic legal systems, rather than in its substantive human rights content. This approach maintains a strict distinction between international law and domestic law, identifying the comparative constitutional issue as being the different ways in which domestic systems bridge the gap between these two different systems. The approach taken is appropriately regarded as *comparative* where the comparison involves norms, each of which is *binding*.[5]

---

3. It is invidious to try to date the modern growth of comparative constitutional law's engagement with human rights but a rough starting point would probably be THOMAS M. FRANCK, COMPARATIVE CONSTITUTIONAL PROCESS: CASES AND MATERIALS (1968), followed by COMPARATIVE HUMAN RIGHTS (Richard P. Claude ed., 1976), both of which demonstrate these characteristics. This tradition has continued to the present day: two of the most widely used American law school casebooks on comparative constitutional law, NORMAN DORSEN ET AL., COMPARATIVE CONSTITUTIONALISM: CASES AND MATERIALS (2d ed. 2010) and VICKI JACKSON & MARK TUSHNET, COMPARATIVE CONSTITUTIONAL LAW (3d ed. 2014), well illustrate some of these tendencies. A significant proportion of each concerns the interpretation of constitutional rights; in each, the material considered relevant primarily comprises domestic constitutional interpretations by constitutional courts or cognate bodies. The European Court of Human Rights is accorded a sort of honorary status of "European constitutional court" for these purposes. Apart from this exception, there are relatively few references to international law materials, and where they occur they are treated primarily as equivalent to domestic sources.

4. *See, e.g.,* AALT WILLEM HERINGA & PHILIPP KIVER, CONSTITUTIONS COMPARED: AN INTRODUCTION TO COMPARATIVE CONSTITUTIONAL LAW 159–88 (3d ed. 2012).

5. This seems particularly the case as regards scholars from civil law-influenced backgrounds who tend to resist this blurring. *See, e.g.,* MICHAL BOBEK, COMPARATIVE REASONING IN EUROPEAN

Second, international human rights law has also come, more recently, to have considerable importance in comparative constitutional law, particularly in systems based in the common law, where international human rights law is drawn on in judicial decisions as an *interpretative* resource—rather than a binding norm—in the course of adjudicating disputes concerning domestic constitutional law. How far, for example, do domestic courts consider international human rights law when interpreting domestic Bill of Rights provisions, what we might call the "indirect application" of international human rights law? The growth in practice of domestic courts engaging in "indirect application" has contributed to a view emerging among some comparative constitutional law scholars that international human rights law is to be regarded as a subset of, and contributing to, the development of a human rights jurisprudence that has become transnational. There is, in this context, little emphasis on strict separation of sources into national and international, monist and dualist systems, binding and non-binding in domestic constitutional law.[6] This second approach now dominates comparative constitutional law and has led to several studies of particular issues, such as comparative studies of the meaning and enforcement of socioeconomic rights across several jurisdictions,[7] and methods of judicial reasoning in human rights cases,[8] in which international law is shown to have been regarded by several domestic judiciaries as one of several normative systems that are to be included in the interpretative exercise.

This brief survey shows that, within the field of comparative constitutional law thus defined, there are no studies, so far as I am aware, attempting to apply the comparative method to the interpretation of international human rights *as such* in different domestic legal systems. So, for example, although there are many comparative studies of the movement to secure women's rights in different domestic systems,

SUPREME COURTS 34 (2013) ("In most of the categories identified . . . as mandatory uses of foreign law [including international law], there is no comparison going on at all."). In a survey of "the use of foreign precedents by constitutional judges," the editors adopt a similar position: "The use of international case law has also been excluded from the research," the editors write, arguing that a clear distinction should be drawn between "the optional and purely voluntary dialogue between courts" and the application of binding international law. Only references to non-binding international law were included. THE USE OF FOREIGN PRECEDENTS BY CONSTITUTIONAL JUDGES 4–5 (Tania Groppi & Marie-Claire Ponthoreau eds., 2013).

6. Two recent studies exemplify this approach. *See* VICKI C. JACKSON, CONSTITUTIONAL ENGAGEMENT IN A TRANSNATIONAL ERA 10–11 (2010) ("This book is concerned less with defining those situations in which international law, as such, is internally binding than with exploring the possibilities of international law serving as a reflective or persuasive resource in the interpretation of domestic constitutions themselves . . . , including the degree to which aspects of international law should be regarded as in a sense constitutional."); ERIN DALY, DIGNITY RIGHTS: COURTS, CONSTITUTIONS, AND THE WORTH OF THE HUMAN PERSON 150 (2013), 150 (describing how "the once rigid lines between international and municipal law have begun to blur").

7. *See, e.g.,* EXPLORING SOCIAL RIGHTS: BETWEEN THEORY AND PRACTICE (Daphne Barak-Erez & Aeyal M. Gross eds., 2007).

8. *See, e.g.,* REASONING RIGHTS: COMPARATIVE JUDICIAL ENGAGEMENT (Liora Lazarus, Christopher McCrudden & Nigel Bowles eds., 2014).

these effectively tend to treat international norms, such as CEDAW, as hardly worth
distinguishing from the national norms.

B. International Human Rights and International Law

If we turn now from comparative constitutional law to the field of general international law, there are two strands of international law scholarship that are of particular relevance to our study.

The first is the strand of international legal scholarship that has traditionally been
concerned with the incorporation of international law into domestic law, and has
developed a sophisticated set of concepts with which to analyze how this is accomplished in different domestic legal systems. This is the point at which international
law scholarship comes most closely into contact with comparative constitutional
law, which, as we have seen, has similar interests. The approach is comparative, but
instead of focusing on the substantive interpretation of the relevant international
law, and whether, for example, the interpretation differs significantly because of
whether it has been incorporated or not, this field of scholarship is more concerned
with distinguishing the techniques of incorporation and the differences in the legal
status of the international law norms depending on which techniques of incorporation have been adopted. It is primarily concerned, then, with differences in the
authority that international law norms have been accorded, rather than with their
substance.[9]

A second scholarly development of importance in international law *is* more concerned with substantive similarities and differences in the meaning of the international legal norms as interpreted by relevant international actors. This international
law scholarship has effectively split into two competing approaches. In one approach,
which I suggest is the dominant, indeed one can say orthodox, approach, international legal scholarship incorporates diverse materials, including from national legal
systems, primarily to illustrate, or to bring about, the coherence of the international
human rights system.

In contrast, a second approach challenges this orthodox approach and tends
to focus on what has been termed "fragmentation." International law has been
described as "fragmenting," meaning that it is losing its coherence amid the pleth-
ora of institutions responsible for interpreting these norms. Fragmentation emphasizes the absence of consensus in practice in the interpretation of the substance of
international law.[10] This fragmentation, however, is primarily seen as emerging at
the international level itself, and is less concerned about identifying fragmentation at the domestic level. We are now seeing the (re-)emergence of an approach to

---

9. A classic study, much of it concerned with human rights interpretation, is SHAHEED FATIMA,
USING INTERNATIONAL LAW IN DOMESTIC COURTS (2005).

10. *See, e.g.,* SARAH JOSEPH, JENNY SCHULTZ & MELISSA CASTAN, THE INTERNATIONAL
COVENANT ON CIVIL AND POLITICAL RIGHTS: CASES, MATERIALS, AND COMMENTARY xi (2000).
A good recent example is BEN SAUL ET AL., THE INTERNATIONAL COVENANT ON ECONOMIC,
SOCIAL AND CULTURAL RIGHTS: COMMENTARY CASES AND MATERIALS (2014), in particular
the Introduction.

international law that emphasizes the multiplicity of different, and sometimes competing, international regimes. This literature often sees the substantive legal norms that international legal regimes develop as differing in significant respects.

The primary focus of the "fragmentation" literature is on international law in general, but there is also considerable interest in particular areas of international law, including human rights. International human rights law is seen as also subject to fragmentation; indeed, it is often seen as a principal example of the phenomenon. There have been studies, for example, examining differences in the treatment of religious dress by the ECtHR and the UN Committee on Human Rights.[11] Attention has been given to how particular areas of international human rights law have developed differently from core aspects of general international law (for example, differences between general international law and international human rights law in how customary law is developed and recognized).[12]

Although focused on international law, both general and specific, the fragmentation literature borrows its basic methodology from comparative law; it involves comparing, for example, how and why different international law bodies have taken similar or contrasting approaches in interpreting relatively similar norms. The difference between this international law scholarship and comparative law scholarship (including comparative constitutional law) is that the focus of the former is on comparing "international" institutions (broadly defined to include prominent regional organizations, such as the ECtHR) rather than on comparing domestic institutions.[13]

In the context of the implementation of CEDAW, for example, we see excellent examples of this second type of international law scholarship, with both coherence- and fragmentation-oriented approaches in evidence. Recently, a *Commentary* on CEDAW has been published that exhibits the features of a classic international law analysis, in which the dominant focus is on the interpretation of the text of CEDAW by international bodies, primarily the Committee established to oversee its implementation, the Committee on the Elimination of all Forms of Discrimination Against Women. The Commentary brings together the Committee's interpretations, introduces the reader to interpretations of CEDAW by other international and regional human rights bodies (such as the European Court of Human Rights and the Inter-American Court of Human Rights), systematizes them according to the particular Article of the Convention, and aims to produce a coherent account of the existing interpretative practice. Occasionally (perhaps in this Commentary somewhat more than in equivalent Commentaries on other international law instruments),

---

11. Amélie Barras, *Transnational Understandings of Secularisms and Their Impact on the Right to Religious Freedom—Exploring Religious Symbols Cases at the UN and ECHR*, 11 J. Hum. Rts. 263 (2012).

12. *See, e.g.,* Anthony D'Amato, *Human Rights as Part of Customary International Law: A Plea for Change of Paradigms*, 25 Ga. J. Int'l & Comp. L. 47 (1995).

13. Few of the many highly regarded commentaries on the major international human rights treaties pay any attention to domestic interpretations of the treaty, and in those commentaries that do, references to domestic case law occupy very little space. *See, e.g.,* Saul et al., *supra* note 10.

there are occasional references to a domestic court's interpretation or application of CEDAW, but there is no attempt to survey these decisions systematically.

The academic literature on CEDAW also contains attempts to address the issue of fragmentation, and recently there has been a significant set of studies that compare CEDAW with other multilateral (international and regional) regimes, with a view to establishing significant differences between the interpretation of CEDAW and other international or regional regimes attempting to further women's equality, particularly that of the European Union,[14] or between CEDAW and other international law regimes outside the human rights field that appear to be cutting across CEDAW, such as areas of international economic law.[15]

C. "Comparative International Law" Introduced

Into this already crowded field of human rights scholarship, another approach is currently being developed, which has been termed "comparative international law." Scholars working in this field of study have identified a gap between scholarship on comparative constitutional law and international law scholarship. This new field of study explores *comparatively* how different *domestic* institutions interpret the same or broadly similar *international* law norms (e.g., whether the United States and the United Kingdom have distinct interpretations of international investment arbitration law). This would include comparisons between international bodies interpreting international law and domestic courts interpreting constitutional and other domestic rights that are seen to be the close *equivalent to* the international legal requirements, in the sense that the domestic standards satisfy the obligation to have already or to adopt for the first time such laws or other measures as may be necessary to give effect to the norms recognized by the international standards.[16] In the international *human rights* context, this is a surprisingly underdeveloped approach. There is only one major study, so far as I am aware, attempting to apply

---

14. *See* Simone van der Post, *Positive Measures in Employment Law: Different Approaches under CEDAW and EU Gender Equality Legislation*, 2 EUR. GENDER EQUALITY L. REV. 21 (2011); Ingrid Westendorp & Antonia Waltermann, *The Essence of Discrimination Against Women: An Interpretation by CEDAW and the European Union, in* THE WOMEN'S CONVENTION TURNED 30: ACHIEVEMENTS, SETBACKS, AND PROSPECTS 33 (Ingrid Westendorp ed., 2012); Lisa Waddington & Laura Visser, *Temporary Special Measures under the Women's Convention and Positive Action under EU Law: Mutually Compatible or Irreconcilable?, in* THE WOMEN'S CONVENTION TURNED 30: ACHIEVEMENTS, SETBACKS, AND PROSPECTS, *supra* at 95; Anja Wiesbrock, *Equal Employment Opportunities and Equal Pay: Measuring EU Law Against the Standards of the Women's Convention, in* THE WOMEN'S CONVENTION TURNED 30: ACHIEVEMENTS, SETBACKS, AND PROSPECTS, *supra* at 227; Dagmar Schiek & Jule Mulder, *Equality and Economic and Social Life Including Implications for the European Union, in* THE WOMEN'S CONVENTION TURNED 30: ACHIEVEMENTS, SETBACKS, AND PROSPECTS, *supra* at 303.

15. Jennifer Sellin & Nishara Mendis, *Women's Right to Health and International Trade—Special Reference to the GATS and the TRIPS Agreement, in* THE WOMEN'S CONVENTION TURNED 30: ACHIEVEMENTS, SETBACKS, AND PROSPECTS, *supra* note 14, at 249.

16. *See, e.g.,* International Covenant on Civil and Political Rights art. 2(2), Dec. 16, 1966, 999 U.N.T.S. 171.

the comparative method to the interpretation of international human rights law as such in different *domestic* legal systems, and that is a very recent study of how selected domestic jurisdictions have interpreted CEDAW.[17]

III. FIELDS OF INQUIRY OF COMPARATIVE INTERNATIONAL HUMAN RIGHTS

What emerges from the discussion so far, therefore, is that both the existing international law and comparative constitutional law literature have strengths and weaknesses in seeking to understand the phenomenon of domestic interpretation of international human rights law at the domestic level, and that the new field of comparative international law is a welcome additional perspective that can be brought to bear. But what of comparative international *human rights* law scholarship? What does it involve? In this section, I consider the fields of inquiry of comparative international human rights law, attempting to specify precisely where comparative international human rights analysis adds value to existing approaches. In the next section, I consider the extent to which comparative international human rights law is sui generis even within the field of comparative international law, and what the implications are if it is.

A. Multilayered Governance

Before proceeding to a discussion of fields of inquiry, there is one key point that needs to be made. It has been clear for some time that the standard dichotomy between the domestic level and the international level no longer captures the multiplicity of governance structures that we find in practice. The term that is used to capture this phenomenon is "multilayered" governance, and the spatial metaphor continues in the adoption of other terms that seek to describe the relationships between institutions that are involved at the various layers. So, for example, it is now common in the legal literature to speak of "vertical" and "horizontal" relationships, which describe the relationship between institutions that are or are not hierarchically structured.[18] We would speak of the "vertical" relationship that exists between the devolved government in Scotland and government of the United Kingdom, sitting in London. In contrast, we may speak of other institutions, not in a hierarchical relationship with each other, as in a "horizontal" relationship, for example the horizontal relationship between the devolved government in Scotland, and the devolved government in Wales. Although relationships between institutions and governments are often more complex than this simple dichotomy presumes, it is useful for heuristic purposes, and the terminology of "vertical" and "horizontal" will be adopted in the subsequent discussion.

17. *See* WOMEN'S HUMAN RIGHTS: CEDAW IN INTERNATIONAL, REGIONAL AND NATIONAL LAW (Anne Hellum & Henriette Sinding Aasen eds., 2013).

18. *See, e.g.,* Thomas Cottier, *Multilayered Governance, Pluralism, and Moral Conflict*, 16 IND. J. GLOBAL LEGAL STUD. 647 (2009).

B. Necessary and Sufficient Conditions

To qualify as "comparative international human rights" all three of the following conditions must be present: (1) there must be an element of international human rights law, (2) there must be domestic "use" of this international human rights law, and (3) there must be a comparison between two or more of these domestic uses of international human rights law. For the purposes of this chapter, "international human rights law" includes human rights treaty law developed and applied at the international level, such as in various United Nations bodies, and human rights treaty law developed and applied by regional human rights bodies, such as the European Court of Human Rights. International human rights law also includes customary international human rights law.

C. Domestic Interpretation of International Human Rights

The principal focus of this chapter is on a particular subset of the second category of comparison suggested above, that is, horizontal comparisons of the ways in which different domestic bodies have interpreted international human rights norms as such. The prime example of what is included is a horizontal comparison between *domestic* courts interpreting *international* human rights law (treaty or customary), for example comparing how the Canadian courts interpret the concept of "jurisdiction" in human rights treaties, with the interpretation of equivalent provisions by the United Kingdom Supreme Court or the United States Supreme Court;[19] or comparing the extent to which national courts consider nonstate actors to be subject to international human rights obligations;[20] or comparing how different national courts exercise their responsibilities in applying the human rights aspects of international criminal law.[21]

The principal focus on judicial interpretation should not be taken as excluding the potential focus on other units of analysis, for example nonstate actors at the state level and transnationally, various international actors, and other state actors such as legislatures, executives, and administrative agencies. Indeed, one of the actors most studied comparatively are national level human rights institutions, given the task of interpreting international human rights law at the domestic level.

Although not traditionally included with the scope of "comparative law," another area of comparison included in this chapter is a vertical comparison between domestic bodies within the same jurisdiction in the way they interpret international human rights law, for example, comparing how the US federal courts interpret international human rights law with how the California Supreme Court interprets it, or comparing how national human rights agencies interpret international

---

19. *See, e.g.,* Marko Milanovic, Extraterritorial Application of Human Rights Treaties: Law, Principles, and Policy (2011).

20. *See, e.g.,* Andrew Clapham, Human Rights Obligations of Non-state Actors (2006).

21. *See, e.g.,* Paul Roberts, *Comparative Law for International Criminal Justice, in* Comparative Law: A Handbook 339 (Esin Örücü & David Nelken eds., 2007).

human rights law with how domestic courts interpret international human rights law.

We can now identify more clearly what comparisons are and are not included in the field of comparative human rights. We can distinguish between: (1) horizontal comparisons of international and regional human rights bodies, (2) horizontal comparisons of national human rights bodies, and (3) vertical comparisons of international human rights bodies with regional human rights bodies, and with national human rights bodies.

D. Horizontal Comparisons

This chapter does not consider that the first of these, that is, horizontal comparisons of the way in which different international bodies interpret international human rights norms, constitutes comparative international human rights law. This particular horizontal comparison is the primary focus of attention in the "fragmentation" literature, from which "comparative international law" seeks to distinguish itself. Comparing, for example, how the International Court of Justice interprets particular human rights with how the International Criminal Court interprets the "same" rights, under treaty or customary international law, is primarily an issue of international law "fragmentation." Also not included are horizontal comparisons between "regional" bodies, comparing, for example, how the ECtHR and the Advisory Committee on the Framework Convention interpret freedom of religion,[22] or comparing the interpretation of the ECtHR with that of the Inter-American Human Rights Court relating to the "same" concepts in human rights law, such as the notion of the "person."[23] So too, horizontal comparisons between "regional" courts' interpretation of international human rights law are not included, where a comparison is drawn, for example, between how the European Court of Human Rights receives and interprets international human rights law[24] compared with the approach adopted by the Court of Justice of the European Union,[25] or compared with how the Inter-American Court receives and interprets the "same" international human rights law, such as

---

22. *See, e.g.,* S.E. Berry, *A Tale of Two Instruments: Religious Minorities and the Council of Europe's Rights Regime*, 30 NETH. Q. HUM. RTS. 10 (2012) (comparing approaches taken by the Advisory Committee on the Framework Convention on National Minorities with that of the European Court of Human Rights in the area of freedom of religion).

23. *See* Piet Hein van Kempen, *The Recognition of Legal Persons in International Human Rights Instruments: Protection Against and Through Criminal Justice?, in* CORPORATE CRIMINAL LIABILITY: EMERGENCE, CONVERGENCE, AND RISK 355 (Mark Pieth & Radha Ivory eds., 2011).

24. *See* MAGDALENA FOROWICZ, THE RECEPTION OF INTERNATIONAL LAW IN THE EUROPEAN COURT OF HUMAN RIGHTS (2010).

25. *See* Christopher McCrudden, *Using Comparative Reasoning in Human Rights Adjudication: The Court of Justice of the European Union and the European Court of Human Rights Compared*, 15 CAMBRIDGE Y.B. EUR. LEGAL STUD. 383 (2013); HANNEKE SENDEN, INTERPRETATION OF FUNDAMENTAL RIGHTS IN A MULTILEVEL LEGAL SYSTEM: AN ANALYSIS OF THE EUROPEAN COURT OF HUMAN RIGHTS AND THE COURT OF JUSTICE OF THE EUROPEAN UNION (2011).

that regarding freedom of expression,[26] or prisoners' rights.[27] Nor, in the context of CEDAW, are we concerned with comparing the treatment of women's rights by different international committees overseeing different human rights treaties.[28]

E. Vertical Comparisons

I have stipulated that two or more state jurisdictions must be involved for it to be regarded as truly "comparative" in my understanding of the term. Therefore, the third type of comparison distinguished above, viz. vertical comparison between international bodies interpreting international human rights law (treaty and customary) and one particular domestic court interpreting international human rights law (treaty and customary), will not be included in the field of "comparative international human rights law." For example, how the UK Supreme Court interprets a particular human right protected under customary international law compared with the interpretation of the same right under customary international law by the International Court of Justice will not be included, nor will comparisons between one jurisdiction's approach to the interpretation of human rights compared with that of the Human Rights Committee be included.[29] But it would be appropriate to include a comparison between multiple domestic courts and a regional or international body.

F. Constitutional and Statutory Rights

Just as several comparisons are not included because they are already included within what the fragmentation literature would consider, several other understandings of comparative human rights law are also not included as they are essentially the subject matter of comparative *constitutional* law. As a result, only a subset of the second category of comparison sketched out above (horizontal comparisons of national human rights bodies) is included. Of course, constitutions are influenced

26. *See, e.g.,* Antoine Buyse, *Tacit Citing: The Scarcity of Judicial Dialogue Between the Global and the Regional Human Rights Mechanisms in Freedom of Expression Cases, in* The United Nations and Freedom of Expression and Information: Critical Perspectives (Tarlach McGonagle & Yvonne Donders eds., 2015).

27. *See, e.g.,* Piet Hein van Kempen, *Positive Obligations to Ensure the Human Rights of Prisoners: Safety, Healthcare, Conjugal Visits and the Possibility of Founding a Family Under the ICCPR, the ECHR, the ACHR and the AfChHPR, in* Prison Policy and Prisoners' Rights: The Protection of Prisoners' Fundamental Rights in International and Domestic Law (Peter J.P. Tak & Manon Jendly eds., 2008).

28. For a comparison of the views of the UN Human Rights Committee and CEDAW, see R.C. Oostland, Non-discrimination and Equality of Women: A Comparative Analysis of the Interpretation by the UN Human Rights Committee and the UN Committee on the Elimination of Discrimination Against Women 184–216 (2006) (unpublished PhD dissertation, University of Utrecht), *available at* http://dspace.library.uu.nl/handle/1874/9832.

29. *See, e.g.,* The International Covenant on Civil and Political Rights and United Kingdom Law (David Harris & Sarah Joseph eds., 1995).

by international law (and vice versa), but that is not the project on which comparative international human rights law is intended to focus. The comparative study of constitutional rights protections that are merely *equivalent* to international and regional rights, such as socioeconomic rights, will also not be included, even where the international standards are used as the baseline for assessing the different approaches adopted nationally.[30]

Comparisons of how ordinary domestic statute law seeks to protect rights equivalent to international human rights, such as the right to private life, insofar as it applies to state and public bodies, will not be included. So, too, domestic law that protects equivalent rights between private persons, including domestic anti-discrimination law, for example, is not included as it falls more clearly into comparative law in the traditional way in which it has been conceptualized above. A horizontal comparison between domestic constitutional law regimes preventing discrimination, for example comparing the approach taken by the United States Supreme Court on a particular right with that taken by the Indian Supreme Court, where no international or regional human rights law issues arise, will not be included. Although not included as the primary object of study, these understandings of "human rights" have links with those issues that are included, and would therefore have to be kept in mind in the course of a comparative international human rights law study.

G. Shared Meta-principles

Although several other comparisons may be at the margins of comparative international human rights law, seeming to fall more squarely into comparative constitutional law or "fragmentation," I suggest that, in the human rights context at least, excluding these comparisons entirely from the field of inquiry weakens the explanatory richness that the project of comparative international human rights law seeks to achieve. In particular, horizontal comparisons between domestic courts interpreting meta-principles that appear to be shared between the different levels and jurisdictions should be included. For example, there is now significant domestic reference to "human dignity," even where the domestic court does not advert to the fact that the meta-principle is also present in international human rights law. A comparative examination of this phenomenon should be included.[31] However, where the comparison is only between interpretations of such meta-principles by international and regional bodies, it would not be included.[32]

---

30. *See* PAUL O'CONNELL, VINDICATING SOCIO-ECONOMIC RIGHTS: INTERNATIONAL STANDARDS AND COMPARATIVE EXPERIENCES (2012).

31. *See, e.g.,* Christopher McCrudden, *Human Dignity and Judicial Interpretation of Human Rights*, 19 EUR. J. INT'L L. 655 (2008); DALY, *supra* note 6.

32. *See, e.g.,* Jure Vidmar, *Judicial Interpretations of Democracy in Human Rights Treaties*, 3 CAMBRIDGE J. INT'L & COMP. L. 532 (2014).

H. Equivalent Standards

So, too, *vertical* comparison between international bodies interpreting international human rights law (treaty and customary) and domestic courts interpreting constitutional and other domestic rights that are equivalent to the international rights, might also usefully be included. Thus, for example, how the Inter-American Court interprets the right to freedom of expression under the IACHR might usefully be compared with the approach taken by the United States and the UK Supreme Courts to freedom of speech under domestic law. Although these additional comparisons appear to be less related to international human rights law proper, they are necessary for a fuller understanding of the reasons for similarities and differences in the interpretation of international law, not least because they are thought to satisfy the obligation to have already or to adopt such laws or other measures as may be necessary to give effect to the rights recognized by the international standards.

I. Transnational Human Rights Law

It is more uncertain whether *transnational* human rights law should be included, in the sense of human rights legal standards that apply across two or more legal jurisdictions but are not international or regional within the meaning of these terms that I have proposed previously; the protections under the Alien Tort Statute (ATS) might fit within this controversial category. After some consideration, I suggest that these "transnational" standards should be included. Several of these types of provisions, like ATS itself, are based on a domestic law provision but are regarded domestically as based on international law, so they are sometimes indirect attempts to apply international law, particularly customary international law. They often involve some of the more interesting hybridization between domestic and international law, leading to distinct national interpretations of international law, and thus seem to fit into my general understanding of the project.[33]

IV. IS COMPARATIVE INTERNATIONAL HUMAN RIGHTS LAW DIFFERENT?

The approach taken in this chapter to defining the field of comparative international human rights law has resulted in a rather narrower definition of the field than the editors of this volume have considered useful regarding other fields of comparative international law. The editors offer a provisional definition: "the field of comparative international law entails," they write, "identifying, analyzing, and explaining similarities and differences in the way in which international law is understood, interpreted, applied, and approached by different national *and international actors*."[34]

33. Anthea Roberts, *Comparative International Law? The Role of National Courts in Creating and Enforcing International Law*, 60 INT'L & COMP. L. Q. 57 (2011).

34. *Supra* note 1 (emphasis added).

While we all agree that the primary focus should be on how different national bodies interpret these norms, the editors' "provisional definition" wouldn't exclude from the analysis how different international and regional courts might interpret these norms (without reference to domestic interpretation), particularly when this is likely to have an effect within particular states. And whilst they agree that the focus of the project is not on the fragmentation debate, which tends to look primarily or exclusively at differences between international law fields and interpreters, if an issue is being dealt with by the ECtHR and national courts, then it seems artificial to separate the regional level out.

One possible reason a narrower approach might be justified in the human rights context is that, as we have seen, there already exists a rich comparative constitutional law literature applying to constitutional law (one that often talks about norms and transnational issues), as well as a rich fragmentation literature applying to human rights. In the absence of a clear distinction among the various fields, the likelihood is high that what we have termed comparative international human rights law could easily fuse with comparative constitutional law, or with the fragmentation literature. This would be a matter of regret, in my view, because keeping the three distinct brings out the extent to which different explanations apply to similarities and differences in the context of comparative *international* human rights law than apply in the context of comparative *domestic* human rights law or fragmentation, and it is to this issue of added value that we now turn.

A. Undertaking Comparative International Human Rights Law Analysis: Some Testable Hypotheses

There are several important issues that arise in any attempt to undertake a comparative international human rights law analysis. I shall focus on only three of these. The first, obvious but critical, issue is what hypotheses we are testing when we engage in a comparative international human rights law analysis. My suggestion is that a suitable issue, indeed one that I suggest should dominate comparative international human rights law analysis generally, is whether international human rights law plays similar or different *functions* in different jurisdictions. Similarities (and differences) in the domestic interpretation of international human rights law arise when national bodies adopt the same (or different) views as to how, and in what circumstances, international human rights law is best applied to address what are perceived to be domestic legal problems. The investigation of this hypothesis, that there are different functions of international human rights law at the domestic level, should constitute the core of the study of "comparative international human rights law."

There is an important point that needs to be emphasized at this juncture. This suggestion is not following a crude realist international relations perspective, which suggests that similarities and differences arise from the interests that states have and consider important, and that domestic interpretation of international human rights simply tracks this self-interest. My suggestion is more sympathetic to disaggregating the different domestic actors that make up the state and treating each as having different roles and functions. So whilst my approach emphasizes the important dynamics and concerns of the local context as the primary determinant of similarity and difference between states in the domestic interpretation of international human rights law, it is significantly institutional in its understanding of that context.

What I suggested was the case in the domestic interpretation of CEDAW by domestic courts may be true more generally, viz. that four elements taken together (international + human rights + law + domestic context) may contribute to an explanation of similarity and difference in substantive interpretation at the national level that neither the international law fragmentation literature taken by itself, nor the scholarship of comparative law (and its subset, comparative constitutional law) taken by itself, provides. It is, therefore, a discrete area of study, but one that sits somewhat uneasily among existing scholarly endeavors, poised between the concerns of international law scholarship and the study of "comparative constitutional law." It does not replace these existing approaches; rather it complements and supplements them.

The second, again obvious but important, issue concerns the choice of which area of international human rights law to focus on. This is likely to be affected not only by the interests of the researcher, but also by the availability of research resources. In particular, if the examination (as I suggest it should) attempts to undertake an analysis across a range of jurisdictions, compiling a dataset may prove no easy task. Take the example of undertaking a comparative international human rights law analysis of CEDAW. We might decide that we wanted to test the hypothesis that CEDAW plays a different role in different states from that which it plays at the international level, and that we will analyze CEDAW's domestic judicial interpretation of its provisions to do this. But how is a dataset of domestic cases to be compiled for the purposes of this analysis? There are multiple domestic law datasets, but accessing them, and collating the material is no easy task.[35]

Third, assuming that we have identified a suitable hypothesis, and compiled a suitable dataset, what are the questions we might ask of the dataset to test our hypothesis? The difficulty of undertaking this analysis should not be underestimated. The temptation in this mode of comparison is to see equivalences or differences depending on the predetermined theoretical assumptions that the comparativist brings to the analysis. If one is a Marxist comparativist, one is more likely to see phenomena fulfilling materialist functions. The danger at this stage is that it may be difficult to get beyond the mere assertion that a particular use of CEDAW in Tonga is the functional equivalent of the use of CEDAW in Belgium.

To deal with this as best we can, a structured approach is helpful, using a two-stage approach. The first stage involves asking to what extent "traditional" explanations for similarities and differences at the domestic level, for example those drawn from fragmentation and comparative constitutional law, account for observable differences and similarities. There are four particular issues that we can identify in our current state of knowledge to test this: (1) the process of norm transference and

---

35. *See* Christopher McCrudden, *CEDAW in National Courts: A Case Study in Operationalizing Comparative International Law Analysis in a Human Rights Context* (this volume).

diffusion, seeking to explain similarities and differences as a function of external force, persuasion or acculturation; (2) the legal status accorded by the courts to this international law instrument in their own legal systems; (3) the interpretative methods used by the courts, considering, for example, whether differences emerge between states that are part of different legal families (common law versus civil law, for example), or different legal cultures, or as a result of different institutional characteristics of the interpretative bodies; and (4) the extent to which similarities and differences in interpretation at the international level are reflected in similarities and differences at the domestic level.

To the extent that similarities and differences between jurisdictions across these four issues do not correlate with the differences and similarities in substantive interpretations of an international legal norm, then this indicates that a more systematic second-stage analysis, going beyond "traditional" explanations is necessary.

The second stage requires, I suggest, an analysis of what, more exactly, the different functions of international law are at the domestic level. Arising from my study of CEDAW, it would be useful to test the hypothesis that international human rights law more generally offers domestic bodies, such as courts, a set of consensus-based, purportedly universal legal norms that courts and advocates are able to draw on to address the particular local context in which the issue arises. Does international human rights law operate in a way, or to a degree, that other legal sources do not, for example in helping the domestic court to escape from otherwise troublesome domestic legal constraints? Do courts and advocates in different jurisdictions draw on such norms to address similar or different domestic contexts, resulting in observable similarities and differences emerging between these different jurisdictions as to the meaning and scope of the human right in question?

B. Functionalism

A functionalist account is, of course, prone to criticism, particularly if it is seen as part of a larger "structural-functionalist" understanding of the world in general. It is important, therefore, to stress the relatively modest role I have given to the suggested functionalist account, and to make clear what I am *not* arguing. I am not suggesting that functionalism should be seen as a grand theory that can explain society in all its forms; it provides a limited (but useful) perspective in this particular context, one way of understanding human rights that other approaches may miss, or underestimate. This modesty has three important implications.

I do not, first, account for the development of human rights generally solely through recourse to a functionalist explanation. I do not assume, therefore, that determining the current function of international human rights law provides an explanation of the efficient cause that produced international human rights law in the first place. Mine is not a teleological explanation. Indeed, my functional analysis does not seek to explain why international human rights happened at all, but how it operates and develops today.

Second, I do not downplay the importance of agency in my functionalist explanation, and agency must be accorded appropriate space. Particularly in the human rights context, we are constantly reminded that individual actors matter, in terms of mobilizing human rights, in terms of interpreting human rights, and in terms of implementing them successfully. My functionalist explanation has a significant limitation, therefore, in not being able to explain in what circumstances particular actors choose to exercise their agency, but to the extent that we are dealing with courts and judges this will involve an analysis of judges' understanding of their role and function generally.

Third, the functionalism suggested here is not partisan, in favor or against the human rights project. I do not seek to *justify* the human rights project by reference to the functions they fulfill in particular societies. I do not consider international human rights to be indispensable, in the sense that they are necessary in order to fulfill particular functional prerequisites, and I do consider that the functions currently fulfilled by international human rights may be able to be met by other functional alternatives. I do not, in short, seek to derive any normative argument from the functional explanation I advance. Future work in human rights law might focus on what the *normative* implications are of comparative international human rights law. Where differences are noted, scholars may wish to consider whether one interpretation is *preferable* to the other, in terms of its legitimacy, its degree of compatibility with international law, or its efficiency (in the sense that one standard is likely to be more effective than another standard in practice). In the future it is worth considering what, if anything, the hypotheses developed below might add to normative critique, but such an analysis is outside the purview of what I have described as the core interests of comparative international human rights law scholarship.

C. Do Differences Matter?

Assuming that these hypotheses turn out to be supported by the empirical evidence, as appears to be plausible,[36] what wider implications, if any, may this have? Here, again, the implications may be somewhat different because they arise in the human rights context, as compared with an area such as international economic law, or the law of the sea. In the latter cases, empirical support for these hypotheses might call for action to better inform interpreters at the domestic levels, for example, but the issue would likely be seen primarily as a coordination problem, not an existential one. I suggest that three implications of the results of comparative international law in the particular area of human rights may be of particular importance.

First, the empirical results may well cast an interesting light on the old, and deeply contested territory, of how we should understand the different accounts we have of the evolution of human rights. One of the key issues in the debates between these different histories of that evolution is whether we see continuity or discontinuity. Is there a continuity of values across space and time, which we see currently fraying at the edges? Or has there always been a discontinuity of values across space and time, and we are merely seeing confirmation of this? Or are we observing some sort of co-evolutionary process, where human rights evolve out of a continuing discourse

36. McCrudden, *supra* note 2.

among the various actors and institutions? Thorough comparative international human rights law promises to throw new light on this old debate.

Second, if a comparative international human rights analysis finds a deep pluralism operating in practice, this will be troubling to those who view the ideology of international human rights law as universalistic.[37] Some might well view empirical support for the hypothesis that international human rights law plays different functions in different domestic contexts as constituting an existential threat to the international human rights project. My own view, however, is that rather than challenging the normative foundations of human rights, it urges us on to attempt to produce a normative theory that is more in sync with empirical reality, but that is an issue for another day.

Third, these findings, if confirmed, appear to cast some doubt on recent constructivist accounts of why international human rights standards come to be received into the practice of states, what Harold Koh has termed "norm internalization."[38] Goodman and Jinks, for example, identify three types of social mechanisms:[39] *material inducement* (states are influenced by others applying "material rewards and punishments"),[40] *persuasion* (states are "convinced of the truth, validity, or appropriateness of a norm belief, or practice"),[41] and *acculturation* (a state grows to emulate the practice of other states with which the state wishes to establish or maintain good relationships).[42]

Constructivist accounts have frequently focused on state decisions regarding ratification of international norms, and in particular how states come to decide that they will formally join new or existing treaty regimes, and have paid less attention, thus far, to the important question of how "states" come to internalize these norms *other* than by the decisions of foreign ministries, cabinets, and legislatures. Less attention has, so far, been given to the question of how international norms come into, and are applied by, domestic *courts*.[43]

Comparative international human rights legal scholarship shows how legal norm internalization may also occur through the influence of judicial decision-making. If my suggestions are correct that a significant driver in the judicial adoption of international human rights norms is their utility in addressing *domestic* issues, then the extent to which this judicial norm internalization occurs through social processes of

---

37. *See* David Kennedy, *One, Two, Three, Many Legal Orders: Legal Pluralism and the Cosmopolitan Dream*, 3 N.Y.U. Rev. L. & Soc. Change 641, 649 (2007).

38. *See* Harold Hongju Koh, *Why Do Nations Obey International Law?*, 106 Yale L. J. 2599, 2615–34 (1997).

39. Ryan Goodman & Derek Jinks, Socializing States: Promoting Human Rights Through International Law (2013).

40. *Id.* at 23.

41. *Id.* at 24.

42. *Id.* at 25–26.

43. Helmut Philipp Aust, Alejandro Rodiles & Peter Staubach, *Unity or Uniformity? Domestic Courts and Treaty Interpretation*, 27 Leiden J. Int'l L. 75 (2014).

persuasion and acculturation, in which courts are primarily concerned with relevant *external* and *international* communities, is questionable. Yet relatively little empirical work has been done on norm internalization of international human rights law at the domestic judicial level,[44] and it is to be hoped that the emergence of comparative international human rights law will encourage other scholars to engage in further study of these issues.

V. CONCLUSION

This analysis has presented an analytical and conceptual examination of the value to legal scholarship that might be added by a comparative international human rights law analysis, compared to previous international and comparative constitutional law approaches. It concludes that the emerging field of international comparative law does, indeed, have a (limited) role to play as sketched out previously, one that is both unique and (strangely) somewhat neglected until recently in the human rights field.

---

44. For an early example, see ENFORCING INTERNATIONAL HUMAN RIGHTS IN DOMESTIC COURTS (Benedetto Conforti & Francesco Francioni eds., 1997). *See also* Gabor Halmai, *Domestic Courts and International Human Rights, in* 2 SAGE HANDBOOK OF HUMAN RIGHTS 749 (Anja Mihr & Mark Gibney eds., 2014). For broader studies, focusing on the role of domestic courts in implementing treaties in general, see INTERNATIONAL LAW AND DOMESTIC LEGAL SYSTEMS, INCORPORATION, TRANSFORMATION, AND PERSUASION (Dinah Shelton ed., 2011) and THE ROLE OF DOMESTIC COURTS IN TREATY ENFORCEMENT: A COMPARATIVE STUDY (D. Sloss, ed., 2014).

22

CEDAW in National Courts

*A Case Study in Operationalizing Comparative
International Law Analysis in a Human Rights Context*

CHRISTOPHER McCRUDDEN[*]

I. INTRODUCTION

This chapter is the second of a trilogy of articles and chapters discussing various aspects of a comparative international law study of national judicial use of the Convention on the Elimination of All Forms of Discrimination Against Women (CEDAW),[1] one of the key human rights covenants that go to make up what has been called the international Bill of Rights.

In the first part of my CEDAW trilogy,[2] I presented an analytical and conceptual examination of the value to legal scholarship that might be added by a comparative international human rights law analysis, compared to previous international and comparative constitutional law approaches. It concludes that the emerging field of international comparative law does, indeed, have a (limited) role to play one that is both unique and somewhat neglected until recently in the human rights field. I suggested that the worked example of CEDAW raised interesting lines of inquiry for empirical testing of several scholarly theories[3] and

* This chapter was written whilst I was a Fellow of the *Wissenschaftskolleg zu Berlin* (2014–2015). I would like to thank Veronika Fikak, Benedict Kingsbury, Christoph Möllers, Brendan O'Leary, Daniel Peat, Steve Ratner, Anthea Roberts, Mila Versteeg, participants of the Sokol Colloquium on Comparative International Law, participants at a seminar at Humboldt University, and several anonymous referees, for helpful comments and suggestions on earlier drafts.

1. Dec. 18, 1979, 1249 U.N.T.S. 13 [hereinafter CEDAW or the Convention].

2. Christopher McCrudden, *Comparative International Law and Human Rights: A Value-Added Approach* (this volume).

3. The examples I used were merely illustrative. I did not seek, for example, to relate my findings to the extensive international relations literature on the implementation of international law.

perspectives,[4] sufficient to justify comparative international human rights law scholarship being seen as likely to give rise to insights that might not otherwise have
emerged, and therefore to be considered as an approach worth pursuing in the future.

In the third article of my CEDAW trilogy, already published in the *American
Journal of International Law* (AJIL), I tackled the difficult question of how to explain
the pattern of domestic judicial use that I had identified, and I suggested explanations for this pattern.[5] My tentative conclusion was that what similarities and differences were observable resulted, at least in part, from the *functions* that international
human rights law fulfills in *domestic* jurisdictions, and that these functions may differ from the role that international human rights law plays at the international level.
It was suggested that the observable pattern of references to CEDAW in national
level courts results, to a significant degree, from the combination of the four elements involved in comparative international human rights law: that it is international law; *and* that it concerns human rights; *and* that it is law; *and* that it is being
applied domestically. In that article, I referred only briefly and in summary form to
both the methodology I used and the findings of the study on which this analysis
was based, promising a fuller account elsewhere.

This chapter is the bridge between the first and the third parts of the CEDAW
trilogy, fulfilling the promise in my AJIL article to explain my methodology and my
basic findings in more detail. The chapter is structured as follows. Section II presents a brief outline of CEDAW in order to locate what follows. Section III provides a
detailed analysis of the methodology I adopted in undertaking the study, including
a discussion of the sources I used in compiling a dataset of judicial opinions and
how I formulated the questions used to analyze this dataset. Section IV presents
the basic findings that resulted from this analysis. Section V concludes. There are, in
addition, two appendices. Appendix A sets out the electronic and other databases
and datasets from which my dataset of domestic cases citing CEDAW was drawn.
Appendix B provides citations for each of the cases in the dataset, by jurisdiction.[6]

II. OUTLINE OF CEDAW

The Convention (which goes under the acronym of CEDAW—confusingly because
the Committee that oversees its implementation also goes under this name[7]) was

---

See, e.g., INTERDISCIPLINARY PERSPECTIVES ON INTERNATIONAL LAW AND INTERNATIONAL
RELATIONS: THE STATE OF THE ART (Jeffrey L. Dunoff & Mark A. Pollack eds., 2013).

4. Olga Frishman & Eyal Benvenisti, *National Courts and Interpretative Approaches to International
Law, in* THE INTERPRETATION OF INTERNATIONAL LAW BY DOMESTIC COURTS: UNIFORMITY,
DIVERSITY, CONVERGENCE 317 (Helmut Philipp Aust & Georg Nolte eds., 2016).

5. *See* Christopher McCrudden, *Why Do National Court Judges Refer to Human Rights Treaties?
A Comparative International Law Analysis of CEDAW*, 109 AM. J. INT'L L. 534 (2015).

6. In order to shorten the footnotes and avoid repetition, cases are cited using their number in
Appendix B rather than the full citation.

7. For an overview of the Committee's work, see Andrew Byrnes, The Convention and the
Committee: Reflections on Their Role in the Development of International Human Rights Law

agreed in New York on December 18, 1979. The Convention was opened for signature at United Nations Headquarters on March 1, 1980, and came into force on September 3, 1981. There are currently 188 parties to the Convention and 99 signatories, making it one of the most widely ratified international human rights conventions.

The Convention consists of a preamble and 30 articles, defining what constitutes discrimination against women, and the circumstances in which it is prohibited under the Convention. Discrimination against women is defined as ". . . any distinction, exclusion or restriction made on the basis of sex which has the effect or purpose of impairing or nullifying the recognition, enjoyment or exercise by women, irrespective of their marital status, on a basis of equality of men and women, of human rights and fundamental freedoms in the political, economic, social, cultural, civil or any other field."[8]

States that are parties to the Convention commit themselves to undertake a series of measures to end this discrimination against women in all its forms. This includes a duty to incorporate the principle of equality of men and women into their legal system, abolish all discriminatory laws, and adopt appropriate ones prohibiting discrimination against women. States also commit to establish tribunals and other public institutions to ensure the effective protection of women against discrimination, and to ensure the elimination of all acts of discrimination against women by persons, organizations, or enterprises. The Convention seeks to ensure equality between women and men through ensuring women's equal access to, and equal opportunities in, political and public life—including the right to vote and to stand for election—as well as in the areas of education, health, and employment. States parties agree to take all appropriate measures, including legislation and temporary special measures, so that women can enjoy all their human rights and fundamental freedoms. The Convention affirms the reproductive rights of women, and identifies family relations as a key area in which women's equality must be secured. It provides women with rights to acquire, change, or retain their nationality and the nationality of their children. States parties also agree to take appropriate measures against all forms of trafficking in women and exploitation of women.

Countries that have ratified or acceded to the Convention are committed to submit national reports to the CEDAW Committee, at least every four years, on measures they have taken to comply with their treaty obligations. This originally provided the principal means of attempting to ensure compliance. Since it initially came into force, however, an Optional Protocol was adopted on October 6, 1999,[9] and opened for signature by any state that has signed, ratified, or acceded to the Convention at United Nations Headquarters in New York from December 10, 1999. States that

and as a Catalyst for National Legislative and Policy Reform, 1–12 (March 2010) (presented at the Commission on the Status of Women, 54th session), http://www.un.org/womenwatch/daw/beijing15/interactive_panel_III/Byrnes%20paper.pdf.

8. CEDAW, art. 1.

9. Optional Protocol to the Convention on the Elimination of All Forms of Discrimination Against Women, Dec. 22, 2000, 2131 U.N.T.S. 83.

ratify or accede to the Optional Protocol (currently 105 states) agree to individual or group "communications" against that state party being made to the CEDAW
Committee. In addition, states have agreed to permit the CEDAW Committee to
initiate inquiries into compliance with the Convention by that state.

III. METHODOLOGY

In this section, I discuss the methodology I adopted, explaining several choices
that were made, including my focus on the higher judiciary, the compilation of a
dataset of domestic judgments citing CEDAW and the limits of this dataset for my
subsequent analysis, and how I used existing CEDAW scholarship, and literature
concerning the domestic incorporation of international law in Europe in order to
help define the issues that would form the basis for drawing up the findings that are
presented in Section IV.

A. Focus on the Higher Judiciary

Building on anthropological work on human rights,[10] I sought, initially, to develop
an analytical framework for studying domestic judicial interpretations of CEDAW.
Judges have frequently been thought to serve as one set of the critical "translators"[11]
of international human rights in the domestic context. Such judicial decisions are,
at least in theory, examples of the domestic appropriation of international human
rights, and one potentially important process by which such rights are remade in
the vernacular. In doing so, judges act as one of the sets of actors "in the middle"
who translate the discourses and practices from the arena of international law and
legal institutions to specific situations. Sally Merry regards these translators as a key
dimension of the process of how international human rights law is incorporated into
domestic law. I restricted my analysis to the interpretative functions of the higher
judiciary, as opposed to other domestic actors, given that information concerning
their activities is somewhat easier to obtain, because the decisions of the higher
courts are usually presented in the form of accessible written decisions. Higher-level
courts were the target also because it is they who produce written decisions that find
their way onto searchable databases.[12]

10. *See* Sally Engel Merry, *Transnational Human Rights and Local Activism: Mapping the Middle*, 108
AM. ANTHROPOLOGIST 38 (2006).

11. *See* Susanne Zwingel, *How Do Norms Travel? Theorizing International Women's Rights in
Transnational Perspective*, 56 INT'L STUD. Q. 115, 124 (2012). There is an extensive literature in which
judges have been seen as translators, at least since the path-breaking work of JAMES BOYD WHITE,
JUSTICE AS TRANSLATION: AN ESSAY IN CULTURAL AND LEGAL CRITICISM (1990). Judges are
not the only translators of international human rights norms, of course. *See* Steven R. Ratner, *Does
International Law Matter in Preventing Ethnic Conflict?*, 32 N.Y.U. J. INT'L L. & POL. 591, 623 (2000).

12. A preliminary assessment of a selection of national CEDAW reports was conducted in order to
test whether a systematic analysis of all national CEDAW reports should be conducted. My assessment was that a full analysis would not be likely to add significantly to the identification of cases,
using these other sources.

B. Compiling Domestic Jurisprudence Relating to CEDAW

Given this decision to focus on the higher judiciary, one of the key tasks in embarking on this case study was to compile a list of domestic jurisprudence referencing CEDAW. This did not prove to be an easy task. There is no one repository of such jurisprudence. Instead, several sources, mostly electronic databases, were scoured for such references (Appendix A lists these sources). The resulting list consists of 326[13] national judicial decisions across 55 jurisdictions in which CEDAW was referred to in the reported decision (Appendix B contains a complete list of the cases.) For the purposes of analysis, all the cases mentioned below are drawn from this dataset; no case has been considered that is not included in this list. The purpose of the list is, within certain constraints, to illustrate when CEDAW is referred to in higher-level domestic courts, in order to provide a basis for considering such questions as why CEDAW is referred to, and whether there are significant differences between states in such usage. I read the judgments of most of the cases listed, in which judgments were available online. A few were unavailable, and I relied instead on secondary accounts, but this was in a small minority of cases. The discussion of the cases is, therefore, primarily based on my own, rather than on others' reading of these cases.

The method for selecting cases can be described as "convenience sampling."[14] As Katerina Linos suggests, this has the disadvantage of being the "least rigorous of sampling methods," and the results reported below need to be read in light of this caveat.[15] Nevertheless, whilst acknowledging limitations, my approach is broader that is often used in comparative legal analysis, as I go beyond the analysis of a handful of well-known cases arising from a select few countries. One of the common problems in convenience sampling (a focus on high-profile examples of disagreement) is minimized, even if not eliminated. My more thorough comparative approach is liable to yield examples of less dramatic agreement and disagreement.

Cases were drawn from 55 states. States from each of the major legal families were included (such as common law, civil law, Islamic). States that are traditionally considered as monist as well as dualist, and many that straddle the divide, were included. There are states that are clearly "developed" countries, and countries that are equally clearly "developing" countries. There are states that are federal states, as well as states with a strong central government and no federal distribution of powers, and states that are members of the EU and NAFTA. There are states that are parties to well-developed regional human rights conventions (such as the European Convention on Human Rights), and states that are not.

13. In my AJIL article, I mistakenly specified that there were 325 cases, which did not take into account an additional Japanese case that was drawn to my attention whilst the article was in proof. *See* McCrudden, *supra* note 5.

14. Katerina Linos, *Methodological Guidance: How to Select and Develop Comparative International Law Case Studies*, at 41 (this volume).

15. *Id.* at 41.

All in all, it is suggested that the list of states included could fairly be said to cover a range of very different countries (when considered against criteria often used in comparative legal analysis). There is, however, a significant bias toward those domestic courts whose judgments are included in digital databases. There is also a bias toward English-language sources, but I have sought to counter this by searching some non-English language sources myself, using appropriate search terms. In the case of Russia, China, and Japan, I relied on searches carried out for me by legal scholars from these jurisdictions.[16]

The list I compiled does not include all cases that are known to me referencing CEDAW in judicial tribunals. Several criteria were used to limit inclusion on the list. As mentioned above, the cases are overwhelmingly drawn from what might be called the superior courts in the judicial hierarchy of the state concerned, and not from lower courts or other adjudicatory bodies.[17] There are, for example, many cases in Australia in which various lower tribunals dealing with refugee claims have referred to CEDAW, but these have not been included as there is sufficient evidence available in the Australian superior appellate courts to illustrate this practice. Another criterion used to limit inclusion in the list is that where a tribunal has referred to CEDAW in a particular type of case (say, employment disputes) for a particular reason (say, because the preamble of the legislation in issue refers to CEDAW), only a selection of such cases is included to illustrate this use, rather than including all such cases. In other respects, the types of tribunals included in the list are diverse, including Conseil d'Etat-type bodies, constitutional courts, supreme courts, and labor courts. My focus on the higher courts is not unproblematic. Concentrating on the superior courts makes sense in systems with centralized judicial review, but where there is decentralized judicial review in place, it is probably less useful.

The dataset contains cases in which CEDAW is cited in the reported judgments of the superior courts. This is a significant limitation in several respects. First, although I consider that the dataset is likely to contain a good part of the universe where CEDAW was cited, by definition it does not include cases in which CEDAW could have been considered but was not. The fact that some courts, as we shall see, include summaries of the arguments of lawyers before the court, which sometimes show that CEDAW was argued but not cited by the court, is useful but does not fill this gap. Second, it means that those jurisdictions in which the practice is not to cite such sources in the written opinion are not considered.[18] It is likely, as a result, to underestimate the extent to which arguments based on CEDAW were considered

16. Several colleagues also assisted in attempting to locate relevant case law in Japan, the People's Republic of China, and Russia. I am exceptionally grateful to Gleb Bogush, Akiko Ejima, Nico Howson, Benedict Kingsbury, Mark West, and Alex X. Zang.

17. Sometimes that required a judgment call, and the default position was to include rather than exclude. *See, e.g.,* App. B No. 11, App. B No. 202.

18. Scholarly literature on this is thin, but for a recent attempt to explain why courts may not cite CEDAW in the Egyptian context, see JASMINE MOUSSA, COMPETING FUNDAMENTALISMS AND EGYPTIAN WOMEN'S FAMILY RIGHTS: INTERNATIONAL LAW AND THE REFORM OF SHARI'A-DERIVED LEGISLATION 242 (2011) [hereinafter COMPETING FUNDAMENTALISMS].

by judges. There are, as a result, some jurisdictions, notably China, where no judgments citing CEDAW were identified. This is not to say that CEDAW had no effect
on the judiciary in these jurisdictions, of course, only that there was no public
acknowledgment of CEDAW by these courts. Third, the effect of using citation of
CEDAW as the key variable means that those states that conform more to the practice of citing such sources (such as common law courts) will be over-represented,
even among the universe of jurisdictions in which CEDAW is cited at all. Fourth,
cases involving CEDAW directly or indirectly that are dealt with in tribunals or by
agencies outside the ordinary courts will be under-represented, as is the case, for
example, with regard to Norway.[19]

The dataset comprises cases that involve a wide variety of different subject areas.
There are, for example, cases dealing with affirmative action, electoral law and political party activity, women's health and bodily integrity (including issues such as
female genital cutting), civil procedure, ability to enter and remain in a state other
than one's own (including issues such as refugee status, immigration, and deportation), rape and other forms of criminal sexual assault, children's rights and child
custody issues, sexual harassment, marriage and family relationships, employment,
social security, land ownership and inheritance, abortion and contraception, pregnancy and maternity, violence against women, and customary law and religious
practices.

C. Analyzing CEDAW's Domestic Jurisprudence: Drawing on CEDAW Scholarship to Help Define the Issues

To my knowledge, no previous attempt has been made to develop a comparative
analysis of CEDAW's domestic judicial interpretation across this broad swath of
jurisdictions. A few global surveys of selected domestic CEDAW jurisprudence
have been conducted,[20] sometimes as part of a larger exercise concerning the
domestic judicial use of international human rights instruments, but none have so
far engaged with the range of domestic judicial materials identified for this chapter.[21]

---

19. Anne Hellum, *Making Space and Giving Voice: The CEDAW in Norwegian Law*, in WOMEN'S
HUMAN RIGHTS: CEDAW IN INTERNATIONAL, REGIONAL AND NATIONAL LAW 588, 618–19
(Anne Hellum & Henriette Sinding Aasen eds., 2013) [hereinafter WOMEN'S HUMAN RIGHTS].

20. *See, e.g.,* Andrew C. Byrnes & Marsha Freeman, *The Impact of the CEDAW Convention: Paths
to Equality* (U.N.S. Wales Law Research Paper No. 2012-7), https://papers.ssrn.com/sol3/papers.
cfm?abstract_id=2011655; Andrew Byrnes, The Convention and the Committee: Reflections
on Their Role in the Development of International Human Rights Law and as a Catalyst for
National Legislative and Policy Reform (2010), http://www.un.org/womenwatch/daw/
beijing15/interactive_panel_III/Byrnes%20paper.pdf.

21. *See, e.g.,* Antonios Tzanakopoulos, Int'l L. Ass'n Study Group on Principles on the Engagement
of Domestic Courts with International Law: Preliminary Report (2014); Int'l L. Ass'n, Comm. on
Int'l Hum. Rts. L. & Prac., Interim Report on the Impact of the Work of the United Nations Human
Rights Treaty Bodies on National Courts and Tribunals (2002); Int'l L. Ass'n, Comm. on Int'l Hum.
Rts. L. & Prac., Final Report on the Impact of Findings of the United Nations Human Rights Treaty
Bodies (2004).

My analysis was aided, however, by the burgeoning academic literature on the use of CEDAW at the national level that falls short of the type of more comprehensive comparative approach attempted here. This literature is of four main types.

There is, first, analysis of national judicial implementation of CEDAW in particular states, which may be a generalized analysis of judicial approaches to CEDAW in that state, or concentrated on a particular issue in which CEDAW has been significantly involved at the judicial level. Discussion of one or other type was found on a significant number of states (22) that have ratified CEDAW: Malaysia,[22] Austria,[23] Sri Lanka,[24] Switzerland,[25] Indonesia,[26] Australia,[27] Norway,[28] France,[29] Zimbabwe,[30] Netherlands,[31]

22. See Jaclyn Ling-Chien Neo, *Calibrating Interpretive Incorporation: Constitutional Interpretation and Pregnancy Discrimination Under CEDAW*, 35 Hum. Rts. Q. 910 (2013).

23. See Rosa Logar, *Die UNO-Frauenrechtskonvention CEDAW als Instrument zur Bekämpfung der Gewalt an Frauen: zwei Beispiele aus Österreich*, 1 Frauenfragen 22 (2009).

24. See Savitri Goonesekere, *Gender-Based Violence: The Response of the Sri Lanka Legal System*, in Struggle for Gender Justice: Justice Sunanda Bhandare Memorial Lectures 71, 72 (Murlidhar C. Bhandare ed., 2010).

25. See Regula Kägi-Diener, *Die Bedeutung internationaler Diskriminierungsverbote, insbesondere von CEDAW, für die schweizerische Rechtsprechung*, 1 Frauenfragen 42 (2009).

26. See Sharon Bessell, *Increasing the Proportion of Women in the National Parliament: Opportunities, Barriers and Challenges*, in Problems of Democratisation in Indonesia: Elections, Institutions and Society 219, 232–35 (Edward Aspinall & Marcus Mietzner eds., 2010) (on Constitutional Court decisions regarding quotas for women in elections); Ziba Mir-Hosseini & Vanja Hamzić, Control and Sexuality: The Revival of zina Laws in Muslim Contexts 62–63 (2010); Donald L. Horowitz, Constitutional Change and Democracy in Indonesia 253–54 (2013).

27. See Andrew Byrnes, *The Implementation of the CEDAW in Australia: Success, Trials, Tribulations and Continuing Struggle*, in Women's Human Rights, *supra* note 19, at 323; Isabel Karpin & Karin O'Connell, *Speaking into a Silence: Embedded Constitutionalism, the Australian Constitution, and the Rights of Women*, in The Gender of Constitutional Jurisprudence 22 (Beverley Baines & Ruth Rubio-Marin eds., 2005) [hereinafter Constitutional Jurisprudence].

28. See Hellum, *supra* note 19, at 588.

29. See Hélène Ruiz Fabri & Andrea Hamann, *Domestication of the CEDAW in France: From Paradoxes to Ambivalences and Back Again*, in Women's Human Rights, *supra* note 19, at 531.

30. See Choice Damiso & Julie Stewart, *Zimbabwe and CEDAW Compliance: Pursuing Women's Equality in Fits and Starts*, in Women's Human Rights, *supra* note 19, at 454.

31. See Jaco van den Brink & Hans-Martien ten Napel, *The Dutch Political Reformed Party (SPG) and Passive Female Suffrage: A Comparison of Three High Court Judgments from the Viewpoint of Democratic Theory*, 29 Utrecht J. Int'l & Eur. L. 29 (2013); Marjolein van den Brink, *The CEDAW After All These Years: Firmly Rooted in Dutch Clay?*, in Women's Human Rights, *supra* note 19, at 482; Barbara M. Oomen, Joost Guijt, & Matthias Ploeg, *CEDAW, the Bible and the State of the Netherlands: The Struggle over Orthodox Women's Political Participation and Their Responses*, 6 Utrecht L. Rev. 158 (2010); Margreet de Boer, *Articles 7 and 8: The Added Value of the Women's Convention and the Dutch Case of the Christian Party*, in The Women's Convention Turned 30: Achievements, Setbacks, and Prospects 163 (Ingrid Westendorp ed., 2012) [hereinafter

United Kingdom,[32] Pakistan,[33] Egypt,[34] India,[35] Nepal,[36] Nigeria,[37] South Africa,[38] Colombia,[39] Costa Rica,[40] Guatemala,[41] Canada,[42] Turkey,[43] and

THE WOMEN'S CONVENTION]; Ineke Boerefijn, *Women's Right to Political Participation. The Case of the Reformed Political Party in The Netherlands, in* WOMEN'S HUMAN RIGHTS AND CULTURE/ RELIGION/TRADITION: INTERNATIONAL STANDARDS AS GUIDELINES FOR THE DISCUSSION? 121 (Rikki Holtmaat & Ineke Boerefijn eds., 2009).

32. *See* Sandra Fredman, *The CEDAW in the UK, in* WOMEN'S HUMAN RIGHTS, *supra* note 19, at 511.

33. *See* Shaheen Sardar Ali, *From Ratification to Implementation: "Domesticating" the CEDAW in State, Government and Society. A Case Study of Pakistan, in* WOMEN'S HUMAN RIGHTS, *supra* note 19, at 430 [hereinafter *From Ratification to Implementation*]; Shaheen Sardar Ali, *Navigating Religion, Politics and Cultural Norms: The Arduous Journey Towards Domestication of CEDAW in Pakistan*, 19 J. PEACE, CONFLICT & DEV. 43 (2012) [hereinafter *Navigating Religion*].

34. *See* COMPETING FUNDAMENTALISMS, *supra* note 18, at 150–52, 242–45.

35. *See* Nihal Jayawickrama, *India, in* THE ROLE OF DOMESTIC COURTS IN TREATY ENFORCEMENT: A COMPARATIVE STUDY 243, 256–64 (David Sloss ed., 2009); Madhu Mehra, *India's CEDAW Story, in* WOMEN'S HUMAN RIGHTS, *supra* note 19, at 385.

36. *See* Kabita Pandey, *Judicial Education on the Convention on Elimination of Discrimination Against Women in Nepal, in* WOMEN'S HUMAN RIGHTS, *supra* note 19, at 410.

37. *See* C.C. Nweze, *Domestication of CEDAW: Points to Consider for Customary Laws and Practices, in* WITHOUT PREJUDICE: CEDAW AND THE DETERMINATION OF WOMEN'S RIGHTS IN A LEGAL AND CULTURAL CONTEXT 49 (Meena Shivdas & Sarah Coleman eds., 2010) [hereinafter WITHOUT PREJUDICE].

38. *See* Mokgadi Lucy Mailula, *Gender, Culture and the Law: The South African Experience, in* WITHOUT PREJUDICE, *supra* note 37, at 75.

39. *See* Verónica Undurraga & Rebecca J. Cook, *Constitutional Incorporation of International and Comparative Human Rights Law: The Colombian Constitutional Court Decision C-355/2006, in* CONSTITUTING EQUALITY: GENDER EQUALITY AND COMPARATIVE CONSTITUTIONAL LAW 215 (Susan H. Williams ed., 2009) [hereinafter CONSTITUTING EQUALITY] (on Decision of C-355 of May 10, 2006, declaring a statute criminalizing abortion under all circumstances unconstitutional, in part on the basis of CEDAW); Martha I. Morgan, *Emancipatory Equality: Gender Jurisprudence Under the Colombian Constitution, in* CONSTITUTIONAL JURISPRUDENCE, *supra* note 27, at 75.

40. *See* Alda Facio, Rodrigo Jiménez Sandova & Martha I. Morgan, *Gender Equality and International Human Rights in Costa Rican Constitutional Jurisprudence, in* CONSTITUTIONAL JURISPRUDENCE, *supra* note 27, at 99; Naomi Seiler, Note, *Sterilization, Gender, and the Law in Costa Rica*, 4 YALE HUM. RTS. & DEV. L.J. 109 (2001).

41. *See* Christiana Ochoa, *Guatemalan Transnational Feminists: How Their Search for Constitutional Equality Interplays with International Law, in* CONSTITUTING EQUALITY, *supra* note 39, at 248.

42. *See* Beverley Baines, *Using the Canadian Charter of Rights and Freedoms to Constitute Women, in* CONSTITUTIONAL JURISPRUDENCE, *supra* note 27, at 48; Lucie Lamarche, *The Canadian Experience with the CEDAW: All Women's Rights are Human Rights—A Case of Treaties Synergy, in* WOMEN'S HUMAN RIGHTS, *supra* note 19, at 358.

43. *See* Hilal Elver, *Gender Equality from a Constitutional Perspective: The Case of Turkey, in* CONSTITUTIONAL JURISPRUDENCE, *supra* note 27, at 278.

Bangladesh.[44] This type of country-level analysis is by far the most prevalent; it is of considerable assistance in providing a thick account of the particular national contexts in which CEDAW has come to be used, often going well beyond doctrinal legal issues and considering the social, political, economic, and cultural context.

The second type of literature is that which is also primarily geographically oriented and seeks to analyze the judicial use of CEDAW by comparing two countries,[45] or by analyzing how courts in particular regions have engaged with CEDAW.[46] This literature is potentially of considerable importance in identifying whether particular regions or jurisdictions may be taking significantly different approaches to the interpretation of CEDAW more generally.

The third type of literature departs from the geographical, state-centered focus and analyzes domestic level judicial engagement across several jurisdictions according to a particular issue or theme, such as how CEDAW has been engaged in dealing with issues of religion and culture,[47] trafficking and prostitution,[48] the definition and prosecution of rape,[49] challenges to discrimination in nationality requirements,[50] female circumcision,[51] divorce,[52] and violence against women.[53] This literature is of potential importance in identifying differences between jurisdictions in how CEDAW is interpreted in dealing with these particular issues.

44. See Afra Afsharipour, Note, Empowering Ourselves: The Role of Women's NGOs in the Enforcement of the Women's Convention, 99 COLUM. L. REV. 129 (1999).

45. See, e.g., Eileen Kaufman, Women and Law: A Comparative Analysis of the United States and Indian Supreme Courts' Equality Jurisprudence, 34 GA. J. INT'L & COMP. L. 557 (2006).

46. See, e.g., Sibongile Ndashe & Solomon Sacco, Watch the Courts Dance: Litigating the Right to Non-discrimination on the Ground of Sex, 4 EQUAL RTS. REV. 26 (2009) (sub-Saharan Africa); Mere Pulea, Women's Dignity and Rights: Situating Pacific Experiences, in WITHOUT PREJUDICE, supra note 37, at 107.

47. See Frances Raday, Culture, Religion and Gender: An Overview, in WITHOUT PREJUDICE, supra note 37, at 17.

48. See Marjolein van den Brink & Marjan Wijers, "Because to Me, a Woman Who Speaks in Public Is a Public Woman": 30 Years Women's Convention and the Struggle to Eliminate Discrimination of Women in the Field of Trafficking and Prostitution, in THE WOMEN'S CONVENTION, supra note 31, at 135.

49. IWRAW Asia Pacific, Addressing Rape as a Human Rights Violation: The Role of International Human Rights Norms and Instruments (2007) (unpublished manuscript), https://papers.ssrn.com/sol3/papers.cfm?abstract_id=1146984.

50. See Gerard-René de Groot, Equal Treatment of Women and Men in Nationality Law, in THE WOMEN'S CONVENTION, supra note 31, at 187.

51. See Phyllis Livaha, Eradicating Female Circumcision: Changing a Harmful Social Norm Through the Women's Convention, in THE WOMEN'S CONVENTION, supra note 31, at 279.

52. See Pauline Kruiniger, Article 16 of the Women's Convention and the Status of Muslim Women at Divorce, in THE WOMEN'S CONVENTION, supra note 31, at 363.

53. See Kate Rose-Sender, Emerging from the Shadows: Violence Against Women and the Women's Convention, in THE WOMEN'S CONVENTION, supra note 31, at 453.

Finally, there is the scholarly literature that primarily seeks to explain rather than describe (that is not to say, of course, that the other three sets of literature do not attempt to do this, but usually in the context of rich descriptions). This fourth set of literature seeks to step back from the detail and attempts to advance various theories as to why the patterns to be found in the previous sets of literature are as they are. It is often implicitly or explicitly[54] using the tools of comparative law[55] or another discipline that encourages cross-national comparisons, such as sociology,[56] politics,[57] or anthropology.[58]

D. Domestic Incorporation of International Law in Europe

This literature significantly aided in drawing up a set of issues that would be used to interrogate the dataset. A rather different way of framing the issues, however, is to consider the implications of a different set of literature, the scholarship on the domestic incorporation of international law in Europe. On the one hand, we would expect national judges in these two systems to be especially aware of European Union law and of the European Convention on Human Rights, because their decisions are subject to what we could call, crudely, supranational judicial review, and because these laws are thoroughly embedded within national legal orders, because these two bodies of law have been foundational in legal education within Europe for at least three decades, and because finding out what European Union Law and European Human Rights Law means for any issue is relatively easy to do. Europe's supranational courts have extensive jurisprudence; there is excellent, widely available, scholarship that digests this jurisprudence; and Europe is fully wired, making access to these sources easy.

In both European systems, however, scholars of the European Union and the European Court of Human Rights have shown that domestic invocation of these rules can be spotty. Among an extensive array of such work, we can point to Karen

---

54. *See, e.g.,* Darren Rosenblum, *Internalizing Gender: Why International Law Theory Should Adopt Comparative Methods*, 45 COLUM. J. TRANSNAT'L L. 759 (2007).

55. *See, e.g.,* Judith Resnik, *Comparative (In)equalities: CEDAW, the Jurisdiction of Gender, and the Heterogeneity of Transnational Law Production*, 10 INT'L J. CONST. L. 531 (2012); Anne Hellum & Henriette Sinding Aasen, *Conclusions, in* WOMEN'S HUMAN RIGHTS, *supra* note 19, at 625; Ruth Rubio-Marín & Martha I. Morgan, *Constitutional Domestication of International Gender Norms: Categorizations, Illustrations, and Reflections from the Nearside of the Bridge, in* GENDER AND HUMAN RIGHTS 113 (Karen Knop ed., 2004); Yvonne Donderas & Vincent Vieugel, *Universality, Diversity and Legal Certainty: Cultural Diversity in the Dialogue Between the CEDAW and States Parties, in* THE RULE OF LAW AT THE NATIONAL AND INTERNATIONAL LEVELS: CONTESTATIONS AND DEFERENCE 321 (Machiko Kanetake & Andre Nollkaemper eds., 2014).

56. *See, e.g.,* Zwingel, *supra* note 11, at 115.

57. Neil Englehart & Melissa K. Miller, *Women's Rights in International Law: Legitimacy, Persuasion and Structuration* (APSA 2013 Annual Meeting Paper, unpublished), https://papers.ssrn.com/sol3/papers.cfm?abstract_id=1902066.

58. *See, e.g.,* Sally Engle Merry, *Constructing a Global Law—Violence Against Women and the Human Rights System*, 28 L. & SOC. ENQUIRY 941 (2003).

Alter's, which has shown extensive variation in the invocation of the EU's gender equality law,[59] and there is a similar pattern shown by Rachel Cicowski[60] in the domestic incorporation of EU gender equality law more recently. Marlene Wind has pointed to the Nordic courts' lack of citations of decisions of the Court of Justice of the European Union.[61] Laurence R. Helfer and Erik Voeten have analyzed the varying influence of ECtHR jurisprudence across member states.[62] We already know, therefore, that variation in the judicial application of international and supranational legal norms exists, and that even the most informed, rule of law-friendly judges can shy away from directly relying on international and transnational law that is indisputably a central part of their domestic legal system. We also know why this might be the case—at least to some extent, in Europe—for example, differences in mobilization of rights across different jurisdictions, particular national sensitivities on particular issues that make references to international or supranational norms less acceptable, and different institutional traditions among the national courts. This literature was also drawn on in the attempt to develop a set of issues for analysis.

E. Structure of Analysis

Informed by this literature, the written judgments in the cases included in the CEDAW dataset were analyzed under four broad headings. The first issue was the process of norm transference: how do judges get acquainted with CEDAW, and how influenced are they by the citation of CEDAW elsewhere. The second issue was the extent to which courts appear to have considered the interpretation of CEDAW as an autonomous matter for the domestic court itself, as opposed to regarding the domestic interpretation of CEDAW as a shared enterprise. For example, did the court refer to other tribunals or to the CEDAW Committee as persuasive or binding sources of interpretative authority? The third issue concerned the legal status accorded by the courts to CEDAW in their own legal systems, and the resulting balance between CEDAW's function as a source of legal authority as opposed to a source of norms that should be followed irrespective of their legal status. The fourth issue was the extent to which the cases reflect different understandings of the interpretation of CEDAW by courts across different jurisdictions in cases with similar substantive questions in disputes.

---

59. KAREN J. ALTER, THE EUROPEAN COURT'S POLITICAL POWER: SELECTED ESSAYS (2009), ch. 8.

60. RACHEL A. CICHOWSKI, THE EUROPEAN COURT AND CIVIL SOCIETY: LITIGATION, MOBILIZATION AND GOVERNANCE (2007), chs. 3, 5 (on domestic incorporation of EU equality law).

61. Marlene Wind, *The Nordics, the EU and the Reluctance Towards Supranational Judicial Review*, 48 J. COMMON MARKET STUD. 1039 (2010).

62. Laurence R. Helfer & Erik Voeten, *International Courts as Agents of Legal Change: Evidence from LGBT Rights in Europe*, 68 INT'L ORG. 77 (2014).

F. Caveats

At this point, several caveats must be entered regarding the analysis of the dataset. Social science methodology would call what I did the mining of "dirty" data, meaning that it is highly likely that the data I used as the basis for my analysis includes missing data, wrong data, and nonstandard representations of similar data. It is clear that the "results of analyzing a database/data warehouse of dirty data can be damaging and at best be unreliable."[63] What is presented in this analysis is a way of "doing" comparative international law that is consistent with traditional comparative law approaches of reading cases and carried out on a larger scale than is usual, but has significant limitations.

I have resisted the temptation to present the findings of the data mining in ways that would imply a greater degree of accuracy than I believe to be the case. Instead, I shall use terms that are intentionally imprecise, in order to convey the sense that the findings are significantly impressionistic. Rather than saying "in x out of y cases," or "in x out of y states," throughout this section the analysis will often mention "a significant number of states," "a few," or "some." Rather than being an empirical analysis, it is better thought of as a report of an empirical study, in which the data are not presented directly but rather revealed through my interpretative framework.

IV. FINDINGS

In this section, I present the basic findings of the study, under various headings, which will be recognizable from the analysis of the existing scholarly literature on CEDAW discussed in the previous section: norm transference, the autonomy of norm interpretation, the domestic legal status of CEDAW, and the substantive variation in the interpretation of CEDAW's norms. In several respects, the results are of interest: significant variations between courts in their interpretation of CEDAW occurred relatively infrequently, courts referred relatively seldom to interpretations of CEDAW by other national courts, and there was little evidence of transnational dialogic approaches to judging.

A. Norm Transference

We can usefully distinguish three principal methods by which CEDAW enters the judicial decision, insofar as this can be gleaned from the written judgment:[64] judicial research; existing use internal to the legal system; and arguments of lawyers representing those before the court. I was particularly interested in whether, if at all,

---

63. Won Kim et al., *A Taxonomy of Dirty Data*, 7 DATA MINING & KNOWLEDGE DISCOVERY 81, 81 (2003).

64. This caveat is important, indicating a difficulty in relying on the written judgments and any summaries of arguments put to the court. A full examination would require access to all written material filed and access to transcripts of oral argument, where relevant. In very few jurisdictions is any of this material easily available.

a pattern emerged in which one or more methods were used more or less in particular jurisdictions.

1. JUDICIAL RESEARCH

First, judges may generate a reference to CEDAW from their own research (or that
of their clerk, or cabinet, or internal research section of the court). In the past, we
might have expected a significant difference between common law and civil law
jurisdictions, with the latter being significantly more used to judges raising legal
issues *sua sponte*. In the common law context, there was previously a sense that such
self-generation of legal authority by judges was suspect, if not improper, and this is
reflected in at least two of the judgments, one from the Supreme Court of Nigeria,[65]
and one from the Constitutional Court of Uganda.[66] In the latter case a separate
opinion did refer to CEDAW,[67] although it had not been referred to by representatives of any of the parties before the Court and its use went against the lead opinion,
which took a more restrained approach to judicially-generated authorities.

Such internal debate within courts appears to be relatively rare, and it is now
frequently the case that judges will refer to CEDAW *sua sponte*. A decision of the
Constitutional Court of South Africa reflects the dominant approach, with the
Court considering that there might be circumstances where a court was obliged
to raise the matter on its own and require full argument from the parties.[68] There
are examples where CEDAW is referred to by judges *sua sponte* in both common
law and civil law jurisdictions, with little difference between them being apparent.[69]
These references may or may not arise because of a perceived obligation to refer to
international agreements that have been ratified by the state in which the Court has
jurisdiction, an issue we consider further below. In some cases, notably in Nepal, the
increased use of CEDAW by the judiciary appears to be linked to a judicial training
program focusing on CEDAW.[70]

2. EXISTING USE INTERNAL TO LEGAL SYSTEM

Although there does not appear to be significant divergence between *jurisdictions*
as to whether judges refer to CEDAW *sua sponte*, there does appear to be significant difference within the same jurisdictions, with some *courts* citing CEDAW more
than others (for example, the French Conseil d'Etat cites CEDAW in some cases,
but neither the Cour de cassation nor the Conseil constitutionnel has done so).[71]

---

65. App. B No. 222.

66. *See* App. B No. 284 (Judge Twinomujuni, in the lead judgment, decided not to discuss international human rights conventions—including CEDAW—because no issue was raised by the parties
to that effect.)

67. The opinion was written by Judge Mpagi Bahegeine.

68. *Cf.* App. B No. 294.

69. *See, e.g.,* App. B No. 229; App. B No. 176.

70. Pandey, *supra* note 36, at 410.

71. Fabri & Hamann, *supra* note 29, at 553.

Some *judges* also cite CEDAW more frequently in their judgments than others.[72] The degree to which the choice of whether to cite to CEDAW is personal to the judge rather than jurisdictionally determined is supported further by the fact that, in several cases, citation to CEDAW appears in dissenting[73] or separate[74] opinions, often in cases in which it is the only citation to CEDAW by judges in that case.

Aside from judges referring to CEDAW *sua sponte*, a second principal set of sources that judges referenced for information about CEDAW was "internal" to the domestic legal system.[75] There are three main types of such cited material, each of which referenced CEDAW: previous jurisprudence within that legal system;[76] domestic legislative materials;[77] and material emanating from the executive branch of the government.[78] It is much less usual to find the reference to CEDAW arising from other sources, either citation to jurisprudence from outside the jurisdiction concerned, or from legislation from outside the jurisdiction concerned, although there is evidence of both in a few cases, the bulk of which refer to ECtHR jurisprudence by the court of a state party to the Convention,[79] or to EU legislation by court of an EU member state.[80] In only two cases was there a reference to CEDAW arising from a court outside the legal hierarchy of the court citing CEDAW.[81]

---

72. *See, e.g.,* App. B Nos. 225, 226. *See also From Ratification to Implementation, supra* note 33, at 451 (noting how among the Pakistan judiciary, "CEDAW's champion seems to be Justice Jilani"); COMPETING FUNDAMENTALISMS, *supra* note 18, at 152 (noting that the Egyptian Supreme Constitutional Court's "readiness to invoke international law has been sporadic at best, depending on the inclinations of the Court's Chief Justice at any given time.")

73. *See, e.g.,* App. B No. 158 (Maria Farida Indrati dissenting); App. B No. 15 (Kirby J dissenting); App. B No. 279 (Judges Kantarcıoğlu, Oto, Özgüldür, Kaleli, Perktaş, and Kömürcü, joint dissent); App. B No. 309 (supporting dissent); App. B No. 311 (supporting Ginsburg dissent); App. B No. 4 (Kirby J dissenting); App. B No. 12 (Callinan J dissenting).

74. *See, e.g.,* App. B No. 231; App. B No. 250; App. B No. 220 (concurring opinion); App. B No. 132 (Péter Kovács concurrence); App. B No. 312 (concurrence); App. B No. 284 (concurrence).

75. The sources of references to CEDAW in this context usually are the only or the principal source identified, although in some few cases another principal source is identified as well.

76. *See* App. B No. 249; App. B No. 322; App. B No. 311 (citing Ginsburg in No. 312); App. B No. 139 (citing No. 146); App. B No. 259 (citing Carmichele); App. B No. 135 (citing lower court decision); App. B No. 133 (citing No. 140); App. B No. 257 (citing No. 266).

77. From the legislature, referred to in *travaux préparatoires* or in the text of the statute. *See* App. B No. 116; App. B No. 115; App. B No. 119; App. B No. 114; App. B No. 113; App. B No. 8; App. B No. 142; App. B No. 3.

78. See App. B No. 309 (CEDAW referred to in asylum officers' guidance).

79. *See* App. B No. 161 (Irish Court refers to ECHR).

80. Referred to in Council Directive 2000/78 recitals and CEDAW cited by domestic court in that context. *See* App. B No. 296; App. B No. 299; App. B No. 301.

81. *See* App. B No. 117 (Fiji court cites Indian court's reference to CEDAW); App. B No. 303 (ECtHR's reference to CEDAW).

3. ARGUMENTS OF COUNSEL

There is evidence in some jurisdictions that where lawyers are unaware of CEDAW, or do not bring it to the attention of the court, CEDAW is less often cited.[82] Unsurprisingly, therefore, the third, and final, source of references to CEDAW identified in judicial decisions is counsel representing a party or an intervener in the case.[83] Within this group of cases, however, there are some significant differences. (Usually, CEDAW is referenced by only one party, although sometimes parties on each side of the dispute will cite it.[84])

Although counsel may cite CEDAW, this does not guarantee that the judge in the case will take up the opportunity to apply CEDAW to the relevant dispute. There are cases in which it is evident from summaries of arguments accompanying the decision that counsel has cited CEDAW but the Court simply ignores it without even mentioning in its judgment that the Court had been referred to the Convention,[85] or ignores it after mentioning in the judgment that an argument had been made based on it,[86] or dismisses it as not worth taking up because it is insufficiently related to the issue that the Court must decide,[87] or because the issue can be dealt with entirely on the basis of domestic law,[88] without engaging in any substantive discussion. In another group of cases, however, those representing one or other party or intervener present a judge with an argument referencing CEDAW, and the judge reacts by seriously engaging with the argument presented.

4. VARIATIONS ACROSS AND WITHIN JURISDICTIONS

There appears to be little evidence that jurisdictions of particular types are more prone to any of these types of reactions to CEDAW than others, and there is evidence of engagement and disengagement within the same jurisdictions.[89] Nevertheless, there is a differential uptake of CEDAW in the courts of different regions of the world,[90] and in the different issues to which CEDAW is applied in these different jurisdictions. A prominent example is provided in cases considering

---

82. *See* Goonesekere, *supra* note 24, at 82.

83. *See, e.g.,* App. B No. 235; App. B No. 169.

84. *See, e.g.,* App. B No. 289 (referred to both by counsel for the applicant and the intervener).

85. *See, e.g.,* App. B No. 131 (CEDAW is not mentioned explicitly in the text, but is listed under documents referred to.).

86. *See, e.g.,* App. B No. 160; App. B No. 247; App. B No. 292; App. B No. 191; App. B No. 264; App. B No. 184; App. B No. 21.

87. See, *e.g.,* App. B No. 310.

88. *See, e.g.,* App. B No. 128.

89. *Compare* App. B No. 4 (engagement), *with* Australian Journalists' Association (1988) EOC 92-224 (Australian Conciliation and Arbitration Commission) (disengagement).

90. CEDAW is relatively popular in the South East Asian region (India, Pakistan, Bangladesh, Nepal) and the Pacific region (Vanuatu, Fiji, Samoa, Kiribati, Philippines, Solomon Islands, Tuvalu), and in the African context.

the relationship between CEDAW and female genital cutting, in which US courts have taken a largely identical line,[91] but where cases from other jurisdictions, particularly in Africa where the practice is more widespread, are less common, primarily in sub-Saharan Africa. Controversial rulings on the incompatibility of polygamy with CEDAW norms[92] are significantly restricted to a limited set of jurisdictions. So too, in the United Kingdom context, for example, there is little substantive use of CEDAW other than in the context of refugees.

Within the group of cases in which there is a serious engagement with CEDAW, there is a relatively high proportion in which nongovernmental organizations[93] or government human rights or equality agencies[94] are involved, but not exclusively so.[95] The bulk of cases in which NGOs used CEDAW in argument come from Bangladesh, India, Kenya, and Nepal. In other jurisdictions, such as the United Kingdom, there is evidence that NGOs have relatively little knowledge of CEDAW, and that this affects adversely the take-up of CEDAW by the courts.[96] In contrast, in the Netherlands, the most prominent cases citing CEDAW were set in train as the result of a group of NGOs, headed by the Clara Wichmann Test Case Fund "taking up" the cases "to obtain clarity on the exact nature of the Dutch State's obligations under CEDAW."[97]

91. CEDAW interpreted as prohibiting female genital cutting: App. B No. 304; App. B No. 305; App. B No. 313; App. B No. 314 (interpretation of FGM as persecution in Immigration and Nationality Act, referencing CEDAW Committee); App. B No. 306.

92. *See, e.g.,* App. B No. 261 (Van Reenen: "although the constitutional validity of polygamy has not been subjected to judicial scrutiny as yet . . . it is in conflict with certain international human rights instruments," citing the Committee on the Elimination of Racial Discrimination (CERD), Art 16.).

93. *See e.g.,* App. B No. 19 (writ petition was filed by Dr. Shipra Chaudhry and Ain O. Salish Kendra, a Dhaka-based human rights nongovernmental organization); App. B No. 144 (writ petition was filed by a nongovernmental organization, Sakshi, which provided assistance to victims of violence); App. B No. 182 (application brought by R.M. (a minor through next friend J.K. her mother) and CRADLE, a Non-Governmental Children Foundation as the 1st Interested Party. The second and third interested parties were COVAW (Coalition on Violence Against Women), and FIDA (Federation of Women Lawyers Kenya)); App. B No. 19 (submitted by Bangladesh Legal Aid and Services Trust); App. B No. 177; App. B No. 265 (amicus argument); App. B No. 117; App. B No. 203 (Sapana Pradhan Malla, Meera Dhungana, and Prakash Mani Sharma representing two leading civil society organizations, the FWLD and the Pro-Public, see Ananda Mohan Bhattarai, The Landmark Decisions of the Supreme Court, Nepal on Gender Justice (National Judicial Academy, Nepal, 2010)); App. B No. 147 (submitted by several women's organizations); App. B No. 205 (submitted by several human rights organizations).

94. *See, e.g.,* App. B No. 129.

95. *See, e.g.,* App. B No. 240; App. B No. 255; App. B No. 184; App. B No. 254; App. B No. 317; App. B No. 282; App. B No. 108; App. B No. 5; App. B No. 308; App. B No. 295; App. B No. 288; App. B No. 23.

96. *See* Fredman, *supra* note 32, at 514. By contrast, in App. B No. 184, the public prosecutor who cited CEDAW had attended training, which had included CEDAW. *See* A Digest of Case Law on the Human Rights of Women (Asia Pacific) 58 (Christine Foster et al. eds., 2003).

97. Oomen et al., *supra* note 31, at 167.

There is some evidence from previous research that there is a gender effect, with women judges citing to CEDAW proportionately more than male judges.[98] In my dataset, several male judges cite to CEDAW much more frequently than their colleagues, in particular Justice Kirby of the High Court of Australia,[99] and Justice Tassadaq Hussain Jilani of the Lahore High Court (later appointed to the Pakistan Supreme Court).[100] We cannot say, therefore that male judges do not cite CEDAW. But there is a clear pattern in the cases analyzed for prominent women judges in the highest tribunals to be likely to cite CEDAW more frequently than their male colleagues. We can identify, among others,[101] Justice Ginsburg of the United States Supreme Court,[102] Justice O'Regan of the Constitutional Court of South Africa,[103] Justices McLachlin and L'Heureux-Dubé of the Supreme Court of Canada,[104] Judge Mpagi-Bahegeine of the Constitutional Court of Uganda,[105] and (particularly) Baroness Hale of the Supreme Court of the United Kingdom (formerly the House of Lords sitting as the final appellate court).[106]

5. AUTONOMY OF NORM INTERPRETATION
Once the court is seized of CEDAW, a major question relates to the relationship that the domestic court conceives itself as having with other interpreters of CEDAW.

98. Hellum, *supra* note 19, at 588 (in most cases in which CEDAW was referred to by the Norwegian Anti-Discrimination Tribunal, it was cited by women Tribunal members).

99. *See, e.g.,* App. B No. 4; App. B No. 13 (Kirby J dissenting).

100. *Navigating Religion, supra* note 33, at 43 ("[I]n the reported case law of Pakistan's superior judiciary (five high courts and the Supreme Court) from accession in 1996 through to 2010, there are only four judgments where the court specifically alluded to CEDAW. Two delivered by the same judge.... The third is a judgment of the High Court of Azad Jammu & Kashmir citing the Jilani judgment.") The cases referred to are: App. B No. 225; App. B No. 228; App. B No. 226; App. B No. 227.

101. *See also* App. B No. 25 (Justice Indra Hariprashad-Charles); App. B No. 231 (Justice Flerida Ruth Romero).

102. *See* App. B No. 311 (Ginsburg); *see also* App. B No. 312 (Ginsburg).

103. *See* App. B No. 263 (O'Regan).

104. *See* App. B No. 26 (McLachlin, C.J.); *see also* App. B No. 28 (L'Heureux-Dubé).

105. *See* App. B No. 284 (Judge Mpagi-Bahegeine). She is said to have been "at the forefront in urging compliance" with CEDAW. Henry Onoria, *Uganda, in* INTERNATIONAL LAW AND DOMESTIC LEGAL SYSTEMS: INCORPORATION, TRANSFORMATION, AND PERSUASION 594, 613 (Dinah Shelton ed., 2011).

106. *See* App. B No. 289 (Baroness Hale) ("In other words, the world has woken up to the fact that women as a sex may be persecuted in ways which are different from the ways in which men are persecuted and that they may be persecuted because of the inferior status accorded to their gender in their home society. States parties to the Refugee Convention, at least if they are also parties to the International Covenant on Civil and Political Rights and to [CEDAW], are obliged to interpret and apply the Refugee Convention compatibly with the commitment to gender equality in those two instruments."). *See also* App. B No. 297 (Baroness Hale); App. B No. 302 (Baroness Hale); App. B No. 303 (Baroness Hale).

There are three recurring relationships in issue: those with other nonjudicial domestic bodies in the same jurisdiction, including the executive and legislature; those with the CEDAW Committee, which, as we have seen, oversees the monitoring and interpretation of CEDAW at the international level; and those with other domestic, regional, and international courts. The question is where along a continuum between autonomous interpretation (where the domestic court considers that it alone has authority to interpret CEDAW in the domestic legal context) and deference (where the domestic court considers that another body has the principal interpretative authority, to which it should defer) the domestic court's approach lies.

We see in the cases included in the dataset examples of both orientations, with some reflecting a strongly autonomous approach,[107] and others reflecting a more deferential approach, with other nonjudicial domestic bodies[108] or the CEDAW Committee[109] (particularly illustrated by references to specific CEDAW General Recommendations as important and statements of authoritative interpretation[110])

---

107. *See* App. B No. 209 (Autonomous interpretation or use of CEDAW committee reports; autonomous interpretation of what is required in order to be able to determine whether the plaintiff has established discrimination under national law and under CEDAW; the same approach applies to both, it would seem). *See* App. B No. 213 (Ratification/confirmation: Netherlands Supreme Court applies autonomous view as to whether this provision of CEDAW is directly effective); App. B No. 213 (refers to CEDAW views but rejects them); App. B No. 110 (referred to CEDAW reports: development of recommendations to the government, even in the absence of violation of CEDAW). *But see* App. B No. 17 (views and recommendations of the CEDAW Committee on the position in Austria were not relevant for the examination of the case and did not have to be considered by the national courts: "The determination of the relevant facts and the legal assessment is solely for the Austrian courts.").

108. For a deferential approach toward other domestic bodies and a function of courts in a democracy, see App. B No. 182 ("At the moment one can only conclude that the exclusion was deliberate and we do not consider that it is the function of the court to fill the gaps. It must not be forgotten that modern Constitutions are being negotiated with the people directly or indirectly by way of Constituent Assemblies and Referendums and it would not be proper for the courts to take their places by filling in fundamental gaps in the Constitutions. The life of society has other important actors such as Parliament and other organs which must be left to play their role to the full"); App. B No. 318 (There is no lacuna in the domestic law and therefore CEDAW could not be used to fill nonexistent gaps. The rights and concepts set out in CEDAW need to be given substance by Parliament in accordance with the separation of powers doctrine).

109. *See e.g.*, App. B No. 18 (although CEDAW did not explicitly refer to the prohibition of torture and other ill treatment, the Committee on the Elimination of Discrimination against Women had held that violence against women impaired or nullified their enjoyment of human rights and fundamental freedoms under general international law); App. B No. 314 (interpretation of persecution in Immigration and Nationality Act, referencing CEADW Committee).

110. *See* App. B No. 9 (General Recommendation No. 25); App. B No. 17 (General Recommendation No. 23); App. B No. 20 (General Recommendation No.19); App. B No. 304 (General Recommendation No. 14); App. B No. 305 (General Recommendation No. 14); App. B No. 313 (General Recommendation No. 14); App. B No. 302 (General Recommendation No. 19); App. B No. 28 (General Recommendation No. 19); App. B No. 258 (General Recommendation No. 19); App. B No. 135 (General Recommendation No. 17); App. B No. 147 (General Recommendation No. 19).

being regarded as prominent authorities. It is particularly striking, however, that I identified only one out of over 300 cases in which the domestic court sought to interpret a provision of CEDAW in light of how other states and foreign courts interpreted the same provision. (And in that case, the sources drawn on involve consideration of a mixture of legislation and judicial interpretation in a highly selective group of jurisdictions.)[111] Courts did not tend to refer to the interpretation of CEDAW by other foreign domestic courts, even when this practice is otherwise relatively frequent in the context of the interpretation of national constitutional and domestic statutory provisions. Courts appear, therefore, to be more willing to be seen to be influenced by foreign judicial decisions in the interpretation of national norms than they are in the interpretation of international norms.[112]

Considerable care must be exercised in interpreting this finding.[113] In particular, this finding should not be interpreted as inferring that judges have not been influenced by how foreign courts have interpreted CEDAW, only that there is little or no evidence of this in the written opinions. We know from other sources, however, that on occasion such foreign influences have been significant, but that this influence has not been signaled in the judgments, as in Nepal.[114]

111. *See* App. B No. 9 (whether establishing quotas for female representation amounted to a "special measure" directed at ensuring substantive equality in accordance with the CEDAW. As "special measures" were referred to in the CEDAW and were part of international human rights discourse, note could be taken of affirmative action measures that were permitted or considered elsewhere. For example, the United Kingdom, European Communities, United States, Canadian Charter of Rights and Freedoms, and New Zealand Human Rights Act 1993 (NZ) discussed, in order to arrive at a conclusion, at 59: "The greatest possible caution is appropriate when considering jurisprudence from other places. However, this short excursus indicates that 'special measures' are widely recognised in differing legal systems as a method of redressing inequalities arising from race or sex. While it would be unhelpful and imprudent to treat any of the approaches to special affirmative action measures referred to above as providing a rigid template for the correct method of construing and applying s 7D of the SDA, it is worth observing that automatic or inflexible quotas, even in differing legal systems, seem to run a greater risk of falling foul of general prohibitions on discriminatory acts and can prove more difficult to justify as 'special measures' than more flexible measures with a similar aim.")

112. Several of the jurisdictions in which foreign precedents are used by constitutional court judges in the context of interpreting domestic law do not appear to have done so when interpreting CEDAW. *See* THE USE OF FOREIGN PRECEDENTS BY CONSTITUTIONAL JUDGES (Tania Groppi & Marie-Claire Ponthoreau eds., 2013).

113. *See* David S. Law & Wen-Chen Chang, *The Limits of Global Judicial Dialogue*, 86 WASH. L. REV. 523, 524 (2011) (observing that "judicial opinions are a highly misleading source of data about judicial usage of foreign law;" noting, based on interviews with members of the Taiwanese Constitutional Court, "the existence of a large gap between the frequency with which the court cites foreign law in its opinions and the extent to which it actually considers foreign law;" and concluding that "[a]nalysis of judicial opinions alone may lead scholars to conclude mistakenly that a court rarely engages in comparative analysis when, in fact, such analysis is highly routine.")

114. *See* Pandey, *supra* note 36, at 426 (importance of contributions to training of Nepalese judges by the then-chief justice of India, showing how the Indian judiciary considered CEDAW).

B. Domestic Legal Status of CEDAW

The domestic legal status attributed by domestic courts to CEDAW varies considerably between different states. In practice, we can observe three different types of legal status being accorded to CEDAW. First, in a few states, CEDAW is used in practice as the basis for direct litigation claims—it is given "direct effect." Second, in a significant proportion of states, CEDAW is given indirect interpretative effect, meaning that it is used primarily as the basis for interpreting other provisions of domestic or relevant international law, such as the domestic constitution, other international conventions, applicable customary international law, or legislation that applies in the state concerned. Third, in a few states, the courts give no significant domestic legal status to CEDAW in domestic courts, regarding it as suitable only for domestic legislative or executive action, or viewing it as an obligation that operates only in the international domain.

We can begin with those states that have not ratified CEDAW. We might suppose that such states would be those in which CEDAW has no effect in the courts of that state, on the basis that there is not even an international law obligation to implement a convention that the state has not ratified. We need to distinguish between treaty-based obligations and obligations based on customary international law or *jus cogens*. No domestic court in the dataset appears to consider CEDAW to have become *jus cogens*. Some domestic courts do, however, appear to recognize aspects of CEDAW as representing customary international law, and take it into account where they are required under domestic law to apply customary international law. United States' courts, for example, take CEDAW into account in applying the Alien Tort Claims Act. Quite apart from this, however, we find in practice that some states that have not ratified CEDAW nevertheless, in addition, accord it indirect interpretative effect, particularly in the interpretation of constitutional provisions.[115] One prominent example, again, is the United States, where domestic courts have sometimes taken the position that it is appropriate to take CEDAW into account, despite the fact that the United States has not ratified CEDAW, both in the interpretation of the Constitution, as well as in the interpretation of ATCA.[116]

---

115. *See* Rubio-Marin & Morgan, *supra* note 55, at 138.

116. See App. B No. 307 (CEDAW regarded as relevant even though it had not been ratified by the Senate); App. B No. 312 (no distinction in effects drawn between ratified and unratified conventions, Ginsburg in concurrence); App. B No. 315 (Referring to CEDAW, the Court held that: "The United States has agreed to 'take all appropriate measures, including legislation, to suppress all forms of traffic in women and exploitation of prostitution of women.'" but the United States had only signed, not ratified CEDAW. A court in Botswana has taken a similar position. *See* App. B No. 23 (Amissah P., referring to CEDAW "There is no evidence that Botswana is one of the 100 States that have ratified or acceded to the Convention but I take it that a court in this country is obliged to look at the Convention of this nature which has created an international regime when called upon to interpret a provision of the Constitution which is so much in doubt to see whether that Constitution permits discrimination against women as has been canvassed in this case.") Botswana has actually ratified CEDAW.

In ratifying states, the critical question is often whether the state court regards CEDAW as having direct effect in domestic law. Some courts in ratifying states do accord CEDAW such direct effect,[117] whilst courts in other ratifying states do not accord CEDAW such effect.[118] In some states, domestic courts do not adopt a blanket approach to determining the issue, treating each provision of CEDAW as requiring separate analysis of the degree of specificity of obligation to which the provision gives rise. In yet other ratifying states, courts have taken an inconsistent approach,[119] with courts in a particular state in some cases appearing to deny direct effect, whilst courts in the same state in other cases act as if direct effect was assumed.[120] Even where CEDAW may theoretically form the basis for direct litigation claims, courts in that jurisdiction may, in practice, accord CEDAW indirect interpretative effect (only or as well), or simply ignore it on occasion. This is because CEDAW may be directly effective, but may be below the constitution and other domestic legislation in the hierarchy of sources.[121]

In states where the courts have decided that CEDAW does not have direct effect, or it is ambiguous, then it is effectively up to the legislature to decide whether further direct effect is to be given to CEDAW in domestic law. Where such legislative action has taken place, then the court may, or may not, have regard to CEDAW in the interpretation of that legislation.[122] There are several states, particularly India,[123] Fiji, and Australia, in which legislation has prominently mentioned CEDAW in its provisions, and the courts have regularly engaged with the interpretation of CEDAW as a result. In these contexts, CEDAW has become part of the everyday legal discourse in particular areas of the law.

Where no legislative incorporation has taken place, the courts may as a result decide to accord CEDAW no direct domestic legal status, but more usually CEDAW is accorded *indirect* effect in the interpretation of legislation and constitutional

---

117. *See, e.g.,* App. B No. 199; App. B No. 229 (CEDAW prevailed in Paraguay over contrary provision of domestic law, and amended it); App. B No. 159.

118. *See, e.g.,* App. B. No. 233 (lack of specificity of CEDAW provisions limiting the extent to which they create clear binding norms); App. B No. 212 (CEDAW is not sufficiently specific and therefore this provision is unsuitable for direct application by national courts).

119. In some states the issue has become a central question in litigation with different courts adopting diverging approaches, e.g., the Netherlands. *Compare* App. B No. 213 (CEDAW has no direct effect in this context) *with* App. B No. 214 (CEDAW provision has direct effect) *and* App. B No. 209 (Court holds particular provision of CEDAW to have direct effect).

120. *See* Fabri & Hamann, *supra* note 29, at 549; App. B No. 166; App. B No. 171.

121. *See* App. B. No. 195 (Mexican Constitution provides that all treaties entered into by president of the Republic with the approval of the Senate, shall be the supreme law of the Union. Also, the Plenum of the Supreme Court of Justice has determined that international treaties are below the Constitution and above the general, federal, and local laws.).

122. *See* App. B. No. 167.

123. *See* App. B. No. 142.

provisions. CEDAW has been frequently referred to in certain contexts in the United Kingdom, where no legislative incorporation has taken place. This is because the common law has long considered that the courts should interpret legislation that is ambiguous in such a way that it conforms to the state's international obligations, if it is possible to do so.[124]

This approach has been adopted in a range of Commonwealth courts, although there are both stronger and weaker forms of this approach apparent. Several courts go well beyond the current United Kingdom judicial approach, according CEDAW interpretative weight tout court. This arises where the court considers that domestic constitutional provisions are the method chosen for according Convention rights, even where there is no explicit textual evidence of this,[125] or where there is a constitutional provision according legal weight to unincorporated international conventions.[126] CEDAW may be used, for example, to fill in gaps in the domestic legal coverage,[127] provided there is no clear legislative or constitutional provision to the contrary.[128] Other Commonwealth courts limit this approach to where legislation is ambiguous,[129] strictly interpreted, and resist CEDAW being used to undermine clear legislative provisions.[130] Some Commonwealth state courts resist according ratified, but unincorporated CEDAW, any legal status.[131] Within the same state, different courts may adopt apparently radically different positions.[132] The stronger Commonwealth approach appears to have been significantly influenced by the adoption of the Bangalore Principles and subsequent equivalent statements of

124. *See* App. B No. 129 (words of the ordinance to be construed, if they were reasonably capable of bearing such a meaning, as intending to carry out Hong Kong's obligation under CEDAW rather than being inconsistent with them).

125. *See* App. B No. 28 (per L'Heureux-Dubé and Gonthier JJ.).

126. *See* App. B No. 177 ("This court has regard to international instruments which our country has subscribed to whether or not they have become part of our domestic law, courtesy of art 2 of the 2010 Constitution.").

127. One of the better-known examples is where CEDAW provided the basis for drawing up judicial standards for what constitutes sexual harassment, in the absence of national legislation. *See* App. B No. 147; *see also* App. B No. 117 (drawing on Bangalore Principles; example of court using international law as gap filling even where international convention not incorporated). For a discussion of the Bangalore Principle, see Melissa A. Waters, *Creeping Monism: The Judicial Trend Toward Interpretative Incorporation of Human Rights Treaties*, 107 COLUM. L. REV. 628 (2007).

128. *See* App. B No. 134; App. B No. 179.

129. *See* App. B No. 282.

130. *See* App. B No. 6 (CEDAW unable to be used to get around clear exception in domestic legislation); *see also* App. B No. 321.

131. *See, e.g.,* App. B No. 196; App. B No. 288 (UK has not ratified CEDAW, so point doesn't arise for decision).

132. *See, e.g.,* App. B No. 318 (no lacuna in the domestic law and therefore CEDAW could not be used to fill nonexistent gaps).

principle,[133] which several judges have used to justify according indirect interpretative effect to CEDAW.[134]

Indeed, where CEDAW is taken into account in judicial decisions, this is most frequently the case in a situation where the primary function of CEDAW is indirect, to assist in the interpretation of another legal norm that operates in that legal system, which may be a constitutional provision,[135] a statutory provision,[136] the common law,[137] or an exercise of discretion in sentencing a criminal offender.[138] It is also noteworthy that CEDAW has been drawn on extensively in the interpretation of other international law conventions that the court regards as relevant, in particular the Refugee Convention.[139] In these contexts, courts sometimes refer to the

133. The Zimbabwe Declaration 1994, inter alia, stated: "Judges and lawyers have duty to familiarise themselves with the growing international jurisprudence of human rights and particularly with the expanding material on the protection and promotion of the human rights of women."

134. *See, e.g.,* App. B No. 117 (draws on Bangalore Principles, etc.). *See also* Meena Shivdas & Sarah Coleman, *Promoting the Human Rights of Women and Girls Through Developing Human Rights Jurisprudence and Advancing the Domestication of International Human Rights Standards, in* WITHOUT PREJUDICE, *supra* note 37, at 127.

135. For interpretations of constitutional provisions, see App. B No. 184; App. B No. 254; App. B No. 234; App. B No. 231; App. B No. 208; App. B No. 233a; App. B No. 126; App. B No. 158; App. B No. 192; App. B No. 44; App. B No. 142; App. B No. 138; App. B No. 281; App. B No. 20; App. B No. 146; App. B No. 141; App. B No. 23.

136. *See* App. B No. 116 (interpretation of Fiji Family Law Act 2003, which explicitly refers to CEDAW); App. B No. 115 (same); App. B No. 114 (same); App. B No. 119 (interpretation of Fiji Domestic Violence Decree); App. B No. 174 (interpretation of Mexican Civil Code). For an interpretation of Australian domestic anti-discrimination law, see App. B No. 10; App. B No. 8; App. B No. 3; App. B No. 7. For an interpretation of New Zealand human rights legislation, see App. B No. 216; App. B No. 218. For an interpretation of the (Indian) Protection of Human Rights Act, 1993, see App. B No. 142; App. B No. 146; App. B No. 136. For an interpretation of Canadian Criminal Code, see App. B No. 28. For an interpretation of Hong Kong Sex Discrimination Ordinance, see App. B. No. 129. For an interpretation of United States Civil Rights Act, 1964, Title VII, see App. B No. 309 (dissent); App. B No. 313 (interpretation of US Alien Tort Statute); App. B No. 314 (interpretation of persecution in Immigration and Nationality Act, referencing CEDAW Committee); App. B No. 302 (interpretation of UK Housing Act 1996).

137. For the disapplication of the marital rape exception in common law, see App. B No. 256. For queries regarding whether the previous approach to determining ancillary relief on divorce is satisfactory, see App. B No. 130; App. B No. 258.

138. *See* App. B No. 240 (sexual assault); App. B No. 118; App. B No. 308 (death penalty); App. B No. 6 (domestic violence).

139. *See* App. B No. 294 (discrimination under CEDAW is not enough to ground "persecution" under the Refugee Convention); App. B No. 12 (Callinan J, dissenting); App. B No. 217 ("being persecuted" under Article 1A of the Refugee Convention definition could be defined as the sustained or systemic violation of basic "human rights" (including CEDAW) demonstrative of a failure of state protection); App. B No. 297 (Baroness Hale); App. B No. 286; App. B No. 289 ("In other words, the world has woken up to the fact that women as a sex may be persecuted in ways which are different from the ways in which men are persecuted and that they may be persecuted because of the inferior status accorded to their gender in their home society. States parties to the Refugee

desirability of ensuring a "harmonious" interpretation, one in which national and international law reach results that are compatible with each other.[140]

C. Substantive Variation in the Interpretation of CEDAW's Norms

The number of cases in the dataset in which CEDAW is cited, at just over 320, is a tiny proportion of cases decided by these domestic courts, and of these an even smaller proportion of cases engage in any extended substantive interpretation of CEDAW. In the main, references to CEDAW are cursory, often little more than a mere mention of the Convention, and even then more usually found sandwiched between other international human rights conventions.[141]

1. RELATIVE HOMOGENEITY

Where substantive interpretation of CEDAW is to be found, there is relatively little substantive conflict between domestic courts in the interpretation of CEDAW norms, although making that judgment is significantly subjective. This relative homogeneity of substantive interpretation is to be found both in the conception of rights that is considered to be embodied in CEDAW, and in the substantive result that emerges from the application of CEDAW to particular areas of dispute. Thus, whether the substantive issue is the common law requirement of corroboration in rape cases,[142] or the principles that fairness requires for women in divorce settlements,[143] for example, a relatively similar approach and result is adopted in otherwise widely differing court systems. So, too, whether the conceptual issue is

Convention, at least if they are also parties to the International Covenant on Civil and Political Rights and to [CEDAW], are obliged to interpret and apply the Refugee Convention compatibly with the commitment to gender equality in those two instruments.")

140. *See, e.g.,* App. B No. 210 (desirability of having harmonious interpretation of CEDAW with other international instruments prohibiting discrimination); App. B No. 212 (CEDAW complementing ICCPR and making it more specific); App. B No. 270; App. B No. 248; App. B No. 136 (desirability of ensuring harmonious interpretation of differing national provisions (including those that refer to CEDAW)).

141. *See, e.g.,* App. B No. 234 (CEDAW grouped with ICESCR, Declaration on the Elimination of Discrimination Against Women 1967, and ILO Convention 111).

142. *See* App. B No. 118. For requirement of corroboration issue, see App. B No. 184; App. B No. 285; App. B No. 112 (CEDAW) used to support and justify a Court's decision to remove the corroboration warning requirement for evidence of victims of sexual violence on the ground of gender discrimination). For a court disapplying the marital rape exception in common law, see App. B No. 256. Where a court wishes to avoid holding the corroboration rule unlawful, it is more inclined not to interpret CEDAW at all. *See, e.g.,* App. B No. 184.

143. *See* App. B No. 194 (CEDAW used to defend provisions in favor of women on divorce); App. B No. 130 (queries whether previous approach to determining ancillary relief on divorce is satisfactory); App. B No. 275 (division of property on divorce should recognize contribution of the woman in terms of home work); App. B No. 277 (terms of divorce award by court); App. B No. 274 (divorce settlement of 95% to man held discriminatory). Where the Court wishes to avoid interpreting CEDAW as requiring such principles, there is a tendency to hold that CEDAW simply

whether CEDAW imposes positive obligations on states (it does),[144] or whether the meta-principle of equality is substantive or formal (it is substantive),[145] a similar approach is again adopted throughout the cases surveyed.

This general finding of relative homogeneity of substantive interpretation is not universal, however, and in three main respects we can identify significant substantive interpretative variation:[146] (1) regarding the implications of the requirement that "special measures" should be "temporary" for establishing the limits on permissible affirmative action, (2) regarding the application of CEDAW to customary inheritance laws, and (3) regarding whether "equality" or "dignity" is the appropriate meta-principle that should influence the interpretation of the CEDAW provisions.

2. SPECIAL MEASURES

The first issue involves the meaning of, and limits on, permitted "special measures" (what in domestic jurisdictions are sometimes termed "affirmative action" or "positive action"). Article 4(1) of CEDAW provides: "Adoption by States Parties of temporary special measures aimed at accelerating de facto equality between men and women shall not be considered discrimination as defined in the present Convention, but shall in no way entail as a consequence the maintenance of unequal or separate standards; these measures shall be discontinued when the objectives of equality of opportunity and treatment have been achieved."

A central issue in the interpretation of this provision is the meaning of "temporary." In an important 1998 Swiss case,[147] concerning whether quotas in an electoral context were justified under the Swiss Constitution and CEDAW, the meaning of Article 4(1) was considered. The Court held that the requirement that the measures should be temporary does not necessarily require, as a condition of validity, that a time limit should be put in place at the time of their adoption; it is sufficient if the measures are repealed as soon as they have reached their goal. This is especially true when it is not predictable how much time it will take to reduce the underrepresentation of women. This approach is in marked contrast with later cases in other jurisdictions, in which courts appear to interpret CEDAW as requiring the

---

does not apply. *See, e.g.,* App. B No. 321 (discriminatory aspects of customary law protected by the Constitution).

144. The right requires positive obligations. *See* App. B No. 118; App. B No. 215; App. B No. 209; App. B No. 215; App. B No. 192; App. B No. 226; App. B No. 211; App. B No. 275 (CERD imposes a positive obligation on states to pursue policies of eliminating discrimination against women by, among other things, adopting legislative and other measures that prohibit such discrimination); App. B No. 239 (CEDAW requires the state to take action to prevent violence against women by nonstate actors (including domestic violence)).

145. *See infra* notes 158–162.

146. Another possible candidate may be emerging, regarding the extent to which CEDAW permits "protective" restrictions on women working in particular industries or at particular times. *Compare* App. B Nos. 234, 238; *with* App. B. No. 208.

147. App. B No. 270.

temporary limitation to be built into the structure of the affirmative action system if it is to be compatible with CEDAW.[148] Perhaps most famously in *Grutter v. Bollinger*, Justice Ginsburg, in concurrence, cited CEDAW in support of her argument that the Constitution set a time limit on the affirmative action in issue.[149]

3. INHERITANCE AND SUCCESSION

The second substantive issue concerns the contested matter of the application of CEDAW to inheritance and succession. On the one hand, several courts have used CEDAW to support challenges to inheritance laws that discriminate against girls and women. For example, in a case dealing with the property rights of women in Hindu succession law, the Supreme Court of India held that Hindu women had equal rights with men under Indian legislation, drawing heavily on CEDAW.[150] In a Kenyan case,[151] the court considered a challenge to a customary law rule denying women inheritance rights due to the expectation that they would eventually get married. The court rejected this justification for inequality in inheritance, holding that denying women equal rights to inheritance under Kikuyu customary law violated the Kenyan Constitution and CEDAW.

A different approach to inheritance is adopted in some other jurisdictions.[152] In a challenge to provisions of a law providing succession to property in favor of men on the basis that the provisions were discriminatory and unfair against tribal women, the Indian Supreme Court held that it would not strike down the discriminatory law, although it was suspended in order to guarantee the woman's right to livelihood.[153] In several Nepalese cases[154] the issue was whether a particular statutory provision that distinguished between married daughters and married sons was contrary to CEDAW. The court held that it was not contrary to CEDAW because it was not discriminatory against women: the status of membership of the daughter with the joint family was severed upon her marriage and she had no rights and obligations regarding her birth family but did through her husband's family. The Court observed that it could not be oblivious to social practices and values. CEDAW has also been held *not* to be applicable to discrimination in inheritance of noble titles in Spain, because these were merely symbolic.[155]

---

148. *See, e.g.,* App. B No. 9; App. B No. 129 (attempt to use affirmative action provision in Hong Kong Sex Discrimination Ordinance to defend different scoring systems for school transfers between boys and girls; CEDAW used to limit the interpretation of the section, requiring it to be read as allowing only temporary exceptions to non-discrimination provision).

149. App. B No. 312.

150. App. B No. 136.

151. App. B No. 181.

152. *E.g.,* several African jurisdictions, see Ndashe & Sacco, *supra* note 46, at 26.

153. App. B No. 141. The dissenting judgment of K. Ramaswamy J would have struck down the discriminatory law, arguing that it was contrary to CEDAW.

154. App. B No. 203; App. B No. 207.

155. *See* App. B No. 246; App. B No. 247.

4. DIGNITY AND EQUALITY

As regards the third substantive issue, the question of which meta-principles should influence the interpretation of CEDAW, we should note initially that this issue arises in only a limited range of courts. This is because the predominant approach to interpreting CEDAW is textual, and there is also a significant group of cases in which this textual approach to interpretation is either supplemented with or replaced by an interpretative approach that has been termed "originalist" in some jurisdictions.[156] Only when courts adopt a more teleological approach to interpretation, in which the court attempts to determine the "end" or "teleos" of CEDAW and interpret its provisions in light of that, do general principles of very considerable generality, which in this context I term "meta-principles," come significantly into play.

There are two dominant meta-principles that are frequently identified in cases included in the dataset: (human) dignity, and equality. Courts sometimes identify both dignity and equality as the appropriate animating meta-principles,[157] but more frequently dignity[158] or equality[159] dominates the discussion. There is seldom any (or any extensive) discussion of what either of these meta-principles means, and more usually the court appears to consider their meaning, and the implications to be drawn from them, to be self-evident. This is perhaps more particularly the case regarding "dignity" than "equality." There are two major exceptions to this. The first, in the case of dignity, is when courts use dignity explicitly as a way of linking women's rights to human rights more generally, seeing them as both linked by a common understanding of dignity, thus ensuring that women's rights should be seen as giving rise to equally legitimate claims.[160] The second is in those cases in which a clear distinction is made between formal equality and substantive equality, with the latter being seen as the basis for CEDAW, giving CEDAW an asymmetric and social justice-oriented interpretation.[161]

---

156. *See, e.g.*, App. B No. 211 (originalist approach mentioned); App. B No. 2 (extensive use of *travaux* in order to interpret the meaning of "discrimination" in CEDAW).

157. *See, e.g.*, App. B No. 116; App. B No. 115; App. B No. 269.

158. *See, e.g.*, App. B No. 192; App. B No. 193; App. B No. 205; App. B No. 225; App. B No. 275; App. B No. 276; App. B No. 5 (sexual harassment of women at their places of work was incompatible with their dignity and honor and had to be eliminated, and that position was reflected in the CEDAW); App. B. No. 309 (in dissent).

159. *See, e.g.*, App. B No. 126; App. B No. 158; App. B No. 234; App. B No. 236.

160. *See, e.g.*, App. B No. 146 (Court has held thus: "The human rights for women, including girl child are, therefore, inalienable, integral and an indivisible part of universal human rights. (....) [T]he Government of India ... ratified ... CEDAW and reiterated that discrimination against women violates the principles of equality of rights and respect for human dignity.")

161. *See, e.g.*, App. B No. 242 (CEDAW used to justify employer's childcare payments only to women to remedy de facto inequalities, Art 4); App. B No. 250 (formal and substantive equality); App. B No. 190 (Court draws on CEDAW to uphold quotas provision in elections against attack; CEDAW "required equality which was substantive, not merely formal, and restitutionary in its reach"); App. B No. 311 (in dissent, CEDAW supporting distinction between prohibiting distinctions that are oppressive, and those that aim at advancing de facto equality); App. B No. 3 (CEDAW

V. CONCLUSION

This chapter has a threefold aim, in providing a bridge between the first and third parts of my CEDAW trilogy: first, to illustrate how the more theoretical issues arising from the use of a comparative international human rights law analysis discussed earlier in this volume[162] were brought to bear on, and themselves benefitted from, empirical study of the domestic reception of a major international human rights convention; second, in the interests of transparency, to provide a more detailed account of the basic findings of the study that were only briefly sketched out in the AJIL article, so that readers of that article are able to judge for themselves whether the analysis presented there stands up; and, third, to set out the methodological and conceptual difficulties that the empirical study encountered, so that future work in comparative international human rights law is able to anticipate these challenges and develop strategies to address them, learning from my mistakes and the shortcomings of the approach I adopted.

is asymmetric in protecting against discrimination against women and not men); *but see* App. B No. 29 (male parents also eligible to receive social security for looking after their children equivalent to that which adoptive parents receive).

162. McCrudden, *supra* note 2.

APPENDIX A

SOURCES USED TO COMPILE THE LIST OF CASES

The International Law Reports database contains the full text of the printed
publication *International Law Reports* from Cambridge University Press. The
database is updated four times each year.

International Law Reports is the only publication in the world that is wholly
devoted to the regular and systematic reporting in English of decisions of
international courts and arbitrators as well as judgments of national courts.

International Law Reports covers all significant cases of public international law
from 1919 to the present day, including international boundaries, state and
diplomatic immunity, treaties between states, war, terrorism, and refugee law.

Lexis/Nexis (the following files: LRC (Law Reports of the Commonwealth),
BHRC (Butterworths Human Rights Reports); All Subscribed Indian Cases;
All Subscribed Malaysian Cases; All Subscribed New Zealand Cases.

Westlaw UK: combined UK cases; European Union cases; European Court of
Human Rights cases.

Westlaw International (the following files: Westlaw All State and Federal United
States; Westlaw Hong Kong Cases; Westlaw All Canadian Cases; Westlaw All
Australian Cases).

World Law Information (the following database: [All WorldII Databases]).

European Gender Equality Review (2008–2015) (and previous equivalent
publications),http://ec.europa.eu/social/keyDocuments.jsp?type=0&policy
Area=418&subCategory=641&country=0&year=0&advSearchKey=noelr&
mode=advancedSubmit&langId=en.

Commonwealth Human Rights Law Digest, http://www.interights.org/chr-law-
digest/index.html.

Interrights Database, http://www.interights.org/chr-law-digest/index.html.

International Association of Women Judges, Jurisprudence of Equality Program
Decisions, http://www.iawj.org/JEPcases.html.

CEDAW Legal Case Bank—Global Justice Center Asian Pacific Human Rights
Information Center, www.globaljusticecenter.net/casebank.

Asia-Pacific Human Rights Information Center, http://www.hurights.or.jp/
english/human_rights_and_jurisprudence/womens-rights/.

International Womens' Rights Action Watch Asia Pacific Case Law Database,
http://www.iwraw-ap.org/resources/case-law/gender-equality-laws-around-
the-world/.

ASIA PACIFIC FORUM ON WOMEN, LAW, & DEVELOPMENT, A DIGEST OF
CASE LAW ON THE HUMAN RIGHTS OF WOMEN (Christine Forster et al.
eds., 2003).

Oxford International Law in Domestic Courts, http://opil.ouplaw.com/page/
ILDC/oxford-reports-on-international-law-in-domestic-courts.

Equal Rights Trust Legal Cases Bank, http://www.equalrightstrust.org.

The following national databases were also searched using the equivalent words and phrases in the local language:

French Conseil d'Etat; Constitutional Court of Chile; Spanish Constitutional Court; Supreme Court of Mexico; Colombia Constitutional Court; German Constitutional Court; Italian Constitutional Court; Israeli Constitutional Court; Russian Constitutional Court

In all cases, searches were conducted of the use of the following words or phrases: "CEDAW", "elimination of all forms of discrimination against women", in English or in the language of the database.

In addition, I supplemented the database of judicial decisions with scholarly literature. Not all relevant cases made their way into the database. I do not expect any systematic differences between the literature and court decisions.

THE UN CONVENTION ON THE ELIMINATION OF ALL FORMS OF DISCRIMINATION AGAINST WOMEN: A COMMENTARY (Marsha A. Freeman et al. eds., 2012).

WITHOUT PREJUDICE: CEDAW AND THE DETERMINATION OF WOMEN'S RIGHTS IN A LEGAL AND CULTURAL CONTEXT (Meena Shivadas & Sarah Coleman eds., 2010).

UNITED NATIONS DEVELOPMENT FUND FOR WOMEN, BRINGING EQUALITY HOME: IMPLEMENTING THE CONVENTION ON THE ELIMINATION OF ALL FORMS OF DISCRIMINATION AGAINST WOMEN (Ilana Landsberg-Lewis ed., 1998).

WOMEN'S HUMAN RIGHTS: CEDAW IN INTERNATIONAL, REGIONAL AND NATIONAL LAW (Anne Hellum & Henriette Sinding Aasen eds., 2013).

APPENDIX B

CEDAW IN DOMESTIC JURISPRUDENCE CASE LIST

Note: countries are listed in alphabetical order, with the exception of Spain, which has been listed before the Solomon Islands, South Africa, and South Korea.

1. Australia
[1]   *Applicant A v Minister for Immigration & Ethnic Affairs* [1997] 190 CLR 225
[2]   *AB v Registrar of Births, Deaths & Marriages* [2007] 162 FCR 528
[3]   *Aldridge v Booth* [1988] 80 ALR 1
[4]   *Attorney-General for the State of WA v Marquet* [2003] 217 CLR 545
[5]   *Castles v Secretary to the Dep't of Justice* [2010] VSC 310
[6]   *Ferneley v Boxing Authority of NSW & Minister for Health of Vic.* [2001] 115 FCR 306
[7]   *Gardner v National Netball League Ltd.* [2001] 182 ALR 408
[8]   *Hall, Oliver & Reid v A & A Sheiban Pty. Ltd.* [1989] 20 FCR 217
[9]   *Jacomb v Australian Municipal Admin. Clerical & Services Union* [2004] FCA 1250
[10] *Jordan v North Coast Area Health Service* (No 3) [2005] NSWADT 296.
[11] *McBain v Vic.* [2000] 99 FCR 116
[12] *Minister for Immigration & Multicultural Affairs v Khawar* [2002] 210 CLR 1
[13] *Qantas Airways Ltd. v Christie* [1996] 138 ALR 19
[14] *Thomson v. Orica Australia Pty Ltd* [2002] FCA 939
[15] *U v U* [2002] 211 CLR 238
[16] *Victoria v Commonwealth* [1996] 187 CLR 416

2. Austria
[17] Oberster Gerichtshof [OGH] [Sup. Ct] Nov. 29, 2007, 1Ob 234/07d

3. Bangladesh
[18] Bangladesh Legal Aid & Servs. Trust v. Gov't of Bangladesh, Writ Petitions No 5863 of 2009, No 754 of 2010, No 4275 of 2010, ILDC 1916 (BD 2010)
[19] Chaudhury v. Bangladesh, Writ Petition No 7977 of 2008, 29 BLD (HCD) 2009, ILDC 1515 (BD 2009)
[20] Dolon v. Gov't of Bangladesh, Writ petition No 4495 of 2009, ILDC 1917 (BD 2011)
[21] Malkani v. Sec'y of the Ministry of Home Affairs, Writ Petition No 3192 of 1992

4. Belize
[22] Roches v. Wade (30 April 2004) Action No 132 (S. Ct) 299

5. Botswana
[23] Attorney General v. Dow [1992] BLR 119 (App. Ct. Lobatse)
[24] Mmusi v. Ramantele [2013] 4 LRC 437 (High Ct.)

6. British Virgin Islands
[25] The Queen v. Vernon Anthony Paddy (E. Caribbean Sup. Ct in the H.Ct of J. (Crim.)), [2011] 4 JBVIC 2701, [2011] ECSC J0427-1

7. Canada

[26] Canadian Foundation for Children, Youth & the Law v. Canada, [2004] 1 SCR 76

[27] Chan v. Canada (Minister of Employment and Immigration), [1995] 3 S.C.R. 593

[28] R. v. Attorney General, [1999] 1 SCR 330

[29] Schachter v. Canada, [1988] 52 DLR (4th) 525

8. Chile

[30] Tribunal Constitutional [T.C.] [Const. Ct], 19 June, 2014, Rol de la causa: 2482-13

[31] T.C., 13 Mar., 2014, Rol de la causa: 2503-13

[32] T.C., 14 Aug., 2013, Rol de la causa: 2320-12

[33] T.C., 4 July, 2013, Rol de la causa: 2357-12

[34] T.C., 18 June, 2013, Rol de la causa: 2250-12

[35] T.C., 30 May, 2013, Rol de la causa: 2306-12

[36] T.C., 9 Jan., 2013, Rol de la causa: 2358-12

[37] T.C., 27 Sept., 2012, Rol de la causa: 2102-11

[38] T.C., 3 Nov., 2011, Rol de la causa: 1881-10

[39] T.C., 20 July, 2011, Rol de la causa: 2025-11

[40] T.C., 4 Jan., 2011, Rol de la causa: 1683-10

[41] T.C., 6 Aug., 2010, Rol de la causa: 1710-10

[42] T.C., 27 Apr., 2010, Rol de la causa: 1348-09

[43] T.C., 31 Dec., 2009, Rol de la causa: 1444-09

9. Colombia

[44] Corte Constitucional [C.C.] [Const. Ct], May 10, 2006, C-355/2006

[45] C.C., June 6, 2014, A173-14. Auto 173/14

[46] C.C., May 21, 2013, A098-13. Auto 098/13

[47] C.C., Feb. 28, 2012, A038-12. Auto 038/12

[48] C.C., Oct. 21, 2011, A226-11. Auto 226/11

[49] C.C., Apr. 21, 2010, A069-10. Auto 069/10.

[50] C.C., Dec. 11, 2009, A339-09. Auto 339/09.

[51] C.C., Sept. 19, 2008, A237-08. Auto 237/08.

[52] C.C., Dec. 6, 2006, A360-06. Auto 360/06.

[53] C.C., July 2, 2014, C-419-14. Judgment C-419/14

[54] C.C., June 4, 2014, C-340-14. Case C-340/14

[55] C.C., May 20, 2014, C-288-14. Case C-288/14

[56] C.C., Nov. 7, 2013, T-772-13. Case T-772/13

[57] C.C., Feb. 28, 2013, T-639-13. Case T-639/13

[58] C.C., June 28, 2013, T-386-13. Case T-386/13

[59] C.C., Feb. 13, 2013, SU071-13. Judgment SU071/13

[60] C.C., Feb. 13, 2013, SU070-13. Judgment SU070/13

[61] C.C., Nov. 20, 2013, C-839-13. Case C-839/13

[62] C.C., Aug. 28, 2013, C-579-13. Case C-579/13

[63] C.C., June 13, 2013, C-335-13. Case C-335/13

[64] C.C., Nov. 23, 2012, T-992-12. Case T-992/12

[65] C.C., Nov. 22, 2012, T-982-12. Case T-982/12
[66] C.C., Sept. 11, 2012, T-707-12. Case T-707/12
[67] C.C., Aug. 24, 2012, T-662-12. Case T-662/12
[68] C.C., Aug. 10, 2012, T-628-12. Case T-628/12
[69] C.C., Aug. 10, 2012, T-627-12. Case T-627/12
[70] C.C., Mar. 21, 2012, T-234-12. Case T-234/12
[71] C.C., Feb. 20, 2012, T-109-12. Case T-109/12
[72] C.C., Sept. 13, 2012, C-715-12. Case C-715/12
[73] C.C., Nov. 8, 2011, T-843-11. Case T-843/11
[74] C.C., Nov. 3, 2011, T-841-11. Case T-841/11
[75] C.C., June 30, 2011, T-502-11. Case T-502/11
[76] C.C., July 26, 2011, C-577-11. Case C-577/11
[77] C.C., June 23, 2011, C-490-11. Case C-490/11
[78] C.C., July 22, 2010, T-585-10. Case T-585/10
[79] C.C., May 3, 2010, T-311-10. Case T-311/10
[80] C.C., June 23, 2010, T 226-10. Case T-226/10
[81] C.C., Dec. 7, 2010, T-1015-10. Judgment T-1015/10
[82] C.C., Feb. 2, 2010, T-045-10. Case T-045/10
[83] C.C., Sept. 29, 2010, C-776-10. Case C-776/10
[84] C.C., May 5, 2010, C-319-10. Case C-319/10
[85] C.C., Oct. 15, 2009, T-732-09. Case T-732/09
[86] C.C., July 31, 2008, T-760-08. Case T-760/08
[87] C.C., July 24, 2008, C-750-08. Case C-750/08
[88] C.C., May 28, 2008, C-540-08. Judgment C-540/08
[89] C.C., Oct. 22, 2008, C-1035-08. Judgment C-1035/08
[90] C.C., Nov. 9, 2007, T-946-07. Case T-946/07
[91] C.C., Aug. 24, 2007, T-661-07. Case T-661/07
[92] C.C., Aug. 15, 2007, T-636-07. Case T-636/07
[93] C.C., Aug. 3, 2007, T-605-07. Case T-605/07
[94] C.C., Dec. 5, 2007, T-1052-07. Judgment T-1052/07
[95] C.C., July 25, 2007, C-552-07. Case C-552/07
[96] C.C., Feb. 7, 2007, C-075-07. Case C-075/07
[97] C.C., Sept. 27, 2006, C-804-06. Case C-804/06
[98] C.C., May 10, 2006, C-355-06. Case C-355/06
[99] C.C., Apr. 25, 2006, C-322-06. Case C-322/06
[100] C.C., Oct. 18, 2005, T-1037-05. Judgment T-1037/05
[101] C.C., May 24, 2005, C-534-05. Case C-534/05
[102] C.C., Dec. 7, 2005, C-1300-05. Judgment C-1300/1305
[103] C.C., Dec. 7, 2005, C-1299-05. Judgment C-1299/1205
[104] C.C., Sept. 2, 2004, T-853-04. Case T-853/04
[105] C.C., May 25, 2004, C-507-04. Case C-507/04
[106] C.C., July 14, 1993, T-273-93. Case T-273/93

10. Costa Rica
[107] Calderón v. President of the Republic (1998) 6 BHRC 306 (Voto no. 716-98)
[108] Sentencia n° 02196 de Sala Constitucional de 11 de Agosto de 1992
[109] Sentencia n° 6472 de Sala Constitucional de 18 de Agosto de 1999

11. Czech Republic

[110] Nález Ústavního soudu zed ne 28.02.2012 (ÚS) [Decision of the Const. Ct of February 28, 2012], sp.zn. ÚS 26/11

12. Egypt

[111] Sup. Const. Ct, case No. 23, session of Mar. 18, 1995, year 16, Official Gazette, No. 14, April 6, 1995

13. Fiji

[112] Balelala v. State [2004] FJCA 49; [2005] 5 LRC 365 (Ct. App.)
[113] Fijian Teachers Ass'n v. President of the Republic of Fiji Islands [2008] FJHC 59 (High Ct.)
[114] LK and JVR [2009] FJHC 60 (High Ct.)
[115] NK and ZMR [2009] FJHC 95 (High Ct.)
[116] PP and RP [2009] FJHC 72 (High Ct.)
[117] Prakash v. Narayan [2000] FJHC 144 (High Ct.)
[118] State v. Bechu [1999] FJMC 3; (1999) 3 CHRLD 155 (First Class Magis. Ct.)
[119] State v. SNM [2011] FJHC 26 (High Ct.)

14. Finland

[120] A v. Directorate of Finnish Immigration, 5.12.2005/3219, KHO:2005:87, ILDC 594 (Sup. Admin. Ct. 2005)

15. France

[121] Conseil d'Etat [C.E.] [Council of State], Apr. 30, 1997, no. 176205
[122] C.E., Nov. 27, 2000, no. 219375
[123] C.E., Nov. 7, 2001, no. 230324
[124] C.E., Oct. 15, 2004, no. 241661
[125] C.E., Apr. 20, 2005, no. 264348

16. Greece

[126] Symboulion Epikrateias [S.E.] [Supreme Administrative Court] 2831/2003; S.E. 2832/2003; S.E. 2833/2003; S.E. 192/2004; S.E. 2388/2004; S.E. 1667/2009

17. Guatemala

[127] Corte Constitucional [C.C.] [Const. Ct], 7 de Marzo de 1996, Sentencia no. 936-95

18. Hong Kong

[128] DD v. LKW, [2008] 2 H.K.L.R.D. 523 (C.A.)
[129] Equal Opportunities Comm'n v. Dir. of Educ., [2001] 2 H.K.L.R.D. 690 (C.F.I.)
[130] L v. C, [2007] 3 H.K.L.R.D. 819 (C.A.)
[131] Sec'y for Justice v. Chan Wah [2000] 3 H.K.C.F.A.R. 459 (C.F.A.)

19. Hungary

[132] Alkotmánybíróság [AB] [Const. Ct] Jan. 10, 2011, 1/2011 (I 14), AK 2011: 3

20. India

[133] Anuj Garg v. Hotel Ass'n of India, A.I.R. 2007 S.C. 663 (India)

[134] Apparel Exp. Promotion Council v. AK Chopra, (1999) 1 S.C.C. 759 (India)

[135] Arun Kumar Agrawal v. Nat'l Ins. Co. Ltd., [2010] I.N.S.C. 516, [2011] 1 L.R.C. 304 (India)

[136] C. Masilamani Mudaliar v. Idol of Sri Swaminathaswaminat Haswami Thirukoil, (1996) 8 S.C.C. 525 (India)

[137] Chairman Ry. Bd. v. Das, A.I.R. 2000 S.C. 988 (India)

[138] Gaddam Ramakrishnareddy v. Gaddam Rami Reddy, (2010) 9 S.C.C. 602 (India)

[139] Gaurav Jain v. Union of India, A.I.R. 1997 S.C. 3021 (India)

[140] Hariharan v. Reserve Bank of India, (2000) 2 S.C.C. 228 (India)

[141] Kishwar v. State of Bihar, (1996) 5 S.C.C. 125 (India)

[142] Laxmi Mandal v. Deen Dayal Harinagar Hosp., (2010) D.L.T. 9 (Delhi H.C.)

[143] Mun. Corp. of Delhi v. Female Workers (Muster Roll), (2000) 2 S.C.R. 171 (India)

[144] Sakshi v. India, (2004) 5 S.C.C. 518 (India)

[145] Shiva v. Bandhopadhyaya, A.I.R. 1999 S.C. 1149 (India)

[146] Valsammapaul v. Cochin Univ., (1996) 1 S.C.R. 128 (India)

[147] Vishaka v. State of Rajasthan, (1997) 6 S.C.C. 241 (India)

[148] Vasantha R. v. Union of India, (2001) L.L.J. 843 (Madras H.C.)

21. Indonesia

[149] Const. Ct, 14/PUU-V/2012

[150] Const. Ct, 29/PUU-V/2007

[151] Const. Ct, 12/PUU-VI/2008

[152] Const. Ct, 74/PUU-XI/2013

[153] Const. Ct, 1/PUU-VIII/2010

[154] Const. Ct, 20/PUU-XI/2013

[155] Const. Ct, 10-17-23/PUU-VII/2009

[156] Const. Ct, 6/PUU-VII/2009

[157] Const. Ct, 88/PUU-X/2012

[158] Const. Ct, 22-24 PUU-VI/2008

[159] Nurhatina Hasibuan v Pt. Indonesia Toray Synthetics, No. 651/PDT/1988/PT.DKI (Jakarta High Ct.) (Jul. 2, 1988)

22. Ireland

[160] Equal. Auth. v. Portmarnock Golf Club, [2009] IESC 73 (S.C.) (Ir.)

[161] J.J. v. L. Mc. L., [2013] IEHC 549 (H. Ct.) (Ir.)

23. Japan

[162] Hiroshima Kōtō Saibansho [Hiroshima High Ct.] Nov. 28, 1991, 1406 HANREI JIHŌ 3

[163] Nagoya Kōtō Saibansho [Nagoya High Ct.] Oct. 30, 1996, 707 RŌDŌ HANREI 37

[164] Nagoya Kōtō Saibansho [Nagoya High Ct.] Sept. 4, 2013

[165]   Osaka Kōtō Saibansho [Osaka High Ct.] Sept. 25, 1998, 992 HANREI
        TIMES 103
[166]   Osaka Kōtō Saibansho [Osaka High Ct.] May 16, 2000
[167]   Osaka Kōtō Saibansho [Osaka High Ct.] Sept. 26, 1991, 602 RŌDŌ
        HANREI 72
[168]   Saikō Saibansho [Sup. Ct.] No. 250, 2000 (Gyohi) No. 249
[169]   Tōkyō Kōtō Saibansho [Tokyo High Ct.] Mar. 29, 1991, No. 819
[170]   Tōkyō Kōtō Saibansho [Tokyo High Ct.] May 29, 1996, No. 4034, 694
        RŌDŌ HANREI 29
[171]   Tōkyō Kōtō Saibansho [Tokyo High Ct.] Dec. 22, 2000, 796 RŌDŌ
        HANREI 5
[172]   Tōkyō Kōtō Saibansho [Tokyo High Ct.] Mar. 24, 2005, 1899 HANREI
        JIHŌ 101
[173]   Tōkyō Kōtō Saibansho [Tokyo High Ct.] Feb. 27, 2007, (Gyoko) No. 124
[174]   Tōkyō Kōtō Saibansho [Tokyo High Ct.] Dec. 27, 2011, (Gyoko) No. 2946
[175]   Tōkyō Kōtō Saibansho [Tokyo High Ct.] Mar. 28, 2014 (Gyoko) No. 3821
[175a] Tōkyō Chihō Saibansho [Tokyo Dist. Ct.] May 29, 2013, 2196 HANREI
        JIHŌ 67

24. Kenya
[176]   Kamunzyu v. Kamunzyu, Succession Cause 303 of 1998, Dec. 15, 2005,
        ILDC 1342 (KE 2005) (H.C.K.)
[177]   Fed'n of Women Lawyers Kenya v. Attorney Gen. (2011) 5 LRC 625
        (H.C.K.)
[178]   Estate of Lerionka Ole Ntutu (2008) KLR 1 (H.C.K.)
[179]   Ochieng v. Att'y Gen., Petition No. 409 of 2009, Apr. 20, 2012, ILDC 1913
        (KE 2012) (H.C.K.)
[180]   P.A.O. v Attorney Gen. (2012) eKLR (H.C.K.)
[181]   Re Wachokire, Succession Cause No. 192 of 2000, Aug. 19, 2002 (Thika
        Chief Magist. Ct)
[182]   RM v. Attorney Gen., Civil Case 1351, ILDC 699 (KE 2006) (H.C.K.)
[183]   Rono v. Rono (2005) 1 KLR (G&F) 803, ILDC 1259 (KE 2005) (H.C.K.)

25. Kiribati
[184]   Republic v. Timiti [1998] KIHC 35; HCCrC 43.97 (17 August 1998)
        (High Ct)

26. Latvia
[185]   Sup. Ct, Aug. 23, 2013, SKA-7/2013
[186]   Sup. Ct, Dec. 3, 2010, SKA-527/2010
[187]   Sup. Ct, Dec. 8, 2010, SKC-11706/2010
[188]   Administrative District Court, Dec. 16, 2008, A42619207 A3692-08/3

27. Lesotho
[189]   Masupha v. Senior Resident Magistrate for the Subordinate Court of Berea
        [2013] LSHC 9, 5 LRC 517 (High Ct. (Const. Div.))
[190]   Ts'epe v. Independent Electoral Commission, Appeal Judgment, C of
        A (Civ) No 11/05, ILDC 161 (LS 2005)

28. Malaysia

[191] Fernandez v. Sistem Penerbangan Malaysia & Kesatuan Sekerja Kakitangan Sistem Penerbangan Malaysia [2005] 3 MLJ 681, ILDC 1036 (MY 2005)

29. Mexico

[192] Amparo Directo 276/2013, Noveno Tribunal Colegiado en Materia Penal del Primer Circuito, Semanario Judicial de la Federación y su Gaceta, Novena Época, tomo IV, Enero de 2014, Página 3189

[193] Amparo en Revisión 300/2012, Tercer Tribunal Colegiado en Materia Civil del Primer Circuito, Semanario Judicial de la Federación y su Gaceta, Décima Época, tomo III, Marzo de 2013, Página 1908

[194] Amparo Directo 135/2012, Primer Tribunal Colegiado de Circuito del Centro Auxiliar de la Octava Región, Semanario Judicial de la Federación y su Gaceta, Décima Época, tomo IV, Octubre de 2012, Página 2364

[195] Amparo Directo 799/2008, Tercer Tribunal Colegiado en Materia de Trabajo del Cuarto Circuito, Semanario Judicial de la Federación y su Gaceta, Novena Época, tomo XXIX, Febrero de 2009, Página 2035

30. Namibia

[196] Müller v. President of the Republic of Namibia, [2000] 1 LRC 654 (S. Ct)

31. Nepal

[197] Dhungana v. Nepal (Writ No. 3392 of the Year 2050), 6 N.K.P. 2052, 462 (S. Ct. 1995)

[198] Sapana Pradhan v. Prime Minister (Special Writ No. 64 of the Year 2061) (S. Ct. 2005)

[199] Meera Dhungana v. Office of the Prime Minister (Special Writ No. 64 of the Year 2061) (S. Ct. 2005)

[200] Rama Panta Kharel v. Office of Prime Minister (Writ No. 63-WS-0019 of the Year 2060) (S. Ct. 2008)

[201] Jit Kumari Pangeni (Neupane) v. Prime Minister (Writ No. 64-0035 of the Year 2063) (S. Ct. 2008)

[202] Achyut Prasad Kharel v. Office of Prime Minister (Writ No. 3352 of the year 2061) (S. Ct. 2008)

[203] Meera Dhungana v. Prime Minister (Writ No. 112 of the Year 2062) (S. Ct. 2008)

[204] Prakash Mani Sharma v. GON (Writ No. 064-WO-0230) (S. Ct. 1999)

[205] Pant v. Nepal Gov't (Writ No. 917 of the Year 2064), 138 I.L.R. 500 (S. Ct. 2007)

[206] Mina Kumari Tilija v. Ministry of Home Affairs (Writ No. 1379 of the Year 2048), 11 N.K.P 2048, 749 (S. Ct. 1992)

[207] Meera Kumari v. His Majesty's Gov't (S. Ct. 1995)

[208] Rina Bajracharya v. HMG Secretariat of the Council of Ministers (Writ No. 2812 of the year 2054) BS (S. Ct., 20xx)

32. Netherlands

[209] Rb. Den Haag 7 september 2005, NJ 2005, 473

[210] Rb. Den Haag 30 oktober 2007, KG 2007, 1099

[211]   ABRvS 5 december 2007, LJN 2007, BB9493
[212]   Hof Gravenhage 20 december 2007, LJN 2007, BC0169
[213]   HR 1 april 2011, LJN 2011, BP3044
[214]   HR 9 april 2010, LJN 2010, BK4547
[215]   HR 9 april 2010, LJN 2010, BK4549

33. New Zealand
[216]   Coburn v. Hum. Rts. Comm'n [1994] 3 NZLR 323 (H.C.)
[217]   Mansouri-Rad v. Dep't of Labour [2005] NZAR 60, ILDC 217 (NZ 2004)
        (Refugee Status App. Auth.)
[218]   N.Z. Van Lines Ltd. v. Proceedings Comm'r [1995] 1 NZLR 100 (H.C.)
[219]   Quilter v. Att'y Gen. [1998] 1 NZLR 523 (C.A.)

34. Nigeria
[220]   Mojekwo v Ejikeme [2000] 5 NWLR 402 (C.A.)
[221]   Mojekwu v Mojekwu [1997] 7 NWLR 283 (C.A.)
[222]   Mojekwu v. Iwuchukwu, [2004] 11 NWLR 196 (S.C.)

35. Norway
[223]   Sup. Ct, Nov. 11, 2009, HR-2009-2129-U-Rt-2009-1389
[224]   Agder Court of Appeal, Jan. 12, 2009, LA-2008-70679

36. Pakistan
[225]   Humaira Mehmood v. The State, (1999) PLD (Lah.) 494
[226]   Saima v. The State, (2003) PLD (Lah.) 747
[227]   Sarwar Jan v. Abdur Rehman, (2004) CLC 17
[228]   Suo Moto No. 1/K of 2006, Federal Shariat Court, (2007) PLD (FSC) 1

37. Paraguay
[229]   Invalidity of Legal Fact of Simulation, Re Aliendre v Mendoza & Sanabria,
        Appeal Judgment No 84, Jul. 27, 2006, ILDC 1522 (PY 2006)

38. Peru
[230]   RJSA, widow of R (on behalf of GRS in the capacity of official guardian)
        v. Peruvian Sup. Ct., No 3081-2007-PA/TC, ILDC 969 (PE 2007)
        (Const. Ct.)

39. Philippines
[231]   Romualdez-Marcos v. Comm'n on Elections, G.R. No. 119976, 248
        S.C.R.A. 300 (S.C., 1995)
[232]   Halagueña, et al. v. Philippine Airlines, Inc., G.R. No. 172013, 602 S.C.R.A.
        297 (S.C., 2009)
[233]   Pharm. & Health Care Assoc. of the Phil. v. Health Sec'y Francisco
        T. Duque III, PHSC 1162 (Oct. 9, 2007)
[233a] Sec'y of Nat'l Def. et al. v. Manalo, PHSC 1086 (Oct. 7, 2008)

40. Russia
[234]   Const. Ct, Judgment of Mar. 22, 2012, No. 617-O-O
[235]   Sup. Ct, Judgment of Feb. 12, 2004, No. 49-G03-164
[236]   Alexeevsky Dist. Ct., Belgorod Region, Case N 2-687/2014

[237] Leninsky Dist. Ct., Jewish Autonomous Region, Case N 2-84A/2012
[238] Samara Dist. Ct., Aug. 20, 2012, Case N 2-2613/2012-2311/2012
[239] Essentuki Mun. Ct., Stavropol Krai, Mar. 24, 2011, Case N 10-7/2011

41. Samoa
[240] Police v. Apelu [2010] WSSC 178 (S. Ct.)

42. Spain
[241] S.T.C., Nov. 7, 2011 (152/2011)
[242] S.T.C., July 16, 1987 (128/1987)
[243] S.T.C., Dec. 14, 1992 (229/1992)
[244] S.T.C., Mar. 25, 1993 (109/1993)
[245] S.T.C., June 14, 1993 (187/1993)
[246] S.T.C., July 3, 1997 (126/1997)
[247] S.T.C., May 20, 2002 (115/2002)
[248] S.T.C., July 4, 2005 (182/2005)
[249] S.T.C., July 3, 2006 (214/2006)
[250] S.T.C., Jan. 29, 2008 (12/2008)
[251] S.T.C., Jan. 19, 2009 (13/2009)
[252] S.T.C., June 7, 1994 (173/1994)
[253] S.T.C., Nov. 28, 1994 (317/1994)

43. Solomon Islands
[254] Hatilia v. Attorney General [2012] SBHC 101
[255] Rajapaksha v. Attorney General [2011] SBHC 189
[256] Regina v. Gua [2012] SBHC 118; [2013] 3 LRC 272

44. South Africa
[257] *Bhe v. Magistrate Khayelitsha* 2005 (1) BCLR 1376 (CC) (S. Afr.)
[258] *Carmichele v. Minister of Safety & Security* 2002 (1) LRC 553 (CC) (S. Afr.)
[259] *F v. Minister of Safety & Security* 2011 (5) LRC 133 (CC) (S. Afr.)
[260] *Gumede v. President of the Republic of S. Afr.* 2008 (4) LRC 351 (CC) (S. Afr.)
[261] *Hassam v. Jacobs* 2008 (4) All SA350 C419 (CC) (S. Afr.)
[262] *Hoffmann v. S. Afr. Airways* 2001 (2) LRC 277 (CC) (S. Afr.)
[263] *Kaunda v. President of S. Afr.* 2005 (4) SA 235 (CC) (S. Afr.)
[264] *Kylie v. Comm'n for Conciliation, Mediation & Arbitration*, 2011 (1) LRC 336 (A) (S. Afr.)
[265] *Mayelane v. Ngwenyama* 2012 (1) LRC 608 (A) (S. Afr.)
[266] *S v. Baloyi* 2000 (2) SA 425 (CC) (S. Afr.)

45. South Korea
[267] Const. Ct., 98Hun-Ma363, Dec. 23, 1999
[268] Const. Ct., 97Hun-Ka12, Aug. 31, 2000
[269] Sup. Ct., 2002Da1178, Jul. 21, 2005

46. Switzerland
[270] Bundesgericht [BGer] [Federal Sup. Ct] Oct. 7, 1998, 124 ENTSCHEIDUNGEN DES SCHWEIZERISCHEN BUNDESGERICHTS [BGE] 121

47. Tanzania

[271] *Chilla v. Chilla*, Civil Appeal No. 188 of 2000 (HC) (unreported)
[272] *Ephraim v Pastory*, Civil Appeal No. 70 of 1989 (HC) (unreported)
[273] *Jonathan v. Republic*, Criminal Appeal No. 53 of 2001 (HC) (unreported)
[274] *Mohamed v. Makamo*, Civil Appeal No. 45 of 2001 (HC) (unreported)
[275] *Mtefu v. Mtefu*, Civil Appeal No. 214 of 2000 (HC) (unreported)
[276] *Ndossi v. Ndossi*, Civil Appeal No. 13 of 2001 (HC) (unreported)
[277] *Njobeka v. Mkorogoro*, P.C. Civil Appeal No. 6 of 2001 (HC) (unreported)

48. Turkey

[278] Anayasa Mahkemesi, Esas No. 2010/119, Karar No. 2011/165
[279] Anayasa Mahkemesi, Esas No. 2009/85, Karar No. 2011/49, ILDC 1910 (TR 2011)
[280] Anayasa Mahkemesi, Esas No. 1990/30, Karar No. 1990/31
[281] Anayasa Mahkemesi, Esas No. 1996/15, Karar No. 1996/34

49. Tuvalu

[282] *Tepulolo v. Pou* [2005] TVHC 1, 5 LRC 701 (High Ct.)

50. Uganda

[283] *Mukasa v. Attorney General*, ILDC 1285 (UG 2008) (High Ct., Dec. 22 2008)
[284] *Uganda Ass'n of Women Lawyers v. Attorney General* [2004] UGCC 1, ILDC 1137 (UG 2004) (Const. Ct., Mar. 10, 2004)
[285] *Uganda v. Matovu*, Criminal Session Case No 146 of 2001 (High Ct., Oct. 21, 2002)

51. United Kingdom

[286] *EM (Lebanon) v. Sec'y of State for the Home Dep't*, [2006] EWCA (Civ) 1531
[287] *AMM (Somalia) v. Sec'y of State for the Home Dep't*, [2011] UKUT 445
[288] *Jomah v. Attar, J (A Child)*, [2004] EWCA (Civ) 417
[289] *R. (on the application of HH) v. Westminster City Magistrates' Ct.*, [2012] UKSC 25
[290] *Fornah v Sec'y of State for the Home Dep't*, [2006] UKHL 46
[291] *R (on the application of Aguilar Quila) v. Sec'y of State for the Home Dep't; R (on the application of Bibi and another) v. Sec'y of State for the Home Dep't*, [2011] UKSC 45
[292] *R v. Sec'y of State for Work & Pensions*, [2002] EWHC 191
[293] *R. (on the application of Mansoor) v. Sec'y of State for the Home Dep't*, [2011] EWHC (Admin) 832
[294] *R v. Immigration Appeal Tribunal*, [1999] 2 AC 629
[295] *R. (Khan) v Oxfordshire Cnty. Council*, [2002] EWHC (Admin) 2211
[296] *Regina (Amicus-MSF Section) v. Sec'y of State for Trade & Industry*, [2004] EWHC (Admin) 860
[297] *Regina (Hoxha) v. Special Adjudicator*, [2005] UKHL 19
[298] *HJ (Iran) v. Sec'y of State for the Home Dep't*, [2010] UKSC 31
[299] *Rolls-Royce v. Unite the Union*, [2009] EWCA (Civ) 387

23

The Great Promise of Comparative Public Law for Latin America

Toward Ius Commune Americanum?

ALEJANDRO RODILES*

I. INTRODUCTION

Notions of "Latin American international law" can be traced to the struggle for independence from the Spanish and Portuguese crowns, to the ideas of men such as Simón Bolivar and José de San Martín,[1] and to doctrines such as *uti possidetis*.[2] They have reappeared from time to time, importantly including Alejandro Álvarez's vision of *le droit international américain*,[3] and the role that the great

---

* I thank the participants at the 28th Annual Sokol Colloquium, at the University of Virginia, School of Law, for a fruitful discussion on the ideas elaborated in this chapter. My special gratitude goes to Mila Versteeg and Pierre-Hugues Verdier for very helpful comments on an earlier draft, as well as to Helmut Aust and Juan de Dios Gutiérrez Baylón for inspiring suggestions. I thank María José Flores Ramírez (ITAM) for technical assistance. The usual disclaimer applies.

1. *See* INDALECIO LIÉVANO AGUIRRE, BOLIVARISMO Y MONROISMO (1987).

2. *See* Juan de Dios Gutiérrez Baylón, *La Explicación de la Fecha del Bicentenario ante el Derecho Internacional: México y la Doctrina del Uti Possidetis, in* LA INDEPENDENCIA DE MÉXICO A 200 AÑOS DE SU INICIO. PENSAMIENTO SOCIAL Y JURÍDICO 139 (Comisión Organizadora de los Festejos del Bicentenario y Centenario de la Revolución Mexicana, ed. 2010); *see also* Marcelo G. Kohen, *La Contribution de l'Amérique Latine au Développement Progressif du Droit International en Matière Territoriale,* 137 RELATIONS INTERNATIONALES 13 (2009).

3. *See* Alejandro Álvarez, *Le Droit International Américain, son origine et son évolution* 14 REVUE GÉNÉRALE DE DROIT INTERNATIONAL PUBLIC 393 (1907); Alejandro Álvarez, *Latin America and International Law,* 3 AM. J. INT'L L. 269 (1909). For an excellent analysis of Álvarez's work and vita, see Liliana Obregón, *Noted for Dissent: The International Life of Alejandro Álvarez,* 19 LEIDEN J. INT'L L. 983 (2006).

---

codification projects of the region played in this regard, both in public and private international law.[4]

Another evolution that has much contributed to the region's perception and approach to international law is the Inter-American human rights system. The early years of the long construction of this system (from the late 1940s to the early 1970s) raised the hope of enhanced cooperation among Latin American states. César Sepúlveda, one of the intellectual architects, asserted that the states of the region conceived of common protection of human rights as a vehicle for consolidating democracies, and hence as a means of guaranteeing their peaceful coexistence and fostering their cooperation.[5]

Today, Inter-American human rights law has become the inspiration for a new grand legal project in the region: "*ius constitutionale commune* in Latin America" (ICCLA), sometimes also referred to as "*ius commune americanum.*" Based on the axiom of the protection of fundamental rights of the inhabitants of the region, ICCLA may be seen as a continuation of the ideas expressed by Sepúlveda more than three decades earlier. However, ICCLA differs from those ideas in important ways. Sepúlveda played a pioneering role in the region in promoting the status of the individual in international law and had a clear Latin American vocation. But he also was a generalist who believed in the legitimacy of *one* universal international law. So, although he praised the practical (better protection) and aspirational (stronger cooperation among democracies) virtues of the regional human rights system, he did not advocate a common law of the Americas.[6]

Unlike earlier approaches to international law in Latin America, the impetus for ICCLA comes from constitutionalists who have embraced the internationalization of their field and merged it with international human rights law, not from international lawyers. What one might regard as a manifestation of "the increased penetration of international law into the domestic realm"[7] is, at the same time, an interesting

4. *See* ALEJANDRO ÁLVAREZ, LA CONFÉRENCE DES JURISTES DE RIO DE JANEIRO ET LA CODIFICATION DU DROIT INTERNATIONAL AMÉRICAIN (1913); ALEJANDRO ÁLVAREZ, LE CONTINENT AMÉRICAIN ET LA CODIFICATION DU DROIT INTERNATIONAL. UNE NOUVELLE 'ÉCOLE' DU DROIT DES GENS (1938). As Liliana Obregón mentions, codification already played a pivotal role for Carlos Calvo and Andrés Bello in relation to the Latin American distinctiveness toward international law. However, it is important to note that neither Bello nor Calvo embraced "Latin American international law," limiting themselves to articulating and highlighting the specificities of the region and its contributions to general international law. *See* Obregón, *supra* note 3.

5. *See* César Sepúlveda, *El Panorama de los Derechos Humanos en América Latina: Actualidad y Perspectivas*, 45 BOLETÍN MEXICANO DE DERECHO COMPARADO 1053 (1982).

6. *See* CÉSAR SEPÚLVEDA, DERECHO INTERNACIONAL 531–34, 247–56 (26th ed. 2013) (mentioning that the regional and universal systems harmonically complement each other, and that the ultimate goal is the universal protection of international human rights law. It is also interesting to observe that in his international law textbook—probably the most influential in law school curricula in Mexico until recently—several pages are dedicated to the doctrines of Carlos Calvo, and none to those of Alejandro Álvarez).

7. Anthea Roberts, Paul B. Stephan, Pierre-Hugues Verdier & Mila Versteeg, *Comparative International Law: Framing the Field*, 109 AM. J. INT'L L. 467, 468 (2015).

case of the increasing penetration of constitutional law into the international realm. Although proponents of ICCLA argue that it does not represent a regional version of international law, they do assert that the project is about the protection of fundamental rights, importantly including those of an international origin. According to them, a common public law of the region is emerging through an increased regional judicial dialogue centered on the jurisprudence of an international tribunal, namely the Inter-American Court of Human Rights in San José, Costa Rica (IACHR, or San José Court).[8] Thus, this conception of public law merges national constitutional and international law.[9]

The aim of this chapter is to analyze ICCLA in light of comparative international law. Even conceding that ICCLA is something other than a regional version of international law, its vernacular stems, at least in part, from a particular approach to international law based on human dignity or, in Inter-American parlance, on "the oneness of the human family."[10] This influence may have important consequences for the way international law is conceived and applied within the region. Although the literature on ICCLA does not focus on international law as such, surfacing its approach to international law lies at the core of comparative international law's research agenda.[11] More importantly, comparative international law invites us to inquire into the promises and perils of such a particular approach.[12] Is ICCLA augmenting the fragmentation of international law, or does it contribute to making international law more international by providing Latin American jurists with a powerful conceptual framework for making their version of international law heard on the global plane?[13] Even if one wishes to avoid normative assertions on whether this Latin American approach to international law should be discouraged or encouraged,[14] one must confront the conception of international law that underlies the ICCLA project. As will be argued in the following sections, ICCLA entails a conception of law in

8. *See* Armin von Bogdandy, *Ius Constitutionale Commune en América Latina: Observations on Transformative Constitutionalism*, 109 AM. J. INT'L L. UNBOUND 109 (2015).

9. *See* Armin von Bogdandy, *Ius Constitutionale Commune Latinoamericanum. Una Aclaración Conceptual, in* IUS CONSTITUTIONALE COMMUNE EN AMÉRICA LATINA. RASGOS, POTENCIALIDADES Y DESAFÍOS 3, 21 (Armin von Bogdandy, Héctor Fix-Fierro & Mariela Morales Antoniazzi eds., 2014).

10. Juridical Condition and Rights of Undocumented Migrants, Advisory Opinion OC-18/03, Inter-Am. Ct. H.R. (ser. A) No. 18, ¶ 100 (Sept. 17, 2003) (with further references to its previous advisory jurisprudence). The San José Court's tenet of the oneness of the human family is deeply influenced by the doctrines of its former president, Cançado Trindade, *see* ANTÔNIO A. CANÇADO TRINDADE, TRATADO DE DIREITO INTERNACIONAL DOS DIREITOS HUMANOS, vols. 1–2 (1997).

11. Anthea E. Roberts, Paul B. Stephan, Pierre-Hugues Verdier & Mila Versteeg, *Conceptualizing Comparative International Law*, at 8 (this volume).

12. *Id.* at 28–9.

13. On comparative international law as a project for furthering a more international international law, *see* Martti Koskenniemi, *The Case for Comparative International Law*, 20 FIN. YB. INT'L L. 1 (2009).

14. Cf. Roberts et al., *supra* note 11, at 6.

a time of globalization and pluralism that affects the very notion of "international law." It envisions an emerging Latin American law that shares the larger aspiration of a global public law.

ICCLA has been constructed at two fronts: the academic (or discursive), and the judicial (or operative). Both are part of the same enterprise, and it is impossible to grasp one without the other: the legal philosophy underlying the legal work, and the legal work backing up the legal philosophy. However, methodologically it is best to address them separately. Therefore, I will first describe the ideological and theoretical genesis of this project, which is the product of a trans-regional academic dialogue. It is highly interesting indeed that ICCLA is nurtured by a comparison, at the macro level so to speak, to a German conception of European constitutionalism: *Gemeineuropäisches Verfassungsrecht* (common European constitutional law).[15] This raises the question about the character of ICCLA as a Latin American project inasmuch as its vernacular incorporates a foreign grammar. So understood, ICCLA would join the list of previous Latin American law projects that, as Liliana Obregón observes, construct their identity as regional particularism with European roots and ideals in mind.[16]

But this observation would miss the mark if the legal literature that promotes ICCLA was correct in asserting that a dynamic and pluralistic intra-regional judicial dialogue involving a cross-fertilization of national courts and the San José tribunal provides the basis for this project. Therefore I next will address the main features of this judicial dialogue, considering whether it truly reveals a pluralistic conversation of national and regional actors, or instead denotes a monologue promoted by an international tribunal. I argue that the latter comes closer to the truth, a conclusion that leads to a reconsideration of the pluralistic narrative about ICCLA. This conclusion raises serious doubts about the emergence of a *ius commune* in Latin America, with which I will deal in my concluding remarks.

II. *IUS CONSTITUTIONALE COMMUNE* IN LATIN AMERICA (ICCLA) AND *GEMEINEUROPÄISCHES VERFASSUNGSRECHT*: WE ARE ALL NATURALISTS NOW

The contemporary constitutionalist framing of law in Latin America has its historical background in the advent of new liberal constitutions and constitutional reforms breaking with authoritarian regimes in the region. This evolution began

---

15. This notion was first articulated by Peter Häberle, *Gemeineuropäisches Verfassungsrecht*, 18 EUROPÄISCHE GRUNDRECHTE-ZEITSCHRIFT 261 (1991). *See also* Markus Heintzen, *Gemeineuropäisches Verfassungsrecht in der Europäischen Union*, 32 EUROPARECHT 1 (1997); Christoph Möllers, *Verfassunggebende Gewalt—Verfassung—Konstitutionalisierung*, in EUROPÄISCHES VERFASSUNGSRECHT. THEORETISCHE UND DOGMATISCHE GRUNDZÜGE 227, 266–67 (Armin von Bogdandy & Jürgen Bast eds., 2009); *see infra* note 26 and accompanying text.

16. This is what Liliana Obregón refers to as the "creole legal consciousness." Liliana Obregón, *Completing Civilization: Creole Consciousness and International Law in Nineteenth-Century Latin America*, in INTERNATIONAL LAW AND ITS OTHERS 247 (Anne Orford ed., 2006).

in the mid-1980s and continued up to Mexico's human rights reform in 2011.[17] A common feature of these new constitutions and constitutional reforms is the strengthening of the catalogue of fundamental rights and their means of protection, importantly including international human rights law. Thus openness toward international law by domestic legal systems has been one of the major characteristics of these constitutional transformations.[18] Drawing inspiration from these changes in Latin American political systems, constitutionalists from across the region have embraced and promoted a version of the rule of law that can be characterized as a "constitutional *Rechtsstaat*" ("*Estado constitucional de derecho*").[19] This version rests on the idea of a legal order that functions for and around the protection of fundamental rights as recognized by the constitution. The judicial function occupies a pivotal position in the construction of this idea of the rule of law. This focus is further strengthened by a profound disappointment in various countries in the region with their executive and legislative branches.

This placing of hope in courts, especially in the highest and constitutional tribunals, has led to a belief that the better way to secure protection of rights entails creative legal interpretation and ponderation of principles, as opposed to strict law application.[20] The approaches of national courts in other regions, especially the German Federal Constitutional Court with its emphasis on the principle of proportionality (*Verhältnismäßigkeitsprinzip*), have decisively influenced the articulation of this legal discourse, which describes itself as "Latin American neo-constitutionalism."[21] A look at the authors whose theories and theses have nurtured the conceptual framework of Latin American neo-constitutionalism reveals a predominantly European orientation.[22]

17. For a comprehensive overview, see ROBERTO GARGARELLA, LATIN AMERICAN CONSTITUTIONALISM: 1810–2010. THE ENGINE ROOM OF THE CONSTITUTION 148–95 (2013); *see also* Alejandro Rodiles, *The Law and Politics of the* Pro Persona *Principle in Latin America, in* THE INTERPRETATION OF INTERNATIONAL LAW BY DOMESTIC COURTS: UNIFORMITY, DIVERSITY, CONVERGENCE 153 (Helmut Philipp Aust & Georg Nolte eds., 2016) (with further references).

18. *See* GARGARELLA, *supra* note 17, at 168–69.

19. *See* LUIS PRIETO SANCHÍS, CONSTITUCIONALISMO Y POSITIVISMO (1997). The concept of "Estado constitucional" goes directly back to Peter Häberle's theses on the "*Verfassungsstaat*," developed over the years, which were assembled in a monograph published in Mexico; *see* PETER HÄBERLE, EL ESTADO CONSTITUCIONAL (2001).

20. *See* Luis Prieto Sanchís, *Neoconstitucionalismo y Ponderación Judicial*, 5 ANUARIO DE LA FACULTAD DE DERECHO DE LA UNIV. AUTÓNOMA DE MADRID 201 (2001).

21. Among the vast literature, see the contributions in EL CANON NEOCONSTITUCIONAL (Miguel Carbonell & Leonardo García Jaramillo eds., 2010); EL DERECHO EN AMÉRICA LATINA: UN MAPA PARA EL PENSAMIENTO JURÍDICO DEL SIGLO XXI (César Rodríguez Garavito ed., 2011); NEW CONSTITUTIONALISM IN LATIN AMERICA: PROMISES AND PRACTICES (Detlef Nolte & Almut Schilling-Vacaflor eds., 2012).

22. The Germans Robert Alexy and Peter Häbele, the Spaniard Manuel Atienza, and the Italian Luigi Ferrajoli are among the most influential, together with the US-American Ronald Dworkin and, as the only Latin American, the Argentinean Carlos Nino. For the influence of these thinkers

Fundamental to Latin American neo-constitutionalism is a cosmopolitan idea of law. Because basic rights are viewed as shared values beyond borders (a common culture), the constitutional state is seen as participating in a constitution of rights that transcends the sphere of the national constitution's formal validity. This transnational participation is said to have two aspects: the openness of the national legal system toward international human rights law, in particular the Inter-American human rights system, and the engagement of national judiciaries in the construction of a common law of the region (*ius commune latinoamericanum*) based on the premises of neo-constitutionalism.[23]

It is not quite clear when the discourse of Latin American neo-constitutionalism merged with that of ICCLA. One might say that, as the former gained ground across the region,[24] the consolidation of a *ius commune* in human rights and constitutional principles became the new aspiration of neo-constitutionalists. The theories of Peter Häberle, a German public lawyer and comparatist, on the constitutional state (*Verfassungsstaat*) and culture have been highly influential in the articulation of this Latin American legal discourse.[25] He coined the term "*ius commune americanum*."[26] In an essay written for a congress in Mexico in 2001, he asked the question whether the notion of a common European constitutional law ("*Gemeineuropäisches Verfassungsrecht*") can be applied to America, focusing on Latin America. He first referred to the basic elements of *Gemeineuropäisches Verfassungsrecht* that he elaborated in a 1991 essay of the same title and further developed in his 2001 monograph on European constitutional theory.[27] Starting with the notion of a European legal culture expressed historically in a *ius commune europaeum* in private law that was revitalized through European private international law, Häberle traced the commonality of fundamental rule-of-law principles across national constitutions in Europe, as well as those expressed in European law stricto sensu (European Union law) and lato sensu (that of the Council of Europe and the Organization for Security and Cooperation in Europe (OSCE)). He argued that these principles permit the

on Latin American neo-constitutionalism, *see* Ana Micaela Alterio, *Corrientes del Constitucionalismo Contemporáneo a Debate*, 8 PROBLEMA 227 (2014).

23. *See, e.g.,* Mariela Morales Antoniazzi, *El Estado Abierto como Objetivo del Ius Constitutionale Commune. Aproximación desde el Impacto de la Corte Interamericana de Derechos Humanos*, in IUS CONSTITUTIONALE COMMUNE EN AMÉRICA LATINA: RASGOS, POTENCIALIDADES Y DESAFÍOS, *supra* note 9, 265, 268–69 (with further references).

24. See the various contributions in EL DERECHO EN AMÉRICA LATINA, *supra* note 21.

25. *See supra* note 19.

26. Peter Häberle, *México y los Contornos de un Derecho Constitucional Común Americano: Un Ius Commune Americanum*, in DE LA SOBERANÍA AL DERECHO CONSTITUCIONAL COMÚN: PALABRAS CLAVE PARA UN DIÁLOGO EUROPEO-LATINOAMERICANO 1 (Peter Häberle & Markus Kotzur eds., 2001).

27. Peter Häberle, *Gemeineuropäisches Verfassungsrecht*, 18 EUROPÄISCHE GRUNDRECHTE-ZEITSCHRIFT 261 (1991); PETER HÄBERLE, EUROPÄISCHE VERFASSUNGSLEHRE (2011). Like most of his work, the 1991 essay has been translated into Spanish: Peter Häberle, *Derecho Constitucional Común Europeo*, 79 REVISTA DE ESTUDIOS POLÍTICOS 7 (1993).

identification of a pan-European constitutional culture. Importantly, he asserted that to extrapolate from the common constitutional culture to the common constitutional law, there must exist a shared interpretive approach, in which courts across Europe (national courts and the regional tribunals in Strasbourg and Luxembourg) use the comparative method for identifying the similarities that will consolidate this *corpus iuris.*

In his Mexican essay, Häberle considered whether the "European model" can be transplanted into Latin America. He maintained that it could, based on what he called "the contours of a Latin American identity."[28] This identity is expressed, according to the Bayreuth professor, in those constitutional clauses that refer to regional integration or regional solidarity, as well as by the common frame of reference that these constitutional orders have in the Inter-American human rights system, concretely in the 1969 American Convention on Human Rights (ACHR) and the jurisprudence of the IACHR. He stated that this "Court, together with its jurisprudence, form a partial constitution in the frame of the common constitutional American law."[29] Just as *Gemeineuropäisches Verfassungsrecht* was a project to be built based on a shared legal heritage and common constitutional principles, his 2001 essay offered a manifesto for the construction of *ius commune americanum.*

Latin American neo-constitutionalists have taken up this manifesto. Legal scholars, judges, and academic institutions closely related to their constitutional elites (part of these elites) as well as to the Inter-American human rights system (often the very same professional circle) have promoted this legal discourse intensively in recent years. Prominent universities in Colombia (e.g., Los Andes, Externado) and the Legal Research Institute of the National Autonomous University of Mexico (IIJ-UNAM), as well as its daughter organization, the Ibero-American Institute of Constitutional Law, are the protagonists, together with Heidelberg's Max-Planck Institute for Comparative Public Law and International Law.[30] A series of publications have appeared in recent years, emerging from several conferences organized by some of the above-mentioned academic institutions, along with some of the constitutional and highest courts of the region and the IACHR.[31] This transnational

---

28. Häberle, *supra* note 26, at 22–23.

29. *Id.* at 40.

30. ICCLA is one of the main research projects of this prestigious institute. It forms part, together with the project *ius publicum europaeum,* of the major research area of "comparative public law." This is interesting in the context of the present book. Comparative public law strives to identify similarities in public law institutions and fundamental rights across various national jurisdictions and international legal regimes, in order to articulate the contours of an emerging global public law in which the national/international divide is blurred. This signals the difficulties in distinguishing between comparative international law and comparative constitutional law, according to increasingly popular conceptions of a changing law in times of "structural transformations of the public space." For more information on these intertwined projects, carried out under the leadership of Prof. Armin von Bogdandy, see Max Planck Inst., Comparative Public Law, http://www.mpil.de/en/pub/research/areas/comparative-public-law.cfm.

31. The most important publications being LA JUSTICIA CONSTITUCIONAL Y SU INTERNACIONALIZACIÓN: ¿HACIA UN *IUS CONSTITUTIONALE COMMUNE* EN AMÉRICA LATINA?

partnership indicates, as I have argued elsewhere, that ICCLA is evidence of "law as profession,"[32] that is, of a project of influential Latin American constitutionalists (scholars and judges) who, as globalization advances, have come to embrace the internationalization of their field, as well as European international lawyers with a (German) constitutionalist and comparatist mindset.[33]

Curiously, the contemporary literature on ICCLA is rather oblivious to Häberle's arguments. Yet it restates the same elements and prospects, taking the same European model as its reference.[34] Moreover, theses on the judicial function that have built on Häberle's pan-European constitutionalism, such as the multilevel game of adjudication according to which a mutually reinforcing transeuropean communicative process of rights protection reinforces constitutional justice,[35] are transplanted into the Latin American context by making the obvious analogies between the European and Inter-American human rights systems, as well as between the constitutional courts and highest tribunals of the member states of these regional systems. A possible explanation for the literature's neglect of Häberle's theses on the universal character of Europe's constitutional culture, capable of fostering similar developments in other regions, is an intention to change perceptions. ICCLA's discourse successfully evokes a move in the layers of comparison from the European to the global model of cosmopolitan constitutionalism. Accordingly, *ius commune latinoamericanum* gives the impression of resembling *Gemeineuropäisches Verfassungsrecht* (or *ius publicum europaeum*) while having global constitutionalism as the shared ideal, or *tertium comparationis*.[36]

(Armin von Bogdandy, Eduardo Ferrer MacGregor & Mariela Morales Antoniazzi eds., 2010); IUS CONSTITUTIONALE COMMUNE EN AMÉRICA LATINA: RASGOS, POTENCIALIDADES Y DESAFÍOS, *supra* note 9; *see also* TRANSFORMATIVE CONSTITUTIONALISM IN LATIN AMERICA: THE EMERGENCE OF A NEW IUS COMMUNE (Armin von Bogdandy, Eduardo Ferrer Mac-Gregor, Mariela Morales Antoniazzi, Flávia Piovesan & Ximena Soley eds., 2017). Germany's Konrad Adenauer Foundation provides much funding for these conferences and publications.

32. *See* Rodiles, *supra* note 17, at 173.

33. The importance of this network of professionals for neo-constitutionalism and *ius commune* is openly acknowledged by proponents of these discourses. *See* César Rodríguez Garavito, *Navegando la Globalización: Un Mapamundi para el Estudio y la Práctica del Derecho en América Latina, in* EL DERECHO EN AMÉRICA LATINA, *supra* note 21, 69, 69–71 (mentioning that this trend "is about a set of epistemic, professional and political networks, more or less organized, which have constructed and promoted Latin American neo-constitutionalism."); *see also* PAOLA ANDREA ACOSTA ALVARADO, DIÁLOGO JUDICIAL Y CONSTITUCIONALISMO MULTINIVEL: EL CASO INTERAMERICANO 122–45 (2015) (underlining the importance of the extension of judicial, legal, and academic regional networks in understanding "*ius commune* inter-americano.").

34. Though not with the same emphasis as Häberle, von Bogdandy also refers to the impulse that *ius commune europaeum* may offer to ICCLA. Von Bogdandy, *supra* note 9 at 4–5.

35. Here, the work of the Walter Hallstein Institute for European Constitutional Law at Humboldt-University, Berlin, is illustrative (information available at http://www.whi-berlin.eu/index.html); for a representative essay on European multilevel constitutionalism, see Ingolf Pernice, *Multilevel Constitutionalism and the Treaty of Amsterdam: European Constitution-Making Revisited?*, 36 COMMON MKT. L. REV. 703 (1999) (dedicated to Pernice's academic teacher, Peter Häberle).

36. For the *tertium comparationis* as an ideal, see John C. Reitz, *How to Do Comparative Law*, 46 AM. J. COMP. L. 617, 623 (1998).

But when one looks more closely at the striking similarities between the methods and goals of ICCLA and *Gemeineuropäisches Verfassungsrecht*, this move in the layers of comparison appears to be rather cosmetic; *ius constitutionale commune latinoamericanum* is still predominantly informed by a German ideal of European constitutionalism.

As mentioned above, ICCLA assigns a pivotal role to judicial dialogue. According to this narrative, the emerging law in Latin America is not hierarchical, unfolding from the international (or regional) to the national levels, but rather develops dynamically and horizontally. At the same time, the San José Court, as a regional court concerned with the human rights of all the inhabitants of the region, is seen within this narrative as providing the general framework. No less important, its jurisprudence is regarded as a conceptual apparatus, an axiomatic one, because of the progressive imprint it has acquired over the years—"progressive" in the sense of providing an expansively evolving interpretation of the protection of human dignity. This assumption is based on a normative postulate of how law in Latin American should evolve constructively and interactionally, based on a Habermasian ideal of reciprocal communicative processes.[37] Having no room for legal formalism, it instead recalls the neo-natural thinking of A.A. Cançado Trindade and Häberle. Anti-formalism is not only the *Leitmotif* of the new law in Latin America[38] but also of great operational value. It facilitates the flexible use by national courts of comparisons and legal transplants. These courts are called upon to embrace a cosmopolitan constitutionalism, according to which the ideal constitution is one open to a conception of global public law that blurs the boundaries between international (human rights) law and national (constitutional) law. It represents the simultaneous internationalization of constitutional law and the constitutionalization of international law.[39]

However, as I argue in the following section, a closer look at these judicial interactions reveals not so much a pluralistic dialogue but more of a monologue driven by an international tribunal. Instead of a reciprocal communicative process through which similarities across nations are identified via the comparative method, one can observe a unidirectional and hegemonic discourse at the service of the San José Court. Somewhat ironically, this unfolds in a rather monist fashion. The structure of this discourse has important consequences for the law and politics of ICCLA, as well as for comparative international law.

Is ICCLA capable of transcending its academic ethos and the elite network of legal professionals involved in it? Are Latin American judiciaries embracing global public law and thereby doing away with old categories defining the relationship between national and international law? Or is a new sort of monism emerging in the region? What does this mean for the relation between comparative international law and comparative constitutional law? Are ICCLA, and global public law more

---

37. *See* Jürgen Habermas, Theorie des Kommunikativen Handelns, vols. 1–2 (2011). On its influence for ICCLA, *see* Von Bogdandy, *supra* note 9, at 13.

38. On formalism as the foil of the interpretive turn in the region, see Jorge Esquirol, *The Turn to Legal Interpretation in Latin America*, 26 Am. U. Int'l L. Rev. 1031 (2011); *see also* Rodiles, *supra* note 17, at 170–71.

39. *See infra* note 45.

broadly, also blurring the lines between both research fields? I believe these questions are interrelated and address them in my concluding remarks.

III. ICCLA IN LEGAL PRACTICE: THE REGIONAL
JUDICIAL DIALOGUE

The transitions from authoritarian regimes (whether formal dictatorships or not)
to democracies across Latin America made the independence of the judiciaries
in many of these countries possible, and transformed most of the constitutional
and highest courts in the region into key players within their sociopolitical environments. A critical aspect of this renewed judicial role is the openness of these
domestic courts toward international law, and Inter-American human rights law in
particular. Some of these courts have conceived of the ACHR and other treaties in
this regime as part of their domestic constitutional law. This conception extends
to the jurisprudence of the IACHR. These developments form the framework for
the intra-regional judicial dialogue that is said to prove the emergence of ICCLA
beyond legal doctrine. In the words of Armin von Bogdandy: "[t]he existence of a
Ius Constitutionale Commune becomes most palpable in the interaction of domestic
authorities with the Inter-American Court."[40]

A. Vertical Dialogue: The San José Court
as a Supranational Constitutional Court

Transnational judicial communication in the region is strongly inspired and promoted by the IACHR, and its expansive, at times even intrusive jurisprudence.[41]
Commentators, as well as Inter-American judges, describe this tribunal as a supranational constitutional court of the region.[42] This suggests a vertical dialogue, that
is, from international courts to national ones.

The point of departure for this dialogue is the *Barrios Altos* decision of 2001.
The IACHR declared that the Peruvian amnesty laws adopted during the Fujimori

---

40. Von Bogdandy, *supra* note 8, at 109.

41. *See* Rodiles, *supra* note 17, at 161–63.

42. *See, e.g.,* L. Burgorgue-Larsen, *La Corte Interamericana de Derechos Humanos como Tribunal
Constitucional, in* Ius CONSTITUTIONALE COMMUNE EN AMÉRICA LATINA 421, *supra* note 31; for
a critical account, *see* Ariel E. Dulitzky, *An Inter-American Constitutional Court? The Invention of the
Conventionality Control by the Inter-American Court of Human Rights*, 50 TEX. INT'L L.J. 45 (2015);
see also René Urueña, *Global Governance Through Comparative International Law? Inter-American
Constitutionalism and the Changing Role of Domestic Courts in the Construction of the International
Law,* Jean Monnet Working Paper Series 21/13 (2013). Former judge of the IACHR, Sergio García
Ramírez, has compared on several occasions the function of the San José Court with the mission of
national constitutional courts; *see* Tibi v. Ecuador, Preliminary Objections, Merits, Reparations and
Costs, Judgment, Inter-Am. Ct. H.R. (ser. C) No. 114, ¶ 3 (Sept. 7, 2004) (J García Ramírez conc.);
Dismissed Congressional Employees v. Peru, Preliminary Objections, Merits, Reparations and
Costs, Judgment, Inter-Am. Ct. H.R. (ser. C) No. 158, ¶¶ 4-5 (Nov. 26, 2006) (J García Ramírez
conc.).

era had no legal effect.[43] Later it explained the "generic effects" of this declaration of invalidity, that is, beyond that particular case.[44] The court then asserted the doctrine of "conventionality control," both in its "centralized" and "diffused" versions.[45] Following *Barrios Altos*, "centralized conventionality control" means that the regional court exercises judicial review of domestic norms not only by verifying the compatibility of those norms with the ACHR and other treaties of the system, but by invalidating them whenever deemed contrary to these international agreements.[46] "Diffused conventionality control" is the duty that the regional court seeks to impose on national courts not to apply domestic laws contrary to the various applicable treaties. To perform this task, national judges are required not only to take into account the treaty texts but also the jurisprudence of the San José Court as "the ultimate interpreter of the American Convention."[47]

National courts in Latin America have been very receptive to this mandate.[48] A decision of Mexico's Supreme Court from 2013 illustrates this. It declared that all domestic judges are bound by the jurisprudence of the IACHR in cases involving Inter-American human rights (actually the whole corpus of international human rights, as those not formally part of the regional system are usually interpreted according to the latter),[49] including cases to which Mexico was not a

---

43. Barrios Altos v. Peru, Merits, Judgment, Inter-Am. Ct. H.R. (ser. C) No. 75, ¶ 44 (14 Mar. 2001).

44. Barrios Altos v. Peru, Interpretation of the Judgment of the Merits, Judgment, Inter-Am. Ct. H.R. (ser. C) No. 83, ¶ 2 (Sept. 3, 2001).

45. *See* Eduardo Ferrer Mac-Gregor, *El Control Difuso de Convencionalidad en el Estado Constitucional, in* FORMACIÓN Y PERSPECTIVAS DEL ESTADO EN MÉXICO 151, 172–84 (Héctor Fix Zamudio & Diego Valadés eds., 2010). For this author and current San José judge, the doctrine of conventionality control, as well as several interpretive methods employed by the IACHR and national courts in relation to Inter-American human rights law, are clear manifestations of "the constitutionalization of international law," and ultimately of "the construction of an Inter-American public law." Elsewhere, Ferrer has characterized the doctrine of conventionality control as the "internationalization of constitutional law." *See* Eduardo Ferrer Mac-Gregor, *Reflexiones sobre el Control Difuso de Convencionalidad. A la Luz del Caso Cabrera García y Montiel Flores v México*, XLIV BOLETÍN MEXICANO DE DERECHO COMPARADO 917, 928 (2011).

46. For a critical assessment of conventionality control as a sort of judicial review, see Christina Binder, *The Prohibition of Amnesties by the Inter-American Court of Human Rights*, 12 GERMAN L.J. 1203, 1215–17 (2011).

47. Almonacid-Arellano v. Chile, Preliminary Objections, Merits, Reparations and Costs, Judgment, Inter-Am. Ct. H.R. (ser. C) No. 154, ¶ 124 (Sept. 26, 2006).

48. This is most visible in Argentina, Colombia, Costa Rica, Ecuador, Guatemala, Mexico, and Peru. *See* HUMBERTO NOGUEIRA ALCALÁ, DERECHOS FUNDAMENTALES, BLOQUE CONSTITUCIONAL DE DERECHOS. DIÁLOGO INTERJURISDICCIONAL Y CONTROL DE CONVENCIONALIDAD 642–53 (2014).

49. Other Treaties Subject to the Consultative Jurisdiction of the Court, Advisory Opinion OC-1/82, Inter-Am. Ct. H.R. (ser. A) No. 1, ¶ 39 (Sept. 24, 1982); *see also* Rodiles, *supra* note 17, at 159–60.

party.[50] Eduardo Ferrer Mac-Gregor, who has become one of the most prominent supporters of ICCLA, both in academia and as a judge of the IACHR, emphasizes the role of the doctrine of conventionality control in the construction of *ius commune*:

> We are definitely transiting to an "integrated Inter-American System"—with a dynamic and complementary "conventionality control"—which is progressively constructing an authentic *Ius Constitutionale Commune Americanum* as a substantive and indissoluble core, which preserves and guarantees the human dignity of the inhabitants of the region.[51]

Accordingly, ICCLA can be described as a highly centralized, unidirectional judicial construction in which the IACHR functions as a sort of supranational guardian of the regional constitution of rights. In this sense, René Urueña has observed that "Inter-American constitutionalism is less an exercise of 'comparative international law', than an integrated hierarchical system of norms that are enforced by both international and domestic tribunals."[52]

However, one could describe this relationship as an instance of comparative international law occurring through vertical dialogue, by means of which the IACHR develops a common regional approach to international law. But one should consider whether there are other, emerging, less obvious features of this communication process that could support the pluralistic dialogue described by the ICCLA literature.

Even if regarded as a top-down dialogue—what has been criticized as being rather a monologue[53]—the double role of national courts means that these are not exclusively applying Inter-American law as understood by the IACHR, but also contributing to regional practice.[54] Their decisions eventually may reach an agreement on the interpretation of some particular international norm and thus qualify as subsequent practice within the meaning of Article 31(3)(b) of the 1969 Vienna Convention on the Law of Treaties.[55] But the Inter-American human rights

---

50. Contradicción de Tesis 293/2011. Derechos Humanos contenidos en la Constitución y en los Tratados Internacionales. Constituyen el parámetro de control de regularidad constitucional. Pero cuando en la Constitución haya una restricción expresa al ejercicio de aquéllos, se debe estar a lo que establece el texto constitucional. Y, Jurisprudencia emitida por la Corte Interamericana de Derechos Humanos. Es vinculante para los jueces mexicanos siempre que sea más favorable a la persona, Pleno de la Suprema Corte de Justicia de la Nación [SCJN], Semanario Judicial de la Federación y su Gaceta, Décima Época, tomo I, Abril de 2014, Páginas 143–45.

51. Gelman v. Uruguay, Monitoring Compliance with Judgment, Order of the Court, Inter-Am. Ct. H.R., Separate Concurring Opinion of Judge Ferrer McGregor, ¶ 100 (Mar. 20, 2013).

52. Urueña, *supra* note 42, at 17.

53. *See* Dulitzky, *supra* note 42, at 76.

54. *See* Anthea Roberts, *Comparative International Law? The Role of National Courts in Creating and Enforcing International Law*, 60 INT'L & COMP. L.Q. 57, 61–64 (2011).

55. *See* Special Rapporteur on the Subsequent Agreements and Subsequent Practice in Relation to the Interpretation of Treaties, *Fourth Rep. on the Subsequent Agreements and Subsequent Practice*

discourse mostly has neglected state consent, because it is associated with "state voluntarism" and perceived as contrary to the dynamic nature of human rights treaties, as well as to the structural transformations of public law in the era of globalization.

However, it is important to distinguish between a narrow unidirectional discourse, on the one hand, and the possibilities for judicial dialogue resting on the law of treaties and explained by comparative international law (e.g., the explanation of the dual function of national courts), on the other. Commentators on the Inter-American system who tend to analyze this regime from a generalist perspective, that is, one informed by general international law that takes the law of treaties better into account, insist on the importance of building regional consent, and highlight the role of national courts as state actors in this regard.[56] Yet subsequent state practice plays little or no role in the jurisprudence of the IACHR or in decisions of Latin American national courts interpreting human rights treaties. Domestic courts in the region do not seem to be very aware of their potential to create state practice within the terms of general international law.

B. An Emerging Mixed Dialogue?

One must note recent developments in judicial communication in Latin America that call for reconsidering the vertical and unidirectional character of this dialogue. In this section, I argue that these developments remain informed by the very same premises of the top-down dialogue, and hence can be seen as a strategy for advancing the overarching narrative of ICCLA centered on and spurred by the San José Court.

It is true that the conventionality control promoted by the IACHR, in its "diffused" version, has prompted a more active engagement of national judges in revising domestic norms' conformity with Inter-American law. Not surprisingly, this has led to more national interpretations of the American Convention, which now form part of the intra-regional dialogue. As one commentator mentions, the Court in San José "already uses comparative Latin American law as an interpretative tool of the Convention."[57] In addition, the strong stance of some national courts as champions of human dignity that adjusts to the reality of underdevelopment,[58] in particular the

---

in Relation to the Interpretation of Treaties, Int'l Law Comm'n, U.N. Doc. A/CN.4/694 (Mar. 7, 2016), 36–44 (by Georg Nolte); *see also* Anthea Roberts, *Subsequent Agreements and Practice: The Battle over Interpretive Power, in* Treaties and Subsequent Practice 95, 101 (Georg Nolte, ed., 2013); Christian Djefall, *Dynamic and Evolutive Interpretation of the ECHR by Domestic Courts? An Inquiry into the Judicial Architecture of Europe, in* The Interpretation of International Law by Domestic Courts, *supra* note 17, at 175, 195.

56. *See* Gerald L. Neuman, *Import, Export, and Regional Consent in the Inter-American Court of Human Rights,* 19 Eur. J. Int'l. L. 101 (2008); *see also* Rodiles, *supra* note 17, at 162–63.

57. *See* Dulitzky, *supra* note 42, at 74 (with various references to cases where the IACHR has used national court decisions in order to construe their own interpretations of the ACHR).

58. Corte Constitucional [C.C.] [Constitutional Court], Sala Primera de Revisión, junio 5, 1992, Ciro Angarita Barón, Sentencia T-406/92, Gaceta de la Corte Constitucional [G.C.C.] (vol. único, p. 190) (Colom.).

Colombian Constitutional Court, further suggests that Inter-American judicial dialogue is not a one-way street anymore. Accordingly, an important building block of
ius commune might consist of a "mixed dialogue," following Anne-Marie Slaughter's
early typology of transjudicial communication.[59] This dialogue would consist of references from national-to-regional-to-national jurisdictions.

The same author who highlights the use of "comparative Latin American law"
by the IACHR, however, correctly points out that the San José Court usually cites
only those judgments of Latin American national courts that fit all too well into its
own position and that it reveals no methodology to explain these cross-references.
The practice clearly suggests cherry-picking according to its own interpretive preferences.[60] Furthermore, a genuine pluralistic conversation in which national and
regional judges came together in a network of communication on an equal footing,
so to speak, would only prove to be the case if national-to-national judicial dialogue
also occurred whenever the advancement of human dignity is at stake and involved
the interpretation of international human rights law and related rights. Particularly
interesting would be a scenario where a common understanding of Inter-American
human rights law, or even of universal human rights law, would develop through
cross-references among national courts of the region without evoking the San
José jurisprudence. Of course, whenever national courts construe a norm of the
American Convention following the case law of the IACHR that itself resorted to
national judgments, an indirect national-to-national dialogue would take place, and
arguably a mixed one would come to the forefront. But this would still be too much
centered, in substance, on the jurisprudence of the IACHR. Instances of interpretation of international human rights law by national courts of the region referring
to readings of their peers of exactly the same normative hypothesis are practically
nonexistent.[61]

There are other means through which national courts in the region communicate. Although these represent indirect venues of judicial communication, they can
prove to be very effective in the promotion of a mixed dialogue. First, there is what
can be called "informal dialogue," that is, the sharing of information and best judicial practices, as well as the cross-fertilization of judicial and legal cultures through
a series of workshops and conferences, publications, and online promotion. The
goal of this informal dialogue is to promote a common understanding and interpretive approach to international (human rights) law. These symposia usually involve
the judges and their staff from some of the constitutional and highest courts of the

---

59. *See* Anne-Marie Slaughter, *A Typology of Transjudicial Communication*, 29 U. RICH. L. REV. 99,
111–12 (1994).

60. *See* Dulitzky, *supra* note 42, at 74–77.

61. Latin American constitutional and highest courts do of course refer to decisions by their peers in
other countries but basically on their understandings of similar constitutional principles and provisions. Thus, it is comparative constitutional law, in a strict sense, rather than comparative international law, which is usually employed by Latin American national courts. This usage of comparative
constitutional law goes well beyond the region (most popular remain the US Supreme Court and
the German Federal Constitutional Court).

region, as well as prominent legal scholars, and have become common practice in recent years. The Ibero-American Institute of Constitutional Law plays a leading role in the promotion of this informal dialogue, and its importance for ICCLA is widely acknowledged.[62]

Second and partly as a result of the activities described above, horizontal judicial communication in Latin America has turned to method. Indeed, what most of the national courts in the region share when it comes to interpreting international human rights law are the means of doing it. They may not quote from each other on the specific reading of this or that norm of the American Convention, but they mimic the interpretive cannons and techniques they use.

These are conventionality control, the *pro homine* or *pro persona* principle of interpretation, and the judicial doctrine of *bloque de constitucionalidad* ("constitutional bloc" or *"bloc de constitutionnalité,"* as it has its origin in the French *Conseil Constitutionnel*). Conventionality control and the *pro homine* maxim have both emerged from the Inter-American jurisprudence. As discussed above, conventionality control presupposes in its diffused version that national judges supervise the conformity of national law with the ACHR and other treaties of the system. In certain instances, the regional Court has even demanded that in case of contradiction, the national law should be declared void.[63] The *pro homine* or *pro persona* principle basically states that the most favorable interpretation to the "human person" is to be preferred, enabling the judge to construe the widest expression of the (human) right at hand. It has been used by the IACHR since its earliest decisions and constantly over the years. It is based on Article 29 of the ACHR, that is, the prohibition of restrictive interpretation. The philosophy underpinning this method is informed by a strong distrust of "state voluntarism," thus shifting the paradigm to human dignity, and favoring dynamic and expansive interpretations of international human rights law. This philosophy of legal interpretation has been most clearly articulated by Cançado Trindade, both in his academic writings and in his vast body of individual opinions as former judge and president of the Inter-American tribunal.[64] The doctrine of *bloque de constitucionalidad*, on its part, is the only one of

---

62. For more information on this transnational platform, see Instituto Iberoamericano de Derecho Constitucional, http://www.juridicas.unam.mx/iidc/; on its role for ICCLA, see von Bogdandy, *supra* note 9, at 4.

63. *See supra* note 45 and accompanying text. For the different degrees of diffused conventionality control, see Pablo Contreras, *Control de Convencionalidad, Deferencia Internacional y Discreción Nacional en la Jurisprudencia de la Corte Interamericana de Derechos Humanos*, 20 Ius et Praxis 235 (2014).

64. On the *pro persona* principle, *see, e.g.*, Mónica Pinto, *El Principio Pro Homine: Criterios de Hermenéutica y Pautas para la Regulación de los Derechos Humanos*, *in* La Aplicación de Los Tratados Internacionales sobre Derechos Humanos por los Tribunales Locales 163 (Martín Abregú & Cristian Courtis, eds., 1997); Karlos Castilla, *El Principio* Pro Persona *en la Administración de Justicia*, 20 Cuestiones Constitucionales 65 (2009); for a critical assessment of this interpretive method, see Helmut Philipp Aust, Alejandro Rodiles & Peter Staubach, *Unity or Uniformity? Domestic Courts and Treaty Interpretation*, 27 Leiden J. Int'l L. 75, 96–100 (2014); *see also* Rodiles, *supra* note 17.

these methods developed by a national court, namely the Constitutional Court in Bogotá.[65] According to it, human rights and related principles that are not expressly established in the national constitution are to be integrated into it, whenever they are relevant for concrete instances of constitutional control or judicial review.[66]

These methods are shared by many Latin American national courts, which have been very much engaged in their promotion, including through the sort of informal dialogue described above. It is also important to mention that there exists a trend of merging all these principles and doctrines into a new rights paradigm of constitutional justice.[67] This has been the case of Colombia's Constitutional Court. Its guiding principle in the building of "constitutional blocs" has been the so-called "favorability clause," which is just a different name for the *pro persona* principle, again conceived as a proper means of exercising conventionality control.[68] Very similarly, Mexico's Supreme Court has declared that conventionality control can be properly exercised by national judges only if they simultaneously engage in control of constitutionality, guided by *pro persona*, and that the means of analysis for such a control consists of the following constitutional bloc: fundamental rights of the Mexican Constitution and the relevant jurisprudence of federal tribunals, the human rights contained in treaties to which Mexico is a party, and the jurisprudence

65. *See* Corte Constitucional [C.C.] [Constitutional Court], mayo 18, 1995, Alejandro Martínez Caballero, Sentencia C-225/95, Gaceta de la Corte Constitucional [G.C.C.] (vol. 1, p. 370) (Colom.); for an overview of the vast case law of the CCC where the constitutional bloc has been decisive, see Mónica Arango Olaya, *El Bloque de Constitucionalidad en la Jurisprudencia de la Corte Constitucional Colombiana*, Precedente 79 (2004).

66. *Pro persona* and *bloque de constitucionalidad* have also favored the increasing use of informal international law by Latin American domestic courts, *see* Rodiles, *supra* note 17, at 166 (with further references). It would be an interesting case study to analyze to what extent and why informal law is playing a greater role than customary international law in Latin America, that is, whereas national courts in the region still feel very uneasy with the use of unwritten international law (*cf.* Peter Staubach, The Rule of Unwritten International Law: Customary Law, General Principles, and World Order (forthcoming 2018)), they seem to have no problem with the application of non-binding resolutions of international bodies, best practices, standards, and the like, and independently if these stem from formal international organizations, expert bodies, global NGOs, or informal networks.

67. *See, e.g.*, César Landa, *La Fuerza Normativa Constitucional de los Derechos Fundamentales*, in Justicia Constitucional y Derechos Fundamentales: Fuerza Normativa de la Constitución 17, 26 (Víctor Bazán & Claudio Nash eds., 2012).

68. *See, e.g.*, Corte Constitucional [C.C.] [Constitutional Court], diciembre 7, 2001, Dr. Rodrigo Uprimny Yepes, Sentencia T-1319/01, Relatoría de la Corte Constitucional; Corte Constitucional [C.C.] [Constitutional Court], enero 27, 2004, Dr. Eduardo Montealegre Lynett, Sentencia C-038/04, Relatoría de la Corte Constitucional; Corte Constitucional [C.C.] [Constitutional Court], abril 14, 2005, Manuel José Cepeda Espinosa, Sentencia C-401/05, Relatoría de la Corte Constitucional; Corte Constitucional [C.C.] [Constitutional Court], julio 22, 2009, Jorge Iván Palacio Palacio, Sentencia C-488/09, Relatoría de la Corte Constitucional; Corte Constitucional [C.C.] [Constitutional Court], marzo 3, 2011, Jorge Iván Palacio Palacio, Sentencia T-129/11, Relatoría de la Corte Constitucional.

of the San José Court, including those guiding principles established in cases to which Mexico was not a party to the dispute.[69]

Once these broader dimensions of judicial dialogue are taken into account, it is not difficult to see that a common (or at least widely shared) method of interpretation is emerging from horizontal communication processes among national courts in the region. This indeed is the most distinctive sign of Latin American trans-judicial processes: a mixed dialogue consisting of the combination of a (classical) vertical communication between an international tribunal and domestic courts and a horizontal dialogue among the latter, which emerges indirectly but solidly through informal platforms and the mimesis of method. Mimesis of method has even greater potential for construing common interpretations of international legal norms, as it does not depend on a case-by-case citation of foreign court decisions. It can be built systemically through a shared understanding of how international law should be approached.

Some commentators regard these developments as indicating the need for more diversity within the Inter-American human rights regime, and call for a new integrationist paradigm in which both the San José and national courts should engage in a true dialogue, rather than a monologue.[70] For others, the new panorama already reflects this diversity, which must be acknowledged as a "dynamic evolution game" of a broader Inter-American community of participants, leaving constitutionalists and hierarchical mindsets behind.[71]

These proposals and readings have some force. However, I am less optimistic for the following reasons. First, the dialogue may be explained as a mixed one from an institutional perspective, but it is still heavily centered on San José jurisprudence when it comes to substance. Conventionality control is precisely about regional homogeneity—if not uniformity—in the interpretation and progressivity of fundamental rights as understood by the IACHR. Just as with conventionality control, *pro persona* has a clear Inter-American identity. Although it is possible to find the most favorable interpretation of a right in the national constitution and its autochthonous elucidation, *pro persona* is attached to the idea of a universal and holistic human rights law best represented by an international tribunal, but one that understands the idiosyncrasies of the region.[72] The IACHR has successfully built over the years a reputation as the ultimate guarantor of the human rights of the inhabitants of the region, and its international character endows it with a high degree of legitimacy precisely because it is perceived as detached from national political

---

69. *See* Expediente Varios 912/2010, Pleno de la Suprema Corte de Justicia de la Nación [SCJN], Semanario Judicial de la Federación y su Gaceta, Novena Época, tomo I, octubre de 2011, Núm. de Registro 23183, Páginas 313, Párr.: 24–31.

70. *See* Dulitzky, *supra* note 42, at 7991 (for this "integrated Inter-American model" recourse to techniques known from the European human rights system, as well as European Union and Andean Community law, such as margin of appreciation and preliminary rulings, are seen as new building blocks).

71. *See* Urueña, *supra* note 42, at 29.

72. In this sense already, *see* Sepúlveda, *supra* note 5 and accompanying text.

vices—something that matters even more in a region where the traditional national political actors, that is, the executives and legislatives (including political parties), are so profoundly discredited. Accordingly, *pro persona* is clearly inclined in favor of Inter-American law as interpreted and developed by the regional court. As to the *bloque constitucional*, this doctrine does not only entail the other two methods, but it is also a means for opening national constitutions. For the same reasons as with *pro persona*, the *bloque* becomes a perfect entry point for the regional system, thus functioning as a sort of widely open-textured integration clause determined and redetermined each time by national judges guided by Inter-American jurisprudence.

Hence, the uses of these methods of interpretation by Latin American national courts tend to consolidate the role of the IACHR as a sort of supranational constitutional court. And this relates to the second obstacle to an optimistic reading of these trans-judicial developments. It is difficult to conceive this as a "dynamic and evolutive game" of several stakeholders when the conversations are the result of an intermediated process. Anne-Marie Slaughter observes that "intermediate dialogue" takes place when national courts communicate with each other, but another institution "effectively brokers" the communication. Her examples deal with the Strasbourg and Luxembourg courts, which sort of direct the dialogue among the domestic courts of the states parties to the European Convention on Human Rights and Fundamental Freedoms and of the member states of the European Union.[73] This 20-year-old typology of the European judicial landscape fits clearly into the present Latin American scenario, where national courts have become interlocutors in the Inter-American judicial dialogue, but in a way which is still very much orchestrated in San José. Moreover, this dialogue augments the standing of the regional tribunal. It serves to disseminate important ideas and values that have distinguished the IACHR over the years, thus fostering its rationale. In this sense, Slaughter's observation that intermediate dialogue is also about the overarching court "self-consciously undertaking this dissemination"[74] also applies to the Inter-American context, and it is important as it is useful for demystifying the pluralistic narrative that underlines ICCLA.

But what does this mean exactly for the grand project of *ius constitutionale commune* in Latin America? In the end, one might say that the role of a strong regional tribunal in triggering the advancement of the rule of law in the region cannot but be a welcome development, never mind that its own powers are considerably extended along the way. But this argument does not hold water. First, the improvement of the rule of law in the countries of the region as a consequence of a monologue orchestrated by the San José Court is itself contestable. Second, the insistence of the ICCLA discourse on pluralism is crucial for its own legitimacy, as it couples this project with the "structural transformation of public law" at the global level.[75] So, if

---

73. *See* Slaughter, *supra* note 59, at 113–14.

74. *Id.* at 113.

75. The "Structural Transformation of Public Law" being another research project led by von Bogdandy at Heidelberg's Max-Planck Institute, information available at Leibniz-Project: Structural Transformation of Public Law, http://www.mpil.de/en/pub/research/areas/structctural-transformation/leibniz-project.cfm. On the close relationship among this theme, pluralism,

pluralism falls out as a convincing narrative for ICCLA, the normative project loses much of its force and legitimation as the product of comparative public law in the region.

These two problems are part of what I referred to above as the law and politics of ICCLA, as well as the interrelated question of the relationship between this project and international law. This also touches upon the relation between comparative international law and comparative constitutional law. These are complex practical and theoretical problems. Here, I can only provide some remarks, or points of view, by way of conclusion.

IV. CONCLUSION

Armin von Bogdandy's plaidoyer for ICCLA in a recent symposium of *AJIL Unbound* on "the constitutionalization of international law in Latin America" basically describes *ius commune latinoamericanum* as having great promise for "addressing the enormous social challenges faced by the region through a common discourse on human rights, democracy and the rule of law."[76] This vision is shared by most if not all proponents of this project, in academia and on the benches.[77] This is a symptom of a very understandable anxiety about the rule of law in a region that faces grave problems of inequality, impunity, corruption, and a general distrust in institutions. ICCLA and the methodological program that comes with it have contributed to the strengthening of the legal protection of fundamental rights in the countries where the highest tribunals have embraced this discourse, and where the national legal orders have opened themselves to international human rights law, to international scrutiny, and to the idea of placing human dignity at the center of the constitutional order. However, the very same anxiety has led to an overemphasis on the role of judiciaries and law, at the risk of losing sight of other places of political contestation that are needed for the consolidation of democracy and for the construction of the rule of law.[78]

Moreover, it is important to bear in mind that the cosmopolitan language of ICCLA is understood among a rather small regional constitutional elite; it is quite alien to ordinary judges faced with very different and much more acute day-to-day problems. Thus, a word of caution on the transformative power of this "supranationally embedded and regionally rooted constitutionalism"[79] is called for. Note that

and ICCLA, see von Bogdandy, *supra* note 9, at 6–7, 16. Bogdandy's theses on public law at the global level, which comprises constitutional and international law, have been compiled in a monograph published in Mexico; *see* ARMIN VON BOGDANDY, HACIA UN NUEVO DERECHO PÚBLICO. ESTUDIOS EN DERECHO PÚBLICO COMPARADO, SUPRANACIONAL E INTERNACIONAL (2011).

76. Bogdandy, *supra* note 8, at 110.

77. *See, e.g.,* Eduardo Ferrer Mac-Gregor, *Conventionality Control. The New Doctrine of the Inter-American Court of Human Rights*, 109 AM. J. INT'L L. UNBOUND 93, 99 (2015).

78. In a similar vein, see Roberto Gargarella, *Democracy and Rights in* Gelman v. Uruguay, 109 AM. J. INT'L L. UNBOUND 115 (2015).

79. Bogdandy, *supra* note 8, at 109.

there is real risk of detachment between a transnational academic discourse and the local needs and realities of lower-level judges and law-applying officials. Viewed from this perspective, a conceptual framework of global public law that integrates national and international law[80] is not only of doubtful practical utility but also provides an inaccurate description of the law in these locales.

As a matter of trans-judicial communication, ICCLA occurs, if at all, top-down, that is, basically following the lead of a regional tribunal that conceives itself as a sort of supranational constitutional court, leaving little room for genuine dialogue. This hardens the pragmatic obstacles for the construction of the rule of law within the countries of the region. First, the gap between the regional constitution of rights and the locales in which this open constitution is supposed to operate only deepens when national courts do not participate in the design of that constitution, but instead almost exclusively in its promotion.[81] Second, due to the very same unidirectional discourse, ICCLA has turned into a power instrument at the service of one international tribunal. The major peril behind this is that ICCLA becomes increasingly eulogistic, incapable of critical self-reflection.[82] On the one hand, this is detrimental for the dissemination of the cosmopolitan constitutional culture underpinning this project beyond those who directly participate in the discourse. This in turn broadens the gap noted above. On the other hand, in a monologue that converges around the San José jurisprudence the courts participating in the enterprise are not able to produce *ius commune*. For that, regional and national courts would have to construe in tandem and via the comparative method a regional public law that transcends national and international law. The current state of affairs of judicial interplay in Latin America seems to block the emergence of ICCLA's conception of law in times of pluralism, that is, the pluralist account of transnational public law.

Analyzing *ius commune latinoamericanum* through the lenses of comparative international law is a difficult task as the former is based on the premise that international and national law converge. The methodology of this project is the comparison of fundamental principles of public law from national and international origins: comparative constitutional law and comparative international law at the same time. If this great promise of comparative law for Latin America were to be realized, ICCLA would represent an approach and, most important, a conception of international law in the region that actually conceives it as something else: transnational or global, but not international law in the ordinary sense anymore. The operational view indicates the opposite. The judicial interplays that take place in

---

80. *Cf.* Mattias Kumm, *The Cosmopolitan Turn in Constitutionalism: On the Relationship Between Constitutionalism in and Beyond the State, in* RULING THE WORLD? CONSTITUTIONALISM, INTERNATIONAL LAW, AND GLOBAL GOVERNANCE 258, 263–64 (Jeffrey L. Dunoff & Joel P. Trachtman eds., 2009).

81. Dulitzky also draws attention to the fact that "[a] mechanical application of the Court's case law could even affect the very judicial independence of Latin American judges." Ariel E. Dulitzky, *An Alternative Approach to the Conventionality Control Doctrine*, 109 AM. J. INT'L L.UNBOUND 100, 104 (2015).

82. I make this point elsewhere; *see* Rodiles, *supra* note 17, at 172–74.

the framework of ICCLA represent a monist conception of international law under which Inter-American human rights law as understood by the San José Court occupies the top position in the new hierarchy. This conception has two possible, though unintended, consequences: the weakening of international law on the regional level, and fragmentation on the universal plane. As a final point, let me briefly elaborate on these apparently contradictory scenarios.

The current legal developments in the region falling under the ICCLA label are counterproductive for the very goals that it pursues. As Olga Frishman and Eyal Benvenisti argue, whenever domestic courts converge in a "faithful submission" to international courts, the development of international law can be adversely affected.[83] As these authors explain, in the end convergence around an international tribunal diminishes its authority because the best support national courts actually can provide to them "is grounded on defiance."[84] To the extent that judicial communication continues to unfold top-down, the San José jurisprudence (and with it ICCLA) runs many of the risks identified by these authors: from the alienation of state parties to the American Convention to the lack of capacity to respond to political reactions to the issuance of inefficient or even counterproductive responses to the problems it seeks to address. There are many signs that these sorts of backlashes are already taking place in the Inter-American context. This also explains why Frishman' and Benvenisti's case against convergence resonates with the arguments of scholars dedicated to the Inter-American human rights system, such as Ariel Dulitzky. For him, the integrated Inter-American model will succeed only through a "contested partnership" between the IACHR and the national courts of the region, a proper dialogue that involves divergence.[85]

The weakening of international law within Latin America need not hinder the perception on the international plane of a self-opinionated regional international law. Such a perception would be detrimental to the normative ideal of one universal legal system. The relevant question here is to what extent this universal aspiration is desirable for Latin America.

There are many good reasons for viewing the international legal order as one that usually serves the interests of the most powerful. In his important study of international law in Latin America, Arnulf Becker associates Latin American "particularists" with progressive legal thinking, as opposed to the "universalists" whom he sees in the tradition of political conservativism and of a professional appeasement that "at the cost of depoliticization makes the Latin American discipline of international law irrelevant."[86]

---

83. Olga Frishman & Eyal Benvenisti, *National Courts and Interpretive Approaches to International Law, in* THE INTERPRETATION OF INTERNATIONAL LAW BY DOMESTIC COURTS, *supra* note 17, at 317, 324–28.

84. *Id.* at 326.

85. *See* Dulitzky, *supra* note 81, at 105.

86. Arnulf Becker Lorca, *International Law in Latin America or Latin American International Law? Rise, Fall and Retrieval of a Tradition of Legal Thinking and Political Imagination,* 47 HARV. INT'L L.J. 283, 305 (2006).

This may hold true in certain instances, but I caution against overgeneralization. This would ignore (or caricature) a whole tradition in legal thinking in the region that believes in the legitimacy of one universal international law for an almost existential and by no means apolitical reason. This legitimacy is based on the conception of the international legal order as the common construction of the international community (the other way of looking at this conception is as "lawfare").[87] Hence, particular versions of international law are viewed with strong suspicion because they often reflect attempts by the powerful few at diminishing the common construction.[88] The "universal aspiration" is an international rule of law ideal that has been vehemently defended by less powerful states, including Latin American ones and their international lawyers; it is so because it stands for the struggle for equality in international relations.[89]

This aspect of the international-law dimension of ICCLA has been neglected by the literature that promotes it, in spite of ICCLA also being a project on the constitutionalization of international law. In part, this is because most scholars and legal professionals involved in ICCLA are constitutionalists, especially on the Latin American side where internationalists are practically absent from the debate. But I believe that this is also related to the self-defeating nature of grand Latin American law projects that have had the bad habit of taking integral components of their own legal tradition and culture as their ultimate foil.[90] In this case formalism and the associated hierarchical thinking that has the national constitution at the top of the pyramid are the foils. Latin American formalists favor a vision of one universal legal system, usually conceived in a dualistic relationship with the national order. Anti-formalists, on the other hand, tend more easily to embrace innovative legal thinking such as that embodied in ICCLA; for this, they rely on a flexible conceptual framework that in many ways resembles naturalistic or neo-naturalistic thinking.

The problem with this standard narrative is that it does not critically address what I think to be crucial for understanding ICCLA, and to which comparative international law draws our attention: the importance of transnational epistemic communities in construing attitudes toward international law.[91] Neo-constitutional

---

87. Elsewhere, I elaborate on the importance of not losing sight of how much states from the so-called global south cherish the international legal order with all its shortfalls, precisely because they view it as their common asset. In other words, the crucial question, *whose international law are we talking about*, is subject to an ongoing contestation. See ALEJANDRO RODILES, COALITIONS OF THE WILLING AND INTERNATIONAL LAW: THE INTERPLAY BETWEEN FORMALITY AND INFORMALITY (forthcoming 2018).

88. I thank Juan de Dios Gutiérrez Baylón for drawing my attention to this (while he mentioned that comparative international law is infected with the same Eurocentric virus it tries to combat).

89. On the defense of the rule of international law by less powerful states, see SUNDHYA PAHUJA, DECOLONISING INTERNATIONAL LAW: DEVELOPMENT, ECONOMIC GROWTH AND THE POLITICS OF UNIVERSALITY 172–85 (2011).

90. See Esquirol, *supra* note 38.

91. See Roberts et al., *supra* note 11, at 25–27.

anti-formalists in Latin America form part of a transnational professional elite, embedded in trans-regional networks, and with *Gemeineuropäisches Verfassungsrecht* as a common frame of reference (as the *tertium comparationis*): what they embrace as the new law of the region, which is said to emerge through comparative public law, is better described as a regional version of a European ideal of global constitutionalism. This does not emerge spontaneously via the comparative method, but is articulated in legal literature, and echoed by the San José Court in self-interest, as well as by those national courts converging around the former. There may well be a certain tendency in liberal-progressive political thinking among various proponents of ICCLA. The reconceptualization of Latin American law as one that tries to fight more forcefully the endemic problems of the region, above all inequality, can indeed be seen as a progressive hallmark of this project, which I personally applaud. But seen from this angle, ICCLA is primarily a legal discourse of a professional network (law as profession) that, as were previous Latin American dreams of legal integration,[92] is heavily driven by the anxiety to participate in the dominant legal discourses from the global north.

---

92. *See* Obregón, *supra* note 16.

PART SEVEN

Comparative International Law, Investment, and Law of the Sea

24

Who Cares about Regulatory Space in BITs?
A Comparative International Approach

<blockquote>
TOMER BROUDE, YORAM Z. HAFTEL,
& ALEXANDER THOMPSON*
</blockquote>

I. INTRODUCTION: THE IMPACT OF INVESTOR-STATE DISPUTE
SETTLEMENT ON STATE REGULATORY SPACE

The international investment protection regime provides a particularly interesting area for comparative international law research. In this chapter, part of a larger project, we focus on a narrow yet important slice of this field, providing a comparative, empirical analysis of state approaches to investor-state dispute settlement (ISDS) as they have developed over the last few decades since this area of international law emerged. Concerns regarding ISDS have come to a head most recently in the mega-regional settings of the Transatlantic Trade and Investment Partnership (TTIP), the Trans-Pacific Partnership (TPP), and the European Union (EU)-Canada Comprehensive Economic and Trade Agreement (CETA). However, discontent with bilateral investment treaties (BITs) and their ISDS provisions has been on the rise for years, leading to shifts in investment agreement policies and even to attempts by some governments to extricate themselves from the system. Much of this so-called "backlash" has focused on the impact of binding ISDS arbitration

* This research was supported by a Marie Curie FP7 Integration Grant within the 7th European Union Framework Programme. The authors are grateful for comments received at several presentations at the University of Virginia, the Hebrew University of Jerusalem, University of California-Los Angeles, University of Arizona, Freie Universität Berlin, King's College London, and individually from Anne van Aaken, Todd Allee, Jürgen Kurtz, Iñaki Sagarzazu, Rachel Wellhausen, and the editors of this volume. We also thank Elisabeth Tuerk and UNCTAD for kindly sharing and assisting with their Mapping Guide. Or Avrahami, Alex Fischer, Moshe Goldman, Lea Gutowicz, Liza Holodovsky, Maayan Morali, Keren Sasson, and Tomer Treger provided valuable research assistance. Any errors are solely those of the authors.

provisions found in most BITs and other types of investment agreements.[1] Critics complain that arbitrators produce inconsistent and conflicting decisions, or even worse, that they are biased toward the interests of investors and interpret treaty provisions in ways that excessively constrain host governments' regulatory autonomy, or *state regulatory space* (SRS)—a concept we will develop and operationalize later in this chapter. This has provoked concerns of a "legitimacy crisis" in investment arbitration and calls for reform to reestablish more regulatory space, especially in the areas of economic and social policy.[2]

We propose a comparative exploration of the ways in which states have reacted to their experience with the investment regime, and its (real or perceived) impact on SRS, through the lens of BIT *renegotiation*. Many BITs include relatively straightforward termination and renewal provisions and procedures,[3] providing windows of opportunity for renegotiation, which by and large has been preferred to termination. Renegotiation has thus become an important and increasingly popular means by which states can "recalibrate" the obligations, both substantive and procedural, in their investment agreements.

Consequently, renegotiation is an important juncture for evaluating states' positions on BITs in general, and their diverse cost-benefit considerations regarding constraints ISDS may impose on SRS in particular. First, the preference for renegotiation over outright termination positively indicates that the overall function of BITs, writ large, is not considered illegitimate or entirely undesirable, in contrast with particular substantive and procedural legal attributes of BITs (including ISDS), which may be understood as requiring change and reform. Second, the fact that states can and do renegotiate BITs means they have the ability to pragmatically adjust their provisions over time. If either one or both parties to a BIT are dissatisfied with their original or earlier negotiation outcomes and find BIT provisions outmoded, unfair, ineffectual, or overly constraining of SRS, they are not trapped with their consequences indefinitely. This reflects not only on the legitimacy of those BITs that are renegotiated to one degree or another, but also on the majority of BITs that are extended, renewed, or otherwise not terminated, without any amendment. Renegotiation of ISDS provisions or a lack thereof is an important part of this equation. Third, and consequently, looking at the actual practice of renegotiation—which provisions are altered and amended, and how—provides us with insights into which aspects of BITs are deemed undesirable by states, especially if we focus on those provisions that logically impact SRS (in the present chapter,

---

1. THE BACKLASH AGAINST INVESTMENT ARBITRATION: PERCEPTIONS AND REALITY (Michael Waibel et al. eds., 2010); Todd Allee & Clint Peinhardt, *Contingent Credibility: The Impact of Investment Treaty Violations on Foreign Direct Investment*, 65 INT'L ORG. 401 (2011).

2. Susan D. Franck, *The Legitimacy Crisis in Investment Treaty Arbitration: Privatizing Public International Law Through Inconsistent Decisions*, 73 FORDHAM L. REV. 1521 (2005); U.N. CONFERENCE ON TRADE AND DEV., INVESTMENT POLICY FRAMEWORK FOR SUSTAINABLE DEVELOPMENT (2012).

3. Andrea Carska-Sheppard, *Issues Relevant to the Termination of Bilateral Investment Treaties*, 26 J. INT'L ARB. 755 (2009).

in the context of ISDS). In other words, the practice of renegotiation provides an empirical prism for understanding how discontent with BITs translates into concrete decisions by governments to recalibrate their treaty obligations.

In addressing these issues, this chapter proceeds as follows. In Section II we discuss the ways in which this empirical textual examination of bilateral treaty-making dovetails with the overall idea of comparative international law research. In Section III we address some more general methodological issues pertaining to the renegotiation and termination of BITs, on the basis of previous research. In Section IV we operationalize the concept of SRS in more detail and its relationship with important ISDS attributes as a potential driver of renegotiation preferences, in the process justifying our coding scheme. In Section V we present some results of our analysis relating to different approaches to BIT and ISDS renegotiation. We show that, at least until the late 2000s, most renegotiated ISDS provisions reflect less, rather than more, regulatory space. Nonetheless, there is substantial cross-regional variation in the content and evolution of ISDS provisions. Most notably, while Western European BITs (with at least one party located in Western Europe) have shifted to offering investors easier access to ISDS, Western Hemispheric BITs (with at least one party located in the Americas) lead the way in providing states greater control. These observations underscore the need to comparatively explore variation in the approach of different countries and regions to international investment law. Section VI concludes, with forward-looking thoughts on both this dimension of comparative international law and on renegotiations of ISDS.

II. BILATERAL TREATY-MAKING AND COMPARATIVE INTERNATIONAL LAW RESEARCH

With respect to *comparative international law* as a field of study, and to renegotiation of BITs and ISDS in the context of SRS, this chapter is a preliminary effort to offer empirical evidence based on a new and evolving dataset on renegotiated treaties. We devote most of our attention to ISDS provisions because they shape the legal consequences of all substantive obligations and have a clear effect on the balance between investor interests and SRS in those cases where they are at odds. We recognize that there is a complex interaction between changes in procedural ISDS provisions on the one hand, and the renegotiation of substantive investment protection rules on the other hand, especially with respect to SRS. If states are unhappy with BITs and with arbitration under them, we could expect to see this manifested in efforts to renegotiate ISDS provisions, reducing exposure to complaints and adverse rulings restrictive of SRS. However, if changes are made to the potential scope of substantive investment protection rules to impinge on SRS, we recognize that there might be less change in ISDS as a procedure.[4]

---

4. See Jürgen Kurtz, *Australia's Rejection of Investor–State Arbitration: Causation, Omission and Implication*, 27 ICSID REV. 65 (2012), for a discussion of the relationship between procedural (ISDS) and substantive recalibration in a particular context. For an effort to compare ISDS and substantive provisions across investment agreements, see Tomer Broude, Yoram Z. Haftel & Alexander Thompson, *The Trans-Pacific Partnership and Regulatory Space: A Comparison of Treaty Texts*, 20 J. INT'L ECON. L. 391 (2017).

Our preliminary evidence, presented below, indicates that most (but not all) states have not made a systematic effort over the years to recalibrate their BITs for the purpose of preserving more SRS as far as ISDS is concerned. In fact, many updated BITs either leave ISDS provisions unchanged or render them more "investor-friendly," in terms of litigation. Without investigating the parallel changes in the substance of investment protection rules, this may only reflect comparatively robust support for ISDS, not a lack of concern for SRS. Indeed, the title of this chapter should be understood as a double entendre: BITs restrictive of SRS are most certainly a source of worry, and we do not imply otherwise. Rather, we are interested in tracing comparative patterns in treaty-making and in identifying which parties to BITs have been, more or less, concerned with diminished SRS. Hence, we see this endeavor as a particularly fruitful type of comparative international law research.

Conventional *comparative law* studies are concerned with the differences and similarities between the law that is made and applied within different (ultimately national) jurisdictions.[5] In contrast, as any relevant *international law* textbook would inform us, international legal research examines the law that (primarily) states make and apply to govern international relations. Taking these observations together, it should then surely follow that the idea of *"comparative international law,"* as a newly defined, broadly delimited, and conceptually hybridized field of study,[6] must also encompass comparative inquiries into national, regional, and international trends in particular public international lawmaking settings.

In other words, comparative international law should also be concerned with the differences and similarities that can be discerned in the public international law that various states formally consent to. When states engage in multiple international lawmaking endeavors through bilateral agreements, the variations in treaty norms that emerge should reflect their individual lawmaking preferences more distinctly than the rules of multilateral treaties in which such preferences are watered-down to the most-common denominator by the debilitating power of consensus,[7] even if subjected to dyadic variation among treaty partners.[8] When these numerous treaty obligations are undertaken within the same issue-area of law (such as the prevention of double taxation, trade liberalization, extradition, technical cooperation, etc., and as discussed in this chapter, investment arbitration), a higher degree of nuance and resolution can be pursued in comparing the very specific types of commitments that different states or categories of states may agree to.

---

5. Modern comparative law is commonly considered to date from the promulgation of European codes, but can be traced to earlier eras. *See, e.g.,* Charles Donahue, *Comparative Law Before the Code Napoléon, in* OXFORD HANDBOOK OF COMPARATIVE LAW (Mathias Reimann & Reinhard Zimmermann eds., 2006); in any case it is by and large concerned with the comparison of territorially delimited jurisdictional systems.

6. Anthea Roberts, Paul B. Stephan, Pierre-Hugues Verdier & Mila Versteeg, *Conceptualizing Comparative International Law* (this volume).

7. Andrew T. Guzman, *Against Consent,* 52 VA. J. INT'L L. 747 (2011).

8. National "Model BITs" may provide an even better reflection of states' preferences. We intend to analyze such models in the near future.

Comparatively researching the type(s) of public international law commitments that states make, prospectively and over time, is quite different from asking how states apply and interpret the law that already binds them, detecting differences and similarities in their approaches to formally identical obligations, such as multilateral treaties or customary international law. It is also different from comparative scrutiny of the doctrinal and procedural ways in which states approve their international obligations and subsequently incorporate them into domestic law, as systemically crucial issues,[9] or ratify international agreements.[10] Examining formal treaty commitments as they are made and adjusted through negotiation and renegotiation can provide a rich—non-normative—basis for comparative analyses of state preferences regarding various rule formulations, at a high degree of resolution.[11]

What we propose in this chapter is therefore another, potentially fruitful strand of comparative international law: a comparative analysis of the types of international law commitments that states choose to make in a multiplicity of bilateral settings within the same issue area (investment protection in general, and especially ISDS). In a field of international law that is characterized by a very large number of functionally equivalent[12] bilateral agreements—indeed a veritable normative web complex, to be distinguished from multilateral lawmaking settings that are also worthy of inquiry—a broad-based empirical analysis of existing commitments and their renegotiations should prove capable of drawing lines between different groups of treaty parties and explaining the variance between substantive treaty commitments. In this context, we turn now to briefly discuss comparative dimensions of BIT renegotiation.

III. THE COMPARATIVE LANDSCAPE OF RENEGOTIATED BITS

An empirically-informed comparative grasp of the changing realities of investment treaties requires, first, a list of all renegotiated BITs and the years in which they were signed, entered into force, and re-signed (following renegotiation). We have assembled such a comprehensive list and use it as a basis for the analysis presented below. Given the originality of this data, we begin by elaborating on the definition of renegotiation we employ and on the process by which we produced this list. We also present some basic trends with respect to BIT renegotiation.

---

9. Pierre-Hugues Verdier & Mila Versteeg, *International Law in National Legal Systems: An Empirical Investigation*, 109 Am. J. Int'l L. 514 (2015) (also in this volume).

10. Yoram Z. Haftel & Alexander Thompson, *Delayed Ratification: The Domestic Fate of Bilateral Investment Treaties*, 67 Int'l Org. 355 (2013).

11. See The Rational Design of International Institutions (Barbara Koremenos et al. eds., 2004); Kal Raustiala, *Form and Substance in International Agreements*, 99 Am. J. Int'l L. 581 (2005), for a positive analysis of treaty design more generally.

12. Such situations are, from a legal perspective, "multi-sourced equivalent norms" or MSENs. *See e.g.*, Multi-Sourced Equivalent Norms in International Law (Tomer Broude & Yuval Shany eds., 2011).

We define a renegotiated BIT as *a signed treaty that replaces an existing mutually ratified BIT or a signed (and where relevant, ratified) amendment to an existing mutually ratified BIT*. This definition excludes investment treaties that were signed and subsequently renegotiated before entry into force. In such instances the original treaty text was not legally binding, so a new treaty text is rather more the outcome of a continuation or culmination of earlier negotiations (although in this respect it may reflect changes in attitude by a party or parties).

Among BITs in force, their renegotiation can take three forms, generally speaking. First, governments may keep the old treaty in place, but amend it with a new protocol. In such cases, the changes to the treaty commonly address a small number of specific issues (which may nevertheless be quite important to the parties—and may also be important if they address ISDS, or have an impact on SRS). Second, the parties to an existing BIT may sign an entirely new investment treaty, adding a clause that terminates the prior BIT—BIT replacement. Third, the parties may substitute a BIT with a "free trade agreement" (FTA) that includes an investment protection chapter. Here we include only FTAs that explicitly terminate and replace the BIT, such as the US-Morocco and the Taiwan-Nicaragua trade agreements.[13]

We note that there exist other mechanisms whereby parties may seek to clarify the scope and nature of their BIT obligations on a mutually agreed basis, such as "joint binding interpretations." However, we have not included them as renegotiations for our purposes, if only because they stand on the "gap-filling" borderline of legal indeterminacy, between interpretation and amendment.[14] In other words, such binding interpretations—which are rare in any case—do not presume to amend or alter the preexisting formal commitment, but rather to exclude some of its possible interpretations. As will be noted in Section IV, we do see the inclusion of such interpretative clauses as affecting SRS.

With these criteria, we identified renegotiated treaties in a two-step process. We began with an examination of the United Nations Conference on Trade and Development (UNCTAD) database of all existing BITs, which is updated regularly. Comparing newer records to older ones and to an earlier UNCTAD publication[15]

---

13. We thus exclude instances in which the parties sign an FTA with an investment chapter but do not terminate an existing BIT, such as the China-Peru BIT and FTA. There exist important legal problems in such situations, when old investment protection and ISDS obligations coexist with new ones. See Wolfgang Alschner, *Regionalism and Overlap in Investment Treaty Law: Towards Consolidation or Contradiction?*, 17 J. INT'L ECON. L. 271 (2014), for a discussion of some of these problems when associated with regional agreements.

14. *See* Margie-Lys Jaime, *Relying on Parties' Interpretation in Treaty-Based Investor-State Dispute Settlement: Filling the Gaps in International Investment Agreements*, 46 GEO. J. INT'L L. 261 (2014); Eleni Methymaki & Antonios Tzanakopoulos, *Masters of Puppets? Reassertion of Control Through Joint Investment Treaty Interpretation*, *in* REASSERTION OF CONTROL OVER THE INVESTMENT TREATY REGIME 155 (Andreas Kulick ed., 2017).

15. U.N. CONFERENCE ON TRADE AND DEV., BILATERAL INVESTMENT TREATIES 1959–1999 (2000). It should be noted that UNCTAD's data offerings have been updated and expanded significantly since our original data collection.

allowed us to identify those treaties that have different dates, and are therefore likely to have been renegotiated. This approach offers a plausible "first cut" but is not fully adequate for two reasons. First, it is possible that the dates diverge for reasons unrelated to renegotiation, such as inaccurate reporting or recording of information. Second, the records may be incomplete if states fail to report the signing of a renegotiated treaty or if the BIT was replaced by an FTA that is not recorded in the UNCTAD lists.

To minimize possible errors and to have a more complete dataset, we complemented the initial list with the examination of additional sources. We first searched for the treaties themselves and inspected their texts. Instances in which the old as well as the new BIT (or the amending protocol), or the new treaty with an explicit reference to the old treaty, were available provided a confirmation of the initial record. We then turned to an extensive search of national governmental websites that provide information on BITs and FTAs. Through this survey, we were able to further verify or correct our list as well as to identify renegotiated treaties missing from the UNCTAD records.[16] With this method, we identified 196 *renegotiated* BITs as defined above. With respect to the different forms of renegotiated BITs, about two-thirds are new investment treaties, about one-quarter are amended BITs, and fewer than 7 percent are FTAs with investment chapters. On the whole, we believe that the dataset provides an inclusive and accurate description of currently renegotiated BITs.

A glance over the data provides a number of insights into the phenomenon of BIT renegotiation. First, this is a rather new trend but is becoming more significant over time. The first renegotiation we were able to identify took place in the middle 1980s and led to the amendment of the France-Egypt BIT in 1986. BIT renegotiation became more widespread in the middle 1990s with the renegotiation of five treaties in 1994 and four treaties in 1995. As Figure 24.1 shows, the number of renegotiated treaties then increased steadily, reaching 20 in both 2009 and 2010.

Eighty-six states from all continents were involved in BIT renegotiation. Some states, such as Guinea, Mexico, and the Philippines, have renegotiated only one treaty. Others have renegotiated BITs recurrently, to the point that only 15 states account for half of these outcomes. Figure 24.2 reports the number of treaties renegotiated by the governments of each of these 15 states. The two leaders in such renegotiation patterns are the Czech Republic and Romania, with 23 and 38 renegotiated treaties, respectively. They are followed by Germany and China, each of which renegotiated at least 15 BITs. Interestingly, the top renegotiators come from a number of geographical regions, including Europe, the Middle East, and East Asia.[17]

---

16. We thank Raymond Hicks for sharing information on FTAs with an investment chapter.

17. No country from Latin America or sub-Saharan Africa renegotiated more than three BITs.

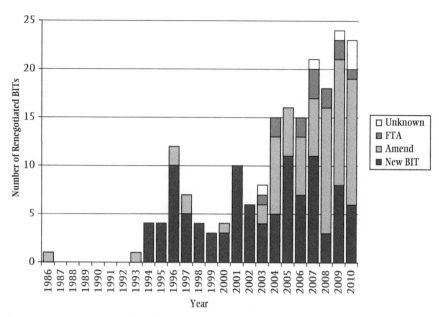

Figure 24.1 Annual number of renegotiated BITs, 1986–2010.

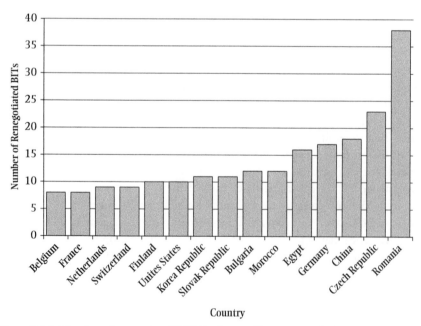

Figure 24.2 Number of renegotiated BITs for the top fifteen renegotiating countries.

IV. COMPARATIVE BIT CONTENT ANALYSIS AND SRS

Elsewhere, two of the present authors have used the data described in the previous section to conduct a broad study of the sources of BIT renegotiation.[18] One of the apparent primary drivers of renegotiation is prior experience of states with ISDS. Specifically governments involved in investment claims are learning from this process about the consequences of these treaties. In turn, they are more likely to pursue changes to their content in order to address their shortcomings and ambiguities. A detailed statistical analysis provided ample empirical support for this claim.

Importantly, however, it has not been argued that the links between actual ISDS experience and BIT renegotiation reflect discontent with ISDS as such or with the global investment regime more broadly. Rather, governments may draw different lessons from their experience with ISDS. In some instances, they may indeed work to constrain the ability of investors to take them to international arbitration and to narrow the legal basis for investment claims (i.e., making their BITs less "investor friendly," or viewed conversely, reducing state exposure to arbitration). In other instances, however, governments may view ISDS as a valuable mechanism that resolves investment disputes in an impartial and efficient manner and will thus work to promote treaties with greater protection of foreign investors. Such lessons may be drawn not only by home governments, who may be expected to promote their outgoing investors' interests, but also by host governments, who might like to reassure foreign investors of their commitment to a fair and transparent business environment. Anecdotal evidence suggests that both logics are at work simultaneously, but a deeper understanding of these dynamics requires a closer look at the content of the treaties themselves. Do the renegotiated treaties offer greater protection to foreign investors from actions taken as expressions of SRS, or do they ensure greater SRS for governments at the possible expense of foreign investors' interests? The two concerns—investor protection and SRS—are not necessarily mutually exclusive (the same renegotiation may both expand jurisdiction, for example, while tightening the text of substantive rights) but they do constitute an important conceptual trade-off.

A comparison of treaty texts can cast light on governments' perspectives regarding their legal obligations. While the intentions of policymakers and negotiators are not always discernable, the content of agreements can serve as their "revealed preference." This is particularly true when one examines changes to existing texts, which result from calculated decisions to modify specific provisions based on practical knowledge of the agreement's consequences.[19] Building on this premise, we have developed a scheme that allows us to better assess states' responses to the changing nature of the global investment regime and to gauge the level of concern they hold with respect to the impact of ISDS on their regulatory autonomy—the

18. Yoram Z. Haftel & Alexander Thompson, *When Do States Renegotiate International Agreements? The Impact of Arbitration*, REV. OF INT'L ORGS., Forthcoming. DOI: 10.1007/s11558-017-9276-1.

19. This can be contrasted with the notion that policymakers were not always fully aware of their potential consequences when they signed the original BITs. *See e.g.*, Lauge N. Skovgaard Poulsen, *Bounded Rationality and the Diffusion of Modern Investment Treaties*, 58 INT'L STUD. Q. 1 (2014).

concept of *State Regulatory Space (SRS)* already mentioned above, which we turn to now in greater detail, as an appropriate conceptual tool to guide our analysis.

SRS refers to the extent of the ability of governments to freely legislate and implement regulations in given public policy domains.[20] If we think of SRS as a continuum, at one extreme states have a great deal of flexibility to pursue policies they see fit, and are thus insulated from external pressure or influence attempts (in the present context, pressure from foreign investors utilizing ISDS). At the other extreme, governments have little room to maneuver and are highly constrained by the ability of foreign investors to challenge their policies under BITs and ISDS, even if not challenged in practice, or even if actual challenges are ultimately unsuccessful (a phenomenon sometimes labeled "regulatory chill").[21] The flipside of lower regulatory space may be better treatment and greater protection of foreign investors,[22] but this is not necessarily the case, and we make no distinct claims in this respect. Our sole interest here is in governmental positions on SRS as affected by ISDS, as reflected in renegotiated BITs. Measuring each BIT on the SRS continuum and comparing the original and renegotiated treaties can thus inform us whether governments have opted to increase, decrease, or keep intact their regulatory space.

To measure SRS, we build on a BIT text coding scheme developed by UNCTAD, with the assistance of several experts.[23] This scheme, labeled "A Mapping Guide" by UNCTAD, examines the most important substantive and procedural provisions of international investment agreements and codes them on the inclusion or exclusion of various elements. The UNCTAD Mapping Guide was designed for comparative purposes, but not necessarily with SRS in mind; indeed, it can be used for a variety of different comparative research goals. Moreover, it is important to note that the UNCTAD Mapping Guide is not concerned with BIT renegotiation, but rather with sorting and comparing BITs and other investment treaties in force at any given time. We have therefore undertaken the coding of a large number of expired BITs that may not be of interest to UNCTAD, and have in any case independently coded all BITs included in our database. In some cases we have also adjusted the coding criteria to better reflect our research interests; in this present chapter these relate to SRS.

At the first stage of this exercise, we coded both the original and the renegotiated treaty texts, following closely the mostly nominal coding rules developed by

---

20. We thus use the term "regulation" broadly to mean "rules issued for the purpose of controlling the manner in which private and public enterprises conduct their operations." *See, e.g.,* GIANDOMENICO MAJONE, REGULATING EUROPE 9 (1996).

21. Lorenzo Cotula, *Do Investment Treaties Unduly Constrain Regulatory Space?*, 9 QUESTIONS INT'L L. 19 (2014); Stephan W. Schill, *Do Investment Treaties Chill Unilateral State Regulation to Mitigate Climate Change?*, 24 J. INT'L. ARB. 469 (2007).

22. Suzanne A. Spears, *The Quest for Policy Space in a New Generation of International Investment Agreements*, 13 J. INT'L ECON. L. 1037 (2010).

23. U.N. CONFERENCE ON TRADE AND DEV., UNIVERSITY MAPPING PROJECT: 2014 FIRST SEMESTER (2014).

UNCTAD. We then transformed the coding in various selected categories into ordinal measures that indicate, in our estimation, more or less SRS. While we have done this for the entire coding scheme, in this chapter we present only data related to ISDS provisions. ISDS provisions are important to study in this respect because they give the rest of the legal obligations "teeth," because they have elicited so much debate among practitioners, and because they exhibit substantial and consequential variation.[24] To be sure, as noted above, we are fully aware that ISDS procedures should not, ideally, be detached from substantive investment law. States' views on ISDS, as a procedural matter, may be affected by the content of their substantive commitments and changes in them. Nevertheless, the analysis provides initial data on these renegotiations. No less importantly, it does provide us with information on state positions toward ISDS as a method of settling investment disputes.

Employing the UNCTAD Mapping Guide as a point of departure, we have classified ISDS provisions in nine categories that are related to SRS, listed in Table 24.1 and described immediately below.[25] The coding of each category ranges from zero (0), for limited SRS (less policy space), to one (1), for greater SRS (more policy space). In this context, along the spectrum of SRS, treaties with no ISDS at all score one in each category. The cumulative measure is then standardized to vary from zero to one, with each of the nine categories weighted equally. Thus, the maximum value of SRS_ISDS is one, reflecting the lowest impact of BITs and other investment agreements upon policy space and SRS. In contrast, ISDS with no qualifications or limitations on the capacity of foreign investors to file investment claims score zero, the highest degree of constraints on SRS. Below is a description of the nine categories and the justification of our coding choices. Some categories are "ordinal" in that the value of SRS is determined according to whether one or more thresholds have been met. Other categories are "cumulative" in that the SRS value is determined by the presence of multiple provisions, which are added together to determine the value.

- *Alternatives to Arbitration*—Ordinal: Even in the shadow of binding investment arbitration, parties always have the option to choose alternative (non-arbitral) dispute resolution procedures, such as conciliation or mediation. There is, however, a qualitative difference between (1) BITs in which such procedures are a mandatory requirement before turning to international arbitration, in which case states have greater opportunity

24. Todd Allee & Clint Peinhardt, *Delegating Differences: Bilateral Investment Treaties and Bargaining over Dispute Resolution Provisions*, 54 INT'L STUD. Q. 1 (2010); J. Pohl et al., *Dispute Settlement Provisions in International Investment Agreements: A Large Sample Survey*, OECD WORKING PAPERS ON INT'L INV. 2012/02 (2012).

25. We have not included reference to state-to-state dispute settlement under BITs. Our focus is only on the characterization of ISDS, wherein the existence or absence of ISDS is not a separate indicator, but rather incorporated separately in each distinct normative category, so that an absence of ISDS would result in SRS_ISDS of 1.

to defend regulatory policies in the face of investor complaints; (2) BITs in which such procedures are not mandatory but explicitly noted as preferable or otherwise desirable; and (3) BITs in which such procedures are not mentioned at all. We consider the first option as most conducive to SRS (other than no ISDS at all), with some difference between the second and third alternatives.

- *Scope of ISDS Claims*—Ordinal: Jurisdiction of ISDS under BITs varies from the very broad (any dispute relating to investment), through specifically enumerated non-treaty bases of jurisdiction (e.g., contract claims), to strict limitation to treaty-based claims, and ultimately, no ISDS at all (least SRS-restrictive). We consider broader jurisdiction to be more restrictive of SRS and narrower scope to be less restrictive.

- *Limitations on ISDS Scope—Limited Provisions Subject to ISDS*— Ordinal: Some BITs delimit the scope of the provisions that may be subject to ISDS, either by prescription or by exclusion. BITs that do not include any such limitations are potentially the most restrictive of SRS. BITs that prescribe some substantive provisions as bases for ISDS are less SRS restrictive. BITs that restrict ISDS to very particular areas (such as the calculation of monetary compensation) are least SRS restrictive, other than BITs that do not include ISDS at all.

- *Limitations on ISDS Scope—Exclusion of Policy Areas from ISDS*— Cumulative: Some BITs exclude defined policy areas from ISDS coverage with the effect of preserving SRS. Such exclusions come in two broad forms: they may relate to particular sectors or issues (e.g., security), or they may provide special mechanisms for taxation or prudential concerns. We assess such exclusions cumulatively and give equal weight to each of these two categories. This is for measurement purposes only and should not be construed as reflecting the relative normative importance of such exclusions.

- *Type of Consent to ISDS*—Ordinal: Where consent to ISDS is express or implied to the point of automaticity, state exposure to investment arbitration (and hence SRS restriction) is maximal. Where case-by-case consent or future consent are required, we assess a much lower degree of SRS restriction, tantamount to an absence of ISDS.

- *ISDS Rules—Forum Selection vis-à-vis Domestic Courts*—Ordinal: Where the default dispute settlement procedure is international arbitration, or where investors have an explicit option to prefer it, we presume that SRS is potentially and more significantly restrained, in comparison to a requirement to start with domestic courts before pursuing international arbitration.

- *Particular Features of ISDS*—Cumulative: We consider three particular features of ISDS included in the UNCTAD Mapping Guide as relevant to SRS. Where investment claims are restricted in time through a type of statute of limitations, SRS is less restricted. The same is true when provisional measures are not entertained, and when ultimate remedies are restricted.

- *Interpretation*—Cumulative: Some BITs authorize parties to be proactively involved in the interpretation of BIT provisions in ways that may expand

SRS. Some BITs allow parties to issue a joint interpretative guidance that may be binding upon arbitral tribunals addressing issues under the same treaty. Other treaties refer certain questions to interpretation by the parties as renvoi, or permit interpretative interventions by parties to the BIT that are not the respondent party. We consider these cumulatively, with every opportunity that BIT parties have to influence the interpretation of their obligations considered as enhancing SRS.

- *Transparency in Arbitral Proceedings*—Cumulative: Arbitral proceedings under BITs are usually not transparent to the public, with closed written and oral proceedings, and an absence of public interventions in the form of amicus curiae briefs. We take the view that such lack of transparency constrains SRS, primarily by making state regulation more susceptible to adverse international arbitral intervention. Thus, we cumulatively reduce the SRS rating of a BIT according to the existence of open written pleadings, oral hearings, or amicus briefs.

Table 24.1. CATEGORIES AND VALUES OF SRS_ISDS

Category	Type	Indicator	Value
Alternatives to arbitration	Ordinal	No clause (compulsory ISDS)	0
		Voluntary recourse to alternatives	0.25
		Mandatory recourse to alternatives	0.75
		No ISDS	1
Scope of claims	Ordinal	Any dispute relating to investment	0
		Listing specific basis of claim beyond treaty	0.33
		Limited to treaty claims	0.66
		No ISDS	1
Limitation on provisions subject to ISDS	Ordinal	No limitations	0
		Limitation of provisions subject to ISDS	0.75
		No ISDS	1
Limitation on scope of ISDS	Cumulative	Exclusion of policy areas from ISDS	0.33
		Special mechanism for taxation or prudential measures	0.33
		No ISDS	1
Type of consent to arbitration	Ordinal	Expressed or implied consent	0
		Case-by-case consent or no ISDS	1
Forum selection: domestic courts	Ordinal	No mention of domestic courts or investor's choice	0
		Domestic court a pre-condition for ISDS	0.5
		No ISDS	1

(Continued)

Table 24.1. (CONTINUED)

Category	Type	Indicator	Value
Particular features of ISDS	Cumulative	Limitation period	0.25
		Provisional measures	0.25
		Limited remedies	0.25
		No ISDS	1
Interpretation	Cumulative	Binding interpretation	0.25
		Renvoi	0.25
		Rights of non-disputing contracting party	0.25
		No ISDS	1
Transparency in arbitral proceedings	Cumulative	Making documents publicly available	0.25
		Making hearings publicly available	0.25
		Amicus curiae	0.25
		No ISDS	1

These categories are the basis of our content analysis of BIT renegotiation with respect to SRS. This exercise first requires (as noted above) the texts of all initial and renegotiated treaties. UNCTAD's database includes many, but not all, such texts. We complemented it with treaties from additional sources, such as the UN Treaty Series, and national databases. We were able to uncover both texts for about 170 of the 196 treaties included in our dataset. In addition, these treaties come in a variety of languages. We tackled this coding challenge by employing coders proficient respectively in five languages: English, French, Spanish, Arabic, and Russian. Several treaties are available in other languages, such as German, Croatian, Finnish, and Romanian, and are therefore currently excluded from the sample, which comprises 160 treaty pairs.[26]

Even though the UNCTAD Mapping Guide is very detailed and provides ample instructions and examples, coding of complex legal texts such as BITs is susceptible to different interpretations and understandings. In order to reduce the risk of coding errors, the three coauthors coded several treaties and arrived at a consensual coding baseline. Each coder then had to code these treaties as well as compare and reconcile his or her coding with this baseline. Only upon completing this training did he or she start coding additional BITs. Furthermore, many of the treaties (especially the non-English language ones) were coded by two research assistants, who later compared and converged on an agreed-upon coding. In any cases of remaining disagreements, the coding was reviewed by the authors, who made the final call. We therefore have confidence that the results of the analysis, reported next, build on accurate data.

26. We intend to continue and expand this dataset by locating missing texts and by coding in additional languages. We are reassured in our results, however, because the 36 BITs excluded from the analysis are spread across regions and time, thereby minimizing the risk of an unrepresentative sample.

V. A COMPARATIVE EMPIRICAL ANALYSIS
OF ISDS PROVISIONS

Using our data, we examine several trends in BIT renegotiation. We first consider global changes in ISDS provisions and then turn our attention to cross-national and regional differences. The number of treaties (denoted n) is reported in parentheses. As this section makes clear, different countries and regions have divergent approaches to this matter.

If we look at the entire sample, the average value of SRS_ISDS for the initial treaties is 0.29. The average value for the renegotiated treaties is only 0.07. Thus, the revised BITs reflect much stronger ISDS and, by implication, much lower flexibility for host governments. This simple observation contradicts the idea of a "backlash" against and a "legitimacy crisis" of the global investment regime. However, a good grasp of this finding requires a more fine-grained analysis of the data. As a first cut, we distinguish between North-South and South-South BITs, which may be driven by distinct logics. Indeed, the decline in state regulatory space is much more pronounced in the former. ISDS has decreased from 0.42 to 0.07 for North-South BITs ($n=73$), but only from 0.12 to 0.08 for the rest of the sample ($n=87$) (but note that SRS is low in this sample to begin with).

An even closer inspection indicates that Western European countries play a key role in the move toward greater investor protection at the ostensible expense of SRS. BITs involving these states show a marked drop in regulatory space: from 0.51 to 0.03 ($n=66$), compared to the rest of the sample that shows a slight decline of 0.02 (from 0.13 to 0.11, $n=94$) in SRS_ISDS. This reality emanates from the fact that Western European governments, which pioneered the BIT movement in the 1960s, did not include any ISDS provisions in their treaties until the 1980s.[27] Thus, 37 initial BITs in the sample (but none of the renegotiated ones) score one on SRS_ISDS, reflecting no ISDS in these treaties. Out of those, a Western European state is a party to 32.

These countries attempted to modernize these treaties in the 1990s and the 2000s by adding far-reaching ISDS provisions (among other design changes). Notably, the low value on SRS_ISDS indicates that newer European BITs provide almost no regulatory space in their ISDS provisions. As Figure 24.3 shows, Germany exemplifies the Western European approach to ISDS. Out of 16 BITs in the sample, 15 included no ISDS provisions in the initial treaty (with China as a notable exception). Furthermore, in 12 treaties the shift was from one extreme to the other, resulting in a score of zero on SRS_ISDS. Only the revised BIT with Ecuador includes meaningful accommodation of regulatory space.

One observes a similar pattern with respect to current and former socialist countries, such as Russia, China, and Romania. These countries concluded numerous investment treaties in the 1980s that allowed for ISDS, but only with respect to compensation. The 1984 BIT that China signed with the Netherlands typifies this approach. Article 9 (3) states that "Disputes concerning the amount of compensation to be

27. LAUGE N. SKOVGAARD POULSEN, BOUNDED RATIONALITY AND ECONOMIC DIPLOMACY: THE POLITICS OF INVESTMENT TREATIES IN DEVELOPING COUNTRIES (2015).

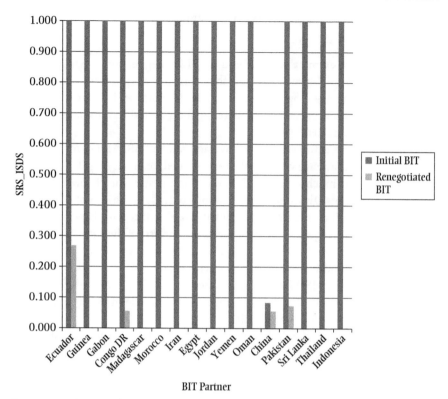

Figure 24.3 State regulatory space for German BITs.

paid when measures of expropriation, nationalization or other similar measures have been taken which cannot be settled [. . .] shall if the investor so wishes be submitted either to the competent court of law of the Contracting Party receiving the investment or to international arbitration."

As these countries changed their economic orientation (either gradually or abruptly) in the 1990s, they negotiated and renegotiated BITs with more sweeping ISDS provisions. This increased coverage is apparent in a decline of 0.17 in SRS_ISDS, from 0.21 to 0.04, in the 18 BITs that fit this category. Romania nicely illustrates this general approach. Figure 24.4 presents the six treaties that it concluded in the 1980s and then renegotiated in the middle 1990s, after turning from communism to capitalism (as we shall see momentarily, Romania changed its approach once more in the 2000s). It is apparent that all six BITs allow much greater investor protection and less SRS in the renegotiated treaties. In line with the discussion above, renegotiated treaties with Western European partners include more sweeping ISDS provisions.

A third group of treaties includes more than 60 BITs signed in the 1990s and then renegotiated in the 2000s by Central and Eastern European countries that have since joined the European Union.[28] Here, we observe almost no change from

28. It is dominated, in particular, by additional protocols to existing BITs signed by the Czech Republic and Romania.

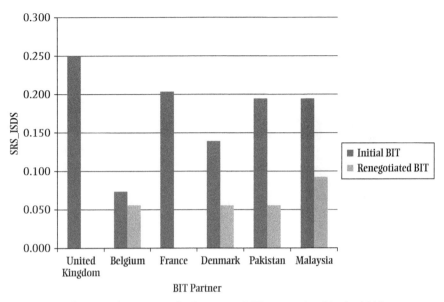

Figure 24.4 State regulatory space for Romanian BITs renegotiated in the 1990s.

a rather low regulatory space in the initial treaties: a very slight increase from 0.054 to 0.058 (n=61). This suggests that these countries did not revise ISDS provisions in their new treaties. Possibly, many of these revised treaties or protocols emphasize issues arising from EU accession and do not address matters related to ISDS. While this group of treaties is seemingly neutral, it actually points to an acceptance of the status quo. To begin with, the average SRS_ISDS of BITs in this category is about 0.05, which indicates a minimal extent of regulatory space. In addition, that these governments went through the trouble of revising their treaties and *could have* renegotiated ISDS provisions, but nevertheless refrained from doing so, suggests they were either uninterested in or unable to tackle this issue. As discussed in previous sections, it is still possible that these updated treaties incorporated substantive provisions with greater regulatory space.

Only one region, the Western Hemisphere (i.e., the Americas), seems to buck the general trend and move toward a higher regulatory space. To the extent that at least one party is located in either North or Latin America, SRS_ISDS slightly increases from 0.20 to 0.21 (n=33), compared to a decrease from 0.31 to 0.04 in the rest of the sample (n=127). Moreover, if both parties belong in this region, regulatory space increases from 0.14 to 0.34 (n=7), compared to a decrease from 0.29 to 0.06 in the rest of the sample (n=153). Most BITs in this region were signed in the 1990s and renegotiated in the second half of the 2000s. The renegotiated agreements contain many limitations and qualifications on the ability of investors to use ISDS, from the exclusion of sensitive policy areas, to time limitations, to the transparency of legal proceedings.

Canada nicely illustrates the Western Hemispheric approach to ISDS provisions. As Figure 24.5 demonstrates, five out of six renegotiated Canadian treaties resulted in substantially greater regulatory flexibility. The sixth agreement—an

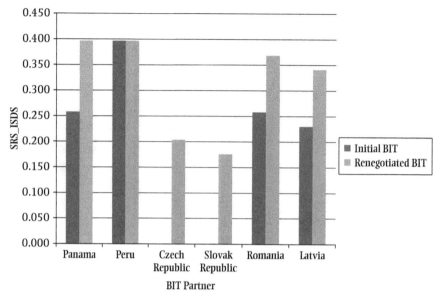

Figure 24.5 State regulatory space for Canadian BITs.

FTA with Peru—remained intact with a high level of SRS_ISDS. It is also apparent that the two agreements with other American partners score higher on SRS_ISDS than those with Eastern European partners. This trend is not only evident in the Canadian (and to a lesser extent American agreements), but also in intra-Latin American ones. In fact, the renegotiated agreements that score the highest on regulatory space in the sample are the 2007 Peru-Colombia BIT and the 2006 Peru-Chile FTA. It appears, then, that the Americas are spearheading the turn to more nuanced and less sweeping ISDS provisions in investment and trade agreements.

Before we turn to our concluding remarks, it ought to be mentioned that we also examined other regions, such as East Asia, the Middle East, and sub-Saharan Africa. Most countries in these regions renegotiated BITs with Northern partners and follow the general trend: that is, high levels of regulatory space in the initial BITs and more investor-friendly renegotiated agreements in the 1990s and 2000s. Unfortunately, only a handful of treaties in our sample are intra-Asian or intra-African, thereby precluding a meaningful empirical analysis of these.[29]

VI. CONCLUSIONS

We use new data on the design of arbitration provisions to offer an empirical analysis of renegotiated investment treaties. Focusing on the concept and measurement of *state regulatory space*, we show that most renegotiations produce treaties with less room for host governments to regulate, as reflected in ISDS provisions. We also describe significant variation across countries and regions, demonstrating the value

29. The dataset includes only five intra-Asian BITS, four intra-Middle East and North African BITs, and no intra-sub-Saharan African BITs.

of a comparative approach to lawmaking and treaty design. Beyond these particular findings, in this chapter we have sought to demonstrate three dimensions of comparative international law research that hold significant potential in the development of the field, perhaps even expanding the original scope of the project.

The first additional dimension is *conceptual*. Comparative international law should address the ways in which international law is made. The premise of the comparative international law project is that states apply and interpret the same international legal norms in different ways, and that an exploration of these differences can illuminate our understandings of state behavior with respect to international law. In our present contribution we have shown that significant variance can also exist among state attitudes toward international law at earlier stages of engagement— stages of lawmaking and law-formation. These differences are manifested in formal state interactions with international law through renegotiation processes and outcomes, even in a highly specialized area of international law such as investment protection that is often considered monolithic or at least monochromatic by non-specialists. It is, therefore, important to devote attention to the comparative patterns of international lawmaking, not only law-taking. This approach has implications for international legal theory. While the examination of differences in state applications of their international legal commitments may seem to express certain weaknesses in the normative power of international law, a demonstration of the intricacy of state preferences with respect to the design and adjustment of their legal commitments over time should actually restore our faith in the seriousness with which states take their legal commitments.

The second additional dimension is *methodological*. Comparative international law must be empirically informed. Comparative international insights can of course be gained through standard doctrinal legal methods of comparison, relating, for example, to underlying legal traditions (civil law, common law, etc.). As this chapter shows, these methods can, however, be augmented by empirical textual analysis based on objectively designed (yet contestable) criteria. Where there are relatively large numbers of treaties in the same subfield of international law (in our case, literally forming this subfield), textual comparisons can provide robust responses to systemic questions, such as the degree to which different states are concerned enough with BIT/ISDS limitations on SRS to take remedial action through renegotiation.

The third additional dimension is truly *comparative*. Comparative international law has a broad range of comparative bases. The findings of our research show that international legal approaches to lawmaking can cut across legal traditions, for example. We have found greater similarities in attitudes toward ISDS in BITs among regional groupings (Western Europe, the Americas) than across legal traditions (indeed, the primary regional groupings include a diverse range of legal systems). We have also seen a variety of path-dependent, historical influences on the formulation of ISDS commitments, changing over time. Thus, comparative international law research must avoid being boxed into preordained categories, seeking instead the most impactful variables and most persuasive hypotheses where lawmaking or law-application is concerned.

25

Africa and the Rethinking of International Investment Law

About the Elaboration of the Pan-African Investment Code

MAKANE MOÏSE MBENGUE & STEFANIE SCHACHERER

I. INTRODUCTION

The year 2015 was a crucial one for Africa regarding the codification of the first continent-wide investment instrument: the Pan-African Investment Code (PAIC). Even though this instrument is not yet officially adopted, it presents an African consensus on the shaping of international investment law. The PAIC is a legal instrument—shaped in the form of an investment model treaty—that has been drafted from the perspective of developing countries and least-developed countries focusing on sustainable development goals. The PAIC contains a number of Africa-specific as well as innovative features, which presumably makes it today a unique legal instrument.

This chapter seeks to present and to contextualize the PAIC by taking a comparative international law approach. Comparative international law focuses largely on similarities and differences between national and regional actors in their approach to international law.[1] With regard to the PAIC, a comparative law analysis allows us to understand how African interests shape different approaches to international investment law and to see how the PAIC challenges core traditional approaches. The analysis leads to the question whether today one can still speak of universal approaches to international investment law. On the one hand, the provisions of the PAIC will be compared to traditional international investment treaty practice in order to understand to what extent the PAIC builds upon these elements. On the other hand, the PAIC provisions will be compared to most recent treaty practice, in particular the Brazilian and Indian treaties, as well as investment chapters in

---

1. Anthea Roberts et al., *Comparative International Law: Framing the Field*, 109 AM. J. INT'L L. 467, 469 (2015).

comprehensive free trade agreements (FTAs), such as the Trans-Pacific Partnership Agreement (TPP) and the Comprehensive Economic and Trade Agreement (CETA) between the European Union (EU) and Canada. This will provide insights as to whether Africa's regional approach differs from current practices of other countries and regions. In addition, comparisons are made with the policy proposals of governmental and nongovernmental organizations advocating for reform in the international investment law regime including the United Nations Conference on Trade and Development (UNCTAD), the Southern African Development Community (SADC), and the International Institute for Sustainable Development (IISD). A comparison to the work of these organizations has the benefit of permitting the innovative character of the PAIC to be appraised.

The chapter is divided into five main sections. Section II provides an overview of bilateral investment treaties (BITs) and other international investment agreements (IIAs) that have been concluded by African states over the last 50 years. Section III illustrates continental initiatives in the context of foreign investment and presents the origins of the PAIC. Section IV addresses the important question as to what extent the PAIC incorporates traditional investment standards and to what extent it breaks with them. Section V explores the aspects of the PAIC that are truly innovative and that reveal the question of a reshaping of international investment agreements. Finally, Section VI examines the PAIC and dispute settlement and, in particular, the controversies around investor-state arbitration.

II. BITS AND OTHER INTERNATIONAL INVESTMENT AGREEMENTS IN AFRICA

African countries concluded the bulk of their still existing bilateral investment treaties mainly in the period from the mid-1990s to the early 2000s. Traditionally, BITs were concluded with capital exporting countries mainly from Europe.[2] Since 2002, the number of signed BITs by African countries declined.[3] Up to the present, African countries have signed about 870 BITs or IIAs, which corresponds to a third of the IIAs signed worldwide.[4] There are 713 agreements with non-African countries and 157 intra-African BITs. Generally the content of the majority of these agreements follows the traditional approaches of treaties elaborated by capital-exporting countries.

Besides BITs, regional investment agreements have emerged within the African continent. Africa's regional integration has been a stated priority agenda for African

---

2. Alfredo Crosato et al., *Africa's Investment Regime: Assessing International Investment Agreements in the Light of Current Trends and Needs in Africa, in* THE GRADUATE INSTITUTE: TRADE AND INVESTMENT LAW CLINIC PAPERS 26 (2016).

3. UNITED NATIONS CONFERENCE ON TRADE AND DEVELOPMENT [UNCTAD], WORLD INVESTMENT REPORT 115 (2014).

4. UNCTAD, International Investment Agreement Database, http://investmentpolicyhub.unctad.org/IIA (last visited Feb. 22, 2016).

governments since the early years of independence.[5] Today, Africa's regional integration is a complex web of various Regional Economic Communities (RECs). In West Africa, there are three RECs: the West African Economic and Monetary Union (UEMOA), the Mano River Union (MRU) as well as the Economic Community of West African States (ECOWAS). Central Africa has two groupings: the Economic Community of Central African States (ECCAS/CEMAC) and the Economic Community of Great Lakes countries (ECGLC). In the Eastern and Southern African sub-regions six groupings co-exist: the Common Market for Eastern and Southern Africa (COMESA), the East African Community (EAC), the Inter-Governmental Authority on Development (IGAD), the Indian Ocean Commission (IOC), the Southern African Development Community (SADC) and the Southern African Customs Union (SACU). North Africa shares two RECs, the Arab Maghreb Union (UMA) as well as the Community of Sahel-Saharan States (CEN-SAD). As a consequence, today of the 55 African countries, 28 retain dual membership, 20 are members of three RECs and the Democratic Republic of Congo belongs to four RECs and 6 countries maintain singular membership.[6]

Most of these RECs adopted legal instruments concerning the regulation of foreign investment.[7] From the 1970s to the 1990s, treaties have been concluded to enhance cooperation and harmonization in the area of investment.[8] More recently, COMESA elaborated a modern investment agreement, which was intended to establish the COMESA Common Investment Area.[9] However, the agreement has not yet entered into force and the region is currently renegotiating its content. The 2006 SADC Protocol on Finance and Investment is another recent text, which is in force in this region. EAC also launched investment initiatives by adopting a model investment code in 2006. Hence, each African REC has at least one instrument relating directly or indirectly to investment. The picture becomes more intricate when one considers that many African states are members of two or more RECs at the same time. Whilst regional economic integration is generally perceived to benefit the economy and thus to foster foreign and domestic investment,[10] the multiple and overlapping commitments arguably make Africa's integration efforts in relation to investment harmonization inefficient. Yet recent developments give hope for more

---

5. Atieno Ndomo, Regional Economic Communities in Africa: A Progressive Overview 8 (2009).

6. Id. at 9.

7. Analysis based on data from UNCTAD, supra note 4.

8. Common Convention on Investments in the States of the Customs and Economic Union of Central Africa, Dec. 14, 1965, 7 I.L.M. 221 (1968); Arab Maghreb Union Investment Agreement, Jul. 23, 1990; Economic Community of West African States, Protocol A/P1/11/84 relating to Community Enterprises, Nov. 23, 1984; Economic Community of West African States, Protocol on Free Movement of Persons, Residence, and Establishment, May 29, 1979, 1906 U.N.T.S. 56.

9. Investment Agreement for the COMESA Common Investment Area, May 23, 2007 [hereinafter COMESA Investment Agreement].

10. United Nations Economic Commission for Africa, Assessing Regional Integration in Africa (ARIA V): Towards an African Continental Free Trade Area 3 (2012).

harmonized economic integration. In the summer of 2015, the regions of SADC, COMESA and EAC launched the Tripartite Free Trade Area (TFTA) that seeks to promote the harmonization of trade arrangements amongst these three RECs.[11]

III. CONTINENTAL INITIATIVES AND THE ELABORATION OF THE PAN-AFRICAN INVESTMENT CODE (PAIC)

At the continental level it is the African Union (AU),[12] which is mandated by its Member States to enhance the political and socio-economic integration of the continent and to promote sustainable development.[13] The most important integration endeavors currently undertaken by the AU are the establishment of the African Economic Community by the year 2034 as well as a Continental Free Trade Area (CFTA).

In the spirit of enhanced economic integration, African Ministers responsible for continental integration decided in 2008 to initiate the work on a comprehensive investment code for Africa, the Pan-African Investment Code (PAIC). The declared aim of the initiative was to attract greater flows of investments into Africa and to facilitate intra-African cross-border investments. It was the intention of the AU and its Member States to elaborate a text that would address Africa-specific needs. African independent experts drafted the text over several years. The groups of experts were composed of representatives coming from the different African RECs mentioned before, from academia as well as the private sector. The process of elaboration can roughly be divided into three phases. Within its first phase, the group of experts compiled African best practices in the field and elaborated a first draft. The next and decisive phase was during the year 2015, where the PAIC text was at experts' level. Two meetings of African independent experts were held in May 2015 in Tunisia and another one in September 2015 in Mauritius. Experts of AU Member States then reviewed the work of the independent experts during a continent-wide meeting in Uganda that took place in December 2015. The third phase started in the year 2016. At a ministerial meeting in Addis Ababa in March 2016, the competent African ministers approved the work of the PAIC. At the last meeting in Nairobi in November 2016, finally, governmental representatives agreed to adopt the PAIC as a non-binding model treaty. It is interesting to underline that this political decision has been made despite the recommendations of the independent legal expert that recommended the PAIC to be a binding instrument. According to the latest information, the AU foresees the official adoption of the PAIC at one of the next ministerial meetings.

11. *See* Southern African Development Community [SADC], Tripartite Cooperation, http:// www.sadc.int/about-sadc/continental-interregional-integration/tripartite-cooperation/ (last visited Mar. 10, 2016).

12. The African Union (AU) is a continental organization consisting of 54 African states (with the exclusion of Morocco). The AU was founded in 2001. Its headquarters are located in Addis Ababa, Ethiopia.

13. Constitutive Act of the African Union art. 3, Jul. 11, 2000, 2158 U.N.T.S. 3.

IV. AN INTROSPECTIVE EXPLORATION OF THE (DIS-)INTEGRATION OF TRADITIONAL INVESTMENT STANDARDS WITHIN THE PAIC

The PAIC contains a couple of innovative features, the most striking ones of which will be examined in greater detail in this section. The PAIC reformulates traditional treaty language, adds new provisions and omits certain provisions completely. The treaty seeks to be balanced and to address specific aspects of African development.

A. Preamble, Objective and Scope of the PAIC

Preambles have a primary significance as to how an IIA will be interpreted in the event of a dispute between the parties or between an investor and a state.[14] Today, new and broader objectives have become more and more relevant, one of which is certainly the objective of sustainable development.[15] In the African context, sustainable development goals are of crucial importance given the important economic, social, and environmental challenges the continent is facing. The preamble recognizes the need for investments for the development of Africa. Such investments should however facilitate job creation, support long-term economic growth, and contribute effectively to the fight against poverty.[16] The preamble also specifically refers to the right of AU member states to regulate all aspects relating to investments within their territories with a view to promote sustainable development objectives.[17] The drafters of the PAIC did not intend to disregard the protection of investors and investments, but stressed the need to achieve an overall balance of the rights and obligations among AU member states and the investors under the PAIC.[18] The preamble emphasizes also the need to promote corruption-free investment and improved laws and regulations that promote transparency and accountability in governance. The PAIC thus promotes *responsible* investment. Another important aspect contained in the preamble of the PAIC is the aim of enhancing African economic and social integration. The PAIC drafters sought to inscribe the Code into larger political ambitions of African socioeconomic integration.

To be consistent with sustainable development objectives as inscribed in the preamble, the PAIC starts off with a first article addressing its primary objective, which is "to promote, facilitate and protect investments that foster the sustainable development of each Member State, and in particular the Member State where the

---

14. Rudolf Dolzer & Margrete Stevens, Bilateral Investment Treaties 20 (1995).

15. UNCTAD, Investment Policy Framework for Sustainable Development (2012) [hereinafter IPFSD].

16. Draft Pan-African Investment Code, pmbl. ¶ 8 (2016) [hereinafter PAIC] (emphasis added).

17. PAIC, pmbl. ¶ 10 (2016).

18. SADC, Model Bilateral Investment Treaty Template with Commentary, pmbl. ¶ 6 (2012) [hereinafter SADC Model BIT].

investment is located."[19] Under the PAIC, investments are only protected when they foster sustainable development. It is also worth noting that the PAIC not only seeks to protect investments, it seeks to first promote investments, then to facilitate investments and finally and only thirdly to protect investments. A specific provision that states the objective of the treaty is rather unusual. However, stating the objective of the treaty in a specific provision can provide added weight to the objective, which in turn has consequences for the treaty interpretation.[20]

With respect to the scope of the PAIC, one aspect is important to highlight. The PAIC by comparison to other IIAs does not only stipulate obligations on states and rights for investors. As its Article 2 states, the PAIC "defines the rights and obligations of Member States as well as investors."[21] This article introduces the very content of the PAIC and refers back to the endeavor stated in the preamble for an overall balance of the rights and obligations among states and investors.

B. Definition of Investment

As the objective of the PAIC is to attract investments that foster sustainable development, the drafting of the definition of an investment that would fall under the PAIC was highly critical. The drafters of the PAIC considered that protected investments should be those businesses that bring constructive economic and social benefits.[22] Henceforth, the PAIC contains an enterprise-based definition. As "an enterprise or a company, (. . .), which is established, acquired or expanded by an investor, including through the constitution, maintenance or acquisition of shares, debentures or other ownership instruments of such an enterprise (. . .)."[23] The assets of the enterprise are included among the covered assets of the investor in an open and indicative list of assets.[24] Other countries such as India and Brazil also opted for the use of an enterprise-based definition.[25] The SADC Model BIT presents the enterprise-based definition as being the most beneficial option for sustainable development.[26] The establishment or acquisition of an enterprise is

---

19. PAIC, art. 1 (2016) (emphasis added).

20. SADC Model BIT, 8 cmt. & art. 1 (2012).

21. PAIC, art. 2 al. 2 (2016).

22. SADC Model BIT, 13 cmt. (2012).

23. PAIC, art. 3.4 (2016) (emphasis added).

24. PAIC, art. 3.4 (2016).

25. Model Text for the Indian Bilateral Investment Treaty, art. 1.4 (2015) [hereinafter Indian Model BIT (2015)]; Investment Cooperation and Facilitation Agreement between the Federative Republic of Brazil and the Republic of Malawi, Braz-Malawi, art. 2, Jun. 25, 2015 [hereinafter Brazil-Malawi CIFA]. For a contrary approach, see Comprehensive Economic and Trade Agreement, E.U.-Can., art. 8.1, Oct. 30, 2016 [hereinafter CETA]; Trans-Pacific Partnership art. 9.1, Feb. 4, 2016 [hereinafter TPP]; Norway Model Bilateral Investment Treaty, art. 2.2 (2015) [hereinafter Norwegian Model BIT].

26. SADC Model BIT, 12–13 cmt. (2012).

in general more likely investments that bear long-term interest in the host state.[27] The drafters of the PAIC followed the recommendation of SADC when they decided on the definition of an investment.

A series of investments are categorically excluded from the scope of the definition under the PAIC.[28] Worth underlining is that the PAIC excludes portfolio investments altogether.[29] It also excludes investments in any sector that is sensitive to the host state's development or that would have an adverse impact on its economy.[30]

Noteworthy is that the PAIC investment definition refers to the full *Salini* test.[31] The PAIC requires an investment to have the characteristics of: "commitment of capital or other resources, the expectation of gain or profit, the assumption of risk, and a significant contribution to the host State's economic development."[32] Today's treaty practice is fragmented regarding the incorporation of the *Salini* test. The US Model BIT was the first treaty text to make reference to it, however always by excluding the significant contribution to the host state's economic development.[33] Alike are the approaches in the TPP and CETA.[34] Other treaties, such as those based on Model BITs from European countries as well as some of Japan's recent BITs adopt the traditional approach of not mentioning the elements of the *Salini* test at all.[35] The Indian Model refers, as does the PAIC, to all four elements.[36] By including the last characteristic of the *Salini* test—the significant contribution to the host state's economic development—the drafters of the PAIC left no doubt

27. *Id.* at 13.

28. Most treaties exclude certain categories. *Cf.* CETA, art. 8.1. (2016); TPP, art. 9.1 (2015).

29. *See also* Brazil-Malawi CIFA, art. 2 (2015).

30. PAIC, art. 4.n.i–iii (2016).

31. Salini et al. v. Morocco, ICSID Case No. ARB/00/4, Decision on Jurisdiction, ¶ 54 (Jul. 23, 2001), 6 ICSID Rep. 400 (2004).

32. PAIC, art. 4.f (2016).

33. United States Model Bilateral Investment Treaty, art. 1 (2012) [hereinafter U.S. Model BIT].

34. CETA, art. 8.1 (2016); TPP, art. 9.1 (2015). *See also* European Union-Singapore Free Trade Agreement, E.U.-Sing., art. 9.1.1, Oct. 17, 2014.

35. *See* Agreement Between Japan and the Islamic Republic of Iran on Reciprocal Promotion and Protection of Investment, Japan-Iran, art. 1.1, May 2, 2016 [hereinafter Japan-Iran BIT]; Agreement Between Japan and Ukraine for the Promotion and Protection of Investment, Japan-Ukr., art. 1.1, May 2, 2015; Federal Ministry for Economics and Technology, Treaty between the Federal Republic of Germany and (...) concerning the Encouragement and Reciprocal Protection of Investments art. 1.1 (2008); Draft Agreement between the Government of the Republic of France and the Government of the Republic of (...) on the Reciprocal Promotion and Protection of Investments art. 1.1 (2006) [hereinafter French Model BIT]; Draft Agreement between the Government of the United Kingdom of Great Britain and Northern Ireland and the Government of (...) for the Promotion and Protection of Investments art. 1(a) (2005); *but see* Agreement between Japan and the Oriental Republic of Uruguay for the Liberalization, Promotion and Protection of Investment, Japan-Uru., Jan. 26, 2015.

36. Indian Model BIT, art. 1.2.1 (2015).

that a covered investment under the PAIC has to have a strong relationship with the development of the host state's economy.

C. Definition of Investor

The definition of an investor under the PAIC appears to be rather basic, stating that an "investor means any national, company or enterprise of a Member State or a national, company or enterprise from any other country that has invested or has made investments in a Member State."[37] However, given the enterprise-based definition of an investment under the PAIC, the crucial point here was to clearly define the notion of a legal person, that is, an enterprise or company. In relation to legal persons, most IIAs rely essentially on three basic criteria to determine the nationality of a company: the concept of incorporation, the concept of the social seat, and the concept of control.[38] A treaty that defines the nationality of a legal entity solely on the basis of the place of incorporation has potentially the largest coverage.[39] References to the place of incorporation are thus mostly coupled with one or more other criteria.[40] Several new treaties require that the legal person in question has in addition to its place of incorporation a "substantial business activity" in the home state.[41] The PAIC builds on this concept and requires a substantial business activity in the member state in which the enterprise or company is located.[42] In order to clarify the content of a "substantial business activity," the PAIC provides for a case-by-case approach by indicating four circumstances that should be taken into account for the assessment of the business activity in question in order to qualify as being "substantial." These criteria are the amount of investment to be brought into the host state, the number of jobs to be created, its effect on the local community, and the length of time the business has been in operation.[43]

D. Rejection of Pre-establishment Commitments

The majority of the existing IIAs only guarantee standards of treatment of foreign investment regarding the post-establishment phase, but there is a growing number of treaties that include commitments with respect to the pre-establishment phase. This is in particular as regards comprehensive FTAs.[44] Recent practice shows that

37. PAIC, art. 4.5 (2016) (emphasis added).

38. DOLZER & STEVENS, *supra* note 14, at 35.

39. UNCTAD, *supra* note 15, at 91.

40. CETA, art. 8.1 (2016), combines the place of incorporation with the criteria of direct or indirect control.

41. TPP, art. 9.1 (2015); Indian Model BIT, art. 1.2 (2015).

42. PAIC, art. 3.1 (2016).

43. PAIC, art. 4.1 (2016).

44. *See* North American Free Trade Agreement arts. 1102 & 1103, Dec. 17, 1992, 23 I.L.M. 289 [hereinafter NAFTA]; *see also* TPP, art. 9.4 (2015).

besides the United States and Canada, the European Union also has sought to include pre-entry commitments in its treaties.[45] Pre-establishment obligations are formulated by including wording to the MFN (most-favored nation) treatment as well as to the national treatment (NT) clauses. That MFN and NT also apply to the pre-establishment phase is usually expressed by language indicating that MFN/NT should apply "with respect to the establishment, acquisition and expansion."[46] The drafters of the PAIC have been aware of current treaty practice but considered that in the context of African countries such provisions may preclude a state from altering domestic law as circumstances may warrant in the light of national sustainable development goals. To this effect, the MFN and NT treatment do not contain any reference to establishment, acquisition, and expansion. Yet to phase out any ambiguities the PAIC states, "for avoidance of doubt, establishment, acquisition and expansion under this Code only apply to the post-establishment phase."[47]

E. Most-Favored Nation (MFN) and National Treatment (NT)

1. CLARIFICATION OF "LIKE CIRCUMSTANCES"

Relative standards of protection such as MFN and NT require a proper basis for comparison of investors or investments. Earlier treaties such as NAFTA or US BITs include the wording of in "like circumstances" or "like situations" in their respective MFN and NT clause.[48] However, the unqualified reference to like circumstances did not lead to consistent case law.[49] This is why some current treaties include an additional criterion for the assessment of the concept of "in like circumstances."[50] Regarding the PAIC, it was the wording contained in the 2007 COMESA Investment Agreement that inspired the drafters.[51] The concept of "in like circumstances" under the PAIC requires on a case-by-case basis, consideration of all the circumstances of an investment such as "its effects on third persons and the local community or on the local, regional or national environment, the health of the populations, or on the global commons. Further such circumstances can be the sector in which the investor is active, the aim of the measure in question or the company size and other factors directly relating to the investment or investor in relation to the measure in question."[52] The list is non-exhaustive, but it ensures that a broad view

45. CETA, arts. 8.6–8.7 (2016); Free Trade Agreement between the European Union and the Socialist Republic of Vietnam, E.U.-Viet., ch. 2, art. 3 & art. 4, sec. 1, Feb. 1, 2016 [hereinafter EU-Vietnam FTA].

46. TPP, art. 9.4 (2015); US Model BIT, art. 4 (2012); NAFTA, art. 1103 (1992).

47. Cf. PAIC, art. 4.4 (2016) (emphasis added).

48. US Model BIT, arts. 3–4 (2012); NAFTA, arts. 1102–1103 (1992).

49. August Reinisch, National Treatment, in INTERNATIONAL INVESTMENT LAW: A HANDBOOK 846, 859 (Marc Bungenberg et al. eds., 2015).

50. TPP, art. 9.4, 9.5 n.14 (2015).

51. COMESA Investment Agreement, art. 17.2 (2007).

52. PAIC, arts. 7.3, 9.3 (2016) (emphasis added).

is taken rather than to question whether the investors are in the same "economic" or "business" sector as several arbitral tribunals did.[53] Furthermore, the additional text ensures that the reasons for any measures can be fully considered, not only their financial impacts.[54]

2. EXCEPTIONS TO MFN

IIAs differ with regard to the exceptions from MFN treatment. Exceptions of regional economic integration organizations (REIOs),[55] taxation,[56] and procedural issues[57] are among the usual ones, but states have used a variety of other explicit derogations from MFN obligations.[58] Whilst such exceptions are most often found in the MFN provision itself, the PAIC contains a specific article stating the exceptions to the MFN clause. The PAIC provides that there is no breach of MFN treatment when an AU member state adopts "any regulatory measure that is designed and applied to protect or enhance legitimate public welfare objectives, such as public health, safety and the environment."[59] In addition, the PAIC precludes measures that are taken "by reason of national security, public interest, and public health or public morals" from being considered as a "less favorable treatment"[60] within the meaning of the MFN provision. A further paragraph contains the classic exceptions on REIOs and taxation matters. It provides that the MFN principle does not oblige a member state to extend to the investor of any other country the benefit of any treatment contained in an existing or future customs union, free trade area, or international agreement to which the investor's home state is not a party, or contained in any international agreement or domestic legislation relating to taxation.[61]

3. EXCEPTIONS TO NT

Compared to the exceptions to MFN, exceptions to NT are much less frequent if not nonexistent. Yet, the drafters of the PAIC considered it to be relevant to include a specific article on the exceptions to NT, following the general NT provision, to ensure African states could take measures to pursue national development

---

53. For an overview of the relevant cases, see Reinisch, *supra* note 49, at 856–60.

54. SADC Model BIT, 21 cmt. (2012).

55. Agreement between The Government of The Republic of Mauritius and the Government of Romania on the Promotion and Reciprocal Protection of Investments, Mauritania-Rom., art. 3, Jan. 20, 2000 [hereinafter Romania-Mauritius BIT].

56. French Model BIT, art. 5 (2006); Agreement between the Government of the Republic of Finland and the Government of the Kyrgyz Republic on the Promotion and Protection of Investments, Fin.-Kyrg., art. 4, Mar. 4, 2003.

57. TPP, art. 9.5.3 (2015).

58. UNCTAD, MOST-FAVORED-NATION TREATMENT 10 (2010).

59. PAIC, art. 8.2 (2016) (emphasis added).

60. PAIC, art. 8.3 (2016) (emphasis added).

61. PAIC, art. 8.5 (2016).

objectives without breaching the NT standard. First, the NT exception clause contains a similar provision as for MFN in respect to the right of a member state to adopt measures that are "designed and applied to protect or enhance legitimate public welfare objectives, such as public health, safety and the environment."[62] Second, AU member states may "grant preferential treatment to qualifying investments and investors in order to achieve national development objectives."[63] For instance, favorable treatment may be addressed to the internal needs of designated disadvantaged persons, groups or regions.[64] Third, the PAIC reserves the right of AU member states to deny an investor the benefits of the PAIC and to grant special and differential treatment by listing two examples: where there is no substantial business activity in that state, or the investor is engaged in activities inimical to the economic interest of member states.[65] This latter clause is very similar to a typical denial of benefits clause, which can be found in many current treaties.[66] Fourth, a categorical exclusion for the application of the NT principle is foreseen for subsidies or grants provided to a government; or second, a state enterprise, including government-supported loans, guarantees and insurance; or third, for taxation measures aimed at ensuring the effective collection of taxes, except where this results in arbitrary discrimination.[67] Finally, the PAIC sets out that the implementation of these exceptions to NT "shall not entitle any investor to compensation for any competitive disadvantages they may suffer."[68]

F. Absence of a Provision on Fair and Equitable Treatment (FET)

FET appears in nearly all of the more than 3,200 IIAs.[69] It is well known that FET has been the most invoked standard in investment disputes.[70] The content of the standard has mainly been developed through arbitral practice, and arguably there is a measurable content of the FET standard.[71] Certain authors argue that the standard

62. PAIC, art. 10.2 (2016) (emphasis added).

63. PAIC, art. 10.3 (2016) (emphasis added).

64. PAIC, art. 10.7 (2016).

65. PAIC, art. 10.4 (2016).

66. CETA, art. 8.16 (2016); TPP, art. 9.14 (2015).

67. PAIC, art. 10.6 (2016).

68. PAIC, art. 10.8 (2016) (emphasis added).

69. The total number is 3,271 IIAs (including 2,926 BITs and 345 "other" IIAs). *See* UNCTAD, *supra* note 3, at 106 (2015).

70. RUDOLF DOLZER & CHRISTOPH SCHREUER, PRINCIPLES OF INTERNATIONAL INVESTMENT LAW 130 (2d ed. 2012).

71. Stephan W. Schill & Marco Jacob, *Fair and Equitable Treatment: Content, Practice, Method, in* INTERNATIONAL INVESTMENT LAW: A HANDBOOK 700, 700–63 (Marc Bungenberg et al. eds., 2015).

remains simply uncertain in content.[72] In the context of sustainable development the question is raised whether the standard hinders the promotion of sustainable development.[73] The reason is that the standard is apt to limit more than other standards the regulatory freedom of host states, including for socially and environmentally sensitive areas.[74] Given the current controversy about this standard, current reform approaches in particular seek to draft clearer and more predictable FET provisions.[75] One of the striking examples is the list of FET violations contained in CETA.[76] This approach is an example of an attempt to mitigate potential for abuse in litigation. However, the FET provision of CETA also includes the concept of legitimate expectations, which reintroduces uncertainty regarding its interpretation.[77] The Indian Model also contains a list stating three aspects of FET.[78] In future disputes we will see whether these provisions prove to better guide arbitral tribunals. A further reform approach toward FET is to avoid any inclusion of the standard in the treaty.[79] This latter option has been used by South Africa and Brazil[80] and is recommended by SADC.[81] In the light of the prevailing uncertainties of interpretation, also in regard of the more precise FET provisions, the drafters of the PAIC decided not to include such a standard. Moreover, this approach is also better suited to guarantee the implementation of sustainable development objectives.

V. TOWARD A RESHAPING AND RESTRUCTURING OF INTERNATIONAL INVESTMENT AGREEMENTS?

A. The PAIC and Investors' Obligations

International investment law is traditionally and until today predominantly concerned with the protection of foreign investors and their investments, which is evidenced by the title of most IIAs as *Treaty Concerning the Promotion and Protection of Investments*. Most investment treaties stipulate reciprocal obligations on the contracting state parties and do not impose any direct legal responsibilities on the

---

72. MUTHUCUMARASWAMY SORNARAJAH, RESISTANCE AND CHANGE IN THE INTERNATIONAL LAW OF FOREIGN INVESTMENT 247 (2015).

73. Roland Kläger, *Fair and Equitable Treatment and Sustainable Development, in* SUSTAINABLE DEVELOPMENT IN WORLD INVESTMENT LAW 237 (Marie-Claire C. Segger et al. eds., 2011).

74. *Id.* at 251, pt. 3.2.

75. *See, e.g.,* TPP, art. 9, annex 9-A (2015); Indian Model BIT, art. 3 (2015); COMESA Investment Agreement, art. 14 (2007).

76. CETA, art. 8.10.2 (2016).

77. UNCTAD, *supra* note 3 at 137; CETA, art. 8.10.4 (2016).

78. Indian Model BIT, art. 3 (2015).

79. Recommended by SADC (*see* SADC Model BIT, 22 cmt. (2012)).

80. *See* Protection of Investment Act 22 of 2015 (S. Afr.); Brazil-Malawi CIFA (2015).

81. SADC Model BIT, 22 cmt. (2012).

investor under international law.[82] As for the majority of traditional and current treaty practice, there is no legal balance between the rights and obligations of investors and those of states under international investment law. At this time, it is safe to affirm that the inclusion of direct obligations on the conduct of a foreign investor has not gained real recognition in investment treaty practice. Yet, there are a few early treaties that include investors' obligations, such as the Community Investment Code of the Economic Community of Great Lakes countries (ECGLC)[83] as well as the Charter on a Regime of Multinational Industrial Enterprises of Eastern and Southern African States.[84] More recent treaties have included, for instance, the obligation of foreign investors to comply with all applicable domestic law and measures of the host state,[85] or to accord priority to workers coming from the concerned state provided they have the same qualifications.[86] The International Institute for Sustainable Development (IISD) was first in adopting an alternative approach in its 2006 Model Investment Agreement.[87] However, most countries remain reluctant to stipulate direct obligations to investors, although it is a legally feasible option to ensure an appropriate balance in the realm of investment treaty practice between the legal protection granted to foreign investors on the one side and their responsibilities toward the societies in which they operate on the other side.[88]

As outlined before, the PAIC is intended to be a *balanced treaty.* In this respect, it contains a specific chapter on the direct obligations of an investor.[89] Such a chapter counterbalances the chapter on the guarantees of treatment for investors and investments. The chapter on investors' obligations contains six provisions entitled: framework for corporate governance, socio-political obligations, bribery, corporate social responsibilities (CSR), obligations as to the use of natural resources, and business ethics and human rights.

Under the PAIC, an investor has to comply with national and international standards of corporate governance for the sector concerned. The investor is required to comply in particular with transparency and accounting standards.[90] The investor

---

82. Karsten Nowrot, *Obligations of Investors, in* INTERNATIONAL INVESTMENT LAW: A HANDBOOK 1154, 1155 (Marc Bungenberg et al. eds., 2015).

83. Community Investment Code of the Economic Community of the Great Lakes Countries art. 19, Jan. 31, 1982.

84. Charter on a Regime of Multinational Industrial Enterprises (MIEs) in the Preferential Trade Area for Eastern and Southern African States art. 17, Nov. 21, 1990, 30 I.L.M. 696 (1991).

85. COMESA Investment Agreement, art 13 (2007); SADC, Protocol on Finance and Investment art. 10, annex 1, Aug. 18, 2006.

86. COMESA Investment Agreement, art. 16 (2007).

87. International Institute for Sustainable Development, Model International Agreement on Investment for Sustainable Development, Part Three, http://www.iisd.org/pdf/2005/investment_model_int_agreement.pdf [hereinafter IISD Model (2006)].

88. Nowrot, *supra* note 82, at 1162.

89. PAIC, ch. 4 (2016).

90. PAIC, art. 19.1 (2016).

is also held to disclose material regarding the financial situation, ownership, and governance of the company, risks related to environmental liabilities, and any other matters as well as to provide information relating to human resource policies, such as programs for human resource development.[91] Furthermore, the PAIC sets out sociopolitical obligations to which the investor is held to adhere, including for instance the respect for cultural values, the noninterference in internal political affairs, and the noninterference in intergovernmental relations.[92] In the same spirit, the investor is prohibited from influencing the appointment of persons to public office or finance political parties.[93] The PAIC further foresees that an investor has to contribute to the economic, social, and environmental progress of the host state with a view to achieving sustainable development and has in any case to ensure that the pursuit of its economic objectives do not conflict with the social and economic development objectives of the host state.[94]

Any act of bribery is generally prohibited under the PAIC.[95] As far as the use of natural resources is concerned, the investor is held not to exploit or use them to the detriment of the rights and interests of the host state and to respect the rights of the local population as well as to avoid land grabbing practices vis-à-vis local communities. Finally, the PAIC addresses principles that should govern compliance by investors with business ethics and human rights in the conduct of their investments, such as to support and respect the protection of internationally recognized human rights; to eliminate all forms of forced and compulsory labor, including the effective abolition of child labor; and to eliminate discrimination in respect of employment and occupation.[96]

Direct obligations for an investor need to be effectively enforced. Options for enforcement are for instance the denial of treaty protection for the investor or the possibility of a state to file counterclaims in an arbitral proceeding. The drafters of the PAIC opted for the possibility of counterclaims as will be presented here below.

B. The PAIC, "Horizontal" Obligations, and Systemic Issues

International investment law was traditionally not concerned with the conservation of natural resources, environmental protection, and social well-being even though these aspects directly relate to any operation of an investment in a host country. Today, the perception has changed and objectives of sustainable development have become universally recognized guiding principles for developing and developed

91. PAIC, art. 19.3 (2016).

92. PAIC, art. 20.1 (2016).

93. PAIC, art. 20.2 (2016).

94. PAIC, art. 22.2, 22.3 (2016).

95. PAIC, art. 21 (2016).

96. PAIC, art. 24 (2016).

states.[97] Thus, in more recent treaty practice societal concerns have prudently been introduced into IIAs.[98] However, according to UNCTAD, there is still a need to harmonize new IIAs with the broader common concerns of a society.[99] Another important aspect is the fact that most IIAs do not interconnect investment protection with other fields of international law such as trade, finance, health, and the environment undermines the systemic coherence of international law.[100]

The PAIC chapter on investment-related issues contains different aspects of policymaking that are concerned with the implementation of a sustainable development objective within African countries.[101] As outlined before, the drafters of the PAIC consider that AU member states should attract *responsible* investors with investments that are not harmful for the environment and bring economic and social benefits to their countries. The provisions of the chapter are addressed to both investors and AU member states, and some provisions are addressed to either the investor or AU member states. Their formulation is binding or hortatory. Some of the subject matters are presented here, such as social and economic development through transfer of technology, environmental protection, and labor policy as well as the preservation of cultural heritage (protection of intellectual property rights and traditional knowledge).

1. Transfer of Technology

The issue of transfer of technology occurs today more and more often in treaty practice. Whereas developing countries seek to encourage the transfer of technology, developed countries often exclude obligations for foreign investors to transfer technology.[102] The PAIC embodies a specific provision dedicated to the transfer of technology.[103] This approach is until now unique in international treaty practice. The PAIC sets out policy objectives as to enhance effective transfer of technology. Investors are encouraged to adopt in the course of their business activities practices that permit the transfer and rapid diffusion of technologies and know-how on reasonable terms in a manner that contributes to the research and development goals of the host state.[104] AU member states are invited to cooperate and facilitate the international transfer of technology by various measures such as providing training for research, engineering, design, and other personnel engaged in the development of national technologies or in the adaptation and use of technologies transferred.

97. Steffen Hindelang & Markus Krajewski, Shifting Paradigms in International Investment Law: More Balanced, Less Isolated, Increasingly Diversified 381 (2015).

98. TPP, art. 9.15 (2015).

99. UNCTAD, *supra* note 3, at 127.

100. UNCTAD, *supra* note 15, at 17.

101. PAIC, ch. 5 (2016).

102. *Compare* U.S. Model BIT, art. 8, al. 1, let. f (2012) *with* Indian Model BIT, art. 1.2.1(iv) (2015).

103. PAIC, art. 29 (2016).

104. PAIC, art. 29.2 (2016).

Finally, AU member states are held to provide assistance in the development and administration of laws and regulations with a view to facilitating the transfer of technology.[105]

2. ENVIRONMENTAL PROTECTION

The right for a host state to adopt environmental measures becomes more and more part of modern IIA practice, and most treaties contain provisions specifically addressing the issue of investment and the environment.[106] Common to many IIAs are so-called "non-lowering of standards" clauses. Such provisions aim to suppress the temptation of host states to lower their environmental standards as an incentive to attract foreign investment.[107] Measures that protect or conserve the environment prominently figure in the general exceptions of many IIAs and assure the host state in its right to regulate in the area.[108] Yet, binding provisions on the protection of the environment in an IIA are rare or even inexistent.[109] The PAIC suggests binding obligations for investors as well as for member states in relation to the environment.[110] Member states are held to ensure that their laws and regulations provide for environmental protection. The investor in turn has to protect the environment, and where the investor's activity causes damages to the environment, he/she has to take reasonable steps to restore it as far as possible. Both the states and the investors are to carry out environmental impact assessments (EIA) in relation to investments. Finally, the PAIC also contains a non-lowering clause stating that any relaxation of domestic environmental legislation in order to attract investments is prohibited.[111] As mentioned before, the PAIC contains specific exceptions to the MFN and NT principles also relating to the environment stating, that when a member state intends to adopt measures for the protection of the environment, the MFN and NT standards are not violated.[112]

3. LABOR ISSUES

Like the environment, labor standards became part of modern IIA practice. Some treaties included references to non-binding codes in the Agreement, such as the *ILO Tripartite Declaration of Principles on Multinationals and Social Policy* or the

---

105. PAIC, art. 29.3 (2016).

106. Lise Johnson & Lisa Sachs, *International Investment Agreements, 2011–2012: A Review of Trends and New Approaches, in* YEARBOOK ON INTERNATIONAL INVESTMENT LAW & POLICY 2012–2013, at 234 (Andrea Bjorklund ed., 2014).

107. *See* NAFTA, art. 1114.2 (1992); U.S. Model BIT, art. 12 (2012).

108. U.S. Model BIT, art. 12.3 (2012).

109. A rare example is SADC Model BIT, art. 14 (2012).

110. PAIC, art. 37 (2016).

111. PAIC, art. 37.1 (2016).

112. PAIC, art. 8.2, 10.2 (2016). For analysis, *see* Section IV, *infra*.

OECD Guidelines for Multinational Enterprises.[113] When labor issues are addressed, the non-lowering clause is also in this context very often used.[114] However, the PAIC contains several more innovative aspects. It foresees a mechanism of consultation and cooperation between the host state and the foreign investor relating to labor and employment objectives. For instance the investor may consult the host state authorities in order to keep manpower plans in harmony with national social development policies.[115] Furthermore, the investor is obliged to comply with international conventions and existing labor policies, and, in particular, not use child labor[116]. In a follow-up provision, the PAIC encourages member states to develop their human resources capacity. Such policies may include incentives to encourage employers to invest in training, capacity building, and knowledge transfer.[117] Special attention has to be paid to the needs of youth, women, and other vulnerable groups.[118]

4. INTELLECTUAL PROPERTY RIGHTS AND TRADITIONAL KNOWLEDGE

Intellectual property rights (IPRs) traditionally fall under the scope of application of IIAs, most obviously as IPRs are a covered investment under most IIAs.[119] The PAIC also provides protection of intellectual property as a form of foreign investment.[120] The PAIC in addition contains a specific provision on IPRs in the chapter on investment-related issues, which provides that member states ensure the enforcement of IPRs in their territory in accordance with the rights and obligations under relevant international instruments.[121] However, the drafters of the PAIC considered it to be crucial to reiterate the right of member states to provide exceptions to the exclusive rights conferred by an IPR, and allow for its use without the authorization of the right holder, under certain circumstances.[122] Such exceptions might in particular be relevant in the context of access to pharmaceutical products and medicine.

113. *See* Free Trade Agreement between the EFTA States and Montenegro, EFTA-Montenegro, art. 35, Sept. 1, 2011; Free Trade Agreement between the United States and the Republic of Korea, U.S.-S. Kor., arts. 19.1–2, June 30, 2007.

114. *See* U.S. Model BIT, art. 13.2 (2012); Agreement between Japan and the Republic of Iran for the Promotion and Protection of Investment, Japan-Iran, art. 22, July 6, 2012.

115. PAIC, art. 34.2 (2016).

116. PAIC, art. 34 (2016).

117. PAIC, art. 36 (2016).

118. PAIC, art. 36.2 (2016).

119. The Treaty for the Promotion and Protection of Investments, Ger.-Pak., Nov. 25, 1959, 457 U.N.T.S. 24, already covered IPRs. For greater detail, see Lahra Liberti, *Intellectual Property Rights in International Investment Agreements: An Overview*, 6 TRANSNAT'L DISP. MGMT. 1, 5–9 (2009).

120. PAIC, art. 4.4(f) (2016).

121. PAIC, art. 25.1 (2016).

122. PAIC, art. 25.2 (2016).

Another consideration of the drafters of the PAIC was to ensure that African traditional knowledge receives adequate protection. In this respect, member states and investors have to protect "traditional knowledge systems and expressions of culture as well as genetic resources that are sought, used or exploited by investors."[123] The notions of "traditional knowledge systems and expressions of culture" has been taken from the UNESCO Convention on the Diversity of Cultural Expression.[124]

VI. THE PAIC AND DISPUTE SETTLEMENT: QUO VADIS?

Recent treaties maintain arbitration of disputes between contracting parties over the interpretation or application of the agreement.[125] There are, however, variations in IIAs concerning the scope of claims that a state can bring against another state. This will depend on whether the given treaty allows, besides the state-state arbitral mechanism, for investor-state arbitration or not.[126] The PAIC opted for the traditional approach with respect to state-state dispute settlement. Its provision starts off by stating, "Member States are encouraged to resolve any disputes regarding the interpretation and application of this Code initially through consultations, negotiations or mediation."[127] If member states wish to settle their dispute through arbitration, the drafters of the PAIC considered that such proceeding shall take place "at any established African public or African private alternative dispute resolution center or the Permanent Court of Arbitration centers in Africa."[128] By ensuring that the arbitration takes place in the continent it is hoped to foster arbitral institutions in Africa.

Besides state-state dispute settlement the current draft of the PAIC foresees the possibility of investor-state dispute settlement (ISDS) as most of the currently existing IIAs do.[129] In contrast to this treaty practice, the issue of ISDS became extremely controversial over recent years and probably constitutes the most controversial issue in today's global reform debate. There are two broad alternatives that exist, either to keep and reform ISDS as some countries have done,[130] or to abandon and replace

---

123. PAIC, art. 25.3 (2016) (emphasis added).

124. Convention on the Protection and Promotion of the Diversity of Cultural Expressions, Oct. 20, 2005, 2440 U.N.T.S. 311 (emphasis added). The convention recognized traditional knowledge systems as part of humanity's cultural heritage and their protection and promotion as an ethical imperative.

125. See Japan-Iran BIT, art. 19 (2016); Indian Model BIT, art. 15 (2015); Norwegian Model BIT, art. 20 (2015).

126. Brazil-Malawi CIFA, art. 13.6, 53 cmt. (2015); SADC Model BIT, art. 28.2 (2012).

127. PAIC, art. 41.1 (2016) (emphasis added).

128. PAIC, art. 41.2 (2016) (emphasis added).

129. UNCTAD, *Investor-State Dispute Settlement: A Sequel* 18, U.N. Doc. UNCTAD/DIAE/IA/2013/2 (2014).

130. Such as the establishment of a tribunal in EU treaties. See CETA, arts. 8.18–43 (2016) & EU-Vietnam FTA, ch.8, sec. 3 (2016). See also Indian Model BIT, art. 14 (2015).

ISDS as some other countries have done.[131] The global debate is perfectly mirrored in Africa, and ISDS did not fail to be the most controversial aspect during the elaboration of the PAIC. In fact, the provisions dealing with ISDS are the only ones in the PAIC text on which no agreement between the drafters could be found. It is well known that South Africa for instance has a clear policy against ISDS.[132] During the PAIC experts' meetings, South Africa together with a couple of other countries argued for the exclusion of ISDS.[133] However, the majority of African countries still see a need for having ISDS in the PAIC in order to render their countries attractive for foreign investors. It is arguably true that foreign investors have poor trust in African judicial systems. Hence the need for ISDS seems, at least for the time being, inevitable. A possible compromise in future negotiations on the PAIC might be that ISDS will be adopted as an optional annex that may or may not be ratified by an AU member state according to its national political agenda relating to ISDS.

Among the countries in favor of ISDS was a consensus to shape provisions on ISDS in a manner as to avoid the shortcomings of this mechanism and to address some of the critics. Consequently, the investor-state provision of the PAIC includes a couple of important reform approaches. First of all the PAIC provides that "disputes arising between investors and Members States under the specific agreements that govern their relations shall be resolved under those agreements."[134] This provision clearly leaves no room for speculation over potential claims based notably on the investor-state contract. In this respect it works as an "anti-umbrella clause."[135]

More critical however is the question of the exhaustion of local remedies. The traditional approach of IIAs, which can be found in most treaties, is to provide for direct access to international arbitration for a foreign investor or at least access after a "cooling-off period."[136] It was long considered that in many countries an independent judiciary cannot be granted and that the defending state might influence the outcome of the process of an investor-state dispute.[137] This view is challenged today. Some authors argue that the situation in most countries has changed and consequently the exhaustion of local remedies should revive.[138] According to UNCTAD, the requirement of dispute resolution before the domestic courts might

---

131. Such as Indonesia and Brazil.

132. *See* Protection of Investment Act 22 of 2015 (S. Afr.).

133. SADC recommends the exclusion of ISDS. *See* SADC Model BIT, art. 29 (2012).

134. PAIC, art. 42.1 (2016) (emphasis added).

135. Recent trends show that umbrella clauses are no longer included into IIAs. *See* UNCTAD, *supra* note 3, at 113.

136. UNCTAD, *supra* note 129, at 18. Some IIAs require pursuing local remedies for a period of time. *See* Agreement between the Belgium-Luxembourg Economic Union and the Republic of Botswana on the Reciprocal Promotion and Protection of Investments art. 12.2, Jun. 7, 2006; Agreement between the Government of the Republic of Korea and the Government of the Republic of Argentina on the Promotion and Protection of Investments, Arg.-S. Kor., art. 8.3(a), May 17, 1994.

137. DOLZER & SCHREUER, *supra* note 70, at 235.

138. SORNARAJAH, *supra* note 72, at 190.

foster sound and well-working legal and judicial institutions in the host state.[139] SADC as well as IISD also consider this approach to be beneficial for host states since the exhaustion of local remedies can prevent frivolous claims and avoid the important costs of international arbitration.[140] Recent treaty practice shows that the requirement of the exhaustion of local remedies remains quite rare with the exception of the Indian Model BIT.[141] The drafters of the PAIC decided to include the requirement for foreign investors to first exhaust local remedies in the member state where their investment is located before a request for arbitration can be submitted.[142] In this way, investor-state arbitration becomes a remedy of last resort under the PAIC.

As regards the conduct of investor-state arbitration, the PAIC sets out that similarly to state-state arbitration, proceedings "may be conducted at any established African public or African private alternative dispute resolution centre or the Permanent Court of Arbitration centres in Africa (or the African Union Court of Arbitration) or African regional court where applicable."[143]

Another crucial aspect of the ISDS provisions of the PAIC is the express possibility for a state to file a claim against an investor in an investor-state arbitration, a so-called counterclaim. In investment arbitration, it is common that the respondent state includes in its defense to treaty claims one or more criticisms of the investor's conduct. However, such arguments are rarely framed as counterclaims seeking affirmative relief.[144] It is noteworthy that the ICSID Convention accepts counterclaims under certain conditions,[145] however in practice tribunals usually deny jurisdiction on counterclaims due to the absence of a clear treaty provision expressly allowing for such claims by the state.[146] The inclusion of express reference to counterclaims thus stresses the consent for the jurisdiction of these claims and renders the existence of consent to counterclaims beyond doubt. Yet, there are very few examples of treaties that contain an express reference to counterclaims. The first was the COMESA Investment Agreement[147] followed by

---

139. UNCTAD, *supra* note 3, at 149.

140. *See* SADC Model BIT, art. 29.4(b) (2012); IISD Model, art. 45 (2006).

141. Indian Model BIT, art. 14.3 (2015).

142. PAIC, art. 42.3 (2016).

143. PAIC, art. 42.4 (2016) (emphasis added). Arbitral proceedings shall furthermore be governed by the UNCITRAL rules.

144. Jean E. Kalicki, *Counterclaims by States in Investment Arbitration*, IISD Inv. Treaty News, Jan. 14, 2013, https://www.iisd.org/itn/2013/01/14/counterclaims-by-states-in-investment-arbitration-2/.

145. Convention on the Settlement of Investment Disputes between States and Nationals of other States art. 46, Mar. 18, 1965, 575 U.N.T.S. 159.

146. *See* Spyridon Roussalis v. Romania, ICSID Case No. ARB/06/1, Award (Dec. 7, 2011); Goetz v. Burundi, ICSID Case No. ARB/01/2, Award (Jun. 21, 2012).

147. COMESA Investment Agreement, art. 28.9 (2007).

SADC.[148] India also included the possibility of counterclaims in its Model BIT.[149] The PAIC provision dealing with counterclaims reads as follows:

> [w]here an investor or its investment is alleged by a Member State party in a dispute settlement proceeding under this Code to have failed to comply with its obligations under this Code or other relevant rules and principles of domestic and international law, the competent body hearing such a dispute shall consider whether this breach, if proven, is materially relevant to the issues before it, and if so, what mitigating or off-setting effects this may have on the merits of a claim or on any damages awarded in the event of such award.[150]

The inclusion of a provision allowing counterclaims by states will ensure the enforceability of investors' obligations contained in the PAIC.[151] It is worth underlining that a state can invoke any violation of any relevant international treaty protecting the environment, human rights, and labor standards under the PAIC provision on counterclaims. The breadth of potential legal bases of a state's counterclaim is thus very large. Allowing such a broad scope for claims for states goes further than the approaches taken by COMESA, SADC, or India. The three latter models foresee that the basis of a counterclaim has to be a breach by the investor of an obligation set out in the actual IIA.[152]

VII. CONCLUSION

Over the last 50 years of international investment law practice, African countries have been perceived as "investment rules consumers." This is partly due to the asymmetry in terms of economic development between African host countries and investors' home countries.[153] African economies did and still do rely heavily on international private capital commitment. In the hope of attracting more foreign investment, African countries concluded numerous BITs with capital-exporting countries by usually accepting the pre-drafted BIT Models of these countries.

Today, however the African RECs became "investment rules providers" with the adoption of modern investment agreements that apply in their respective region.[154] However, regionalism within Africa bears the risk of overlapping legal commitments

148. SADC Model BIT, art. 19, 29.19 (2012).

149. *See* Indian Model BIT, arts. 14.11, 14.2(i)(b) (2015).

150. PAIC, art. 43 (2016) (emphasis added).

151. SADC suggests this enforcement mechanism to create a monetary liability in domestic courts of the host state for a breach of the treaty obligations by an investor. *See* SADC Model BIT, 39 cmt. (2012).

152. Indian Model BIT, art. 14.11 (2015); SADC Model BIT, art. 19.2 (2012); COMESA Investment Agreement, art. 28.9 (2007).

153. Crosato et al., *supra* note 2, at 30.

154. *Id.*

and uncertainty concerning the applicable rules. If the different RECs in Africa develop each their own investment regime, the risk of fragmentation in Africa is high. The PAIC is potentially an instrument that ensures harmonization throughout the African continent as regards the regulation of foreign investments.

As shown in the above analysis the PAIC is intended to be a *balanced instrument*, meaning it seeks to balance between investment protection and non-investment-related public interests. The drafters of the PAIC did not underrate the need for attracting foreign capital into Africa, yet this need should not neutralize the long-term goal of sustainable development. Africa is one of the world's regions that will certainly attract foreign investment in the next years because of its many and precious natural resources. What is at stake now is to regulate which type of investments and investors operating in Africa should be protected under international law. The answer of the drafters of the PAIC is that it has to be investments that foster the bigger interests and needs of African societies, and its economies, and that do not harm the environment. Thus, foreign investment that will be made in Africa in future years shall be an investment, which is *responsible*.

In the comparative international law perspective, the PAIC is a perfect example for identifying similarities and differences between the regional African approach and other national or regional approaches as regards the design of an IIA. As the international investment law regime is going through a period of review and revision, countries, and regions, as well as international governmental and nongovernmental organizations are discussing various reform approaches.[155] The analysis of the PAIC, by comparing these various approaches, made it possible to see which of the traditional provisions contained in an IIA seem to be successful as well as to see provisions that give rise to national or regional adaptation.[156] Several of the ideas that can be found in the PAIC text are what can be called common approaches in the international discussion on reforming the investment law regime as a whole. Such ideas mainly concern the reformulation of certain treaty standards, the inclusion of societal concerns, and the rethinking of the ISDS system. The ISDS provisions of the PAIC seek in particular to strengthen African arbitral institutions.

Africa unlike Brazil is not making a fundamental contestation of the system of IIAs. The PAIC is rather an African tuning or recalibrating of an international investment instrument. However, some aspects in the PAIC are clearly innovative. The inclusion of direct obligations on investors, for instance, or the specific exceptions to the MFN and national treatment standards or the complete omission of a FET standard have not occurred in other IIAs.[157]

As mentioned before, the PAIC will be adopted as a model treaty serving as a guide for individual member state IIA negotiations. Despite its non-binding nature, the elaboration of the PAIC has permitted African countries to deliberate on their vision of the future shape of IIAs. The PAIC reflects the broad consensus of all

---

155. UNCTAD, *supra* note 3, at 121.

156. Roberts et al., *supra* note 1, at 473.

157. With the exception of the single investor's obligation in the COMESA Investment Agreement, art. 13, 19 (2007).

AU member states on precise provisions over foreign investment regulation and endows Africa with a voice in the international debate on the future and reform of the investment regime. As the comparative analysis has shown, more and more diversity exists in the international investment regime as to how IIAs are designed. The PAIC reflects the development that new IIAs are no longer based on either the North American or European model but rather that other regions also engage to shape IIAs according to their level of economic development and social needs. In particular, the strong emphasis on sustainable development goals in the PAIC bears the potential for the PAIC to also become a model for innovation outside of Africa.

26

Not so Treacherous Waters of International Maritime Law

Islamic Law States and the UN Convention on the Law of the Sea

EMILIA JUSTYNA POWELL

I. INTRODUCTION

The United Nations Convention on the Law of the Sea[1] is a widely accepted, all-encompassing international agreement that regulates the law of the sea. UNCLOS addresses a myriad of topics associated with sea governance, including navigational and economic rights, pollution, conservation of marine resources, scientific exploration, and piracy. Importantly, the Convention has taken on increasing significance in the past several decades as states continue to engage in maritime disputes. The multiple-year negotiations that culminated in the UNCLOS Convention were complex and entailed over 150 countries of different cultural, geographical, and legal backgrounds bargaining over an outcome acceptable to most sides.[2] As a result, 167 countries have ratified the treaty, including accessions and successions. What might seem puzzling is that among the ratifiers are 22 Islamic law states (ILS), states that are traditionally skeptical toward international multilateral treaties.[3] What

1. U.N. Convention on the Law of the Sea, *opened for signature* Dec. 10, 1982, 1833 U.N.T.S. 397 [hereinafter UNCLOS or the Convention].

2. *See* NATALIE KLEIN, DISPUTE SETTLEMENT IN THE UN CONVENTION ON THE LAW OF THE SEA (2005).

3. Islamic law is based primarily on religious principles of human conduct. *See* H. PATRICK GLENN, LEGAL TRADITIONS OF THE WORLD: SUSTAINABLE DIVERSITY IN LAW (5th ed. 2014). I define an Islamic law state as a state, a substantial part of whose official legal system is based on the Quran. *See* Emilia Justyna Powell, *Islamic Law States and Peaceful Resolution of Territorial Disputes,* 69 INT'L ORG. 777 (2015); Emilia Justyna Powell, *Islamic Law States and the Authority of the International Court of Justice: Territorial Sovereignty and Diplomatic Immunity,* 4 L. & CONTEMP. PROBS. 79 (2016). I introduce this categorization strictly for empirical reasons while recognizing the contested

Table 26.1. SIGNATURE AND RATIFICATION RATES ACROSS
DOMESTIC LEGAL SYSTEM TYPES

Signature/Ratification Rates				
International Treaty/ Institution	UNCLOS	International Court of Justice (ICJ) Optional Clause*	International Criminal Court (ICC) the Rome Statute	Permanent Court of Arbitration (PCA) the Convention for the Pacific Settlement of International Disputes
Islamic Law	93/82%	18.5%	59.3/26%	3.7/48%
Civil Law	72/79%	41%	81/71%	35/68%
Common Law	84.8/95.7%	32.6%	71.7/67.4%	4.3/58%
Mixed Law	89.5/78.9%	36.8%	63.2/52.6%	1.6/63%

* In the context of the ICJ, the percentages denote rates of states recognizing the compulsory jurisdiction of the Court (signing the Optional Clause).

makes this particularly remarkable is that UNCLOS includes an extensive system of mandatory dispute resolution procedures, turning the act of ratification into a costly commitment—a type of international commitment that ILS usually avoid.[4] Consider data presented in Table 26.1: UNCLOS ratification rates for ILS (82 percent) are higher than for comparable international instruments of an adjudicative nature, such as the Optional Clause of the International Court of Justice (18.5 percent), the Rome Statute establishing the International Criminal Court (26 percent), or the Convention for the Pacific Settlement of International Disputes that establishes the Permanent Court of Arbitration (48 percent). For the most part, signature rates mirror the ratification patterns.

How truly international is international law? In general, relations between the Islamic world and international law have been at times volatile due to the inherent link between Islamic law and Islamic religion.[5] Sharia is to be an all-embracing and

nature of its name as well as its components. Unlike the scholarship on Islamic law, Islamic civilization, etc., my focus is on states' actions in the international arena. I also do not consider the normative issue of whether it is feasible for any state to enshrine principles of sharia in its institutions. I am also keenly aware of the reality that sharia cannot by any means be reduced to a system of laws. *See* WAEL HALLAQ, THE IMPOSSIBLE STATE (2013); and SHAHAB AHMED, WHAT IS ISLAM? THE IMPORTANCE OF BEING ISLAMIC (2015).

4. Emilia Justyna Powell, *Islamic Law States and the International Court of Justice*, 50 J. PEACE RES. 203 (2013). According to Article 287, states have a procedural choice for peaceful settlement if a dispute dealing with interpretation or application of the Convention arises. The main choices include the International Tribunal for the Law of the Sea (ITLOS), the International Court of Justice (ICJ), or an arbitral tribunal (under Annex VII or VIII). See pp. 15–16 for a detailed description of these procedures.

5. Awn S. Al-Khasawneh, *Islam and International Law*, in ISLAM AND INTERNATIONAL LAW 29 (Marie-Luisa Frick & Andreas T. Müller eds., 2013); Charles N. Brower & Jeremy K. Sharpe, *International Arbitration and the Islamic World: The Third Phase*, 97 AM. J. INT'L L. 643 (2003).

comprehensive guidance to each aspect of life, a means that will direct Muslims to favors and blessings granted by God.[6] In fact, in Islamic law there is to some extent limited separation between rules of law and rules of faith.[7] This lack of distance between legal and religious norms trickles through to Islamic international law, or *siyar*. *Siyar*—as a branch of Islamic law that regulates behavior of Islamic states and individuals in the international arena—parallels the Western concept of international law.[8] Islamic maritime law constitutes an integral part of *siyar*, and like all other substantive areas of Islamic law, is to be cherished, applied, and protected by the Muslim world. *Siyar*'s origins lie in the Quran and the Sunna. Thus, just as adherents to Muslim faith are to abide by sharia, so are Islamic tribes, nations, and states. Islamic scholars conceive of *siyar* as deriving from the eternal truth and justice that God gave to humanity. Islamic international law, just as its Western counterpart, pertains to various issues, such as the Islamic world's dealings with non-Islamic entities, treaty obligations, laws of war, maritime exploration, protection of diplomatic agents, and territorial sovereignty. However, what makes the tenets of *siyar* distinct from the Western international law is the fact that the former, like any substantive and procedural branch of Islamic law, carries the added weight of the will of God and his sanctions.[9]

Thus, the concept of *siyar* introduces a particularly "hard case" for international law to have authority vis-à-vis the Islamic world.[10] At the same time, it provides a unique legal framework within the field of comparative international law. Indeed, many countries have conflicting domestic legislation, but ILS might be at times reluctant to shed conflicting domestic law that is based on sharia. Moreover, *siyar* is more than one of the "distinctive contemporary approaches of particular states or regions toward international law, such as US, Chinese, and EU approaches to international law."[11] The uniqueness of *siyar* is that it goes beyond mere differences in interpretation or application of classic international law. It coexists alongside the law of nations. As such, it contravenes

---

6. I choose to employ the term "Islamic law" to describe the religious law of Islam, the sharia. Sharia is, according to Islamic faith, the expression of the will of God for humans, and it is the most perfect, infallible, just, and perpetual system of laws. See WAEL B. HALLAQ, THE ORIGINS AND EVOLUTION OF ISLAMIC LAW (2005); Majid Khadduri, *Islam and the Modern Law of Nations*, 50 AM. J. INT'L L. 358 (1956). I do so recognizing that the nature of sharia runs beyond the relationship between its legal and non-legal components. See MARSHALL HODGSON, THE VENTURE OF ISLAM: CONSCIENCE AND HISTORY IN A WORLD CIVILIZATION (1974).

7. C.G. WEERAMANTRY, ISLAMIC JURISPRUDENCE: AN INTERNATIONAL PERSPECTIVE 30 (1988). *But see* Ira M. Lapidus, *State and Religion in Islamic Societies*, 151 PAST & PRESENT 3 (1996).

8. Mohd Hisham Mohd Kamal, *Meaning and Method of the Interpretation of Sunnah in the Field of Siyar: A Reappaisal, in* ISLAM AND INTERNATIONAL LAW, *supra* note 5, at 64.

9. LABEEB AHMED BSOUL, INTERNATIONAL TREATIES (MU'AHADAT) IN ISLAMIC PRACTICE IN THE LIGHT OF ISLAMIC INTERNATIONAL LAW (SIYAR) 12 (2008).

10. *See* GARY KING ET AL., DESIGNING SOCIAL INQUIRY (1994); Jason Seawright & John Gerring, *Case Selection Techniques in Case Study Research: A Menu of Qualitative and Quantitative Options*, 61 POL. RES. Q. 294 (2008).

11. Anthea Roberts, Paul B. Stephan, Pierre-Hugues Verdier & Mila Versteeg, *Conceptualizing Comparative International Law*, at 5 (this volume).

Hersch Lauterpacht's definition of international law as "the only branch of law containing identical rules administered as such by the courts of all nations."[12]

ILS, for the most part, did not participate in the creation of the overwhelming majority of substantive classical international law doctrines or rules underlying peaceful dispute resolution. Subsequently, institutional features of most international treaties differ from Islamic law and instead embrace Western values. As one international judge noted, "So there is a lot of truth in the fact that international law reflects what is now a predominant culture and that's Western culture."[13] In fact, some scholars have argued that public international law and Islamic international law constitute divergent legal systems,[14] and that the Islamic world—the Middle East in particular—has emerged as "the underclass of the international system, wherein law is utilized in an instrumental manner."[15] As a result, the argument goes, ILS are unlikely to support Western-based international treaties because these treaties often lack legitimacy in the Islamic world.[16]

Does this pessimistic assessment of the relationship between international law and Islamic law adequately describe ILS's perception of UNCLOS? The issue of the relationship between ILS and international treaties is both important and well timed. Sharia continues to be an authoritative symbol in the majority of ILS. Islamic nonstate actors, governments, political parties, as well as Islamic scholarly and intellectual leaders, despite sometimes weighty differences among them regarding the exact meaning and interpretation of sharia, agree that sharia constitutes an important part of the Islamic world. Are these countries indeed acceptant of institutionalized international maritime law?

UNCLOS has been praised as "one of the most important treaties ever elaborated under the auspices of the United Nations."[17] Some scholars have even labeled the Convention as "a comprehensive constitution for the oceans."[18] In the international

---

12. Hersch Lauterpacht, *Decisions of Municipal Courts as a Source of International Law*, 10 Brit. Y.B. Int'l L. 65, 95 (1929), cited by Roberts, Stephan, Verdier & Versteeg, *supra* note 11, at 3.

13. Author's interview with Judge Awn-Shawkat Al-Khasawneh, vice-president of the ICJ and former prime minister of Jordan (Feb. 18, 2015).

14. *See* William Samuel Dickson Cravens, *The Future of Islamic Legal Arguments in International Boundary Disputes Between Islamic States*, 55 Wash. & Lee L. Rev. 529, 532 (1997).

15. Jean Allain, International Law in the Middle East: Closer to Power than Justice xv (2004).

16. In this chapter, I deal only with peaceful settlement among states and not among individuals. ILS have been supportive of the Convention on the Settlement of Investment Disputes between States and Nationals of Other States (the ICSID Convention), and the UN Convention on the Recognition and Enforcement of Foreign Arbitral Awards.

17. Helmut Tuerk, *The Contribution of the International Tribunal for the Law of the Sea to International Law*, 26 Penn St. Int'l L. Rev. 290 (2007).

18. Tommy T.B. Koh, *A Constitution for the Oceans, in* United Nations Convention on the Law of the Sea 1982: A Commentary 11 (Myron H. Nordquist ed., 1985). The UNCLOS Preamble accurately describes the Treaty's prominence in providing "a legal order for the seas and

relations scholarship, there exists a daunting lack of empirical studies focusing specifically on the Islamic world's view of the international law of the sea. There is a fair amount of work that addresses the Islam-international law nexus in the context of specific international treaties and international organizations.[19] However, most of this literature provides a detailed description of the state of affairs, without taking up the question of the underlying logic, causal explanations, and empirical investigation. Additionally, hardly any empirical studies focus on how the Islamic legal tradition relates to international law with regards to maritime law. Considerably more empirical work has been done in other substantive areas of international law, primarily human rights law, laws of war, and diplomatic protection.[20] How does Islam regulate maritime activities? The Islamic world's potential openness to UNCLOS could presumably be immensely beneficial for the international community as a whole. As research demonstrates, being part of international agreements, especially those that include mandatory dispute resolution procedures, has a pacifying effect on ILS. For example, dyads composed of ILS that sign onto the International Court of Justice have the highest probability of ending the issue at stake once an agreement is reached, significantly higher than for Western law dyads. They also exhibit the highest rates of agreement compliance.[21]

Are ILS—as a distinctive category of countries—indeed willing to make a costly commitment to UNCLOS despite the Convention's elaborate dispute resolution procedures? Is there a synergy of sharia and international maritime law that may explain the Islamic world's attitudes toward UNCLOS? This study provides a compelling analysis to address these puzzles by focusing on substantive international and Islamic law of the sea, as well as rules governing peaceful resolution of disputes in both legal systems. I show that unlike other international treaties, substantive provisions of UNCLOS express principles historically present in Islamic law. Additionally, peaceful resolution procedures of the Convention incorporate ILS's desire for flexibility in conflict management as well as Islamic preference for nonconfrontational dispute resolution.

II. THEORY: THE SUBSTANTIVE AND PROCEDURAL CONGRUENCE OF ISLAMIC LAW AND THE UNCLOS REGIME

Why do states choose to be part of only some international agreements but not others? While a skeptical realist might see international treaties, especially treaties

oceans which will facilitate international communication, and will promote the peaceful uses of the seas and oceans."

19. Brower & Sharpe, *supra* note 5; Cravens, *supra* note 14; Urfan Khaliq, *The International Court of Justice and Its Use of Islam: Between a Rock and a Hard Place?*, 2 OXFORD J.L. & RELIGION 98 (2013); Catherine Sims & Emilia Justyna Powell, *Religion in International Law: Francisco de Vitoria, Islamic Law, and the International Court of Justice* (Univ. Notre Dame Working Paper).

20. *See generally* ISLAM AND INTERNATIONAL LAW, *supra* note 5; KRISTINE KALANGES, RELIGIOUS LIBERTY IN WESTERN AND ISLAMIC LAW: TOWARD A WORLD LEGAL TRADITION (2012).

21. SARA MCLAUGHLIN MITCHELL & EMILIA JUSTYNA POWELL, DOMESTIC LAW GOES GLOBAL: LEGAL TRADITIONS AND INTERNATIONAL COURTS (2011).

with dispute resolution provisions, as an idealist's waste of time,[22] other scholars have suggested that countries take on international obligations to "lock-in" favored policies in the face of prospective political uncertainty,[23] to provide costly signals of a commitment to future behavior,[24] or to impose self-constraints when treaties help them solve problems efficiently.[25] Others claim that one of the reasons states sign and subsequently ratify international treaties is that they authentically agree with principles and values these agreements embody. In essence, states' actions on the international arena reflect their domestic ideological and legal biases.[26] This is particularly true in the case of treaties that contain costly commitments, such as compulsory dispute settlement provisions, which oblige treaty parties to use peaceful conflict management mechanisms such as negotiations, mediation, or adjudication.

Because of inherent uncertainty associated with the application of international law, I argue that countries are more supportive of an international treaty if it employs substantive as well as procedural rules similar to that country's own domestic legal system.[27] States perceive international law through their own legal culture.[28] These differences in perception of international law are fundamentally based on how each society understands the nature of law, justice, and conflict resolution.[29] Jouannet calls this process the "selling of each national legal model in order

22. *See* Hans Morgenthau, Politics Among Nations: The Struggle for Power and Peace (1948).

23. *See* Andrew Moravcsik, *The Origins of Human Rights Regimes: Democratic Delegation in Postwar Europe*, 54 Int'l Org. 217 (2000).

24. *See* Edward D. Mansfield & Jon C. Pevehouse, *Democratization and International Organizations*, 60 Int'l Org. 137 (2006).

25. *See* Barbara Koremenos, *If Only Half of International Agreements Have Dispute Resolution Provisions, Which Half Needs Explaining?*, 36 J. Legal Stud. 189 (2007).

26. *See* Powell, *Islamic Law States and Peaceful Resolution of Territorial Disputes, supra* note 3; Mitchell & Powell, *supra* note 21; Beth A. Simmons, Mobilizing for Human Rights: International Law in Domestic Politics (2009); Anne-Marie Slaughter, *International Law in a World of Liberal States*, 6 Eur. J. Int'l L. 503 (1995).

27. Arguments advanced here address the question of why Islamic law states join UNCLOS, which is quite different from the issue of treaties' institutional design. *See* Kenneth W. Abbott et al., *The Concept of Legalization*, 54 Int'l Org. 401 (2000); Barbara Koremenos et al., *The Rational Design of International Institutions*, 55 Int'l Org. 761 (2001); Koremenos, *supra* note 25.

28. Raymond Cohen, *Language and Conflict Resolution: The Limits of English*, 3 Int'l Stud. Rev. 25 (2001); Charles H. Koch, *Envisioning a Global Legal Culture*, 25 Mich. J. Int'l L. (2003).

29. Mohammed Abu-Nimer, *An Islamic Model of Conflict Resolution: Principles and Challenges, in* Crescent and Dove 73 (Qamar-ul Huda ed., 2010). There is a voluminous scholarship, mostly descriptive, on cultural and especially linguistic differences in the context of dispute resolution (In the context of Islamic law, see Uzma Rehman, *Conflict Resolution and Peacemaking in Islam: Toward Reconciliation and Complementarity Between Western and Muslim Approaches*, 50 Islamic Stud. 55 (2011)).

to influence the establishment of international norms and institutions."[30] The more congruence between a treaty and a state's domestic legal system, the more likely is a state to support an international agreement. This mechanism is especially evident with regards to comprehensive international conventions with intricate rules outlining peaceful dispute resolution procedures. Each legal system, or if one prefers a more encompassing concept—each legal tradition—embraces quite divergent approaches to dispute resolution.[31] These unique approaches, or paradigms of conflict resolution, are sometimes deep-seated and strongly ingrained in the fabric of a country, reflecting its domestic legal system, culture, and religion.[32] In fact, in some instances specific legal rules or values embedded in an international treaty can cause certain countries to be "alienated from their own legal traditions."[33] All else being equal, comprehensive international conventions may not accomplish much in terms of decreasing uncertainty about the interpretation of international law. Thus, states must look for other clues to reduce ambiguity in the international realm. Interstate maritime relations—although regulated by UNCLOS—are still tainted by information problems and uncertainty about norms and about behavior of other states.

As history demonstrates, disputes over maritime zones, internal waters, and offshore natural resources are commonplace. Thus, states are likely to engage in structured bargaining within institutional limits established by UNCLOS. This bargaining entails using dispute resolution forums specifically outlined in the Convention, including arbitration and adjudication. When such venues render a decision, the facts of each case are filtered through the procedural rules of a particular adjudicator, and are subject to the process of interpretation. Similarity between domestic law and laws embedded into a treaty provides states with better insight into the intricate system of the treaty's rules. States have incentives to join a treaty created in their own legal image to lessen uncertainty in bargaining.

UNCLOS is a sophisticated agreement, full of legal terms and concepts contained in the total of 320 Articles and 9 Annexes. Part XV of UNCLOS that regulates settlement of disputes comprises 21 meticulously crafted Articles.[34] Legal congruence can provide a useful tool to navigate these laws. The section below shows an important congruence in Islamic and international maritime law.

---

30. Emmanuelle Jouannet, *French and American Perspectives on International Law: Legal Cultures and International Law*, 58 Me. L. Rev. 293 (2006).

31. In the comparative law literature, the technical terms of art for a group of countries that share substantial legal affinity has been "families of law," as coined by René David in the early 1960s (*see* Rene David, Les Grands Systèmes De Droit Contemporains (1964)). More recently, the concept of "legal traditions" as propagated by H. Patrick Glenn seems to have swept the scholarly field in its effort to provide a term for legal constellations (*see* Glenn, *supra* note 3).

32. Cohen uses the term "paradigms of conflict resolution," which I believe accurately describes the fundamental differences in how different legal systems and different cultures approach dispute resolution. Cohen, *supra* note 28, at 26.

33. Al-Khasawneh, *supra* note 13.

34. Information obtained from the UN website: http://www.un.org (last visited Aug. 1, 2017).

A. UNCLOS and Islamic Maritime Law: Substantive Congruence

Law of the sea is present in Islamic law sources in a form highly compatible with international law. The Quran urges Muslims to engage in expeditions on the seas as well as exploiting the rich maritime resources.[35] Also, the Sunna includes many Hadiths, or traditions, that encourage maritime activities such as overseas expeditions and trade activities.[36] One tradition explicitly provides that "a maritime expedition is better than ten campaigns of conquest on land."[37] The Islamic world has also been prolific in compiling written legal documents on maritime law. Despite the fact that there was relatively little room for any international laws in the Middle Ages, Mohammed ibn al-Hasan al-Shaybani, a prominent Islamic jurist of the Hanafite school, wrote an *Introduction to the Law of Nations* at the end of the eighth century, long before the systematization and codification of international law in Europe by Grotius and other prominent Western writers.[38] During the early 900s, the first Islamic law of the sea treatise, the *Treatise Concerning the Leasing of Ships and the Claims Between Their Passengers* was assembled.[39] Other maritime treaties originating between the thirteenth and fifteenth centuries addressed the status of high seas as well as inland and offshore waters.[40] For example, the maritime code of Malacca compiled at the end of the fifteenth century comprehensively regulated commercial and maritime activities.[41]

Early Islamic historical accounts, jurisprudential queries, and treaties demonstrate that Islamic law distinguished between the high seas, the area of the sea beyond the reach of any state's political authorities; maritime belts, where state authorities had certain but limited privileges; and inland waters, which were subject to administration by the state. Most important, Islamic religious sources and

---

35. The Quran comprises rules that God revealed to the Prophet Muhammad. The Sunna literally means "the path taken or trodden" by the Prophet Muhammad (GLENN, *supra* note 3). Judicial consensus (*ijma*) and analogical reasoning (*qiyas*) constitute subsidiary sources of Islamic law.

36. Several Western scholars assert that the Islamic world during the classical period (827–1252) was apprehensive of the sea (JAMES HORENELL, WATER TRANSPORT: ORIGINS AND EARLY EVOLUTION (1946)). However, a vast majority of Muslim historians disagree with this view, arguing that the fear of the sea was propagated by the political rulers such as provincial governors and caliphs, and was absent in the original Islamic law sources, such as the Quran and the sunna (HASSAN S. KHALILIEH, ISLAMIC MARITIME LAW (1998)). Schools of Islamic jurisprudence also differed on this issue, with some of them approving the high seas travel, while others rejected it.

37. KHALILIEH, *supra* note 36.

38. HUGO GROTIUS, ON THE LAW OF WAR AND PEACE was published in 1625.

39. Robert Lopez, *The Trade of Medieval Europe: The South, in* THE CAMBRIDGE ECONOMIC HISTORY OF EUROPE FROM THE DECLINE OF THE ROMAN EMPIRE 306 (Edward Miller et al. eds., 2d ed. 1987).

40. Some of these documents dealt with very specific issues such as the importance of the ship's name, and the duties and rights of ship owners, crew, and passengers.

41. Ram Prajash Anand, *Maritime Practice in South-East Asia Until 1600 A.D. and the Modern Law of the Sea*, 30 INT'L & COMP. L.Q. 445 (1981).

political authorities have refrained from claiming any permanent legal dominion over the high seas. Even the existence of a conflictual relationship between an ILS and a non-ILS was never considered "an obstacle to the freedom of navigation."[42] Such an approach was reflective of modern international law to a much larger extent than the contemporaneous view of the Western world. In the Middle Ages, several European states frequently made wide claims over vast areas of the ocean that led to limited freedom of navigation.[43] In fact, some scholars propose that freedom of the seas "was lost and forgotten in Europe after the disintegration of the Roman Empire."[44] Terms such as "mare nostrum" (our sea) and "mare clausum" (closed sea) expressed the Western approach that a complete freedom of the seas constituted a significant impediment to international politics.[45] It was not until the second half of the nineteenth century that the freedom of the seas doctrine as well as other modern norms of maritime international law were formulated to further the needs of European commercial interests.

In sum, the substantive Islamic maritime law and practice have been since the beginning highly compatible with modern international law of the sea as expressed in UNCLOS. Section 1 of the Convention outlines principles governing the status of high seas, stipulating that "the high seas are open to all States" (Article 87) and "shall be reserved for peaceful purposes" (Article 88). The freedom of high seas encompasses several activities such as navigation, over flight, and scientific research. Additionally, the Convention forbids any state to "validly purport to subject any part of the high seas to its sovereignty" (Article 89). In many ways, Islamic law of the sea was several centuries ahead of the Western world's regulation of maritime activities.

B. UNCLOS and Islamic Maritime Law: Procedural Congruence

UNCLOS dispute resolution procedures incorporate ILS's desire for nonviolent dispute resolution, as well as flexibility in conflict management. States have been given an unprecedented choice of settlement venues should a dispute regarding the interpretation or application of the Convention arise: the International Tribunal for the Law of the Sea (ITLOS), the International Court of Justice (ICJ), or an

---

42. KHALILIEH, *supra* note 36.

43. For example, maritime republics such as the Republic of Venice and the Republic of Genoa declared a mare clausum policy in the Mediterranean Sea. Also Nordic states and England attempted to control sea travels via establishing passage rates and monopolies on fishing rights.

44. RAM PRAKASH ANAND, ORIGIN AND DEVELOPMENT OF THE LAW OF THE SEA 440 (1982).

45. The term "mare nostrum" originally was used by Romans to describe the status of the Mediterranean Sea after the conquest of Sicily, Sardinia, and Corsica during the Punic Wars (264 to 146 A.D.). Mare clausum is an exception to *mare libris* (free sea, which is open to navigation to all states' ships). The mare clausum principle started to lose its significance in the late eighteenth and early nineteenth centuries due to the needs of the Commercial and Industrial Revolutions. *See* ANAND, *supra* note 44, at 137.

arbitral tribunal (under Annex VII or VIII).[46] Countries are allowed to choose one of these options a priori and they can specify their rank order of these procedures. The unparalleled flexibility of Article 287—the "choice of procedure" article— came as the result of "states' inability, during UNCLOS III, to agree on a single third-party forum to which recourse should be had when informal mechanisms failed to resolve a dispute."[47] If a state party chooses not to make an Article 287 declaration, the default dispute settlement procedure is Annex VII arbitration.

It is important, however, to place Article 287 in the overall context of the Convention's general rules on peaceful settlement, especially the preceding Article 279 that urges state parties to "settle any dispute between them concerning the interpretation or application of the Convention by peaceful means" in accordance with the UN Charter's mandate of peaceful settlement. The Convention also gives priority to any existing compulsory dispute settlement mechanisms that are binding on the disputants (Article 282). Thus, if the disputing parties have previously agreed to give jurisdiction to a specified settlement venue that entails a binding decision, such as the ICJ or the International Maritime Organization, then neither party can object to that venue's adjudicative prerogatives. Additionally, UNCLOS grants precedence to informal dispute settlement mechanisms, such as negotiations or other diplomatic means (Article 283).[48] Among all other non-binding methods, the Convention gives particular attention to conciliation, encouraging its use by disputing states. Inherently, the goal of conciliation proceedings is not to focus on strict application of law, but "to promote an amicable settlement."[49]

The wide choice of settlement procedures within the UNCLOS framework is truly unparalleled. As a general pattern, international treaties either do not call for obligatory resolution of disputes, or include reference to only one or a few settlement venues.[50] In the particular context of maritime law, the analogous rules of the 1958 Geneva Conventions on the Law of the Sea constituted merely an optional protocol adapted by around 30 states. In contrast, UNCLOS dispute resolution provisions constitute an integral part of the Convention and are inseparable from

---

46. In the Annex VII arbitration, the list of arbitrators "experienced in maritime affairs" is submitted by each state party (UNCLOS, Annex VII, art. 2). In the spirit of flexibility, the Convention lays down no requirements concerning legal qualifications of the arbitrators. Annex VIII arbitration is designed to deal with highly specialized disputes such as those over fisheries or navigation. This type of arbitral tribunal may be composed of technical experts from specialized agencies and organizations, who may be better qualified than general judges to deal with highly technical maritime issues. The arbitrators are to be experts in the fields of fisheries, protection of the marine environment, marine scientific research, and navigation. UNCLOS, Annex VIII, art. 2.

47. John E. Noyes, *The Territorial Tribunal for the Law of the Sea*, 100 AM. J. INT'L L. 119 (1998).

48. The disputants can at any time abandon the UNCLOS settlement techniques and resort to any peaceful method of their own choice.

49. J.G. MERRILLS, INTERNATIONAL DISPUTE SETTLEMENT 191 (2011).

50. Andrew T. Guzman, *The Cost of Credibility: Explaining Resistance to Interstate Dispute Resolution Mechanisms*, 31 J. LEGAL STUD. 303 (2002).

its substantive maritime laws. UNCLOS dispute resolution provisions, denoted as a "cafeteria" approach to compulsory settlement,[51] or a "package deal,"[52] are unlike any other maritime regulation.

Sharia's principles of dispute resolution are highly similar to these of the UNCLOS Convention. Islamic law places emphasis on moral and just relations between states and calls for peaceful resolution of interstate disputes. At the same time, however, Islamic law puts a premium on apology, acknowledgment, reconciliation, and compassion as vital outcomes of any dispute settlement process. Reminiscent of international non-binding third-party methods such as conciliation or mediation, *sulh*, a non-formal amicable settlement between the disputants with help from a third party, was the Prophet Muhammad's favored method of managing conflict.[53]

The use of *sulh*, and more generally the prominence of reconciliation, has its origins in pre-Islamic tribal law. Peaceful and long-lasting settlement of all intertribal contentions was necessary to successfully deal with survival in the harsh realities of nomadic desert life: it helped ensure tribes' continued existence by preventing disputes from turning into warfare. Interestingly, these informal reconciliation methods are still used at local and village level disputes in several ILS. Some examples include informal conflict resolution procedures such as jirga and shura in Afghanistan, *sulh* in Jordan, or traditional justice system and community-sponsored conciliation in rural Morocco.[54] In some of these countries, mediation between disputants is also encouraged officially by the courts.

All states—Islamic or not—have the option to resolve disputes via a variety of means across the entirety of issues covered by UNCLOS. Yet, while Western legal systems embrace or even promote courts, Islamic law prioritizes nonconfrontational informal dispute resolution. Islamic law's preference toward informal modes of resolution carries over into the international arena. As research demonstrates, ILS naturally gravitate toward the non-binding third-party methods such as mediation and conciliation in resolution of their disputes. These methods not only

---

51. Alan E. Boyle, *Dispute Settlement and the Law of the Sea Convention: Problems of Fragmentation and Jurisdiction*, 46 INT'L & COMP. L. Q. 40 (1997).

52. JOHN COLLIER & VAUGHAN LOWE, THE SETTLEMENT OF DISPUTES IN INTERNATIONAL LAW: INSTITUTIONS AND PROCEDURES 86 (2009).

53. George Sayen, *Arbitration, Conciliation, and the Islamic Legal Tradition in Saudi Arabia*, 24 UNIV. PA. J. INT'L ECON. L. 905 (2003). The Quran teaches, "The recompense for an injury is an injury equal thereto (in degree): but if a person forgives and makes reconciliation, his reward is due from God: For God loveth not those who do wrong." Sura XLII, Verse 40.

54. Leila Hanafi, *Moudawana and Women's Rights in Morocco: Balancing National and International Law*, 18 ILSA J. INT'L & COMP. L. 515 (2011–2012); DANIEL PHILPOTT, JUST AND UNJUST PEACE: AN ETHIC OF POLITICAL RECONCILIATION (2012); Ali Wardak, *Building a Post-war Justice System in Afghanistan*, 41 CRIME, L. & SOC. CHANGE 319 (2004); Jirga in Afghanistan consists of local elders and important male figures "that make consultative but binding and non-appealable decisions" Mahammad Hashim Kamali, *References to Islam and Women in the Afghan Constitution*, 22 ARAB L. Q. 270 (2008). Shura constitutes a method of collective consultation, which is grounded in the traditions of the Prophet Muhammad, who recommended placing a matter before the followers for consultation should other legal sources be silent on an issue.

promote reconciliation between the disputing states through flexible out-of-court procedures, but also enable these countries to solicit help from an Islamic inter-mediary and to potentially include sharia principles in the process of settlement.[55] UNCLOS, unlike many international treaties, offers a wide option of settlement venues, and thus fulfills ILS's desire for flexibility in dispute resolution. Two stipula-tions of the Convention: Article 283, which gives priority to informal dispute set-tlement mechanisms, and Article 284, which promotes conciliation, make dispute resolution under UNCLOS particularly attractive to the Islamic world. In addition to negotiations and non-binding third-party methods, the Convention provides states with a choice of two courts: ITLOS and the ICJ. Importantly, ILS are, accord-ing to the Convention, free to choose any form of settlement resolution in any *order* they wish, which plays a fundamental role in Islamic law. Although the Quran acknowledges and fully permits the use of adjudication, Muslims as well as ILS are encouraged to choose negotiations and the non-binding methods first, and then resort to adjudication as the last step. According to Mohammed AlQasimi, "resort-ing to a court is the final step, which is not recommended by the Quran"; at the same time, however, even though negotiations and non-binding third-party methods are preferable, "there is nothing, be it in the Quran or in the Saying of the Prophet, there is nothing which prohibits adjudication as a method of solving disputes."[56]

Interestingly, adjudication has been historically present in Islamic maritime law and practice. Early accounts of maritime cases, jurisprudence, and commercial treaties dating from the eleventh to fifteenth centuries demonstrate that adjudica-tion, loosely defined, was an important method of settlement. The *Bahrain-Qatar* dispute over the Hawar Islands and four other territories—which naturally raised issues of maritime delimitation—constitutes an informative example of how ILS approach international courts. [57] The long-standing contention was finally settled by the ICJ in a 2001 judgment that awarded each side a part of the disputed territory.[58] Interestingly, the parties resorted to the ICJ only after Quran-supported informal reconciliation efforts in the late 1980s and 1990s failed to provide a solution accept-able to both sides. In the words of one international advocate, the *Bahrain-Qatar* dispute is a prime example of disputants calling upon the ICJ as a last resort venue, precisely because prior attempts at mediation had failed.[59]

---

55. Powell, *Islamic Law States and Peaceful Resolution of Territorial Disputes, supra* note 3.

56. Memorandum of conversation with Mohammed AlQasimi, Vice Dean, College of Law, United Arab Emirates University (Mar. 12, 2013).

57. Maritime Delimitation and Territorial Questions between Qatar and Bahrain (Qatar v. Bahrain), Judgment, 2001 I.C.J. 87 (Mar. 16). The protracted contention was over several territories: the Hawar Islands, the island of Janan/Hadd Janan, the shoals of Quit'at Jaradah and Fasht ad Dibald, and Zubarah, a town site on the northwest coast of Qatar. *See* CONSTANZE SCHULTE, COMPLIANCE WITH DECISIONS OF THE INTERNATIONAL COURT OF JUSTICE 234–35 (2004).

58. Bahrain kept the Hawar Islands and Quit'at Jaradah. The Court determined that Qatar had sov-ereignty over Zubarah, Janan/Hadd Janan, and the Fasht ad Dibald.

59. Author's interview with an anonymous international lawyer who has appeared repeatedly in the ICJ's cases as a state advocate (Oct. 2013).

Islamic maritime laws are highly compatible with UNCLOS. I argue that the synergy between sharia and international law has the power to attract ILS to the Convention. Thus, in contrast with many other international treaties, ILS's rates of support for UNCLOS should be at least comparable to those of non-ILS. Since its beginnings, international law has leaned heavily on Western, mainly European, conceptions of law originating from the civil and common legal systems.[60] States representing Western legal traditions participated actively in the process of the creation of substantive international law, and were able to implant their legal rules into the international legal system. As a result, for the most part, international law as well as international venues for peaceful dispute resolution reflect Western legal values. As one international practitioner noted, "Islamic law should not be brought in to help interpret general principles of international law. International law is international law. Islamic law is Islamic law."[61] Thus, in most cases, it is civil and common law countries that sign and ratify international treaties. UNCLOS, however, is different. Based on my theory, I propose the following hypotheses:

Hypothesis 1: ILS are at least as likely as civil and common law states to sign and ratify UNCLOS.

An interesting feature of the UNCLOS Convention is that it allows the ratifiers to comment on its substantive and procedural provisions. States can place declarations and restrictions on the Convention. For example, according to Article 310, states can make declarations or statements concerning the application of the Convention at the time of joining the treaty, which do not exclude or modify the legal effect of the Convention's provisions. Additionally, UNCLOS enables the ratifiers to identify the dispute resolution forum of their choice (Article 287) and to exempt specific types of disputes from the compulsory settlement provisions (Article 298). In sum, declarations and restrictions deal with particulars of each ratifying state's commitments in the framework of the Convention and can customize states' obligations.[62] This mechanism provides an important "modification tool" to UNCLOS joiners, because different countries face different levels of uncertainty in the context of the Convention. These clauses enable countries to respond individually to their own specific risks by choosing from the available range of design options to engineer their own treaty commitment.[63] For example, upon ratification, Canada exempted itself, inter alia, from the compulsory dispute resolution provisions relating to its law enforcement

---

60. For description of domestic legal systems, see the Research Design section of the chapter.

61. Anonymous ICJ state advocate, *supra* note 59.

62. The literature on the design of international agreements demonstrates that during treaty negotiations, states pay close attention to both substantive treaty standards, such as the depth/precision of rules, as well as to procedural issues, including monitoring provisions (Emilie M. Hafner-Burton et al., *Emergency and Escape: Explaining Derogations from Human Rights Treaties*, 65 INT'L ORG. 673 (2011); Koremenos et al., *supra* note 27.

63. Peter B. Rosendorff & Helen V. Milner, *The Optimal Design of International Trade Institutions: Uncertainty and Escape*, 55 INT'L ORG. 829 (2001).

activities within its exclusive economic zones;[64] Algeria declared that it would not submit any disputes arising out of the Convention to the ICJ, unless there was a specific agreement between all disputants outside the framework of UNCLOS.[65]

ILS have been traditionally careful in drafting their international commitments, showing a high propensity to customize their treaty obligations. This is especially the case in the context of any international dispute mechanisms, where an international court's rulings "often conflict with and seek to displace well-established or assumed interpretations of legal rules or social norms."[66] For example, ILS optional declaration clauses at the ICJ are substantially longer in comparison with clauses of other countries, reflecting the tendency of ILS to embed more reservations in their commitments to the World Court.[67] Because the Quran obliges the faithful to keep their promises, all contracts and treaties are subject to the pacta sunt servanda rule.[68] Such obligation is binding in relation to other Muslims and nonbelievers. This rule, ipso facto, encourages careful and detailed contractual design, as ILS have important incentives to ensure that their obligations and rights are clearly stated. Based on characteristics of Islamic law and the nature of UNCLOS declarations and restrictions, I propose the following hypothesis:

> *Hypothesis 2:* ILS are more likely than civil and common law states to place declarations and restrictions on UNCLOS.

III. RESEARCH DESIGN

To evaluate my theoretical arguments linking congruence of international and Islamic maritime law to ILS behavior toward UNCLOS (signature, ratification, placing declarations/restrictions), I use information taken from the UNCLOS website page specifying the "Status of the Convention and of the related Agreements" as of July 21, 2011.[69] In this time period, 161 (82 percent) of 193 states in the world ratified or acceded to the Convention. *UNCLOS Signature* and *UNCLOS Ratification* status constitute my dependent variables that directly relate to Hypothesis 1. Table 26.2 stratifies signature and ratification decisions by countries' domestic legal traditions, focusing on four major legal traditions in the world: civil law,

---

64. UNCLOS Declaration of Canada (Nov. 7, 2003), http://www.un.org/Depts/los/convention_agreements/convention_declarations.htm.

65. UNCLOS Declaration of Algeria (June 11, 1996), http://www.un.org/Depts/los/convention_agreements/convention_declarations.htm.

66. Karen J. Alter et al., *How Context Shapes the Authority of International Courts*, 79 L. &. CONTEMP. PROBS. (2016).

67. MITCHELL & POWELL, *supra* note 21.

68. S.E. RAYNER, THE THEORY OF CONTRACTS IN ISLAMIC LAW: A COMPARATIVE ANALYSIS WITH PARTICULAR REFERENCE TO THE MODERN LEGISLATION IN KUWAIT, BAHRAIN, AND THE UNITED ARAB EMIRATES (1991).

69. U.N. Division for Oceans Affairs and Law of the Sea, http://www.un.org/Depts/los/index.htm.

Table 26.2. UNCLOS SIGNATURE/RATIFICATION STATUS: CIVIL, COMMON, AND
ISLAMIC LAW STATES, DETAILED STATISTICS

UNCLOS Signature and Ratification	Civil law		Common law		Islamic law		Mixed law		Total	
	Sign.	Rat.	Sign.	Rat.	Sign.	Rat.	Sign.	Rat.	Sign.	Rat.
No	27 (26%)	24 (23%)	6 (13%)	2 (4%)	2 (7%)	5 (18%)	2 (10%)	4 (21%)	37 (19%)	35 (18%)
Yes	75 (74%)	78 (77%)	40 (87%)	44 (96%)	26 (93%)	23 (82%)	18 (90%)	16 (79%)	159 (81%)	161 (82%)
Total	102 (52.5%)		46 (23.5%)		28 (14%)		20 (10%)		196 (100%)	

Table 26.3. UNCLOS DECLARATIONS AND RESTRICTIONS

	UNCLOS Declarations and Restrictions	
	Mean	Range
Civil Law	2.3	(0–30)
Common Law	1.2	(0–12)
Islamic Law	2.5	(0–9)
Mixed Law	.9	(0–7)

common law, Islamic law, and mixed law.[70] The data fit with my theoretical expectations, demonstrating that ILS are comparable to states from other legal traditions in terms of their levels of support for UNCLOS. In fact, signature rates are the highest for ILS (93 percent). As for ratification, ILS with an 82 percent ratification rate come in second place, after common law states (96 percent).

The number of *UNCLOS Declarations/Restrictions* is the second dependent variable that I use to test Hypothesis 2. I gathered original data from the UNCLOS website, which lists all stipulations states add to their Convention commitments.[71] Usually, countries place declarations and restrictions upon ratification, formal confirmation, accession, or succession to a treaty.[72] Table 26.3 displays information regarding the number of declarations and restrictions placed on UNCLOS across domestic legal traditions. ILS place, on average, the highest number of restrictions and declarations (mean 2.5), higher than common law (1.2), civil law (2.3), or

70. Please see the next page for a detailed description of domestic legal systems.

71. U.N. Division for Oceans Affairs and Law of the Sea, Declarations and Statements, http://www.un.org/Depts/los/convention_agreements/convention_declarations.htm.

72. Accession is an act through which a state agrees to be legally bound by a treaty. The legal effects of accession are the same as for ratification. However, accession is not preceded by an act of signature. Succession in the context of an international treaty takes place when one state replaces another state in the responsibility for the international relations of territory.

Table 26.4. ISLAMIC LAW STATES IN UNCLOS

Islamic law state	Signature	Ratification	Restrictions and declarations
Afghanistan	1	0	0
Algeria	1	1	5
Bahrain	1	1	0
Comoros	1	1	0
Egypt	1	1	9
Gambia	1	1	0
Indonesia	1	1	0
Iran	1	0	8
Iraq	1	1	2
Jordan	0(a)*	1	0
Kuwait	1	1	1
Lebanon	1	1	0
Libya	1	0	0
Malaysia	1	1	9
Maldives	1	1	0
Mauritania	1	1	0
Morocco	1	1	5
Nigeria	1	1	0
Oman	1	1	7
Pakistan	1	1	3
Qatar	1	1	1
Saudi Arabia	1	1	7
Sudan	1	1	4
Syria	0	0	0
Tunisia	1	1	8
UAE	1	0	0
Yemen	1	1	2
Total: 27	25	22	71

* accession

mixed law states (0.9).[73] Table 26.4 provides additional information on specific ILS that have signed/ratified the Convention as well as the number of declarations and restrictions placed by these countries. Out of all ILS, only Syria has not signed the Convention (Jordan joined via accession), and Afghanistan, Iran, Libya, Syria, and

73. Interestingly, ILS have the smallest number of objections to UNCLOS. In fact, to this day no ILS has placed an objection regarding any UNCLOS stipulation. Non-ILS have objected, albeit rarely, to several provisions of the Convention.

United Arab Emirates have not ratified the Convention. Fourteen (14) ILS place at least one declaration or restriction on their UNCLOS commitment, ranging from 1 (Kuwait, Qatar) to 9 (Egypt and Malaysia).

The main variable of interest, *Islamic Law*, is used along three other dichotomous variables (*Civil Law, Common Law, Mixed Law*) to capture a state's domestic legal tradition. Following my previous work, I define an Islamic law state as a state a substantial part of whose *official legal system is directly* based on the Quran, however interpreted by the state. This definition does not hinge on religion or political preferences of citizens, but rather on whether a country officially and directly applies sharia as a substantial part of personal, civil, commercial, or criminal law. Again, as mentioned in the introduction, this study does not consider the normative question of whether Islamic law as integrated in modern state governance accurately reflects the traditional sharia. That said, I acknowledge a strong debt to scholarship that ponders these seminal issues.[74] With these caveats in mind, I believe that introducing the ILS category can help shed light onto the Islamic world's preferences on the international arena, particularly in the context of empirical approaches. The ILS category differs from other seemingly related definitions, such as "Islamic states," "Arab states," or "Muslim states," all of which emphasize a particular defining feature of "Islam-ness." For example, the category "Muslim states" usually denotes countries with a majority Muslim population, and the term "Islamic states" is often used to describe countries with particularly religious populations.[75] Thus, although fitting in the "Muslim states" category, Turkey with its overwhelmingly Muslim population cannot be classified as an Islamic law state as defined here because its official legal system is secular. I base my coding on Powell and Sara Mitchell's categorization of ILS, as well as other subsidiary sources.[76]

The non-Islamic legal traditions include *Civil Law, Common Law, and Mixed Law.* The civil legal tradition, rooted in the laws of the Roman Empire, largely relies on the written letter of law (codes), which meticulously regulates each substantive and procedural area of law. Common law, originally stemming from the laws of the British Isles, embraces the doctrine of stare decisis, or precedent, and has historically relied to a much smaller extent on the written letter of law. The mixed legal system combines elements from two or more legal traditions.[77]

---

74. *See* HALLAQ, *supra* note 3; Hodgson *supra* note 6; NOAH FELDMAN, THE FALL AND RISE OF THE ISLAMIC STATE (2008); Lapidus, *supra* note 7.

75. *See* Maurits Berger, *Islamic Views on International Law, in* CULTURE AND INTERNATIONAL LAW 110 (Paul Meerts ed., 2008). To remedy the fuzziness of the "Muslim states" category, some scholars choose to use a more precise term of "Muslim majority states." *See* Anver M. Emon, *Shari'a and the Modern State, in* ISLAMIC LAW AND INTERNATIONAL LAW: SEARCHING FOR COMMON GROUND? 52 (Anver M. Emon et al. eds., 2012).

76. *See* Sara McLaughlin Mitchell & Emilia Justyna Powell, *Legal Systems and the Peaceful Resolution of Territorial Disputes,* 69 J. POL. 397 (2007); MITCHELL & POWELL, *supra* note 21. Other sources include the CIA World Factbook, https://www.cia.gov/library/publications/the-world-factbook/, and HERBERT M. KRITZER, LEGAL SYSTEMS OF THE WORLD: A POLITICAL, SOCIAL, AND CULTURAL ENCYCLOPEDIA (2002).

77. In this chapter, I argue that it is not only possible, but also conceptually useful to classify legal traditions into categories that share important characteristics. This process of classification should be based on identifying fundamental elements of a legal system, through which "the rules to be applied

My analyses control for several additional factors that, according to the literature, matter in how countries view UNCLOS and international treaties in general. UNCLOS deals with rights of coastal as well as landlocked states.[78] However, as several scholars have observed, landlocked countries have not gotten equitable treatment in the Convention. For example, UNCLOS awards regulatory power over the natural resources of coastal seas to coastal states. Importantly, upon pressure from coastal ratifiers, Article 297 of the Convention excludes from adjudication certain disputes relating to coastal states' sovereign rights, such as marine research or fisheries.[79] At the same time, landlocked ratifiers do not receive any exclusive allocation of ocean natural resources.[80] Eric Posner and Alan Sykes argue that countries with longer coastlines benefit the most from the Convention and the landlocked countries gain very little.[81] To control for this factor, I use the variable *Length of Coastline*, obtained from the CIA World Fact Book, which measures the total length of the boundary between the land area (including islands) and the sea.[82] Next, since UNCLOS impacts the interests of oil and gas producing states, I account for offshore petroleum deposits. Offshore oil and gas deposits are extracted from rock formations beneath the seabed and most often affect the environment of the continental shelf. The variable *Off-Shore Petroleum* codes the number of offshore oil and natural gas deposits. In constructing this variable, I use Peace Research Institute Oslo (PRIO) Petroleum data v 1.2.[83]

The variable *Capabilities* is based on the national capabilities index (CINC score) as developed by J. David Singer, Stuart Bremer, and John Stuckey.[84] Research demonstrates that powerful countries are less supportive of international treaties,

---

are themselves discovered, interpreted and elaborated" René David & John E.C. Brierley, Major Legal Systems in the World Today 20 (1985). However, all legal scholars agree that legal traditions are internally intricate and complex.

78. UNCLOS repeatedly refers to landlocked states. For example, the Convention Preamble talks about taking into account "special interests and needs of developing countries, whether coastal or land-locked."

79. The use of conciliation is obligatory in some instances. However, the coastal state's exercise of its rights may not be questioned, and the parties to a dispute are not bound by the conciliation commission's report J.G. Merrills, International Dispute Settlement 172 (2011).

80. Bernard H. Oxman, *The Territorial Temptation: A Siren Song at Sea*, 100 Am. J. Int'l L. 830 (2006).

81. Eric A. Posner & Alan O. Sykes, *Economic Foundations of the Law of the Sea*, 104 Am. J. Int'l L. 569 (2010).

82. Information available on the CIA website at: https://www.cia.gov/library/publications/the-world-factbook/fields/2060.html.

83. Lujala Päivi et al., *Fighting Over Oil: Introducing a New Dataset*, 24 Conflict Mgmt. & Peace Sci. 239 (2007), http://www.prio.no/Data/Geographical-and-Resource-Datasets/Petroleum-Dataset/Petroleum-Dataset-v-12/. I combine the number of offshore oil and natural gas polygons for each state.

84. David J. Singer et al., *Capability Distribution, Uncertainty, and Major Power War, 1820–1965*, in Peace, War and Numbers 19 (Bruce Russet ed., 1972).

especially treaties with dispute settlement mechanisms.[85] Weak states, on the other hand, see impartial adjudication as a means of protection against stronger states.[86] As UNCLOS includes very elaborate dispute resolution provisions, I expect weaker states to be more supportive of the Convention. The *Democracy* variable captures the democratic legalist perspective, which asserts that democracies' respect for judicial processes and rule of law carries over into international relations. Thus, democracies should be more likely to support international institutions and treaties.[87] I employ the Polity IV data set.[88] Finally, *ICJ Optional Clause* and *ICJ Compromissory Clause Treaties* variables measure a state's relationship with the ICJ, the main judicial organ of the United Nations. The first variable is dichotomous and captures whether a country has accepted the ICJ's compulsory jurisdiction.[89] The second variable is a yearly count measure of the total number of treaty memberships with compromissory clauses for each state.[90] Whether or not a state accepts the jurisdiction of the ICJ—either on a compulsory or compromissory basis—constitutes a good measure of the state's overall commitment to international law, and in particular to international peaceful dispute resolution mechanisms. Accepting the authority of the ICJ constitutes a costly commitment, and my expectation is that states committed to the ICJ should also be more likely to express their support for UNCLOS.

IV. EMPIRICAL ANALYSES

To test my hypotheses, I estimate the following two sets of models: logit models (UNCLOS Signature and UNCLOS Ratification; Table 26.5), and negative

---

85. Richard B. Bilder, *International Dispute Settlement and the Role of International Adjudication*, INTERNATIONAL LAW: CLASSIC AND CONTEMPORARY READINGS 233 (Lynne Rienner ed., 1998); James Smith, *Inequality in International Trade? Developing Countries and Institutional Change in WTO Dispute Settlement*, 11 REV. INT'L POL. ECON. 542 (2004).

86. Gary L. Scott & Crag L. Carr, *The ICJ and Compulsory Jurisdiction: The Case for Closing the Clause*, 81 AM. J. INT'L L. 57 (1987).

87. Beth A. Simmons, *See You in "Court"? The Appeal to Quasi-judicial Legal Processes in the Settlement of Territorial Disputes*, in A ROAD MAP TO WAR: TERRITORIAL DIMENSION OF INTERNATIONAL CONFLICT 205 (Paul F. Diehl ed., 1999).

88. Monty Marshall & Keith Jaggers, Polity IV Project: Political Regime Characteristics and Transitions, 1800–2015 (2016), http://www.systemicpeace.org/polityproject.html.

89. Accepting compulsory jurisdiction signifies a state's acknowledgment of the ICJ's adjudicative powers in all legal disputes regarding interpretation of a treaty, of other international obligations, or any question of international law. This variable has two categories: (1) a state accepts the compulsory jurisdiction with or without reservations or (0) a state does not recognize the Court's jurisdiction. Almost all states in the time frame of my analyses place reservations on their declarations; thus introducing a categorical dependent variable (ICJ acceptance without reservations, ICJ acceptance with reservations, no ICJ acceptance) is not empirically justified.

90. A state may recognize the Court's jurisdiction through compromissory clauses in bilateral or multilateral treaties. Via a compromissory clause, parties to a treaty agree that if a dispute of a given type arises, it will be submitted to the ICJ, either immediately, or after another means for settlement fails.

Table 26.5. Logistic Regression: UNCLOS Signature and Ratification (1982–2006)

	Estimates		Predicted probabilities	
	UNCLOS signature	UNCLOS ratification	UNCLOS signature	UNCLOS ratification
Common Law	3.20*(1.69)	1.90*(1.03)	.95	.94
Civil Law	—	—	.72	.80
Islamic Law	1.75*(.98)	1.09*(.694)	.91	.91
Mixed Law	1.67*(1.03)	.958(.920)	.90	.88
Length of Coastline	.000(.000)	.000*(.000)	25perc(56): .69 75perc(2470): .71	25perc(56): .68 75perc(2470): .76
Off-Shore Petroleum	−.018(.090)	−.058(.108)	25perc(0): .73 75perc(19): .62	25perc(0): .82 75perc(19): .578
Capabilities	29.71(46.84)	−28.49(33.63)	25perc(.0002): .68 75perc(.003): .70	25perc(.0002): .82 75perc(.003): .81
Democracy	−.244***(.089)	−.049(.067)	Min(0): .84 Max(10): .35	Min(0): .83 Max(10): .74
ICJ Optional Clause	.86*(.60)	.146(.518)	No: .72 Yes: .85	No: .80 Yes: .82
ICJ Compromissory Clause Treaties	.045*(.026)	.063**(.028)	Min(0): .54 Max(78): .93	Min(0): .58 Max(78): .98
Constant	.720*(.498)	.146(.485)		
	N=160 Wald Chi2(9)=11.63 Prob>chi2=.2349	N=160 Wald Chi2(9)=11.82 Prob>chi2=.1423		

NOTE: robust standard errors in parentheses; *p<.10, **p<.05, ***p<.01

Table 26.6. Negative Binomial Regressions: UNCLOS Declarations
and Restrictions (1982–2006)

	Estimates	Predicted probabilities
Common Law	−.028(.619)	1.58
Civil Law	—	1.36
Islamic Law	1.01***(.376)	3.87
Mixed Law	−1.01(.641)	.58
Length of Coastline	−.000(.000)	25perc(56): 1.38 75perc(2470): 1.37
Off-Shore Petroleum	.131**(.058)	25perc(0): .99 75perc(19): 19.82
Capabilities	−1.79(12.27)	25perc(.0002): 1.39 75perc(.003): 6.89
Democracy	−.031(.034)	Min(0): 1.52 Max(10): 1.14
ICJ Optional Clause	.066(.282)	No: 1.36 Yes: 1.50
ICJ Compromissory Clause Treaties	.033***(.008)	Min(0): .77 Max(78): 11.29
Constant	−.472*(.304)	
	N=160 Wald Chi2(9)=42.32 Prob>chi2=.000	

NOTE: robust standard errors in parentheses; *p<.10, **p<.05, ***p<.01

binomial models (UNCLOS Declarations and Restrictions; Table 26.6). I use logit models because of the dichotomous nature of *Signature* and *Ratification* dependent variables. Models' estimates are followed by substantive effects: predicted probabilities in Table 26.5, and expected counts in Table 26.6.[91] Hypothesis 1 expressed my expectation that ILS are at least as likely as civil and common law states to sign and ratify the UNCLOS Convention. In both models, the *Civil Law* dummy constitutes a reference category. Coefficients for the *Islamic Law* variable are positive and statistically significant in the signature and ratification models. Predicted probabilities demonstrate that ILS are very likely to both sign and ratify UNCLOS. The likelihood of signature for these states is 0.91, slightly lower than for common law states (0.95), higher than for mixed law states (0.90), and significantly higher than for civil law states (0.72).

91. Predicted probabilities are calculated using Clarify, Version 2.0. *See* Gary King et al., *Making the Most of Statistical Analyses: Improving Interpretation and Presentation*, 44 Am. J. Pol. Sci. 347 (2000).

592 COMPARATIVE INTERNATIONAL LAW

I observe very similar patterns in the context of UNCLOS ratification. Predicted probability of ratification for ILS is again high (0.91), a bit lower than for common law states (0.94), and higher than for civil law states and mixed law states (0.80 and 0.88 respectively). Importantly, the Islamic world's commitment to UNCLOS is comparable with that of ratifiers representing other legal traditions. These patterns are quite different from what we observe in the context of other substantive areas of international law and other treaties with compulsory dispute settlement provisions. Again, as Table 26.1 demonstrates, ILS, as a group, are not as supportive of the ICJ's compulsory jurisdiction, and constitute the smallest group among the joiners of the Rome Statute (the ICC), as well as the Convention for the Pacific Settlement of International Disputes (PCA). For ILS, uncertainty concerning interpretation of legal rules and the overall legal structure of the ICJ, the ICC, or the PCA is much greater than for Western law states. This uncertainty is largely elevated in the context of UNCLOS because of the substantive and procedural congruence between Islamic and international maritime law.

The results concerning clauses that states add to the Convention are interesting. Consistent with Hypothesis 2, ILS are more likely to include declarations and restrictions. Upon ratification, Islamic ratifiers put to use these instruments' ability to customize particulars of their UNCLOS commitments. Traditionally relatively cautious in drafting their international agreements, ILS have, on average, 3.87 UNCLOS declarations/restrictions. This number is lower for countries representing other legal traditions. For example, the expected count for common law states is more than two times lower (1.58), almost three times lower for civil law states (1.36), and 6.6 times lower for mixed law states (0.58). These results support existing research, such as the finding that ILS embed more reservations in their commitments to the ICJ.[92]

Control variables provide additional insights into states' view of UNCLOS. More democratic states are less likely to sign the Convention (Table 26.5). As previous research shows, democracies sign only those international commitments that they are likely to keep in the future.[93] It appears that UNCLOS does not fall into this category. The *Democracy* variable is statistically insignificant in the ratification model and both of the negative binomial models. I am unable to statistically tease out the relationship between state strength and levels of support for UNCLOS. The variable *Capabilities* is statistically insignificant in all four models. The *Length of Coastline* affects the likelihood of UNCLOS ratification. The longer a state's coastline, the more likely this state is to ratify the Convention. This finding supports Posner and Sykes who conjecture that while states with the longest coastlines benefit most from the Convention, "landlocked states benefit very little."[94] The number of *Off-Shore Petroleum* deposits, albeit insignificant in the signature and ratification models,

92. MITCHELL & POWELL, *supra* note 21.

93. Kurt T. Gaubatz, *Democratic States and Commitment in International Relations*, 50 INT'L ORG. 109 (1996); Brett Ashley Leeds, *Domestic Political Institutions, Credible Commitments, and International Cooperation*, 43 AM. J. POL. SCI. 979 (1999).

94. Posner & Sykes, *supra* note 81, at 596.

impacts the way that states structure their UNCLOS commitments. Countries with offshore oil and natural gas reserves place a higher number of declarations and restrictions. In both cases, the increase in expected counts is substantial, indicating these states' aptitude to carefully stipulate their UNCLOS commitments. For example, Brazil, a state with 22 offshore petroleum deposit sites, places nine restrictions/ declarations on UNCLOS, several of which relate to its offshore activities. One of Brazil's stipulations, for instance, states: "The Brazilian Government understands that in accordance with the provisions of the Convention the coastal State has, in the exclusive economic zone and on the continental shelf, the exclusive right to construct and to authorize and to regulate the construction, operation and use of all kinds of installations and structures, without exception, whatever their nature or purpose."[95]

I find that a state's relationship with the ICJ can influence its attitude toward UNCLOS. Countries that recognize the ICJ's compulsory jurisdiction (*ICJ Optional Clause*) are more likely to sign the Convention. However, this variable has no statistically discernible effect on the propensity to ratify UNCLOS nor to place declarations and restrictions on the Convention. Recognizing the ICJ's compromissory jurisdiction (*ICJ Compromissory Clause Treaties*), on the other hand, influences states' propensity to sign, as well as ratify UNCLOS. Substantive effects are quite large. The likelihood of UNCLOS signature for a state that is a part of 78 treaties with compromissory ICJ clauses is 0.93, compared with 0.54 for a state that does not recognize the ICJ's compromissory jurisdiction. Very similar patterns emerge in the context of UNCLOS ratification (predicted probabilities 0.98 and 0.58 respectively). Interestingly, states that recurrently recognize the ICJ's compromissory jurisdiction are also more likely to place declarations and restrictions on their UNCLOS commitments. The expected count of declarations/restrictions increases for states that are part of 78 compromissory ICJ treaties increases from 0.77 to 11.29. This result demonstrates that states that are more open to international adjudication are also more careful in drafting their international commitments.

V. CONCLUSION

Far too frequently, points of convergence and departure between Islamic law and international law have been either overplayed or simply dismissed, leading to a dichotomous division of the scholarship. Dismissing areas of divergence between these two legal systems does not push the scholarship forward and undermines meaningful intercultural conversations. There is an increasing need for the Western world to cooperate with the Islamic world on issues of conflict and peace. For these dialogues to be successful, a much more thorough consideration of the Islamic legal tradition is critical. It is not true across the board that Islamic law and international law constitute two separate entities, with not much in common. The reality is that despite the fact that a complete convergence between these two legal systems is not possible,

95. UNCLOS Statement of Brazil (Dec. 22, 1988), http://www.un.org/Depts/los/convention_ agreements/convention_declarations.htm.

Islamic law can substantially contribute to the development of the law of nations.[96] Islamic maritime law is highly similar to international law, and this congruence is made evident via the Islamic world's openness to UNCLOS. As Mohammed AlQasimi stated, "There is a book called *Al-Siyar Al-Kabir*, written by Shaybani. This is the counterpart to Grotius' book *On the Law of War and Peace*. So this is the main source for Islamic international law. It contains very similar principles and ideas about the nature of relations between Islamic states and other states." [97] There are many dimensions of deep commensurability between Islamic and international law, some of which reach deep into the heart of peaceful interstate coexistence.

The focus on ILS in the context of international maritime law and UNCLOS sheds light on international law's authority more generally. International law—especially in areas of substantive and procedural convergence with Islamic law—is able to garner acceptance even among its Islamic audience that arguably operates in the framework of strong domestic counter norms that might leave little space for modern international law. Islamic law's edicts are grounded in religious beliefs and are potentially hard to topple by any secular legal system—domestic or supranational. Islamic international law falls directly into the category mentioned in the Introduction to this volume as a case where "differences in the way in which international law is interpreted and applied might affect what is identified as international law."[98]

However, my arguments are not meant to negate the impact of strategic considerations, which indeed play a fundamental role in states' decisions to sign agreements. Any country's behavior emerges as a result of a variety of factors and influences coming together. Power, material gains, regime type, geographic location, etc., all shape to some extent states' preferences and actions. Global politics reveal how truly complex interstate relations are, and no explanation should be bound by a focus on one single factor, while holding back all the other potential streams of influence. Islamic law and its relationship to international law constitute only one of these influences for the Islamic world.

96. Al-Khasawneh, *supra* note 5; Gamal M. Badr, *A Survey of Islamic International Law*, 76 Am. Soc. Int'l L. Proc. 56 (1982).

97. AlQasimi, *supra* note 56.

98. Roberts, Stephan, Verdier & Versteeg, *supra* note 11, at 8.

Index

Figures and tables are indicated by "f" and "t" following page numbers. Cases are under either deciding tribunal or country where court is located